RICHARD I

Also in the Yale English Monarchs series

RICHARD I

John Gillingham

YALE UNIVERSITY PRESS
NEW HAVEN AND LONDON

For Tom, who knows about heroes

Copyright © 1999 by John Gillingham

Set in New Baskerville by Fakenham Photosetting Ltd, Norfolk
Printed in Great Britain by St Edmundsbury Press

Library of Congress Cataloging-in-Publication Data

Gillingham, John.
Richard I/John Gillingham.
(Yale English Monarchs)
Includes bibliographical references and index.
ISBN 0–300–07912–5 (alk. paper)
1. Richard I, King of England, 1157–1199.   2. Great Britain—History—
Richard I, 1189–1199.   3. Great Britain—Kings and rulers—Biography.
I. Title.   II. Series.
DA207.G473   1999
942.03′2′092—dc21
[B] 99–22273
CIP

A catalogue record for this book is available from the British Library.

10 9 8 7 6 5 4 3 2 1

CONTENTS

ILLUSTRATIONS

PLATES

MAPS

PREFACE

In a series of English Monarchs the life of Richard I presents peculiar problems. For many years he was simultaneously one of the most famous of all kings of England and one of the least studied. Most famous as a legendary hero; least studied because his career both falls between the stools of all traditional academic histories – of England, of France, of the Crusades – and has never attracted the interest of historians of society and government, to the development of which he has been thought to contribute nothing. As king of England he notoriously spent only six months of a ten-year reign in England. On crusade he spent not much more than a year in Outremer, and was unable to recapture Jerusalem. On his way back from crusade he was taken prisoner in Austria and spent over a year in captivity, while his continental dominions were subjected to a series of attacks. Within five years of his death the French part of that 'Angevin Empire' stretching from Scotland to the Pyrenees which he had inherited from his father Henry II, one of the 'great' kings of English history, had been largely overrun by the king of France. When Churchill, in his *History of the English-Speaking Peoples*, wrote: 'His life was one magnificent parade, which, when ended, left only an empty plain', he was reflecting the general consensus among English-speaking historians.

On the other hand, as a study of monarchy the reign of Richard I has much to offer. No other medieval king of England had so many enemies in so many different parts of the world and was, in consequence, commented upon from so many different *and hostile* points of view. In Capetian France, in Germany, in Italy and in the Low Countries as well as in the Middle East, authors who in some sense represented the interests of their lords, King Philip Augustus, Emperor Henry VI and Saladin, wrote about Richard in ways which, true or not, tell us much about contemporary ideas of rulership in both the Christian and Muslim worlds. No other ruling king of England was ever observed so closely from 'the other side of the hill' as Richard was by writers who were themselves attached to Saladin's staff. This makes it possible to see Richard I's performance as king from a unique perspective. Much less remarkable, though still significant, is the fact that in his own lifetime he came to be perceived by authors who were his own subjects as a ruler in heroic mould. In consequence for many centuries after his death he was regarded as the model of good kingship. The last quarter of the twelfth century – and especially the 1190s – has rightly been recognized as 'a golden age' of historical writing in England. Some of the finest – the most detailed and well informed (Roger of Howden and Ralph of

Diceto), most critical (William of Newburgh), most secular and satirical (Richard of Devizes), most original (Gerald de Barri) – of medieval English historians were Richard's contemporaries and wrote about him. Few, if any, kings of England offer so many different approaches to people's ideas of what it meant to be a king.

This is not a book about Richard's inner life. His relationship to his mother, for example, could well have been central to his life in many ways, but it is not a subject about which contemporaries wrote except in the most general terms, so we know virtually nothing about their thoughts on the matter – let alone about the 'reality' of that relationship, or about any other close personal relationship. It is possible to argue that there is no sign in the surviving evidence that contemporaries thought he was homosexual; it is not possible to argue that he was not homosexual. I am concerned with the former, not at all with the latter. It is less a question of what I think he was 'really' like, but rather of the many different ways in which contemporaries portrayed him. It is less a question of whether I think he was 'a hero' or 'a villain', but rather of why so many – even of his enemies – presented him in a heroic light, and why others saw him as arrogant and treacherous.

Nor is this book a study of 'The Government of Richard I'. This is a subject on which much vital spadework still remains to be done, and which I am not competent to do. In 1935 Lionel Landon knew of 565 charters issued by Richard I as king. Dr Nicholas Vincent has now collected well over a thousand! Although the records of the English exchequer for Richard's reign have been well edited, the same is emphatically not true of the records of the Norman exchequer on which Dr Vincent Moss is now working. A full-scale attempt to study Richard's government is best left until we have good scholarly editions of the records of that government. Such a study will throw much new light on the structure of government and administration during his reign, but very little on his capacity as a king. Although the formulae of charters can be made to reveal something of conventional ideals of kingship, they cannot tell us whether or not a particular ruler was thought to live up to those conventional ideals. Charters and other chancery documents can help us to reconstruct the ruler's itinerary and his entourage; they can tell us where a king was, identify some of those who were with him, and to whom he was dispensing favours; but whether it made sense for him to spend time in England, or in his continental dominions, or on crusade, whether he chose his advisers well and rewarded them properly – all these were matters of opinion. Fiscal records can sometimes tell us how much revenue a ruler collected, and how; they also throw light on how much he spent, and on what. But whether he was generous or miserly was a matter of opinion. Kings could be very rich, as records show Edward II to have been in 1326 and Richard II in 1399. It did them little good. A king's glory, as the exchequer expert Richard FitzNigel, promoted bishop of London in the first council of Richard I's reign, put it in the preface to *The Dialogue of the Exchequer*, 'lay not in hoarding treasure but in spending it as it should be spent'. But how should it be spent? That too was a matter of opinion. Kings were sustained politically, or brought down, by contemporary opinion. Central to this political biography therefore is an analysis of contemporary opinion, and of the literary sources, both Latin and vernacular, which give us access to those opinions.

I have been thinking about these problems on and off for more than twenty-five years. In my first serious stab at the subject, *Richard the Lionheart* (1978), I focused on Richard in France, above all in Aquitaine. This was on the quite sensible grounds that he spent some two-thirds of his political life in France. On the other hand it resulted in underplaying two other aspects of his career – precisely those for which he became most famous. The first was his leadership of the Third Crusade – for which he became a legend. The second was his allegedly negligent government of England – for which English historians since the seventeenth century have found it hard to forgive him. In this book, chapters 3–6, dealing with the years in Aquitaine before his accession to the throne, do not do much more than add footnotes to the earlier study, but in chapters 1–2, 7–19 I hope to offer a substantially more detailed analysis of the reign of Richard as king of England.

Writing about Richard I involves some practical problems. During the ten years of his reign he played a major part in the histories of England, France, Germany, Sicily, Cyprus and the kingdom of Jerusalem. It would help if his biographer knew a little bit about the histories of all these countries, and could read all the relevant languages. I fear that my doubtless inadequate and inconsistent transliteration of Arabic personal names will irritate all those who understand the subject. Since I cannot read Arabic I have had to rely entirely on translations for sources written in that language.

In many other ways I have relied upon friends and colleagues. It was when I met Hans Eberhard Mayer in Munich that I first became interested in the subject of the crusades and in Richard's role in them. Over the years I have owed much to his generosity. I am indebted to the London School of Economics and Political Science, both for funding travel which allowed me to visit many of the places in France which otherwise I might not have seen, and for graciously facilitating the early retirement which made writing this book possible. It is clear from the work of Ivan Cloulas and the Association de la Route historique des Plantagenêts that Coeur de Lion is alive and well in France. I owe a debt of gratitude to Christopher Falkus who first invited me to write a book – or two – on Richard the Lionheart; to Jinty Nelson for organizing the King's College London Colloquium on the 800th anniversary of Richard's accession in 1989; and to the organizers of conferences at Caen and Thouars on the 800th anniversary of his death, especially to Frédérique Chauvenet and Martin Aurell. From my former student, Richard Benjamin, tragically killed in a car accident, I learned much about the pleasures of history. From my former teacher, J. O. Prestwich, I learned – and happily continue to learn – much both about Richard I and about how to read twelfth-century narratives. From Jane Martindale I learned – and continue to learn – about Aquitaine. I am particularly grateful to Jim Holt and to David Carpenter for sharing with me the fun of disgreeing with one another. Among the friends and colleagues who over many years have been kind enough to send me relevant books, offprints and/or unpublished work and have in this way ensured that I could never quite forget Richard, I would like to thank Marianne Ailes, Nick Barratt, Peter Edbury, Claude Fagnen, John France, Ruth Harvey, Richard Heiser, Tom Keefe (sadly missed), Olivier de Laborderie, Simon Lloyd, Emma Mason, Hannes Möhring, David Morgan, Vincent Moss, Jonathan Phillips, Dominique Pitte, Dan Power, Matthew Strickland, Ralph Turner, Nick Vincent. Thanks also must go to my publisher Yale University Press; to Robert Baldock for taking on an awkward project with a combination of decisiveness and patience; to Alex Nesbit for seeing it swiftly through the Press; and in particular to Beth Humphries, my copy-editor, for taking immense pains with a shambles of a text. From those whom I should have thanked, but have stupidly omitted, I ask only that they should forcibly point this out to me.

LIST OF ABBREVIATIONS

Actes	*Recueil des actes de Philippe Auguste*, i and ii, ed. H.-F. Delaborde, C. Petit-Dutaillis and J. Monicat (Paris, 1916–43)
Ambroise	Ambroise, *L'Estoire de la guerre sainte*, ed. G. Paris (Paris, 1897), cited by line number to facilitate reference to the forthcoming translation by Marianne Ailes as well as to that by M. J. Hubert and J. La Monte, *The Crusade of Richard Lionheart* (New York, 1941)
Annales angevines	*Recueil d'Annales angevines*, ed. L. Halphen (Paris, 1903)
ANS	*Anglo-Norman Studies*
Ansbert	*Historia de Expeditione Friderici*, ed. A. Chroust (MGH SRG, 1929)
Baha al-Din	Beha ed-Din, *What Befell Sultan Yusuf*, trans. C. W. Wilson (Palestine Pilgrims Text Society, xiii, London, 1897)
BIHR	*Bulletin of the Institute of Historical Research*
Born	*The Poems of the Troubadour Bertran de Born*, ed. W. D. Paden, Jr, T. Sankovitch and P. H. Stäblein (Berkeley, 1986)
Boussard	J. Boussard, *Le Gouvernement d'Henri II Plantagenêt* (Paris, 1965)
CCM	*Cahiers de civilisation mediévale*
Chron.	Roger of Howden, *Chronica*, ed. W. Stubbs (4 vols, RS, 1868–87)
Chron. Maj.	Matthew Paris, *Chronica Majora*, ed. H. R. Luard (7 vols, RS, 1872–84). This contains within it a useful edition of Roger of Wendover's *Flores Historiarum*
Coggeshall	*Radulphi de Coggeshall Chronicon Anglicanum*, ed. J. Stevenson (RS, 1875)
DA	*Deutsches Archiv*
Devizes	*The Chronicle of Richard of Devizes*, ed. and trans. J. T. Appleby (London, 1963)
Diceto	*Radulfi de Diceto Decani Londiniensis Opera Historica*, ed. W. Stubbs (2 vols, RS, 1876)
Edbury	P. W. Edbury, *The Conquest of Jerusalem and the Third Crusade. Sources in Translation* (Aldershot, 1996)
EHR	*English Historical Review*
Foedera	*Foedera, conventiones, litterae*, i, part 1, ed. T. Rymer, A. Clarke, F. Holbrooke, J. Caley (London, 1816)

Gabrieli	F. Gabrieli, *Arab Historians of the Crusades* (London, 1969)
Gerald, *Opera*	*Giraldi Cambrensis Opera* ed. J. S. Brewer, J. F. Dimock and G. F. Warner (8 vols, RS, 1861–91). Separate works are cited as follows. Figures in parentheses refer to Rolls Series volume number.
Gerald, *Descrip.*	*Descriptio Kambriae* (6)
Gerald, *Expug. Hib.*	*Expugnatio Hibernica. The Conquest of Ireland, by Giraldus Cambrensis*, ed. and trans. A. B. Scott and F. X. Martin (Dublin, 1978)
Gerald, *Princ.*	*De Principis Instructione* (8)
Gerald, *Top.*	*Topographia Hibernica* (5)
Gervase	*The Historical Works of Gervase of Canterbury*, ed. W. Stubbs (2 vols, RS, 1879–80)
Gesta	Roger of Howden, *Gesta Henrici II et Ricardi I*, ed. W. Stubbs (2 vols, RS, 1867)
Gillingham, *Coeur de Lion*	J. Gillingham, *Richard Coeur de Lion. Kingship, Chivalry and War in the Twelfth Century* (London, 1994)
HGM	*Histoire de Guillaume le Maréchal*, ed. P. Meyer (3 vols, Paris, 1891–1901). Cited by line number.
HSJ	*Haskins Society Journal*
Ibn al-Athir	Ibn al-Athir, *el-Kamil*, in *Recueil des historiens des croisades: historiens orientaux*, ii, part 1 (Paris, 1887)
Imad al-Din	Imad al-Din *Conquête de la Syrie et de la Palestine par Saladin*, trans. H. Massé (Paris, 1972)
Itin.	*Itinerarium Peregrinorum et Gesta Regis Ricardi* in *Chronicles and Memorials of the Reign of Richard I*, i, ed. W. Stubbs (RS, 1864). Cited by book and chapter to facilitate use of the translation by Helen Nicholson, *Chronicle of the Third Crusade* (Ashgate, 1997) as well as to the edition of the *Itinerarium Peregrinorum* itself, ed. H. E. Mayer, *Das Itinerarium Peregrinorum* (Stuttgart, 1962)
JMH	*Journal of Medieval History*
Kessler	U. Kessler, *Richard I. Löwenherz. König, Kreuzritter, Abenteurer* (Graz, 1995)
Landon	*The Itinerary of King Richard I*, ed. L. Landon (Pipe Roll Society, London, 1935)
Lyons and Jackson	M. C. Lyons and D. E. P. Jackson, *Saladin: The Politics of the Holy War* (Cambridge, 1982)
Magna Vita	Adam of Eynsham, *Magna Vita Sancti Hugonis*, ed. D. L. Douie and H. Farmer (2 vols, Edinburgh, 1962)
Map	Walter Map, *De Nugis Curialium. Courtiers' Trifles*, ed. and trans. M. R. James, C. N. L. Brooke and R. A. B. Mynors (OMT, Oxford, 1983)
MGH SRG	Monumenta Germaniae Historica. Scriptores rerum Germanicarum in usum scholarum

MGH SS   Monumenta Germaniae Historica. Scriptores
MRSN   *Magni Rotuli Scaccarii Normanniae*, ed. T. Stapleton (2 vols,
                London, 1840–4)
Nelson, *Coeur*   J. L. Nelson, *Richard Coeur de Lion in History and Myth*
  de Lion   (London, 1992)
Newburgh   William of Newburgh, *Historia Rerum Anglicarum*, ed. R.
                Howlett in *Chronicles of the Reigns of Stephen, Henry II and
                Richard I*, i and ii (RS, 1884). Cited by book and chapter to
                facilitate reference to *History of William of Newburgh*, trans. J.
                Stevenson, 1856 (repr. Felinfach, 1996)
Norgate   K. Norgate, *Richard the Lionheart* (London, 1924)
OMT   Oxford Medieval Texts
Philippidos   William the Breton, *Philippidos*, in *Oeuvres de Rigord et de
                Guillaume le Breton*, ed. H. F. Delaborde, ii (Paris, 1885)
Powicke   F. M. Powicke, *The Loss of Normandy* 2nd edn (Manchester,
                1961)
PR   Pipe Roll
Prestwich   J. O. Prestwich, 'Richard Coeur de Lion: *rex bellicosus*', in
                Riccardo Cuor di Leone nella storia e nella leggenda (Accademia
                Nazionale dei Lincei, Problemi attuali di scienza e di cul-
                tura, ccliii, Rome, 1981); repr. in *Richard Coeur de Lion in
                History and Myth*, ed. J. L. Nelson (London, 1992)
RHF   *Recueil des historiens des Gaules et de la France*
Rigord   Rigord, *Gesta Philippi Augusti* in *Oeuvres de Rigord et de
                Guillaume le Breton*, ed. H. F. Delaborde, i (Paris, 1882)
RS   Rolls Series
Selected Letters *Selected Letters of Pope Innocent III concerning England*, ed. C. R.
                Cheney and W. H. Semple (London, 1953)
Sicard   Sicard of Cremona in Salimbene de Adam, *Cronica*, ed. G.
                Scalia (Bari, 1966)
Sig. Cont.   *Sigeberti Continuatio Aquicincta*, MGH SS, vi (written by
                Andreas of Marchiennes)
Torigny   *The Chronicle of Robert of Torigni* in *Chronicles of the Reigns of
                Stephen, Henry II and Richard I*, ed. R. Howlett, iv (RS, 1889)
Vigeois   'Chronica' in *Novae Bibliothecae Manuscriptorum Librorum*, ed.
                P. Labbe (2 vols, Paris, 1657), ii, 279–329. Since there is a
                better edition of Book 1 of Geoffrey in an unpublished
                thesis, P. Botineau, 'La Chronique de Geoffroi de Breuil,
                prieur de Vigeois' (Paris, 1964) and a more accessible one
                of Book 2 in *RHF*, xviii, 211–23, I have cited this chronicle
                by the common numbering of book and chapter.
Warren   W. L. Warren, *Henry II* (London, 1973)
WB   William the Breton, *Gesta Philippi Augusti* in *Oeuvres de Rigord
                et de Guillaume le Breton*, ed. H. F. Delaborde, i (Paris, 1882)

Chapter 1

THE BEST OF KINGS, THE WORST OF KINGS

Unique among the kings of England Richard I played an active leading role in the great events of world history, in his case the struggle for control of the Middle East between two world religions, Islam and Christianity. By contrast, all other kings of England who ruled as well as reigned, no matter how clever, ambitious, able or power-hungry they may have been, confined their ruling and their campaigning to the north-western corner of Europe. No earlier or later king took on a challenge remotely comparable with the task of taking a fleet and an army to the eastern end of the Mediterranean and there facing, even facing down, an adversary as formidable as the great Saladin. Not surprisingly Richard I was for long seen as the greatest of English kings. According to Ranulf Higden, the fourteenth-century author of a world history which was both learned and popular, the Bretons boasted of their Arthur just as the Greeks of Alexander, the Romans of their Augustus, the English of Richard and the French of Charlemagne.[1] Higden was not making a case for Richard, he was merely taking it for granted that this was how the English thought of him. Or consider a short list of important dates recorded in the fourteenth-century Bordeaux *Livre des coutumes*:

AD 542	In this year died Arthur King of Greater Britain.
AD 827	In this year died Emperor Charlemagne
AD 813	In this year died Count Roland
AD 1199	In this year died Richard king of England.[2]

This then was the company which Richard kept: Alexander, Augustus, Roland, Charlemagne, King Arthur.

In the last two or three hundred years orthodox opinion has judged Richard more harshly. 'He was certainly one of the worst rulers England

---

[1] *Polychronicon Ranulphi Higden*, ed. C. Babington and J. R. Lumby (9 vols, RS, 1865–86), v, 336.
[2] *Archives Municipales de Bordeaux*, v: *Livre des coutumes*, ed. H. Barckhausen (Bordeaux, 1890), 396.

has ever had.'[3] That certainty was based on a consensus among the best and most influential historians which goes back at least as far as David Hume and Edward Gibbon. For Hume, Richard was 'so much guided by passion and so little by policy', 'negligent', 'undesigning, impolitic, violent'. 'No man, even in that romantic age, carried personal courage and intrepidity to a greater height', hence his subjects 'had reason to apprehend, from the continuance of his reign a perpetual scene of blood and violence'.[4] For Gibbon, 'if heroism be confined to brutal and ferocious valour, Richard will stand high among the heroes of the age'.[5] The great nineteenth-century scholar, William Stubbs, believed that 'all allowances being made for him, he was a bad ruler; his energy, or rather his restlessness, his love of war and his genius for it, effectually disqualified him from being a peaceful one; his utter want of political common sense from being a prudent one'.[6] For the most influential twentieth-century English historian of the crusades, Sir Stephen Runciman, although Richard was 'a gallant and splendid soldier' he was also 'a bad son, a bad husband and a bad king'; for the most influential French one, René Grousset, he was 'ce paladin impolitique et brutale'.[7] In the second half of the twentieth century, the view that Richard was a bad husband and a careless ruler who neglected his duty to provide properly for the succession to the throne was reinforced when homosexuality came to be added to the list of his characteristics. A recent study has concluded that 'as a crusade leader, Richard was a dismal failure', that 'he was no hero, but a man who merely

[3] J. A. Brundage, *Richard Lionheart* (New York, 1974), 258. One of England's worst kings: J. J. Norwich, *The Kingdom in the Sun* (London, 1970), 141. Cf. 'Richard I has always been viewed as one of the worst kings of England', G. Regan, *Lionhearts. Saladin and Richard I* (London, 1998), 230.

[4] D. Hume, *History of England*, 1871 repr. of 1786 edn, i, 261, 263, 265, 279. 'It is Hume who is read by everyone. Hume is the historian whose views and opinions invariably become our own', wrote the nineteenth-century professor of history at Cambridge, William Smyth, cited ibid., p. x.

[5] E. Gibbon, *The History of the Decline and Fall of the Roman Empire*, 1906 repr., vi, 350.

[6] He was also, in Stubbs's view, 'a man of blood, whose crimes were those of one whom long use of warfare had made too familiar with slaughter: a bad son, a bad husband, a selfish ruler and a vicious man', *Itin.*, pp. xvii, xxi, xxvii.

[7] S. Runciman, *A History of the Crusades*, iii (Cambridge, 1954), iii, 75. R. Grousset, *Histoire des croisades*, iii (Paris, 1936), 2. It has, of course, to be remembered that Runciman was a 'hellenophile with a Gibbonian vision of the crusades as a story of Christian folly and fanaticism', R. Irwin, 'Saladin and the Third Crusade: a Case Study in Historiography and the Historical Novel', in M. Bentley, *Companion to Historiography* (London, 1997); and that Grousset believed in a civilized French colonial settlement in the Levant which was disrupted by such crusading enthusiasts as Richard of England. However a German scholar, biographer of Richard's contemporary, has recently concluded that Richard 'war kein grosser König', P. Csendes, *Heinrich VI* (Darmstadt, 1993), 129.

wanted to fight hand-to-hand forever'.[8] He who once was the best of kings, became the worst of kings. How can we explain these two opinions?

What matters here is, above all, Richard's commitment to the crusades. English historians who have judged him harshly have tended to do so on the grounds that his enthusiasm for the crusade led him to neglect his kingdom; French ones on the grounds that his conduct on crusade was brutal and stupid, notably his slaughter of the Muslim prisoners taken at Acre. Those who in the past compared him to Alexander, Augustus, Charlemagne and King Arthur did so because he led a crusade. It was the Third Crusade, his crusade, which made him famous throughout the world of Latin Christianity, and in Islam too. Men who were themselves at the siege of Acre believed that they were present at a great moment of history, one they compared with the siege of Troy. In the eyes of Western authors, Saladin's capture of Jerusalem and the collapse of the Latin kingdom of Jerusalem in 1187 had been the result of an intercontinental struggle, when soldiers from two parts of the world, Asia and Africa, combined to attack the third, Europe.[9] The siege of Acre was Europe fighting back. There the sense of Christian solidarity was such that even such inveterate enemies as the Pisans and Genoese could work together in the common enterprise. Thanks to his crusade Richard moved on a world stage where all who supported him could admire his brilliant generalship, his personal prowess and courage; where all who loathed him could see his arrogance and his ruthlessness. It was when describing Richard's first glimpse of the beleaguered city of Acre and of the surrounding hills covered with the tents and pavilions of Saladin's soldiers – 'men who had it in their hearts to harm Christianity' – that Ambroise, the *jongleur*-historian of the Third Crusade, for the first time gave him that name by which he is remembered: 'coeur de lion'.[10] Indeed a series of dramatic episodes in the crusade came to be perceived and presented both in literature and in decorative art as a personal duel between two individuals, Richard and Saladin. It was on the crusade that Richard entered the world of legend, where he has remained ever since. What is claimed to be the oldest pub in England is called The Trip to Jerusalem Inn and, allegedly, dates from 1189. 'But our King did well at Acre,' wrote T.S. Eliot.[11] As John Prestwich has put it, 'we cannot understand the Richard of history if we disregard the qualities which made

[8] M. Markowski, 'Richard Lionheart: Bad King, Bad Crusader?', *JMH*, xxiii (1997), 351–65. The fact that, as Markowski puts it, 'from his day to our own writers and legends have lionized him tells much more about those writers and audiences than about Richard'. True, and it is above all the writers and audiences of his day that I deal with here.

[9] *Itin.*, Preface and Bk 1, chs. 32, 38.

[10] Ambroise, 2310–20.

[11] T. S. Eliot, Choruses from 'The Rock', *Collected Poems, 1909–1962* (London, 1963), 180 – a reference I owe to Kate Ashdown.

him the Richard of legend'.[12] This Richard himself understood. When setting out on crusade he took Excalibur with him.

But the crusade is – and was – controversial. In religious terms the aim
of the Third Crusade was to recover the Holy City. This Richard did not do.
Was the crusade – was he – therefore a failure? There were people at the
time who said so. At the end of his *L' Estoire de la guerre sainte*, Ambroise
addressed them. 'Time and again many ignorant and foolish people say
that they [the crusaders] achieved nothing in Syria because Jerusalem was
not reconquered. But they have not investigated the matter properly. They
criticize what they do not know and speak of places where they did not set
foot.' Ambroise's own rejoinder was couched in appropriately religious
terms. 'We who were there, who saw it and knew it at first hand, we who suffered there, we dare not lie about those who, as we saw with our own eyes,
suffered for the love of God. . . . [Those who died there] will be at the right
hand of God in the heavenly city of Jerusalem, for people such as they
conquered that other Jerusalem.'[13] Few modern historians have much
sympathy for this line of argument. For them Richard was the crusader who
failed to recover Jerusalem but who did massacre thousands of prisoners at
Acre.[14]

Setting religious and moral considerations aside, it might be argued that
if Richard could not recapture Jerusalem, none the less he conquered
Cyprus. In religious terms the island mattered little, but strategically it was
infinitely more important than Jerusalem. Modern historians have often
argued that in giving such a high priority to Jerusalem, Saladin made a
strategic mistake. But not Richard. Whenever possible he chose options –
the conquest of Cyprus, the recovery of the coastal cities of Palestine, a
campaign against Egypt – which made strategic sense and which brought
substantial and lasting gain for the shattered Christian foothold in the
Middle East. Had he headed straight for Jerusalem, he might have taken
it, and for an instant his reputation would have been immensely higher.
But it could not have been held for long. To a remarkable degree most,
though not all, contemporaries and near contemporaries adopted
non-religious criteria in assessing his conduct of the crusade. Even monks

---

[12] J. O. Prestwich, 'Richard Coeur de Lion: *Rex Bellicosus*', in *Richard Coeur de Lion
in History and Myth*, ed. J. L. Nelson (London, 1992), 16.

[13] Ambroise, 12,224–56. In Ambroise's view, 3,000 of those who now sat at God's
right hand had died of illness and famine at the siege of Acre, and 100,000 died
because as crusaders they had chosen a life of celibacy (see below, 89). Roger of
Wendover's curious story of Richard buying back from Saladin the relics which the
latter had captured when he took Jerusalem was presumably another attempt to
show that in religious terms the crusade had some success, *Chron. Maj.*, ii, 378–9.

[14] 'Cet acte de barbarie iniouïe, perpétré de sang-froid, produisit dans tout l'Islam
un effet désastreux', R. Grousset, *Histoire des croisades* iii, 61–2. Grousset went on to
argue that it was stupid as well as barbarous.

recognized and admired his prowess and his conquests. Aubri de Trois-Fontaines, for example, a Cistercian of the next generation whose allegiance to the French crown led him to take a decidedly critical view of many of Richard's actions, wrote up his performance on crusade as a catalogue of great deeds of command and courage on land and sea. 'These are the great deeds which are remembered in praise of Richard. First he captured Messina, then he conquered Cyprus, which the Latin Christians still hold, then the naval battle in which he sank the great ship from Alexandria ... then the relief of Jaffa'.[15]

Yet it is unlikely that anyone ever went on crusade in more extraordinary circumstances than Richard did, or when the more prudent thing would have been to stay at home. His problem was that he came to the throne in 1189 having been betrothed for the last twenty years to Alice, a sister of the reigning king of France, Philip Augustus. During those twenty years Alice had been in the custody of Richard's father, Henry II, and Henry had not been able to resist the temptation to seduce her. Rightly or wrongly Richard decided that this made it impossible for him to marry her. But to send her back to her brother after twenty years would be an enormous insult to the honour of the French royal house, and inevitably it would result in a demand for massive territorial compensation backed by the threat of war. He could not possibly go on crusade and leave King Philip behind with a free hand to take his justified revenge. On the other hand, looking beyond France and England, how could he not go on crusade? In western Europe there had been a huge emotional response to the fall of Jerusalem. This was everywhere perceived as a crisis of Christendom.[16] Recovery from the disaster was possible, but would almost certainly get more difficult as time passed. How could he, the first prince north of the Alps to respond to the crisis, to take the cross, fail to make it his first priority? He was in an impossible situation.

In the short run he was able, by great deviousness, to manoeuvre a way through – in the opinion of an admiring younger contemporary he possessed 'the eloquence of Nestor, the prudence of Ulysses'.[17] So the two kings, Richard and Philip, went on crusade together. But this could do no more than postpone the problem. When he repudiated Alice in Sicily, then presented Philip with a *fait accompli* by marrying Berengaria of Navarre in Cyprus – an English royal wedding in Cyprus! – the king of France was humiliated and bitterly angry. While the great siege of Acre continued, Philip dared not leave, but as soon as it had been brought to a successful conclusion, he abandoned the crusade and returned home

---

[15] *Chronica Albrici Monachi Trium Fontium*, MGH SS, xxiii, 869.

[16] On the significance of 1187 in crusading history see C. Tyerman, *The Invention of the Crusades* (London, 1998), 26–8.

[17] *Itin.*, Bk 2, ch. 5.

determined to make Richard pay. His difficulty was that by the moral standards of the time it was not an easy matter to attack the property of someone who was away on crusade. He therefore had to present Richard as a thoroughly nasty and unscrupulous man, as likely as not to betray to the Muslims the Christendom he was so ostentatiously pretending to defend. Philip's official biographers, Rigord of St-Denis and William the Breton, explained that illness had forced him to return (naturally they did not mention that Richard too had been ill at the siege of Acre – indeed more seriously so, according to the information which reached Saladin) and said that Richard's conduct had been suspicious, leading to stories that he had poisoned the French king and betrayed Christianity. Then rumours were spread thoughout the whole west that Richard had bribed Saracen murderers – Assassins – to kill Philip's ally, Conrad of Montferrat, the lord of Tyre. For a while Philip went nowhere without an armed guard to let it be known that he feared that the long knives of Richard's Assassins could reach out from Syria and strike even in France. Philip in effect established a black propaganda factory at Paris in order to create the image required by his invasion of Richard's lands.[18] When the returning crusader was arrested in Austria and then held in prison for over a year this too could only be justified by accusing Richard of having committed great crimes. The German emperor Henry VI and the duke of Austria also found it convenient to exploit the stories and rumours disseminated by the king of France. German and Austrian chroniclers took on board a view of Richard which portrayed him as arrogant, ruthless and treacherous.

Richard's supporters, encouraged by the king himself, naturally responded in kind to Philip's campaign of defamation. Hence in his own lifetime he became a deeply controversial figure at the centre of a violent propaganda war. Historians and commentators writing in Austria, Germany, the Low Countries, Italy and Outremer, as well as in France and England, all participated in this struggle over Richard's reputation. In a lament composed soon after his death the troubadour Giraut de Borneil observed that 'of this king I hear that if two people mourn him, the third undoes their work'.[19] When the dust had settled, most experienced politicians, even many in France, saw through the French king's attempt to justify the unjustifiable. Joinville in his *Life of Saint Louis* presents Louis's counsellors holding up the choices which Richard made while on crusade as the right ones, a model for Louis IX to follow, and contrasted his conduct with that of Louis's own grandfather: 'as soon as Acre had been taken, King Philip returned to France, an action for which he was much

---

[18] Kessler, 191–9.
[19] *The* cansos *and* sirventes *of Giraut de Borneil: A Critical Edition*, ed. R. V. Sharman (Cambridge, 1989), 475, 478.

blamed'.[20] As this anecdote reveals, those who went on crusade themselves appreciated Richard's achievement. The contemporary political resonance of the criticism faded, but the legend remained. In Italy, Germany and Spain as well as in France and England, Richard remained a figure of legend, a heroic champion of a holy war.[21]

But the product of the 1190s international war of information and disinformation within western Christendom was to be a rich seam of material for modern historians to mine, though they have not always recognized it for what it was. Gossip had been sent spinning into circulation and generated stories far too good for chroniclers to discard. Here, for example, is an account of Richard plotting against Philip's life as told by one version of the Old French Continuation of William of Tyre, a source commonly regarded as a reliable one for events in Outremer:

> Richard committed a great and horrible crime by scheming to kill the king of France without laying a finger on him. While the king of France was lying ill King Richard went to call on him. As soon as he arrived he enquired after his illness and how he was. The king replied that he was at God's mercy and felt himself severely afflicted by his illness. Then King Richard said to him, 'As for Louis your son, how are you to be comforted?' The king of France asked him, 'What about Louis my son that I should be comforted?' 'It is for this', said the king of England, 'that I have come to comfort you, for he is dead.'

In fact Louis, who had been left behind in France, was not dead. The story continues with Philip ordering his galleys and returning to France after consulting his advisers and doctors – 'he thought to cause you so much anguish while you are ill that you would never get up again'.[22]

If modern English historians have blamed him for neglecting his king-

---

[20] Jean de Joinville, *Histoire de Saint Louis*, ed. N. de Wailly (Paris, 1868) 28, 199; in *Chronicles of the Crusades*, trans. M. R. B. Shaw (Harmondsworth, 1963), 183, 304. For another parallel between Richard and Saint Louis see the comment that 'Peasant identification with the state tended to be with the person of the idealized trustworthy ruler, often figures from the past like Richard I of England or Louis IX of France', C. Wickham, 'Gossip and Resistance among the Medieval Peasantry', *Past and Present*, clx (1998), 22.

[21] 'Il buono re Ricciardo', in *Il novellino*, ed. G. Favat (Genoa, 1970), 302–3. M. H. Jones, 'Richard the Lionheart in German Literature of the Middle Ages' and D. Hook, 'The Figure of Richard I in Medieval Spanish Literature', both in Nelson, *Coeur de Lion*; C. Edwards, 'The Magnanimous Sex-Object: Richard the Lionheart in the Medieval German Lyric' in *Courtly Literature: Culture and Context*, ed. K. Busby and E. Kooper (Utrecht Publications in General and Comparative Literature, xxv, Amsterdam, 1990).

[22] Edbury, 108–9. Runciman wondered whether this might not have been 'a piece of heavy buffoonery' on Richard's part; at any rate he treated it as a story which went

dom, this was not how contemporary commentators saw it. They praised him for going on crusade – though some, perhaps with the wisdom of hindsight, felt that he had been too generous to his brother John. If anything, they criticized him for too much government rather than too little. Those such as Ralph of Coggeshall and Roger of Howden who lived through the heavy financial demands of the last years of Richard's reign had good reason to lament his 'insatiable cupidity' and a country 'reduced to poverty' by the oppression of judicial and forest eyres.[23] Yet they acknowledged that the money was raised in order to fight wars in which the king had justice on his side – thus although the heavy demands he made on his subjects meant that he was a flawed hero, they saw him none the less in heroic light, just as Ambroise had done. Historians writing a little later and who had not had to pay Richard's taxes found it even easier to see the hero. For Roger of Wendover and Matthew Paris superlatives were in order. Richard was most wise, most victorious, most merciful (*sapientissimus, victoriosissimus, clementissimus*). On a visit to Paris, Henry III invited Louis IX to a banquet in a room hung with shields, among them Richard's shield, and was jokingly accused of discourtesy. Below that shield how could the French dine except trembling with remembered fear?[24] The design on the shield shown on Richard's second seal is the one which ever since then has been the royal coat of arms.[25] Nothing more graphically illustrates the point that it was Richard who became the model of English kingship. In a poem purporting to be written during Richard's lifetime – but probably a *post factum* exercise in prophecy – Geoffrey of Vinsauf begins by addressing England: 'Queen of kingdoms while King Richard lives, whose glory spreads afar a mighty name, you to whom is left the world's dominion, your position is secure under so great a helmsman.... Your king is the star with whose radiance you shine; the pillar whose support gives you strength; the lightning which you send against foes', etc. etc.[26]

A line in a poem composed early in the reign of Edward I, 'Behold he shines like a new Richard', shows that it was Richard who set the standard to which kings were expected to aspire.[27] Equally he was the standard by

round while Philip was still at Acre, helping him to make up his mind to go home, Runciman, *History*, iii, 52. But for the unreliability and late date of this source, see P. W. Edbury, 'The Lyon *Eracles* and the Old French Continuations of William of Tyre', in *Montjoie: Studies in Crusade History in Honour of Hans Eberhard Mayer*, ed. B. Keder, J. Riley-Smith and R. Hiestand (Aldershot, 1997).

[23] Coggeshall, 92; *Chron.*, iv, 62–3.

[24] *Chron. Maj.*, ii, 354; iii, 213; v, 478f.

[25] A. Ailes, *The Origins of the Royal Arms of England* (Reading, 1982).

[26] The translation here is based on that in *Poetria Nova of Geoffrey of Vinsauf*, trans. M. F. Nims (Toronto, 1967), 28–31. For Geoffrey's more famous lament on Richard's death see below, 321.

[27] *Thomas Wright's Political Songs of England*, ed. P. Coss (Cambridge, 1996), 128.

which they might be adjudged to have fallen short. The author of the *Life of Edward II* wrote:

> For our King Edward has now reigned six full years and has till now achieved nothing praiseworthy or memorable. How differently began King Richard's reign: before the end of his third year he had scattered far and wide the rays of his valour. In one day he took Messina, a city of Sicily, by force, and he subdued the land of Cyprus in a fortnight. Then how he bore himself at Acre and in other foreign parts history vividly relates in the Latin and French tongues. Oh! If only our King Edward had borne himself so well![28]

In the *Short Metrical Chronicle* Edward I's failure to make good his vow to go on crusade is contrasted with his predecessor's achievement; Acre fell in 1291, exactly one hundred years after Richard had captured it. By this date Richard had come to represent the English nation, a man whose wars were demonstrations of English superiority over other nations, especially the French.[29] Yet although the wars launched by Edward I led to a jaundiced view being taken of kings of England in fourteenth-century Scotland, Richard's reputation survived. In the words of John of Fordun, he was 'that noble king so friendly to the Scots' in whose reign there was 'so hearty a union between the two countries ... that the two peoples were reckoned one and the same'.[30]

Indeed it was a Scottish historian, John Major, who in 1521 was the first to date the activities of Robin Hood and Little John to 1193–4 when Richard was in captivity on his way back from crusade.[31] Although other dates for Robin Hood had already been suggested or implied, this was the one which caught on, probably because Richard was himself a legend, as much a figure of romance as of history. According to a fourteenth-century English romance, itself based on a now lost thirteenth-century French version, Richard was capable of reaching down a lion's throat and tearing out its heart.[32] Hence in Shakespeare's *King John* (Act I Scene i), when Lady Faulconbridge tells her son Philip that his father was not her hus-

---

[28] *Vita Edwardi Secundi*, ed. N. Denholm-Young (Edinburgh, 1957), 39–40.

[29] For discussion of this, and for Richard as a patriotic leader of the 'doughty knights of England', a king who in Sicily builds a siege-castle 'of timber made in England', see T. Turville-Petre, *England the Nation. Language, Literature and National Identity, 1290–1340* (Oxford, 1996), 120–4, 130–1.

[30] John of Fordun, *Cronica Gentis Scotorum*, ed. and trans. W. F. and F. H. Skene (Edinburgh, 1871), ii, 269–71.

[31] J. Major, *Historia maioris Britanniae* (1521), trans. A. Constable, *A History of Greater Britain* (Scottish History Society, x, 1892), 156–7.

[32] *Der mittelenglische Versroman über Richard Löwenherz*, ed. K. Brunner (Vienna, 1913), ll. 880–1,100. See below, 263.

band but King Richard, Philip, the play's hero, sees no cause to blame his mother:

> Madam, I would not wish a better father ...
> He that perforce robs lions of their hearts
> May easily win a woman's.[33]

As Philip Faulconbridge's sentiments indicate, sixteenth-century historians continued to regard Richard as a great king. Polydore Vergil, though writing in self-consciously humanist Latin, was entirely medieval in his praise of Richard's qualities as a ruler and man, commenting that if some thought him proud that was just his greatness of spirit. Holinshed followed Vergil closely and commended Richard as 'a notable example to all princes'.[34] John Foxe, despite his violently anti-papal stance, approved of the crusade and praised him not only as a great warrior but also as a noble, forgiving, bounteous and witty individual.[35] Early in James I's reign John Speed saw Richard as 'a noble prince, of judgement, of a sharp and search-ing wit' whose rule 'showed his love and care of the English nation as also of Justice itself'. He lamented 'the fatal accident which brought the black cloud of death over this triumphal and bright shining star of chivalry' and prevented him returning to Jerusalem, 'for which all Christendom hath at this hour reason to be sorrowful'.[36]

The first to dissent from the opinion which had dominated English historical writing for more than 400 years and to begin the work of establishing a new orthodoxy was the courtier-poet and historian, Samuel Daniel. In his brilliant *Collection of the Historie of England* – in my view the first great history of medieval England – he wrote of Richard that 'he exacted and consumed more of this kingdom than all his predecessors from the Normans had done before him, and yet deserved less than any, having neither lived here, neither left behind him any monument of piety or of any other public work, or ever showed love or care to this Commonwealth, but only to get what he could get from it'. Although he considered Richard undeserving except for his valour, he acknowledged that he 'got the opinion and love of his subjects in such sort as they strain even beyond their ability to recover and preserve him'.

---

[33] For an analysis of this play's image of model king and model subject see O. de Laborderie, 'Du Souvenir à la réincarnation: l'image de Richard Coeur de Lion dans la *Vie et Mort du Roi Jean* de William Shakespeare', in Nelson, *Coeur de Lion*, 141–65.

[34] Polydore Vergil, *Anglicae Historiae*, Liber xiv (1649 edn), 340; R. Holinshed, *The Chronicles of England, Scotland and Ireland* (London, 1807, reprint of 1586 edn), 266, 270–1.

[35] John Foxe, *Acts and Monuments* ii, part 1 (1854 edn), 302–3, 317, 319.

[36] John Speed, *The Historie of Great Britain* (London, 1611), 473, 477, 481.

Never had prince more given with less ado and less noise than he. The reason whereof was his undertaking the Holy warres, and the cause of Christ, with his suffering therein; and that made the clergie, which then might do all, to deny him nothing: and the people, fed with the report of his miraculous valour, horrible incounters in his voyage abroad, (and then some victorie in France) were brought to bear more than otherwise they would have done.

Daniel was much too good a historian not to realize that in his judgement on Richard I, in claiming to see through contemporary opinion to the 'historical truth' that lay concealed behind it, he was simultaneously at his most original and at his most anachronistic. So, in a remarkable passage, he immediately apologized to the past for taking such liberties with it. 'Pardon us, Antiquity, if we miscensure your actions, which are ever (as those of men) according to the vogue and sway of times, and have only their upholding by the opinion of the present: we deal with you but as posterity will with us (which ever thinks itself the wiser) that will judge likewise of our errors according to the cast of their imaginations.'[37]

Earlier, in the 1590s, Daniel had lavished praise on Richard I.[38] Why then did he now knowingly adopt the anachronistic approach which he had condemned when he saw it practised by others? As he was a courtier attached to the queen's privy chamber, writing his history between 1612 and 1618 and dedicating this part of it to Anne of Denmark, 'it being for the most part done under your roof during my attendance upon your sacred person', it seems likely that his new criticism of Richard was in part a reflection of arguments current at court at the time. James I, in debt, was resisting those influential voices urging him to become the leader of a continental Protestant 'crusade' against Spain. Daniel's criticism of Richard for gathering mighty treasures with 'tyrannical severity' in England only to consume them in projects abroad was one which suited the interests of James I's court.

Naturally so radical a reinterpretation of England's most heroic king, the one whose reputation was most deeply embedded in legend, did not at once carry all before it. Sir Richard Baker, for example, in 1641 still saw Richard as 'valiant, wise, liberal, merciful, just and which is most of all, religious. A prince born for the good of Christendom'.[39] None the less several changes allowed Daniel's line to become the standard one. Setting aside

---

[37] S. Daniel, *The Collection of the Historie of England* (London, 1621), 101–2, 107. I do not, of course, mean that no English historian before Daniel had ever found anything to criticize in Richard. I do mean that he was the first to take a fundamentally negative view of the king.

[38] In the first edition of his *Civile Wars* he praised Richard for his conquests and for bringing England out of 'raw and wailing infancy' into the first strength of youth, Daniel *Collected Works* 5 vols, ed. A. B. Grosart (London, 1885–96) ii, 16–17.

[39] R. Baker, *A Chronicle of the Kings of England* (London, 1641), 67.

contemporary opinion became much easier once the Protestant Reformation allowed John Foxe to write that 'scarcely any testimony is to be taken of that age, being all blinded and corrupted with superstition'. Crusading gradually went out of fashion in Protestant England. By 1639 Thomas Fuller could write that 'superstition not only tainted the rind but rotted the core of this whole action'.[40] Fuller's comment that Richard was 'more prodigal of his person than beseemed a general' took on an increasingly critical edge the more unusual it became for army commanders to take part in battles themselves. Similarly his view that as a result of ordering the massacre at Acre Richard 'suffered much in his repute' was a portent of modern opinion.[41] As Richard's virtues as a crusading king who, unlike modern commanders, was willing to risk his own life as well as those of his soldiers, came to be less and less appreciated, so Daniel's innovative perception of him as a king who neglected his kingdom and wasted its resources abroad was all the more readily taken up. By 1675, after some rehabilitation of Richard III, Sir Winston Churchill could describe Richard I as 'the worst of all the Richards we had', 'an ill son, an ill father, an ill brother and a worse king'; 'that which renders him most unworthy the affections of his subjects was not only making himself a Stranger to them, but leaving them to be governed by a Stranger'.[42] This line was followed by the most influential eighteenth-century historians. Laurence Echard emphasized the motif of a king who was never there.[43] Paul Rapin could find in Richard no other virtue than 'a brutish fierceness' which together with an insatiable love of money, pride and lust meant that England 'where he never was above 8 months during the whole course of his reign was very unhappy under his government'.[44] Inevitably David Hume, for whom the crusades were 'the most signal and most durable monument of human folly that has yet appeared in any age or nation', had no sympathy for the greatest of English crusaders. While admitting that 'the English pleased themselves with the glory which the king's martial genius procured them', he none the less concluded that Richard's 'impetuous and vehement spirit' was 'better calculated to dazzle men by the splendour of his enter-

---

[40] Cited in C. Tyerman, *England and the Crusades 1095–1588* (Chicago, 1988), 5. See ibid., 341–70 for a fine analysis of the waning of the crusading ideal in England.

[41] T. Fuller, *The Historie of the Holy Warre* (3rd edn, Cambridge, 1647), 123, 127.

[42] W. Churchill, *Divi Britannici* (London, 1675), 215–16. There he retained Daniel's consciousness of judging the past by present standards – 'however Posterity has forbore to blur his Memory, yet the present Age has no such cause to admire him'.

[43] 'Tho' he had many noble Qualifications yet England suffered severely under his Government, through the constant occasions he had for money, and the great rapacity of his Justiciaries during his absence from England, where he never spent above 8 months of his whole reign', L. Echard, *The History of England* (London, 1707), 229.

[44] Paul Rapin de Thoyras, *History of England* (London, 1732), 257.

prises, than either to promote their happiness or his own grandeur by a sound and well-regulated policy'.[45] And it was Hume's interpretation which was to remain the orthodoxy for the next 200 years. Even Sir Walter Scott would sum up Richard's reign as 'furnishing themes for bards and minstrels but affording none of those solid benefits to his country on which history loves to pause'. The perception of Richard as a king who neglected his kingdom came to be so powerful that the early twentieth-century historians who worked in most detail on his reign, Kate Norgate and Maurice Powicke, challenged it only by implication. The 'Little England' view of Richard was summed up by A.L. Poole in the Oxford History of England. 'He used England as a bank on which to draw and overdraw in order to finance his ambitious exploits abroad.'[46] A biography published in 1974 acknowledged that 'judged by the standards of his own times and own class of knightly rulers and warriors, Richard was indeed a fine monarch and a very great man, for he exemplified virtues which they most admired and for them his vices and failings lay in areas of minor importance' but it then went on to assert that the clergy and bourgeoisie of the time thought differently. 'The clergy deplored Richard's moral failures; the bourgeoisie were appalled by the insanity of his fiscal policy.'[47] Even children who in the 1950s still played at 'being' Richard the Lionheart in games in school playgrounds had to be put right. 'Richard was not a good king. He cared only for his soldiers.'[48]

This negative judgement still remains the view of late twentieth-century pundits who wish to shape popular opinion.[49] For example in a short article on 'The Evergreen Role of Robin Hood', Barry Norman pointed out that the cinema 'presents R. Hood as superhero by insisting that Richard the Lionheart, whom he supported, was a good thing while Prince John was a thoroughly bad egg. In fact Richard was a rotten monarch ... while John, though admittedly a touch careless with the Crown Jewels in the Wash, was probably a better king than his brother.'[50] As this suggests, the sixteenth-century invention of Richard's association with Robin Hood was in time to give powerful reinforcement to the notion of Richard as an

---

[45] History of England (as n. 4), 162, 279; W. Scott, Ivanhoe (London, 1933), 455.

[46] A.L. Poole, From Domesday Book to Magna Carta (2nd edn, Oxford, 1955), 350.

[47] Brundage, Richard Lionheart, 263. Brundage took the view that 'modern academic historians are much more likely to be sympathetic to the reservations felt by the clergy and the merchants'.

[48] L. Du Garde Peach, Richard the Lionheart (Ladybird History Book, London, 1965), 46. For the playground scene, A. Bridge, Richard the Lionheart (London, 1989), 244.

[49] I set out to challenge that perception with my Richard the Lionheart (1978, 2nd edn, 1989); I like to think with some success. However by focusing there on Richard as duke of Aquitaine and on his involvement in French politics, I in effect side-stepped, rather than tackled head on, the popular perception of him as a king of England who went on crusade.

[50] Radio Times, 15–21 February, 1997.

absentee king, with Robin as the people's champion protecting them against oppression – doing, in other words, what the king ought to have been doing. Above all else, this is the Hollywood Richard. Indeed Errol Flynn's Robin Hood (1938) was explicitly presented as 'the outlaw who showed Richard his duty to his country'. In Walt Disney's *Robin Hood* (1973), going on crusade is 'crazy' and is explained as the consequence of a basically good Richard being hypnotized by Prince John's serpentine adviser Sir Hiss. And in the twentieth century the name 'Coeur de Lion' was no longer to be explained in terms of a strong right arm and a healthy appetite, but in terms of absenteeism. 'Whenever he returned to England he always set out again immediately for the Mediterranean and was therefore known as Richard Gare de Lyon.'[51]

Whatever we now think of going on crusade, the aim here is to study Richard as a twelfth-century ruler, as a king who depended for his successes and failures on the opinions of his contemporaries, on their assessment of whether or not he was living up to the expectations they had of him. Inevitably only the opinions of those who wrote them down are in some measure accessible to us. Often they were trying to shape opinion rather than merely reflect it. Thus central to this enquiry are two interrelated matters: Richard's reputation and the formation of the conflicting opinions that lay behind it.

[51] W. C. Sellar and R. J. Yeatman, *1066 and All That* (London, 1930), 23.

Chapter 2

THROUGH MUSLIM EYES

So fierce was the propaganda war against and for Richard within Western Christendom that, in a curious way, it is quite possible that the most detached judges of his character and abilities were opponents who belonged to an entirely different culture: Muslims, indifferent to this internal Christian struggle. No fewer than three contemporary Muslim historians, Imad al-Din, Baha al-Din and Ibn al-Athir, watched the struggle between Richard and Saladin with great interest. Two of them, Imad al-Din and Baha al-Din, were peculiarly well placed to assess the king of England's political personality. Attached to Saladin's headquarters staff, they were immersed in the day-to-day struggle to help their master formulate and execute diplomatic and military policy designed to defeat Richard. Baha al-Din in particular was very close to Saladin.[1] They had the best of all possible reasons to observe Richard's manoeuvres closely and assess him realistically. Is there any other king of England, any other medieval ruler of any country, whom we can see through the eyes of such well-informed observers on 'the other side of the hill'? Of course, as Saladin's admirers both Imad al-Din and Baha al-Din had good reason to present Richard as a formidable enemy. How else to explain their lord's defeats at Acre, Arsuf and Jaffa? But it might still be worth noticing just what it was they thought made him formidable. The stance of the third historian, Ibn al-Athir of Mosul, was quite different. He took a decidedly cool, sometimes critical, view of Saladin and for centuries has enjoyed the reputation of being one of the finest of Islamic historians.[2] Great champion of Islam Saladin

---

[1] Imad al-Din, as chancellor, was responsible for drafting treaties and for Saladin's official correspondence (hence his highly rhetorical style); not surprisingly his history is not as frank as Baha al-Din's. For example, Imad al-Din's comment on Richard's great victory in battle at Arsuf (see below, 177–8) was that had the Franks not been able to take shelter in the town they would have been destroyed, Imad al-Din, 344. Baha al-Din, however, made no attempt to conceal the scale of the defeat. He enjoyed a more confidential relationship with Saladin – as indeed on occasion he liked to make clear. For example: 'On that day' (22 September 1191) 'I too was seized by an indisposition that prevented me attending him throughout the whole day. In spite of the important matters he had on his mind, he sent three times during the day to inquire how I was', Baha al-Din, 299–300.
[2] H. A. R. Gibb, 'The Arabic Sources for the Life of Saladin', *Speculum*, xxv (1950), 58–72.

undoubtedly was, but in Ibn al-Athir's eyes he was also the schemer who had overthrown the Zengid dynasty of Mosul. Perhaps it was for this reason that he called Richard, not Saladin, 'the most remarkable man of the age'.[3] Here too there still remains the question: what was it about Richard that the historian of Mosul thought so remarkable?

Inevitably they saw him above all as a leader in war – in many respects as a Christian counterpart to Saladin. Thus it is necessary to read their views of Richard in the light of their presentation of Saladin. 'With him,' wrote Baha al-Din of Saladin, 'to wage war in God's name was a veritable passion; his whole heart was filled with it, and he gave body and soul to the cause. He spoke of nothing else; all his thoughts were of instruments of war; his soldiers monopolised every idea.'[4] As Richard approached the siege of Acre, this same author introduced him as 'a very powerful man among the Franks, a man of great courage and spirit. He had fought great battles and showed a burning passion for war.'[5] Then, when Richard disembarked at Acre, he commented on his 'extreme daring' as well as on his 'good judgement, wide experience, and insatiable ambition'.[6] Richard's modern biographers have often observed that even Muslims criticized his excessive daring. This is based on a conversation between Richard's trusted adviser, Hubert Walter, and Saladin himself. Hubert Walter praised Richard's prowess, chivalry and generosity:

> 'Sire, I say with pride
> That my lord is the finest knight
> On earth ...'
> The sultan heard the bishop through
> And answered: 'Well I know 'tis true
> That brave and noble is the king,
> But with what rashness doth he fling
> Himself! Howe'er great prince I be
> I should prefer to have in me
> Reason and moderation and largesse
> Than courage carried to excess.'[7]

---

[3] Ibn al-Athir, 43.

[4] Baha al-Din, 24; Gabrieli, 100. (When the passage cited is also in the extracts translated in Gabrieli's *Arab Historians of the Crusades* I shall generally cite the latter since it is much more widely available than other versions.) Of course in other passages Baha al-Din is at pains to emphasize that Saladin possessed many other and quite different qualities.

[5] Gabrieli, 213.

[6] Baha al-Din, 249. Regrettably I cannot read Arabic, so one of the shortcomings of this book is my reliance on translations from that language. For example, the words which Wilson translated as above were translated by Gabrieli as 'the King was indeed a man of wisdom, experience, courage and energy', Gabrieli, 214.

[7] Ambroise, 12, 134–52.

But this is an imaginary conversation composed by Ambroise: in other words, it is a comment from one of Richard's followers, not from a Muslim opponent. There is certainly good evidence that on occasion Richard's counsellors thought him excessively daring.[8] But did Muslims share this view?

It would be surprising if Saladin's admirers did. Baha al-Din portrays the sultan not only as a man with a burning passion for war, but also as one who possessed immense personal bravery. 'The Sultan was the bravest of the brave. When we were close upon the enemy the Sultan insisted on making a reconnaissance round their army once or twice every day. At the height of the fighting he used to pass between the lines of battle accompanied by a young page leading his horse.' On one occasion Saladin's advisers thought he was risking his own life all too readily. 'We tried to make him give up this project since he would have but a very small number of men with him while the Franks had all mustered at Tyre and thus he would be running great risk. The Sultan paid no heed to our remonstrances.' His answer to those who blamed him, 'the bulwark of Islam', for risking his own life, was: 'the worst that can befall me is the most noble of deaths'.[9] All three Muslim historians report a famous episode when Richard, out riding on patrol, almost fell into their hands. Only the sacrificial bravery of one of his followers, who persuaded their attackers that he, not Richard, was the king, saved him from being captured. Whether Richard was being too rash or not, they do not say. What they do make plain is his purpose in riding away from the safety of his main army. He had gone to protect the wood collectors and foragers, that is to defend those who had been assigned a duty that was both essential and, when enemy forces were nearby, very dangerous.[10]

On another occasion Baha al-Din portrays Richard riding out at night in order to reconnoitre the position of a major Muslim army. This was in June 1192 when Saladin, in Jerusalem, had sent for reinforcements and an army commanded by his half-brother was on its way from Egypt. If at all possible the junction of the two Muslim forces had to be prevented. When Richard was informed by Bedouins in his pay that the army of Egypt had camped for the night at an oasis where it was vulnerable to attack, 'he did not believe it; but he mounted and set out with the Bedouin and a small escort. When he came up to the caravan, he disguised himself as a Bedouin and went all around it, till he was satisfied that quiet reigned there and everyone was fast asleep.' He then launched a devastating dawn attack and routed the army meant to relieve Jerusalem. 'This was a most disgraceful

---

[8] Even that Richard boasted of going against their advice: see below, 316.

[9] Baha al-Din. 21–7; Gabrieli, 97–102.

[10] Baha al-Din, 302; Imad al-Din, 347 (and again some weeks later) 373; Ibn al-Athir, 52.

event,' wrote Baha al-Din. 'It was long since Islam had sustained so serious
a disaster. Never was the Sultan more grieved or rendered more anxious.'[11]
Whether or not Richard really did ride around the Egyptian camp at night
is not, in the context of his reputation in Muslim eyes, as important as the
fact that his enemies believed that this was the sort of thing he did. And
they believed this because he sometimes did.

Consider the events of 1 August 1192. Saladin had made an unexpected
advance and had captured the town of Jaffa; only the citadel still held out.
Richard's galleys arrived. What happened next is described by Baha al-Din,
himself – as he makes clear – in the thick of things. 'At daybreak we heard
the sound of Frankish trumpets. The sultan sent for me at once and said:
"Relief has come, it is true, by sea, but there is a strong enough force of
Muslim troops on the beach to prevent their landing." ' Saladin was wrong.
'As soon as the king heard that the citadel was still holding out he made all
speed for the shore, and his galley – it was painted red, its deck was covered
with red awning and was flying a red flag – was the first to land. In less than
an hour all the galleys had landed their men under my own eyes. They
then charged the Muslims, scattering them in all directions and driving
them out of the harbour. I galloped off to tell the Sultan.'[12] Saladin then
withdrew as far as Caesarea. Three days later, realizing that a night march
would give him an opportunity to take Richard by surprise while the latter
still had very few troops with him, he retraced his steps.

> He resumed his march that same evening, pushed on until daybreak,
> and appeared unexpectedly before Jaffa. The king of England was
> encamped outside the walls of the city, and had only seventeen knights
> with him and about 300 footsoldiers. At the first alarm this accursed man
> mounted his horse, for he was brave and fearless, and possessed excel-
> lent judgement in military matters. Instead of retiring into the city,[13] he
> maintained his position in face of the Moslem troops who surrounded
> him on all sides except towards the sea, and drew up his own men in
> order of battle. The sultan, anxious to make the most of this
> opportunity, gave the order to charge. But the Franks displayed such
> determination in the face of death that our troops lost heart, and
> contented themselves with surrounding the camp though at some
> distance from it. I was not at this fight, being ill and staying behind with
> the baggage, but I learned from a man who was there that they had at
> most seventeen horsemen – some counted only nine – and perhaps as
> few as three hundred infantry, though some say a thousand or more.
> The sultan was furious and went from squadron to squadron, promising

---

[11] Baha al-Din, 343–5. See below for a fuller narrative, 207.
[12] Baha al-Din, 368–70.
[13] The point being that he had too few men with him to be able to hold the walls.

rich rewards if they would return to the charge, but no one responded. When the sultan saw the temper of his men, he realised he could not possibly stay there, outfaced by a handful of men, for that would have been a grievous blow to his reputation. So he left the battlefield in anger. I have been assured by men who were there that on that day the king of England, lance in hand, rode along the whole length of our army from right to left, and not one of our soldiers left the ranks to attack him.[14]

What these two incidents reveal is that Richard's daring was a potent weapon. In June 1192 it had enabled him to get good, precise information; in August it instilled fear. In these stories the Richard of legend appears – a legend in his lifetime, a legend in the minds of his enemies.[15]

They did not fear, however, only his soldierly qualities. They feared also his political and diplomatic skills. 'See the cunning of this accursed man. To obtain his own ends he would employ first force and then smooth speaking. God alone could protect the Muslims against his wiles; we never had among our enemies a man bolder or more crafty than he.' According to Imad al-Din, 'each time that he concluded a pact he broke it, each time he gave his word, he wriggled out of it, each time we told ourselves "he will be true", he betrayed us'.[16] But what emerges very clearly from the narratives of Imad al-Din and Baha al-Din – something that the image of the legendary Richard does not lead us to expect – is that throughout his stay in Palestine it was Richard who initiated the talks. He was the one who was constantly seeking diplomatic contacts. He sent envoy after envoy to Saladin's camp. He was, seemingly, as keen to talk about peace as to make war. Obviously the negotiations were sometimes as much for the furtherance of war as of peace. More than once the Muslims were convinced that Richard was negotiating only in order to gain time. 'We', wrote Baha al-Din, 'were afraid that these talks were like the former ones – nothing but a means employed by the king to gain time – and by this time we were well acquainted with his methods'.[17] This was a game the Muslims understood perfectly well; after all they played it themselves often enough. Equally both sides knew that one of the purposes of the peace talks was information. 'The object of these frequent visits from the ambassador was to ascertain the state of our spirits, and to learn whether we were inclined to resist or give way; we on our side were induced to

[14] Baha al-Din, 36, 375–6. Ibn al-Athir heard a story of Richard coolly taking a meal in full view of the Muslim army, 64.

[15] It is true that Saladin's troops were already in a sullen mood when they refused to charge at Jaffa. This, however, only emphasizes the double importance of troop morale and the contribution which stories of this sort made to its maintenance or its undermining.

[16] Baha al-Din, 359; Imad al-Din, 354.

[17] Baha al-Din, 383–7. I.e. his methods of gaining time.

receive the enemy's messages by the very same motive that prompted them.'[18]

Even so it is striking that it was consistently Richard who took the initiative, and who put forward new proposals. In June 1191, soon after his arrival at Acre, Richard sent an envoy to Saladin. 'A messenger came to us with the following message: It is the custom of kings when they happen to be near one another to send each other mutual presents and gifts. Now I have in my possession a gift worthy the sultan's acceptance, and I ask permission to send it to him.'[19] From then on the exchange of gifts became common.[20] Richard's uncertain health – he suffered from malarial fever – played a part in this. In Baha al-Din's words, 'the king constantly sent messengers to the sultan for fruit and snow, for all the while he was ill he had a great longing for pears and peaches. The sultan always sent him some, hoping by means of these frequent messages to obtain the information of which he stood in need.'[21]

More remarkable still was an aspect of Richard's diplomatic style which clearly took them aback. On 18 June 1191 (ten days after his arrival at Acre) an envoy arrived in the Muslim camp 'to express the king of England's desire for an interview with the sultan'. Saladin refused. 'It is not customary for kings to meet, unless they have previously laid the foundations of a treaty; for after they have spoken together and given one another the tokens of mutual confidence that are natural in such circumstances, it is not seemly for them to make war upon one another. It is therefore absolutely essential that the preliminaries should be arranged first of all.'[22] Richard asked for a 'summit meeting' again in November 1191; again in vain.[23] But what Richard did get was a number of meetings

---

[18] Baha al-Din, 257.

[19] Ibid., 256–7. Saladin's brother, al-Adil, accepted on the sultan's behalf, 'provided he will accept a gift of equal value from us'.

[20] King Philip also received gifts from Saladin, though only when he was on his way back to France and Saladin wanted to find out something about his plans do the sultan's biographers think it worth mentioning, Baha al-Din, 271; Imad al-Din, 328. According to Roger of Howden, during the siege of Acre Saladin 'frequently sent the kings of England and France pears from Damascus, plenty of other local fruits, and other small gifts in the hope of persuading them to make peace', Gesta, ii, 171; Chron., iii, 114. Howden did not reach Acre until July, by which time the pattern initiated by Richard was established.

[21] Baha al-Din, 379. There is a marked contrast between Richard's keenness to obtain food and drink from them and King Philip's fear of poison.

[22] In November 1191 Saladin also drew attention to the difficulty of finding an interpreter trusted by both sides, Baha al-Din, 252, 351; Imad al-Din, 309.

[23] In fact a meeting between Richard and Saladin never took place, though in June 1191 one may have been close, Baha al-Din, 256, 321. It is not surprising that Baha al-Din's tone is one of surprise. In the negotiations of 1191–2 Richard made proposals of a kind never before seen in Frankish–Muslim relations. See M. A. Köhler, *Allianzen und Verträge zurischen fränkischen und islamischen Herrschem im Vorderen Orient* (Berlin, 1991), 354.

with al-Adil, Saladin's brother, his most influential and trusted adviser (and, thanks to his political skills, his successor). The first of these meetings took place on 5 September 1191. On this occasion al-Adil rejected Richard's proposals with scorn.[24] In the weeks that followed Richard negotiated through al-Adil whom he referred to as 'my friend and brother'.[25] On 8 November they met again. 'When the king of England came to visit him in his tent, he met with the most honourable reception at his hands; then the king took him to his quarters and had a repast served consisting of such dishes peculiar to his country as he thought would be most agreeable to his palate. Al-Adil partook of them, and the king and his suite ate of the dishes provided by al-Adil.' The latter 'had brought with him all sorts of dainties and delicacies, various kinds of drinks and beautiful gifts and presents fit for one prince to offer another. They parted from one another with mutual assurances of perfect goodwill and sincere affection.'[26] According to Imad al-Din, 'they talked quietly together for a long time' before Richard left, accompanied – and it is a point worth noting – by al-Adil's secretary.[27] They did not meet again until September 1192, when peace was finally concluded. Then al-Adil came to Jaffa, and though Richard was very ill, he insisted on seeing him.[28]

Another Muslim with whom, according to Baha al-Din, Richard took the trouble to get closely acquainted was al-Adil's chamberlain, Abu Bekr. At one stage Abu Bekr gave Saladin the gist of a private conversation he had had with Richard – what had been said 'when he had happened to be alone with the king'.[29] In their study of Saladin, Lyons and Jackson noted that Richard 'throughout his stay on the Coast was conspicuous for the contacts that he made with individual Muslims'.[30] An episode which illustrates this more vividly than any other took place on the afternoon of 1 August 1192 – within a few hours of his daring landing on the beach at Jaffa. Richard invited Abu Bekr and other leading Muslims to visit him. They found him in the company of several of the prisoners taken at Acre, high-ranking Mamelukes 'who were treated with great cordiality by the king, and whom he often summoned to his presence. He spoke half seriously and half in jest. Among other things he said: "This sultan is mighty, and there is none mightier than him in the land of Islam. Why then did he run away as soon as I appeared? By God I was not even properly armed for a fight. See, I am still wearing my sea boots." Then again he said: "Great and good God, I did not think he could have taken Jaffa in two months, and yet he did it in two

---

[24] Baha al-Din, 287; Imad al-Din, 339–40.
[25] Baha al-Din, 304, 307–8, 310–11; Imad al-Din, 378.
[26] Baha al-Din, 320.
[27] Imad al-Din, 353.
[28] Baha al-Din, 384.
[29] Ibid., 371–2, 377–80.
[30] Lyons and Jackson, 351-52.

days." '[31] What is striking here is the tone which Richard, even at such a juncture, is said to have adopted: half serious and half in jest. Teasing Saladin about the events of the morning, teasing himself for underestimating Saladin earlier. In fact the evidence suggests that this was the tone which Richard struck from the outset of his negotiations. Hence Baha al-Din's report that when Richard first suggested an exchange of gifts, al-Adil 'who knew full well what tone to take, replied jokingly'.[32] This is the context for Richard's most famous peace proposal – the scheme for a marriage between al-Adil and his sister Joan. Somewhat to the surprise of his advisers Saladin accepted the proposal at once. But Baha al-Din explains why: 'he knew it was nothing but mockery and trickery on his part'. When Joan refused to marry a Muslim, Richard suggested that al-Adil might like to become a Christian. Doubtless more jesting, but also, in Baha al-Din's judgement: 'By this means he left the door open for future negotiations.'[33] That Richard so often sought to meet his enemies face to face suggests a man confident of the force of his own personality, of his ability to speak persuasively, of his diplomatic skill at high-level meetings.

But the evidence, above all from Baha al-Din, of the relaxed and even friendly relations between Richard and some of Saladin's counsellors and lieutenants also creates a problem. How then are we to understand the accusations of perfidy? In part, no doubt, they regarded him as perfidious, because he was a Frank and that is what all Franks were: masters of perfidy.[34] In part also, no doubt, because the stereotype was quickly confirmed by two events that occurred early in the crusade. The first was Richard's occupation of Cyprus. It was difficult to explain how he could have conquered the island so quickly except, perhaps, by deceiving and capturing its ruler.[35] The second, and much more important, event was the massacre of so many of the prisoners taken when Acre surrendered. There can be little doubt that one of the root causes of this catastrophe was mutual distrust.[36] Both these events preceded Richard's first meeting with al-Adil. Presumably one intended outcome of the face-to-face meetings made at his request was the creation of trust where none had existed before. As

[31] Baha al-Din, 371–2.

[32] Ibid., 257.

[33] Ibid., 304, 307–8, 310–11. Indeed since these joky marriage proposals involved discussion of the territorial endowment of the happy couple they proved to be a helpful point of entry for further and ultimately successful negotiations.

[34] See, e.g., Ibn al-Athir, 46–7. Ibn al-Athir also says that Conrad feared Richard's perfidy, 51. However it seems they decided that Richard was less perfidious than Conrad of Montferrat (see below, 187).

[35] Imad al-Din, 292; and, following him, Ibn al-Athir, 43. However, Baha al-Din's brief references to the conquest of Cyprus do not mention deceit. Indeed in general Baha al-Din is much less insistent on Richard's perfidy than Imad al-Din.

[36] Of course another root cause was the relative Christian indifference to Muslim loss of life. For more detailed consideration of this, see below, 170.

Saladin, before any such meeting had taken place, had commented: 'tokens of mutual confidence are natural in such circumstances'. Richard worked hard to maintain an atmosphere of mutual confidence. 'Incessantly he assured us of his friendship for al-Adil and of the sincerity of his feelings,' wrote Imad al-Din; but Saladin's chancellor, always more suspicious than Baha al-Din, was not convinced. For him such messages were 'the arrows of felony and perfidy'.[37] But at times the Muslims responded with similar language. 'Since you trust us with such trust, and since one good turn deserves another, the sultan will treat your sister's son like one of his own sons' was a message which went from Saladin to Richard in July 1192.[38] At least there were no further massacres.

Doubtless Richard's cultivation of these contacts with the Muslim world was primarily the result of political calculation. It would be impossible to demonstrate that the warlike crusader was also genuinely interested in Muslim culture. Two episodes mentioned only in Muslim sources are, however, at least worth mentioning for the light they throw on perceptions of his character. The loot captured when Richard overwhelmed the Egyptian army in that dawn attack included notes made by the geographer and traveller, al-Harawi. On discovering that these notes did not contain any military secrets Richard might have been expected to destroy them as useless gibberish. Instead he had the author identified and sent him a personal message saying that if he visited the crusaders his property would be returned. The invitation was not accepted; this was one initiative which Richard took which led nowhere.[39] Then there was, according to Ibn al-Athir, a feature of the meeting with al-Adil on 8 November 1191 which recalls Richard's own reputation as a troubadour. The king 'asked al-Adil if he could arrange for him to hear some Arabic singing. Al-Adil had a woman brought before him who accompanied herself on the guitar. She sang before the king of England – and to his great satisfaction.'[40]

The friendly relations between Richard and leading Muslims, the attempt to create trust, had the effect of creating distrust between him and his fellow-crusaders. As Baha al-Din discovered, when Richard first proposed a meeting with Saladin, 'the Frankish princes in a body expressed strong disapproval, on the ground that it would imperil the Christian cause'.[41] This observation is fully borne out by Christian sources. Indeed for all his heroic and – at the time – world-renowned deeds of war, the openness of Richard's contacts with the Muslim world was to provide fertile ground for the rumour and innuendo which would be used to justify his subsequent capture and imprisonment by his co-religionists.

[37] Imad al-Din, 378.
[38] Baha al-Din, 355.
[39] Lyons and Jackson, 351–2.
[40] Ibn al-Athir, 53. In the French translation 'guitare'.
[41] Baha al-Din, 256.

Chapter 3

AQUITAINE, 1157–72

The political personality of the ruler who so impressed the Muslims had been very largely shaped in France, above all in Aquitaine, the land of his mother, Eleanor of Aquitaine, where Richard had spent most of his youth and where he had been duke since 1172. Since his father, King Henry II, was a Frenchman from Anjou it was necessary to go a long way back in Richard's family tree to find an English ancestor – to one of his great-grandmothers, Edith, the wife of King Henry I. This English link, slight as it was, was none the less well known to the men who frequented the princely courts of Europe, for in their world family connection was all-important. It shaped the destinies not just of individuals but of entire provinces and kingdoms. One contemporary student of these matters, the learned historian Ralph of Diceto, dean of St Paul's, traced Richard's ancestry through Edith to the Anglo-Saxon kings of Wessex, the line of Alfred the Great and Cerdic, and then, through them, back to Woden and Noah.[1] But remarkable though his English forefathers were, with the old Germanic god of war among their number, they seem to have meant little to Richard himself – and this despite the fact that he was born in England, on 8 September 1157 at Oxford, presumably in the royal palace of Beaumont. When he jokingly referred to the story that he was descended from the devil he meant no disrespect to his ancestor Woden. He was refer-ring to an Angevin legend, a version of the story of Mélusine. She was a lady of unearthly beauty who married a count of Anjou and bore him four chil-dren. Everything about her and about her marriage seemed to be perfect, apart from one disquieting fact: she hated going into churches and she absolutely refused to be present at the consecration of the Host. Jealous voices reminded the count of this again and again; eventually he decided to put her to the test. He summoned her to attend church and then, at the moment of consecration, just as she was about to leave, four armed men stopped her. But as they seized her by the mantle, she shook it from her shoulders, folded two of her children in her arms and floated away through a window, never more to be seen by her husband and the two children she had left behind.[2] The point is that Richard's closest family

[1] Diceto, i, 299.
[2] Gerald, *Princ.*, 301.

associations, whether real or legendary, were with western France and not with England or Normandy.

Few weddings can have had so dramatic a political effect as that between Richard's parents. It was to have consequences which dominated much of his adult life. It took place in May 1152, just eight weeks after Eleanor's first marriage, to King Louis VII of France, had been annulled. Since she had inherited the vast duchy of Aquitaine, covering something like one-third of the area of modern France, she brought a tremendous accession of wealth and prestige to her new husband.[3] Very naturally, Louis was alarmed and angered by Eleanor's choice. Henry was already count of Anjou and duke of Normandy. He had inherited Anjou from his father, Geoffrey Plantagenet.[4] Normandy had come to him via his mother Matilda. Married to Eleanor, and ruling Aquitaine as her husband, he would be considerably more powerful than the king of France himself. Even though as count and duke he owed allegiance to the king, for Louis this was an uncomfortable prospect, an inversion of the right order of things.[5] The fact that Henry as grandson of King Henry I also had a strong claim to the throne of England only made Louis's alarm the greater. After the divorce he had continued to style himself duke of Aquitaine, and to regard his ex-wife as his ward. But she was a thirty-year-old woman, duchess in her own right and, to the chagrin of her ex-husband, she pleased herself. Two years later King Stephen of England was persuaded to recognize Henry as his heir, and in December 1154 he was crowned king at Westminster. He was now the most powerful ruler in Europe, richer even than the emperor, and completely overshadowing his nominal lord, the king of France. While Eleanor and Louis had been married, it had been King Louis who was by far the greatest figure in the kingdom. Why then had he decided to divorce her?

They had been married in 1137 when her father, Duke William X of Aquitaine, had died suddenly, and without sons, while on a pilgrimage to

[3] The best study of Eleanor is J. Martindale, 'Eleanor of Aquitaine', in Nelson, *Coeur de Lion*, 17–50; repr. in Martindale, *Status, Authority and Regional Power* (Aldershot, 1997). Also useful are the essays in *Eleanor of Aquitaine: Patron and Politician*, ed. W. W. Kibler (Austin, Texas, 1976), especially that by E. A. R. Brown, 'Eleanor of Aquitaine: Parent, Queen and Duchess'.

[4] Although there is near-contemporary warrant for the name 'Plantagenet' applied to Geoffrey – *Chroniques des comtes d'Anjou*, ed. L. Halphen and R. Poupardin (Paris, 1913), 170 – its use as a family name goes back no further than the fifteenth century, and the story of the 'sprig of broom' is much later still.

[5] Helpful for setting the general political scene in France at this period are J. Dunbabin, *France in the Making 843–1180* (Oxford, 1985), E. M. Hallam, *Capetian France 987–1328* (London, 1980) and K. F. Werner, 'Kingdom and Principalities in Twelfth-Century France', in *The Medieval Nobility*, ed. and trans. T. Reuter (Amsterdam, 1979); S. Reynolds, *Fiefs and Vassals* (Oxford, 1994), ch. 7 'The Kingdom of France 1100–1300'; G. Duby, *France in the Middle Ages* (Oxford, 1991).

Compostella. Eleanor's uncle Raymond, count of Tripoli, was ruler of one of the crusader-states and too far away either to help her or to threaten to take her inheritance for himself. It was a sensible alliance for a fifteen-year-old heiress deprived of a father's or an uncle's protection. Moreover contemporaries believed that, as a husband, Louis VII gave her love as well as protection. But as time went by the marriage turned sour. Louis became an extremely devout and ascetic man. The story went around that once, when he was seriously ill, he was advised by his doctors that it would improve his chances of survival if he were to sleep with a woman. An attractive young lady was taken to him but Louis would have nothing to do with her, saying that he would rather die than commit the sin of adultery, even for medicinal purposes only.[6] Eleanor, on the other hand, was said to be beautiful and lively; she was certainly headstrong and, at Antioch, indiscreet. Whether or not there was any truth in them, the fact remains that rumours about her affairs became common gossip. In time they reached legendary, almost Messalina-like proportions. She, wrote Michelet, was the real Mélusine.[7] Not surprisingly she is said to have complained that Louis was more like a monk than a king.[8]

That the two were incompatible was clear by the late 1140s but this of itself would not have brought about the annulment.[9] The principal function of marriage was to produce heirs and this their marriage had failed to do. After an early miscarriage she bore Louis just two children in fourteen years, and both of them were girls. Despite Eleanor's own history, the lesson to be learned from recent events in England and Normandy was that it was virtually impossible for a daughter to keep a hold on her inheritance. If Louis VII were to prevent a repetition of Stephen's reign from happening in France then he needed sons. In 1154, after the clergy had put an end to his marriage to Eleanor, he married Constance of Castile. She too, however, bore only girls and then died, in childbirth, in 1160. The need for a male heir to the throne of France was now desperate and it took Louis only five weeks to find a third wife, Adela of Champagne. Eventually, in August 1165, a son was born. The mood of the Parisians, when they heard the news for which they had been waiting so long, was recalled years later by Gerald de Barri, then a student living in a rented room on the Île de la Cité. One warm summer's night, he was abruptly awoken when all the bells of the city began to peal. Through his window he could see the flickering light of flames. His first thought was that Paris was on fire – an

---

[6] Gerald, *Princ.*, 132. Also in Gerald, *Opera*, ii, 216–17.

[7] E-R. Labande, 'Pour une Image véridique d'Aliénor d'Aquitaine', *Bulletin de la société des antiquaires de l'ouest*, 4th series, ii (1952), 175.

[8] Newburgh, Bk 1, ch. 31.

[9] 'Love, Marriage and Politics in the Twelfth Century', in J. Gillingham, *Richard Coeur de Lion. Kingship, Chivalry and War in the Twelfth Century* (London, 1994), 251–2.

ever-present threat when wood was the chief building material. He rushed
to the window. But the fires were bonfires and the bells told not of danger
but of joy. The narrow streets were crowded and it was not long before
Gerald had discovered the cause of the exultant bedlam. 'By the grace of
God there is born to us this night a King who shall be a hammer to the
King of the English.' The child was given the name of Philip.[10] In the
course of time he and Richard were to become fellow-crusaders and bitter
enemies.

It is not difficult to imagine Louis VII's exasperation at the time of
Richard's birth in 1157, when he still had no son of his own. In fourteen years
Eleanor had not produced an heir to his kingdom, but in the first five years of
her second marriage she had had four children and three of them were boys:
William, who died in 1156, Henry and Richard. Altogether Henry II and
Eleanor had eight children, the last of whom, John, was born in 1167. Henry,
it was clear, was no monk. In 1157 he was a solidly built man of twenty-four,
twelve years younger than his wife. He was to be a great king, for thirty-five
years the master politician of Western Christendom, able to overwhelm or
outmanœuvre all his rivals. Only at the end, when in the grip of his last illness,
was he defeated. He was an intelligent and well-educated man who enjoyed
argument and conversation, whether in French or Latin. Hunting was an
important component of the aristocratic lifestyle, but few can have been
more addicted to the pursuit than Henry. He liked nothing better than to be
in the saddle and away before the crack of dawn.[11] He must often have been
seen plainly dressed in hard-wearing hunting clothes; yet one of his courtiers,
Walter Map, observed that 'he is always robed in precious stuffs, as is right'.[12]
He hated sitting still, and remained constantly on the move, restless and
seemingly tireless, preferring to call for needle and thread to mend his own
clothes rather than do nothing.[13] Walter Map attributed what increasingly
came to be felt, by Richard as well as by virtually everyone else, as the most
exasperating aspect of Henry's political style to his mother's teaching:

> He should spin out all the affairs of everyone, hold long in his own hand
> all posts that became vacant, collect the revenues of them, and keep
> aspirants to them hanging on in hope: and she supported this advice by
> an unkind parable: an unruly hawk, if meat is often offered to it and
> then snatched away or hid, becomes keener and more inclinably obedi-
> ent and attentive.[14]

[10] Gerald, *Princ.*, 292–3.
[11] For the view that so much hunting can have left Henry with neither time nor
energy for thinking and planning about government and law, see B. Lyon, 'Henry
II: A Non-Victorian Interpretation', in *Essays in Medieval History Presented to G. P.
Cuttino*, ed. J. S. Hamilton and P. Bradley (Woodbridge, 1989).
[12] Map, 116–17.
[13] *Magna Vita*, i, 113–19.
[14] Map, 478–9.

Since he ruled dominions stretching from England's border with Scotland in the north to the Pyrenees in the south, Henry II had to travel further and faster than most ruling princes. Despite the rumour that he could fly, all this really meant for Henry was that he was in the saddle so much that he suffered from sore legs.

It was inevitable that for Richard and his brothers and sisters their father was a distant figure, always in a hurry. It seems likely that as small children they stayed in the relative security of England while Henry spent most of his time abroad, immersed in what was always to be the central concern of his life: governing his continental dominions. In a letter written in the summer of 1160 Archbishop Theobald of Canterbury asked the king to return to England. Among other arguments he reminded Henry of his children. 'Even the most hard-hearted father could hardly bear to have them out of his sight for long.'[15] But the letter failed to achieve its object. Not until January 1163 did Henry again set foot in England, after an absence of four and a half years. There is not much, at this stage of his life, to suggest that Henry was fond of his children. In May 1165 the queen took Richard and his elder sister Matilda (born in 1156) to Normandy; a fortnight later King Henry crossed the Channel in the other direction, leaving his family behind while he mounted a major campaign, albeit an unsuccessful one, against the Welsh.[16] Everything about his later life shows that Richard was much closer to his mother than to his father. But Eleanor too had to travel a great deal, and in his earliest years it was almost certainly Richard's nurse who provided love and security on a day-to-day basis. Twelfth-century romances show that for a noblewoman to suckle her own child implied a quite exceptional degree of love. Richard was handed over to a wet-nurse called Hodierna and he seems to have remembered her with affection. More than thirty years later, when he became king, he granted her a generous pension.[17] She became a wealthy and, in her own part of the world, a famous woman – perhaps the only wet-nurse in history to have a place named after her: the Wiltshire parish of Knoyle Hodierne.[18]

As with all royal children, sons as well as daughters, one of Richard's chief functions in his parents' eyes was to undertake the role of a pawn in the diplomatic game: the game in which he would excel. Since diplomacy largely revolved around the family relationships of princely dynasties, chil-

---

[15] *Letters of John of Salisbury*, ed. W. J. Millor and H. E. Butler, i (London, 1955), no. 121. All attempts to get to grips with the question of relations between particular parents and particular children in this period are hampered by lack of evidence. Cf. R. V. Turner, 'Eleanor of Aquitaine and her Children: an Inquiry into Medieval Family Attachment', *JMH*, xiv (1988), 321–35.

[16] Torigny, 225. The sheriffs of London had met some expenses for Richard in 1163; PR 9 Henry II, 71.

[17] PR 2 Richard I, 118; PR 3–4 Richard I, 118, 281.

[18] Norgate, 2–3.

dren had to expect to be betrothed early – and occasionally even married early. In 1158 and 1159 two betrothals were made which were to have an influence on the rest of his life. The earlier of the two was the betrothal of his elder brother, Henry, to Margaret, Louis VII's first daughter by his second wife. At the time Henry was three years old while Margaret was still a baby. But she was old enough to be assigned a dowry, a stretch of land which lay between the rivers Seine, Epte and Andelle, known as the Norman Vexin. It was agreed that this would be handed over to the Angevins when the marriage itself took place. Until that date Louis was to retain the Norman Vexin while Margaret was to be kept in Henry's custody. In September 1158 Henry travelled to Paris and then took the little girl back to Normandy with him. The point of this betrothal was that the castles of the Vexin controlled communications between Paris and Rouen. Long ago the Vexin had been divided into two along the line of the river Epte: on the east bank the French Vexin held by the king of France, on the west the Norman Vexin held by the duke of Normandy. In 1145, however, Count Geoffrey of Anjou and his son Henry had granted the Norman Vexin to Louis VII in return for his acquiescence in their conquest of Normandy. Now Henry II wanted it back. Possession of its castles, Gisors, Neaufles, Dangu and a dozen others was essential if he was to sleep secure in Rouen. By November 1160 he had decided that Henry and Margaret were old enough to be married; Henry was now five and Margaret a couple of years younger. Immediately after the ceremony the castles of the Norman Vexin were handed over – much to King Louis's chagrin.[19]

By then Richard too had been betrothed. Early in 1159 Henry II travelled south through Poitou and Saintonge until he came to Blaye on the Gironde. There he met Raymond-Berengar IV, count of Barcelona. Since Raymond-Berengar was married to the queen of Aragon and ruled that kingdom in his wife's name, he might have taken the title of king, but refused to do so, saying that it was better to be known as the greatest count rather than the seventh-greatest king. Henry and he made a treaty of alliance, agreeing that Richard should be betrothed to one of the count's daughters and that, when married, they should be granted the duchy of Aquitaine.[20] The reason for this betrothal was that Henry was planning a campaign against Count Raymond V of Toulouse and since the rich and powerful Raymond-Berengar was already at odds with Toulouse he made a natural and formidable ally. As Eleanor's husband, Henry II had taken over the old claim of the dukes of Aquitaine to Toulouse. Eleanor's grandfather, William IX of Aquitaine, had married Philippa, the only child of Count William IV of Toulouse. Philippa was ousted by her uncle, William IV's younger brother, but in the eyes of her descendants she had been the rightful countess of Toulouse and

---

[19] Torigny, 208.
[20] Ibid., 200; Newburgh, Bk 2, ch.10.

periodically they went to war to reassert that claim. Toulouse would be a rich prize and it would have been foolish to allow the claim to drop. Traditionally looked upon as the capital of the former Visigothic kingdom of Aquitaine, it seemed to belong to Aquitaine. As the focus of roads linking the Atlantic ports of La Rochelle, Bordeaux and Bayonne with the flourishing maritime trade of the Mediterranean, Toulouse was an important commercial centre. Care was taken to ensure that the river Garonne remained open to shipping all the way from Bordeaux to Toulouse; swamps were drained and the forests lining the river banks were cleared.[21] Thus financially and strategically his wife's claim made good political sense to Henry II. Naturally, however, the present count of Toulouse was not going to be dispossessed without a fight. As husband of Louis VII's sister, Constance, Raymond of Toulouse could count on help from his brother-in-law. The massive expedition launched in the summer of 1159 was the biggest military effort ever made by Henry II. Although he failed in his main aim of forcing the count of Toulouse to submit, he did succeed in capturing Cahors and the Quercy.[22] As for Richard's betrothal, nothing came of it. The girl whom he was to have married vanishes from the pages of history and we do not even know her name. But this short-lived diplomatic episode was certainly not without significance. It marked the beginning of Richard's association with Aquitaine.

In area the duchy of Aquitaine was larger than Henry's Norman and Angevin lands put together. As counts of Poitou the dukes had long ruled Poitou and Saintonge, and had been recognized as overlords by the counts of Angoulême, La Marche and Périgord and by the viscounts of Limoges. Then with the acquisition of Gascony in the mid-eleventh century they became rulers of Bordeaux and overlords of a number of counties and lordships extending from the mouth of the Garonne to the Pyrenees, in area about twice the size of Poitou. To the east lay border regions – Berry and Auvergne – where even the dukes' nominal suzerainty was at times doubtful. In Poitou the inhabitants spoke a northern French dialect; to the south, from Saintonge onwards, the vernacular was Limousin, a dialect of Provençal or Occitan, the language of troubadour poetry and very different from the French of the north, the Langue d'Œuil, as opposed to the Langue d'Oc of the south. Further south still, towards Navarre, the inhabitants spoke Basque, a language which no one else could understand.[23]

[21] On the claim, J. Martindale, 'Succession and Politics in the Romance-speaking World c. 1000–1140', in *England and her Neighbours: Essays in Honour of Pierre Chaplais*, ed. M. Jones and M. Vale (London, 1989), 34–7; repr. in Martindale, *Status, Authority and Regional Power*; on the economic geography, Warren, 82–8; on maintenance of the Garonne, J. H. Mundy, *Liberty and Political Power in Toulouse 1050–1230* (New York, 1954), 4, 48.

[22] R. Benjamin, 'A Forty Years War: Toulouse and the Plantagenets, 1156–96', *Historical Research*, lxi (1988), 271.

[23] R. Collins, *The Basques* (Oxford, 1986), 234–48.

According to an old story, the devil, intending to win the souls of the Basques, tried to learn their language, but after seven years of unremitting study had mastered only three words. At first, as counts of Poitou, the dukes had been chiefly involved in northern French politics but once they also became counts of Gascony their interests turned more and more to the south, towards Toulouse and towards Spain, where they took a leading part in the Holy War against the Muslims. The subsequent shift of focus southwards meant that the dukes of Aquitaine became yet more distant and therefore seemed more insignificant to those influential writers whose field of vision was restricted to the Anglo-Norman realm on either side of the Channel.

Richard, an Angevin on his father's side, was a southerner on his mother's. In his own lifetime the most vividly remembered of his maternal ancestors was his great-grandfather, Duke William IX (1071–1126). William was a crusader, much admired for his prowess, generosity and handsome appearance. He was the first known troubadour and, as such, a key figure in the history of European literature. He was also a man whose attitude to life amused, astonished and alarmed his contemporaries. The trouble with him, according to the contemporary English historian, William of Malmesbury, was that he took nothing seriously, that 'he turned everything into a joke and made his listeners laugh uncontrollably'.[24] The sheer craftsmanship of his lyrics, however, makes it clear that he took the business of composing verse and music very seriously indeed. Aquitaine was the most civilized province in France. Ebles of Ventadour, the only other troubadour known from William IX's time, came from the Limousin, and most of the outstanding song-writers of the next generation – Cercamon, Marcabru, Jaufré Rudel, Bernard de Ventadour – lived and worked within the borders of Aquitaine. When four Poitevin knights were taken prisoner by Richard's Angevin grandfather Count Geoffrey Plantagenet, they won their release by composing and singing a song in praise of their captor. In the history of European music the twelfth century is a key period of development, when the unison of Gregorian chant gave ground to polyphony – much to the disgust of conservative intellectuals like John of Salisbury, who complained of 'the wanton and effeminate sound produced by caressing, chiming and intertwining melodies, a veritable harmony of sirens'. And in twelfth-century music there is no place more famous than the abbey of St Martial's in Limoges. The manuscripts of St Martial's contain both church music and many of the earliest

---

[24] William of Malmesbury, *Gesta Regum Anglorum*, vol. 1, ed. and trans. R. A. B. Mynors, R. M. Thomson and M. Winterbottom (Oxford, 1998), c. 439. For comment see J. Martindale, '"Cavalaria et Orgueil": Duke William IX of Aquitaine and the Historian', in *The Ideals and Practice of Medieval Knighthood*, ii, ed. C. Harper-Bill and R. Harvey (Woodbridge, 1988), 87–116; repr. Martindale, *Status, Authority and Regional Power*.

troubadour lyrics, with their accompanying melodies.[25] In the visual arts Limoges was the great European centre of enamel work. In sculpture there are the magnificent and intricately carved façades of the church of Notre-Dame-la-Grande in Poitiers and of the cathedral at Angoulême. Perhaps even more revealing are the astonishing carvings which adorn many of the small Romanesque churches of the Saintonge, for whereas the façades of important churches, under the patronage of princes like the duke of Aquitaine or the count of Angoulême, may well be the work of internationally famous masters, these village churches illustrate the strength of a purely local tradition of superb craftsmanship.[26]

The duchy of Aquitaine was not just the most civilized province in France, it was also a region of great wealth – it would have had to be to support so much fine art. The learned English historian Ralph of Diceto described its economy in glowing terms:

> Aquitaine overflows with riches of many kinds, excelling other parts of the western world to such an extent that historians consider it to be one of the most fortunate and flourishing of the provinces of Gaul. Its fields are fertile, its vineyards productive and its forests teem with wild life. From the Pyrenees northwards the entire countryside is irrigated by the River Garonne and other streams; indeed it is from these life-giving waters [*aquae*] that the province takes its name.[27]

Its main exports were salt and wine. Salt, one of the indispensable ingredients of life, was produced along the whole length of the duchy's Atlantic coast. The main varieties were 'Bay Salt' from the Bay of Bourgneuf in the north in the Marches between Poitou and Brittany, the salt of Brouage, panned on the sheltered shores behind the isles of Oléron and Ré, and, in the far south, the salt of Bayonne. However, for the twelfth century we are much better informed about the rapidly expanding wine trade. There is plenty of evidence for the planting of new vineyards in the Bordelais and even a Poitevin was prepared to admit that Bordeaux wine was of superb quality, but at this date by far the most important wine-exporting region was further north, in Aunis and Saintonge.[28] A fine white wine was produced around Niort, St Jean d'Angély and La Rochelle and then shipped overseas from La Rochelle. This port, founded as late as the 1130s, very

---

[25] On the contribution of the courts of the south to the development of music see the early chapters of C. Page, *Voices and Instruments of the Middle Ages* (London, 1987).

[26] L. Seidel, *Songs of Glory. The Romanesque Facades of Aquitaine* (Chicago, 1981).

[27] Diceto, i, 293–4.

[28] C. Higounet, *Bordeaux pendant le haut moyen âge* (Bordeaux, 1963), 246–58. R. Dion, *Histoire de la vigne et du vin en France des origines au XIXe siècle* (Paris, 1959); X. de Planhol, *An Historical Geography of France* (Cambridge, 1994), 228–9.

quickly came to enjoy all the characteristics of a boom town.[29] Its modern quays were well suited to accommodate the new large ships, known as cogs, which in the course of the second half of the twelfth century came to dominate the maritime trade of the Baltic, North Sea and Channel coasts. With these ships the merchants of La Rochelle could compete in the markets of England and Flanders with wines produced nearer at hand in the Paris basin and the Rhineland. So successfully did they break into the English market that they soon put the native vineyards out of business. After all, as one late twelfth-century writer put it, English wine could be drunk only with closed eyes and through clenched teeth. This growing export trade was of great importance to the duke of Aquitaine. By protecting the producers and merchants and by imposing tolls and customs dues he could profit from it – doubly so if he ruled over the English and Norman ports into which the wine was imported. These revenues, unknown and incalculable though they are, helped to make the duke one of the greatest and most powerful princes in western Europe.[30]

The marriage of Henry of Anjou to Eleanor and his accession, two years later, to the throne of England had brought together under a single sceptre peoples and provinces which hardly knew each other. In the century since 1066 England and Normandy had become two parts of a single political society, linked rather than separated by the Channel, the main road of the Anglo-Norman realm. Men and women crossed easily from one side to the other; many wealthy families held lands in both England and Normandy; and even though sharp-eared language snobs were soon able to mock French 'spoken after the manner of Marlborough', people at the upper levels of society spoke the same language, Anglo-Norman French, on both sides.[31] But very few Englishmen came to know Aquitaine; that is why Ralph of Diceto took the trouble to include a lengthy description of the duchy and its inhabitants in his chronicle. Only those who were sufficiently moved by piety or curiosity to go on a pilgrimage to the celebrated shrine of Santiago de Compostella, on roads which took them through Aquitaine, can have learned anything at all about the land which was to be the chief concern of Richard's life. The cult of *Santiago Matamoros*, St James the slayer of Moors, was growing in popularity throughout the twelfth century and, like the wine trade, it was beginning to forge links between England and the south-west. Henry I's most lavish monastic foundation, at Reading, where he was buried and where Henry II, in 1156, buried his first-

---

[29] On La Rochelle's place in the wine trade, R. Favreau, 'Les Débuts de la ville de La Rochelle', *CCM*, xxx (1987), 23–8. William the Breton called it 'the town of Bacchus', *Philippidos*, xii, 821.

[30] Martindale, 'Eleanor', 24–8.

[31] I. Short, 'Patrons and Polyglots: French Literature in Twelfth-Century England', *ANS*, xiv (1991), 229–49.

born son William, was dedicated to St James. Although its collection of relics contained many choice items, such as pieces of Aaron's rod and Christ's foreskin, the *pièce de résistance* was undoubtedly the hand of St James, brought to England from Italy by Richard's grandmother, the Empress Matilda.[32] In 1173 an abbot of Reading became archbishop of Bordeaux, and in 1181 Henry II endowed a hospital of St James for the benefit of poor pilgrims, also in Bordeaux.[33]

By the mid-twelfth century pilgrims were sufficiently numerous to merit a guidebook. It was written by a clerk who knew Poitou well. He advised visitors what roads to take and pointed out the sights they should see on the way. Some of these can still be seen – for example, the church of St-Hilaire-le-Grand in Poitiers, or the lower church of St Eutropius, who was believed to be a descendant of Xerxes of Persia, in Saintes. Others have vanished, like the rich abbey of St Jean d'Angély where the head of St John the Baptist had been venerated ever since its miraculous discovery in the mid-eleventh century. In Blaye, on the northern bank of the Gironde, the pilgrim could look upon the tomb of Roland, the hero of the *Chanson de Roland*, the most famous of all the *chansons de geste*. In reality Roland had been killed in a Basque ambush at the Pass of Roncesvalles but in twelfth-century legend he died gloriously, fighting for Christendom in the great war against the infidel. The nearer the pilgrim approached the Pyrenees the deeper he penetrated a countryside where almost every landmark had some kind of association with Roland. In the abbey church of St Seurin at Bordeaux, for example, he could see Roland's horn, the sound of which might have summoned reinforcements to Roncesvalles but which Roland, more careful of his reputation than of his life, had refused to blow until it was too late. In this landscape, which Richard learned to know well, the idea of a holy war against the Saracens must have seemed very real and very close at hand.

The guidebook also provides useful information about the people who lived in the regions through which the pilgrim would have to pass. In Poitou they are tough and warlike, skilled with lances and bows and arrows, brave in the battle-line, swift in the chase, elegant in dress, handsome, articulate, generous and hospitable. In Saintonge, however, they speak in a rustic fashion. In the Bordelais the language is still worse. As for the Gascons, they are gossipy, licentious, and poorly dressed; although they eat and drink far too much they don't sit at table but squat around a fire; they share the same cup and when they go to sleep they share the same rotting straw, master and mistress, servants and all. The Basques and Navarrese are much like the Gascons – only worse. They all eat out of one big pot like

---

[32] K. Leyser, 'Frederick Barbarossa, Henry II and the Hand of St James' , *EHR*, xc (1975).
[33] Torigny, 255.

pigs at a trough, and when they talk it sounds like a dog barking. When they want to warm themselves in front of a fire they are not ashamed to lift up their kilts and display their private parts. They treat their women like mules and they fornicate with animals; indeed in this respect they are so jealous that they go so far as to attach chastity belts to their mares and mules.[34] It is sadly obvious that as the author of the guidebook moved further south into regions more and more unfamiliar to him so his prejudices became more and more vitriolic. As for the pilgrims they would probably not know a great deal about the societies through which they passed for they rarely strayed far from their fixed itinerary of shrines and hostels; like tourists they saw little except monuments and hotels. For most Englishmen and Normans even Poitou lay deep in the unfamiliar south. Thus Aquitaine remained a far-off, unexplored country and its inhabitants were well known for their fickleness and treacherousness. No right-thinking Englishman would trust them an inch.

But it is misleading for us to share those prejudices, to think of Aquitaine as one vast political wilderness where tenants rebelled against their lords, nephews fought against their uncles, and all done with a passionate ferocity which left little or no room for effective ducal government – although this does still tend to be the way in which historians describe Aquitaine. It is easy enough to point to famous feuds such as that between Ebles II of Comborn (in the Limousin) and his uncle Bernard, during the course of which Ebles raped his aunt in front of witnesses and which ended when his uncle castrated and murdered him.[35] But to generalize from such sensational particulars as these is to ignore both common sense and political geography. It is as nonsensical as measuring the power of English kings solely in the light of unusual incidents occurring on the Scottish marches. All princes had to face the problems posed by distant and turbulent borderlands. The relatively peaceful and well-governed 'home counties' of the duke of Aquitaine, from Poitiers westwards to the sea at Talmont, then down the coast to Bordeaux and up the valley of the Garonne as far as Agen, comprised an area as large as midland and south-eastern England and included some of the most prosperous and commercially developed parts of the whole duchy. It is true that late twelfth-century English historians such as Gerald de Barri and Richard of Devizes wrote of Aquitaine as a region almost impossible to govern – but this was precisely in order to praise Richard for governing it well.[36]

[34] J. Vielliard, *Le Guide du pèlerin de Saint-Jacques de Compostelle* (Macon, 1938), 16–32, 62, 66, 78. On this see C. Hohler, 'A Note on Jacobus', *Journal of the Warburg and Courtauld Institute*, xxxv (1972). For discussion of the cult of Roland at Bordeaux, Higounet, *Bordeaux*, 142–3.
[35] Vigeois, Bk 1, ch. 25.
[36] Gerald, *Top.*, 195–6: Devizes, 76.

There was, however, a special problem for the ducal government and one with which Richard was to become familiar at an early age. This lay in the fact that castles held by two great aristocratic families, the Lusignans and the counts of Angoulême, could at times hinder land communications between the duke's three administrative capitals, the old Roman and episcopal cities of Poitiers, Saintes and Bordeaux. The lands and castles belonging to the Taillefer counts of Angoulême and their vassals at Jarnac, Bouteville, Archiac, Barbezieux and Montignac, as well as Angoulême itself, lay across the roads which linked Poitiers and Saintes with Bordeaux. The lands and castles belonging to the Lusignans and their vassals at Couhé, Vouvant, Château-Larcher and Frontenay, as well as Lusignan itself, lay across the roads which linked Poitiers with Saintes and the great port of La Rochelle. The facts of political geography alone are sufficient to suggest that there might have been many occasions when the duke of Aquitaine found himself at odds with the Taillefers and the Lusignans. Indeed feuds with these families had been part of the staple political diet of the early twelfth-century dukes.[37] Although the Lusignans were nothing like as rich or powerful as the counts of Angoulême, who ruled what was in effect an independent principality in the heart of Aquitaine, Lusignan seems to have been the storm centre of a revolt which broke out early in 1168. This may reflect King Henry's more immediate concern with rebels whose main fortress was only fifteen miles south-west of Poitiers, or it may simply be that in 1168 Count William of Angoulême was overshadowed by the more vigorous personality of the new head of the house of Lusignan, Geoffrey de Lusignan. He now stood on the threshold of a long and turbulent career which was to earn him a great reputation as a knight both in Europe and on crusade and to help lift his dynasty out of the ranks of the barons of Poitou and place it firmly among the leading princes of Christendom.[38] At this date, however, the Lusignans were no match for Henry II, now at the height of his powers. They had to look on while he laid waste their estates together with those of their supporters and captured and dismantled the great castle of Lusignan itself.[39] Only the fact that Henry had so many other calls on his energy and resources enabled them to survive.

---

[37] For the political geography see J. Boussard, *Le Gouvernement d'Henri II Plantagenêt* (Paris, 1956) and, above all, two unpublished doctoral theses: J. Martindale, 'The Origins of the Duchy of Aquitaine and the Government of the Counts of Poitou' (D.Phil., Oxford, 1964) and R. C. Watson,'The Counts of Angoulême from the Ninth Century to the Mid-thirteenth Century' (Ph.D., University of East Anglia, 1979).

[38] On the Lusignans see S. Painter, 'The Houses of Lusignan and Châtellerault, 1150–1250', *Speculum*, xxx (1955) and idem, 'The Lords of Lusignan in the Eleventh and Twelfth Centuries', *Speculum*, xxxii (1957), both repr. in *Feudalism and Liberty: Articles and Addresses of Sidney Painter*, ed. F. A. Cazel (Baltimore, 1961).

[39] Torigny, 235–6.

In March 1168 Henry was summoned north by the news that negotiations with Louis VII had reached a crucial stage. For some time now Henry had been thinking about the future of his dynasty and his lands. He wanted to arrange a family settlement – no easy matter with so many children and such widespread territories to consider, and when any arrangement would need the consent of Eleanor's ex-husband if it were to be valid. Knowing Louis's concern for the Holy Land, Henry let it be known that all he really wanted was to put his own house in order, provide for his children, and then be off on crusade in his lord's company. Henry's plan was for his eldest son to take his patrimony, i.e. all of those lands which he himself had inherited (Anjou, Maine, Normandy and England), while Richard should have his acquisition: the duchy he had acquired by virtue of his marriage.[40] Louis had now provisionally agreed to a settlement and Henry's presence was required to ratify it. The terms included clauses recognizing Richard as duke-designate of Aquitaine and arranging a betrothal between him and Louis's daughter Alice. Nothing was said about the Angevin claim to Toulouse, though the Capetian line on this question was clear enough: it could only be settled by a judgment in the court of the king of France.[41] Before going north to meet the French king, Henry left Poitou in the hands of Queen Eleanor with an experienced commander, Earl Patrick of Salisbury, at her side as her military adviser. The rebels seized the chance to return to Lusignan in force and begin to rebuild it. When Henry heard of this he turned back again, deputing some of his officials to continue the discussions with Louis. The French king seems to have taken this as an insult and, if he had not already been in touch with the Poitevin rebels, he very soon was. He met their envoys at Bourges. An alliance was quickly forged. Both parties agreed not to make peace without the other's consent. Louis promised to help the Poitevins recover their losses, while they handed over hostages as a guarantee that they would keep their side of the bargain.

By early April Henry, concerned above all to secure his family settlement, was prepared to make restitution to the Poitevins in order to salvage it. But in the meantime Louis had taken a step back by withdrawing his consent to the betrothal of Richard and Alice. While these talks were continuing on the Norman border, a clash in Poitou between the men of Geoffrey de Lusignan and Earl Patrick resulted in the earl's death. Although making war was a fairly routine element in the life of an active nobleman, it was very rare indeed that one was killed; partly because, in the face of danger, a noble could don his expensive and effective armour, his helmet and coat

[40] For a brief discussion of the problems involved, Gillingham, *The Angevin Empire* (London, 1984), repr. in *Coeur de Lion*. The third son, Geoffrey, had already been betrothed to Constance, heiress to Brittany.

[41] For this plan and the following events the principal source is one of John of Salisbury's newsletters, *Letters of John of Salisbury*, ii, ed. W. J. Millor and C. N. L. Brooke (Oxford, 1979), no. 272.

of mail; and partly because his opponents did not try to kill him – if he should be so unfortunate as to be at their mercy they preferred to capture him and ransom him, a profitable way of bringing financial pressure to bear on his friends and family. In twelfth-century warfare it was only the poor who were expected to die, so the death of Earl Patrick came as a great shock to everyone.[42] The Poitevins claimed that they had been attacked while peace talks were in progress and that though they had naturally defended themselves they had certainly not intended to kill the earl. But the earl's followers – among them his young nephew William Marshal – told a very different story. They said that he had been ambushed while unarmed and slain by a thrust in the back. William, though himself without a helmet, fought like a lion to avenge his uncle's death but was eventually overborne by weight of numbers as well as by another sword thrust from behind – and carried off into captivity. Years later that journey still remained vivid in his memory. Fearing King Henry's anger his captors kept under the cover of woodland, moving stealthily from one secret hide-out to another, dragging William along with his wound unbandaged and still bleeding. The whole episode left its mark on William's mind. For him the Poitevins were and always would be faithless traitors.[43]

The death of Earl Patrick in these confused and possibly scandalous circumstances inevitably embittered relationships and made peace even harder to achieve. A further conference at La Ferté-Bernard in July 1168 met in an atmosphere of mutual suspicion and broke up with nothing achieved. For a future duke of Aquitaine there was additional cause for disquiet in the presence of envoys from Gascony as well as from Poitou, Brittany, Wales and Scotland in the French camp.[44] It seemed that both parts of his duchy were now in a state of unrest. The war went on throughout the second half of 1168. As usual in his dealings with Louis VII, Henry seems to have held the upper hand. He was much richer than Louis, able – as the French king was not – to hire large armies of mercenaries and to reduce his leading vassals, the counts of Flanders, Boulogne and Blois, for example, to a position of neutrality by paying them substantial pensions. The contrast between the two kings was ruefully noted by Louis himself in a remark he made to Walter Map:

'Your lord the King of England, who lacks nothing, has men, horses, gold, silk, jewels, fruits, game and everything else. We in France have nothing but bread and wine and gaiety.' This saying I took note of, for it was merrily said, and truly.[45]

---

[42] M. Strickland, *War and Chivalry. The Conduct and Perception of War in England and Normandy 1066–1217* (Cambridge, 1996).

[43] *HGM*, 1623–881.

[44] *Letters of John of Salisbury*, ii, no. 279; Torigny, 237.

[45] Map, 450–1.

After more difficulties peace was finally achieved in January 1169 at Montmirail. Henry II renewed his own homage to Louis and then watched his two elder sons do homage: Henry for Normandy, Anjou and Maine, Richard for Aquitaine. The betrothal of Richard and Alice was at last finalized; she was to come without a dowry.[46]

Where Richard was during this year of military and diplomatic manoeuvring we do not know, but it is a reasonable guess that he was with his mother, since Aquitaine was her duchy and it was by her wish that it was to be made over to him.[47] His father too must have been well satisfied with the Peace of Montmirail. In return for his family settlement he had agreed to be reconciled to the Poitevin rebels and make good the losses which they had suffered since the beginning of the war. But this was a promise which Louis had no means of enforcing. Whether he knew it or not the French king had effectively abandoned his allies. Henry had set his house in order but had no thoughts of setting off on crusade. Instead he was determined to punish the rebels. In his own mind he was free to turn against them, despite the terms agreed at Montmirail, because he and they had not exchanged a kiss of peace.

The spring and early summer of 1169 Henry spent in the south, taking and demolishing many of the castles from which the rebels had defied his authority. The counts of Angoulême and La Marche submitted, while, in a notorious incident, one of their allies, Robert de Seilhac, died – or so it was believed – as a result of the harsh treatment he received in Henry's prison.[48] Despite the fact that Richard and his elder brother had performed homage to Louis VII for their lands, it was obvious that their father had in no way relinquished control. But, like it or not, he nearly had to in August 1170, when he was very seriously ill. Believing that death was at hand he confirmed the territorial dispositions made at Montmirail and asked to be buried at the monastery of Grandmont in the Limousin, one of the monks of which had played an important part in the peace negotiations. On his recovery he made a pilgrimage to the shrine of Rocamadour in the Quercy.[49] These and other indications – the marriage of his daughter Eleanor to Alfonso VIII of Castile, a projected campaign in the Auvergne, a claim that the archbishopric of Bourges rightfully belonged to the duchy of Aquitaine – show that the southern parts of his dominions continued to be very much in his mind in these months.[50] Even after the murder of Thomas Becket in his own cathedral on 29 December 1170, there were churches in Aquitaine which still turned

[46] Torigny, 240; *Letters of John of Salisbury*, ii, no. 288, 636–49, esp. 648–9 for the 'no dowry' agreement.

[47] 'by his mother's wish', Vigeois, Bk 1, ch. 67.

[48] Torigny, 241–2; Vigeois, Bk 1, ch. 66; A. Richard, *Histoire des comtes de Poitou 778–1204* (2 vols, Paris, 1903), ii, 150; Norgate, 8, n.1.

[49] *Gesta*, i, 6–7; Torigny, 247–8; *Letters of John of Salisbury*, ii, nos 287–8.

[50] *Gesta*, i, 10–11; Torigny, 247.

to Henry for help and protection. In March 1171 the monks of St Martial's, Limoges, though perhaps with some embarrassment, asked for, and were sent, aid in putting down a revolt of their townsmen at La Souterraine, a revolt which had the backing of Count Audebert of La Marche.[51]

Soon after this incident Richard emerges from the obscurity which had surrounded his movements in the two years since he knelt in homage at Montmirail. We see him now in the company of his mother. Together he and Eleanor laid foundation stones for the monastery of St Augustine in Limoges in 1171. It was presumably in the late 1160s and early 1170s that he learned his love for both the language and music of Aquitaine and the great trust in his mother's political abilities which he was to demonstrate on numerous occasions in later years. And at last, in June 1172, when he was fourteen years old, the great day came when Richard was formally installed as duke of Aquitaine. In the abbey church of St Hilary in Poitiers where, four years earlier, Earl Patrick of Salisbury had been buried, he took his seat in the abbot's chair to receive from the hands of the archbishop of Bordeaux and the bishop of Poitiers the sacred lance and banner which were the insignia of the ducal office. But as duke he was to be more than just the count of Poitou. So Richard moved on to Limoges and there he was again proclaimed duke in a ceremony witnessed by the Limousin chronicler Geoffrey of Vigeois, who at that date was one of the monks of St Martial's.[52] The climax of the ceremony came when the ring of St Valerie was slipped on to Richard's finger. In twelfth-century legend St Valerie was the martyred saint who personified Aquitaine and her story as told at Limoges – where she had lived and died and where her 'thousand-year-old' body was still preserved – was intended to show that Limoges was a more venerable city than Poitiers. Three years earlier Richard had performed homage to King Louis at Montmirail but now that he had worn the ring of St Valerie he could claim that he held his duchy in indissoluble union with the people of Aquitaine and the saints who watched over them. The two ceremonies at Poitiers and Limoges were a ritual expression of Aquitaine's *de facto* independence from the king of France.[53] By the same token they might also be taken to mean that Richard's right to his duchy was independent of his father's will. But whatever the symbolic significance of these ceremonies may have been, for the moment Henry still retained the reins of power.

[51] Vigeois, Bk 1, ch. 66; Richard, *Histoire des comtes*, i, 158–9.

[52] Vigeois, Bk 1, ch. 67. There is some disagreement over the date. Richard, *Histoire des comtes*, ii, 150, dated it to 1170, and has been followed by a number of authors. I, like Norgate, prefer 1172 since Geoffrey of Vigeois refers to the 1173 meeting at Limoges between Henry II and Raymond of Toulouse as happening 'anno sequenti'.

[53] For the significance of the rituals, Richard, *Histoire des comtes*, ii, 150–3; H. Hoffman, 'Französische Fürstenweihen des Hochmittelalters', *DA*, xviii (1962).

Chapter 4

WAR WITHOUT LOVE, 1173−4

In the spring of 1173 Richard attended a great court held at Paris by Louis VII. This was the year in which he came to man's estate, for it was at about this time that King Louis knighted him – and by knighting him encouraged him to take up arms against his father.[1] For Richard's presence in Paris meant that he had sided with his mother and his older brother Henry against their father in what a contemporary poet called 'the war without love'.[2]

A few weeks earlier, in February 1173, Henry II had met Count Humbert of Maurienne at Clermont-Ferrand in the Auvergne to finalize the details of the betrothal between his youngest son John and the count's daughter and heiress presumptive. The occasion was made even more splendid by the presence of King Alfonso II of Aragon and Count Raymond V of Toulouse, who had asked him to act as an arbitrator in their long-standing quarrel. Just at the time when, in Rome, Pope Alexander III was preparing to canonize the murdered Thomas Becket it seemed that the prestige of Becket's old opponent was reaching still greater heights. To show the world how many princes felt it worth their while to dance attendance on him, Henry invited them and also the king of Navarre to a court he planned to hold in Limoges at the end of the month. There, on 25 February 1173, before them all, Count Raymond knelt and did homage for the county of Toulouse, first to Henry II, then to his eldest son Henry, and finally to Richard.[3] The ceremony seemed designed to express the solidarity of the united Angevin family over the old enemy of Toulouse. But for the old King the wheel of fortune was about to turn. Hitherto he had been a vigorous and aggressive prince, disturbing without compunction – as Walter Map put it – the peace of half of Christendom. From now on he was to be more and more on the defensive, until in the end he would be, in William of Newburgh's words, 'sick to death of war'.[4]

---

[1] *Gesta*, i, 63.

[2] *Jordan Fantosme's Chronicle*, ed. R. C. Johnston (London, 1981), line 20.

[3] *Gesta*, i, 35–6; Vigeois, Bk 1, ch. 67, who gives the date. The dean of St Paul's was much impressed by the splendour of the court at Montferrand, but in view of the explicit statement of both Howden and Vigeois seems to be wrong in implying that Richard did not receive Raymond's homage later that month, Diceto, i, 353.

[4] Map, 484; Newburgh, Bk 3, ch, 14.

It started when Count Humbert of Maurienne gave his daughter into Henry's custody and asked him what provision he was intending to make for her future husband.[5] Five-year-old John was, of course, as yet John Lackland. In Kate Norgate's words, the question 'stirred up a trouble which was never again to be laid wholly to rest till the child who was its as yet innocent cause had broken his father's heart'.[6] Henry replied that John would be given the three castles of Chinon, Loudun and Mirebeau. This proposal enraged young Henry. He had done homage for Normandy and Anjou at Montmirail and he had been crowned king of England in 1170. Yet he had never been assigned any lands from which he might maintain himself and his queen in their proper estate. He was now eighteen years old and wanted to be master in his own household. In November 1172 he had met his father-in-law on the Norman border and it was believed that Louis VII had urged him to demand what was rightfully his. The Young King, as he was called, must have known that it would not be easy to persuade his father to give up any of his power and revenues. The Old King, after all, was not yet forty. The proposal to transfer Chinon, Loudun and Mirebeau to a mere child was surely just a trick giving Henry II an excuse to keep these three important castles in his own hands for many years to come. Young Henry, as count of Anjou, angrily refused to give his consent to the plan. Instead he demanded that at least part of his inheritance should be handed over to him at once: either England or Normandy or Anjou. The Old King would not do it and from then on he and his eldest son could not talk without quarrelling.

Henry II would have been an unusually stupid man not to realize that there were bound to be difficult moments in the relationship between him and his heir. But he is unlikely to have foreseen the next blow. Count Raymond came to him privately and told him that Eleanor and his other sons were also plotting against him. So, at any rate, Geoffrey of Vigeois – on the spot – thought, though since Henry left Richard and Geoffrey with Eleanor, it may be that he was mistaken about the contents of a confidential conversation.[7] At any rate Henry left Limoges in haste on the pretext of a hunting party, giving instructions that his castles should be put in a state of war-readiness. He headed north, taking his eldest son with him.[8] But at Chinon, while his father slept, the Young King slipped away by night and fled to the court of King Louis. Henry II had left Richard and Geoffrey in their mother's care. If she had been included in Count Raymond's warning, Henry presumably believed that though his wife might join in a little family intrigue against him, she would not want to carry her opposition to

[5] For the events of this paragraph, *Gesta*, i, 34–5, 41. Torigny, 255.
[6] K. Norgate, *England under the Angevin Kings* (2 vols, London, 1887), ii, 134.
[7] Vigeois, Bk 1, ch. 67.
[8] *Gesta*, i, 41–2.

the point of war – particularly if that were to involve her in an alliance with her ex-husband. Whatever his calculations may have been, of one thing we can be sure: he was grievously mistaken. Eleanor sent Richard and Geoffrey to join their brother at the French king's court while she herself summoned the Poitevins to arms.

It was an astonishing decision. When the learned dean of St Paul's searched back through ancient and modern history for parallels to the revolt of 1173-4, he found more than thirty examples of sons rebelling against their parents, including some from the recent history of both Anjou and Poitou, but he cites no case of a queen rebelling against her husband. In a letter penned on behalf of the archbishop of Rouen by a famous stylist, Peter of Blois, Eleanor was reminded that it was a wife's duty to submit, a reminder backed up by the threat of ecclesiastical sanctions. 'For we know that unless you return to your husband you will be the cause of a general ruin.'[9] Twelfth-century English historians, writing during Eleanor's own lifetime, were understandably cautious when they came to analyse her role in the revolt. They tended both to hold her responsible and to avoid responsibility for this judgement by choosing words such as 'so it was said'.[10] In his *Gesta Henrici*, written soon after the event, Roger of Howden put the blame on Louis VII but added that some believed that Eleanor and her uncle, Ralph de Faye, the seneschal of Poitou, were also responsible. In the early 1190s when he revised his account, and when Eleanor was once again a power to be reckoned with, he preferred to omit all mention of her role.[11] Ralph was undoubtedly an influential counsellor. He was involved in the most important questions of policy – negotiations for the marriage of royal children: Eleanor in 1170 and John in 1173.[12] But in view of Eleanor of Aquitaine's masterful political activity in later years it seems superfluous to look for a power behind the throne. If the initiative did not come from their mother it is hard to see either Richard, at fifteen, or Geoffrey, at fourteen, being persuaded to rebel by a man behind the scenes.

It was her own decision, no one else's. But it has remained as puzzling to modern historians as it was shocking to contemporaries. Eleanor's last child, John, had been born in December 1167. The evidence, scrappy though it is, gives no hint of a meeting for more than two years, between the autumn of 1170 and the end of 1172 when they held their last Christmas court together at Chinon.[13] Henry remained overall policy-maker but it looks as though Eleanor had been left to supervise the day-to-day running of her duchy and effectively in sole charge of her second son.

---

[9] Diceto, i, 355–66; *RHF*, xvi, 629–30.

[10] Gervase, i, 242, 'dicebatur'; Diceto, i, 355, 'sicut dicitur'; Newburgh, Bk 2, ch. 27, 'connivente, ut dicitur, matre'.

[11] *Gesta*, i, 42, 'ut a quibusdam dicebatur'; *Chron*, ii, 46.

[12] See, for example, *Letters of John of Salisbury* ii, no. 212.

[13] Torigny, 255; *Gesta*, i, 35.

But here we enter the land of romance and legend. It has been said that at the court of Poitiers 'the gilded youth of Poitou and Aquitaine breathed an air that seemed to belong to some tale of chivalry'. Here there were music and dancing, tournaments and troubadours, talk of knight-errantry and courtly love. At the centre of this joyous court life stood the figure of Eleanor, 'dominating all around her by that intellectual radiance, that love of literature and fine language which was her hall-mark'.[14] All very different, it is implied, from the sober court of Henry II where lawyers and administrators liked to spend their nights discussing the wording of the latest royal writ.[15]

Occasionally literary historians have gone even further and have suggested that courtly love was much more than just a fashionable and pleasant way of passing time. They have seen it as a revolutionary and subversive moral doctrine. To glorify the love felt for another man's wife was to flout contemporary notions of obedience and authority, the authority of the Church as well as the authority of the husband. By undermining these two bastions of a male world, courtly love was, in effect, threatening the existence of the whole social order. The historians who have taken this line have identified Eleanor and her eldest daughter, Marie, countess of Champagne (1140-98), as the outstanding patrons of this dangerous movement. The contemporary rumours that Eleanor had been an adulteress made it possible to believe that she preached what she practised. Marie is said to have been a frequent visitor to her mother's court at Poitiers and to have brought with her the greatest poet in France, Chrétien de Troyes. Among Chrétien's works was a romance, *Lancelot*, written at Marie's request, which took as its hero a man who had an illicit affair with the wife of his lord, King Arthur. In addition Eleanor and Marie appear to be central figures in a treatise entitled *De Amore* written by Andrew, a chaplain at the court of Champagne in the early 1180s. This celebrated treatise, still usually known as 'The Art of Courtly Love', lies at the origin of the legend of the courts of love; tribunals before which lovers were supposed to bring their quarrels in order to have them adjudicated by authorities in the art of love like Eleanor of Aquitaine and her

---

[14] R. Pernoud, *Eleanor of Aquitaine* (London, 1967), 151, 155. The romanticizing 'Eleanor industry' has continued unabated, promoted by, amongst others, a former prime minister of France and mayor of Bordeaux, J. Chaban-Delmas, *La Dame d'Aquitaine* (Monte Carlo, 1987), as well as by specialists in medieval literature, who are understandably much better on the legend and literature than on the life, e.g. D. D. R. Owen, *Eleanor of Aquitaine* (Oxford, 1993). As Martindale points out, the industry is based mostly on 'an unreflecting empathy' or on 'an author's views on women and their idealised position in society', Martindale, 'Eleanor', 35–8.

[15] Not that there is any evidence Henry joined in these discussions, see Gillingham, 'Conquering Kings: Henry II and Richard I', in *Coeur de Lion*.

daughter.[16] One such dispute was settled by Marie with a verdict apparently asserting that true love cannot exist between man and wife. No one any longer seriously believes that Marie and Eleanor actually did preside over such tribunals.[17] It is accepted that the courts of love were a fiction, an intellectual game. But it is still widely believed that it was a game which was avidly played at Poitiers whenever Marie, 'her' chaplain Andrew, and Chrétien de Troyes came to visit Eleanor. As a result of this belief Eleanor retains her place as the woman who, above all others, symbolizes the new social and cultural pattern of courtly love. She stands for the civilization of the south, of the *Midi*, the home of the troubadours, against the sterner, rougher, cruder world of the North, represented, in this image, by her husband, the King of the North Wind, whose authority she is subtly undermining and against whom she will soon break out in open rebellion. On this view, in the tension between Richard's parents which may have been developing from the late 1160s onwards, there was not just the clash of temperaments, there was also the conflict of two cultures. It would be hard to imagine a more complex and bewildering environment for an adolescent to grow up in.

If it were true. The trouble is that the revised version of the legend of the courts of love is as ill-founded as the old one. Nowhere is there any evidence to show that the Countess Marie, Chrétien de Troyes and Andrew 'the Chaplain' ever visited the court at Poitiers – or anywhere else, since Eleanor was certainly not continuously at Poitiers during these years. *De Amore* was not written until about 1186, by which time Andrew had probably left Marie's service. The two verdicts which he attributes to Eleanor make it obvious that, in these passages at least, his intention was a satirical one. In the first case Eleanor gave a judicial decision condemning consanguineous marriages – of which she had made two. In the second case she judged the problem of a woman who had to choose between a mature knight of complete probity and a young man devoid of worth. According to Andrew, Eleanor's verdict was that a woman would act less wisely if she chose the less worthy one. Since Eleanor, at the age of thirty, had separated from a husband of her own age in order to marry a nineteen-year-old, Andrew's audience can hardly have missed the irony, particularly if – as seems possible – the book was written at the French royal court. The Countess Marie's denial of the existence of love in marriage is 'dated' to May 1174 – the one date in the whole book – when Eleanor was her

---

[16] Andreas Capellanus, *On Love*, ed. and trans. P. G. Walsh (London, 1982) who points out that there is no justification in the manuscripts for the conventional title 'The Art of Courtly Love' – which he terms 'tendentious'.

[17] J. F. Benton, 'The Court of Champagne as a Literary Center', *Speculum*, xxxvi (1961). I find Benton's arguments more persuasive than those of J. H. M. McCash in 'Marie de Champagne and Eleanor of Aquitaine: a Relationship Re-examined', *Speculum*, liv (1979).

husband's prisoner. The intellectual game was being played not by Eleanor in the years 1169–73 but by Andrew 'the Chaplain' in the late 1180s. And if Andrew's approach was humorous and satirical can we afford to believe that the 'new concept' of love in adultery was ever at any time seriously advocated?[18]

But the most serious fault with the modern legend of Eleanor of Aquitaine is the contrast drawn between her and her husband. Eleanor, it is true, was a patron of literature and art, but so were most princes and certainly Henry II was. Artists sought his favour more often than they sought his wife's, which is hardly surprising since he had more power and patronage to dispense. Even Bernard of Ventadour, the poet of lyrical love, composed for Henry more often than for Eleanor.[19] But perhaps this too should not surprise us. Although the rumours of the queen's supposed adulteries were real enough and, given the prevailing double standard in sexual matters, much more shocking than most of the stories of the king's mistresses, none the less if either of them ever had a romantic love affair it is likely to have been Henry rather than Eleanor. As late as 1191 the tomb of Rosamund Clifford – Henry's 'Fair Rosamund', who died in 1176 – was still covered in silk cloth and tended by the nuns of Godstow Priory in accordance with the terms of Henry's benefaction to their nunnery.[20] The legend of Eleanor is doubly misleading. It does justice neither to Henry's interest in literature nor to Eleanor's own personality. For it is clear that she was an extraordinary woman; only not in the manner of legend. The legend must go – but at the same time we must be careful not to let the queen out with the asses' milk.

Some writers have said that Eleanor was driven to violence by Henry's adulteries, culminating in his open attachment to Rosamund Clifford. This, again, is to give too much weight to later legends which attribute Rosamund's death to the fury of a jealous queen who, according to one version, tore the king's mistress's eyes out or, according to another, gave her a choice between poison and the knife.[21] An alternative explanation has been sought in political rather than personal emotions, the theory that her revolt

---

[18] There are similar problems involved in evaluating Chrétien de Troyes's *Lancelot*.

[19] P. Dronke, 'Peter of Blois and Poetry at the Court of Henry II', *Medieval Studies*, xxxviii (1976), 186–8. For Eleanor and Bernard de Ventadour, see Martindale, 'Eleanor', 37–8. For links between Henry II and Chrétien's early romances, *Cligés* and *Erec and Enide*, see *Chrétien de Troyes. Arthurian Romances*, trans. W. W. Kibler (Harmondsworth, 1991), 5–6.

[20] *Gesta*, ii, 231–2; *Chron.*, iii, 167–8.

[21] 'Aliénor ne s'est pas vengée en assassinant Rosemonde. Elle a fait mieux. Elle a soulevé le Poitou', E-R. Labande, 'Pour une Image véridique', 208–9. Love transformed into jealousy was also the motive favoured by Pernoud: 'Henry had broken faith: he had prized lechery above creative sharing, and now the joy of courtly love was gone for ever', Pernoud, *Eleanor*, 151. The stories of Fair Rosamund are treated thoroughly in Owen, *Eleanor*, 114–48.

reflected her resentment at being reduced to insignificance by Henry II's own dominant personality.[22] This is certainly a more plausible general background to the revolt but it does not explain why Eleanor rebelled in 1173 and not at any other time. Doubtless the timing of the revolt can be partly understood in terms of the flaring up of the Young King's dissatisfaction at Limoges. But he was a feckless young man and likely to be kept in a state of frustration for a long time to come. So why did Eleanor decide that this was the moment to precipitate a family crisis and begin 'la guerre senz amur'? It may be that there is a clue to this in something else that happened at Limoges. The homage sworn by Raymond of Toulouse was a great triumph for Henry II, but did Eleanor see it in that light? As duchess of Aquitaine she had inherited the ducal claim to Toulouse, but at Limoges Raymond had not only done homage to the dukes of Aquitaine, he had also done homage to the Young King. Did this mean that Aquitaine was going to be permanently subordinated to the ruler of the Anglo-Norman realm? The possibility must have made Eleanor's ancestors turn in their graves. Nor can it have been pleasing to the Poitevin nobles.[23] One of them, Hugh of Chauvigny, is reported to have hated all Englishmen. The death of Earl Patrick of Salisbury was still an episode which aroused harsh feelings on both sides.

The list of Eleanor's subjects who followed her into rebellion is headed by Count William of Angoulême, Geoffrey and Guy of Lusignan and their cousin Geoffrey de Rancon, lord of Taillebourg, and by William, called 'the archbishop', lord of Parthenay.[24] Since Ralph de Faye was a member of the house of the viscounts of Châtellerault this means that with the one exception of the viscount of Thouars — who had earlier suffered badly as the result of a quarrel with Eleanor — she had been joined by all the leading barons of Poitou and the Angoumois. But equally striking is the fact that the rest of Aquitaine, including regions as turbulent as La Marche, the Limousin and the whole of Gascony, took virtually no part in the revolt. In the Limousin we know that the lords were caught up again in yet another round of the long-drawn-out feud between Viscount Aimar V and his uncles.[25] It is probable that elsewhere, too, local interests took priority over the problems of the Angevin family.[26]

---

[22] Warren, 120-1.

[23] 'Politically she may have resented the absorption of Aquitaine into the "Angevin Empire", Martindale, 'Eleanor', 33. In a forthcoming study Jane Martindale will make the point that she could also have objected to Count Raymond's homage on the grounds that it constituted an acceptance of his right to rule the county and hence was a repudiation of her own claim to Toulouse – one for which her husband had been willing to fight in 1159.

[24] Gesta, i, 46–7. On the lords of Parthenay see G. T. Beech, *A Rural Society in Medieval France: the Gâtine of Poitou in the Eleventh and Twelfth Centuries* (Baltimore, 1964).

[25] For details of what Geoffrey of Vigeois saw as 'a serious enmity involving many nobles', Vigeois, Bk 1, ch. 68.

[26] A possible exception was Arnold de Boville at Castillon-sur-Agen. *Gesta*, i, 101. See below, 52.

Meanwhile Richard and his brothers at Paris in the spring of 1173 took an oath not to make peace with their father except with the consent of the king and barons of France.[27] A formidable coalition of princes was assembled, William, king of the Scots, and the counts of Flanders, Boulogne and Blois, all ready to invade Henry's territories and counting upon the support of rebels scattered throughout his dominions. But in this, the first great crisis of his reign, the Old King remained supremely cool, waiting for his enemies to show their hand before committing his own forces in sudden and decisive pounces. Above all he used his immense cash resources to hire large numbers of mercenaries. These soldiers were generally known as *routiers* and were often assigned an ethnic identity as Brabançons, but sometimes Navarrese or Basques or Germans, not so much to indicate their precise place of origin as to express the fact that they were foreigners and spoke a language which was not understood. As professional soldiers they had a great reputation for ruthlessness both in battle and in ravaging the countryside.[28] With this fearsome military instrument at his disposal Henry waited for the invasion. In July 1173 Richard and his brothers took part in an attack on eastern Normandy made under the command of Philip of Flanders. At the siege of Drincourt, however, Philip's brother, Matthew of Boulogne, was wounded by a crossbow bolt. When he died a few days later Philip called off the invasion.[29] If this was Richard's first experience of war it bore an ironical similarity to his last. Other attacks also petered out and by the autumn King Louis and the Angevin princes were sufficiently depressed to put out peace feelers. At a conference at Gisors Henry offered terms to his sons. To Richard he offered half the revenues of Aquitaine and control of four castles; similar proposals were put to Henry and Geoffrey. He was willing to submit these terms to arbitrators to vary as they thought fit, but only on condition that he was to retain full power and jurisdiction. He was prepared to bargain about money, but not about power. On Louis VII's advice the three brothers rejected these proposals.[30] The war continued. Early in November Henry led his Brabançons in a thrust to the south of Chinon, threatening the lands of Ralph de Faye. He captured the castles of La Haye, Preuilly and Champigny.[31] He also captured his wife. According to Gervase of Canterbury, she was in male clothing when taken.[32] It may well have been the news of his mother's capture which stirred Richard to take his first independent political action. Up to this

---

[27] *Gesta*, i, 43–4.
[28] Newburgh, Bk 2, ch. 27. Strickland, *War and Chivalry*, 291–329.
[29] *Gesta*, i, 49.
[30] Ibid., 59.
[31] Ibid., 62–3.
[32] Only Gervase reports this (i, 242), adding that she lacked 'stability' – an especially grave shortcoming in the eyes of a monk. Other contemporaries are notably discreet, saying nothing whatever about Eleanor's movements and capture.

point, still only sixteen years old, he had remained very much a background figure, drawn along in the wake of his elder brother, and both of them overshadowed by their protector, King Louis of France. But with his mother arrested it was now up to him to take charge of the rebellion in Poitou.[33]

His first move was to threaten La Rochelle. But the town remained steadfastly loyal to the Old King and shut its gates against him. Its citizens presumably believed that their interests would be better served if Henry won, for he stood for the preservation of a single sovereign authority ruling in Poitou, England and Normandy, in other words over both ends of La Rochelle's trade, over wine-growers and wine-drinkers. But there were many who were jealous of the new town's phenomenal rise and who looked upon it as a sink of iniquity where the *nouveaux riches* wallowed in the luxury obtained from trade. If La Rochelle was against Richard then Saintes was for him. When, in 1150, the citizens of La Rochelle had asked the bishop of Saintes for permission to build a new parish church to accommodate the growing number of worshippers, they had met with a refusal. In the end they had to go over the bishop's head, obtaining the authorization they wanted from the pope. The old episcopal city of the Saintonge, proud of its venerable past, its Capitol, its amphitheatre and its Roman walls, looked askance at the bustling intruder and feared that La Rochelle's gain would be its loss.[34] So successfully indeed did the bishops of Saintes oppose the claims of their rival that it was not until the seventeenth century that La Rochelle was allowed to have a cathedral of its own. In these circumstances it was only appropriate that in 1174, while his father occupied Poitiers, Richard should set up his headquarters in Saintes and turn the cathedral into an arms depot. In seeing the importance of La Rochelle Richard had shown a good, if over-ambitious, grasp of strategy, but he was still no match for his father. It was not just that the Old King possessed the greater resources — which he did — but he was also able to overwhelm his enemies by sheer speed of movement. He arrived at Saintes while Richard thought he was still celebrating Whitsun at Poitiers and took the city gates by storm. Richard and a few followers escaped downstream to Geoffrey de Rancon's castle at Taillebourg while the bulk of his troops were driven back into the cathedral, where they held out for a few days.[35] In the interests of speed and surprise Henry had brought no artillery train

---

[33] In the opinion of an annalist at St Aubin, Angers, many Poitevins supported Richard less out of liking for him than out of hatred for his father, *Annales angevines*, 38. Given Richard's age this is hardly surprising. This author too has nothing to say on the subject of Eleanor's role in the revolt.

[34] On the rivalry between La Rochelle and Saintes, and the former's role in the revolt, see Favreau, 'Les Débuts', 8–9. Richard the Poitevin, *RHF*, xii, 420.

[35] *Gesta*, i, 71; Diceto, i, 380. The retreat to Taillebourg is reported in the margin of one version of the Annals of St Aubin, *Annales angevines*, 38 – though chronological error suggests that this note was not written down at the time.

with him from Poitiers so Richard was quite safe in the great fortress of Taillebourg, but he had lost his military stores as well as the services of the 60 knights and 400 archers captured in Saintes. As a result during the rest of the summer he could make little headway against the officials whom Henry left in charge of Aquitaine when he once again turned his attention to the north. Richard struggled stubbornly on, but the effective end of the civil war came on 13 July when William the Lion, king of Scots, was captured at Alnwick, just one day after – as few contemporaries could resist pointing out — Henry had done public penance at Canterbury for those hasty words which had led to Becket's murder.

The continuing resistance of the young duke of Aquitaine delayed the progress of peace talks between the kings of England and France but on 8 September they were able to agree to a truce until Michaelmas (29 September), the terms of which specifically excluded Richard.[36] Free from all other threats of war, Henry could concentrate on subduing Richard. As his father approached, Richard retreated steadily, never once daring to stand his ground against him. Angered when he heard that Louis and the Young King had deserted him, the news none the less convinced him that the cause was lost. On 23 September he entered his father's presence. Weeping, he threw himself flat on his face at Henry's feet and begged forgiveness. His father raised him up and gave him the kiss of peace. Thus everything went smoothly when the peace conference reconvened at Michaelmas at Montlouis, between Tours and Amboise. Like his brothers Richard agreed to accept rather less than he had been offered the previous autumn: half the revenues of Aquitaine, but this time only two residences, and apparently unfortified ones. Financially Henry treated his sons generously but he retained full power throughout his dominions.

For the rest of the king's subjects the treaty of Montlouis meant, by and large, a return to the status quo as it was fifteen days before the outbreak of war. Loyal barons who had lost lands and castles had them restored. Most of Henry's prisoners were freed without ransom and given their lands back. But however much he desired peace and, with peace, an opportunity to make good war's heavy drain on his financial resources, there were limits to Henry's clemency. Rebels might get their lands back but all fortifications which they had raised since the beginning of the war were to be demolished. In the coming months and years the question of castles was to remain in the forefront of everyone's mind. The end result of Henry's policy was that ruined castles were to be seen throughout his dominions, visible reminders of the Old King's power and the penalties meted out to rebellious lords.[37] For those who had contributed to Henry's victory there were rewards. The town of La Rochelle was granted a 'commune': that is,

---

[36] This paragraph follows *Gesta*, i, 76–9.
[37] *HGM*, 2202–21.

it was given rights of self-government and allowed to choose its own mayor.[38]

However, the treaty of Montlouis said not one word about Eleanor. Her rebellion had been the most damaging of all blows to the Old King's cause and pride; and she would be punished accordingly. She was to remain Henry's captive for as long as he chose. In effect she would be held as a hostage for the good behaviour of her sons; [39] above all for the good behaviour of the new duke of Aquitaine.

[38] Favreau, 'Les Débuts', 23-4.
[39] Martindale, 'Eleanor', 34.

Chapter 5

DUKE OF AQUITAINE, 1174–83

Richard's obstinate resistance in 1174 may well have impressed his father. At any rate in January 1175 he sent him to Aquitaine with orders which went beyond the terms of the treaty of Montlouis. Most castles were to be reduced to the state they were in fifteen days before the outbreak of war; but others were to be razed to the ground.[1] To Henry it may well have seemed a sensible way of killing two birds with one stone – chastizing rebels and at the same time providing his second son with useful experience. To help Richard carry out this task Henry gave him full control over the duchy's armed forces and instructed local officials to put their revenues at his disposal. The twin tasks of 'pacifying' Aquitaine and punishing rebels were to dominate Richard's life for at least the next eight years. In executing them he acted as his father's agent – as is clear from the written reports that he sent his father, which Roger of Howden then included in his history of 'The Deeds of King Henry'. Without them we would have very much less information about Richard's activities as duke. It has to be borne in mind though that these reports comprise little more than lists of 'missions successfully accomplished' – setbacks do not warrant inclusion. In the first such report we learn that that rebel castles have been reduced and that, after a siege of nearly two months, Arnold de Boville's castle of Castillon-sur-Agen and its garrison of thirty knights had surrendered in August 1175. In a very concise report, room was found to draw attention to the use of siege artillery. Castillon's site was a notoriously strong one and Richard was presumably proud of this, the first of many sieges he would conduct.[2]

But by the spring of 1176 Richard found himself faced by a formidable coalition of enemies, beyond what he could deal with by himself. At its head were the sons of the count of Angoulême, their half-brother Viscount

---

[1] Henry himself marched into Anjou to carry out a similar policy and sent Geoffrey to do the same in Brittany, *Gesta*, i, 81–3

[2] Ibid., 101. Howden refers to 'Castelloneum supra Agiens' which Boussard, 514 and Warren, 565 follow Stubbs in identifying as Castillon-sur-Dordogne. But see Norgate, 19, n.1 for identification as Grand-Castel, a little above Agen on the Garonne; J. Andrieu, *Histoire de l'Agenais* (Agen, 1893), i, 38–42. When Henry II had taken it – in less than a week – in 1161 its capture 'had astonished and terrified the Gascons', Torigny, 211. However only Howden mentions the siege of 1175.

Aimar of Limoges, Viscount Raymond II of Turenne, whose sister had married Count William of Angoulême, and the lords of Chabanais and Mastac. To seek help against this league of nobles Richard went to see his father in England.[3] This revolt was not simply a continuation of the war of 1173–4. Apart from the sons of the count of Angoulême, the rebels of 1176 were an entirely different group from the rebels of 1173–4. Whereas in the earlier revolt fighting had centred on the northern parts of the duchy, Poitou and the Saintonge, in 1176 it was focused further south and east, in the Angoumois and the Limousin. Indeed when Richard marched against Angoulême he made this move after taking counsel with the barons of Poitou. We must look elsewhere for an explanation.

Norman and English chroniclers also report another event, apparently unconnected with the war, an event which occurred not in 'turbulent Aquitaine' but far away in the quiet countryside of Surrey. Shortly before Christmas 1175 Reginald, earl of Cornwall, an illegitimate son of Henry I, died at Chertsey and was buried in Reading Abbey, his father's foundation.[4] He left no son, just three daughters. According to English custom the estate should have been divided between the daughters. But Henry II took into his own hands the county of Cornwall and all the earl's estates in England, Wales and Normandy and kept them to provide for his youngest son John, allowing only a small portion to go to Reginald's daughters. The earl had ruled Cornwall almost as an independent principality, separate from the royal administration of the English shires, and Henry was doubtless glad of the opportunity to integrate it into his system of government – especially since at this period production of tin from the Cornish mines was booming. With the twelfth-century expansion of the European economy there was an increasing demand for tin for domestic use in pewter and for ecclesiastical use in bell-metal. All this concerns Aquitaine because Earl Reginald's eldest daughter, Sarah, had been given in marriage to Aimar of Limoges while he was a minor in Henry II's custody. For the viscount it was an illustrious connection; in Limoges men saw Earl Reginald as a great and influential figure, a man who had helped Henry II to the English throne. And when it became clear that the earl would have no sons, it became a marriage which aroused high expectations – expectations which were disappointed when the king took Cornwall for himself.[5] Up to this point Aimar had remained loyal to the Old King. He had helped to entertain Henry and a vast gathering of kings and nobles for seven days at Limoges in February 1173 and had held aloof from the revolts of 1168 and 1173–4. In 1176 he suddenly changed his line. He went over to opposition and on

---

[3] *Gesta*, i, 114–15.
[4] Ibid., 105.
[5] Vigeois, Bk 1, ch. 56; G. R. Lewis, *The Stannaries* (Cambridge, Mass., 1906), appendices J and L.

and off pursued this new policy until his death in 1199. But it is certain that even in the thirteenth century the viscounts did not forget their Cornish connection.[6] In 1175–6 Henry II's obsessive concern for John, revealed again and again in the last sixteen years of his reign, drove Aimar of Limoges to rebellion. When he became king, Richard – too generous to John perhaps – failed to find a means of reconciling Aimar, and in the end it was while laying siege to one of the viscount's castles that he received his fatal wound.

In April 1176 Henry II responded generously to Richard's request for the resources to meet this additional threat. On his return to Aquitaine he was able to recruit mercenaries on a large scale. They were much needed since one of the leading rebels, Vulgrin of Angoulême, had not only put his castles in a state of readiness but took the field with a force of Brabançons with which, according to Diceto, he ravaged Poitou. Richard defeated them in a battle between St Maigrin and Bouteville towards the end of May.[7] Vulgrin's castles still held out but Richard ignored them and turned against Viscount Aimar. Advancing into the Limousin he captured the castle of Aixe, thus prising open the approach to Limoges along the line of the river Vienne. Limoges, like many other towns in the twelfth century, was growing up around two distinct nuclei. On the one hand there was St Stephen's Cathedral and the bishop's palace; locally this centre was known as the city, the *civitas* or the *urbs*. On the other was the abbey of St Martial and the castle of the viscount; this was called the citadel, the *castrum*. The citadel seems to have been the most populous part; here were the workshops which produced the famous Limoges enamels. Within the citadel there was constant bickering between abbot, viscount and townspeople – grown so rich that they obeyed no one, remarked Geoffrey of Vigeois ruefully – and yet also a sense that they were bound together in

---

[6] T. D. Hardy, *Rotuli Litterarum Clausarum* (Record Commission, 1833), 429, 437.
[7] The date – 'immediately after Whitsun' – and place of battle from Howden, *Gesta*, i, 120. St Maigrin and Bouteville lie south and west of Angoulême. However another – and more detailed – account of a defeat suffered by Vulgrin's Brabançons in 1176 is given by the dean of St Paul's, Diceto, i, 407. He sites the battle 'near Barbezieux' – a place which could certainly be described as lying between St Maigrin and Bouteville – but also says that the victors at Barbezieux were Bishop John of Poitiers and Theobald Chabot commanding the army of Poitou in the absence of Richard, then in England with his father. For Diceto, the victory and the minimal losses suffered by Bishop John's forces showed the wisdom of relying on God's servants rather than on secular power. Given that Howden clearly had an 'official' report in front of him and that Diceto, writing some years later, had sought and obtained information from Bishop John (Diceto, i, 5–6), a plausible explanation of these discrepancies might be that Richard defeated the Brabançons at Barbezieux and that Diceto confused the site of this engagement with that of an earlier one in which the bishop and Chabot had forced the Brabançons to leave Poitou before Richard, returning from England, pursued them south of Angoulême.

opposition to their neighbour, the bishop's city. The two main parts of Limoges were separated geographically and by the fact that each had its own enclosure. Whenever there was fighting around Limoges one permanent complicating factor was the rivalry between city and citadel. During the troubles of 1173–4 the inhabitants of the citadel seized the opportunity to turn their enclosure into a proper circuit of walls, a move which was probably aimed against the city rather than against ducal authority, though clearly it was taking advantage of the latter's temporary weakness.[8]

In June 1176 Richard laid siege to Limoges; after a few days' resistance Aimar's citadel capitulated. By the end of the month the duke was back in Poitiers, where he met his brother Henry. The Young King had been pressing for permission to go on a pilgrimage to Compostella but Henry II, believing that this was just an excuse to get away from his watchful eye, had instead ordered him to help suppress the rebellion in Aquitaine. After holding a council with the barons of Poitou, Richard and Henry marched into the county of Angoulême. Having cleared the field of Vulgrin's troops Richard now intended to strike at the Taillefer castles, presumably accepting the fact that this would drive Vulgrin's father, Count William, to take his son's part. Châteauneuf, the castle controlling the key bridge across the river Charente west of Angoulême, on the main road from Poitiers to Bordeaux, fell after a fortnight's siege. At this point Henry packed up and left. He had been a reluctant ally and may well have resented playing second fiddle to his younger brother. In any event he never had much stomach for serious campaigning. Undeterred by the Young King's defection, Richard pressed on. He captured Moulineuf after a siege of ten days and then turned to Angoulême itself. Here, gathered within its walls, were the enemies who had so far eluded his grasp: Count William of Angoulême and Vulgrin, Aimar of Limoges, the viscount of Ventadour and the lord of Chabanais. Seemingly mustered for a last-ditch stand, they in fact conceded defeat after only six days. Count William surrendered all his chief castles, Bouteville, Archiac, Montignac, Lachaise and Merpins, as well as the town of Angoulême. Richard took hostages from them and then sent them and other members of their league to England to sue for mercy at his father's feet. Henry II received them at Winchester on 21 September, but postponed consideration of their case until he himself should come to Normandy. In the meantime he sent them back to his son in Aquitaine.[9]

The Old King, like his eldest son, sometimes toyed with the idea of going to Compostella. Moreover in the years 1176–7 he was taking a keen

[8] *Gesta*, i, 120. On the topography and power structures at Limoges, G. Verynaud, *Histoire de Limoges* (Limoges, 1973), 26–8.

[9] *Gesta*, i, 121. Howden was copying the telegraphic style of the 'official report' sent to Henry II, so it seems likely that the phrase *pravo usus consilio* (taking bad advice) to describe the Young King's departure was his own comment. For the place and date of Henry II's court, Diceto, i, 414.

interest in the competing politics of the Spanish kingdoms and he may well
have instructed Richard to ensure that the great road south from Bordeaux
to the Pyrenees was kept open for travellers of all sorts: pilgrims, traders
and couriers. Richard and his Brabançons carried out this task with an
efficiency which must have shattered many observers accustomed to a
more leisurely way of doing things. He celebrated Christmas Day 1176 at
Bordeaux. By 9 January 1177 he had besieged Dax, which had been held
against him by the viscount of Dax and Count Centulle of Bigorre, and
taken it; he had besieged Bayonne, which the viscount of Bayonne had
held against him, and taken it; he had marched right up to 'the Gate of
Spain' at Cize and there he had captured and demolished the castle of St
Pierre. This lightning campaign undertaken in the depths of winter while
most people were still celebrating Christmas had the desired effect. The
leaders of the Basque and Navarrese communities swore that they would
keep the peace and allow pilgrims to pass unmolested. Richard returned to
Poitiers and from there, on 2 February, sent envoys to his father reporting
his success and announcing that he had pacified all parts of Aquitaine.[10] It
was an exaggeration. At the end of the campaign he had dismissed his
Brabançons. No longer paid, they had to live somehow and since they
could make a good, professional job of plundering and devastating this was
always their preferred solution to the problem of unemployment. For several months, under the command of William le Clerc, a defrocked priest
and a well-known captain of mercenaries, they wrought havoc in the
Limousin. Eventually, stirred by the preaching of Abbot Isambert of St
Martial's, the nobles and populace organized a militia to combat them.
Carrying a cross brought back from Jerusalem before them, the 'army of
peace' caught up with the Brabançons at Malemort, near Brive, and
relieved their outraged feelings in an orgy of slaughter.[11]

Some months earlier, while Richard was still in the foothills of the
Pyrenees, a crisis had blown up in the rich, flat pasture land of western
Berry, the most north-easterly part of Aquitaine. The duke's position here
was weak since he possessed no lands or castles of his own and he had to
rely solely on his rights as the acknowledged overlord. Strategically it was
an important area. From Bourges Capetian forces could launch a quick
strike against Tours and Poitiers. For this reason Henry II was always on the
lookout for excuses and opportunities to intervene in Berry. In 1170 he
had made a bid to capture Bourges itself but withdrew when Louis VII
came up with an army. Then, towards the end of 1176, Ralph of Déols, lord
of Châteauroux, died, leaving a three-year-old daughter, Denise, as his only
child. Henry claimed custody but her kinsmen fortified their castles and

[10] *Gesta*, i, 131–2.

[11] Vigeois, Bk 1, ch. 70; *Chroniques de Saint-Martial de Limoges*, ed. H. Duplès-Agier
(Paris, 1874), 59, 189.

refused to hand her over. This was a rebuff which could not go unpunished, especially since the income of the lord of Déols was reputed to be equal to the ordinary revenues of Normandy. Henry was busy in England so he at once ordered his eldest son to take an army from Normandy and Anjou and occupy the lordship with all speed.[12]

After some initial success, however, the Young King's campaign ground to a halt and Henry decided that he would have to take a hand himself. It was time to clarify the confused political situation in Berry. In June 1177 he sent envoys to Paris bearing demands which were clearly intended to bring matters to a head. Louis VII was to honour the agreements he had made concerning the marriages of his daughters Margaret and Alice. He was to hand over the French Vexin (as the remainder of Margaret's dowry) and endow Alice with Bourges.[13] Louis responded to these totally unjustified demands by arguing that it was Henry who had broken the agreement by keeping Alice in his custody for far too long. In addition he persuaded a papal legate to publish the fact that he had been instructed by Pope Alexander III to lay all of Henry's dominions under an interdict unless the marriage was celebrated in the near future. For more than a year Alexander, at the French king's request, had been putting discreet pressure on Henry either to return Alice to her father or marry her to Richard.[14] Now that the threat of interdict had been made public Henry began to negotiate more seriously. In August he crossed to Normandy in force and summoned his sons to a family conference. By September, after meetings with the legate and King Louis, a new agreement had been reached at Nonancourt. Problems relating to Châteauroux and other lands in dispute in Berry and Auvergne were referred to a panel of arbitrators; Richard was to marry Alice; finally both Louis and Henry agreed to go on crusade and, in the meantime, made a mutual non-aggression pact.[15] In three ways these complex diplomatic manœuvrings had touched Richard closely: as Alice's husband-to-be; as overlord of western Berry and the Auvergne; and finally as a future crusader, for it was probably in Normandy in September 1177 that he first heard a papal legate preach of the perils facing the Christian kingdom of Jerusalem. It may have been at this time that the name Saladin began to mean something to him.

After the sealing of the treaty of Nonancourt it was time for Henry II to carry out the promise made at Winchester the previous September and deal with William and Vulgrin of Angoulême, Aimar of Limoges and the other defeated rebels. He sent Richard on ahead while he travelled south through Berry, where once again his eldest son was making heavy weather

---

[12] *Gesta*, i, 127, 132, 195-6; Diceto, i, 425; Torigny, 274.

[13] *Gesta*, i, 168-9.

[14] *Gesta*, i, 180-1; Landon, 223-4.

[15] *Gesta*, i, 190-4.

of the task assigned to him. The Old King was soon in possession of Denise of Déols, and sent her to Chinon for safe-keeping.[16] Then he took his army to the Limousin. Richard and he spent about a month there 'punishing the rebels as each deserved'.[17] What he meant by this vague phrase, Howden does not tell us.[18] Robert of Torigny, however, reports that Richard took possession of the citadel of the viscount of Limoges as punishment for the support he had given to the count of Angoulême.[19] There is no direct evidence for Angoulême itself but we know that in 1199 Count Ademar was still trying to recover lands which had once been held by his father Count William and 1177 is the most likely date for their confiscation by the Angevins. The presence of Henry and his sons, together with their army, made a considerable impression on the Limousin. It was probably October 1177 that Walter Map had in mind when he referred to the king's forces devastating the region and noted that some who delighted in evildoing ravaged everything in sight, saying 'This is not robbery or violence; we are bringing peace and obedience.'[20]

In mid-November Henry II returned to Berry for a fruitless conference with Louis VII at Graçay on the subject of their conflicting claims to Auvergne. Since the barons of Auvergne are reported to have stated that their province belonged of old to the duchy of Aquitaine, the Old King was being remarkably easygoing in allowing the dispute to be referred to another commission of enquiry.[21] This suggests that he had bigger fish to fry – and indeed he had. He hurried back to the Limousin and completed a piece of business, negotiations for which must already have been in train. At his favourite monastery of Grandmont, where in 1170 he had wanted to be buried, he met Count Audebert of La Marche. La Marche was a huge fief held of the duke of Aquitaine, but the counts had always been more or less independent. Their possessions dominated the roads leading north from Limoges to Poitou and Berry. Count Audebert had taken part in the rebellion of 1168 and had encouraged the revolt of the townspeople of La Souterraine in 1171, but he had now decided to leave his native soil. His family life had ended in disaster. He had suspected his wife of having a lover, had killed the man on Easter Day and repudiated his wife. When,

---

[16] For her later history see N. Vincent,'William Marshal, King Henry II and the Honour of Châteauroux', *Archives* (forthcoming).

[17] *Gesta*, i, 194–6. Howden also states that the king brought charges against those who had sided with his sons and against him in 'the time of war' – his usual formula for 1173–4. But the Limousin was not much involved then. Moreover the punishment of Aimar of Limoges suggests that it was the war of 1176 that was meant.

[18] Since both father and son were in the Limousin, no written report was made and so Howden was without his usual source of information.

[19] Torigny, 275.

[20] Map, 96–7. Though it is also possible that the comment refers to the ravaging of the Limousin in 1182.

[21] *Gesta*, i, 196.

later on, his only son died, it was taken to be a sign that he had killed the supposed lover unjustly. Apart from a daughter who was believed to be barren he had no other near kin and in a state of acute depression he determined to sell up and go to the Holy Land. For Henry II this was an opportunity not to be missed, particularly convenient since he had just laid his hands on the lordship of Déols. So in December 1177 in exchange for an immediate cash payment of 15,000 *livres angevines* (6,000 marks) and forty pack animals – clearly intended to be used for the long pilgrimage to Jerusalem – Henry acquired the whole county of La Marche. Since it was believed to be worth 20,000 marks it was an amazing bargain, but one which was available only to a purchaser with immense cash reserves. It transformed the entire structure of power in eastern Aquitaine. Inevitably it was a transaction which disturbed many of Audebert of La Marche's neighbours, and especially his distant kinsmen, the Lusignans and Taillefers.[22] But there was nothing they could do. Henry took the homage of the barons and knights of La Marche and then returned to Angers to celebrate Christmas. It was one of the greatest feasts of his reign. His sons were there and so was a concourse of knights so huge that it reminded men of his coronation.[23] Unquestionably there was a great deal to celebrate.

As princes maintaining the peace within their dominions, the Angevins could generally rely on the support of the Church. Not always, of course, and at Limoges they had bruised local pride. In February 1178 the canons of St Stephen's had secretly elected as bishop Sebrand Chabot, a man whom they knew would be unacceptable to the king. So when the cat was let out of the bag in September, they were driven out of the city by Richard's agents and the cathedral was closed for twenty-one months.[24] This apart we know nothing of Richard's activities in 1178 until the end of the year.[25] According to reports which Howden received the following

[22] Ibid., 196–7. The story of the count's misfortunes was told by the Limousin chroniclers, Vigeois, Bk 1, ch. 70, and *Chroniques de Saint-Martial*, 188–9. The 6,000 marks made a big impression: the amount was recorded by Vigeois and Bernard Itier as well as by English and Norman authors. Although Labbe's edition of Vigeois gives 5,000 marks, most manuscripts have 6,000. According to Torigny, 274–5, Henry paid 6,000 marks for land worth 20,000 marks 'as the king himself said'. Diceto, i, 425 also gives 6,000 marks – and his informant, Bishop John of Poitiers, was there. On the Lusignan claim see Painter, 'The Lords of Lusignan', 33.

[23] Torigny, 276.

[24] Archdeacon of Thouars, dean of Poitiers, Sebrand belonged to a family which had joined the revolt of 1173, Vigeois, Bk 1, ch. 70. A Chabot had helped him in 1176 so there may have been no particular reason for Richard to share his father's dislike of Sebrand Chabot, but presumably he disliked the secrecy, and carried out his father's orders. Diceto, ii, 4–5 inserts the story under 1180, when Vigeois, Bk 1, ch. 72, shows that Sebrand, though not yet fully restored to Henry's favour, had managed to return to Limoges.

[25] After 1177 Roger of Howden spent less time at Henry II's court and so he had access to Richard's reports less often than before.

summer, late in 1178 Richard had taken a large army to Dax where he found, to his great delight, that the townspeople had captured an old opponent, Count Centulle of Bigorre, and held him in prison. He was then persuaded to release him by Alfonso II, king of Aragon and count of Barcelona (1162–96). Apparently Alfonso came to visit Richard and agreed to stand surety for his friend's behaviour, guaranteeing that he would do nothing against the will of the duke of Aquitaine or his father. As a further precaution Richard made the count of Bigorre surrender Clermont and the castle of Montbron.[26] The description of the count as Alfonso's 'friend' suggests that there was more to this incident than simply the curbing of an unruly vassal. Alfonso II, himself a troubadour and patron of troubadours, was in these years bidding fair to become 'Emperor of the Pyrenees'. He had succeeded his father as a five-year-old in 1162, but in the mid-1170s was beginning to flex his muscles. In 1173 Marie, viscountess of Béarn, entered a nunnery, leaving Béarn to be governed in the name of her small son by a regent appointed by Alfonso II – even though her lands included some estates which, theoretically speaking, were within the duchy of Aquitaine. In the last couple of years the pace of Alfonso's advance had quickened. After a long struggle Raymond V of Toulouse had eventually, in 1176, resigned all his rights over Provence. In 1177 Alfonso had taken over Roussillon and in March 1178 had renewed an old alliance with Castile – an aggressive alliance directed against the little mountain kingdom of Navarre. In addition he had, by virtue of a marriage alliance, attached the count of Bigorre to his cause, granting him possession of the strategically vital Val d'Aran in 1175.[27] With his influence spreading over the Pyrenees – Béarn, Bigorre, Roussillon and Provence – Alfonso II was a formidable neighbour, a potential threat to the dukes of Aquitaine as well as to the kings of Navarre and counts of Toulouse. There can be little doubt that when Richard led his army to Dax it was part of a campaign intended to counter the northward expansion of Aragon.

He then returned to hold his Christmas court at Saintes. By then fresh trouble was brewing in the Angoumois. It looks as though Count William of Angoulême was already making his preparations for a pilgrimage to Jerusalem, leaving his eldest son Vulgrin as effective head of the family. Possibly Richard had summoned him to Saintes to do homage and Vulgrin had refused, not willing to accept the losses recently inflicted upon his

---

[26] *Gesta*, i, 212–13. This report then goes on to cover the dramatic events of the first five months of 1179.

[27] For a succinct account of Alfonso, 'a militant young king', see T. N. Bisson, *The Medieval Crown of Aragon* (Oxford, 1986), 35–7; P. Tucoo-Chala, *La Vicomté de Béarn et le problème de sa souveraineté* (Bordeaux, 1961); C. Higounet, 'La Rivalité des maisons de Toulouse et de Barcelone pour la prépondérance méridionale', *Mélanges d'histoire du moyen âge dédiés à la mémoire de Louis Halphen* (Paris, 1951). Alfonso was probably persuaded to withdraw his claim to be overlord of all Béarn.

family. His resistance was stiffened by an alliance with Geoffrey de Rancon, who held large estates in Poitou and in the Saintonge – as well as an important fief, the lordship of Marcillac, as a vassal of the counts of Angoulême. The Rancon family had participated in the revolts of 1168 and 1173–4 and, like the Taillefers, may well have been disturbed by the advance of Angevin power in the valley of the Charente, from Saintes eastwards through Cognac towards Angoulême. Geoffrey de Rancon's great castles at Taillebourg and Pons were well sited to disrupt communications between Bordeaux, Saintes and La Rochelle; and it was against one of these, Pons, that Richard launched his first attack early in 1179. But although he had mustered a large army, the siege went badly for him. Evidently Geoffrey de Rancon had anticipated the attack and laid in plenty of supplies. By Easter week it must have been clear to Richard that he was making no headway against a well-conducted defence and that in terms of political psychology it was risky to stake his reputation on one big success. Leaving the larger part of his forces behind to maintain the blockade of Pons he marched north past Cognac and laid siege to Richemont. After three days the castle capitulated and was demolished. In the next three weeks the same treatment was handed out to four more castles: Genzac, Marcillac, Grouville and Anville.[28] But then, instead of returning to the siege of Pons, he led his army in May 1179 to the enterprise which was to establish him once and for all as an acknowledged expert in the vital art of siege warfare: the capture of Taillebourg.

Taillebourg is situated on the right bank of the river Charente, perched on an outcrop of light-coloured rock. It still overlooks a bridge and in those days there was also a causeway to take the traveller over the marshy ground beyond. Indeed, since there were no fords and no other bridge, it controlled the only crossing of the Charente between Saintes and Tonnay-Charente. In contemporary opinion it was an impregnable fortress; indeed Richard himself had taken refuge there five years earlier when driven out of Saintes by his father. Protected on three sides by a sheer rock face and massively fortified on the fourth, its garrison had every reason to feel confident. No one – or so Diceto believed – had ever dared to attack it before. But on 1 May Richard brought up siege machines and began to bombard the walls, concentrating on the fourth side where a small town nestled at the foot of the citadel.[29] At the same time he set his troops to ravage the surrounding fields and vineyards. Partly out of over-confidence

---

[28] *Gesta*, i, 213.

[29] This account of the capture of Taillebourg is based on Diceto, i, 431–2, though his dates differ slightly from those given by Howden, *Gesta*, i, 213. Torigny also emphasizes the strength of the site, 281–2. Howden's laconic report merely says that Richard laid siege to the *castellum* on 3 May and it fell three days later; by omitting all reference to the town it would appear that in the manner of official reports this was both accurate and misleading.

and partly as a result of the double pressure of having to sit still under a bombardment while their property was burned and looted under their noses, on 8 May the garrison made a foray against Richard's camp, placed temptingly close to the walls. This was precisely what Richard was waiting for. His men counterattacked. After a fierce struggle at the gates they were able to force their way in at the heels of the retreating defenders. The garrison withdrew into the citadel, leaving the town and the bulk of their supplies to be plundered at will. Three days later the citadel itself capitulated. So great an impression did the capture of Taillebourg make that Geoffrey de Rancon at once surrendered Pons. Richard then dismantled both castles. Having seen his ally overwhelmed in this startling fashion, Count Vulgrin decided that discretion was the better part of valour. He handed over the keys to Angoulême and Montignac and their walls too were razed to the ground. After an arduous five-year apprenticeship in the disciplines of war the twenty-one-year-old duke had produced his masterpiece. At the moment of crisis, in the hand-to-hand fighting at the gates of Taillebourg when the decision could have gone either way, Richard had thrown himself into the thick of the mêlée. When he took his news to his father in England he was given a conqueror's welcome.[30]

*

During the years from 1175 to 1179 the power of the duke of Aquitaine had surged to a level never before attained. La Marche, Limoges and the lordships of the Pyrenees had been brought to recognize his authority. Even the most powerful of the duke's subjects, the counts of Angoulême, who for generations had been accustomed to act as though they were independent princes, had twice conceded defeat, in 1176 and 1179. The fact that Count Vulgrin, shortly before 1179, had married Elizabeth, daughter of Hugh, lord of Amboise, suggests that the marriage had been arranged to suit the Angevins, for Hugh was one of their trusted men. A connection like this, to a family from the Touraine, was an abrupt departure from the time-honoured pattern of Angoulême marriage alliances which linked the counts to the lords of Périgord, the Limousin, La Marche and the Saintonge.[31] In one well-remembered case Eleanor's father, Duke William X, had tried to insist that he should have the right to arrange the marriage of the probable heiress to the viscount of Limoges, but the nobles of the

---

[30] The dean of St Paul's described the demolished castles as dens of thieves, and says that Henry greeted Richard *cum honore maximo*, Diceto, i, 432. According to Robert of Torigny, 282, Richard went to visit the shrine of St Thomas as well as to see his father.

[31] I owe this point to the kindness of Dr Rowan Watson.

Limousin, fearing 'the Poitevin yoke', successfully resisted this demand and she was given instead to a count of Angoulême.[32]

The marriage of Eleanor to Henry II transformed the situation. Able to call upon the financial and military resources of his whole empire, the new duke was a political bulldozer possessed of a weight which could flatten opponents and their castles. In 1156 Henry II had taken young Aimar V of Limoges out of the custody of his uncles and had arranged his marriage to Sarah of Cornwall.[33] But like all bulldozers he was ponderous and slow to turn. Despite his phenomenal energy the sheer size of his dominions inevitably meant that it could be months or even years before he was free to deal with a distant crisis or give his officials the support they needed against a major local potentate. After 1174, however, Henry hoped that the presence of his sons in different parts of the empire would in some measure provide the mobility, flexibility and speed of response which alone he could not give. Early in 1177, when commanding his eldest son to cope with the business of Déols, he said that he, when alone, had lost none of his rights and that it would be a disgrace if they were to lose anything now that there were several of them to rule.[34] The Young King failed to live up to his father's hopes. He was generous, courteous and chivalrous. No one attended more tournaments than he did. Young knights loved him for he gave them pleasure and livelihood. But in politics and in real war he was a child, incapable of concentrating for long. Unable to see beyond the short-term gain he went from whim to whim, reacting without thought to whatever gossip he happened to have heard last. In the summer of 1177, when his wife was pregnant, she left him and returned to her father's court.[35]

Richard by contrast may well have exceeded his father's expectations. The combination of the father's resources and occasional presence with Richard's determination and burgeoning military skills had, it seems, pacified even the more independent parts of the duchy. In the aftermath of Taillebourg a number of the leading nobles of Aquitaine decided that the time had come for a pilgrimage to Jerusalem. For some it may have been a penance imposed by a church which, in its desire for peace and undisturbed enjoyment of its material wealth, could often be counted upon to lend the weight of spiritual sanctions in support of the sword of power wielded by princes. Others may have been relieved to leave behind, for a while at least, the sight of their ruined castle walls, a nagging reminder of the defeats they had suffered. Led by old Count William of Angoulême and his stepson Aimar of Limoges, they left on 7 July, joining Audebert of La

[32] Vigeois, Bk 1, ch. 48.
[33] Ibid., ch. 56.
[34] *Gesta*, i, 132.
[35] Ibid., 169.

Marche on the road to Jerusalem. Barely a month later Count William died at Messina; and in the next year Audebert ended his days at Constantinople. For a period of two years from the summer of 1179 to the summer of 1181 we know nothing of Richard's movements. In part this was due to Henry II's presence on the continent from April 1180 to July 1181; in part it doubtless reflects the subdued mood of the Angoumois and the Limousin with so many of the wealthiest and most influential nobles away on pilgrimage. Aimar of Limoges arrived back at Christmas 1180 and Henry was reconciled with Sebrand Chabot at Grandmont the following Lent.[36]

But on 29 June 1181 there occurred an event the consequences of which were to shatter the peace of Aquitaine. As usual it concerned a death and a disputed inheritance. Count Vulgrin of Angoulême died, leaving no child but an infant daughter, Matilda. This, in Geoffrey de Vigeois's words was to be 'the cause of great calamity for our country'.[37] In Richard's view, Vulgrin's daughter should inherit the county of Angoulême and he, as duke and overlord, should have custody of her. But the inheritance customs of western France held out far greater prospects to the brothers of the dead man than Richard was prepared to allow.[38] A duke of Aquitaine in the style of 1176 and 1179 was not going to have much time for customs which reflected the political realities of earlier days. Naturally this was not how Vulgrin's brothers, William and Ademar, saw it. They claimed the county and when driven out by Richard they fled to their half-brother, Aimar of Limoges. Here, shortly before Vulgrin's death, Richard had given offence by once again insisting that the walls of St Martial's should be pulled down.[39] The rebels were soon joined by the count of Périgord and the viscounts of Ventadour, Comborn and Turenne, the most prominent members of that network of intermarriage and cousinage which characterized Limousin and Angoumois society. Richard's disregard for their cherished customs of inheritance threatened them all, directly or indirectly, and provided a cause to which all could rally in defence of the right order of their world.

At this point the king of France, the traditional defender of men's rights throughout the kingdom, chose to become involved. But it was no longer Louis VII, a king who in the last few years had been a sick man, chiefly concerned to ensure the undisputed succession of his son and then end his

---

[36] Richard's one recorded campaign in Aquitaine in 1181 took him to Gascony. It seems that the heir to the viscounty of Lomagne, south of Agen, refused to pay him homage. Richard's reply was to send an army to occupy Lectoure, the chief town of the viscounty, until in mid-August the recalcitrant heir came to heel and in return was dubbed a knight at St Sever, Vigeois, Bk 1 chs. 71–2.

[37] Ibid., ch. 72.

[38] J. Yver, 'Les Caractères originaux du groupe de coutumes de l'ouest de la France', *Revue historique de droit français et étranger*, 4th series, xxx (1952).

[39] Vigeois, Bk 1, ch. 72.

days in peace. Now the king was Philip II. Although only fifteen at the time of his father's death (18 September 1180), he soon showed himself to be a cunning and unscrupulous politician – very different from Louis. But if his reputation as one of the great kings of French history is anything to go by, then the means he used were justified by the end: the destruction of the Angevin empire. Later on a story was told of his early years as a young and untried king. At a council meeting of his barons one day he sat apart, chewing a hazel twig and apparently lost to the world. When challenged to say what was on his mind, he replied that he had been wondering whether it would ever be given to him to make France great again, as it had been in the days of Charlemagne.[40] Ironically, in the early stages of his reign Philip relied heavily upon aid from Henry II and his sons, the family which he was to do so much to tear apart. Late in 1181 indeed Richard, at his father's command, joined his brothers Henry and Geoffrey in a campaign against Stephen, count of Sancerre. The purpose of the expedition was to help young Philip establish himself on the throne by freeing him from what he saw as the overbearing influence of the house of Champagne.[41] But as the rebellion of William and Ademar of Angoulême gathered substance Philip saw his opportunity. He accepted the homage of Angoulême. Now wrote Bertran de Born, the poet of the Limousin resistance to Richard, 'we will know for sure whether King Philip takes after his father or follows in the footsteps of Charlemagne'.[42]

The years 1182–3 were to be the make-or-break crisis of Richard's rule in Aquitaine, faced as he was by so many enemies. Characteristically he seized the military initiative, launching a surprise attack on Puy-St-Front, the count of Périgord's fortress at Périgueux, on 11 April 1182. He captured the citadel but he had only a few troops with him and couldn't hold it for long, so he pushed on past Excideuil into the Limousin, driving straight into the heartland of the rebel cause and devastating the country as he went. This aggressive move suggests that he had already asked for his father's help and was confident that it would soon be forthcoming. By mid-May the Old King had arrived. He summoned the leading rebels to a conference at Grandmont.[43] Presumably at this meeting he heard those charges against Richard which a little later were to reach the ears of some English chroniclers. Gervase of Canterbury reports that 'the great nobles of Aquitaine hated him because of his great cruelty'. The dean of St Paul's heard that he 'oppressed his subjects with unjustified demands and a

---

[40] Gerald, *Princ.*, 293–4 (Bk 2, ch. 25).

[41] Diceto, ii, 9; Gervase, i, 297.

[42] Born, 176–83, no. 10, 'Pois Ventedorns'. Bertran added that once a king has said yes (as Philip had in giving Angoulême to Taillefer), it is not right that he should say no – perhaps reminding Philip and the rebels of Richard's nickname, 'Oc e Non' (Yea and Nay), and hence urging them to be just as decisive.

[43] Vigeois, Bk 2, ch. 2.

régime of violence'. Roger of Howden, as usual, gives a more detailed account. 'He carried off his subjects' wives, daughters and kinswomen by force and made them his concubines; when he had sated his own lust on them he handed them down for his soldiers to enjoy. He afflicted his people with these and many other wrongs.'[44] But Henry II was not impressed by complaints of this kind. He and Richard shared the same view of ducal rights. Henry sent a message to his eldest son to come and help and then he joined Richard in the business of subduing the Limousin. First they systematically attacked and occupied the chief strongholds held by Viscount Aimar and his vassals: Excideuil, St Yrieix and Pierre–Buffière. Then they turned on the count of Périgord and laid siege to Puy-St-Front. Here, on 1 July, they were joined by the Young King and such was the over-whelming strength of their combined forces that both Aimar of Limoges and Elie of Périgord decided to sue for peace. Aimar promised to give no more help to his half-brothers of Angoulême and handed over his first- and third-born sons as hostages. Elie surrendered his fortress and Richard demolished its walls.[45]

The events of the summer of 1182 show, beyond all doubt, that while they stood united the Angevins were masters of their huge dominions. A family of princes responding to their father's directives, and pulling together when any one of them was challenged, was an unbeatable instrument of government. But there were problems. What would happen when their father died? Would the Young King step into the Old King's shoes? Would he then command his younger brothers? Should they owe allegiance and obedience to him? Or would they go their separate ways, each ruling an independent principality? Richard and his elder brother would give very different answers to these questions. Yet somehow, against the pressure of these unavoidable and underlying tensions, Henry II had to find ways of preserving family unity, of upholding his system of government. Had he done so – as did his exact contemporary Frederick Barbarossa – he would have ended his days like Barbarossa, a much-admired king. Henry, however, failed, and so ended his days disliked, humiliated and defeated. The immediate problem was to satisfy his eldest son. As the one who might one day step into his father's shoes he was also the one who stood most in his father's shadow. Richard had Aquitaine; Geoffrey had Brittany; but it was the Old King, not the young one, who held Anjou, England and Normandy. Though in time Henry would succeed to a far greater inheritance than either brother, he did not have the

---

[44] Gervase, i, 303; Diceto, ii, 19; Gesta, i, 292. When Howden rewrote this passage in the early 1190s he made no mention at all of the rebels' accusations against Richard, and referred instead to the damage Richard suffered at the hands of the Young King's Aquitanian allies, Chron, ii, 274.

[45] Vigeois, Bk 2, ch. 2; Gesta, i, 288.

patience to wait. He wanted to rule now – and in Aquitaine he thought he saw an opportunity. The rebels of 1182 had been defeated, but they had weighed up one of their conquerors – and they also saw an opportunity.

The Young King had passed through Limoges and St Yrieix on his way to join his father and brother at Puy-St-Front. At Limoges he had ostentatiously donated a cloak embroidered with the words *Henricus Rex* to the monks of St Martial's.[46] On this and many other occasions he would have been able to gauge the strength of local feeling against Richard's imperious rule. A new field of activity seemed to be opening up for him if only he had the courage to grasp the nettle. But however frustrated he was, however jealous of his younger brother's reputation as a successful soldier, it cannot have been an easy decision. If he went to war against Richard, which side would their father take? As he edged ever closer to the point of no return, to an open commitment to the rebels, the Young King's life came to bear the marks of a man tormented by uncertainty and doubt. He was not sure of the loyalty of his own household. The most famous knight in his following, William Marshal, was suspected of being Queen Margaret's lover. But the Young King was incapable of taking a firm line. He could neither put a stop to the gossip nor put William on trial. At Christmas, William Marshal, loudly protesting his innocence, left his master's service and rode off in search of fresh tournaments. Some months earlier, in the autumn of 1182, young Henry had once again asked his father to give him a principality, Normandy, so that he could make proper provision for his own knights. When Henry II again refused, he stormed off to France, saying that he was going to go to Jerusalem. Eventually his father persuaded him to return to Normandy but not before Philip of France had learned something of his brother-in-law's troubles and half-formulated schemes.[47]

As the Young King wavered between the three options of remaining dutifully at his father's side, going to Jerusalem, or marching into Aquitaine, he was certainly tempted by messages from the rebels offering to recognize him as their duke, but he may also have been egged on by Geoffrey of Brittany. For Geoffrey, although he seems to have taken no part in suppressing the revolt, had also been in the Limousin during that summer. On the Feast of St John (24 June) he had met his father at Grandmont 'together with certain nobles', as Geoffrey of Vigeois puts it.[48] It would be interesting to know who these nobles were; or even to know whether the chronicler's choice of phrase was due to ignorance or a desire for brevity or for the sake of discretion. But, however innocent his presence at

[46] Vigeois, Bk 2, ch. 2.
[47] *HGM*, 5095–848; *Gesta*, i, 289–9, 296. D. Crouch, *William Marshal* (London, 1990), 45–6.
[48] Vigeois, Bk 2, ch. 2.

Grandmont may have been, we do know that by the winter of early 1183 Geoffrey was playing a very devious game indeed. It is not easy to see why. His eldest brother Henry had cause to feel frustrated, but for a third son Geoffrey of Brittany was extremely well endowed. Perhaps the answer is as simple as the one given by some contemporary writers. 'Geoffrey, that son of treachery ... that son of iniquity' is how Roger of Howden sums up his character, while Gerald of Wales gives a more elaborate description of a prince 'overflowing with words, smooth as oil, possessed, by his syrupy and persuasive eloquence, of the power of dissolving the apparently indissoluble, able to corrupt two kingdoms with his tongue, of tireless endeavour and a hypocrite in everything'.[49] By the autumn of 1182 war had broken out again in Aquitaine.[50] The Taillefer brothers were still able to find support within the Angoumois, notably from the lords of Archiac and Chalais. Encouraged by this, Viscount Aimar decided to hire mercenaries in Gascony and denounce the peace terms so recently agreed.

The Young King's opportunity was getting nearer, but if he were to show his hand at last, he needed an excuse, a justification for the war which would make sense in his father's eyes and might just lead him to condone the attack on Richard. This justification was provided by the castle of Clairvaux, and the scheme very nearly worked. Richard had been rebuilding and strengthening Clairvaux and his motives for doing so have long puzzled historians, since it was a step which could be interpreted as an infringement of his elder brother's rights.[51] Early in 1183 the Limousin troubadour, Bertran de Born, anxious to bring the Young King into the rebel camp, composed a political song, a *sirventes*, which included the following lines:

> Between Poitiers and l'Ile Bouchard and Mirebeau and Loudun and Chinon someone has dared to build a fair castle at Clairvaux, in the midst of the plain. I should not wish the young King to know about it or see, for he would not find it to his liking; but I fear, so white is the stone, that he cannot fail to see it from Mateflon.[52]

Despite its geographical inaccuracy, the song, politically speaking, was right on target, designed as it was to show that the duke of Aquitaine was building a castle in the middle of the lands of the count of Anjou. What was Richard doing? Was he strengthening his border where it faced the great

---

[49] *Gesta*, i, 297–8; Gerald, *Top.*, 200, written in the late 1180s; repeated in *Princ.*, 178–9. For indications of a violent dispute between Henry II and Geoffrey in 1181 or 1182, J. Everard, 'The "Justiciarship" in Brittany and Ireland under Henry II', *ANS*, xx (1997), 102.

[50] Vigeois, Bk 2, ch. 6.

[51] Torigny, 302.

[52] Born, 182–3.

Angevin arsenal and treasury at Chinon, which would one day come into the hands of his feckless elder brother? Possibly, but the site of Clairvaux suggests an explanation much nearer at hand. It lay only about six miles west of Châtellerault, and documents from the 1130s indicate that the castellan of Clairvaux at that time was a vassal of the viscount of Châtellerault. These viscounts were among the most important barons of Poitou. Eleanor's father, Duke William X, had married one of their daughters; another member of the family had been William IX's most famous mistress. Their castle at Châtellerault controlled the strategically vital Tours–Poitiers road at the point where it crossed the river Vienne. In 1184 Richard was to return to this area, founding a new town and castle at the bridge over the river Creuse at St Rémi de la Haye, about twelve miles on the other side of Châtellerault. This time the new foundation was to the viscount's detriment and was expected to anger him. All this suggests that when he started work on Clairvaux Richard anticipated the viscount's hostility rather than his brother's. But the problem with Clairvaux was that although it lay in Poitou a count of Anjou could claim to hold it. Like the more important castles of Loudun and Mirebeau it was one of the territorial gains made in the late tenth century at the expense of the count of Poitou. Unlike these cherished Angevin possessions, however, Clairvaux had been held by relatively unimportant vassals and by the 1130s they seem to have become more closely attached to the viscounts of Châtellerault.[53] If Richard had heard about the old Angevin claim when he began work on a castle within the political orbit of Châtellerault he may have thought that the years of co-operation with his father meant that it could be disregarded. But whatever his view it gave the Young King some reason to hope that he might be able to win over his father, Henry of Anjou, to an Angevin cause.

Towards the end of 1182 Richard was summoned from his war in the Angoumois to attend his father's Christmas court at Caen. It was intended as a splendid demonstration of the power and solidarity of the Angevin family, the greatest court ever held in Normandy. Besides all his sons Henry II was accompanied by a daughter, Matilda, and her husband, the greatest of the German princes, Henry the Lion, formerly Duke of Saxony and Bavaria, but now driven into exile and on his way to the shrine at Compostella. No Norman baron was to hold a court of his own that Christmas; they would all celebrate with the king. More than a thousand

---

[53] The interpretation of Richard's building of Clairvaux is based on parallels with the inquest into the building of Saint-Rémy-sur-Creuse printed in *Archives historiques du Poitou*, viii, 39–53, and on what can be gleaned of the earlier history of Clairvaux from C. Chevalier, 'Cartulaire de l'abbaye de Noyers', *Mémoires de la Société archéologique de Touraine*, xxii (1872), 402, 476, 486, 505–6, 528–9, 626; and idem, 'Documents concernant le prieuré de St Denis en Vaux', *Archives historiques du Poitou*, vii, 347. For his other town foundations in Aquitaine, see M. Beresford, *New Towns of the Middle Ages* (Gloucester, 1988), 351–2, 636.

knights jostled in the ducal castle and halls of Caen.[54] Among the knights
who were in Normandy late in 1182 was Bertran de Born. The troubadour
was quarrelling with his brother Constantine over the family castle at
Hautefort in the border lands between Périgord and the Limousin, and he
probably hoped to persuade either or both Henry II and Richard to take his
side. In a courtly song Bertran says that only the conversation and beauty of
the Duchess Matilda prevented him from dying of boredom at the dull and
vulgar Norman court. 'Her breast makes night seem day, and if you could
see further down the whole world would glow.'[55] But it is highly unlikely
that, if Bertran had stayed in the north until after Christmas, he would have
found the rest of the trip so dull. The Young King was there and the
troubadour had high hopes of him. Someone had to overturn the present
political arrangements in the Limousin if he was ever to lay his hands on
Hautefort. In the next few weeks, as the Angevin court moved south from
Caen, the tensions came to the surface and in Bertran de Born the muddle,
the bickering and the bitterness would have found a fascinated observer.

Henry II planned to provide a legal framework for the continuance of his
empire by asking both Richard and Geoffrey to do homage to their elder
brother; doubtless he also hoped that this clear recognition of his seniority
would do something to allay the Young King's sense of frustration. Geoffrey
agreed readily enough. Brittany had long since been in some way subject to
Normandy. At Le Mans he performed the required homage. But Richard at
first refused, arguing that he was as nobly born as his brother. Ten years
after the court held at Limoges in 1173 Henry II had again raised the spectre of Aquitaine being permanently reduced to a subordinate role in the
Angevin empire. After a while the Old King persuaded Richard to change
his mind and he agreed to do homage so long as it was spelt out that
Aquitaine should belong to him and his heirs for ever. Now it was the Young
King who drew back and, doubtless to their father's immense exasperation,
refused to accept Richard's homage.[56] Homage on these terms was totally
incompatible with the engagements he had by now entered into with the
rebels. But without some explanation his refusal to accept Richard's
homage must have seemed incomprehensible and so, on 1 January 1183,
the whole muddled story was blurted out. In the words of Roger of Howden:

the young King, of his own accord and under no compulsion, laying his
hands on the Holy Gospels in the presence of a large crowd of clerks and

[54] *HGM*, 5693–714; Torigny, 304; Map, 488.
[55] 'Casutz sui de mal en pena', Born, no. 8, 160–7, Some lines in 'Ges de disnar',
no. 9, 168–73, imply that either Henry II or Richard introduced Bertran to Matilda.
[56] *Gesta*, i, 291–2; only the dean of St Paul's, in an account very sympathetic to
Henry II, makes explicit that Aquitaine was to belong to Richard and his heirs,
Diceto, ii, 18.

laymen, swore that from that day onward and for the rest of his life he would be loyal to King Henry, his father and his lord, and would serve him faithfully. Moreover since he did not wish to have preying on his mind any malice or grudge by reason of which his father might later be offended, he revealed that he had pledged himself to support the barons of Aquitaine against his brother Richard and said that he had done this because Richard had fortified the castle of Clairvaux though it really belonged to the Angevin patrimony which he should inherit from his father.[57]

The dispute over Clairvaux was easily solved. Grudgingly but fairly quickly Richard was induced to hand the castle over to his father. This done, it soon became obvious that Clairvaux had been no more than a pretext and that the real problems lay elsewhere.

At Angers the Old King called Henry, Richard and Geoffrey together and compelled them to swear a compact of perpetual peace. But any oath of peace, if its terms were to be at all realistic, needed to include the Aquitainian rebels. So it was agreed that they would reassemble to confirm their peace compact at Mirebeau and that the rebels would be invited to attend this meeting. Henry II sent Geoffrey to the Limousin to arrange a truce and to ensure that the discontented barons would come to the peace conference. Geoffrey, however, once on the loose, did nothing of the kind. Instead he joined the rebels. The Young King, who clearly knew what Geoffrey was plotting, then suggested that he should follow his brother, again supposedly as a peace-maker. Moreover he persuaded his father to agree that if the terms imposed on the rebels the previous summer were not acceptable to them now – as obviously they were not – then they would be granted a fresh hearing in the king's court.[58] This, of course, was intolerable to Richard. He had resigned Clairvaux; he had agreed to do homage to his brother; and now it looked as though all the work of 1182 was going to be undone. As the news of the quarrel between the Old King's sons spread, those who had been defeated the year before took fresh courage, while others like Geoffrey of Lusignan, who had previously been too cautious to join the revolt, now decided that their moment had come. Presumably some of those who were still loyal to Richard kept him informed of the deteriorating political situation, and of the contacts between his brothers and the rebels. While Henry II talked of peace and

[57] *Gesta*, i, 294.

[58] Ibid., 295; with somewhat different details in Diceto, ii, 18, who suggests that in the end Richard, infuriated by his brother's demand that he should swear fealty on some holy relics, angered his father by arguing that he was the lawful successor of his mother just as the first-born son was of his father, i.e. he claimed that after his father's death he would hold Aquitaine directly from the king of France, not as part of the Angevin dominions, Norgate, 50, n.1.

allowed first Geoffrey and then Henry to pull the wool over his eyes, Richard's duchy was slipping away from him. Finally he could contain his frustration no longer. After an angry scene with his father he left the court without permission and rode in haste to Poitou to fortify his castles and towns.[59]

The Young King meanwhile had obtained Henry II's leave to go to the Limousin on his mission of peace. He sent his wife to the court of Philip Augustus and joined Geoffrey at Limoges early in February.[60] There they were met by Viscount Aimar, who had with him a large force of Gascon *routiers* under a chief called William Arnald. The forbidding presence of these mercenaries was sufficient to persuade the inhabitants of the citadel that they too would be well advised to join the revolt. The abbot of St Martial's, the leader of the 1177 'crusade' against the Brabançons and well known for his loyalty to the dukes of Aquitaine, took refuge in the abbey town of La Souterraine. A second contingent of *routiers* under William's uncle, Raymond le Brun, was making its way north to reinforce Aimar. Geoffrey had a fine company of knights with him at Limoges and had also mustered mercenaries in Brittany with orders to attack Poitou from the north-west. All in all the rebels had assembled a very considerable fighting force. But Richard was in no mood to sue for peace. He hunted down the Breton forces, executing all those who fell into his hands and organizing retaliatory raids on Geoffrey's estates. Then he seized the initiative in a dramatic fashion, just as he had in April 1182. At the head of a small cavalry force he rode almost non-stop for two days and nights and on 12 February he fell upon Aimar's *routiers* as they attacked the church of Gorre a dozen miles to the west of Limoges, believing him to be still somewhere beyond Poitiers. Richard himself 'manfully' killed William Arnald, and though the exhaustion of his horses meant that Viscount Aimar managed to escape, many of the *routiers* were captured, dragged to Aixe, where some were drowned in the river Vienne, others put to the sword and the rest blinded. So far as Geoffrey of Vigeois was concerned it was a fate that all such evildoers deserved.[61]

By now Henry II himself was on his way to the Limousin, following his sons in the forlorn hope of finding a peace formula. Presumably he had

---

[59] *Gesta*, i, 291–2; Diceto, ii, 18–19. The sequence of events is not entirely clear, partly because Howden first gave a brief account of what happened, and then added an explanation of why it happened which involved going back over some incidents again. For Geoffrey of Lusignan at Limoges, *HGM*, 6408–13.

[60] *Gesta*, i, 296.

[61] Howden reports the fighting between Richard and Geoffrey's Brabançons, ibid., 292–3; the campaigning in the Limousin is reported in Vigeois, Bk 2, ch. 6. From this, and from Bertran's poems, it seems that Geoffrey was heavily committed in the south so whether he had time to go to Brittany himself, as Howden says, is a moot point, Norgate, 51, n.5. Indeed Howden himself cut this from his own revised version of events, *Chron.*, ii, 274.

already set in motion the machinery which the next month would array a large army under his command, but when he approached Limoges he still had only a few men with him. In the citadel of St Martial's everyone's nerves were on edge. As Henry II drew near, a watchman, mistaking the king's small band for a raiding party organized by the citizens of the epis-copal city, sounded the alarm. The men of St Martial's swarmed out to drive off their enemies. In the confusion that reigned before one of the Englishmen in the citadel recognized the royal banner, one of Henry's household was wounded and the king himself had a narrow escape. Henry then withdrew to the relative safety of Richard's stronghold at Aixe. Here, that same evening, he was visited by the Young King, who tried to explain and excuse what had happened. But Henry was shocked and angry and would not listen, so his son went back to his friends in Limoges. At Aimar's command the inhabitants of St Martial's took an oath of allegiance to the Young King and then prepared to stand siege. Since the citadel's walls had been razed in 1181, ramparts of earth, stone and wood had to be erected from the fabric of a number of churches which were hastily demolished for the purpose. Not for another fortnight, however, did Henry and Richard have a force sufficiently large to encir-cle St Martial's. For the moment they had to be content to occupy the episcopal city and from there keep a watchful eye on their enemies. The two Henrys, father and son, spent the next few weeks in a fruitless series of negotiations, emotional reconciliations, quarrels, scuffles, promises made and broken. Once more, according to Howden, the Old King had a narrow escape when his horse lifted its head and was hit by an arrow that otherwise would have struck its rider in the chest. In describing these incidents Howden became more and more critical of the deceits of both the Young King and Geoffrey, and of the way they allowed their followers to endanger the lives of their father's envoys.[62] At times the Young King may genuinely have regretted the path he had chosen but he was now too far along it to be able to draw back. It seemed to Howden that his offers of reconciliation were mere blinds intended to win for his brother Geoffrey's forces a free hand to terrorize the region. Then a force of Brabançons sent by his brother-in-law Philip Augustus arrived on the scene – the opening shot in a campaign which the king of France was to wage for the next thirty years. They took St-Léonard-de-Noblat by storm, massacred its inhabitants, and then swept on past Limoges to capture and sack Brantôme. Yet more mercenary bands, hired by Viscount Aimar and Raymond of Turenne, were devastating the southern

---

[62]Vigeois, Bk 2, ch. 7; *Gesta*, i, 296–9. Howden's detailed account of events in the Limousin in spring 1183 suggests that he himself was there for a while before being sent back to Normandy in May, ibid., 299–300.

Limousin.[63] Bertran de Born used the confusion to turn his brother out of Hautefort. The whole countryside was in uproar.

When their main army arrived on 1 March, Henry and Richard made no attempt to chase the widely scattered bands of plundering *routiers*. Instead they concentrated their energies on subduing the rebels' capital, the citadel of St Martial's. Henry II's headquarters remained the bishop's city; Richard occupied St Valerie, cutting off the citadel from the Pont St Martial over the Vienne. For both sides it was to prove an arduous siege. Inside the citadel the Young King quickly ran short of money. He and Aimar had engaged every *routier* chief who offered his services, fearing that he would go over to Henry II if they didn't. It was a sensible policy – if they could afford it. But for obvious reasons his father had cut off the Young King's allowance. He obtained a 'loan' from the burgesses, but this did not last long. So he was driven to seize the chalices, plate and other treasures which belonged to the shrine of St Martial. Having emptied the citadel of gold and silver he left Limoges and went off in search of new sources of pay for his mercenaries. He plundered Grandmont and then the abbey of La Couronne near Angoulême.[64] But the citadel, under the command of Geoffrey of Brittany, Viscount Aimar and Geoffrey de Lusignan, still held out. The besieging forces grew discouraged. Many of them were quartered in tents and they suffered badly from the cold, wet weather. Some left after only a fortnight and, as time went by, it became harder to maintain the blockade. Finally, in late April or early May, Henry II decided to raise the siege. It looked very much as though Henry II and Richard were beginning to lose their grip on the war. This was a major crisis.

Neighbouring princes were marching into Aquitaine in order to play their part in what was rapidly developing into a showdown on the scale of 1173–4. On the Young King's side were Philip of France, Hugh, duke of Burgundy, and Raymond, count of Toulouse. For Raymond, whose county had been held as a fief of Aquitaine since 1173, the replacement of Richard by his elder brother held out the prospect of release from a galling sense of subordination. On the other hand Raymond's rival in the great struggle for Provence, Alfonso II of Aragon, came in on Richard's side. What Richard himself was doing at this stage is unclear. Geoffrey of Vigeois's focus on events in the Limousin, in and around his beloved St Martial's, may well mean that he did not report campaigns elsewhere in Aquitaine. For example, in Bertran de Born's 'Ieu chan, que l reys m'en a preguat', a song seemingly written while the outcome of the struggle was still uncertain, the poet says that Richard has 'Angoumois by force and

---

[63] Vigeois, Bk 2, chs 8–11. Neither Rigord nor William the Breton mentions Philip's intervention. This is not surprising in view of Henry's generosity towards Philip, highlighted by Rigord, 34–5.

[64] Vigeois, Bk 2, chs 12–16.

freed all Saintonge as far as Finisterre'. Even allowing for poetic licence this implies that Richard had scored some successes not otherwise reported. Moreover, although fully committed to the rebel cause Bertran cannot entirely withhold his admiration for Richard's determination. He never deviates from his path and if his allies don't sell him out he will be more ferocious than any wounded boar.[65] But at Limoges itself the Young King was free to go over to the attack. Although he was driven away by the defenders of the city of St Stephen's with derisive shouts of 'We do not want this man to reign over us', he was able to capture the castle of Aixe, which was so lightly garrisoned that it must have been abandoned by Henry and Richard. Three days later, on 26 May, the Young King fell ill. For a little while longer his health held up sufficiently for him to plunder one more shrine, at Rocamadour, and then at Martel, on 11 June, he died.[66]

It was the end of the rebellion. Although his hesitations had alarmed some of them and although his acute shortage of money remained an embarrassment right up to the end, yet the rebels had committed themselves to him.[67] Whatever the origin of the revolt, by early 1183 it had been transformed into a struggle to make him duke of Aquitaine in place of the 'tyrannical' Richard. Owing to his lack of resources he had always been to some extent a figurehead, but he had become an indispensable one. He was the justification for the war, particularly in the eyes of neighbouring princes whose intervention might have been decisive but who understandably did not feel involved in the quarrel over the succession to Angoulême. As soon as they heard of his death, Hugh of Burgundy and Raymond of Toulouse returned home. Like the king in chess, the Young King had possessed very little power of his own, yet without him it was impossible to carry on the game.

[65] Born, no. 14, 204–13. An allusion to 'the pawns of La Vallée having run away scared' – La Vallée being in Anjou – seems to imply that it was written after Henry II had raised the siege of the citadel of Limoges, and while Bertran had high hopes of winning.

[66] Vigeois, Bk 2, chs 16–19; *Gesta*, i, 300–1, and (for participation of Alfonso) 303.

[67] For frustration with the Young King's leadership, and the view that Geoffrey would have provided better, 'D'un sirventes', Born, no. 11, 184–9.

Chapter 6

THE UNCERTAIN INHERITANCE,
1184–9

The structure of Angevin rule in Aquitaine had been severely shaken by
the Young King's intervention, but once he was gone it was not difficult to
pick up the pieces. On hearing of his death Viscount Aimar and Geoffrey
de Lusignan left Limoges in order to accompany his body as far as
Grandmont. As the cortège approached Uzerche on its way north, the
chronicler Geoffrey and a few monks from the priory of Vigeois, standing
on a hill, watched it go by on the road below. It was, observed Geoffrey, a
fine day.[1] Since it was good campaigning weather, Henry II and Richard
seized the opportunity to return to Limoges, to lay siege to Aixe and the
citadel. On 24 June Aimar of Limoges surrendered. He promised to lend
no more support to his half-brothers in Angoulême. The citadel's newly
built walls were razed to the ground. Then, while Henry II headed back to
Anjou, Richard and Alfonso of Aragon besieged Bertran de Born in
Hautefort. The castle was believed to be impregnable but after seven days
it was taken on 6 July and restored to Constantine de Born.[2] Alfonso then
returned to Barcelona, leaving Richard to devastate the estates of the count
of Périgord and his friends.[3] Eventually all the rebels submitted and
accepted peace terms. Some of their castles were demolished and others
retained in the king's hand. Count Geoffrey was punished by being
deprived of all his fortresses in Brittany. But although Angevin rule in
Aquitaine was fully restored, Richard's own position remained uncertain.
The revolt had come close to success and it may well have shaken Henry
II's confidence in his son's ability to rule Aquitaine. If Richard were to

---

[1] Vigeois, Book 2, ch.19.
[2] Ibid., ch. 18. According to Geoffrey, Bertran had ousted his brother 'through
treachery'. Losing Hautefort left the troubadour with a grudge against Alfonso,
though in the song 'Qan vei pels vergiers despleiar' he mockingly forgave him on
the grounds that he 'was forced to do it by the lord of Poitou; and a king who
expects pay from a lord must earn it the hard way', Born, 280–1.
[3] According to Howden, Henry II rewarded Alfonso lavishly, *Gesta*, i, 303.
According to Bertran, Alfonso went home with the king's money instead of using it
to ransom his captured men, Born, 278–9. All this suggests that Alfonso's contribution to the war of 1183 amounted to far more than just the capture of Hautefort;
see Benjamin, 'A Forty Years War' 277–8.

resign the duchy then some interesting prospects would open up. For the moment, however, the Old King was content merely to resume control of those castles which he had granted to Richard before the outbreak of the war.[4] Doubtless, at any rate for a while, his son could bear this loss of authority with patience in view of his new position as Henry's chief heir.

At Michaelmas 1183 Henry showed his hand. He summoned both Richard and John to Normandy and ordered Richard to hand over Aquitaine in return for John's homage. If Richard was to step into his dead brother's shoes then why should not John – for as yet John was still Lackland – step into Richard's shoes? It seemed to be an easy and natural solution. But this is not how it appeared to Richard. He had not worked and fought for eight years in order to give Aquitaine away. It was for Aquitaine that he had, in Bertran de Born's words, 'gained and given and spent so much wealth, and dealt and received and withstood so many a blow, and endured so much hunger, so much thirst, and so much fatigue from Agen as far as Nontron'.[5] In any case if he gave up Aquitaine he would be just as dependent on his father as his older brother had been.[6] He asked for two or three days' grace so that he could consult with his friends and when this was granted, he took his leave. At nightfall he rode straight for Poitou, pausing only to send an envoy to his father with the message that he would never allow anyone to take his place as duke of Aquitaine. This must mean that ducal castles were once again under his control. From now onwards Henry began to pay a price for the fact that he had only occasionally visited Aquitaine, and had only very rarely drawn Poitevins and other southerners to his court. In emergencies Richard had needed his father's support – and his father had given it, but so far as the general day-in day-out management of patronage and government was concerned, he had evidently enjoyed a free hand. While his father kept his distance, it had been Richard who spent ducal revenues, Richard whose court was the focal point of southern political and social life. It was Richard, therefore, not his father, who won the loyalty of the majority of politically minded Aquitanians. To add to Henry's troubles he was constantly being pestered by King Philip's claim that now that the Young King was dead, his widow's marriage portion – Gisors and the other castles of the Norman Vexin – should be returned to France. Eventually at a conference held on the frontier between Gisors and Trie on 6 December 1183 Philip agreed to let Henry keep the Norman Vexin on condition that he pay Margaret an annual pension of 2,700 *livres* and on the understanding that he grant it to whichever of his sons married Alice. Since Alice had long

---

[4] *Gesta*, i, 302-4.

[5] In 'Qan la novella flors', Born, 286-7.

[6] In a song probably written early in 1183, 'D'un sirventes', Bertran described a king who lives on an allowance doled out by another as a king of fools, ibid., 186-7.

been betrothed to Richard the vagueness of the phrase 'to whichever of his sons married her' suggests that Henry may have been toying with the idea of marrying her not to Richard but to John. In this event Philip might well have approved of any plan which would make proper provision for his half-sister and her husband, whether it was Aquitaine or even something more. At the same conference Henry II did homage to Philip for all his continental possessions.[7] It looks as though he was deliberately emphasizing the legal basis of his right to order the affairs of Aquitaine. But if it came to conflict between father and son over possession of the duchy, law would matter less than the personal ties and loyalties made – or not made – in the years since 1175.

Throughout the winter of 1183–4 the Old King continued his efforts to prise Richard away from all or part of Aquitaine, but neither threats nor blandishments had any effect. At last, in a fit of anger, he gave John permission to invade the duchy and try to take it by force. Richard, of course, had been preparing for some such move. He had held his Christmas court at Talmont, north of La Rochelle, and distributed gifts on a lavish scale.[8] But princely generosity could not buy every lord's loyalty. It was safer to hire soldiers as well and it is at this time that we first come across the name Mercadier, a name that from now on was to be closely linked with Richard's. In 1183 Mercadier was just the commander of yet another of the bands of *routiers* which were busily spreading havoc in the southern Limousin, but in the next fifteen years he became the most famous professional soldier in Europe. Instead of flitting from one employer to another he remained constant in Richard's service and was with him still at the end at Chalus. Perhaps this was because Richard paid better than all rival employers, but over so long an association other bonds must have developed. This is clear from words which Mercadier himself dictated in 1196: 'I fought for him strenuously and loyally. I never opposed his will but was prompt in obedience to his orders. In consequence of this service I gained his respect and was placed in command of his army.' He first appears acting under Richard's orders in February 1184 when he led a force which sacked Excideuil – a stroke directed against Aimar of Limoges, who was presumably hoping to profit from the quarrel between Henry II and his son.[9]

In fact the expected invasion of Aquitaine did not materialize until some time after Henry had sailed to England in June. At the end of that month his officials were able to meet a Portuguese princess at La Rochelle and

---

[7] *Gesta*, i, 304–6, 308. See Rigord, 27f. For an important study analysing Henry's neglect of Aquitanians, see N. Vincent, 'King Henry II and the Poitevins', *CCM* (forthcoming).

[8] *Gesta*, i, 311; Vigeois, Bk 2, ch. 28.

[9] Vigeois, Bk. 2, chs 25, 28; Mercadier's words cited by Powicke, 232.

escort her safely across Poitou. This delay suggests that he had not intended his angry words to be taken literally, but at least one of his sons was capable of making trouble, while claiming to be doing no more than carrying out his father's wishes. John was still only sixteen years old so it is probable that the real initiative for the invasion came from the unscrupulous Geoffrey, now apparently restored to his duchy. Richard and Geoffrey had been formally reconciled in the summer of 1183 but the memory of the struggle for Limoges obviously still rankled. The two younger brothers carried out raids into Poitou while Richard retaliated with raids against Geoffrey's lands in Brittany. When news of this war reached Henry II in the autumn of 1184 he summoned all three to England. The fact that they obeyed the summons shows that the Old King was still in effective control of the whole of his empire. In December Richard, Geoffrey and John were publicly reconciled at Westminster.[10] Throughout the second half of 1184 Henry II had been seeking a solution to the problem of the succession. Immediately on his arrival in England he gave orders for Eleanor's release from custody. She was present at the important council meetings at the end of the year and it would be surprising if her voice was not heard in the discussions about the future of Aquitaine – all the more so since she could be expected to have some influence over her children, and particularly over Richard. Henry's mind was still working on the possibility of marrying Alice of France to another of his sons. He welcomed an embassy from the emperor, Frederick Barbarossa, and agreed to a proposal for a marriage alliance between Richard and one of the emperor's daughters. The princess in question, however, died later that year. Henry kept Richard and John in England over Christmas, but sent Geoffrey to Normandy 'to hold it in custody'.[11] Was this a veiled threat to Richard? A reminder that he should not take it for granted that he would in time succeed to England, Normandy and Anjou? If Richard insisted on keeping Aquitaine, would he have to give up his claim to inherit the rest? That Henry was now thinking of Richard's keeping his duchy is suggested by the plans he was making to install John as king of Ireland, but what price would the Old King demand in return for this concession? Richard was alarmed. Immediately after Christmas he obtained permission to return to Aquitaine and we next hear of him once again at war with Geoffrey.[12]

Henry held Richard responsible for this further outbreak, which was in flagrant defiance of his recent ban. In April 1185 he crossed to Normandy and began to muster an army, but he soon found a more effective means of dealing with his insubordinate but formidable son. He sent for Eleanor

[10] Diceto, ii, 28-9; *Gesta*, i, 311, 319-20.

[11] *Gesta*, i, 313, 319-21. For discussion of which of Barbarossa's daughters may have been intended, and of Henry II's intentions, Kessler, 34-5.

[12] *Gesta*, i, 334, 337.

to join him and when she arrived, a message went to Richard, requiring him to surrender Aquitaine to his mother, the lawful duchess. In view of Richard's affection for his mother, this was a trump card. He laid down his arms, ordered his castellans to obey Eleanor's commands and returned, like a dutiful son (*sicut filius mansuetus*), to his father's court.[13] But for Richard too this was a triumph: the full rehabilitation of his mother to all her rights as duchess of Aquitaine.[14] It could only mean that his own future as duke was doubly assured. In the meantime Henry, Eleanor and Richard acted as joint rulers. On occasion a fortunate, or exasperated – since charters had to be paid for – beneficiary would receive no fewer than three charters each confirming him in the legitimate enjoyment of the same right.[15] The real power in Aquitaine, in the sense of the power to appoint men or collect and transfer money, still lay with Henry – as thus far it always had when he was on the continent and chose to exercise it. But, by the time the Old King returned to England in April 1186, Richard's position as heir apparent had been strengthened. In the previous month Henry and Philip had held another conference at Gisors, confirming the settlement reached in December 1183, but this time, instead of promising that Alice would marry one of his sons, Henry agreed that she should be married to Richard.[16] Geoffrey of Brittany had no illusions about the significance of this agreement. Any expectations he may have had of inheriting a larger share of the Angevin empire were fading fast. His one hope now lay with Philip and he went to visit him in Paris, the traditional move for all discontented sons of Henry II. The rumour that he used his notoriously smooth tongue to get himself recognized as seneschal of France suggests that he was aiming at Anjou, since this was a title claimed by the counts of Anjou.[17]

While Geoffrey was intriguing against him in Paris, Richard was occupied with an invasion of Toulouse. His father had given him a plentiful supply of money and there was considerable justification for the war. Not only had Count Raymond V supported the Young King in 1183, but early in the next year his son Raymond VI had led some *routiers* into the Limousin, possibly acting in collusion with Viscount Aimar, since it seems to have been in response to this act of aggression that Mercadier struck at Excideuil in February 1184. It may well be that the count of Toulouse and his son had taken advantage of Richard's difficulties in 1184–5 to recover

[13] Ibid., 337–8.

[14] As Diceto was to observe, 'the eagle of the broken covenant', i.e. Eleanor, 'shall rejoice in her third nesting', i.e. (counting male births only) Richard, 'for in all things he strove to bring honour to his mother's name', Diceto, ii, 67–8.

[15] J. C. Holt, 'Aliénor d'Aquitaine, Jean sans Terre et la succession de 1199', *CCM*, xxix (1986), 95–100.

[16] *Gesta*, i, 343–4.

[17] Ibid., 350; Newburgh, Bk 3, ch. 7; Gerald, *Princ.*, 175–6 (Bk 2, ch. 10).

the disputed territory of Quercy.[18] Unfortunately Geoffrey of Vigeois died in 1184, some months after being hit on the head by a piece of falling masonry, and without his chronicle to guide us we are hopelessly ignorant of events in this part of the world after the February of that year.[19] Richard's counterattack in 1186 seems to have gone very well indeed. In April 1186 he met King Alfonso at Najac-de-Rouergue and made a new treaty with his old ally.[20] Count Raymond dared not risk battle against Richard's massive army; nor did the pleas for help which he sent to King Philip meet with any response.[21] Presumably Philip judged that for the moment he had no means of putting pressure on either Henry or Richard which would be both legitimate and effective.

Once again it was an unexpected death which altered the situation. In a tournament at Paris in August 1186 Duke Geoffrey was trampled to death. Philip, as overlord of Brittany, at once claimed custody of Geoffrey's two daughters, and threatened to invade Normandy if Henry II did not hand them over. Having forced the Old King on to the defensive, Philip was able, in subsequent negotiations, to demand that Richard stop his harassment of Toulouse. In October the two kings agreed on a truce until January 1187 but whether or not this was supposed to include the war in Toulouse is not clear. One indication that Richard was still maintaining a more aggressive attitude than his father lies in the fact that when the constable of Gisors killed a French knight in a skirmish which occurred after the truce had been made, he thought it wiser to take refuge with Richard. By February 1187 at the latest, however, Richard had left the south and was in Normandy to welcome his father on his arrival from England. Two meetings with Philip during the spring resulted in the truce being prolonged until midsummer but otherwise served only to widen the gap between the two sides.[22] In addition to demanding custody of Brittany, the king of France had yet again raised the question of Alice's marriage and the Norman Vexin. It looks as though the agreement of March 1186 had failed to establish beyond all possibility of argument whether or not the Angevins could keep the Vexin if Alice remained unmarried. Unquestionably, if either Richard or John had married her, it would have added plausibility

[18] Vigeois, Bk 2, ch. 28. For the identification of 'Pairaco' as Payrac, 50 kilometres north of Cahors, and for discussion of the question of when the counts of Toulouse recovered territory lost in 1159, see Benjamin, 'A Forty Years War', 276–7.

[19] He reports the accident himself, Vigeois, Bk 2, ch. 25.

[20] In the treaty both men promised to make war against Count Raymond, either in person or, if absent, to send 200 knights in their place. For the text of the treaty and discussion of its terms and date (April 1185 in the manuscript) see Benjamin, 'A Forty Years War', 277–84.

[21] Gesta, i, 345, 347. Presumably based on reports which Richard sent back to his father – in which no mention is made of the contribution of King Alfonso.

[22] Ibid., 350, 353–5, ii, 5. Diceto, ii, 43–4.

to Philip's claim that this vital territory was his sister's marriage portion and, as such, might one day be returned to France. If, on the other hand, Henry II wished to maintain that the Vexin belonged of old to Normandy and was therefore his by hereditary right, it was safer not to confuse the issue by marrying Alice to one of his sons.[23] Whatever the legal rights and wrongs, so long as the Angevins actually held Gisors they were negotiating from a position of strength and could reasonably hope that one day a king of France would be forced to concede their case. The fate of Alice, more than twenty-five years in the king of England's custody without ever being married, has puzzled modern historians just as much as contemporary ones. Gossip said that the Old King had seduced her and that Richard would not marry his father's mistress.[24] It may very well be so, but after 1183 diplomatic calculation could also have persuaded both of them that it was better if Alice did not marry an Angevin. Moreover, by simply keeping her in their power they were holding all their options open and preventing Philip from marrying her to someone else and so forging a new alliance. As a policy it was unscrupulous but probably effective, though certainly not without some disadvantages. For example, it meant that whenever the king of France wanted to stir up trouble, he always had a legitimate grievance to hand.[25]

The early summer of 1187 was filled with the bustle of preparations for war. Since Philip was challenging Henry II's right to hold Alice, Brittany and the Vexin, it was up to him to take the initiative. He could choose where to strike, while Henry had to disperse his forces in an attempt to guard the whole of his long frontier. In June Philip made his move. He

[23] Gervase, i, 346; Rigord, 77–8.

[24] In addition to Howden's account of what was said in 1191 (see below, 142), the seduction story is told by Gerald, *Princ.*, 232 (Dist. III, c. 2) and alluded to by William the Breton, *Philippidos*, iii, 631–7, iv, 126–9. Andreas of Marchiennes, writing in the mid-1190s, observed that 'Henry had kept her always with him and never handed her over to his son Richard. On this subject many things are said, but I think it improper to include uncertain gossip in a true history (*verba ventosa et dubia in veraci historia*)', *Historia regum Francorum*, MGH, SS, xxvi, 211. Cf. Richard 'was suspicious about that custody', Devizes, 26. According to the *Chronica monasterii de Melsa*, ed. E. A. Bond (3 vols, RS, 1866–8), i, 256 she bore Henry a son who was dead by 1190. Although this is a late fourteenth-century chronicle it is curiously well informed about Angevin matters 200 years earlier, probably deriving from stories told by Robert of Thornham, cf. C. Tyerman, *England and the Crusades 1095–1588* (Chicago, 1988), 65.

[25] For a good discussion of the problem see Kessler, 38–44. She points out that while the Young King was still alive Henry's reluctance to see Alice married must have been motivated by something other than the Vexin problem. There is no pre-1189 evidence for the gossip, but a liaison between Henry and his ward between 1180 and 1183 would explain much that is puzzling in Henry's policy towards France in those years – including his remarkable generosity to Alice's brother at the start of his reign.

marched into Berry. By prior arrangement the lord of Issoudun and, further north in the Loire valley, the lord of Fréteval opened their castles to his troops. In Berry, where Angevin and Capetian possessions lay intermingled, it was hard to be loyal to one allegiance only. This was particularly true for the lord of Issoudun, since he was Robert of Dreux, King Philip's cousin. Richard and John barred any further advance by holding Châteauroux long enough to permit their father to come up with the main Angevin army and force Philip to raise the siege. But Philip, his prestige at stake in this first open challenge to the Angevin position, could not afford to retreat. Instead, on 23 June he drew up his forces in battle array. Henry II did likewise. The scene was set for a pitched battle.[26]

At the last minute both sides drew back. It would have been very surprising had they chosen to fight. Pitched battles were rare; between kings they were very rare indeed. In his whole life Henry II never fought a battle; nor did Philip until 1214 and although that battle, at Bouvines, turned out to be the victory which crowned his career he did his best to avoid it. Philip's reluctance helps to explain why even so famous a soldier as Richard never fought a battle in Europe, with the possible exception of his encounter with Vulgrin of Angoulême's mercenaries in 1176 – but that was probably a slaughter rather than a battle. Warfare was not normally about battles. It was about laying waste enemy territory, about the pursuit of a retreating army, about sieges. Most battles occurred as a result of sieges when, as at Châteauroux in June 1187, a besieging army found itself faced by a relieving army. But even in these circumstances a full-scale pitched battle between two more or less evenly matched armies, with well-armed knights and infantry on both sides, was an extraordinary event. Battles were, quite simply, far too risky. In the confusion of battle an accident might decide the issue one way or another and the fortunes of a single day might undo the patient work of months or years. Though comparatively few knights were actually killed on the battlefield, the prince who committed his cause to battle was also putting himself in jeopardy, since the surest way to win a battle was to capture or kill the opposing commander, as Harold was killed at Hastings. Most of the time sensible princes deliberately took steps to avoid so chancy a business.[27] The armies arrayed in the fields outside Châteauroux contained many nobles who knew each other well, who had met at tournaments or on pilgrimages, who were cousins or neighbours. Even if, for once, the kings had not been bluffing when they drew up their armies, these men were reluctant to attack each other. Moreover a papal legate had arrived, sent by Urban III with instructions to settle the quarrels of north-west Europe and prepare men for a crusade. With his

[26] Rigord, 78-9; *Gesta*, ii, 6-7.
[27] J. Gillingham, 'Richard I and the Science of War in the Middle Ages', in *Coeur de Lion*, 211-26.

moral support a group of nobles and clergy from both sides tried to work out peace terms. This proved to be impossible. For as long as there was an alternative neither Philip nor Henry was prepared to make any concession to the other, and there was, of course, an alternative: not peace, not war, but a truce. The requirements of the crusade and the tensions of being brought to the brink of battle both pointed to the need for a long, rather than a short, truce. Two years was the period finally agreed upon. The armies separated and Philip was left in possession of Issoudun and Fréteval.

But that day Philip gained something more significant than temporary control of a couple of lordships. When he went back to Paris Richard went with him. 'Philip so honoured him,' wrote Roger of Howden, 'that every day they ate at the same table, shared the same dish and at night the bed did not separate them. Between the two of them there grew up so great an affection that King Henry was much alarmed and, afraid of what the future might hold in store, he decided to postpone his return to England until he knew what lay behind this sudden friendship.'[28] This does not mean – as some modern writers have assumed – that Richard and Philip were having a homosexual affair. It was common for people of the same sex to share a bed. For example, Henry II and William Marshal did so.[29] The *jongleur* who reported this had no fears that his audience would misunderstand him. He meant to imply that the Old King trusted William, that they were close politically, not sexually. If men exchanged a kiss it was a gesture of friendship or of peace, not of erotic passion. It is an elementary mistake to assume that an act which has one symbolic meaning for us today possessed that same meaning 800 years ago. When Richard and Philip rode to Paris together, it was an act of political defiance – as Henry II knew only too well. Gestures of this kind were part of the vocabulary of politics; an astute politician like Philip used them to great effect. When Geoffrey of Brittany was buried it was said that Philip had been forcibly prevented from throwing himself into the grave.[30] Now in the summer of 1187 Henry sent messenger after messenger to Richard asking him to return and promising to grant him everything that was justly his. Feigning obedience, Richard left Paris but then turned and swooped on Chinon. He seized all the coin in the castle treasury and carried it off to spend on re-stocking and repairing the castles of Aquitaine. Henry's response was to send yet more messengers and at long last he was able to persuade his son to come to see him. Richard admitted that he had listened to the advice of people who were deliberately trying to sow dissension between them. Then at Angers he did homage to his father, swearing on the Gospels that he would be faithful to him against all men.[31]

[28] *Gesta*, ii, 7.
[29] *HGM*, 8984.
[30] Gerald, *Princ.*, 176 (Bk 2, ch. 10).
[31] *Gesta*, ii, 9.

What had caused this sudden breach between father and son? Why had Richard first of all defended Châteauroux against Philip and then ridden away in his company? Almost certainly the explanation lies in the highly charged atmosphere of a battlefield on the eve of battle. Richard seems to have played an important part in the peace and truce talks, and as he went to and fro between the armies his father may have begun to wonder just what these exchanges meant. Was his son willing to accept terms which he would find unacceptable? Possibly there were moments when Henry persuaded himself that he was being betrayed. Moreover, if Richard discussed peace on the assumption that he would be the heir to all his father's dominions then he may have reactivated very real differences of opinion which had lain dormant since the spring of 1185.[32] Those nerve-racking hours, with the armies drawn up in battle array in sight of each other, can hardly have been the best of times for a calm discussion of the problem of the succession. Presumably this is why Philip chose precisely that moment to raise again the spectre which was to haunt the Old King's last years.

At Châteauroux on 23 June 1187 Henry II and Philip had been confronted with the problem of whether or not to commit their forces to battle – the most difficult and terrible decision to face an army commander – and they had drawn back. A few days later, on the morning of 3 July, in a camp at Saffuriya in Galilee another king, the king of Jerusalem, after a night of doubt and conflicting advice, took the opposite decision. A powerful Muslim force was besieging his city of Tiberias and he gave the order to advance to its relief knowing full well that by leaving his camp he was risking battle.[33] He did not reach Tiberias. Marching in fierce summer heat and unrelentingly harassed by Muslim mounted archers, the army was forced to halt at Hattin, in a waterless region, in the hope of being able to continue next day.[34] The Christian soldiers spent a thirsty and sleepless

---

[32] Whatever was actually said at Châteauroux, the two most detailed versions of the negotiations, by Gervase and by Gerald de Barri, are both very hostile to Henry II and consequently present Richard in a favourable light. According to Gervase, to secure the truce and to rescue his father from a hole into which he had dug himself by his own deceits, Richard was willing to abase himself before Philip. He was clearly very impressed by what he believed Richard would do for his father, Gervase, i, 370–3, 377–82, 432. Since Canterbury monks had business of their own at the king's court in France in the summer and autumn of 1187, his account is presumably based on information supplied by them. According to Gerald, Henry sent a letter to Philip suggesting that Alice should marry John and inherit all the continental dominions except Normandy. He too credits Richard with securing the truce, Gerald, *Princ.*, 232–3 (Bk 3, ch. 2).

[33] R. C. Smail, 'The Predicaments of Guy of Lusignan, 1183–87' in *Outremer*, ed. B. Z. Kedar, H. E. Mayer and R. C. Smail (Jerusalem, 1982).

[34] B. Z. Kedar, 'The Battle of Hattin Revisited' and C. P. Melville and M. C. Lyons, 'Saladin's Hattin Letter', both in *The Horns of Hattin*, ed. B. Z. Kedar (London, 1992), 190–212.

night, their eyes smarting from the smoke which blew into their camp as the enemy systematically set fire to the dry scrub around them. When morning came the king, Guy of Lusignan, could see what he must have known already. His exhausted army was completely surrounded. Inspired by the presence of their most sacred relic, the Holy Cross, the Christian soldiers put up a tremendous fight. But the outcome of the battle was a foregone conclusion. On 4 July the army of Jerusalem was annihilated. Guy of Lusignan and the Holy Cross were captured. Those Templars and Hospitallers who survived the battle itself were executed immediately afterwards. As the élite troops of the Christian army these monk-knights could not be allowed to live to fight another day.

With practically all its fighting men either killed or captured, the kingdom of Jerusalem lay helpless at the feet of the invader. In an attempt to appease the wrath of God and save Jerusalem itself, the defenders of the Holy City indulged in extraordinary rituals of penance. Mothers shaved the heads of their daughters and then made them undress to take cold baths in public on the Hill of Calvary. It was in vain. On 2 October the Muslim army marched into the city. The al-Aqsa mosque was restored to Islam. It is symptomatic of the greater tolerance of the Muslims that the Jewish community was allowed to return to Jerusalem and four Christian priests were permitted to hold services in the Church of the Holy Sepulchre. Ever since 1099, when the first crusaders captured the Holy City and massacred the people who lived there, Jews and Muslims alike, the Christians had always treated Jerusalem as though it belonged to them alone.

Guy of Lusignan had been beaten by a greater man. The Muslim leader was Al-Malik al-Nasir Salah ed-Din Yusuf; in the West he was known as Saladin.[35] Whereas Guy had only arrived in the Middle East in 1180 and at the time of his defeat had been king of Jerusalem for less than a year, Saladin had ruled Egypt since 1169 and Syria since 1176. His legendary reputation in the Muslim world as the liberator of Jerusalem has at times obscured the fact that he was an ambitious, skilful and experienced statesman. He had received his political education in the household of Nur al-Din, ruler of Syria from 1154 to 1174 and in those years the crusaders' greatest enemy. From Nur al-Din Saladin learned to appreciate the importance of *jihad*, the holy war against the unbelievers, as the powerful religious force which alone was capable of uniting the divided Muslim world. Like Nur al-Din, Saladin became the champion of Islamic orthodoxy and unity, the patron and friend of poets and preachers whose eloquence was pressed into the service of the *jihad* – and its leader. Although as a general he may be faulted, in diplomatic skill and political understanding he towered head and shoulders above his Middle Eastern rivals, Muslim and Christian alike.

[35] Lyons and Jackson, 255–66.

No man knew better than he the value of a generous gesture. Guy of Lusignan was by no means the handsome fool he has often been made out to be, but his grip on the crown was precarious and the resources of his kingdom were depleted. Against the mighty Saladin he had very little chance. By the end of 1187 only three coastal towns – Tyre, Tripoli and Antioch – were left in Christian hands. Inland a handful of castles still held out. Many garrisons had surrendered quickly because they knew they could rely on Saladin to keep his word to spare their lives. Outremer – 'the land beyond the sea' – was on the verge of extinction, less than a hundred years after the men of the First Crusade had called it into life. Since the failure of the Second Crusade in 1148 the young men of Western Europe had been reluctant to go east, but the news of the disaster at Hattin and the fall of Jerusalem changed all that.

In the autumn Richard took the cross at Tours, in the new cathedral which was rising in place of the old one where, sixty years earlier, his great-grandfather, Fulk V of Anjou, had lain prostrate before the high altar to receive the cross on the way to becoming king of Jerusalem. Now another Angevin had responded to the call for help. North of the Alps he was the first prince to announce that he was going on crusade.[36] He acted in haste, without seeking his father's permission.[37] According to Bertran de Born, 'He who is count and duke and will be king has stepped forward, and by that his worth has doubled.' Whether this thought filled the father of the 'duke who will be king' with as much enthusiasm as it did Bertran may perhaps be doubted. Canterbury monks at court in Normandy witnessed Henry's stunned reaction to the news of his son's action; for several days he would see scarcely anyone.[38] As for Philip, the prospect of seeing the man who was supposed to marry his sister go off on crusade for an indefinite period seems to have been too much for him. Immediately after Christmas, despite the truce, he gathered a large army and threatened to invade unless Henry either returned Gisors or forced Richard to marry

[36] Contemporary English historians were virtually unanimous in noting, sometimes more than once, that he was the first to take the cross, quite often praising him for setting a noble example: Diceto, ii, 50; Devizes, 5; Newburgh, Bk 3, chs 23, 25; *Radulfi Nigri Chronica*, ed. R. Anstruther (London, 1851), 95; Ambroise, 60–5, 185. Gerald, *Expug. Hib.*, 206–9, written at a time when he still hoped Henry II would lead a triumphant crusade, then repeated in *Princ.*, 239–40 (Bk 3, ch. 5). Andreas of Marchiennes was also impressed, *Sig. Cont.*, 425; cf. his *Historia regum Francorum*, MGH SS xxvi, 211. In the light of the enthusiasm shown by others, the fact that Roger of Howden did no more than note that he took the cross, *Gesta*, ii, 29, suggests that at this stage he was unusually unsympathetic towards Richard.

[37] Diceto, ii, 50 'without awaiting [his] father's advice or wishes'; 'without consulting [his] father', Newburgh, Bk 3 ch. 23. It is arguable that had Richard asked his father's permission and it had been refused, he would have been in an even more awkward position, Kessler, 48.

[38] Born, no. 36, 'Nostre seingner somonis el mezeis', 386–7; Gervase, i, 389.

Alice. The two kings held another conference on the border between Gisors and Trie on 21 January 1188. But instead of talking about Gisors, they talked about Jerusalem. They listened to an impassioned sermon delivered by the archbishop of Tyre and were moved to take the cross themselves. According to Roger of Howden and Gervase of Canterbury, as they did so, the shape of a cross could be seen outlined in the sky above their heads.[39]

As long ago as 1172 Henry II had promised to mount a crusade and ever since then he had done nothing about it – though he had given a good deal of financial aid to the stricken kingdom.[40] Philip was as reluctant as Henry, but the two kings were now swept along by the tide of public opinion. In every way possible preachers and troubadours stirred up enthusiasm. Men who did not take the cross received gifts of distaff and wool, implying that they were no better than women. According to Muslim reports, the preachers used visual aids: 'Among other things they made a picture showing the Messiah, and an Arab striking him, showing blood on the face of Christ – blessings on Him! – and they said to the crowds: "This is the Messiah, struck by Mahomet the prophet of the Muslims, who has wounded and killed him."' In another picture, Jerusalem was painted showing the Church of the Resurrection with the Messiah's tomb. 'Above the tomb there was a horse, and mounted on it was a Saracen knight who was trampling the tomb, over which his horse was urinating. This picture was sent abroad to markets and meeting places. Priests carried it about, groaning "Oh, the shame." In this way they raised a huge army, God alone knows how many.'[41]

The rewards offered to those who took the cross were considerable. On the most mundane level, repayment of any debts they owed was postponed until their return; while they were on the crusade their property was taken under the protection of the Church. More important, they were granted a plenary indulgence which freed them from the terrors of purgatory and hell, and held out to them the promise of eternal life in heaven. In the words of St Bernard of Clairvaux, the most successful saint of the twelfth century.

> O mighty soldier, O man of war, at last you have a cause for which you can fight without endangering your soul; a cause in which to win is glorious and for which to die is but gain. Are you a shrewd businessman, quick to see the profits of this world? If you are, I can offer you a bargain

[39] *Gesta*, ii, 29–30; Gervase, i, 406.

[40] H. E. Mayer, 'Henry II of England and the Holy Land', *EHR*, xcvii (1982). For Henry's reluctance see Tyerman, *England and the Crusades*, 40–56; a kinder interpretation of Henry's crusading intentions is offered in Jonathan Phillips, *Defenders of the Holy Land* (Oxford, 1996).

[41] Gabrieli, 182–3, 208–9.

which you cannot afford to miss. Take the sign of the cross. At once you will have indulgence for all the sins which you confess with a contrite heart. The cross is cheap and if you wear it with humility you will find that you have obtained the Kingdom of Heaven.[42]

Unlike his father, Richard was genuinely committed to the crusading cause. He was a soldier and no war could bring greater prestige than the war against the Saracens, the war in the Holy Land, the emotional centre of the Christian world. On this battleground no act of bravery, no deed of chivalry, would go unrecorded. But it would be a mistake to think that Richard was indifferent to the attractions of a plenary indulgence. While at Messina, *en route* for the Holy Land, he seems to have been overcome by a sense of the wickedness of his life. He summoned all the archbishops and bishops who were with him in Sicily and flung himself to the ground at their feet. Then, naked and holding three scourges in his hands, he confessed his sins.[43] Whatever his sins, a man subject to such fits of remorse would have been well aware that a crusade was a religious act as well as a great military adventure. At Beaulieu Abbey near Loches he would have seen the piece of stone from the Holy Sepulchre which his notoriously savage ancestor Count Fulk the Black was believed to have bitten off while kneeling down to pray there on one of his three pilgrimages to Jerusalem.[44] And to a penitent soldier a crusade was even better than an unarmed pilgrimage. As the troubadour Pons de Capdeuil put it, 'What more can kings desire than the right to save themselves from hell-fire by mighty deeds of arms?'[45]

Crusades required organization as well as enthusiasm. At the conference on 21 January it had been agreed that the men of the king of France should wear red crosses, the men of the king of England white crosses and the men of the count of Flanders green crosses. Later that month other decrees were issued at Le Mans, where Richard had joined his father and a host of barons from Anjou, Maine and Touraine. These included arrangements for the collection of a crusading tax known as the Saladin Tithe, details of the financial privileges to be enjoyed by the crusaders and a set of rules of conduct which they were supposed to observe. They were not to swear or gamble, and the only women who were to be allowed on crusade were washerwomen of good character (for crusaders were supposed to be neatly, though not ostentatiously dressed). According to Roger of Howden, the fact that crusaders were exempted from paying the Saladin Tithe meant that the publication of the edict of Le Mans was followed by a great rush to take the cross.[46]

[42] Cited in H. E. Mayer, *The Crusades* (2nd edn, Oxford, 1988), 34.

[43] *Gesta*, ii, 146–7. See below, 265–6.

[44] *Chroniques des comtes d'Anjou*, 50–1.

[45] C. A. F. Mahn, *Die Werke der Troubadours*, i (Berlin, 1846), 355.

[46] *Gesta*, ii, 30–2; Newburgh, Bk 3, ch. 23.

But early in 1188, perhaps even while Richard was attending the crusading conference at Le Mans, a rebellion broke out in Aquitaine.
According to Ralph of Diceto, the signal for revolt was given when Geoffrey
de Lusignan killed one of the duke's closest advisers. Geoffrey was then
joined by his old associates, Ademar of Angoulême and Geoffrey de
Rancon, and together they ravaged some of Richard's lands. Ademar had
become the undisputed head of the Taillefer family after the death of his
brother William a few years earlier. It looks as though Richard had some
time before this given up his insistence that Angoulême should be
inherited by Vulgrin's daughter Matilda. None the less, old grievances like
the Taillefer claim to La Marche were still outstanding and Richard may
have added new ones by demanding a high price in return for agreeing to
recognize Ademar as count. We possess only one piece of information to
support the general statement that Richard went through the rebels' lands
with fire and sword, capturing and demolishing their fortresses, and this
suggests that Geoffrey de Rancon's castle of Taillebourg was once again at
the centre of events. As in 1179, however, it fell before Richard's
onslaught. The rebels were forced to sue for peace, and they received it –
but only on condition that they too took the cross.[47] In the case of Geoffrey
de Lusignan at least, this enforced vow was speedily fulfilled, since he
reached Outremer during the summer of 1188.[48]

No sooner was this revolt put down than Richard became involved in a
new war with Count Raymond of Toulouse. The two of them had been at
daggers drawn ever since 1183, and in recent months, as incident followed
incident, tension had built up to a new peak. Raymond was accused of
arresting some Aquitanian merchants as they crossed his lands and then
either imprisoning, blinding, castrating or killing them. In the course of
one of Richard's retaliatory raids he captured an important man, Peter
Seillan, a member of the family which governed the city of Toulouse on the
count's behalf and one of his closest advisers. Since Richard held Seillan
responsible for much of the trouble he refused to release him, either for a
ransom or in exchange for prisoners taken by Count Raymond, even
though these now included two of King Henry's household knights, who
had apparently wandered into the territory of Toulouse on their way back
from the shrine of Compostella. But Raymond was equally intransigent: he
refused to free the pilgrims except in return for Peter Seillan. King Philip
travelled south in an attempt to make peace, but faced with such stub-
bornness on both sides he was forced to return with nothing accomplished.
His irritation at this failure to control his warring vassals increased in the
spring of 1188 when Richard, no longer distracted by rebellion, launched

---

[47] *Gesta*, ii, 34; Diceto, ii, 54. Taillebourg mentioned only by Gerald, *Princ.*, 245
(Bk 3, ch. 7).
[48] *Itin.*, Bk 1, ch.11.

his Brabançons in a massive attack on Toulouse. This time it was not a question of skirmishing along the border, but of a major reoccupation of territory lost since 1183. Within a short time Richard had captured no fewer than seventeen castles and with garrisons installed in Cahors and Moissac was firmly in control of the Quercy.[49] As his army approached the walls of Toulouse itself the townspeople seized the opportunity to emancipate themselves from comital authority. With his whole political position in western Toulouse crumbling, Raymond again appealed for help to his overlord, King Philip, and this time his appeal was answered. According to Howden, Philip complained to Henry about his son's conduct, to which Henry replied that none of these things had been done with his advice or approval and he certainly could not justify any of them.[50] If this was the line which Henry took in public, it is not surprising that it should be rumoured that he had encouraged and given financial support to both the rebels and the count of Toulouse. According to Dean Ralph it was this which turned Richard against his father.[51]

Arguing that Richard's attack on Toulouse was a breach of the treaty of January 1188 – which Richard denied[52] – Philip invaded Berry for the second time in twelve months, probably confident that since Henry II disclaimed responsibility for his son's actions he was unlikely to move swiftly

[49] The *casus belli* is set out by Howden, *Gesta*, ii, 34–6, probably on the basis of Richard's dispatches; Diceto, ii, 55; Rigord, 90.

[50] *Gesta*, ii, 36.

[51] That Henry encouraged Richard's enemies is reported as rumour by Diceto, ii, 55 and as fact by Gerald, *Princ.*, 244–5 (Bk 3, ch. 7). In Gerald's opinion Henry intended to prevent Richard from going on crusade. Although in the form we have it Gerald's *De Principis Instructione* was not completed until much later, the underlying plan of Books 2 and 3 is to make Henry's attitude to the crusade the cause of the tragic fall of a once-great king. See K. Schnith, 'Betrachtungen zum Spätwerk des Giraldus Cambrensis: *De Principis Instructione*' in *Festiva Lanx* (Munich, 1966). This suggests that Books 2 and 3 (i.e. not just Book 1) were being composed early in Richard's reign. On the chronology of composition and on Gerald's passion for the crusade see R. Bartlett, *Gerald of Wales 1146–1223* (Oxford, 1982), 69–70, 77–86. True, Gerald was 'blinkered and wildly partisan' but this does not quite mean that this work is entirely 'worthless for the purpose of interpreting events', Warren, 618.

[52] Howden reports that Richard told his father that the count of Toulouse had refused to be included in the truce and peace which he and the king of France had made. According to Howden, John Cumin, archbishop of Dublin took Richard's message to his father, and since he was an old acquaintance of Howden's it is likely that the archbishop was the historian's source for Richard's explanation, *Gesta*, ii, 40. It is certainly the case that Raymond of Toulouse did not take the cross, and in that sense could be said to have excluded himself from the terms agreed in January 1188. Philip, however, regarded Toulouse as part of the kingdom of France; hence Diceto's observation that Philip objected to Richard attacking his kingdom 'without having defied him', Diceto, ii, 55. Gervase also took a sympathetic view of Philip's attitude, i, 432.

to his assistance. He took with him a full train of siege artillery with sappers and engineers. On 16 June he captured Châteauroux and this time it fell into his lap so easily that men talked of treason. A few ducal castles held out but, apart from these, the whole of Berry was prepared to recognize Philip's authority. Further north, and a few miles west of Fréteval, which Philip had held since the previous June, the lord of Vendôme switched his allegiance to France.[53] Richard hurried back to the defence of his north-eastern frontier. His father, shaken by the speed of the collapse and alarmed by the imminent threat to Loches and other key castles in the Angevin heartland, hastily mustered an army in England.[54] It included a large force of Welsh infantry soldiers who were soon to win a fearsome reputation for themselves. Narrowly escaping shipwreck in a tremendous storm in the Channel, Henry reached Normandy on 11 July.[55] On learning of Henry's movements Philip withdrew from Berry in order to defend his border with Normandy. Thus Richard was free to recover much of the lost terrain unhindered by the presence of a hostile field army. But the central fortress of Châteauroux itself, under the command of Philip's most famous knight, William des Barres, resisted all his efforts to capture it. Indeed in one mêlée outside the gates Richard was thrown from his horse and rescued only by the strong arm of a sturdy butcher.[56] In the meantime, however, Henry II had made no attempt to invade France; not relishing the prospect of another confrontation like that at Châteauroux in 1187, he preferred to keep his army encamped within Normandy. This enabled Philip to seize the initiative again. Leaving his Norman border in the capable hands of his cousin, the warlike bishop of Beauvais, he advanced westwards from Vendôme, along the valley of the Loire. At Trou, though he was unable to take the castle, he captured forty knights and burned down the town. Richard at once countered Philip's thrust by moving into the Loire valley himself. He captured Les Roches, a fortress halfway between Trou and Vendôme.[57] Philip then returned to Paris, while Richard, keeping abreast of him, rode on to Normandy.

Only after his son's arrival at his camp did Henry II rouse himself from the passivity of the last month. He had done little except reiterate his protests against Philip's invasion of his dominions. But the king of France had shown a contemptuous disregard for Henry's complaints. At the end of one conference he cut down the famous elm which marked the border and was the traditional meeting place of kings of France and dukes of

---

[53] Rigord, 90–2.
[54] For the recent discovery of a remarkable writ of summons in which Henry promised Châteauroux itself to William Marshal if he would serve the king faithfully with as many knights as he could, see N. Vincent, 'William Marshal'.
[55] *Gesta*, ii, 39–40; Gervase, i, 433.
[56] This incident is reported only by Gervase, i, 434.
[57] *Gesta*, ii, 45. Rigord, 92.

Normandy. In his view peace conferences were a waste of time; the old elm had outlived its usefulness. Clearly if Henry's protests were to be taken seriously he would have to match his words with deeds. On 30 August 1188 the Angevin army crossed the border near Pacy-sur-Eure and marched towards Mantes, where Philip was believed to be staying. Richard was involved in a skirmish with some French knights, among them his old opponent William des Barres. What really happened is anyone's guess but it seems that each accused the other of cheating. According to Howden, William des Barres surrendered to Richard and was released on parole − standard practice in both tournaments and war − only to break parole and escape on a squire's rouncy. The incident was famous enough for William the Breton many years later to take the trouble to provide a long alternative account in Latin verse in order to explain the setback suffered by the man whom he portrayed as 'the glory of French knighthood'. According to this, when Richard found that he could not win by fair means he cheated by plunging his sword into William's horse.[58] Clashes like this one, between individual knights or groups of knights, often seem to be the main ingredient of medieval war as described by contemporary chroniclers. It made good sense for the writers to celebrate the deeds of prowess of their aristocratic patrons, but such knightly combats, whether chivalrously conducted or not, were in fact only a very small part of war. As Henry's army advanced towards Mantes it burned and looted everything in its path. What this meant is made crystal clear by the description of an army on the march in the *Chanson des Lorrains*:

The march begins. Out in front are the scouts and incendiaries. After them come the foragers whose job it is to collect the spoils and carry them in the great baggage train. Soon all is in tumult. The peasants, having just come out to the fields, turn back, uttering loud cries. The shepherds gather their flocks and drive them towards the neighbouring woods in the hope of saving them. The incendiaries set the villages on fire and the foragers visit and sack them. The terrified inhabitants are either burned or led away with their hands tied to be held for ransom. Everywhere bells ring the alarm; a surge of fear sweeps over the countryside. Wherever you look you can see helmets glinting in the sun, pennons waving in the breeze, the whole plain covered with horsemen. Money, cattle, mules and sheep are all seized. The smoke billows and spreads, flames crackle. Peasants and shepherds scatter in all directions.[59]

[58] *Gesta*, ii, 46; *Philippidos*, iii, 431−565. In this version William des Barres recognized Richard by the lions on his shield, ll. 445−6. For discussion of the insignificance of this for the heraldry of the 1190s, see Ailes, *Origins of the Royal Arms of England*, 67−71.

[59] Quoted in A. Luchaire, *Social France at the Time of Philip Augustus*, trans. E. H. Krehbiel (London, 1912), 261.

This was the classic method of waging war. 'This is how war is begun: such is my advice,' said Count Philip of Flanders in 1174. 'First lay waste the land.'[60] That evening, on 30 August 1188, Henry's army returned to Ivry loaded down with plunder. Next day, having seen his father stirred into action at last, Richard headed back to Berry, promising his father that he would serve him well and faithfully.[61]

The war continued into the autumn but increasingly half-heartedly on both sides. The needs of harvest and vintage, the expense of keeping large numbers of men in arms and the reluctance of some of the leading French nobles to fight against princes who, like themselves, had taken the cross, all combined to persuade Philip, despite his dramatic gesture at Gisors, to ask for another peace conference. Richard and the two kings met on 7 October at Châtillon-sur-Indre, on the border between Touraine and Berry. Philip had an advantage on occasions like this since he alone represented France while the Angevins were represented by two princes whose interests diverged somewhat and whose differences could be, and were, skilfully exploited by the Capetian king. Philip consistently offered to return his conquests in Berry on condition that Richard's conquests in Toulouse were handed back to Count Raymond. While both Angevins would naturally have liked to get their own way in both regions it is likely that the Quercy meant more to Richard than it did to Henry. Philip, however, seems to have overplayed his hand, demanding that Henry surrender Pacy-sur-Eure as security while the exchange was being carried out and causing the English king to break off the conference in indignation.[62]

So far as Richard was concerned, if his father was eventually going to insist that he give up his conquests then it was at least possible that he would get better terms if he approached Philip directly and offered to abide by the judgment of the French court. Philip would doubtless be gratified by an explicit recognition of his position as overlord of Aquitaine and Toulouse and might well concede something in return. This, at any rate, was the offer which Richard made to the king of France while the latter was disbanding his mercenaries at Bourges. Although Richard claimed that he took this initiative in the hope of bringing about peace – presumably so that the crusade could get under way – his father did not like it at all, presumably on the grounds that the general position of the Angevins would be weakened if they admitted the principle that their disputes could be set-

---

[60] *Jordan Fantosme's Chronicle*, l. 450.

[61] *Gesta*, ii, 46. The devastation caused by this raid was long remembered on both sides of the border. As William Marshal remembered it, it was a model of chivalrous warfare and, naturally, launched on the marshal's advice, *HGM*, 7782–852. See 'War and Chivalry in the *History of William the Marshal*', in Gillingham, *Coeur de Lion*, 231–2.

[62] *Gesta*, ii, 48–9.

tled in their overlord's court.[63] This was the beginning of the final breach between Henry and his son. Once Richard had begun to negotiate directly with Philip it was relatively easy for the king of France to play upon his fears, and above all on the fear engendered by the common gossip that the Old King wanted to disinherit him and confer the crown upon John.[64] Why had John not taken the cross? Soon Richard and Philip were in agreement and, at Richard's suggestion, a new conference between the kings was arranged.[65] In order to have peace and Philip's support in his bid to be recognized, once and for all, as heir to the throne, Richard was now, whatever his previous attitude had been, keen to marry Alice – or at any rate was prepared to say that he was.

The three men met at Bonsmoulins on 18 November. Henry II was understandably disconcerted when Richard and Philip arrived together. The atmosphere was very tense. On the first day of the conference all parties were able to keep a grip on themselves and talk calmly. On the second the strain began to tell. Some sharp words were exchanged. By the third day they were quarrelling openly and at times so fiercely that the knights standing around went for their swords. Philip had opened the proceedings by again suggesting an exchange of conquests, but Richard opposed this, arguing that it would mean that he gave up lands, including the Quercy, which brought him an annual revenue of 1,000 marks or more, in return for estates in Berry which, though they were fiefs attached to Aquitaine, were in fact held by other lords and so were of very little direct financial benefit to him. It is possible that this difference of opinion was pre-arranged and intended simply to minimize the extent of the co-operation between Richard and Philip as a preliminary to the new proposal which they now made and which presumably had been worked out between them. Philip offered to return all his gains of the last year on two conditions: that Henry give Alice in marriage to Richard and make his barons, both in England and on the continent, swear an oath of fealty to Richard as heir. According to Diceto, the Old King rejected this, saying that he would not be seen to give way to compulsion. According to Gervase, Henry refused to give a direct answer but spoke evasively 'as was his custom'. 'Now at last,' said Richard, 'I must believe what I had always thought was impossible.' He turned to Philip and, going on his knees before him, did homage for Normandy, Aquitaine, Anjou, Maine, Berry and his conquests in Toulouse. Saving only the fealty which he owed to his father he swore

---

[63] Ibid., 49. Only Howden says Richard made this offer.

[64] In these circumstances it was no wonder, according to Gervase, that Richard should turn for help to Philip, Gervase, i, 435.

[65] William Marshal, doubtless reflecting the view held in Henry's household, believed that Richard and Philip had come to terms prior to the meeting at Bonsmoulins, HGM, 8065–175; Diceto, ii, 57, for the view that the conference was 'procured by Richard'.

allegiance to Philip against all men. In other words, in return for this act of homage, the king of France was prepared to restore all of his gains while permitting Richard to keep all of his. After this shattering denouement little more could be done at Bonsmoulins. The kings agreed to meet again in mid-January 1189 and made a truce to last until then.[66] As William Marshal remembered it, he had advised Henry to send after his son and try and bring him back, as he had been brought back before. William and Bertrand de Verdon were then sent in pursuit of Richard. They arrived at Amboise where he had stayed the night, but he had already left in a hurry. They were told that no one had ever seen him so anxious to call out his people; during the night he had had at least 200 letters written and sent out. He was not going to be brought back; they should not waste their time riding after him.[67] However, it looks as though Henry did not quite give up hope. According to Gervase, the Old King went to Aquitaine himself while sending his chancellor, his illegitimate son Geoffrey, to ensure that his castles in Anjou were securely held. Presumably Henry still hoped to be able to command the loyalty of many Aquitanians – perhaps those whom he had recently encouraged to revolt – but according to the *History of Willliam the Marshal*, though he rode to Le Dorat, he achieved nothing there.[68]

It may be that Henry II was not plotting to make John his heir.[69] Certainly, so far as we can see, he took no steps to promote the interests of his younger son, apart from not insisting that he take the cross. The Old King may have been obsessed by the problems that had arisen after he had recognized young Henry as his heir and determined not to make the same mistake again.[70] But it would not have been the same mistake. Richard was not Henry. In character he was very different from his dead elder brother. He was now thirty-one years old and a soldier and politician of great experi-

[66] My account of the conference is based on Gervase, i, 435 and Diceto, ii, 58, confirmed in its essentials by Rigord, 92–3 and by Howden, whose much briefer version highlights just how much Philip was prepared to promise in return for Richard's homage, *Gesta*, ii, 50.

[67] *HGM*, 8217–54. So Marshal let Henry know that his son had indeed betrayed him, 'La traïson fause e amére', ibid., 8258.

[68] Gervase, i, 436. *HGM*, 8285–9. And William of Newburgh believed that in the war of 1189 the forces of Aquitaine chose to follow Richard, Newburgh, Bk 3, ch. 25. Some of the most famous knights did, see *HGM*, 8632–4, 8705–10, 8811–14 for Andrew de Chauvigny, Philippe de Colombiers and Aimeri Odart.

[69] But many contemporaries believed he was: *Radulfi Nigri Chronica*, ed. Anstruther, 95; Gerald, *Princ.*, 232; Ambroise, 102; Newburgh, Bk 3, ch. 25. Many modern historians have shared this view. Kate Norgate thought that only Henry's partiality for John could explain 'his endless shifts', Norgate, 70. Another possibility is that Henry was exploiting John by using him as a trump card to be played against Richard, Kessler, 22.

[70] As suggested by Gervase, i, 436 and later by Howden, *Chron*, ii, 355. Kessler, 45, points out it was the father who took the initiative, seeking to unsettle and undermine a son generally recognized as the rightful heir (e.g. Rigord, 93).

ence.[71] When entrusted with government he did not make a mess of it.[72] If deprived of his rights he would make a much more serious opponent than the Young King had. In Philip of France moreover he had – as Henry II all too slowly learned – an ally vastly different from the Louis VII of the 1170s. The costs of treating Richard in this fashion were far greater than the gains to be made from keeping him in suspense about his future. In W. L. Warren's words, 'Henry had adopted the tactic of trying to discipline Richard by keeping him in uncertainty and had then become caught in the toils of his own deviousness.'[73] The tactic worked for a while but it was madness to remain obstinately wedded to it while his son's frustration increased and while men pressed for an end to political uncertainty in order to permit the launching of the crusade. Looking back from after the battle of Bouvines, 1188 came to be seen as the start of a great and, in the end, a disastrous war.[74]

At last the Old King's touch had deserted him. As he kept the last Christmas of his life at Saumur, he can hardly have failed to notice how many of his barons stayed away, a sure sign that they were preparing to transfer their allegiance to Richard and Philip. In these cheerless circumstances Henry fell ill and was unable to attend the peace talks in January 1189. His enemies believed that the sickness was just another of his delaying tactics and so they renewed the war as soon as the truce expired. They were at once joined by the Bretons rising in rebellion against the king who had done much to limit their independence.[75] Henry sent envoy after envoy to Richard in the hope of calling him back to his side, but not even when he used an ambassador as distinguished as the archbishop of Canterbury was his son to be persuaded. According to Gervase, although Henry now regretted offending his son, Richard no longer believed anything he said.[76] Many years later William Marshal recalled being sent to Paris by Henry – presumably the Old King hoped to drive a wedge between

---

[71]In the second edition of his *Topographia Hibernica* written shortly before Henry's death (see below, 267), Gerald composed a sustained contrast between the two brothers, entirely in Richard's favour and ending with the words that 'neither ancient nor modern times have ever seen two sons born of the same prince and yet so different from one another', Gerald, *Top.*, 198.

[72]Quite apart from the rhetoric of Gerald's praise for Richard's government of Aquitaine, there is the evidence of the establishment of five new ducal *prévôtés* in Poitou by 1189; ten in 1174, fifteen by 1189. See R. Hajdu, 'Castles, Castellans and the Structure of Politics in Poitou, 1152–1271', *JMH*, iv (1978), and Gillingham, 'The Angevin Empire', *Coeur de Lion*, 42, 78.

[73]Warren, 622–3.

[74]*HGM*, 8079–81, 8185–8.

[75]*Gesta*, ii, 61.

[76]Gervase, i, 438–9; cf. Newburgh, Bk 1, ch. 25. Gervase also had his doubts about Henry's illness at this date, though he was certainly ill from March onwards, *HGM*, 8292–6; Gerald, *Princ.*, 259.

the allies – and finding on arrival that they had been forestalled. Richard's agents were already there, among them one of his most trusted advisers, his chancellor William Longchamp, so Henry's schemes came to nothing.[77] Not until after Easter was King Henry well enough to attend a conference, but even then nothing was achieved. Finally a papal legate, John of Anagni, arrived in northern France on a peace-making mission and he was able to obtain an undertaking from both kings that they would abide by the decisions of an arbitration panel consisting of himself and four archbishops: Rheims, Bourges, Rouen and Canterbury. At Whitsun they all assembled near La Ferté-Bernard in Maine, twenty-five miles north-east of Le Mans. Both sides came fully armed and on their guard. There Philip and Richard laid down three conditions upon which they were prepared to make peace. Alice should be married to Richard. Henry should acknowledge Richard as heir to the kingdom of England. John should take the cross. Richard indeed added that there was no way that he would go to Jerusalem unless his younger brother went with him. Henry rejected these terms. John of Anagni threatened to lay an interdict on France if Philip did not come to terms with Henry, but Philip was unmoved and observed that the legate's money bags were obviously full of English silver.[78] With that the conference came to an end and Henry withdrew to Le Mans.

But Philip and Richard did not withdraw to the frontier. Instead they launched a successful surprise attack on La Ferté-Bernard. Then, in quick succession, other castles to the north-east of Le Mans – Montfort, Maletable, Beaumont and Ballon – were handed over to Richard. On 12 June, after a feint in the direction of Tours, Richard and Philip suddenly swooped on Le Mans itself. Henry II fled northwards towards Normandy, abandoning the town in which he was born.[79] Hard on his heels came the pursuit, and at the head of the pursuers was Richard. They caught up with Henry's rearguard, which was under William Marshal's command and, in William's opinion, would have overwhelmed them had not William himself saved the day. He turned and rode straight at Richard. Because they had both anticipated not a fight, but a long, hard ride, neither of them was wearing a hauberk. As William levelled his lance Richard suddenly saw the danger he was in. 'By God's legs' – one of his favourite oaths – 'do not kill me, Marshal. That would be wrong, I am unarmed.' 'No, let the Devil kill

---

[77] HGM, 8313–34. It was at this time, Marshal claimed, that Henry promised him the heiress to Striguil, ibid., 8303–6.

[78] Gervase, i, 446–7; Gesta, ii, 66–7; only in his later revision did Howden say that Henry made a counter-proposal, that Alice should marry John, Chron., ii, 363. If the king did suggest anything of the kind, he must have been at the end of his tether, since cool reflection would have told him that at this stage Philip was in no position to accept it, and making the offer would only serve to confirm the rumours about his plans for John. See Norgate, 86.

[79] Gesta, ii, 67; Diceto, ii, 63; Gerald, Princ., 283 (Bk 2, ch. 24).

you,' retorted William, 'for I won't.' Then, adjusting his aim, he ran his lance through Richard's horse. The story of the Lionheart's narrow escape was told by William Marshal himself and since William never suffered from modesty it may have been improved in the telling.[80] But within a few weeks Richard was loading Marshal with honours, lands and responsibility, and an incident such as this, combining skill at arms with sound political common sense, could well have impressed him. At all events the pursuit came to a sudden halt and Henry was able to make good his escape in peace.

But the Old King was far from being at peace. Instead of pushing on to Normandy to muster an army and then return to Maine in force, he switched direction and went home to die. With just a handful of followers he rode to Chinon, the castle of his ancestors, and stayed there, ill and exhausted, while Richard and Philip overran Maine and Touraine. On 3 July Tours itself, the strategic key to the whole empire, fell. Next day Henry, though in such agony that he could hardly sit on his horse, met Philip and Richard at Ballon and there agreed to the terms which they dictated. He would pay Philip 20,000 marks and in all things submit to his judgement. Alice was to be handed over to a guardian nominated by Richard; after his return from crusade she was to be restored to him. Henry's subjects, both in England and on the continent, were to swear allegiance to Richard. The starting date of the crusade was fixed for Lent 1190 when both kings and Richard were to muster at Vézelay. If Henry failed to abide by these terms his barons were to transfer their allegiance to Philip and Richard.[81] According to Gerald de Barri, who gives the most vivid, if not the most reliable, account of these days, Henry was then required to give Richard the kiss of peace. As he pretended to do so he hissed in his son's ear, 'God grant that I may not die until I have had my revenge on you.'[82]

The conference over, Henry was carried back to Chinon on a litter and there, on 6 July 1189, he died. He had not obtained his revenge. Indeed his last hours had been made even more bitter by the news that John had deserted him.[83] The news of the fall of Le Mans had convinced him that his

[80] *HGM*, 8831–50; Gerald, *Princ.*, 286 (Bk 3, ch. 25).

[81] *Gesta*, ii, 68–70. The terms of the treaty avoid saying that Richard will marry Alice; cf. Diceto, 63, n. 1, according to which it was agreed that after 'the return' she will be given in marriage as advised by the king of France. On what all this might mean see Kessler, 61–2.

[82] Gerald, *Princ.*, 296 (Bk 3, ch. 26). And, says Gerald, on returning to Philip, Richard amused the whole court with an account of the manner in which he and his father had made peace.

[83] Gerald, *Princ.*, 295 (Bk 3, ch. 24); *Radulfi Nigri Chronica*, 95; *HGM*, 9068–98. In his revised chronicle Howden gives a more elaborate account of John's contribution to the misery of Henry's death, *Chron.*, ii, 366, but it is already implicit in the more contemporary and laconic *Gesta*, ii, 72.

father's ship was sinking. From Chinon Henry's body was carried to Fontevraud and laid in the abbey church.[84] When Richard arrived at Fontevraud he strode directly into the church, saying nothing. He stood for a while at the head of the bier, showing no emotion.[85] Then he turned away. He was king now and there was work to be done.

[84] According to Howden, Henry's corpse bled from the nose when Richard arrived 'as though his spirit was angered by his approach' and Richard wept as he accompanied the body to Fontevraud, *Gesta*, ii, 71, *Chron.*, ii, 367. Howden's tale, though probably inaccurate in stating that Richard shared his father's last journey, reflects the feeling that Richard had caused his father's death: cf. Gerald, *Princ.*, 305 (Bk 3, ch. 28). In Chrétien's *Yvain*, the hero of the poem killed a knight and then found himself trapped in the same room as the corpse. When its wounds began to bleed profusely everyone knew that the killer – 'the murderer, the traitor', as the widow called him – was somewhere there. Fortunately for Yvain he had just been given a ring which made him invisible, Chrétien de Troyes, *Arthurian Romances*, 307–9.

[85] This is based on the description of the scene given in *HGM*, 9292–303. According to Chrétien, when Erec's royal father died, 'this weighed upon Erec much more than he showed people outwardly, but grieving is uncourtly on the part of a king and it does not befit a king to show grief', *Arthurian Romances*, 117. The Augustinian canon William believed that by his conduct at his father's funeral, Richard made up in some measure for the way he had treated him in life, Newburgh, Bk 3, ch. 25. 'Bury richly the king my father,' he commanded, according to William Marshal, *HGM*, 9358–60. For the potential significance of this instruction see below, 325.

Chapter 7

DUKE OF NORMANDY, KING OF ENGLAND, 1189

As Richard turned away from his father's body he called over two of the dead king's most loyal followers, William Marshal and Maurice of Craon. 'So, Marshal, the other day you tried to kill me and would have done so had I not turned your lance aside.' This accusation wounded William's knightly pride and he replied indignantly that had he wanted to kill Richard, nothing could have stopped him. 'Marshal, you are pardoned. I bear you no malice.' Indeed far from punishing William and the others who had stayed with the Old King until the end, and who on this account had awaited his son's arrival in the abbey church with some trepidation, Richard praised and rewarded them. When the chancellor told him that Henry had given Marshal the hand of Isabel de Clare, heiress to the lordship of Striguil in the Marches of Wales, to the county of Pembroke and to the immense lordship of Leinster in Ireland, Richard interjected, 'By God's legs! He did not, he only promised to do it. But I give her to you now.' William rushed to Dieppe, fell off a gangplank in his haste to get aboard ship, and married the girl as soon as he was in London.[1] Richard's well-calculated act of generosity had, in effect, made William a millionaire overnight. In the ability of kings to bestow gifts on this scale lay much of their power; the careful management of the vast system of patronage was an essential part of the art of kingship. At the same time he sent Gerald de Barri, cousin of the Lord Rhys of Deheubarth, by far the most powerful of the native Welsh princes, on a mission 'to keep the peace' in Wales. Richard presumably – and entirely correctly – anticipated that Rhys might try to recover lost Welsh territory as soon as he heard that the Old King was dead.[2] This suggests that when Richard made William Marshal a great landowner in South Wales he was alert to strategic geography as well as to the generosity of good lordship.

---

[1] *HGM*, 9304–409, 9469–550. Clearly this story was told in a way meant to point a contrast between the new ruler's generous and decisive action and his father's custom of promising without delivering. Nicholas Vincent has recently unravelled the story of some of these promises, Vincent, 'William Marshal'.

[2] Gerald, *De Vita Sua* (*Opera*, i), 80–1, 84. See Gillingham, 'Henry II, Richard I and the Lord Rhys', *Peritia*, x (1996), 225–36.

Among the other promises which Henry II had made but had not yet ful-filled was the gift of the hand of Denise of Déols and Châteauroux to Baldwin of Béthune.[3] In fact Châteauroux (though not Denise herself) had actually been in the possession of the Old King's enemies since June 1188 and it was of vital strategic importance in the defence of Aquitaine. For this reason Richard had already promised the heiress to one of his most accomplished and trusted knights, Andrew de Chauvigny. Baldwin, however, was a knight well known for his prowess and sense of honour. Fifteen years later, when John had lost Normandy and a group of English landowners who had held estates in Normandy requested permission to perform homage to Philip for their Norman lands, he asked Baldwin for his advice. The petitioners had told John that though their bodies might be with the king of France their hearts would be with him. Baldwin made short work of this argument. 'If their bodies are against me and their hearts for me and those hearts whose bodies are against me were to come into my hands, I would throw them down the privy.' Richard in 1189 could ill afford to lose a man of this calibre, so Baldwin was assured that he would be given adequate compensation for the loss of Châteauroux. In due course he too married a rich widow and, in consequence, became count of Aumâle. Both Andrew de Chauvigny and Baldwin of Béthune went on cru-sade as two of Richard's closest companions-in-arms, and Baldwin was to serve his king as a hostage in Germany. When Richard returned to England in 1194 he said that he owed more to Baldwin than to any other man.[4] Knights like William Marshal, Baldwin of Béthune and Maurice de Craon were to be celebrated in the song and verse of minstrels for the way in which they approached contemporary ideals of courtly and chivalrous excellence.[5] It was such men as this that Richard drew to his side.

Strategic considerations immediately forced themselves on Richard's attention. The fall of Tours on 3 July had been the final blow which had brought Henry II to his knees. The position at Tours was extremely com-plicated. Although it lay within the Angevin dominions, the two main churches there, the cathedral and the abbey of St Martin, each possessing its separate urban settlement, were both closely attached by tradition and privilege to the French crown. The kings of France cherished this special relationship and found it useful. In 1167, for example, when he was at war with Henry II, Louis VII had written to the abbot and treasurer of St Martin's:

---

[3] On this Vincent, 'William Marshal'.

[4] *HGM*, 9374–98, 10,117–36; *Histoire des ducs de Normandie et des rois d'Angleterre*, ed. F. Michel (Paris, 1840), 99–100. Within a few days of arriving in England where she had long been held, Richard had given Andrew his heiress, *Gesta*, ii, 76.

[5] R. Harvey, *Moriz von Craûn and the Chivalric World* (Oxford, 1961), 50–3. On Maurice as seneschal of Brittany, Everard, 'The Justiciarship in Brittany', 105.

We wish to be informed about the King of England's intentions. Will he be advancing into Poitou or returning to the Norman sea-coast? If you are certain about this send us the information by letter to be returned with our sergeants. If the matter is uncertain, send such news as you have through one of them and retain the other until you are able to give us further information.[6]

In the light of letters like this it is hardly surprising that Richard felt that something had to be done about Tours – and quickly. He met Philip in the chapter house of St Martin's and they came to an arrangement which was designed to remove the causes of friction between the abbey and the counts of Anjou.[7] From Philip's point of view the agreement would prevent the abbey's wealth in men and money being used in a war against him; from Richard's point of view harmonious relations with the Church would make it less likely to operate as an espionage centre on behalf of the kings of France.

From the Loire valley Richard went to Normandy. At Rouen on 20 July he was girded with the ducal sword and received an oath of fealty from the clergy and people of the duchy. Now his first concern was to provide for his family. He gave his niece Matilda to Geoffrey, son and heir of the count of Perche; doubtless strategic considerations played a part here too since this alliance strengthened his border in a vital area, on the north-eastern edge of Maine – precisely where he and Philip had broken through a few weeks earlier. He confirmed his brother John's possession of those estates which his father had given or promised him: the county of Mortain in Normandy and £4,000 worth of land in England. He sent instructions telling the clergy of York to elect his half-brother Geoffrey as archbishop; this too was in accordance with his father's wishes.[8] On 22 July he rode out of the great border castle of Gisors for another conference with King Philip and – at any rate according to Philip's historian, Rigord of St Denis – the wooden bridge collapsed under him, tumbling the new duke and his horse into the ditch.[9] Rigord saw this as an omen that Gisors would not for much longer be prepared to accept Richard as its lord. Once again the king of France claimed the Norman Vexin, but dropped his demand for the time being

---

[6] Cited in J. C. Holt, 'The End of the Anglo-Norman Realm', *Proceedings of the British Academy*, lxi (1975), 35.

[7] The document recording the agreement was drawn up in July 1190 in the name of both kings, but in it Richard refers to a meeting 'antequam idem regnum fuissem adeptus', *Actes*, i, no. 361 (Landon no. 259). The strategic importance of this agreement was first emphasized by Holt in the article cited in the previous note. The problem of Tours was, however, far from being solved in 1189–90.

[8] *Gesta*, ii, 73.

[9] Rigord, 97.

when Richard expressed his willingness to marry Alice.[10] In addition to the 20,000 marks promised by Henry II, Richard agreed to pay 4,000 marks as a contribution to his ally's costs in the recent campaign. In return Philip restored the lands which he had conquered, including Châteauroux, but excluding Graçay and Issoudun. Apart from this territorial loss and the concession of more or less non-existent rights in the Auvergne, Richard had inherited the whole of the Angevin continental empire – and in November 1188 at Bonsmoulins he had not rated Graçay and Issoudun very highly.[11] After all the doubts of Henry's last years and after the chaos of the last few weeks, Richard must have felt reasonably satisfied with this outcome. In any case while Andrew de Chauvigny held Châteauroux the frontier in Berry would be in safe hands. Another fine soldier, Robert earl of Leicester, lord of Pacy and hence a key figure in the defence of the Norman frontier, was given back estates which Henry II had confiscated.[12]

Ever since his father's death Richard had been engaged in a sustained exercise in image manipulation. Undeniably he had sinned in taking up arms against his father. For this sin he needed absolution – and he obtained it from the archbishops of Canterbury and Rouen as soon as he entered Normandy at Sées.[13] More doubtful was the question of honour. Had he acted dishonourably? Had not William Marshal told Henry of Richard's 'false and bitter treachery' in 1188?[14] Yet he had publicly pro-claimed his opposition to his father at Bonsmoulins in his father's presence and at a time when Henry was still at the height of his power. In this was he to be compared with those who pretended to be loyal but who betrayed precisely at the moment when their support was most needed? Treachery was a question of timing. Thus he made an example of Gui de Vaux, Ralph of Fougères and Juhel III de Mayenne, three prominent barons who had belatedly joined the war against his father. He seized their estates and announced that this was the appropriate reward for all who abandoned their lord in his time of need. Platitudes of this sort were intended to give the message that the new king was a man with a keen sense of honour. In Roger of Howden's words, 'he honourably retained all those servants of the king his father whom he knew to be loyal and who had loyally served

---

[10] He did not say so when he wrote the *Gesta*, but later, after he had got to know Philip better, Howden commented that Richard saw that if he had agreed to Philip's demands it would have been to his eternal shame, *Chron.*, iii, 4.

[11] *Gesta*, ii, 73–4. See above, 95.

[12] *Gesta*, ii, 75.

[13] Later, when Richard was a prisoner in Germany, the dean of St Paul's recon-sidered the question. Perhaps after all Richard had needed further punishment from God in order to bring him to a proper state of contrition for his attack on his sick father, but in 1189 the dean, in Normandy himself, seems to have been satis-fied, writing that Richard made up for the way he had treated his father by the honour in which he held his mother, Diceto, ii, 67–8.

[14] *HGM*, 8258. See above, 96 n. 67, for the circumstances.

his father. He restored them to the posts which they had long held from his father, to each as they deserved. But he despised those clerks and laymen who had deserted his father and gone over to him, and these he dismissed from his service.'[15] What mattered most to Richard was honour – or at any rate his reputation for honour, especially at the most critical moments such as the decision to take up arms against his father or, later, the decision to make peace with Saladin. In one of Bertran de Born's songs, 'Nostre seingner somonis el mezeis' – almost certainly composed in 1188 – we are told that Richard 'desires honour (*pretz*) more than any man, Christian or infidel. He seeks honour and success so intently that his reputation constantly grows and improves.' In a single stanza about Richard, Bertran uses the word *pretz* no fewer than seven times in only nine lines.[16] In 1189 Richard wanted to draw a sharp distinction between his disobedience and others' treachery. But he made one glaring exception. John had been, in Howden's words, 'the occasion, or rather the immediate cause, of his father's death'.[17] Yet his younger brother's treachery was rewarded.[18]

While still at Fontevraud Richard had sent orders that his mother should be released from the strict surveillance under which she had again been placed by Henry, probably towards the end of 1188. Once free, her main task had been to ensure that Richard would be welcomed as a prince who restored justice after the arbitrary and oppressive rule of the Old King. Confiscated estates were restored. When reporting Robert of Leicester's recovery of his estates, Howden had commented that the duke restored to their lawful estates all those whom his father the king had disinherited. The prisons were emptied. Those who were in gaol by due process of law were required to find sureties that they would stand trial, but those who had been imprisoned merely because the king or his judges had ordered it were freed unconditionally. Eleanor wrote that she knew from her own experience how delightful it was to be released from confinement. According to the William of Newburgh, writing years later and in a more jaundiced frame of mind, the only result was that evildoers were free to transgress more confidently in the future.[19] However, in 1189 the policy achieved its purpose. Richard, according to Gervase, 'spoke kindly to all who came to him. Hence he was at first much loved.'[20]

---

[15] *Gesta*, ii, 72, 107. Gerald de Barri who had immediately been taken into Richard's service (see above, 101) was one of the clerks who had stayed in his father's service to the end.

[16] Born, 386–7. The song relates to the kings taking the cross. But seven times in nine lines? Is someone protesting too much, Bertran and/or Richard?

[17] *Gesta*, ii, 72.

[18] Richard's motives can only be guessed at. But conventional ideals of filial piety and brotherly love presumably played a part.

[19] *Gesta*, ii, 74–5; Newburgh, Bk 4, ch. 1.

[20] Gervase, i, 451.

From the conference with Philip he rode to Barfleur to take ship to England. He had not been in any rush to take possession of England. His succession to the throne was now beyond all question. After all the anxieties, in the end it had turned out to be the first time for centuries that a son had been his father's undisputed heir. Both he and John embarked at Barfleur, but they sailed in different ships and put in at different ports, Richard landing at Portsmouth and John at Dover.[21] Was this intended? It may be that Richard wanted to prevent John from sharing in the joyous welcome being prepared for the new king. In a contrived piece of theatre Richard enacted the part assigned to him by his own propaganda by arriving in England with one of the Old King's most unpopular ministers, Stephen of Tours, the parvenu and unchivalrous seneschal of Anjou, in tow and ostentatiously loaded down with chains.[22] Such, it was implied, was to be the fate of all those powerful men who had dominated Henry II's administration and had enriched themselves at his subjects' expense. Even the laments composed upon the death of Henry were transformed into songs of welcome.[23]

Post hanc tibi vesperam	After this eventide and by virtue of a
Facto letiori	more joyful event a new day-star
Dabit diem prosperam	ascending will bring a time of
Casu repentino	prosperity by a sudden change at
Novus surgens lucifer	sunrise.
Ortu matutino.	
Spe salubris gratie	In the hope of healing grace rejoice!
Gaudeas militie	You are about to receive the flower
Florem susceptura	of chivalry, whose word has a truth
Cuius verbi verita	that comes from the heart, whose
Mente proditura	tireless munificence cannot be
Indefessa largitas	exhausted but when he has given
Nescit fatigari	much thinks he has given little.
Sed cum multa dederit	The courteous count declares himself
Pauca putat dari.	to be fit for you; love, with dread,
Comes comis nuntiat	will ally his men to you. Richard
Parem tibi fore	of Poitou the future king of
Cui socios sociat	England.[24]

---

[21] *Gesta*, ii, 75. This detail is obscured in Howden's later summary, *Chron.*, iii, 5.

[22] On Stephen of Tours (or of Marçay) see J. Boussard, *Le Comté d'Anjou sous Henri Plantagenêt et ses fils 1151–1204* (Paris, 1938), 114–17; *Gesta*, ii, 71–2; *HGM*, 8015–24, 9178–204; Devizes, 4–5.

[23] *Gesta*, ii, 75–6. At this point even the prosaic Howden breaks into warm praise of a new sun king, noting that very few were grieved at the death of the old one.

[24] Translation of these lines from the anonymous song 'In occasu sideris' is based

Amor cum timore.
Ricardus Pictavie
Rex futurus Anglie.

When Richard landed at Portsmouth on 13 August 1189 he was greeted with enthusiasm. People found it all too easy to believe that a new king meant a fresh start and an easier life. Looking back after Richard's death, the stern Cistercian moralist Ralph of Coggeshall was to say that at the beginning of his reign Richard appeared to be the mirror of kings[25] – not bad for a son who had just hounded his father to death! The image-building campaign had worked.

On Sunday, 13 September he was crowned in Westminster Abbey. In Roger of Howden's description of the ceremony we have the first detailed account of a coronation in English history. At the heart of the service lay not the crowning of the new ruler but his anointing. All his clothes were stripped off except his breeches and his shirt, which was open to show his chest. Baldwin, the archbishop of Canterbury, then anointed him with holy oil on his head, chest and hands. This act was believed to confer upon the new ruler the divine sanction for his king-ship. After the anointing Richard was dressed in ceremonial robes and then crowned. In later coronation services it was the archbishop who took the crown from the altar in order to place it on the king's head, but in 1189 Richard himself picked up the crown and handed it to the archbishop. Whether or not this was an innovation it was a characteristic gesture of self-help. He then mounted the throne and sat there while mass was celebrated. After the service came the coronation banquet. The clergy, in due order of rank, dined at his table, while the laity, earls, barons and knights, had separate tables. They all feasted splendidly.[26] Some idea of the scale of the occasion may be gathered from the fact that at least 1,770 pitchers, 900 cups and 5,050 dishes had been bought in preparation for it.[27] It was just the kind of pageantry in which Richard delighted. The words of a song believed to have been sung for the coronation of this most musical king reiterate the theme of the dawning of a new age.

on that in *Music for the Lion-hearted King. Music to Mark the 800th Anniversary of the Coronation of Richard I of England*, Gothic Voices, dir. Christopher Page (Hyperion CDA66336, 1989).

[25] Coggeshall, 91. Of course from Ralph's standpoint the better the start, the sadder the fall from grace. But even modern historians convinced of Richard's incompetence as a ruler have believed in the contrast between his honour and 'the double-dealing and financial unscrupulousness that had characterised many of his father's actions', J. T. Appleby, *England without Richard* (London, 1965), 20.

[26] *Gesta*, ii, 80–3.

[27] PR 1 Richard I, 21, 30, 216.

Redit aetas aurea	The age of gold returns
Mundus renovatur	The world's reform draws nigh
Dives nunc deprimitur	The rich man now cast down
Pauper exaltatur.	The pauper raised on high.[28]

But while the feasting went on inside the palace, a riot developed outside. Some Jews, bringing gifts for the new king, had tried to enter, but the Christian crowd at the gates would not have this. They fell upon the Jews, killing some and wounding others. The trouble then spread to the city of London, where it continued throughout the night. Jews were killed, their houses plundered and burned down. Next day Richard had some of the rioters arrested, three of them hanged and a Jew who in fear of his life had agreed to be baptized a Christian he encouraged to return to his religion. He then sent letters to every shire ordering that the Jews should be left in peace.[29] According to the early thirteenth-century Anonymous of Laon, he sent envoys to Normandy and Poitou to prevent anything similar happening there.[30] The Jews were under his special protection. Whether or not his dealings suggest he was unusually tolerant, like many kings of the time, he regarded them as a valuable source of revenue.[31] Despite his efforts, there were more anti-Jewish riots in the next few months: at Lynn, Norwich, Lincoln, Stamford and elsewhere. Men were full of the crusading spirit. They longed to see Jerusalem and the Holy Cross, and they looked with anger upon the descendants of the people who had clamoured for the crucifixion of Christ. Besides, going on crusade was an expensive business and the loot taken from Jews could help many a poor but pious man on his way. This wave of popular anti-Semitism reached its height at York in March 1190, by which time Richard had already left the country. About 150 Jews managed to escape the mob and take refuge in the castle. But urged on by a fanatical hermit the mob besieged the place. When the Jews realized that they could not hold out much longer most of them committed suicide,

---

[28] For a suggested emendation of the text – as well as for the music – see Gothic Voices, *Music for the Lion-hearted King.*

[29] *Gesta*, ii, 83–4. Newburgh, Bk 4, ch. 1. The dean of St Paul's may have felt some shame at London's handling of the Jews; at any rate he blamed 'foreigners' for the riot, Diceto, ii, 69.

[30] *RHF*, xviii, 707. The author is thought to have been an English-born Premonstratensian canon. The substantial Jewish community in Normandy continued to enjoy peace and prosperity, N. Golb, *The Jews in Medieval Normandy* (Cambridge, 1998), 356–9.

[31] H. G. Richardson, *The English Jewry under Angevin Kings* (London, 1960), 164–5. Philip Augustus preferred to begin his reign by expelling the Jews, confiscating their land and cancelling debts owed to them – while keeping 20 per cent of the value of the cancelled debts for himself. After his early return from crusade – a time when his devotion to Christianity was in doubt – he had more than eighty Jews found guilty of ritual murder at Brie and burned at the stake. Later still, to Rigord's dismay, he allowed them to return to Paris, Rigord, 15–16, 24–33, 119, 141.

having first killed their wives and children. The rest, relying on the besiegers' promises that they would be spared if they accepted Christian baptism, came out of the castle and were massacred.[32]

Meanwhile, in mid-September 1189, Richard had attended to the business of the realm at a great council held at Pipewell Abbey near Corby in Northamptonshire. He removed Ranulf Glanville from the justiciarship and appointed two men in his place, William de Mandeville, count of Aumale and earl of Essex, and Hugh du Puiset, a man with thirty-five years' experience of ruling the bishopric and palatinate of Durham.[33] He appointed four new bishops – Godfrey de Luci to Winchester, Richard FitzNigel (author of *The Dialogue of the Exchequer*) to London, Longchamp to Ely, Hubert Walter to Salisbury – and made a number of other senior ecclesiastical appointments, including new abbots at Selby and Glastonbury.[34] This too was meant to point the contrast with the previous regime, for Henry had been notorious for keeping major churches vacant so that he could pocket their revenues.[35] The four new bishops were, wrote Richard of Devizes, 'men of no little virtue and fame'.[36] The same could not be – and was not – said of the archbishop elect of York. It was rumoured that, despite his illegitimate birth, he was hoping for higher things. Once, it was reported, he had put the lid of a golden bowl on his head and asked his friends whether a crown wouldn't suit him. After all, William the Conqueror had started life as William the Bastard; indeed later in this same year another illegitimate son, Tancred of Lecce, was to make himself king of Sicily. That there was some substance to these rumours is indicated by the fact that he earlier, as bishop elect of Lincoln, preferred to resign the see rather than be ordained, since once he was a priest he would be ineligible for all secular office including the office of kingship. It may be that Richard was aware of Geoffrey's ambitions, and that this reinforced the filial piety with which, in July, he had ordered the canons of York to elect his half-brother. Some of them objected on the grounds that the warlike Geoffrey was a man of blood, conceived in adultery and born of a whore. He was none the less elected and the validity of the election was confirmed, at Richard's request, by a papal legate. On 23 September, though still loudly proclaiming his reluctance, Geoffrey was ordained a priest. Within a month he had refused to accept Richard's nominations as

---

[32] R. B. Dobson, *The Jews of Medieval York and the Massacre of March 1190* (Borthwick Papers, xlv, York, 1974); see also H. Thomas, 'Portrait of a Medieval Anti-Semite: Richard Malebisse', *HSJ*, v, (1993) 1–15, for the career of one of the leaders of the mob at York, a knight who joined John's rebellion, and whose career began to prosper once John was king.

[33] William de Mandeville was another of those who had stayed with the dying Henry II to the end, *HGM*, 8782, and who was now promoted by Richard.

[34] *Gesta*, ii, 85.

[35] Newburgh, Bk 3, ch. 26; Coggeshall, 97.

[36] Devizes, 7.

dean and treasurer of York and had plunged into the quarrels with the canons of his cathedral which were to last the rest of his life.[37]

The most difficult ecclesiastical business with which Richard had to deal, and the one which affords us a remarkable eyewitness description of a king at work in the management of disputes – a central aspect of the art of king-ship – was the neurotic quarrel between the Cistercian archbishop of Canterbury, Baldwin of Ford, and the Benedictine monks of his cathedral priory. The story is told in passionate detail by one of the participants, the chronicler Gervase of Canterbury. In his opinion the archbishop was a greater enemy to Christianity than Saladin. Baldwin's plan, first adum-brated in 1186, to found a collegiate church at Hackington in honour of the martyrs St Thomas and St Stephen, had at once been interpreted by the monks of Christ Church as an attack on their own position and prestige. Their desperate struggle to scupper Hackington led to endless conferences and appeals to the courts of both king and pope. By January 1188 the monks had been confined within their own monastic buildings, and they stayed there for a year and a half, kept alive, Gervase said, only by the kind-ness of those people of Canterbury, including Jews, who provided them with food. Liturgical service in the cathedral had been largely abandoned. The quarrel gave Gervase many opportunities to see both Henry and Richard at close quarters. He came to regard Henry as a procrastinator and a double-dealer, a man on whose word it was absolutely impossible to rely.[38] Hence, in the words of David Knowles, the king himself became 'one great obstacle to peace'.[39] Once Henry was dead, the parties managed to agree a truce of sorts and the gates of the monastic enclosure were reopened.

As soon as he had been crowned Richard made strenuous efforts to bring the two parties to agree to abide by the decision of an arbitration panel which he would choose. However, in October matters deteriorated when Baldwin appointed as prior Roger Norreys, a monk whom his brother monks regarded as a traitor since he had escaped from the locked enclo-sure (allegedly through the sewers) and had gone over to the archbishop's side. Eventually, at the end of November, king and court, including Queen Eleanor and all the bishops, travelled to Canterbury in a major effort to bring the dispute to a conclusion. Richard was determined to do this with-out papal intervention and a legate who had travelled all the way from Rome for the same purpose was not allowed to cross the Straits of Dover.[40]

[37] Gerald, *Vita Galfridi* (*Opera*, iv), 368, 373–5, 379; *Gesta*, ii, 88, 91, 100. D. L. Douie, *Archbishop Geoffrey Plantagenet and the Chapter of York* (York, 1960).

[38] Gervase, i, 372, 382, 392, 418, 420, 435, 439.

[39] M. D. Knowles, *The Monastic Order in England* (Cambridge, 1940), 322.

[40] Stubbs's introduction to his edition of the Canterbury Letters, *Chronicles and Memorials of the Reign of Richard I*, ii, repr. in his *Historical Introductions to the Rolls Series*, ed. A. Hassall (London, 1902), 384–411, provides the best narrative of the dispute. Richard's attitude to the legate led Stubbs to the view that the new king

Gervase gives a vivid account of the next few days and of the king's close personal involvement in the negotiations. Pressed by the king, the monks at last agreed to accept arbitration if the archbishop agreed in advance to call a halt to Hackington and to depose Prior Roger. Richard put this to Baldwin, saying that he himself would remove Roger and demolish Hackington if Baldwin did not agree. However, he then accepted Baldwin's argument that it was hardly fair that he should submit to arbitration having already conceded the two main points, so he returned to the monks and asked them whether, if the archbishop conceded those two points, they in turn might be prepared to accept Baldwin's decision based on his own Cistercian sense of justice on the other matters in dispute. The monks reluctantly agreed, on condition that some of their charters of privilege were publicly read out. Richard then whispered something to Baldwin, before turning again to the monks and telling them that they should not be alarmed if, when the agreement was announced, words were chosen which were designed to avoid humiliating the archbishop. By this time it was late in the day. In the gloom of the chapter house even the king in his glittering robes was barely visible. Confused and worried, the monks listened as Walter of Coutances, the archbishop of Rouen and one of the great fixers of the time, announced that a way of peace had been found. 'It is our judgement that the archbishop has the power to found a church wherever he pleases and appoint any prior he chooses. Let the monks beg mercy of the archbishop and he will remit his anger against them.' The monks were shattered. They had trusted the king and he had tricked them. One of them tried to speak, but fell silent when the king commanded them all to kneel. In the dark the monks, betrayed and browbeaten, knelt and asked pardon of the archbishop. At last Baldwin spoke. He remitted his anger and asked that if he had offended them, they would forgive him. Then before the monks had a chance to say anything the bishop of Rochester rose and announced that the college at Hackington would be demolished and the hated prior deposed. 'Let us now enter the church, sing a Te Deum and exchange the kiss of peace.' And so it was done. Next day a formal record of the agreement was drawn up.[41] A king, using a combination of ingenuity, tact and the power of majesty, had pushed men to compromise who hitherto had found nothing less likely. Stubbs observed that Richard had achieved the desired result without descending to 'chicanery or bullying' and concluded that in his handling of the Canterbury dispute 'he stands in pleasant contrast to his father in respect both of his openness and his firmness. He would not suffer the law of the land to be overridden by a rescript from Rome. He condescended to none of what S.

'showed himself even more determined than his father that his rights and dignities should not be infringed', 407.

[41] Gervase, i, 474–81.

Thomas called his father's mousetraps: the tricks by which that astute king managed to put his adversaries in the wrong without committing himself to a decided course.'[42] Despite his high praise for the king here, so powerful was the learned consensus within which Stubbs worked that he was not in the least tempted to revise his overall view of Richard's kingship.

Another matter to be dealt with in the autumn of 1189 was the safety of England's frontiers. When Henry II had refused to go on crusade in 1185, he had said, according to Diceto, that he was staying to defend his kingdom from the barbarians, from attack by the Welsh and Scots.[43] And in 1189, just as Richard had anticipated, Lord Rhys had attacked as soon as he heard the news that Henry was dead. He captured Laugharne and Llanstephan and laid siege to Carmarthen.[44] From the council at Pipewell Richard sent John, the new lord of Glamorgan, with a large army to face down Rhys, while Richard himself went on to Worcester where he met 'the other Welsh kings' in late September.[45] It was presumably here that he received their promise not to attack England while he was on crusade.[46] In October John brought Rhys to Oxford but Richard refused to meet him and so Rhys returned angrily to his own lands.[47] Presumably Richard had already been informed of the terms which John had made with Rhys – the Welsh annals refer to a *pax privata* – and had no intention of ratifying them.[48] As a result Rhys continued his war, capturing St Clears at

---

[42] *Chronicles and Memorials*, ii, cxiv. *Historical Introductions*, 434.

[43] Diceto, ii, 8, 34.

[44] Gervase, i, 457; Gerald, *Itinerarium* (*Opera*, vi), 80 – this despite Gerald's claim that the peace-keeping mission on which he had been sent had been successful; *De Vita Sua*, (*Opera*, i) 80–1, 84.

[45] *Annales Cambriae*, ed. J. Williams ab Ithel (RS, 1860), 57; *Gesta*, ii, 87–8. For evidence that it was Richard and not, as previously thought, John, who met Welsh kings at Worcester, see Gillingham, 'Henry II, Richard I and the Lord Rhys', 225–36. Who they were is not known for sure but one was probably Dafydd of Gwynedd. Although Howden called the Welsh rulers 'kings', their own preferred style was now prince, see D. Crouch, *The Image of Aristocracy in Britain 1000–1300* (London, 1992), 85–93; H. Pryce, 'Owain Gwynedd and Louis VII: the Franco-Welsh Diplomacy of the First Prince of Wales', *Welsh History Review*, xix (1998), 21–4.

[46] Devizes, 7.

[47] *Gesta*, ii, 97. In his revised history Howden heightened the significance of Richard's refusal by adding that Henry II had been accustomed to meet Rhys, *Chron.*, iii, 23. Was this an implicit criticism of Richard – as most modern historians have assumed – or of Henry II? In the light of the wasted meetings which he recorded in 1184 Howden may have come to believe that conferences with the Welsh – whom, in any case, he regarded as a poor and savage people – were a waste of time. References to Henry's 'customary practice' are usually critical in tone.

[48] *Annales Cambriae*, 57. See Norgate, 25–6. Since Gerald was released from his crusade vow and attached to the staff of Longchamp before Richard left England, it looks as though he had continued to act as a government adviser on Welsh affairs during the autumn of 1189.

Christmas, and other castles in south-west Wales in subsequent years. This must have been a matter of concern to the two most powerful English magnates in the region: William Marshal as lord, if not yet earl, of Pembroke and John as lord of Glamorgan. However, so far as we can tell, the Welsh rulers kept the promises they had made in 1189; for whatever reason, not even Lord Rhys and his sons intervened in English politics when John raised the standard of revolt in 1193-4.

In November 1189 Richard's other brother Geoffrey was sent to the Tweed to meet William 'the Lion' king of the Scots and escort him to England. William and his brother, Earl David of Huntingdon – who had already been prominent in the ceremonial of Richard's coronation – found the English court at Canterbury. In a famous and important document, the Quit-claim of Canterbury, dated 5 December 1189, Richard gave back to William the castles of Roxburgh and Berwick which William had been forced to surrender to Henry II in 1175, and he formally acknowledged Scotland's independence from England. In the words of the Melrose Chronicle this agreement freed Scotland 'from the heavy yoke of domination and servitude'. For this William paid 10,000 marks.[49] In the future Richard would be much admired in Scottish historical writing. Many modern English historians, feeling that Scotland should be ruled from Westminster, have taken a different view, and have preferred to follow Gerald's description of the Quit-claim as 'a piece of vile commerce and a shameful loss to the English crown'.[50] But the Quit-claim not only helped to pay for Richard's crusade, it also ensured that when John rebelled in 1193-4 the Scots did not invade England. Indeed King William even made a substantial contribution to Richard's ransom. How great a diplomatic triumph Richard scored in 1189 can be seen by comparing 1193-4 with those occasions when the Welsh and Scots took full advantage of turmoil in the English establishment, during Stephen's reign, in 1173-4, and again in 1215-16. Given what Richard achieved at Canterbury in 1189 – the restoration of peace between archbishop and monks, and peace on his northern border – it is hardly surprising that Roger of Howden should note that when the council broke up everyone went home 'praising the king's great deeds'.[51]

From Canterbury Richard went to Dover and then crossed to Calais on 12 December. It would be more than four years before he returned to England. His priority was still the crusade. In troops, war equipment and money Richard was to outshine all the other leaders of the crusade. In consequence he played the commanding role; the Third Crusade was very

[49] *Gesta*, ii, 81, 97-8; A. O. Anderson, *Early Sources of Scottish History* (repr., Stamford, 1990), ii, 322.
[50] Gerald, *Princ.*, 156.
[51] *Gesta*, ii, 99.

much his crusade. This was not just because he ruled over large territories; it was also because among these territories were some where the administrative system was particularly well developed. Above all this is true of England, and the surviving records of government finance, notably the rolls of the court of the exchequer, the Pipe Rolls, give some indication – though certainly an incomplete one – of the massive scale of Richard's preparations.[52] His officials had gone from port to port commandeering the biggest and best ships they could find. All the details we have about this operation come from England – the Cinque Ports alone supplied at least thirty-three ships – but Normandy, Brittany and Aquitaine were also required to contribute. The normal arrangement was for Richard to pay two-thirds of the cost of a ship, leaving the remaining one-third as a crusading obligation imposed upon others. The king also paid the wages of the crews, at the rate of 2d a day for sailors and 4d for the steersmen. In the financial year beginning at Michaelmas 1189 Henry of Cornhill, who dealt with more naval business than any other senior royal official, spent over £5,000 on ships and wages. In addition the ships had to be provisioned and laden with war supplies – 50,000 horseshoes from the ironworks of the Forest of Dean, for example.[53] As the ruler of a seaborne empire Richard was to be the first crusader king to equip and take his own fleet to Outremer.[54]

Vast sums of money had to be found. One of his first actions on arriving in England had been to send officials to all the royal treasuries to count and take into safe-keeping the silver accumulated by his father.[55] However massive Henry's treasure may have been, Richard needed more, especially since 24,000 marks were owed to Philip.[56] How was more money to be raised? It was very doubtful whether Richard could successfully impose another tax to pay for the same crusade which the Saladin Tithe had been designed to finance. Other methods seemed more promising. The

[52] 'Few commanders understood better than Richard the importance of mobilizing money and spending it to the best effect', Prestwich, 11–12.
[53] For a full survey of the preparations in England see Tyerman, *England and the Crusades*, 66–83.
[54] When the decision to take the sea route was taken is uncertain. Henry II had originally intended to go overland (Diceto, ii, 51–4). According to Gerald, at that date – early 1188 – Richard was already planning to go by sea (*Princ.*, 245). It may be that Henry II also changed his mind, probably as a result of contacts with William II of Sicily and the Genoese. See H. Möhring, *Saladin und der dritte Kreuzzug* (Wiesbaden, 1980), 71–2, 77–8.
[55] In 1189 Howden estimated the treasure at £900,000. Later he amended this to 'more than 100,000 marks'. Possibly, as Stubbs suggested, £900,000 was a mistake for £90,000 – i.e., 135,000 marks, *Gesta*, ii, 76–7, *Chron.*, iii, 8.
[56] The first Pipe Roll of the reign records the transfer of 25,000 marks across the sea, PR 1 Richard I, 5.

country's wealth was concentrated in the hands of a relatively small number of people, all of them closely bound to the king by legal and political ties. In consequence it paid the king to soak the rich, to exploit their relationship with him rather than try to impose a widespread public tax. One opportunity of this kind had occurred in August when the bishop of Ely died intestate, for this meant that the king was entitled to seize the bishop's moveable wealth: 3,000 marks in coin, as well as gold and silver plate, precious cloth, grain, horses and other livestock.[57] This is the kind of action Gerald de Barri had in mind when he pointed out that the Angevins relied more upon irregular profits than upon a steady income. 'The King is like a robber permanently on the prowl, always probing, always searching for the weak spot where there is something for him to steal.'[58]

Then there was the fact, central to the political structure of twelfth-century England, that ambitious men were willing to offer large sums for privileges, places and offices of profit. After his coronation Richard set systematically to work. In Howden's words, 'he put up for sale everything he had – offices, lordships, earldoms, sheriffdoms, castles, towns, lands, the lot'. Thus in a series of massive bargains Godfrey de Luci, bishop of Winchester – the richest see in England – made an offer for the sheriffdom of Hampshire with custody of Winchester and Porchester castles, paid £3,000 for two manors claimed by the church of Winchester and offered 1,000 marks to have possession of his own inheritance.[59] To be appointed sheriff was, in a twentieth-century phrase, to be given a licence to print money. Twice a year the sheriff had to render an account at the exchequer but this apart he was given almost a free hand to wield power in his shire. Power, naturally, meant profit. But just as he had been appointed, so also he could be removed at the king's will. In Worcestershire, for example, Robert Marmion was removed and fined £1,000, presumably for misconduct. It may be an indication of the scale of profits which could be made by an unscrupulous sheriff that Marmion was able to pay 700 marks within a year. He was succeeded by William Beauchamp, who offered 100 marks for the job. Ranulf Glanville himself relinquished the sheriffdom of Yorkshire; his steward, Reiner, who had acted as his deputy in Yorkshire, was fined 1,000 marks.[60] The new sheriff was John Marshal, William's brother. Ranulf Glanville's son-in-law, Ralph of Arden, was removed and fined more than 1,000 marks. His replacement was William Longchamp's brother. Of the

[57] Diceto, ii, 68. Cf. Henry II's seizure of the goods of Archbishop Roger of York, Diceto, ii, 12.

[58] Gerald, *Princ.*, 316.

[59] Devizes, 7–9. Details in the Pipe Roll confirm this, except for the shrievalty – which Godfrey did not, in fact, obtain, PR 2 Richard I, 136, 151.

[60] According to Richard of Devizes, Glanville had to pay a fine of £15,000. The level of the fine was presumably related to his position as chief justiciar rather than to his local authority as sheriff.

twenty-seven men who had been sheriffs at the end of Henry II's reign, only five retained their office. In East Anglia the sheriffs carried on much as before; everywhere else there was replacement and reshuffling, and every transaction brought in money. The new appointments were men of experience in government, not strangers to the realm. This hardly suggests – as was once supposed – that Richard was uninterested in administrative problems and lacked his father's supposed genius for solving them.[61] A recent systematic study of Richard's sheriffs by Dr Richard Heiser has investigated them all, not just the most famous cases which came to the attention of the chroniclers. His conclusion is that 'prudence and foresight characterized Richard's placement of sheriffs, not carelessness and reck-lessness', and that 'Richard's handling of these officials shows that he understood and appreciated their significance, demonstrating that he was a monarch who was interested in the proper and efficient functioning of his English kingdom'.[62] That offices as well as titles, charters and privileges should be bought and sold was all perfectly usual. It was simply that those transactions which were normally spread over several years were now concentrated into just one in order to meet the demands of an overriding need: the crusade.[63] By these methods Richard raised enormous sums of money fast.[64]

[61] For the evidence which suggests that Richard himself was involved in the appointment of sheriffs, Richard Heiser, 'The Sheriffs of Richard I: Trends of Management as Seen in the Shrieval Appointments from 1189 to 1194', *HSJ*, iv (1992), 111–12. On the basis of a systematic study, 'The Sheriffs of Richard Lionheart: A Prosopographical Survey of Appointments, Politics and Patronage, 1189–99' (unpub. Ph.D. thesis, Florida State University, 1993) Richard Heiser concluded that Richard I 'was as much an administrative king as his father and great-grandfather'.
[62] R. R. Heiser, 'Richard I and His Appointments to English Shrievalties', *EHR*, cxii (1997), 1–19, 11. For the context in which Richard's dealings with sheriffs should be seen, E. Amt, 'The Reputation of the Sheriff, 1100–1216', *HSJ*, viii (1996–9), 95–7.
[63] A study of offers of more than £100 for an heir or heiress during the years between 1180 and 1212 revealed that whereas in all years but two the sum of accumulated debt owed to the crown under this heading normally exceeded the amount of cash paid into the treasury, in 1189–90 the amount paid in came to twice the amount owed – a remarkable variation on the usual pattern: T. K. Keefe, 'Proffers for Heirs and Heiresses in the Pipe Rolls: Some Observations on Indebtedness in the Years before the Magna Carta (1180–1212)', *HSJ*, v (1993), 99–109. The other unusual year was 1196–7.
[64] The exchequer audited £31,089 in 1190, twice as much as in the previous exchequer year. N. Barratt, 'The English Revenues of Richard I' (forthcoming, in 1999 conference proceedings to be published by the Archives du Calvados, Caen). Not until 1204–5 was this sum exceeded. However, so far as total crown revenue from England is concerned, these are misleading statistics since they omit the unknown but probably very large sums raised under such heads as the Saladin Tithe in 1188–9 and the king's ransom in the mid-1190s.

In recent centuries there has been a historical school of thought strongly critical of Richard's management of English affairs at the start of his reign. Once the act of going on crusade was itself seen as 'neglecting England', it was probably inevitable that Richard's preparatory measures would also be seen in a negative light as 'the reckless expedients of a negligent king'.[65] Since contemporaries did not view the crusade in that light they also saw his preparations differently. A famous passage in Howden's *Gesta Ricardi* has, however, often been regarded as containing critical and – since it was written in 1189 or 1190 – strictly contemporary comment.

> The king removed from office Ranulf Glanville, the justiciar of England, and almost all the sheriffs and their officers; the closer they had been to his father, the more he oppressed them. Anyone who did not have as much as he demanded was immediately arrested and sent to jail where there was weeping and gnashing of teeth; then he appointed other sheriffs in their place. And everything was put up for sale, offices, lordships, earldoms, sheriffdoms, castles, towns, lands, the lot.

Howden then illustrated his general point by citing the cases of three churchmen, Hugh du Puiset of Durham, Godfrey of Winchester and the redoubtable Abbot Samson of Bury St Edmunds, who succeeded in buying what they wanted, before concluding that 'in this manner the king acquired a huge amount of money, more than any of his predecessors is known to have had'.[66]

Whether Howden meant these observations as criticisms is less clear-cut. On the first point, was he applauding or regretting the fate of the sheriffs? He was much less enamoured of Glanville than some of the justiciar's modern admirers. Learned in the law he may have been, but Howden also regarded him as a nasty and corrupt judge.[67] At the end of Henry II's reign, the justiciar and his kinsmen had seemed to be all-powerful in England; Howden may well have approved cutting the Glanville family connection down to size. On the second point, to what extent did he believe that Richard was selling off the rights of the crown, the 'family silver'? According to William of Newburgh, writing eight or nine years later, this was the impression which many people had at the time – even the king's friends. When they chided him on this account he replied light-heartedly,

---

[65] In the four months he spent in England in 1189 he 'did almost everything possible to break up the firm and orderly government that his father had imposed on the country', Appleby, *England without Richard*, 36–7. His arrangements in 1189 were 'shambolic', D. A. Carpenter, 'Abbot Ralph of Coggeshall's Account of the Last Years of King Richard and the First Years of King John', *EHR*, cxiii (1998), 1225.

[66] *Gesta*, ii, 90–1.

[67] Ibid., i, 314–16. According to Richard of Devizes, 5, Glanville was under suspicion of having exploited the Old King's trust.

'I would sell London if I could find a buyer'. Stories of this kind fuelled
gossip about the state of Richard's health and led to speculation that he
himself did not expect to return from crusade; hence his apparently
indiscreet and immoderate gifts and sales gave the impression that he
cared very little about the future of the monarchy. This, as it seemed, was
a closing-down sale and there were all sorts of bargains to be had. But,
Newburgh continued, it later became obvious that Richard, far from being
foolishly careless of the rights of the crown, had in fact been most skilfully
and subtly tempting the acquisitive rich to empty their purses.[68] This was
already apparent to Richard of Devizes writing in 1193. According to him
the jokes which the king cracked in 1189 should have served to remind
people of the English proverb: 'the clever man who tries his hand at business buys for twelve pence and sells for one and a halfpence'.[69] By allowing
the acquisitive to think they were getting bargains Richard may well have
been indulging in some sharp practice but it was not abandoning royal
rights. Doubtless some people felt they had been deceived. Howden
reports that by Christmas 1189 Hugh du Puiset had realized that it was not
the king's zeal for justice but his thirst for cash which had led to Hugh's
appointment as justiciar. If there is, as has been thought, a 'jaundiced
point of view' in Howden's account of the 'sale', this could be because
Howden, as a royal clerk who acted as intermediary between king and
bishop of Durham, a bishop who made some of the most spectacular mis-
calculations, was himself one of those deceived.[70] On the other hand it
must be noted that the tone of Howden's account of Richard's Canterbury
court in December 1189 is very positive indeed.[71]

Another contemporary comment which has sometimes been regarded as
critical is Diceto's laconic remark that Richard 'considered a few aspects
of the government of the kingdom with a few people' before he left
England having made himself a richer king than any of his predecessors.[72]
This may be critical, but critical of what? The dean's account of events in

[68] Newburgh, Bk 4, ch. 5.

[69] Devizes, 9.

[70] For the relationship between Howden and du Puiset in these months see D.
Corner, 'The *Gesta Regis Henrici Secundi* and *Chronica* of Roger, Parson of Howden',
BIHR, lvi (1983), 132–9. He argues that the passage about the sale was written after
January 1190, when Howden felt that he no longer had a secure place under the
new regime.

[71] *Gesta*, ii, 99.

[72] Diceto, ii, 73. Immediately before the opaque phrase cited above, Diceto mentioned John's marriage; immediately after it he mentioned William de Mandeville's
death. This might indicate that when he referred to 'a few aspects' he had either
John or Longchamp in mind, or both. But he might have meant something else
altogether. Almost certainly the few who were consulted would have included
Eleanor. She had been present at most of the great assemblies of 1189 and contemporary chroniclers were in no doubt about the influence she exercised.

England in 1190–1 is a remarkably discreet one, so it is hard to know. Was it a veiled criticism of the role of his own friend, William Longchamp, now the king's chancellor? Was it an allusion to Richard's support for John's marriage to Isabel of Gloucester? If Howden and Diceto did express criticism in 1189 it was very muted. The views of Ralph of Coggeshall are striking. Writing in 1195, he was puzzled by the fact that Richard had been captured. It had to be a just judgment of God – but for what? He could not think; it was a mystery. In a context in which Coggeshall was searching for things for which Richard deserved God's punishment, it did not occur to him to think of either the king's treatment of his brother or his promotion of Longchamp.[73]

Among historians writing during Richard's lifetime only one is a severe critic of the measures he took before departing on crusade: William of Newburgh. He took Richard to task for two reasons. First, in a chapter entitled 'The King's Love for his Brother', he blamed him for his generosity to John, for bestowing on him so many gifts that he seemed to possess almost one-third of the kingdom (in addition to what he already had in Ireland and Normandy) and for giving him in marriage Isabel of Gloucester, his cousin in the fourth degree. This imprudent and unlawful generosity, wrote William, led to many evils since it encouraged John's ambition and led him into treachery.[74] On this subject even Richard of Devizes, a historian with an immense admiration for Richard, recorded some doubts. Such was the generosity with which he treated John, he wrote, that 'many people said, both in public and in private, that if John's innate characteristics were not suppressed, his lust for power might lead him to drive his brother from the throne'.[75] As is obvious, these were not strictly contemporary criticisms. Both Richard of Devizes and William of Newburgh had the wisdom of hindsight. John had been made phenomenally powerful in England. Even before the coronation Richard had granted him the counties of Derby and Nottingham, and the honours of Tickhill, Wallingford, Peverel, Lancaster, Marlborough and Ludgershall (the last four with the castles). On 29 August he had seen to it that he married – at long last and in defiance of the archbishop of Canterbury's prohibition on grounds of consanguinity – Isabel of Gloucester whose inheritance included Bristol and the Marcher lordships of Glamorgan and Newport. In December a papal legate recognized the marriage as lawful pending an appeal to Rome and lifted the interdict which Archbishop

[73] Though John was on Coggeshall's mind since a few lines earlier he had referred to John's plotting – and had done so sufficiently trenchantly for him to tone this passage down later (when John was king). Coggeshall, 52.

[74] Newburgh, Bk 4, ch. 3. Followed in this by Poole, *Domesday Book to Magna Carta*, 349.

[75] Devizes, 6.

Baldwin had placed on John's lands; in the same month Richard made him a further grant of the four counties of Cornwall, Devon, Somerset and Dorset. This was probably to complete his father's wish that John should have £4,000 worth of land in England.

Whatever William of Newburgh and Richard of Devizes may have thought later, Richard probably had little choice in 1189. Not to carry out this act of filial piety would have been just as dangerous. In any case John was not simply a subject. He was an Angevin prince. True, he had his lordship of Ireland, but he might have hoped for Anjou or Aquitaine or Brittany. With hindsight two contemporary historians were convinced that John had been treated with dangerous generosity, but in 1190 it might have been argued that he had been pensioned off with the wealth appropriate to his status but with very little power – as John himself doubtless thought.[76] It is significant that he was not given custody of the most important castles in his counties. That he would make trouble as soon as Richard was at a safe distance was all too likely, but what alternative was there? It is not easy to see how Richard could have insisted upon John going on crusade with him – and even this would have had its own risks. In so far as John was dangerous, it was in alliance with Philip Augustus. If Philip was on crusade, it was better that John should stay at home. Richard was aware of the potential trouble his brother might cause. At a family conference in Normandy in March 1190 Richard had John swear an oath not to enter England for the next three years except with his express permission. He later changed his mind; according to Howden, this was on his mother's advice.[77] Wherever John was he could be a disruptive force. The combined power, influence and political skill of their mother and the ministers whom Richard appointed should have been sufficient to keep him in check. Indeed the generous grant of estates in England enabled them to prevent John going over to Philip Augustus at the beginning of 1192 by enabling them to make the threat that they would confiscate his English lands if he did.[78] Moreover by marrying him to the bride promised him by his father, Richard had at least ensured that John would find it harder to make trouble by marrying Alice of France. And, though not without some alarms, he was kept in check until the extraordinary and totally unforeseeable news came that Richard was a prisoner in Germany – news which transformed John's prospects overnight.

William of Newburgh's second criticism of Richard was that without the advice and consent of the magnates he left the administration of the

[76] Indeed it is even arguable that the mistake lay in not giving John enough power, Barratt, 'English Revenues'.

[77] *Gesta*, ii, 106. Archbishop Geoffrey of York also had to promise to stay out of England.

[78] See below, 229.

country to his chancellor, William Longchamp, bishop of Ely, whom he described as 'an obscure foreigner of unproven ability and loyalty'.[79] Here a combination of hindsight and monastic morality – William strongly disapproved of churchmen exercising secular power – has led him to do less than justice to Longchamp's record as it was known in 1189.[80] He had been a clerk in Henry II's chancery before entering Richard's service, in which he had already distinguished himself for diligence and loyalty. He was also the author of a treatise on civil law, a man of considerable culture and learning, much admired by the learned dean of St Paul's. It was predictable that Richard's decision to give custody of both the Tower of London and the royal seal of absence to Longchamp was likely to upset Hugh du Puiset, who would certainly have thought they should have gone to him once he was left as sole justiciar following the death of William de Mandeville.[81] The two bishops found it impossible to work together, so in March 1190 Richard altered the arrangement, limiting Bishop Hugh's authority to the lands north of the Humber and appointing Longchamp as justiciar for the rest of England. Even this apparently clear division of authority failed, however, to prevent tension. Hugh was gradually outmanoeuvred and by June Longchamp was supreme: as chancellor, justiciar and papal legate he held a more powerful combination of offices than any earlier royal servant.[82] After de Mandeville's death Richard experimented with a number of schemes for the government of England, schemes which could readily be adjusted while he remained within his dominions, but once the time for leaving on crusade had been reached, it was Longchamp who enjoyed Richard's trust. Above all it must have been important for the king to choose someone he could trust – which tended to limit his choice to people he had learned to know well, not just since July 1189. Not everyone criticized the appointment. Under '1189' Coggeshall merely noted that Richard committed England to the *industria* of Longchamp.[83] The appointment turned out to be misjudged, since Longchamp's faults meant he was unable to survive the political turbulence whipped up by John in 1191, but there is no reason to think that this, as opposed to the chancellor's quarrel with the bishop of Durham, was foreseeable in 1189. In the early months of 1190

[79] Newburgh, Bk 4, ch. 5.

[80] William's hostility to bishops in secular politics is well brought out in N. Partner, *Serious Entertainments. The Writing of History in Twelfth-Century England* (Chicago, 1977), 88–92.

[81] According to *The Handbook of British Chronology* (3rd edn, 1986), 450, 460, de Mandeville as earl of Essex died on 14 November 1189 and as count of Aumale on 12 December.

[82] Roger of Howden reflects Hugh du Puiset's view, *Gesta*, ii, 101, 106, 108. The administrative arrangements of 1189 are discussed and defended in F. J. West, *The Justiciarship in England 1066–1232* (Cambridge, 1966), 67.

[83] Coggeshall, 28–9.

Richard had seen Longchamp co-operate closely with experienced associate justiciars: William Marshal, Geoffrey FitzPeter, William Brewer, Robert of Whitefield and Roger FitzReinfrey. In any case Richard's contingency plans proved sufficient to cope with the problems of 1191 (see below, 227, 229). When he returned from prison, Longchamp returned with him, remaining his chancellor until he died in 1196. The record of his life in politics and administration was a good one, spoiled only by his failure in 1191.

Modern historians who have followed William of Newburgh in benefiting from the wisdom of hindsight, have generally been those whose instincts told them that a king of England should stay in England. But this is not how people felt in 1189. Contemporaries were unanimous in believing that Richard's highest duty was to attempt the recovery of Jerusalem. It was primarily a religious duty, but not just that. The tottering kingdom of Jerusalem was looked upon as a family inheritance. Its queen, Sybilla, was a cousin, a member of the junior branch of the house of Anjou. As she and her husband Guy de Lusignan – one of Richard's Poitevin subjects – fought to save her inheritance, it was the duty of the head of the senior branch of the family, first Henry II, now Richard, to do all he could to help.[84] That there would be problems was obvious. They would just have to be faced. The absence of an effective and legitimate ruler, whether it was because the king was a child, or mad, or feeble-minded, or in prison, or on crusade, always created severe difficulties for the political and social system, but they were not necessarily insoluble. During the absence of Louis VII and Eleanor on the Second Crusade, Ralph of Vermandois and Suger of St Denis had managed to govern the kingdom of France, though it is worth noting that Suger, like Longchamp, had to face a campaign led by the king's ambitious and stay-at-home brother, Robert of Dreux, to topple him.[85] It was easy enough for Richard to foresee that his brothers might prove troublesome while he was away, particularly since he had no legitimate children and John at least might well hope to inherit the crown. But if he went on crusade, difficulties there were bound to be. In fact had he managed to return reasonably quickly after the end of his crusade, it would have been apparent to all that the arrangements he made in 1189–90 and modified from Sicily in 1191 had worked extremely well. It was only the totally unpredictable event of his imprisonment in Germany that allowed John to do serious damage to the fabric of the Angevin empire. It is incumbent on critics of Richard's arrangements to show what more could have been done to keep John loyal, to hold in check those characteristics of his that as early as 1193 Richard of Devizes had already identified as his 'little ways' (*innatos mores*).[86]

[84] Prestwich, 6–7.
[85] L. Grant, *Abbot Suger of St-Denis* (London, 1998), 156–78. But Suger held on. Undoubtedly this 'aged and sanctimonious' abbot had far more experience of French politics than Longchamp did of English.
[86] Devizes, 6, with apologies to A. A. Milne.

Chapter 8

FRANCE AND SICILY, 1190

On 30 December 1189 Richard met Philip in conference near Nonancourt. The two kings swore to protect the goods of all crusaders and to act in good faith towards one another. The king of France would help the king of England to defend his land exactly as he would want to see Paris defended if it were besieged; the king of England would help the king of France to defend his land just as he would wish to defend Rouen if it were besieged. The barons of both kings swore to remain true to their allegiance and to keep the peace while their lords were abroad.[1] Philip may have hoped that Richard's promise to act in good faith meant that he would in due course marry Philip's sister, but he must already have had a shrewd suspicion that Richard would act in bad faith. In a song which can be dated to 1188 Bertran de Born called Richard a perjuror for swearing to Philip that he would marry his sister Alice when he was also betrothed to the king of Navarre's daughter.[2] It seems certain that he had no intention of marrying Alice. Once his father was dead there was nothing to stop him from doing so, had he wanted to. Instead he continued to promise that he would, only not yet, and in the meantime he made various temporizing arrangements. He had needed Philip's help in order to secure his succession and so he had lied to him. Once on the throne and committed to the crusade, he had to maintain the pretence. If he repudiated Alice now the crusade would collapse while he was forced to defend his dominions against the attacks of a furious French king. So, in a manner worthy of his father, he continued with a series of half-lies and half-truths.[3] It was certainly fortunate for Richard that not only had Philip too taken the cross, but that in the atmosphere after the fall of Jerusalem it was a commitment which even the most reluctant of crusaders could hardly wriggle out of. But so grievous a suspicion between the kings of England and France hardly boded well for the future of their joint crusade. Fortunately the survival of the kingdom of Jerusalem did not depend upon the kings of England and

---

[1] *Gesta*, ii, 104–5.

[2] Born, no. 35, 'S'ieu fos aissi', 380–1.

[3] The judgement of King Philip's historian on Richard's policy here – 'At the least it seems insincere' – is notably restrained, J. Bradbury, *Philip Augustus, King of France 1180–1223* (London, 1998), 78. For the argument that he managed to avoid a direct lie on oath, Kessler, 62–5.

France alone. Ever since September 1189 a steady stream of crusaders had been arriving in the Holy Land. Most important of all, the old emperor, Frederick Barbarossa, though the last of the kings to take the cross, had been the first to set off. He left Regensburg in May 1189 and, following the Danube route, had made slow but steady progress. By Easter 1190 he had crossed the Bosporus and was now in Asia Minor.

During the first six months of 1190 Richard toured his continental dominions. As seneschal of Normandy he reappointed William FitzRalf, a well-tried servant who had held the office since 1180 and was to retain it until his death in 1200.[4] In Anjou the position is less clear. Stephen of Tours had been replaced by Payn de Rochefort, but by May 1190 Stephen was back at Richard's court and he may have received his old office back for the period of the king's absence. Whoever the seneschal was, there was no sign of trouble in Anjou while Richard was away. In Aquitaine two seneschals were appointed: in Poitou, Peter Bertin, formerly provost of Benon, and a man with long experience in the service of the duke; in Gascony Élie de la Celle, a member of a distinguished administrative family.[5] (Possibly this was the model which Richard had in mind when he divided England into the lands north and south of the Humber with a justiciar in charge of each part. Whereas in England the experiment failed through the personal animosities of Hugh du Puiset and William Longchamp, in Aquitaine there were no such problems.) Given the turbulent reputation of the province very few difficulties actually arose there and those that did were efficiently coped with by Richard's seneschals.

During May and early June Richard was in the far south. He visited Bayonne and hanged the lord of the Pyrenean castle of Chis for the crime of highway robbery.[6] Though many of this lord's victims had been pilgrims on their way to Compostella it is hard to believe that it was devotion to the cult of St James alone that brought Richard into the Pyrenees. In view of the humiliating defeats he had recently inflicted on Raymond of Toulouse he could hardly expect the south-eastern frontier of Aquitaine to remain at peace for long after his departure on crusade. The fact that all the great princes of France had taken the cross except for Count Raymond was a sinister sign that was all too easy to read. The obvious answer was to renew and strengthen the alliance with the great enemy of Toulouse, King Alfonso II of Aragon – the alliance which had served Richard well in the crisis of 1183, and which had enabled him to recover the homage of Béarn by February 1187 at the latest. With this alliance came the friendship of King Sancho VI of Navarre, since at this date Navarre and Aragon were drawing together in opposition to King Alfonso VIII of Castile, and were soon to

---

[4] *HGM*, 9710–14.
[5] Boussard, *Comté d'Anjou*, 114–17; Landon, nos 216, 217, 219, 223.
[6] *Chron.*, iii, 35. Landon, no. 291.

make a formal treaty. It is against this background that we must see Richard's marriage to Sancho VI's daughter, Berengaria of Navarre.

The circumstances of their wedding were, to say the least, odd.[7] Richard was to spend the winter of 1190–1 in Sicily on his way to Outremer. Berengaria arrived at his court at Messina at the end of March 1191 and they were eventually married in Cyprus in St George's Chapel, Limassol, on 12 May. On the face of it Sancho of Navarre seems to have been extraordinarily rash to send his daughter so far in search of a husband who was himself moving eastwards, all the more so since it was not until March 1191 that Philip finally agreed to release Richard from his promise to marry Alice, and Berengaria had probably left home in November or December 1190. It would be strange indeed if Sancho had regarded a crusader betrothed to someone else as the ideal husband for his daughter. He must surely have demanded far-reaching assurances and, with the best will in the world, the negotiations which preceded Berengaria's departure from Navarre must have been complex and prolonged. The question is: who conducted these negotiations and when did they begin? Because Berengaria was taken to Sicily by Eleanor of Aquitaine, historians used to assume that it was Eleanor who conducted the negotiations and that she did so during the summer and autumn of 1190, when Richard had already embarked on the first stage of his journey to Outremer: thus the oft-repeated charge against Richard, that he went on crusade still unmarried and without giving a thought to the problem of an heir. But there is evidence that points to a much earlier date. The soldiers in Richard's crusading army seem to have believed that he had formed an attachment to Berengaria while he was still count of Poitou. Above all there is Bertran de Born's 1188 song loudly reminding Philip of the shame he has to endure now that Richard is betrothed to the king of Navarre's daughter. Since Richard clearly had no intention of marrying Alice it is likely that, in his mind, he was firmly committed to marrying Berengaria. But what about the mind of Sancho VI? At Bonsmoulins in November 1188 and perhaps again in July 1189 Richard had given the impression that he would marry Alice. He had certainly intended Alice's brother to think so. Could Sancho afford to trust so devious a liar?

At Candlemas 1190 (2 February) Richard held court at La Réole on the banks of the Garonne. The court was attended by many of the greater lords of Gascony, archbishops, bishops, abbots as well as secular magnates like the counts of Béarn and Armagnac. It is possible that they had come simply to welcome their lord for the first time since he had become duke of Normandy and king of England, yet the presence of Henry, son of Henry the Lion, duke of Saxony, at La Réole suggests that important questions of

[7] For what follows see 'Richard I and Berengaria of Navarre', in Gillingham, *Coeur de Lion*, 119–39.

foreign policy may also have been on the agenda. A very similar court had
assembled twenty years earlier at Bordeaux to settle the marriage between
Richard's sister Eleanor and young Alfonso VIII of Castile. All these are no
more than straws in the wind. Much more striking is the evidence which
shows that, from La Réole, Richard sent a writ to England summoning
Archbishop Baldwin of Canterbury and some other bishops to a council
meeting in Normandy in mid-March, or rather to an important family conference, for as well as the bishops – whose advice on questions of marriage
law would doubtless be useful – Richard also summoned his brothers John
and Geoffrey, his mother Eleanor, and Alice. The question of Richard's
betrothal to Alice must have been discussed at this meeting though the
chroniclers tell us nothing about it. Of its nature this was confidential business. It was at this meeting, however, that both John and Geoffrey were
forced to take an oath not to enter England within the next three years, so
family politics was very much on Richard's mind.

A few days after presiding over this conference, on 16 March 1190, he
met King Philip again. Crusade preparations were behind schedule, so
their departure date was postponed until 24 June, the feast of St John the
Baptist. No sooner had they taken this decision than news arrived that
Isabella of Hainault, Philip's queen, had died in childbirth on the day
before.[8] This was further reason to delay the departure, though there were
some who took it as a sign that God was becoming impatient. It cannot
have been easy to persuade Sancho of Navarre to send his daughter to be
married somewhere abroad in these ambiguous and hazardous circumstances, especially if Richard had once before offered marriage and then
withdrawn it, or seemed to withdraw it. In February and March 1190
Richard may have found that he needed more time to complete such intri-
cate negotiations. Probably it was not until May and early June, when he
again visited Bayonne and was close to the Navarrese border, that he had
the opportunity for a face-to-face meeting with Sancho and was at last able
to bring the matter to a satisfactory conclusion. It was a splendid match for
the daughter of a minor Spanish king – if it had not been, it is hard to
imagine how Sancho could ever have agreed to such an extraordinary
arrangement. But it was also a very useful diplomatic marriage for Richard.
It helped to secure his distant southern frontier and it provided his
seneschals in Aquitaine with an ally upon whom they could call for reinforcements should there be a rebellion or trouble with Toulouse in his
absence. Now at last Richard was ready to go. But far from going on crusade without a thought for the problem of the succession it rather looks as
though the opposite was the case: he had postponed his departure until
most of the problems surrounding his marriage had been resolved. He
then waited in Sicily until Philip had yielded and until Berengaria had

[8] *Gesta*, ii, 104–5; Diceto, ii, 73–4, 77.

arrived. Richard's first priority was the crusade, but he was by no means a fanatic who rushed in without preparation.

From Bayonne he returned to Anjou. There, at Chinon, he issued disciplinary regulations for the sailors of the crusading fleet, the main part of which was now about to sail to its first rendezvous near Lisbon at the mouth of the Tagus. Among the provisions of this naval law were the following:

> Any man who kills another shall be bound to the dead man and, if at sea, be thrown overboard, if on land, buried with him. If it be proved by lawful witnesses that any man has drawn his knife against another, his hand shall be cut off. If any man shall punch another without drawing blood he shall be dipped in the sea [keelhauled?] three times. Abusive or blasphemous language shall be punished by fines varying according to the number of offences. A convicted thief shall be shaved like a champion, tarred and feathered and put ashore at the first opportunity.[9]

Richard then went on to Tours, where he received the staff and scrip which were the traditional attributes of the pilgrim. According to Roger of Howden, writing with hindsight, when Richard leaned on it, the staff broke. If anything at all like this happened, it made no difference.[10] Richard rode out of Angevin territory and joined forces with Philip of France at Vézelay on 2 July.[11] By then they must have planned to join their respective fleets at Genoa and Marseille and then rendezvous at Messina, the deep-sea port

---

[9] *Gesta*, ii, 110–11. The ordinance was issued 'Teste me ipso'. On this formula see J. C. Holt, 'Ricardus rex Anglorum et dux Normannorum', in *Magna Carta and Medieval Government* (London, 1985), 29–30.

[10] *Chron.*, iii, 36–7. In the *Gesta*, composed while the crusade was still in progress, he noted that Richard received staff and scrip without incident at Vézelay, *Gesta*, ii, 111. Quite likely Richard went through the same ritual at both Tours and Vézelay, Ambroise, 303–64.

[11] Details of his itinerary from Tours to Vézelay, and from there on to Lyon and Marseille, are not in Ambroise's *Estoire de la guerre sainte*, but are given by Richard de Templo, author of the *Itinerarium Peregrinorum et Gesta Regis Ricardi*, a work that is substantially a Latin translation of Ambroise, dating from some thirty years later, *Itin.*, Bk 2, chs. 8–10. In ch. 10 the first person plural form, 'we crossed', is used and so it has been suggested that he may, as a young man, have gone on the Third Crusade himself. So he may, but this kind of identification – *Wirgefühl* – with crusading forces occurs commonly in Christian sources, and the details of the itinerary may come from a separate work composed by someone else altogether. Except where there is reason to think Richard de Templo was translating a slightly better manuscript of Ambroise than the only one now surviving, I shall treat his additional material on the crusade as evidence of what was recollected thirty years later – and recollected through a haze of legend building. The extant MS of Ambroise has some obvious gaps – see, for example, below, 215 n. 85, and M. L. Colker, 'A Newly Discovered Manuscript Leaf of Ambroise's *L'Estoire de la Guerre Sainte*', *Revue d'histoire des textes*, xxii (1992).

widely recognized as the point of departure for the best crossing to Outremer.[12] At Vézelay the two kings concluded a vitally important agreement. They were going to war to win land and plunder as well as glory and, according to Ambroise, they 'swore a mutual oath that whatever they conquered together they would share loyally'.[13] Here Ambroise implies that the agreement applied only to those acquisitions they made jointly. This was to be Richard's view. But, unlike the naval law, no official text of this crucial agreement survives, only summaries and passing allusions in letters and narrative sources. What precisely was agreed was to be endlessly disputed. Finally, on 4 July 1190, three years to the day after the battle of Hattin, their armies began to move off. Richard's crusade had begun.

From Vézelay the two kings rode to Lyon, where more crusaders joined them. Here, according to Ambroise, the crusading army encountered its first setback. The rear was delayed for three days when a wooden bridge over the Rhône collapsed under the weight of those trying to cross. Mercifully, though a hundred or so fell into the river, only two were drowned – or rather, as Ambroise in characteristically pious phrases, put it:

> I mean but two discovered were,
> To be more certain none would dare,
> The water there so fiercely surges
> That little which falls in emerges.
> If these be dead in the world's sight
> They stand before God clean and bright:
> 'Twas on His path they set their feet;
> They shall have mercy, as is meet.[14]

Again according to Ambroise, there were a good 100,000 men at Lyon. This may be ten times too many.[15] All that is certain is that the army was a very large one – there are indications that it was as large as a twelfth-century army could be. According to Roger of Howden, when the

---

[12] D. Matthew, *The Norman Kingdom of Sicily* (Cambridge, 1992), 74–5, 137.

[13] Ambroise, 365–70; Richard de Templo's version of this is 'a treaty to share equally everything that would be acquired by right of war, *jure belli*', *Itin.*, Bk 2, ch. 9. William of Newburgh, like Ambroise, gave an English version in which the agreement applied only to those acquisitions made jointly, Newburgh, Bk 4, ch. 21. In 1198 Innocent III summed up the French view of the agreement as a pledge to share 'all acquisitions made after the start of the Jerusalem journey', *Selected Letters*, 6.

[14] Ambroise, 473–80.

[15] Ambroise, 419. Quite apart from the usual problem of the essentially rhetorical treatment of high numbers, it may well be that the eyewitness on whom Ambroise relied, possibly Ambroise himself, did not join Richard's company until it reached Messina. Apart from the broken bridge episode he has nothing to say between the departure from Vézelay and arrival at Messina.

kings reached Lyon they decided to separate because the countryside could not support their joint army.[16] Philip made his way to Genoa. For 5,850 marks he had hired a Genoese fleet to convey his army to Outremer. They were to provide transport for 650 knights and 1,300 squires with their horses; there was to be food and fodder for eight months, wine for four months.[17] The comparatively small size of Philip's force was largely a consequence of the fact that many French princes were making their own way to Acre; indeed many had already gone. The contrast between this and Richard's much larger and more centrally controlled force reflects the contrasting structures of their two kingdoms.[18]

On 31 July Richard reached Marseille, where he expected to find his huge fleet of over a hundred ships waiting for him.[19] But on this day the fleet was still approaching the Straits of Gibraltar. The main flotilla, sixty-three ships under the command of Robert de Sablé and Richard de Canville, had reached the Tagus safely, but while waiting for the arrival of the thirty ships of William de Fors of Oléron's squadron, crews and passengers visited Lisbon and ran riot. In an excess of religious zeal they attacked the city's Muslim and Jewish population, burned down their houses and plundered their property. There was, however, no element of religious discrimination in the freedom with which they raped women and stripped vineyards bare of fruit. Eventually the exasperated king of Portugal shut the gates of Lisbon, trapping several hundred drunken men inside the city and throwing them into gaol. By the time this had been sorted out and the overdue squadron arrived, it was already 24 July and a further two days passed before the whole fleet was ready to start coasting around Spain. The upshot of it all was that by the time they reached Marseille – three weeks late on 22 August – Richard had already left.[20] After waiting a week he had divided the force which had marched from Vézelay into two. One contingent, led by Archbishop Baldwin of Canterbury, Ranulf Glanville and Glanville's nephew, Hubert Walter, the recently elected bishop of Salisbury, sailed directly to Outremer – presumably in hired ships – and arrived at Tyre on 16 September.[21]

[16] *Gesta*, ii, 112. Howden joined the army at Marseille.

[17] *Codice diplomatico della repubblica di Genova*, ed. C. Imperiale di Sant'Angelo (3 vols, Genoa, 1936–42), ii, 366–8.

[18] However, it must be remembered that by the time they had reached the rendezvous at Messina, if not before, Richard's force was comprised of men from every part of his empire: 'Ço erent Norman e Peitevin, Gascon, Mansel e Angevin, e de Engleterre en i aveit assez plus que l'em ne saveit', Ambroise, 743–7. The implication that the English were there in greater numbers than any other group, together with Richard's royal title, explains why the contemporary shorthand for his whole force was often 'English'.

[19] For details of the fleet numbers and cost, Tyerman, *England and the Crusades*, 81.

[20] *Gesta*, ii, 115–22.

[21] Ibid., 115; *Epistolae Cantuarienses*, in *Chronicles and Memorials of the Reign of Richard I*, ed. W. Stubbs (RS, 1865), ii, 328–9, trans. Edbury, 171.

The second contingent, Richard's own company, embarked in ten large ships (known as busses) and twenty galleys, also hired, then coasted eastwards in a more leisurely fashion.[22] He visited Genoa, where Philip was lying ill in a house near the church of St Lawrence; according to Richard of Devizes the French king suffered from seasickness.[23] Richard spent five days at Portofino and while he was there the two kings had the first of their many disagreements. Philip sent a message, asking Richard for the loan of five galleys. Richard offered three, which Philip refused. It was a small matter, but it boded ill for the future of the crusade.

Richard sailed on down the coast of Italy, occasionally going ashore to stretch his legs. But although he landed at the mouth of the Tiber, only a few miles from Rome, he did not bother to visit the pope, Clement III.[24] Indeed a cardinal who was sent to meet him was told in no uncertain terms just what the king thought of the greed of the papacy. Apparently it had cost Richard 1,500 marks to persuade the pope to make William Longchamp legate for the English Church. The gospel preached in Rome was the gospel according to the mark of silver – or so contemporary satirists insisted. It was not that Richard was in too much of a hurry to visit Rome; he made this plain by staying ten days at Naples and five days at Salerno, mostly doing some sightseeing.[25] If he consulted any of Salerno's medical authorities Howden does not mention it.

While at Salerno, he heard the news for which he had been waiting. His fleet, after staying at Marseille for a week to re-fit, had been sighted and was now approaching Messina. So he pushed on and crossed the Straits of Messina on 22 September. Earlier that day he had had a narrow escape. Passing through a small village on an overland journey from Mileto with just one companion, he heard the cry of a hawk coming from a house. Believing that only noblemen had the right to own hawks, he pushed his way in and seized the bird. At once he was surrounded by a crowd of angry villagers and when he refused to give it back they attacked him with sticks

[22] It is at this point that Roger of Howden's crusade journal begins. Howden stayed on with the army after having brought Hugh du Puiset's complaints against Longchamp to the king at Marseille, Corner, 'The *Gesta Regis*', 135.

[23] Devizes, 15.

[24] Diceto, ii, 84.

[25] At Naples Richard went to see the remains of the four sons of Aymon, heroes of French poetry, 'standing in furs and bones' in the crypt of the abbey of San Gennaro. The epic *Quatre Fils Aymon* (better known as *Renaud de Montauban*; my thanks to Marianne Ailes for this identification) tells the story of Renaud of Montauban and his three brothers against whom Charlemagne waged a relentless war until Renaud began to expiate his sins by going on a pilgrimage to the Holy Land. In his wars against Toulouse Richard may have visited Montauban. The rest of Howden's account of Richard's Italian journey is the journal of a literary and historical tourist, wondering at sites associated with Virgil, Lucan and Robert Guiscard, *Gesta*, ii, 112–15, 124–5.

and stones. One man drew a knife and Richard struck him a blow with the flat of his sword only to see the blade snap. So the crusader king was reduced to pelting villagers with anything he could lay his hands on in order to escape from the very awkward situation into which his carelessness had landed him.[26] Next day he exchanged pettiness for pomp, orchestrating a grand entry into Messina. He arrived, wrote Howden:

> with many busses and other great ships and galleys, in such magnificence and to such a noise of trumpets and clarions that a tremor ran through all who were in the city. The king of France and his men, and all the chief men, clergy and people of Messina stood on the shore, wondering at what they had seen and heard about the king of England and about his power.[27]

This was how to make an impression. As Ambroise observed, it was the proper custom of great princes to enter a city in great state. Whether it was tactful on this occasion is another matter. According to Ambroise, 'the Grifons were angry and the Lombards grumbled because he came into their city with such pomp and circumstance'.[28] Philip had arrived a week earlier, had done so quietly and had been assigned quarters in the royal palace. That he too was unhappy is indicated by the fact that after a brief conference with Richard, he announced his intention of leaving for the Holy Land that same day. But no sooner had he sailed from the harbour than the wind shifted and, much to his dismay, Philip was forced to return to Messina and to further meetings with the king of England. However, while Philip stayed in the palace, Richard set up camp with his army along the shore.

Entirely by chance, they had arrived in Sicily at a critical moment in its history. The kingdom of Sicily – a kingdom which included much of southern Italy as well as the island itself – was a fertile and prosperous land where goats had not yet done their work of destruction. Besides corn – Sicily was still one of the great granaries of the Mediterranean world – there were oranges and lemons, cotton and sugar cane in abundance.[29] It was a land to tempt a conqueror and had already been conquered several times in its turbulent history, most recently by the Normans – cousins of

---

[26] *Gesta*, ii, 125.

[27] *Gesta*, ii, 125–6.

[28] Ambroise, 555–604. Grifon was his term for Greeks; Lombard for those inhabitants who observed the Latin rite (Lombards having been established in Italy since the sixth century). Since Philip had entered with just one ship it would have been hard not to outshine him; moreover Ambroise believed that Philip, by avoiding the crowd gathered on the shore to watch his arrival, had disappointed the curious.

[29] Matthew, *Norman Kingdom*, 71–85; D. Abulafia, *The Two Italies* (Cambridge, 1977).

the men who conquered England – in the decades between 1060 and 1090. For men from the north the most remarkable thing about Sicily was neither its wealth nor its highly developed system of government, but the diversity of its population. Greek, Muslim and Latin (both Lombard and Norman) lived side by side, each with their own language and religion. The court at Palermo spoke Norman French and issued decrees in Latin, Greek and Arabic. These very different communities had lived together fairly well, though a recent and more sustained Christian effort to convert Muslims was beginning to provoke resentment. Even so, the Muslim traveller Ibn Jubayr who visited Sicily in 1184 remarked on the relative absence of discontent among the island's Muslim population and noted with interest that Christian women were beginning to follow Arab fashions: they wore veils when they went out of doors and they never stopped talking. The blend of cultures produced a unique civilization. At Palermo, Monreale and Cefalù the visitor can still see superb examples of its art and architecture.

But in 1190 Sicily stood on the eve of another conquest. Its trouble had been brought about by a dispute over the succession to the throne following the death of King William II in November 1189. He had no children and his heir was his thirty-five-year-old aunt, Constance. But she was married to a German, Henry of Hohenstaufen, Frederick Barbarossa's eldest surviving son and heir. Few people in Sicily wanted a German king, and Pope Clement III had a terrifying vision of what would happen to the papacy if it came to be completely surrounded by the territories of one over-mighty ruler. So pope and Sicilian barons conspired together against Constance and her German husband. The crown passed to Tancred of Lecce, an illegitimate cousin of William II. He was, in the most literal sense of the words, an ugly little bastard, whose enemies never tired of poking fun at his dwarfish figure. He looked, so they said, like a monkey with a crown on its head. His hold on the throne was anything but secure. On the island a Muslim revolt broke out, while on the mainland rebel barons joined forces with an invading German army. No sooner had he overcome these threats than he was faced by the problem of having an enormous army of crusaders encamped within his unsettled kingdom.[30] They were supposed to be going to Jerusalem but who could tell what damage they might do *en route*? Only a few years later, in 1204, a crusading army allegedly on its way to Jerusalem had sacked the greatest city in the Christian world, Constantinople, and with that blow destroyed the Byzantine empire. According to Sir Maurice Powicke, 'the thought of Richard before Constantinople makes the heart leap'.[31] For Tancred the sight of

[30] Matthew, *Norman Kingdom*, 286–9; Norwich, *Kingdom in the Sun*, 356–61; E. Jamison, *Admiral Eugenius of Sicily* (London, 1957), 80–5.
[31] Powicke, 105.

Richard before Messina was enough to make his heart sink. There were family matters on which Tancred and Richard were far from seeing eye to eye. King William II had been married to Richard's sister Joan. When he died a dower should have been assigned to his widow. But Tancred did not trust her: he kept her in close confinement and withheld the dower.[32] Richard was not going to stand for this. Immediately after his arrival, he sent envoys to Palermo, and Tancred agreed to release Joan. She reached Messina on 28 September and, according to Howden, when Philip saw her he looked so cheerful that in no time at all it was rumoured that he was going to marry her.[33] Richard was less pleased. Although Tancred had given Joan some money, a million *tari* according to Richard of Devizes, he was still holding on to her dower.[34] Moreover William II, in his will, had left a large legacy, including money, gold plate, one hundred war galleys and vast quantities of grain and wine, to his father-in-law, Henry II.[35] But as Henry died a few months before William, Tancred regarded this part of the will as null and void. Richard took a different view. The bequest had been intended to help finance Henry's crusade. Now here was Richard, Henry's heir and a crusader. Naturally he claimed the money and the galleys.[36] In the meantime, on 30 September, he seized the fortified monastery of Bagnara on the mainland side of the Straits of Messina and established Joan and her household there.[37]

To add to the complications the crusaders and the – mainly Greek – population of Messina soon took a violent dislike to each other. According to Ambroise the latter were to blame.

> For the townsfolk, rabble, and the scum
> Of the city – bastard Greeks were some,
> And some of them Saracen-born
> Did heap upon our pilgrims scorn
> Fingers to eyes, they mocked at us,
> Calling us dogs malodorous.
> They did us foulness every day:

[32] Part of his problem was that her dower, the county of Monte Sant'Angelo, lay in the area most immediately threatened by invading Germans.

[33] *Gesta*, ii, 126. By this time Howden believed that after a series of meetings Richard and Philip were again on good terms.

[34] Devizes, 17. *Taris* were tiny coins (30 to the local ounce) made of 16⅓ carat gold, P. Spufford, *Money and its Use in Medieval Europe* (Cambridge, 1988), 167–9.

[35] *Gesta*, ii, 132–3; Devizes, 17.

[36] According to Gerald, Richard had been negotiating with William II about a crusade fleet as early as 1188, *Princ.*, 245.

[37] *Gesta*, ii, 127.

> Sometimes our pilgrims they did slay,
> And their corpses in the privies threw.
> And this was proven to be true.[38]

Almost certainly it was rising food prices which lay behind all this trouble. The presence of a large army stretched the resources of the region, and prices went up in response to the increased demand. But this is not how the crusaders saw it. They put the blame on the greed of the local shopkeepers. Soon the crusaders and the notoriously turbulent Messinesi were virtually at war. On arrival in Sicily Richard found himself confronted by two serious problems: Tancred and the Messinesi. By 8 October he had solved both.

On 2 October he occupied the nearby Greek monastery of San Salvatore and turned it into a supply dump for the stores from his ships. He had decided to winter in Sicily.[39] Holding both Bagnara and San Salvatore he now controlled both sides of the straits. To the worried Sicilians this looked like the first move in an armed takeover of the whole island.[40] Next day fighting broke out and Richard found he was unable to put a stop to it. Alarmed by the prospect of losing control of the situation he invited King Philip and Tancred's governors of Messina, Admiral Margarit and Jordan del Pin, as well as the archbishops of Messina, Monreale and Reggio, to a conference in his lodgings on 4 October.[41] But while they were trying to reach agreement, presumably on the problems of food prices and army discipline, a confused clamour of shouts and the clash of arms brought their discussion to an abrupt end. The lodging of one of the barons of Aquitaine, Hugh of Lusignan, was being attacked. Richard at once left the conference and ordered his men to arm themselves. He was now determined to settle the matter by force. Rather than allow this kind of rioting to go on indefinitely he would seize control of Messina. The Messinesi had gathered on high ground, preparing – so Howden believed – a treacherous attack, but they were driven back when 'the king himself with just a handful of men advanced up a slope so steep that no one had thought it possible'.[42] The gates of the city were broken down and the troops stormed in with Richard

---

[38] Ambroise, 549–58. On the other hand he admitted that they were worried by conversations between 'our pilgrims' and their wives, 611–12.

[39] For the winter closure of shipping, J. H. Pryor, *Geography, Technology and War. Studies in the Maritime History of the Mediterranean 649–1571* (Cambridge, 1988), 87–9. In the treaty with Tancred drawn up on 6 October Richard spoke of being held up by 'rough winds, waves and weather', *Gesta*, ii, 133–4.

[40] *Gesta*, ii, 127. Indeed Richard of Devizes composed a long set piece in which the king – 'that terrible lion' – was represented as having already decided to take Messina in retribution for the way his followers were being treated, Devizes, 19–22.

[41] *Gesta*, ii, 127–8, 138. Both Howden and Ambroise believed that Margarit and Jordan were in fact stirring up trouble, Ambroise, 671–4. On Margarit see Möhring, *Saladin*, 149–52.

[42] *Gesta*, ii, 128–9; cf. 'Ke tel gerrier n'aveit el monde', Ambroise, 686.

at their head. Many were killed in the street fighting, including twenty-five of the king's own household troop. To Howden's indignation, King Philip and his men refused to help their fellow-pilgrims; instead, while the fighting raged around them, they strolled about the city as though they were at home. Ambroise even accused Philip's men of defending the port from an attack by Richard's galleys, killing two rowers in the process.[43] On the landward side, where Richard was directing operations, his men were more successful. English, Normans, Poitevins, Gascons, men from Maine and Anjou – they were, wrote Ambroise with a proud sense of solidarity in the shared enterprise, people who had taken many a town. It was all over so quickly, as he put it, that it would have taken longer for a priest to say matins than it took the king of England to capture Messina. After the fighting came the plundering – the customary reward for those who risked their lives in an assault.

> And ye may know of surety
> That much was lost of property
> When they successfully attacked
> The town. It speedily was sacked;
> Their galleys were destroyed and burned,
> Which were not poor or to be spurned.
> And there were women taken, fair
> And excellent and debonair.[44]

When King Philip saw Richard's banners waving above the walls and towers of Messina, he was furious and, no doubt, humiliated since the people of Messina must have believed that his presence within their walls guaranteed their safety. He demanded that the banners should be taken down and his own hoisted up in their place. To plant a banner in a captured town was to stake a claim to a share in its government and its plunder. If Richard was claiming that Messina was now his, to do with as he liked by virtue of the right of conquest, then Philip was reminding him of the agreement they had made at Vézelay. Richard finally allowed his banner to be hauled down and replaced by the standards of the Templars and Hospitallers in whose custody Messina should remain until Tancred had met his terms.[45] Ambroise believed that it was this quarrel over the banners

---

[43] *Gesta*, ii, 129; Ambroise, 779–86. The bitterness this caused in Richard's camp is vividly illustrated by the fact that many years later his envoys to the curia told the pope that 'the king of France had been the first to inflict injury, in that at Messina where, being called on to furnish aid in meeting an attack of King Tancred's men against [us], he not merely failed to give it, but with his own hand killed three of [our] men with a cross-bow', *Selected Letters*, 6–7. Cf. Coggeshall, 33.

[44] 'Plus tost eurent il pris Meschines

C'uns prestres n'ad dit ses matines. (Ambroise, 741–5, 809–10, 813–20)

[45] *Chron.*, iii, 58. In his original crusade journal, the *Gesta*, Howden made no mention of either Philip's protests or this arrangement.

Which in the French King did create
Envy that time will ne'er abate.
And herewith was the warring born
Whereby was Normandy sore torn.[46]

But though he gave way on the legal formalities, Richard made sure that he still kept control of the situation. He took hostages from the wealthier citizens of Messina and began to build a wooden castle on a hill overlooking the town. He called the castle Mategriffon, meaning 'Kill the Greeks'.[47]

If he were to recover Messina, Tancred had very little choice. By 6 October his council had agreed terms with Richard. In addition to the million *tari* he had handed over with Joan, Tancred now agreed to pay another 40,000 ounces of gold. Half of this was in lieu of Joan's dower; the other half served both to satisfy Richard's other demands and as the settlement to be bestowed upon one of Tancred's daughters when she married Richard's three-year-old nephew, Arthur of Brittany, whom Richard designated as his heir should he die without issue. If the marriage did not take place through Richard's or Arthur's fault, then 20,000 ounces would be returned. In return Richard acknowledged that his claim on Tancred had been met in full and promised that for as long as he was in Sicily he would give Tancred military aid against any invader.[48] Here, at least, Tancred had gained something: an ally against Henry of Hohenstaufen, now King Henry VI of Germany. According to Rigord of St Denis, Tancred had earlier tried to persuade Philip to agree to a similar marriage alliance, but the French king had refused to be drawn into a treaty which would jeopardize his friendship with Henry VI.[49] Since Richard, like his father, maintained close family and political ties with Henry the Lion, the duke who was the chief German opponent of the Hohenstaufen in the 1180s and 1190s, he, rather than Philip, was Tancred's natural ally. Forty thousand ounces of gold was a heavy price to pay for the temporary assistance of a crusading army.[50] The diplomatic asset of Richard's friendship was perhaps more valuable. When Henry VI entered Italy the next year his projected invasion of Sicily was thrown into disarray by a revolt in Germany organized by Henry the Lion's son, Henry –

[46] Ambroise, 827–30.

[47] *Gesta*, ii, 138.

[48] Ibid., 132–8. Although, as here, Henry VI is treated as the most likely invader, an Almohad attack on Sicily, perhaps in support of the war of their co-religionists, was also a possibility, see Möhring, *Saladin*, 192–207.

[49] Rigord, 106. But he had, of course, recognized Tancred as the lawful king, and been assigned the palace in Messina as his quarters. It may be that the alliance with Henry VI existed only after Philip's return from crusade.

[50] Richard sailed from Messina on 10 April 1191 and Henry VI invaded Tancred's kingdom on 29 April.

the same prince who had attended Richard's court at La Réole in Gascony in February 1190. So far as Richard was concerned the immediate advantages of the treaty were obvious, particularly since Joan was willing to see her 20,000 ounces spent in the service of the crusade. As for the marriage alliance between his nephew and Tancred's daughter, depending on the outcome of the impending German invasion of Sicily, either Tancred's kingship was finished, or his would be an alliance worth having. Either way Richard and/or his nephew kept the 20,000 ounces. Moreover, when he designated Arthur as his heir presumptive, Richard was probably already aware of Berengaria's imminent departure from Navarre. He did not expect to die without issue.[51]

By 8 October the differences between Richard and Philip had also been settled by the simple expedient of Richard giving Philip one-third of all the money he received from Tancred.[52] In an effort to prevent further disturbances, the three kings fixed the price of bread at a penny a loaf, stabilized the price of wine, and laid down that no merchant should make a profit of more than 10 per cent on a deal. Whether or not this price freeze was rigidly enforced, the crusaders were able to spend a further six months in Sicily without any more serious trouble. According to Ambroise, Richard won great admiration from the Sicilians by ordering that plunder taken in Messina should be returned.[53] Another cause of dissension, this time within the army, was gambling and the debts which some soldiers were refusing to meet on the ingenious grounds that as crusaders they naturally enjoyed the crusader's privilege of a moratorium on repayment of debt. It was decided that the moratorium would apply only to those debts contracted before the start of the crusade. Philip and Richard banned all gambling by ordinary soldiers and sailors except when their officers were present. Soldiers who disobeyed this order were to be stripped naked and whipped through the army on three successive days, while sailors were to be keelhauled three days running. Knights and clergy, however, could play for up to 20 shillings a day, on pain of a fine if they exceeded this limit. Kings were specifically permitted to gamble away as much as they pleased. A financial and disciplinary committee was established to enforce these regulations and to control the army's common chest, the fund which took over and administered half the possessions of those who died while on crusade. Among its members were the

[51] But for the impact of the treaty on events in England see below, 227.

[52] In the French camp it was argued that Philip should have received a half, but that *pro bono pacis* he was content with a third, Rigord, 106. However years later Philip's envoys complained to Pope Innocent that they had not received the half which was their due, *Selected Letters*, 6.

[53] Ambroise, 1029–32. Howden believed that after the capture of Messina the reputation of the English was high, *Gesta*, ii, 139, cf. Devizes, 16–17.

masters of the Temple and the Hospital, Duke Hugh of Burgundy, Robert de Sablé and Andrew de Chauvigny.[54]

If Richard was impatient to be on his way he gave little sign of it. Indeed he may long ago have decided to wait in Sicily until his bride arrived. But many of the other crusaders were far less patient. They

> said it was wrong
> To linger. They made loud laments
> Because it cost them much expense.[55]

Richard calmed their complaints by a generous distribution of gifts. Philip too was able to lavish substantial cash sums upon his followers, since Richard had given him a share of Tancred's gold. The presence of the crusading army no longer posed a threat to Tancred and this persuaded some Muslims to submit to him.[56] So the time passed quietly and pleasantly enough.[57]

Richard took the opportunity to meet Joachim of Fiore, the Cistercian abbot who believed that he had discovered the concealed meaning of the Bible, especially of the Book of Revelation. This discovery led him to see a pattern in history and enabled him to predict the future of the world. Richard was intrigued and asked Joachim to come and talk to him. The abbot divided world history into three ages: the Age of the Father, the Age of the Son and the Age of the Spirit. The Third Age was to be the culmination of human history, a time of love, joy and freedom when God would be in the hearts of all men. The empire and the Church of Rome would have withered away. In their place there would be a community of saints who had no bodily needs; therefore there would be no wealth, no property, no work. Complicated calculations had revealed to Joachim that the Third Age was nigh. It would come some time between 1200 and 1260. What particularly interested Richard was Joachim's identification of Saladin as the sixth of the seven great persecutors of the Church in the Second Age. Joachim prophesied that Saladin would soon be driven out of the kingdom of Jerusalem and killed; that the infidels would be slaughtered and the Christians would return once more to the Holy Land. 'And God', he said, 'has decreed that all these things will be done through you. Persevere in

---

[54] *Gesta*, ii, 129–32.

[55] Ambroise, 1053–6. Some had arrived at Messina before the kings and had already had a long wait.

[56] Rigord, 106–7; *Gesta*, ii, 141.

[57] Roger of Howden, however, as an experienced clerk and envoy, could probably be more usefully employed and the content of pages 137–46 of the *Gesta Regis* suggests that he was sent to Rome, where – amongst other things – he was able to help transact some more business relating to Durham and York, before returning to Messina by Christmas, probably by 19 December, *Chron.* iii, 71, *Gesta*, ii, 142–3.

the enterprise you have begun and He will give you victory over your enemies and glorify your name for evermore.' However confident Richard was,
to listen to these fervent words was doubtless reassuring. Yet it was salutary
to be reminded that Saladin's defeat did not mean the end of all their
troubles. After Saladin would come the seventh persecutor, Antichrist, who
would rule for three and a half years. According to Joachim, Antichrist had
already been born at Rome, was now fifteen years old and would be elected pope before revealing his true self to the world. This prophecy made
Richard question the abbot's calculations. Perhaps the present Pope,
Clement III, whom Richard disliked, was Antichrist? But Richard himself
held other theories. In his view Antichrist was to be born in Egypt or
Antioch and would rule the Holy Land. After his death there would be a
period of sixty days during which people whom Antichrist had seduced
would be given the opportunity to repent of their sins. Joachim did not,
however, alter his system to take account of Richard's prejudices or ideas.
On the whole the churchmen in Richard's entourage seem to have been
interested in, rather than impressed by, Joachim's ideas.[58] Most of them,
after all, were practical down-to-earth men chosen by a king who wanted
bishops who knew how to command men and supply armies. None the less,
Joachimite patterns of thought were to remain influential. In particular the
idea of a Third Age, to be reached after a period of violent upheaval, was
to have a permanent appeal.[59]

Meanwhile the winter closure of the sea lanes meant that in the Holy
Land the Christian army, hemmed in by Saladin, was running dangerously
short of provisions. They had to contend not only with Muslim attacks but
also with the threat of starvation and the diseases associated with mal-
nutrition. Whenever a horse was killed it was at once surrounded by a
crowd of jostling soldiers, each fighting to obtain a piece of the flesh;
nothing was wasted, they ate head, intestines and all. Men were seen down
on their hands and knees, eating grass. In Sicily Richard's immense supply
of stores was under guard in the monastery of San Salvatore; his ships were
beached and undergoing repairs. Richard celebrated Christmas 1190 in
magnificent style in his castle of Mategriffon. King Philip was his guest and
all who were there marvelled at the splendour of the gold and silver plate,
at the variety and abundance of meat and drink.[60]

---

[58] *Gesta*, ii, 151–5.

[59] And they clearly fascinated Roger of Howden himself, for when he later revised
this section of his journal, he first altered Joachim's crusade prophecy to make it fit
with what he now knew had happened, and then added considerably to the account
he gave of the Antichrist. Towards the end of his own life, in 1201, he noted that
learned men believed that the devil had been loosed upon the world, *Chron.*, iii,
80–6, iv, 161–2.

[60] Ambroise, 1081–108.

Chapter 9

THE CONQUEST OF CYPRUS

By February 1191 the army in Sicily was getting impatient. Building siege machines, though useful preparatory work, was not what they had left home for. Only Richard's generosity in distributing gifts to all and sundry held the troops together. The enforced idleness was getting on Richard's nerves too. In this restless atmosphere it was easy for a trivial incident to be blown up out of all proportion. One day when Richard was out riding with knights from his and Philip's household, they met a peasant with a supply of canes. At once they took the canes and arranged an impromptu tournament. Richard clashed with his former opponent, William des Barres, and as old antagonisms came to the surface the knightly contest quickly degenerated into a brawl in which no one else was allowed to intervene. Richard tried to throw William to the ground but he hung on grimly to his horse's neck and could not be shifted. Finding himself unable to win, Richard completely lost his temper and ordered William never to show his face in his presence again; from now on he would look upon him as an enemy. Richard indeed forced Philip to send William away and not until the eve of the French King's departure from Sicily did he relent and allow William to return to his lord's – and the crusade's – service. Even then Richard gave way only after Philip and all the leading men in the army had gone down on their knees before him. Yet at the same time as he was reluctant to be reconciled with des Barres, Richard showed himself to be anything but a reluctant giver. 'He gave many of the ships which had come from England to the king of France and his men; he distributed treasures in profusion to earls, barons, knights and sergeants. None of his predecessors had given so much in a year as he gave in this February; by this we believe he has earned God's favour for "God loveth a cheerful giver"' (2 Cor. ix. 7).[1]

As if this unmatchable generosity were not irritating enough for Philip, he now had to face the humiliating business of Richard's repudiation of his sister. By late February Eleanor and Berengaria, accompanied by Count Philip of Flanders, had reached Naples and Richard sent galleys to meet them there and convey them to Messina. But although Count Philip

---

[1] *Gesta*, ii, 155–7.

was allowed to embark, Eleanor and Berengaria were not. Tancred's officials said that their escort was too large to be accommodated in an already
overcrowded city and sent them to Brindisi. This was obviously not the
real reason, so Richard went to see Tancred to demand an explanation.
The two kings met at Catania on 3 March and spent five days together.
According to Roger of Howden, Tancred finally confessed to Richard that
he had been listening to Philip's insinuations. The French king apparently had warned Tancred that Richard's word was not to be relied upon;
that he had no intention of keeping the treaty they had made last
October and instead was planning to deprive Tancred of his kingdom.[2]
This is a curious story: however well informed Roger of Howden was, he
is unlikely to have overheard the private conversation of two kings. None
the less the fact that Eleanor and Berengaria were kept away from Messina
suggests that Howden is doing more than simply repeating anti-French
gossip.

Tancred was understandably nervous about the crusaders but had
nothing to fear from Philip's small force. His problem was Richard and the
Angevin army. Although they were now allies, Richard's assault on
Messina, and the circumstances in which the alliance had been forged,
were hardly such as to dispel all Tancred's doubts. Yet it was vital that he
read Richard's intentions correctly. The king of Sicily's insecurity was fertile ground for Philip's diplomatic skill – these were just the kinds of fears
he had played upon when separating Henry II from his sons. What Philip
wanted is clear enough: he wanted to save his sister's honour. She had now
been betrothed to Richard for more than twenty years and to be cast aside
after so long would be an intolerable insult. As the news came that Eleanor
and Berengaria had crossed the Alps and were travelling southwards
through Italy, Philip's concern grew. But their journey may have raised his
hopes of drawing Tancred over to his side. For Tancred too had news
which gave him cause for grave concern. Henry VI had left Germany and
was heading in the direction of Sicily. It is not hard to imagine Tancred's
feelings when he learned that Eleanor and Henry VI had met at Lodi, not
far from Milan, on 20 January 1191.[3] Doubtless she reassured Henry VI
that Richard would be leaving Sicily – and the field clear for him – as soon
as he could. But Tancred could not be sure of that. Was the king of
England planning to throw in his lot with the king of Germany? These
were the fears which Richard had to dispel when he met Tancred at
Catania and, eventually, he succeeded. The two kings exchanged gifts as a
token of their renewal of friendship. Richard gave Tancred the sword
Excalibur which had once belonged to King Arthur. Tancred's gift was

---

[2] Ibid., 157–9.
[3] *Die Regesten des Kaiserreiches unter Heinrich VI*, ed. J. F. Böhmer and G. Baaken
(Cologne–Vienna), *Regesta Imperii* IV/3, no. 116.

more prosaic, but conceivably more useful: four large transport ships and fifteen galleys.[4]

The French king had been playing a dangerous game. Once Tancred was convinced that he had nothing to fear from Richard, then Philip became the victim of his own intrigue. He protested his innocence, claiming that the whole thing was a put-up job, a scheme devised by Richard to give him an excuse for breaking his promise to marry Alice. For two reasons, however, Philip's defence does not ring quite true. First, because Tancred's agents had prevented Berengaria from leaving Naples – an unnecessary complication if it was just a charade. And, secondly, because the count of Flanders, on his arrival in Sicily, took Richard's side against King Philip – which suggests that he did not believe the French king's story. At all events, Philip was now isolated and in a weak bargaining position. Richard drove home his advantage. He had no wish, he said, to discard Alice but he could never marry her since she had been his father's mistress and had borne him a son. It was a grim accusation, but Richard claimed that he could summon many witnesses able to testify to its truth. In the face of this terrible threat to his sister's honour Philip gave up his struggle to save her marriage.[5] In return for 10,000 marks he released Richard from his promise. Other clauses in the treaty between the two kings drawn up at Messina in March 1191 regulated most of their outstanding differences, above all the question of Gisors and the Norman Vexin. This disputed territory was to belong to Richard and his male descendants, but would revert to Philip and his heirs if Richard were to die without a legitimate son. If Philip died without a surviving male heir it would be regarded as a part of Normandy. Elsewhere the treaty was based on the status quo. Richard confirmed Philip's rights over Issoudun, Graçay and Auvergne, while Philip confirmed Richard's rights over Cahors and the Quercy.[6] For Philip this treaty was a humiliation. In a gesture which

[4] *Gesta*, ii, 159. According to this report, at first Richard would accept nothing more than 'a certain small ring'. On this gift exchange see M. Warren, 'Roger of Howden Strikes Back: Investing Arthur of Brittany with the Anglo-Norman Future', *ANS*, xxi (1998).

[5] *Gesta*, ii, 160. Although Henry II has been defended against this accusation, for example Warren, 611, it is difficult to discount Howden's explicit statement that this was what Richard told Philip, and difficult to believe that Richard simply invented the story in order to extricate himself from an unwelcome marriage. For this it would have been sufficient to have witnesses testify that she had had a child, and that he was not the father (cf. 'I never had carnal knowledge of her': *Philippidos*, iv, 129); he did not have to name his own father as the child's father. However tense Richard's relations with his father had been before the latter's death, it is hard to see why he would invent an unnecessary lie now. See Kessler, 40.

[6] Landon, 228–32 for text and discussion of the treaty of Messina. Curiously, Howden's summary of the treaty states that Richard agreed to return the Vexin to Philip, *Gesta*, ii, 161 (repeated *Chron.*, iii, 99). For many reasons this cannot be

perfectly expressed his feelings he chose to set sail from Messina on 30 March, just a few hours before Eleanor and Berengaria arrived.[7] In Rigord's view, the quarrel between the two kings began when Richard rejected Alice.[8] It might be more accurate to say this was the moment when their quarrels turned into bitter hostility. From now on, in Ulrike Kessler's phrase, Philip's crusade was directed not so much against Saladin as against Richard.[9]

Three days' rest was enough for the seventy-year-old Eleanor. Then she set off on the long journey back to Normandy, leaving Berengaria in the care of Richard's sister Joan. Richard of Devizes, who almost certainly never saw her, dismissed Berengaria as 'more sensible than attractive'.[10] Ambroise, who probably did, is much kinder. She was Richard's 'beloved, a wise maiden, a fine lady, noble and beautiful, with no falseness or deceit in her'.[11] For William of Newburgh – who also never saw her – she was 'a maiden famous for beauty as well as wisdom' and he described her arrival in Sicily in terms which show that he expected Richard to find pleasure in the marriage – as well as a remedy against fornication.[12] These conventional phrases tell us nothing about his or her sexuality – apart, perhaps, from the fact that it was assumed to be conventional.[13]

The wedding, however, had to be postponed, not through any reluctance on Richard's part but because it was Lent. Still, though Richard could not marry in Lent, he could at least travel. Now that Berengaria had arrived, there was no reason why he should delay any longer in Sicily. So he prepared to go. The castle of Mategriffon was dismantled and stowed away, in sections, aboard ship. On 10 April 1191 Richard's huge fleet, now numbering over 200 vessels, left Sicily behind.[14] The fleet carried not merely men, horses and arms, but treasure, heavy siege equipment and victuals. It included war galleys and skiffs, vessels designed for combat,

right, above all because in later years when putting their king's case to the pope, Philip's envoys do not claim that Richard had broken his promise to do so, *Selected Letters*, 6–7. See Kessler, 72–3. It may be that Howden, who loved documents, did not see a copy of the text of this treaty until he was shown one when he was on the way back to France together with King Philip; in which case he was shown a forged document. He did not finish writing up his crusade journal in the form we have it until summer 1192, *Gesta*, ii, 150). See also Bertran de Born's sardonic comment on Philip's generosity in giving Richard Gisors, Born, no. 42.

[7] *Gesta*, ii, 161.

[8] Rigord, 107–8 omits all mention of the treaty.

[9] Kessler, 75.

[10] 'puella prudentiore quam pulchra', Devizes, 25. But he was presumably aiming at alliteration rather than accuracy.

[11] Ambroise, 1140–43.

[12] Newburgh, Bk 4, ch. 19.

[13] For further consideration of their marriage, see below, 263.

[14] According to Richard of Devizes, Berengaria – sensible young woman – 'was still a virgin – perhaps', Devizes, 35.

reconnaissance and assaults on beaches. Richard of Devizes, who liked precise figures, said it comprised 156 ships, 24 busses and 39 galleys, in all 219. On the basis of his figures for 'men per ship' Richard would have been in command of 17,000 soldiers and seamen – an immense force for the period.[15]

On the third day out of Messina, Good Friday, 12 April, a storm blew up.[16] Richard was able to keep the greater part of the fleet together; at night-time a light was kept burning at the mast-head of the king's ship as a guide to the others.

> This fleet of mighty ships and men
> He guided, as the mother hen
> Doth guide toward the feed her brood,
> Such was his native knightlihood.[17]

But when they reached their first rendezvous at Crete on 17 April some twenty-five ships were missing, among them the great ship carrying both Joan and Berengaria. With a strong following wind Richard sailed on to Rhodes, which he reached on the 22nd. He stayed there for ten days; he was ill, he had to wait for his galleys to catch up, he had to find out where the missing ships were, and he wanted news of the 'tyrant of Cyprus'.[18] In fact some of the missing ships, among them Joan and Berengaria's, were well ahead of the main fleet; on 24 April they reached the south Cypriot coast near Limassol, where three of them (but not Joan and Berengaria's) were driven aground and their cargoes plundered. Some of the crew and passengers were drowned, including Roger Malcael, the king's vice-chancellor and seal-bearer. Those who reached dry land were imprisoned and their money taken.[19] By the time the 'tyrant' of Cyprus, Isaac Ducas

---

[15] Devizes, 28, 35. For the calculation, Tyerman, *England and the Crusades*, 66. For analysis of the fleet and a discussion of numbers, Prestwich, 7–8.

[16] *Gesta*, ii, 162. From this point on Howden's account of Richard's voyage and conquest of Cyprus lacks all precise dates – with one exception – until 1 June. That exception is the date of Richard's marriage and the coronation of his queen. Given Howden's practice of giving precise dates, especially for the royal itinerary, when he can, this suggests that he was not an eyewitness of the major events between 12 April and the beginning of June; probably because the ship in which he sailed was not in that part of the fleet over which Richard regained control. It seems, however, that Ambroise's ship was, so what follows will be chiefly based on his account.

[17] Ambroise, 1247–50. For further praise of Richard's outstanding qualities as a naval commander, Devizes, 35.

[18] Ambroise, 1269–312. Strong wind and high waves meant that the galleys, with the low freeboard which made them susceptible to being swamped, had to proceed cautiously, following Richard 'terre a terre', as Ambroise put it. See Pryor, *Geography, Technology and War*, 69–71.

[19] *Gesta*, ii, 162–3. When Roger Malcael's body was washed ashore, the seal, which the vice-chancellor always wore on a chain round his neck, was recovered. With his

Comnenus, arrived at Limassol on 2 May some of the stranded crusaders had fought their way out of the fort in which they had been detained and, with the help of a well-timed landing party, had managed to join their fellows in the ships standing offshore. Meanwhile their whereabouts had been discovered and reported back to Richard. On 1 May (a day before Isaac's arrival at Limassol) he sailed from Rhodes.[20] The speed with which Joan and Berengaria were tracked down, and the fact that despite their fears of Isaac they stayed there, strongly suggests that Limassol had been given as a rendezvous before the fleet left Messina. According to Ambroise, when Richard received news that Philip's presence at the siege of Acre meant that things were moving there, he sailed against the wind to Cyprus: 'He already had another plan in mind'.[21] The plan, in all probability, was the conquest of Cyprus.[22]

Cyprus, for centuries a part of the Byzantine empire, had since 1184 been ruled by Isaac Comnenus, a member of the former imperial family, in opposition to the Angelus dynasty now in power in Constantinople.[23] To anyone who knew the situation of the Christians in Outremer, dependent for their survival and reinforcement on the long supply line from southern Italy, the strategic importance of Cyprus was obvious. If Latins held this prosperous island they could use it both as a source of renewable supply and as a springboard for future crusades. The long-term future of the kingdom of Jerusalem would be infinitely improved. All this must have become plain to Richard while he was in Sicily, if not long before.[24]

Isaac must have known about the great east-bound army wintering in Sicily. The unannounced appearance of a massive armed force on his shores would have been tantamount to an act of war; when a small band of

chancery background, this is just the sort of detail which Roger of Howden would have heard. Only Richard de Templo gives a date for the shipwreck – 'the eve of St Mark the evangelist' *Itin.*, Bk 2, ch. 30. In this form it could have been in the version of Ambroise which he translated, but some caution is required, and the date must be treated as probable rather than certain.

[20] Ambroise, 1315–18.

[21] Ibid., 1340–7.

[22] That the conquest of Cyprus was 'in Richard's mind from the outset' is asserted by Saladin's secretary, Imad al-Din, 291. He was, of course, writing after the event. Among modern historians, it was first suggested as a possibility by Brundage, *Richard Lionheart*, 100–1; the arguments that make it probable were set out by Prestwich (in Nelson, *Coeur de Lion*, 8–9) and then developed in greater detail by Kessler, 127–50.

[23] P. W. Edbury, *The Kingdom of Cyprus and the Crusades 1191–1374* (Cambridge, 1991), 3–4.

[24] The master of the Hospital, Garnier of Nablus, a native of Outremer, had been with Richard at Messina in December 1190; earlier, as master of the Hospitallers in England, he had attended the council at Pipewell/Geddington in September 1189, Landon nos 41, 54, 346. For his career see J. Riley-Smith, *The Knights of St John in Jerusalem and Cyprus c. 1050–1310* (London, 1967), 107–8.

crusaders inflicted casualties on his subjects and then did not sail away – a clear sign that they expected to be reinforced soon – he must have suspected what was coming. It seems to have been at this time that he turned for help to Saladin, and tried to forge the alliance which so much scandalized the Westerners.

> And it was told of them as fact
> That they had sealed their friendship's pact
> By drinking one another's blood.
> 'Twas proved that this was no falsehood.[25]

When Richard arrived on Monday, 6 May he found that Isaac had stripped Limassol bare of everything that could be moved and used it to fortify the beach: doors, benches, chests, planks, blocks of stone, abandoned hulks of old ships.[26] According to Ambroise, Richard sent an envoy to Isaac, demanding redress and restoration of the goods taken. The envoy was rebuffed, allegedly with the mysterious but presumably derisive phrase 'Tproupt sire!'[27] As it turned out, Isaac had miscalculated disastrously, but few military enterprises are more dangerous than trying to force a landing in the presence of the enemy. As Ambroise put it, 'we were at a disadvantage, for we were coming from the sea, in tiny boats, battered by waves, all on foot, weighed down by our arms, while they were on their own land'. Undaunted, Richard and his men – 'nos savions plus de guerre' – piled into their ships' boats and rowed for the shore. As soon as they were in range, crossbowmen and archers opened fire on the defenders, forcing them to move. Then, with Richard at their head, the assault troop jumped into the shallow water and charged up the beach. After some fierce fighting the Cypriots (Greeks and Armenians) retreated. Rather than risk a pursuit in unknown and hilly country, the crusaders occupied the abandoned town and port of Limassol, finding there a very satisfying quantity of foodstuffs.[28]

Howden and Ambroise give very different versions of what happened

[25] Ambroise, 1391–4. For the date of alliance see Möhring, Saladin, 186–7. In Richard de Templo's elaboration of Ambroise's account Isaac was accused of yet further falsehood, treacherously inviting Joan and Berengaria ashore, Itin, Bk 2, ch. 31.

[26] Limassol itself, like all other towns on the island then, was unwalled, Edbury, The Kingdom of Cyprus, 14.

[27] Ambroise, 1447–62. Histories composed in mid-thirteenth-century Outremer include narratives of Richard's conquest of Cyprus, translated in Edbury, 100–4, 176–8. They occasionally provide details such as place names which derive from knowledge of the island's geography, but such details are set within stories incompatible with Ambroise's account, so I have ignored them here. They are, however, useful evidence for the way Richard's conquest was regarded there fifty years later.

[28] Ambroise, 1503–64; cf. Gesta, ii, 163–4, Chron., iii, 107.

next. According to the former, Isaac regrouped and pitched camp about five miles from the town, announcing that he would give battle the next day. But Richard sent out scouts, ascertained the enemy's whereabouts, moved his men silently into position, and attacked their camp while they were still asleep. Isaac himself just managed to escape but had no time to dress first. According to Ambroise, Richard spent the night disembarking his horses, having them exercised, and then personally leading a cavalry attack of at most fifty knights. Such was Isaac's numerical superiority that a clerk, Hugo de la Mare, advised Richard to retreat, only to be told 'Sir clerk, you get on with your writing. Forget about fighting and leave the chivalry to us, by God and Saint Mary.' After this exchange the king's attack, 'faster than a bolt of lightning', inevitably swept all before it. Whatever the differences, two ideas are common to both accounts. The first is that Isaac was taken by surprise (according to Ambroise it had not occurred to him that Richard had brought warhorses with him, or would be in a position to use them after they had been at sea for a month). The second is that the capture of their camp brought in a vast quantity of booty, including treasure, livestock, horses (in better condition than ours, observed Ambroise), arms and Isaac's imperial standard, embroidered in cloth of gold, which Richard immediately decided to present to the abbey of Bury St Edmunds.[29] However it happened – and Ambroise's version of events was almost certainly composed by someone closer to the scene of action than Howden was – two such victories within twenty-four hours were quite enough to persuade many of the local landowners that it was better to submit at once. They came to Richard's camp and handed over hostages. By 11 May the ranks of those still loyal to him had thinned out to such an extent that Isaac decided to sue for peace.

On that same day another group of visitors came to Limassol. At their head was the king of Jerusalem, Guy of Lusignan, and his brother Geoffrey, Richard's old enemy. But the Lusignans were no longer the turbulent lords of Poitou. Guy and Geoffrey had come as suppliants, asking for Richard's support against the political manœuvres of King Philip – who had arrived in Acre on 20 April – manœuvres which were designed to push Guy off the throne and replace him with Conrad of Montferrat. After a year in captivity Guy had been released by Saladin in June 1188 on condition that he took no further part in the fighting. Guy, of course, had no difficulty in finding a clergyman who would release him from the oath he had sworn to Saladin. Unfortunately for him, while he was in prison, Conrad of Montferrat's defence of Tyre had made him the hero of the hour and Conrad had no doubt that he would make a much better king than Guy. Under his energetic command the defenders of Tyre had made good use of the few weeks' breathing space granted them when, in September 1187,

[29] *Gesta*, ii, 164; Ambroise, 1565–694.

Saladin, having already captured nearly all the cities and castles of the kingdom of Jerusalem, decided to lay siege to Jerusalem rather than to the
great coastal fortress of Tyre. Saladin entered the Holy City on 2 October,
the anniversary of Mahomet's ascent into heaven from Jerusalem. It was a
brilliant stroke of propaganda skilfully utilized by Saladin's chancery in the
jubilant letters which they circulated throughout the Muslim world. After
Mecca and Medina, Jerusalem was the most holy place in Islam and its
recovery ensured that Saladin's name would never die.

For his army it was the emotional climax of the campaign of 1187.
Unfortunately, it was not the end. Now Saladin pushed his weary soldiers
to lay siege to Tyre. But by November the city's fortifications were in
first-rate shape and his army had to face the tedious and uncomfortable
prospect of a long-drawn-out blockade. If Tyre could survive the winter
then it could serve as a beachhead for Christian reinforcements. In
terms of military strategy it was a much more important city than
Jerusalem, for once the Franks had lost the coast they could not hope
to keep or recover the Holy Sepulchre. In later years there must have
been moments when Saladin regretted that he had made a political
rather than a military decision in September, but it is easy to be wise
after the event and in the autumn of 1187 his momentum must have
seemed irresistible.

Tyre survived. On 1 January 1188 Saladin called off the siege. Conrad of
Montferrat sensed that his star was in the ascendant. He began to behave
as though he were the real ruler of the kingdom, and when Guy was
released refused to hand back Tyre. Guy found that he was a king without
a kingdom and, in Conrad's eyes indeed, not even a king any more. Guy
took an important initiative by laying siege to Acre but as time went by his
position became increasingly difficult. He was king of Jerusalem by virtue
of the fact that he had married Sibylla, the heiress to the kingdom. In the
autumn of 1190, however, he lost both his wife and his two daughters, victims of one of the epidemics which were a normal part of life in the
unhealthy atmosphere of an army camp. With Sibylla dead, could Guy still
claim to be king? Guy believed that as the anointed king he should retain
the kingdom, but in legal terms the circumstances of his anointing and
coronation in September 1186 were highly dubious.[30] In that case perhaps
Sibylla's younger sister, Isabella, should inherit her rights. It seemed to
Conrad that Isabella ought to be queen and that he was just the sort of man
to be her husband. True, it was rumoured that at least one of Conrad's two
previous wives – one Italian, one Greek – was still alive, but then army
gossip was notoriously unreliable. It was true also that Isabella had a hus-

[30] B. Z. Kedar, 'The Patriarch Heraclius' in *Outremer. Studies in the History of the
Crusading Kingdom of Jerusalem presented to J. Prawer*, ed. B. Z. Kedar, H. E. Mayer and
R. C. Smail (Jerusalem, 1982), 196–8; Gillingham, 'Love, Marriage and Politics', in
Gillingham, *Coeur de Lion*, 244–6.

band already, Humphrey of Toron; he was unquestionably alive, indeed he was there in the camp outside Acre. But then there were churchmen in the camp too and wherever there were churchmen, marriages could be broken. If the archbishop of Canterbury would not annul the marriage – and Baldwin, who arrived in October 1190, did in fact refuse to do so – then Conrad could try the archbishop of Pisa, who might be attracted by the possibility of securing an extension of Pisa's commercial privileges in Outremer. So Isabella was abducted from her tent outside Acre and persuaded – by her mother – that her marriage to Humphrey was invalid. Despite Humphrey's protests, the marriage was annulled. On 24 November Isabella was wedded to Conrad. In canon law the marriage was both incestuous, because Isabella's sister had once been married to Conrad's brother, and bigamous, because her marriage to Humphrey was wrongly dissolved – as was later established by a papal commission. Legally a farce, the proceedings were none the less thought to make good political sense on the grounds that the kingdom needed a tough ruler with the skills and driving force which Humphrey of Toron clearly lacked. For some months an open confrontation and the danger of an armed clash between Conrad and Guy was avoided because Conrad and Isabella went back to Tyre, leaving Guy at Acre. But with King Philip's arrival at Acre all that changed. Conrad returned to the siege of Acre and was recognized as 'king elect' by Philip.[31]

Inevitably Richard agreed to help Guy. Sybilla, after all, was Richard's cousin, and even after her death he had continued to regard her husband as the rightful king. As duke of Aquitaine he probably still considered himself the Lusignans' lord and protector. Indeed there was already one Lusignan in his army, Guy and Geoffrey's nephew, Hugh. Perhaps just as important, by now it was only natural that he and Philip should take opposing sides. Guy of Lusignan and his party, Humphrey of Toron among them, did homage to Richard.[32] Next day, 12 May, Richard and Berengaria were married in the chapel of St George at Limassol and then Berengaria was crowned queen by John, bishop of Evreux.[33] By holding the wedding here it may have been hoped to avoid the awkwardness that would have accompanied a wedding at the siege of Acre; easier to present Philip with a *fait accompli*. So in a Cypriot town a queen of England was crowned by a bishop of a Norman see. Richard was king of England, but he was also much more than that, and those whose lives became bound up with his found that they had to range widely through the whole of Christendom. In assigning to Berengaria a dower which, while Eleanor lived, comprised all

[31] See below, 157.
[32] Ambroise, 1701–27; *Gesta*, ii, 165. Also with Guy were Bohemund, prince of Antioch, and Leo, an Armenian who became prince of Armenia in 1197.
[33] *Gesta*, ii, 166–7.

his rights in the whole of Gascony south of the Garonne, Richard was doubtless fulfilling one of the terms of the marriage settlement negotiated with Sancho of Navarre.[34]

Soon afterwards Isaac confirmed the peace terms which his envoys had offered and swore allegiance to Richard. In return Richard sent back some of the plunder he had won, including three of Isaac's magnificent tents which the 'emperor' pitched in the place of the peace conference, the 'parlement', between his and Richard's negotiators. The terms which Isaac accepted were so stiff, however, that it is unlikely he had any intention of keeping them.[35] Probably he hoped only to gain time and obtain some idea of Richard's plans. At any rate he left abruptly, once again abandoning his tents and equipment.[36] Richard is said to have been pleased by this indication that Isaac did not consider himself bound by the terms of the agreement.[37] It gave him the justification he needed for conquest. He acted, wrote Howden, 'as a circumspect and prudent man'. Part of his army he handed over to Guy of Lusignan with instructions to pursue and, if possible, capture Isaac. The rest were embarked in the galleys, half of which, under his command, sailed one way round the island, while the other half, commanded by Robert of Thornham, sailed round in the opposite direc-

[34] E. Martène and U. Durand, *Veterum Scriptorum et Monumentorum Amplissima Collectio*, i (Paris, 1924) cols 995–7. After Eleanor's death the very considerable dower estates she had been assigned in England, Normandy, Maine, Touraine and Poitou were to revert to Berengaria. However, Richard's successor saw no need to abide by the terms of this agreement. On this see I. Cloulas, 'Le Douaire de Bérengère de Navarre, veuve de Richard Coeur de Lion, et sa retraite au Mans', *CCM* (forthcoming).

[35] According to Ambroise, he had agreed to pay 3,500 marks in compensation, to lead 500 mounted men against the Muslims in Syria and, as a guarantee of his loyalty, to hand over his castles, which would be returned to him if he served faithfully, Ambroise, 1775–832. As given by Howden, the terms were even harsher; he would supply more troops, pay 20,000 marks' compensation and hand over his daughter, his only child, to be married as Richard decided, *Gesta*, ii, 165.

[36] Ambroise, 1833–50. According to Ambroise, Isaac was advised to flee and to continue the fight for Cyprus by Paien of Caiphas, an adherent of Conrad of Montferrat. Once Richard had thrown his weight behind Guy of Lusignan, it was in Conrad's interest to prevent Richard arriving at Acre with the resources of Cyprus at his disposal. If Conrad had sent Paien to Isaac with this aim, the plan clearly misfired. By marrying Isabella, Conrad had married the daughter of a Comnena, hence his new kinship with Isaac Comnenus. On this see Kessler, 146–7.

[37] The surviving sources for the conquest of Cyprus are all pro-Richard, and it would be naïve to accept them at face value. If there is anything to Ambroise's Paien of Caiphas story (see previous note), it could be that Paien warned Isaac against Richard's double-dealing. Saladin's secretary believed that Richard took Cyprus by treachery, Imad al-Din, 292. Amongst others, Conrad's envoys to Saladin could easily have supplied that information.

tion.[38] As they circumnavigated the island they captured coastal towns and castles as well as enemy ships. At Famagusta Richard was met by Dreux de Mello and Philip of Beauvais, acting as envoys from the king of France and urging him to move on at once to Acre. Richard and Guy are unlikely to have been impressed by King Philip's choice of his cousin the bishop of Beauvais as envoy since he had been deeply involved in legalizing the wedding of Conrad and Isabel.[39] According to Ambroise, the interview was an angry one.

> The half of Russia's wealth he'd spurn
> Before to Syria he would turn
> Till he had crushed the Cypriot
> From whose isle rich supplies are got.[40]

From Famagusta the crusaders' army moved into the interior, making for Nicosia, the island's chief town. According to Ambroise, in view of the danger of ambush, Richard took command of the rearguard. Isaac obliged with an attempted ambush and was again forced into flight. Once Nicosia had fallen, more and more Cypriots came to offer submission. There is good evidence that Isaac as a ruler had been disliked and feared, and this opinion was exploited and developed in a propaganda war of conquest. Typical of the stories about Isaac which were now being put into circulation and which were intended to show him up as a tyrannical usurper was the one that told how he cut the nose off a noble who was honest enough to advise him to submit.[41]

Isaac, however, still held out out in the great castles perched high in the mountains of northern Cyprus: Buffavento, Kantara and St Hilarion (or *Dieu d'Amour* as the Franks called it, claiming that it was the Castle of Love built for Cupid by Venus, queen of Cyprus, a legend appropriate to the castle's romantic site). Presumably he calculated that eventually Richard would have to move on to the Holy Land. Isaac could then come out of hiding and take over the island once again. It was not an unreasonable hope but it came to nothing when Guy of Lusignan captured the coastal

---

[38] *Gesta*, ii, 166. Although Howden said that Richard had galleys with him when he landed at Limassol, according to Ambroise it was not until after Richard's wedding that his well-armed and magnificently equipped galleys 'for which he had waited so long' arrived, Ambroise, 1745–8. If in his haste he had sailed from Rhodes in bad weather (ibid., 1318–50), this would explain why his galleys arrived later. Only after they, with their inshore fighting capacities, had come could he begin a campaign of conquest.

[39] Ambroise, 4129; Edbury, 96.

[40] Ambroise, 1899–902. Cf. Gervase, ii, 88 for the belief that Philip had been playing false in urging Richard to leave Cyprus.

[41] Ambroise, 1907–62.

fortress of Kyrenia and, within it, Isaac's daughter.[42] When Isaac heard the news of her capture he was beside himself with grief. He surrendered on 1 June 1190, making – or so it was said – only one condition: that he should not be put in irons. Richard accepted this, and then had silver chains made especially for him.[43] The story of this incident was widely circulated; it was 'calculated to produce both amusement and awe'.[44]

In area Cyprus was only about the size of East Anglia, but the mountainous terrain ought to have made conquest difficult. Isaac's love for his daughter was a piece of luck for Richard, but the whole campaign had been finely conceived and methodically carried out as a combined operation using both naval and land forces – the vital capture of Kyrenia, for example, had been the result of a siege 'by land and sea'.[45] The conqueror reaped tremendous rewards. In addition to the spoils of war and the property confiscated from those who had fought against him, Richard imposed a 50 per cent capital levy on every Cypriot. In return he confirmed the traditional laws and customs of the island. But from now on these laws were to be enforced by Angevin officials backed by Angevin garrisons. As an outward sign of the new order Richard required all loyal Greeks to shave off their beards; they were obliged to look like Westerners. Two Englishmen, Robert of Thornham and Richard de Canville, were put in charge of the government of the island.[46] But not all the Cypriots submitted. A kinsman of Isaac's led a revolt. Robert of Thornham suppressed it, captured and hanged its leader.[47] The rebellion may have persuaded Richard to dispose of his rights over Cyprus sooner rather than later. He sold them to the Templars for 100,000 Saracen bezants (dinars), 40,000 of which were

[42] Ibid., 1967–2006. Guy's crucial success occurred while Richard was ill at Nicosia. For the importance of Kyrenia, 'the location of Isaac Comnenus' treasury and probably the best fortified place in the island at that time', see Edbury, *The Kingdom of Cyprus*, 13.

[43] Ambroise, 2014–46; Gervase, ii, 88. But at least Isaac was spared mutilation, his most likely fate had he fallen victim to internal Byzantine politics. For the date, *Gesta*, ii, 167. Richard de Templo gives 'the Wednesday after the feast of St Augustine' (31 May), *Itin.*, Bk 2, ch. 40.

[44] Prestwich, 3. Ambroise, 2057–9 added a moving description of Isaac's reunion with his daughter.

[45] Ambroise, 1972.

[46] *Gesta*, ii, 167–8; Ambroise, 1945–8. Richard de Canville died soon afterwards.

[47] *Gesta*, ii, 172–3. The late fourteenth-century *Chronicle of Meaux Abbey* contains further details about Richard's provisions for the government of Cyprus and, in view of the association between the abbey and Robert of Thornham, it is not impossible that these have some slight basis in his reminiscences, including the story that by hanging the rebel Robert angered Richard. Allegedly the latter's view was that even hanging someone who claimed to be king was an affront to royal dignity, *Chronica Monasterii de Melsa*, ed. E. A. Bond (RS, 1866), i, 258–60.

paid at once.[48] For Stubbs this was no way to treat an expansion of empire. Richard, he wrote disparagingly, 'had no scheme of territorial aggrandisement such as gave a unity to the whole life of his father and of his competitor Philip' and so 'the rich and tenable acquisition of Cyprus was cast away even more easily than it was won'.[49] But although Cyprus later came to be thought of as a possession of the English crown, this is not how Ambroise saw it at the time. 'All this the king of England conquered for the service of God and to put at the disposal of His land.'[50]

In terms of military strategy in the service of the Holy Land the conquest of Cyprus turned out to be a master stroke. Though reasonably safe from attack (not until 1571 did Cyprus fall to the Turks), it lay so close to the eastern shores of the Mediterranean that a man standing on the hills around Stavrovouni could see on the horizon the cedar-covered mountains of Lebanon. The news of Richard's success cheered the troops besieging Acre.

> The king, by taking Cyprus, had
> Made all the army to be glad
> For therefrom would they food derive
> To keep the mighty host alive.[51]

Very likely this had been in Richard's mind from the outset of his crusade, but this is not the impression given by the man in the best position to know, the king himself. In a newsletter sent to Longchamp written on 6 August he summarized what happened after he left Messina:

As we were continuing our pilgrimage journey, we turned to Cyprus (*in Cyprum divertimus*) where we hoped to find the refuge of those of our number who had been shipwrecked. But the tyrant who – revering

---

[48] Edbury, 112. According to another version Richard was at the siege of Acre when the Templars spoke with him and bought the island, *Recueil des historiens des croisades. Historiens occidentaux* (5 vols, Paris, 1844–95), ii, 189. They may well have spoken to him then, but that the sale was completed before Roger of Howden (who is silent on the subject) left Acre to return to England seems unlikely. This was at the beginning of August. Richard himself made no reference to a sale in a letter he wrote on 6 August 1191; his words indeed imply that Cyprus was still his, Edbury, 178–9, from *Epistolae Cantuarienses*, in *Chronicles and Memorials of the Reign of Richard I*, ed. W. Stubbs (RS, 1865), ii, 347. Rigord, 118 confirms the sale and puts the price at 25,000 marks; given the French king's claim to half of Cyprus, the French court may have kept a close interest in the terms of the sale.
[49] Stubbs, *Historical Introductions*, 321. (*Itin.*, i, xxv).
[50] Ambroise, 2081–2. For later English views see Edbury, *The Kingdom of Cyprus*, 11–12. Handel's 1727 opera, *Riccardo Primo, Rè d'Inghilterra*, focuses on Richard's exploits on Cyprus – information I owe to the kindness of Tim Hochstrasser.
[51] Ambroise, 2367–70. For a similar recognition of the importance of supplies from Cyprus, Coggeshall, 31–2; Sicard, 21.

neither God nor man – had usurped the name of emperor, hurriedly brought a strongly armed force to bar us from the port. He robbed and despoiled as many as possible of our men who had suffered wreck and imprisoned those dying of hunger. Not unnaturally we were spurred to revenge (*vindictam*). We did battle with our enemy and, thanks to divine assistance, obtained a quick victory. Defeated and fettered, we hold him together with his only daughter. We have subjected to ourselves the whole island of Cyprus with all its strongpoints.[52]

Here, while saying nothing about his intentions, Richard presents the conquest as a punitive act and as a turning away from the path of the crusade, 'our pilgrim journey' (*iter peregrinationis*). By 6 August, whatever had actually happened, it made sense to present it in these terms. According to Howden, at Acre Philip demanded half of everything Richard had taken from Cyprus as well as half of the island itself on the grounds that this was what they had agreed at Messina. Richard replied that their agreement applied only to acquisitions made 'in the land of Jerusalem' but that he would acquiesce if Philip gave him half of the county of Flanders, as well as half of what he had got after the deaths of both Philip of Flanders and the castellan of St-Omer. Howden's version of the renewed agreement reached after this spat was that it should apply in the land of Jerusalem.[53] Or did it apply to gains made 'on the Jerusalem journey'? There were ambiguities, possibly the result of deliberate fudges, in the original agreement, and in its subsequent renewals at Messina and Acre. If Philip was to have half of what Richard acquired on crusade, in 'God's service', then it may have suited Richard to present the conquest of Cyprus as an unforeseeable response to shipwreck rather than as a planned component of the crusade. By 6 August Philip was on his way back to France, taking with him his version of his rights and lawful claims. It made sense for Richard to ensure that those governing his dominions heard his version, and if he had planned the conquest of Cyprus, he had good reason to be economical with the truth.[54]

[52] *Epistolae Cantuarienses*, 347, trans. in Edbury, 179.
[53] *Gesta*, ii, 171. Innocent III's précis of the French case referred only to half the treasure taken from Cyprus; the English case was that Philip obtained satisfaction on this and all other matters before he left Outremer, *Selected Letters*, 6–7. Philip of Flanders died at Acre on 1 June 1191 and by the terms of a treaty he had made with Philip of France in 1180, his death meant that the French king could claim to be the new lord of Artois.
[54] Prestwich, 8. English contemporaries accepted the 'unintended' version, e.g. Coggeshall, 31. In William of Newburgh's version of the quarrel between Richard and Philip, Richard explains that he went to Cyprus 'non ex intentione, sed incidenter ... causa ulciscendae divertisse', Newburgh, Bk 4, ch. 21. Such turns of phrase suggest he may have used Richard's letter of 6 August, see J. Gillingham, 'Royal Newsletters, Forgeries and English Historians: Some Links between Court and History in the Reign of Richard I', *CCM* (forthcoming).

Chapter 10

THE SIEGE OF ACRE, 1191

For two years all eyes in both the Muslim and Christian worlds had been focused on Acre. Men never forgot their first sight of the siege of Acre. 'When on our way there from Tyre we sighted it from the top of a hill, we tried to guess as nearly as we could the number of those engaged. The lord of Sidon said there were five hundred thousand; I said six hundred thousand.'[1] As Richard approached Acre, he saw, in Ambroise's words, 'the flower of the world encamped around it'. According to Baha al-Din, around Acre there were gathered 'all the forces of the coast, of Jerusalem, Damascus, Aleppo and Egypt and the other Muslim countries. The city itself was held by the most renowned emirs in the army, the bravest champions of Islam.'[2] Baha al-Din Qaragush, one of Saladin's most experienced commanders and his outstanding military architect, had been placed in charge of the defence of the city. If it fell it would be a tremendous blow to the prestige of the victor of Hattin and liberator of Jerusalem.

Yet when two years earlier, in August 1189, the defeated Guy of Lusignan had risked taking an army through difficult and enemy-held country to lay siege to Acre, it had looked for all the world like an act of great folly.[3] Once their initial attempt to scale the walls had failed, it was clear that an army the size of Guy's had no hope of taking Acre, which had been, until it fell to Saladin in July 1187, the largest town and chief port in the kingdom of Jerusalem. When Saladin came to the relief of this great city Guy would be trapped between the Acre garrison and the might of the main Muslim army. His political opponents liked to write Guy off as a simple man but not even they had thought he could be as stupid as that. And yet it had worked, as in Guy's apparently hopeless position nothing else could have worked. Guy set up camp on the hill of Toron, three-quarters of a mile east of Acre, and although he was unable to take the city, Saladin was equally incapable of dislodging him. Reinforcements from the west came in. A Pisan fleet attempted a sea blockade. They were

---

[1] The 'I' here was Balian, lord of Ibelin, talking to Saladin's biographer, Baha al-Din, 21.

[2] Ambroise, 2313; Baha al-Din, 21, 259–60.

[3] There is a good analysis of the siege in R. Rogers, *Latin Siege Warfare in the Twelfth Century* (Oxford, 1992), 212–35, and an excellent narrative from the Muslim point of view in Lyons and Jackson, 295–330.

able to hold a stretch of coast just north of Acre and keep open the sea communications without which Guy was doomed, but could not prevent the occasional Muslim supply ship getting through. To protect their position from attack both from the garrison and from Saladin's field force, the Christians dug a double line of trenches across the peninsula on which Acre stood. From now on Acre was subjected to a close landward blockade. From behind their trenches the crusaders' artillery bombarded the city walls while the garrison replied in kind. Occasionally a major assault was launched when mobile siege towers or battering rams were employed and the siege artillery brought up much closer to the walls; but at these times the besiegers' engines were vulnerable to the incendiary weapons – Greek fire – of the defenders. Thus a position of stalemate was reached. Generally Saladin remained in his camp in the hills at Shafar'am about seven miles away from the Christians, moving up to Tell Ayadiah (two and a half miles away) when the garrison needed closer support. Both sides settled down to a struggle of attrition, a combination of artillery duel and trench warfare. That Saladin should remain nearby throughout the entirety of the siege is an extraordinary testament to his appreciation of its vital importance. In the spring of 1190 and again in 1191 when the sea became navigable again, both sides were able to bring in further reinforcements and supplies. Two Egyptian fleets fought their way in, but the galleys with which Saladin had hoped to contest Christian dominance of the eastern Mediterranean became immobilized there because the crews were needed to man the walls in an increasingly desperate struggle. Even Ambroise learned to admire the Muslim defenders of Acre for holding out 'when they beheld how the whole world was coming to destroy them'.[4] As months turned into years and men – and, on the Frankish side, women – fought and died, as the tales of suffering and heroism grew, so the stakes and the tension grew higher and higher.[5]

Philip Augustus reached Acre on 20 April 1191. His arrival had been keenly anticipated. As Baha al–Din put it, 'the enemy took every opportunity of informing us that they were expecting the king of France to arrive very shortly. He held a very high rank among the Christians and all the besiegers' forces would have to put themselves under his orders as soon as he arrived. This king, accompanied by his principal officers, came at last with six ships laden with provisions and as many horses as he considered necessary.' His force was so much weaker than the Muslims had been led to believe that they were much encouraged.[6] In rapidly deciding to recog-

<hr>

[4] Ambroise, 5072–4.

[5] One favourite story among the besiegers of Acre was of a woman who was so enthusiastic that, when mortally wounded, she begged that her body would be thrown into the moat so that even dead she could help to fill it in.

[6] All Muslim sources make this point: Baha al-Din, 240 (Gabrieli, 212); Imad ad-Din, 289–90; Ibn al-Athir, 41.

nize Conrad of Montferrat as king, Philip took an important and inevitably divisive political step.[7] This apart, he was content to set up his siege engines and continue the work of filling in the city's ditches and bombarding its walls. Although the garrison succeeded in burning some of his artillery, his efforts were so successful, wrote Rigord, that Acre would have fallen into his hands had he not courteously chosen to delay the final assault until after Richard's arrival.[8] By 5 June the pressure on the city was so great that Saladin moved camp from Shafar'am to Tell Ayadiah.[9]

On 5 June Richard set sail from Famagusta. He made his first landfall near the great castle of the Knights of St John at Margat. This castle was to be Isaac's prison. Then he sailed south, reaching Tyre next day. The garrison of Tyre, however, acting on instructions from King Philip and Conrad of Montferrat, refused him permission to enter the town.[10] So Richard spent the night encamped outside the walls and on 7 June continued on his voyage to Acre. According to Sicard of Cremona, he was in command of twenty-four galleys guarding the rear of his convoy when they fell in with a huge three-masted ship coming from Beirut laden with supplies and reinforcements for the garrison of Acre. Howden claimed that it was carrying as many as 1,500 élite warriors; doubtless an exaggeration, but one which reflects a perception of the ship's awesome size.[11] Large sailing ships riding high out of the water and of a tonnage many times that of attacking galleys could not easily be stopped if they had a favourable wind.[12] But in Baha al-Din's words, 'providence ordained that the wind should fall'. This enabled Richard's galleys to close with the great ship and, after a fierce and prolonged struggle, to sink it. Sicard, though in general one of Richard's critics, credits him with the determination and inspiration to drive the galley captains to renew their attacks despite the losses sustained as a result

---

[7] In a privilege for the Venetians issued on 7 May 1191 at Acre (otherwise all his charters were issued at Tyre) Conrad who had previously been styled 'lord of Tyre' now took the title *rex electus*, with the authority and consent of King Philip, Philip of Flanders, and the dukes of Burgundy and Austria. For discussion of the charter, H. E. Mayer, *Die Kanzlei der lateinischen Könige von Jerusalem* (2 vols, Hanover, 1996), ii, 443–4, 474–6, 479–80. Philip's choice had probably been made long before, in November 1190 when his cousin, the bishop of Beauvais, helped Conrad to marry Isabella.

[8] Rigord, 108. Howden believed he did no more than put his machines in place, *Gesta*, ii, 169.

[9] Baha al-Din, 246–7. By then he probably knew that Richard had completed his conquest of Cyprus.

[10] *Gesta*, ii, 168. Possibly Richard preferred to spend the night outside Tyre, but that is not how Howden presents it.

[11] Sicard, 22; *Gesta*, ii, 168–9. According to Baha al-Din, 249–50, there were 650 soldiers aboard; 700 according to Imad al-Din, 299, so it was very large indeed.

[12] Pryor, *Geography, Technology and War*, 120–1. On one occasion four large Christian ships claimed to have held off 150 galleys.

of the great ship's high freeboard and missile firepower. In Saladin's camp
it was believed that when the captain saw that defeat was inevitable, he
scuttled his ship rather than see valuable supplies and siege equipment fall
into enemy hands. How great a loss this was to the Muslims is clear from
Baha al-Din's claim that Saladin took the news 'with perfect resignation to
God's will'. For Imad al-Din, it was a critical turning point.[13] Even after this
triumph, according to Ambroise, Richard still worked. As he approached
Acre he put much thought into how it could be conquered. He 'looked
and studied, continually drawing and re-drawing his plans'.[14] On arrival on
8 June he was, of course, given a joyous welcome. First the conquest of
Cyprus and the certain prospect of a much more secure supply line; now
the unexpected psychological boost of a victory at sea. The celebration in
the crusader camp lasted well into the night as the army danced and sang
by the light of torches and bonfires. By this same light the depressed
Muslims could see 'what a vast amount of equipment he had brought with
him; his arrival put fear into their hearts'.[15]

Philip's recognition of Conrad as king meant that as much time had to
be spent on politics as on war. According to Howden, both Pisans and
Genoese offered Richard their service, but he would not accept that of the
Genoese since they had already pledged their allegiance to Philip and
Conrad.[16] Confident of Richard's support Geoffrey de Lusignan, on his
brother's behalf, accused Conrad of treason but – again according to
Howden – no one dared lay a hand on him for fear of a tumult in the city.
Conrad subsequently fled to Tyre, believing, wrote Baha al-Din, that if he
remained at Acre he would be arrested and Tyre given to Guy.[17] Even at
the height of the struggle against Saladin the two kings were contending
against each other. Philip had offered pay of three bezants (gold pieces) to
any knight who would join his service, only to be outbid by Richard, who
offered four.[18] The rivalry of the kings was reflected in the histories within

[13] According to Ambroise, 2141–299, nearly all on the ship drowned but Richard
saved about thirty-five, emirs and engineers; if the ship had got through, Acre
would never, he wrote, have been taken. Whatever the numbers involved, indeed
whatever the precise date of the sinking (Muslim sources give a slightly later date),
both sides agreed on the importance of this naval battle.
[14] 'Li rois esguarda e sorvit/ E toz jorz porvit e porvit', Ambroise, 2331–2, 2350–4.
[15] Baha al-Din, 249 (Gabrieli, 213–14).
[16] Gesta, ii, 170. Actually so had the Pisans, but now they switched sides (yet again).
[17] Ibid., ii, 170–71; Baha al-Din, 254; Imad al-Din, 304–5. According to Ibn al-
Athir, 51, Conrad feared Richard's perfidy. The Muslims date the news of his flight
to 25 June. The vagueness of Howden's dating of events at Acre between 10 June
and 3 July may indicate that he was not there at the time.
[18] Ambroise, 4575–99, 4686–90; according to Richard de Templo, Itin., Bk. 3, ch.
4, this was pay per month – an implausibly low rate for knights. For more realistic
rates (though in implausible circumstances) see Gesta, ii, 176. Presumably it is dif-
ferential pay rates which lie behind Howden's report that Richard took into service

their realms. Authors loyal to Richard minimized King Philip's efforts and Philip's biographers did the same for Richard's. It was imperative that Philip's biographers portray Richard as a reluctant, unreliable and deceitful crusader; only in this way could they hope to provide any sort of moral justification for their king's subsequent invasion of a fellow-crusader's lands. Thus in Rigord's version, Richard's only contribution to the siege was the sinking of the great ship (and even this is matched by the sinking of another 'similar' supply ship 'by us' off Tyre). After his arrival at Acre Richard is either deceitfully uncooperative or just one of the 'fideles Dei' who helped the king of France.[19] In the light of this historiographical rivalry it seems better to base any assessment of the two kings' perfomance on crusade on the evidence of contemporary Muslim opinion, in this respect non-partisan.

Richard arrived, Saladin's men gloomily noted, with twenty-five ships, 'each one as big as a citadel'.[20] But these twenty-five comprised just a part of Richard's fleet. Most of his transports, carrying many barons and their following, together with much of his siege equipment, were still at Tyre, delayed by the Arsur wind, and did not arrive until several weeks later.[21] For this reason he did not fall in with Philip's suggestion that they launch an immediate joint assault, and the subsequent French attack failed.[22] Presumably his troops would have helped to defend the outer trenches against the diversionary attack on their lines which was made by the Muslim field army as soon as it heard the signal – drum beats – from the walls of Acre. That day it was Geoffrey de Lusignan who won the greatest praise.[23] Gradually the bombardment was intensified as Richard brought

those men whom Philip dismissed, as a result of which Philip's unguarded siege-engines were burned, ibid., 170.

[19] Rigord, 108–10, 115.

[20] Baha al-Din, 248–9 (twenty-five ships, Gabrieli, 213), Imad al-Din, 297. Since Ambroise, 2120–8, 2343–8, also made a point of the size and quality of Richard's galleys, is it possible that in addition to his war galleys, he also had something akin to the 'great galleys' of later centuries? On the great galley, Pryor, *Geography, Technology and War*, 43–54.

[21] Ambroise, 4610–15, 4704–36. According to the dean of St Paul's, whose chaplain was among the crusaders, when the fleet left Cyprus it comprised 13 large ships called busses, 100 other transport ships and 50 galleys: Diceto, 93.

[22] Ambroise, 4600–90. Saladin's historians report major attacks on 14 and 18 June, the first of which petered out as the troops became exhausted in the midday heat. Rigord, in his determination to show how enthusiastic a crusader Philip was, dates the French attack to the day after Richard's arrival. He also says that Richard agreed to help, but then let the side down by changing his mind at the last minute, Rigord, 108–9. Naturally Rigord's account of Richard's lack of co-operation does not mention the explanation given by Ambroise.

[23] The convention was that when one king launched an assault on Acre, the other guarded their camp, *Gesta*, ii, 173. On Geoffrey de Lusignan – no finer knight since the days of Oliver and Roland, Ambroise, 4655–67.

up his siege machines to join those already erected by Philip, Hugh of
Burgundy and the Templars and Hospitallers.[24] Slowly but surely the walls
of Acre were being battered down. By 24 June the garrison was desperate.
According to Baha al-Din, 'They told us they were utterly exhausted, being
forced to be on the walls without rest to oppose the attacks of the enemy
which had been incessant since the arrival of the king of England.'
However, Richard fell gravely ill, and this, in Imad al-Din's opinion,
allowed the defenders of Acre a breathing space, the chance to rest and
make some repairs.[25] Philip also fell ill. The chroniclers called their illness
Arnaldia or *Léonardie*, a fever which caused their hair and nails to fall out.
It was probably a form of scurvy or trench mouth. At one point Richard's
life was thought to be in danger, but as soon as his condition began to
improve he insisted that he be carried to the front line in a litter so that he
could continue to direct siege operations and display his skill with a crossbow.[26]

   Richard's illness had also interrupted his diplomacy. On 18 June he had
sent an envoy to Saladin, suggesting that the two of them should meet.
Saladin's response was that he would do this only after a preliminary agreement had been reached. The envoy tried again, suggesting that they
should meet alone except for an interpreter. Again this was turned down,
but it was agreed that he and Saladin's brother al-Adil should meet.[27]
Saladin's entourage then heard nothing for a while, and they suspected
that the other Frankish princes had opposed the scheme. However the
envoy reappeared with a message from Richard. 'Do not believe the
reports which have been spread. Only my illness has caused the delay. I am
answerable only to myself for what I do. No one has any authority over me.'
An exchange of gifts was then proposed by Richard, and on 1 July his envoy
returned bringing a Muslim prisoner whom he gave to Saladin. As Baha al-
Din knew well, 'the object of these frequent visits was to ascertain the state
of our morale and we were induced to receive the enemy's messages by the
same motive that prompted them'. On 4 July three envoys were allowed to
visit the Muslim market. Naturally they were meant to be impressed by the
7,000 cookshops and 1,000 baths that serviced Saladin's army (there were,
of course, none of the wine shops and brothels that serviced the Christian
camp).[28]

---

[24] According to Ambroise, Richard's artillery hurled stones he had specially
brought from Sicily and he erected a belfry, Ambroise, 4799–800, 4781–6; cf.
Devizes, 43. But for doubts on this point see Rogers, *Latin Siege Warfare*, 225.
[25] Baha al-Din, 253, 255; Imad al-Din, 307. Occasionally a messenger was able to
swim through the Frankish lines; otherwise the garrison kept in touch with Saladin
by using carrier pigeons.
[26] In this he followed Philip's example, Ambroise, 4820–2, 4935–40, 4970–2.
[27] On the significance of this see above, 27.
[28] Baha al-Din, 252, 256–7, 263; Imad al-Din, 309–10. Imad al-Din described in

But it was not the morale in Saladin's field army (which was indeed being considerably reinforced in late June and early July) that mattered. Another major attack on Acre was launched after Philip's miners had brought down a section of the walls next to the Accursed Tower, a key point in the city's defences. The difficulties encountered in mounting assaults over rubble-filled ditches meant that this attack was beaten off, and the French sustained heavy losses.[29] Even so the garrison was exhausted. They were getting little or no sleep since they were forced by their relative lack of numbers to remain permanently at arms whereas the crusaders now had enough men to be able to alternate their assault troops, allowing some to rest while fresh men took their place, while keeping their trenches and ramparts permanently manned against Saladin's diversionary attacks. Next day one of he garrison commanders, al-Mashtub, came out under a flag of truce to discuss terms of surrender. He asked that the lives of the defenders should be spared, pointing out that quarter was granted to the Franks when they asked for it, but Philip's reply (at any rate as the interpreter expressed it) sent him back in fury to the city.[30] That night a number of emirs slipped out of Acre in a small boat. On 4 and 5 July Saladin planned both dawn and night attacks, but to no avail.[31] On the 5th Richard's miners set fire to their mine and in the following night a large part of the wall collapsed. This brought the garrison to further negotiations. On 7 July the French again suffered casualties in an attack near the Accursed Tower.[32] According to Ambroise, Richard offered first two bezants, then three, then four to anyone who could bring him back a stone from the tottering tower.[33] Still the garrison held out, sending a message to Saladin on 7 July that they would fight to the death.[34]

characteristically ornate language the activities of the prostitutes who had flocked to do business with the crusaders:

> Tinted and painted, desirable and appetising, bold and ardent, with nasal voices and fleshy thighs ... they offered their wares for enjoyment, brought their silver anklets up to touch their golden earrings ... made themselves targets for men's darts, offered themselves to the lance's blows, made javelins rise towards shields .... They interwove leg with leg, caught lizard after lizard in their holes, guided pens to inkwells, torrents to the valley bottom, swords to scabbards, firewood to stoves ... and they maintained that this was an act of piety without equal, especially to those who were far from home and wives. (trans. based on Gabrieli, 205–6)

[29] Ambroise, 4867–908. It looks as though Howden was (again?) at Acre. In the first of a number of precisely dated entries he dates this attack to 3 July, *Gesta*, ii, 173–4, though it seems to be the same assault as that which Saladin's historians dated 2 July.

[30] Baha al-Din, 258–62. If Richard was still unwell this might explain why Baha al-Din's account refers only to Philip's tactless language; cf. *Gesta*, ii, 172, 174.

[31] Imad al-Din, 312–14; Baha al-Din, 263–4; *Gesta*, ii, 174.

[32] *Gesta*, ii, 174–6.

[33] Ambroise, 4941–64.

[34] Baha al Din, 264–5 (Gabrieli, 220).

Their courage was tremendous and compelled admiration even in the
Christian camp. But courage alone was no longer enough. Negotiations
were resumed, both with Saladin and the defenders. Saladin offered to
restore the Holy Cross and to release one of his prisoners for every one of
the garrison, but the Franks demanded the liberation of all prisoners and
the restoration of the whole of the lost land.[35]

On 11 July Richard's forces and the Pisans attacked again, and came so
close to success that the defenders decided it was time to give up. 'The
breach in the walls was now very large and they feared that every one of
them would be put to the sword if the city were carried by storm.'[36] On 12
July besiegers and besieged agreed terms. The garrison surrendered the
city and all it contained: stores, artillery and ships. It is no great exaggeration to claim that the capture of the Egyptian galley fleet was 'as important
as the capture of Acre itself' since it marked the end of 'Saladin's
attempted challenge to Christian dominance at sea' – the last time in the
Middle Ages that an Egyptian sultan contested what was increasingly an
'Italian lake'.[37] Since the crews did not burn their ships, it must be assumed
that in negotiations the crusaders insisted that they would accept the city's
surrender only if the fleet was handed over intact. The lives of the garrison,
and those of their wives and children, were to be spared in return for a
ransom of 200,000 dinars, for the release of 1,500 prisoners (plus one or
two hundred named individuals) and for the restoration of the Holy Cross.
In addition Conrad was to receive a commission of 10,000 dinars for his
good offices as a mediator.[38] When he heard of the conditions Saladin was
horrified, but it was too late – Frankish banners were already waving over
the city. Acre had fallen at last. Two days later Saladin withdrew to
Shafar'am and began negotiations to clarify the terms.[39]

On 13 July Acre and its contents, including the prisoners, were divided
between the kings of France and England.[40] After some days spent prepar-

[35] Imad ad-Din, 317–18; Baha al-Din, 266.

[36] Baha al-Din, 266 (Gabrieli, 222).

[37] Pryor, *Geography, Technology and War*, 125–30. Sicard of Cremona put the
number of captured galleys at seventy: Sicard, 22.

[38] Imad al-Din, 318. Howden, *Gesta*, ii, 178, says 200 named individuals, and he
does not mention the payment for Conrad (which may have been a secret agreement between Conrad and the garrison – for Howden's suspicions of their contacts
see ibid., 173–4) but otherwise his figures agree with Imad al-Din's. Baha al-Din,
266–7, puts Conrad's commission at 4,000 dinars and says the Franks were to have
600 prisoners returned to them.

[39] Baha al-Din, 268–9.

[40] Initially the prisoners taken at Acre had, according to Howden, been offered
freedom if they would accept baptism into the Christian faith. Many of them
allegedly took up this offer – but as soon as they were released, they crossed over to
Saladin's lines. After this Philip and Richard said that there should be no more bap-
tisms, *Gesta*, ii, 179.

ing the city and re-consecrating its churches, Richard, Berengaria and Joan moved into the royal palace on 21 July.[41] Two days earlier the counts and barons who belonged to the camp of neither king had held a protest meeting outside the walls. It had become clear to them that no formal provision was going to be made to reward them despite the fact that some of them had been at the siege for as long as two years. The kings promised satisfaction, but did nothing as the days passed by. Eventually many disgruntled crusaders sold their arms and went home.[42] The kings had other – as they saw it, far more pressing – things on their minds. On 20 July, probably in order to bring pressure to bear on Saladin, Richard tried to persuade Philip that they should issue a joint statement of intent to remain there for three years, or until the city and land of Jerusalem were recovered. Perhaps intentionally this had the effect of forcing Philip's hand. On 22 July he acknowledged that he was planning to go home. He had a very good reason for wanting to be back in France as soon as possible. Count Philip of Flanders had died at Acre on 1 June 1191, and the rich lands of Artois, his share of the count's inheritance, was understandably a much more inviting prospect than an army camp in the company of a richer and more powerful partner. If he wanted to be sure of Artois, then to Artois he must go.[43] When pressed by his nobles to stay, he let Richard know that he would think of doing so only if he were given half of Cyprus. Once again Richard refused and the quarrel which ensued settled the matter. Philip would go.[44]

His impending departure left Conrad in the lurch. On 26 July he prostrated himself at Richard's feet and begged pardon for the offences he had committed against Guy of Lusignan. Next day the two claimants put their cases before the two kings, and on 28 July, in Richard's palace, the kings delivered their verdict. Guy would remain king for his lifetime but, whether or not he married again and had children, the throne would then pass to Conrad and Isabella and their heirs. In the meantime the kingdom's revenues would be shared between them. Conrad was to hold a large

[41] Ibid., 179–82. Philip took possession of the Temple, *Chron.*, iii, 123.

[42] *Gesta*, ii, 181. Sicard of Cremona was particularly severe on the two kings' unblushingly unjust treatment of all those 'from the Roman Empire or elsewhere' who had struggled and suffered at Acre for so much longer than either Philip or Richard, Sicard, 22–3. Among those who left was Duke Leopold of Austria.

[43] Neither Rigord nor William the Breton, desperate to justify in moral terms their king's early return from the crusade, mention the Flanders inheritance. However, it was not just Richard's admirers who saw this as one of Philip's motives. Andreas of Marchiennes was explicit that it was Philip's cupidity which made him abandon the crusade, setting an example followed, he lamented, by many timid soldiers, *Historia regum Francorum*, MGH SS, xxvi, 212, cf. *Sig. Cont.*, 427–8. It is also clearly implied by the Austrian chronicler who was one of Richard's fiercest critics, Ansbert, 100.

[44] *Gesta*, ii, 181–3.

northern county consisting of Tyre and – if he could recover them – Sidon and Beirut. Geoffrey of Lusignan was granted the lordship of Jaffa and Ascalon in the south. Now that his nephew Hugh IX 'le Brun' was a grown man there was less scope for Geoffrey at home in Poitou, especially while Richard maintained his policy of excluding the Lusignans from La Marche. Jaffa and Ascalon, however, if they could be reconquered would be more than sufficient to compensate Geoffrey.[45] On 29 July

> Philip, against the advice and counsel of his princes, asked Richard for leave to go home. This was granted. He then swore on the Gospels and in the view of all the people that he would neither do any harm to the king of England's lands and subjects nor permit any to be done by anyone; on the contrary he would see to their peaceful safekeeping and would defend them against enemy attack to the best of his ability just as he would wish to see Paris defended should it be attacked.[46]

He then appointed Duke Hugh of Burgundy commander of the French forces and gave his half of Acre to Conrad. On 30 July the Muslim prisoners were divided between Richard and Philip and on the 31st Philip left Acre for Tyre, taking his prisoners with him.[47] He was accompanied as far as Tyre by Conrad of Montferrat, who had no wish to remain in an army dominated by the lord of the Lusignans. On 3 August the king of France embarked at Tyre and sailed for home.

In a few hectic days of politics at the end of July 1191 all the contentious issues everywhere had been settled. In reality, of course, none of them had been. Philip was going home a humiliated, and therefore a dangerous man. He had been humiliated at Messina when Richard repudiated his sister, and now he had been humiliated again. Perhaps if all 'his' nobles had chosen to go back with him, it might not have been too bad. But only Peter of Nevers did; most, including the most famous knight among them, William des Barres, as well as the most powerful prince, the duke of Burgundy, chose to stay with the crusade. Whatever Philip's men may or may not have said – and, according to Howden, they begged Philip to stay for the sake of the dignity of the crown of France – there is no doubt that in choosing to stay they criticized him for going.[48] There is no doubt too

[45] Ibid., 183–4. On 1 August Richard gave the order to march to Ascalon.
[46] Ibid., 184.
[47] Ibid., 185. Why did Philip not leave them with the duke of Burgundy in Acre? What purpose, other than complicating Richard's negotiations with Saladin, can have been served by taking them to Tyre? Perhaps in the hope of compensating Conrad for raising his hopes in May and dashing them in July.
[48] Ibid., 183. 'Truly I say that most severely/ they blamed him, and they very nearly/ denied their king and lord – so great/ had grown their discontent and hate', Ambroise, 5285–8. Howden and Ambroise are, of course, far from unbiased.

that Philip knew this. His envoy to Pope Innocent III referred to the shame he had incurred in returning to his own realm. He blamed it on Richard, saying that Richard had compelled him to go by seducing from his allegiance his knights and even his kinsmen.[49] This was another way of saying that he could not bear the way the combination of Richard's money and prowess were putting him in the shade, particularly since, as king of France, he liked to think of himself as Richard's superior.[50] Perhaps only Saint Louis could have put up with so galling a situation. Richard, of course, was well aware that once Philip was in Paris he might try to occupy Gisors and the Norman Vexin as well as Artois. To an unscrupulous and angry politician it was a crusade-sent opportunity, a temptation not to be resisted. Why should he keep his oath when Richard had not married Alice?[51] In these circumstances it would have been naïve of Richard to put any faith in Philip's promise, and he did not. A group of Richard's men, among them Roger of Howden, quickly caught up with Philip's galleys and coasted back to Europe in their company.[52] There can be little doubt that they were going back to give warning of the expected attack and ensure that preparations were made to counter it.

Philip's early biographers, Rigord and William the Breton, did their best to defend their lord and explain his departure. According to Rigord, Philip suspected Richard of treachery because he was exchanging gifts and envoys with Saladin, and this fact, together with his illness, made him decide, reluctantly, to leave; only when he was back in the west did his health

But Andreas of Marchiennes wrote of 'frightened rabbits' (see above, n. 43) and Sicard of Cremona, for all his hostility to Richard, wrote eloquently of the shame that was attached to Philip's return home: 'repatriavit cum obprobrio immenso, ubique sibi in faciem acclamato: Vah, qui fugis et terram Domini derelinquis', Sicard, 23.

[49] *Selected Letters*, 6. Cf. Jacques de Vitry, *History of Jerusalem*, 113–14; Edbury, 108–9. Neither Howden nor Ambroise mentions Philip losing the allegiance of one of his own kinsmen at Acre, but Innocent's letter tends to lend some credibility to Richard of Devizes's story of Henry of Champagne going over to Richard after Philip had refused to afford him a loan unless he pledged the county of Champagne as security, Devizes, 43–4.

[50] As pointed out by, for example, Coggeshall, 33–4. German chroniclers take a more sympathetic view of the uncomfortable situation in which Philip found himself. See below, 226.

[51] On the question of whether Richard had ever explicitly sworn to marry Alice, see Kessler, 62–6.

[52] It was once believed that in preparation for the impending attack he sent back his most professional soldier, Mercadier. This is the implication of a letter dated 1 August 1191, Landon, no. 359. However, the letter was written not by Richard in Acre but by a forger in Paris in the 1840s. See R. H. Bautier, 'La Collection de chartes de croisade dite "Collection Courtois"', in *Comptes rendus des séances de l'Académie des Inscriptions et Belles-Lettres* (Paris, 1956); also Gillingham, *Richard the Lionheart*, 301.

improve. However, since he had the best interests of the crusade at heart, he took only three galleys with him, committing the rest of his army and treasure – enough, according to William the Breton, to pay 500 knights for three years – to Duke Hugh of Burgundy.[53] In fact at best he had left behind his share of the ransom of the prisoners of Acre and this had yet to be received. In order to tide Hugh of Burgundy over until the ransom had been collected, Richard had to lend him 5,000 marks. Indeed by taking his prisoners to Tyre and there handing them over to Conrad, Philip had made the task of collecting the ransom more difficult. Even in Capetian France, despite Philip's immense contribution to the extension of royal authority, his crusading record remained a permanent slur upon his reputation. In his life of Philip's grandson, St Louis, Jean de Joinville harked back to the contrast between the rival kings: between Philip who 'returned to France, for which he was greatly blamed' and Richard who 'remained and performed great feats of arms'.[54]

Richard must have felt that Philip's going was not all loss. If Howden is right, Richard could have given him half of Cyprus had he actually wanted Philip to stay. But, in the vivid phrase of the Winchester chronicler, Richard of Devizes, Philip had been to Richard like a hammer tied to the tail of a cat. Though his responsibilities and the demands made upon his treasure chest were increased, with both Philip and Conrad gone, at least there could be no doubt now who was in charge at Acre.[55] It was, for example, now up to Richard to see that Saladin implemented the terms of the treaty made by his officers at Acre. This was not going to be easy, partly because Saladin also had his problems. After making so many financial and military demands upon his emirs in the years since 1187 it was probably impossible for him to bring together so much money and so many prisoners by the stipulated date, a month after the fall of Acre. Some of the details of both the treaty and the subsequent negotiations are obscure. Not surprisingly there are differences between the Christian and Muslim accounts of what happened. Except in one respect, however, there seems no reason not to accept Baha al'Din's version. According to this, the two sides kept exchanging messages until on 2 August the Christians accepted Saladin's terms, i.e. that at the end of the thirty-day period after the capitulation of Acre they would be satisfied with a first instalment: the Holy Cross, all the prisoners and half the money. The king of England's envoys were shown the Cross to satisfy themselves that it was really there; they pros-

[53] Rigord, 116–17; William the Breton repeated the rumour that Philip had been poisoned, WB, 193.

[54] Joinville, *Chronicles of the Crusades*, trans. M. R. B. Shaw, 304–5.

[55] Devizes, 78. It does not, of course, follow that everyone was happy about this. For those who wished to stay with the crusade but who earlier had thrown in their lot with Philip and/or Conrad, Richard's assumption of power may well have seemed arrogance.

trated themselves on the ground before it till their faces were covered in dust.

On the due date, 11 August, Saladin said that the Christians could have the first instalment on one of two conditions. Either they must release all those captured at Acre, and accept hostages for the remainder of what was due or, if they would not release them, then they must give Saladin hostages to be kept until the rest was paid and the garrison freed. They refused, demanding that Saladin pay what he had promised and be content with their solemn promise that their prisoners would be released as soon as the remainder of the money had been handed over. This Saladin rejected. He feared that the Christians might go back on their word once they had received a first instalment which contained so high a proportion of what they wanted. Neither side trusted the other and so both were looking for guarantees which the other would not give. Almost certainly the difficulties which surfaced on the day the first instalment was due were aggravated by the fact that Richard was then in no position to hand over all the Acre garrison even if he had wanted to do so. The prisoners whom Philip had taken to Tyre were not yet back in Acre.[56] On 5 August a delegation headed by Hubert Walter and Robert, count of Dreux had been sent to Tyre to fetch them back. To their dismay they found that Philip had already left, and Conrad was unwilling to comply.[57] It took the sending of a second delegation headed by the duke of Burgundy and carrying with them Richard's threat that he would go to Tyre himself and take Conrad's lordship from him, before the marquis came to heel. Not until 12 August was Burgundy back at Acre with Philip's share of the prisoners.

Negotiations continued until 20 August.[58] In Richard's camp, men believed that, as Baha al-Din half acknowledged, Saladin was spinning out the negotiations as a delaying tactic. The longer he could pin Richard down in Acre, the harder the crusaders' task would be. Since the beginning of the month their ships had been loaded with artillery, ammunition and victuals in readiness for the march south.[59] As time passed and still they could not leave, suspicions mounted and tempers became frayed. Skirmishing between the armies continued and, on 19 August, a rumour – possibly deliberately manufactured – spread through the Frankish camp: Saladin, it was said, had killed his prisoners.[60] According to Baha al-Din,

---

[56] This holds good whether we take Baha al-Din's date (11 August) for payment of the first instalment or Howden's (9 August), *Gesta*, ii, 187.

[57] Ibid., 186. Conrad said he would hand over Philip's half of the prisoners in return for half of the Holy Cross, wrote Ambroise, 5421–35.

[58] According to Howden, the late arrival of the prisoners from Tyre had led to Richard agreeing to postpone the due date until 20 August, *Gesta*, ii, 186–7.

[59] Ibid., 185.

[60] Ibid., 189.

Richard had sworn that his prisoners would be enslaved if the sultan failed to fulfil the agreed conditions.[61]

He now broke the solemn promise he had made, openly revealed the intentions he had hitherto disguised and carried out what he had anyway planned to do as soon as he had received the money and the prisoners. This is what his co-religionists told us later. On the afternoon of 27 rajab/20 August he and all the Frankish army marched to occupy the middle of the plain. Then they brought up the Muslim prisoners whose martyrdom God had ordained, more than three thousand men in chains. They fell upon them as one man and slaughtered them in cold blood, with sword and lance. Our scouts had informed Saladin of the enemy's manoeuvres and he sent reinforcements to the advance guard, but by then the slaughter had already occurred. As soon as the Muslims realized what had happened they attacked the enemy and battle raged, with casualties on both sides, until night fell. The next morning the Muslims wanted to see who had fallen, and found their martyred companions lying where they fell, and some they recognized. Great grief seized them, and from then on the only prisoners they spared were people of rank and men strong enough to work. Many reasons were given to explain the massacre. One was that they had killed them in reprisal for their own prisoners whom Muslims had previously killed. Another was that the king of England had decided to march to Ascalon, and did not want to leave so many prisoners behind in Acre. God alone knows what his reason really was.[62]

Richard himself summarized the events of 20 August in a letter of 1 October to the abbot of Clairvaux. 'The time limit expired and, as the treaty to which Saladin had agreed was entirely made void, we quite prop-

[61] Although this threat seemed natural to a Muslim, living in a society which kept slaves, it is much less likely to have been made by late twelfth-century western Europeans who, through no particular virtue of their own, happened to live in a society which did not. There was room for misunderstanding here. If Richard and his fellow-Christians insisted that in case of default the prisoners would be at their mercy 'in life and limb' (as they might well have done), this could have been taken to mean that the prisoners would be enslaved – see, for example, Baha al-Din's account of King Philip's negotiation with al-Mashtub, 262. Compare Ambroise's phrase to describe the prisoners taken at Darum in May 1192 after they had surrendered unconditionally, *sanz contredit chaitifs esclaves*, Ambroise, 9351. Sicard of Cremona, however, did argue that the prisoners should have been enslaved, Sicard, 23.

[62] Baha al-Din, 272–4 (Gabrieli, 223–4). Cf. Imad al-Din, 328–30. Two days after the battle of Hattin, Saladin had killed all the Templars and Hospitallers who were in his hands without giving them any chance of being ransomed. According to Imad al-Din, he watched the slaughter with a joyful face, and looked upon it as an act of purification, cited Gabrieli, 138–9.

erly had the Saracens that we had in custody – about 2,600 of them – put to death. A few of the more noble ones were spared, and we hope to recover the Cross and certain Christian captives in exchange for them.'[63] Although St Bernard of Clairvaux had written 'The Christian glories in the death of a pagan, because thereby Christ himself is glorified', in this letter written to St Bernard's successor the tone is matter-of-fact rather than jubilant.

Of all Richard's deeds this is the one most bitterly condemned by modern historians. It has been called both barbarous and stupid and has been cited to show that there were no depths to which he could not sink in a fit of anger or to relieve his supposed frustrations. [64] No doubt he was angry. But this does not necessarily mean he 'was beside himself with rage'. Anger was part of the standard repertory of kingship; hence it was often – though not always – a controlled emotion.[65] Unquestionably the other Christian leaders were involved in the decision and its execution, above all the duke of Burgundy on behalf of the king of France.[66] Even William the Breton said that Richard's anger was just, and carefully associated Philip with the decision.[67] Indeed the early versions of the Old French Continuations of William of Tyre place the massacre at a time when Philip was still at Acre and associate him with it; in later versions Richard gets the greater credit when he 'took pity on the people whom he saw weeping and lamenting because Saladin had deceived them'.[68] From the moment the garrison of Acre agreed terms of surrender their lives had been treated as a bargaining counter. On 20 August Richard deprived himself of this counter, and, as a result, the money which had been collected for the ransom Saladin now distributed among his troops. But Richard had to move on. A bargaining counter which tied him to Acre was hardly an asset.[69] Could the crusaders afford to march away leaving only a garrison to

---

[63] *Chron.*, iii, 131. Howden gives a list of 'the more noble ones' who were spared, *Gesta*, ii, 189–90. As a chancery clerk he was doubtless glad to see 'Kahedin qui erat scriptor in Accon' among them.

[64] Grousset, *Histoire des croisades*, iii, 61–2.

[65] As in the case of the anger which Richard expressed against Conrad on 7 August, *Gesta*, ii, 186–7. 'When public displays of anger are located in eleventh- and twelfth-century political narratives, they do not provide evidence of emotional instability; instead they reveal the position occupied by displays of anger in a relatively stable, enduring discourse of disputing, feuding and political competition', S. D. White, 'The Politics of Anger', in *Anger's Past*, ed. B. H. Rosenwein (Ithaca, New York, 1998), 127–52, 142.

[66] *Gesta*, ii, 189; Ambroise, 5513–42. Later an unnamed Frankish prisoner told Saladin that it was the king alone who was responsible for this abominable act, Baha al-Din, 279–80. But he was a man of high rank pleading for his life.

[67] *Philippidos*, iv, 218–24. Richard's anger is also referred to by Rigord, 117–18, by Ansbert, 99, and by Jacques de Vitry, *History of Jerusalem*, 113.

[68] Edbury, 107–8. For the earlier version see *Chronique d'Ernoul*, ed. L. de Mas-Latrie (Paris, 1871), 276–7.

[69] Saladin retained his bargaining counters by sending his prisoners to Damascus.

guard nearly 3,000 Muslims? Merely to feed so many men would be difficult enough since, on Saladin's orders, the countryside around Acre had
been thoroughly devastated. Presumably Richard could simply have freed
them all in return for the payment of the first instalment, but in that case
he would have lost the confidence of his army for allowing himself to be
outmanoeuvred by Saladin.[70] By the 20th the prisoners had become an
embarrassment rather than an asset and it seems that Richard and his
fellow-soldiers had no compunction in ridding themselves of them in a
fashion that was brutally efficient.

How did contemporary or near-contemporary Christian authors deal
with the massacre? Almost without exception they regarded it as the
natural consequence of Saladin's failure to abide by the terms agreed and
they either approved or referred to it in neutral tones.[71] Ambroise speaks
of 'Christianity avenged' and has in mind vengeance for the many thousands who had died at the siege of Acre.[72] But most think more in terms of
military advantage than vengeance. One Frenchman, Jacques de Vitry,
believed that Philip treated his prisoners less harshly than Richard did, and
then added, 'yet the king of England did more to injure and weaken the
enemy by slaying many thousands of them who had they lived might have
done much harm to the Christians'.[73] This was the judgement of a man
who was to be bishop of Acre from 1216 to 1228. The Cistercian monk
Ralph of Coggeshall thought that the news that Saladin had failed the
people of Acre led to the coastal towns of Haifa, Caesarea, Arsuf, Jaffa,
Gaza and Ascalon falling into Richard's hands; their citizens abandoned
them rather than trust Saladin to help.[74] William of Newburgh makes the
same point, emphasizing still more strongly the anger of the citizens at
being let down by Saladin. These Christian monks, in the timeless fashion
of soldiers and their commanders through the ages, thought of the military
advantages won by slaughter.[75]

Richard might have considered sending his to Cyprus, though transport difficulties
and the Cypriot rebellion (see above, 152) may have made this an unrealistic option.
   [70] Presumably in the atmosphere of distrust Saladin would not have allowed
Richard to take the first instalment in return for freeing all the prisoners except
those 'more noble ones' whom Richard did not kill – who inevitably were precisely
the ones Saladin most wanted released.
   [71] William of Newburgh approved, Bk 4, ch. 23; neutral, Diceto, ii, 94–5. Cf. the
Spanish *Gran Conquista de Ultramar*, ch. ccxxiii, cited in Hook, 'The Figure of
Richard I', 125.
   [72] Ambroise, 5536–615. After the truce of summer 1192 he believed that there
were Muslims keen to take revenge on pilgrims visiting the 'Holy Places', but that
Saladin's council ensured that nothing of the sort was allowed to happen, ibid.,
11,971–12,012.
   [73] De Vitry, *History of Jerusalem*, 112–13.
   [74] Coggeshall, 33–4.
   [75] The one exception I have noticed is Sicard of Cremona. In his view, when
Saladin failed to pay the promised money the prisoners should have been enslaved,

How did Muslims regard the slaughter? Unquestionably it angered them, and was remembered. After they recaptured Acre in 1291 a later Egyptian chronicler, Abu l-Mahasin, wrote:

> It is marvellous to observe that Almighty God permitted the Muslims to conquer Acre on the same day and at the same hour as that on which the Franks had taken it. After the famous siege of 1191 they promised to spare the lives of the Muslims and then treacherously killed them. When God permitted the Muslims to reconquer the city, the Sultan gave his word to the Franks and then had them slaughtered as the Franks had done to the Muslims. Thus Almighty God was revenged on their descendants.[76]

A comment made long after the event, inspired by an anniversary and by the coincidence (according to the Muslim calendar) of dates is one thing; contemporary reaction is another. Baha al-Din reports that Saladin was 'furious at the massacre'. The few Christians who had the misfortune to be captured by Saladin between 28 August and 10 September were put to death and on at least one occasion he allowed his troops to cut the bodies to pieces 'to satisfy their thirst for revenge'.[77] Like his Christian contemporaries Baha al-Din believed that the massacre had significant military repercussions, writing that on the day Acre fell, 'I happened to be on duty in the Sultan's tent ... and I begged him to think of the future fate of the cities of the coast, and of Jerusalem itself, and to turn his attention to delivering the Muslim captives in Acre'. He subsequently noted that Saladin knew it would be impossible to hold Ascalon, so he evacuated and demolished it, 'convinced that his soldiers would be afraid to shut themselves in the city with the remembrance of Acre and the fate of its garrison fresh in their minds'.[78] On 4 September negotiations between the two sides were resumed, and on the 5th Richard and al-Adil met face to face.[79] From then on the courteous exchanges of June and July were resumed and enhanced. Contacts became closer and significantly more friendly. So they continued throughout Richard's stay in the East.

---

not killed, and he condemned Richard's orders as against law and justice (*contra fas et licitum*). He also noted that in his treatment of his Christian captives, Saladin did not return evil for evil, Sicard, 23.

[76] Gabrieli, 349.

[77] Baha al-Din, 278–81, 295. Cf. Ibn al-Athir, 49. Of course Saladin had sometimes had prisoners executed before the massacre at Acre, e.g. Baha al-Din, 29.

[78] Baha al-Din, 268, 296; cf. Imad al-Din, 346. See below, 179 n. 19.

[79] Baha al-Din, 287–8; Imad al-Din, 339–40. Once negotiations were resumed the question of the treatment of prisoners was put on the agenda (e.g. Baha al-Din, 323; Imad al-Din, 351) and from then on, whatever the formal arrangements, they were generally in safer hands. But only generally. Saladin's secretary reports that some of the prisoners taken on a raid near Jaffa on 1 March 1192 were too feeble to walk and so they were beheaded, which encouraged the others to walk faster, Imad al-Din, 375.

Chapter 11

TOWARDS JERUSALEM

On 22 August Richard pitched his tents outside the trenches of Acre, leaving his wife and his sister behind in the city. For three days he waited for the whole army to assemble. Elderly laundresses 'who washed clothes and heads and were as clever as monkeys when it came to getting rid of lice' were the only camp-followers whom Richard would allow to accompany the army on its march. This added to the reluctance of some of the soldiers to leave a city that had become, in Ambroise's eyes, a shameful den of sin and lust.[1] On 25 August the march to Jaffa began.[2] Richard's strategy was clear: first conquer the coast as far as Ascalon.[3] The great harbour fortress of Ascalon was the key to the vital road which linked Egypt and Syria and, as such, a key to Jerusalem. If both Egypt and Syria were in hostile hands and supplies could flow freely between them, there could be no hope of retaining Jerusalem. But if Ascalon were held by an aggressive soldier who posed a constant threat to the supply line, then, though difficult, it might just be possible to hold Jerusalem. Presumably this was why, as early as 28 July, Geoffrey de Lusignan had been granted the county of Jaffa and Ascalon – not just because he was Guy of Lusignan's brother but because he was one of the fighting heroes of the siege of Acre.[4] Whether Richard would be allowed to pursue his strategic goal was an entirely different matter. There were many in the army who wanted to go as directly as possible to Jerusalem, pray at the holy places of the city and then return home, their pilgrimage completed. If asked about the future of Jerusalem, they would doubtless have said that God would provide – as he had, they felt, provided for the future of the city after the First Crusade.[5] For the moment, however, that debate could be postponed. Whichever way it

---

[1] *Gesta*, ii, 190; Ambroise, 5669–86, 5693–8.

[2] This was the last entry which Roger of Howden made in his crusade journal before going north to join up with Philip's party on the way home, Corner, 'The *Gesta Regis*', 140; cf. D.M. Stenton, 'Roger of Howden and "Benedict"', *EHR*, lxviii (1953), 579.

[3] Ambroise, 5548–9. This had already been announced at the beginning of August, *Gesta*, ii, 185–6. See Prestwich, 9–10.

[4] Ambroise, 4657–66, where he is compared with Roland and Oliver.

[5] For the argument that this was the right approach see Markowski, 'Richard Lionheart: Bad King, Bad Crusader?' 351–65.

went, first they had to take Jaffa, on the road to Ascalon and the port near-est Jerusalem.

At Acre the Franks had faced military problems essentially the same as those they would have faced in any siege of a similar town in Europe. They had been safely entrenched behind their own line of fortifications and the renowned Turkish cavalry had never had a real opportunity to demon-strate its skill.[6] But from now on the men from the West would be facing something quite different. The Turks were essentially mounted archers, though they each carried a small round shield and a lance, sword or club as well as their bow. All their weapons, however, were lighter than those used by the Frankish knights and in hand-to-hand fighting between equal numbers, the Franks held the advantage. The Turks therefore used the speed and agility of their horses to stay at a distance while sending in a rain of arrows upon their enemies. They used the bow while riding at speed with such dexterity that even in retreat they could turn in the saddle and shoot at their pursuers. They used their mobility to encircle the enemy and assail him from all sides at once. Only when their archery had reduced the enemy to a state of near helplessnesss did the Turks shoulder their bows and ride in for the kill.

The chief tactical weapon of the Franks was the charge of their heavily armoured knights. Holding reins and shield in his left hand, the knight held a lance rigid beneath his right arm, using the horse's forward momentum to give power to the blow delivered by the lance. The weight of the charge was such that no other cavalry could stand up to it. It had been said that a Frank on horseback could make a hole through the walls of Babylon. After the initial impact they were likely to fight with sword and mace rather than lance, driving home the advantage won by the charge. Generally speaking, if they succeeded in delivering a charge against the main body of their more lightly armed enemy, they won the battle. It was as simple as that – or as difficult. If the timing of the charge was fractionally wrong, the elusive Turkish cavalry was able to scatter, leaving the Franks beating against thin air. And once the charge had been delivered the Franks, having lost their tight formation, became vulnerable to counterattack. The Turkish horse-archers swarmed all round their enemy like gnats round a man's head. To try to drive them away with a charge was all too often like using one's hand to beat off the gnats. The only observable result was a temporary agitation in the swarm:

[6] The classic analysis of the two styles of cavalry warfare is that of R. C. Smail, *Crusading Warfare 1097–1196* (Cambridge, 1956), 75–83, 112–15; see also J. France, *Victory in the East: A Military History of the First Crusade* (Cambridge, 1994), 147–9, on Turkish tactics and armour.

When to pursue them one essays
Their steeds unrivalled like a swallow
Seem to take flight, and none can follow.
The Turks are so skilled to elude
Their foemen when they are pursued
That they are like a venomous
And irksome gadfly unto us.
Pursue him, he will take to flight
Return, and he renews his spite.[7]

The Turks would turn repeatedly and harass the ponderous knights to their doom. Thus the charge had to be held back until exactly the right moment – and it was not easy to be patient when under non-stop fire. Except at close range the light Turkish bow did not have the power to fire an arrow capable of piercing a coat of mail and wounding the body of the wearer, but it could penetrate far enough to stick in the mail, so that knights under Turkish attack were often said to resemble hedgehogs or porcupines. More serious than his undignified appearance was the fact that the knight was liable to have his less well-armoured horse killed under him. It was in this situation that the foot-soldier came into his own. The knights and their horses had to be protected until the moment to charge came. The job of protecting them was given to the infantry, both spearmen and archers. They were drawn up in a defensive screen, surrounding the knights like a wall and forcing the Turks to stay out of effective archery range. If the Franks were to survive in this kind of warfare then the qualities they needed were steadiness and discipline.

The march to Jaffa was to be a classic demonstration of Frankish military tactics at their best.[8] They marched close to the seashore, their right flank protected by the sea and by the fleet. The capture of the Egyptian fleet at Acre meant there was nothing to fear from that quarter. The knights were organized in three divisions with their left flank protected by infantry. Since this meant that the foot-soldiers had to bear the brunt of the ceaseless Turkish attack, Richard divided them into alternating halves: one half marched on the left, while the other took things easy, marching beside the baggage train between the knights and the sea. Saladin, too, marched south, on a parallel course, keeping the main body of his troops at some distance from the Franks and sending in bands of skirmishers to harass them continually. Richard's men were under orders to ignore all provocations and to keep marching in close formation. No one was to break ranks. Saladin naturally concentrated on the rearguard, where the infantry was

[7] Ambroise, 5653–62.
[8] Analysed in J. F. Verbruggen, *The Art of Warfare in Western Europe during the Middle Ages* (Woodbridge, 1997), 232–9; and by Lyons and Jackson, 334–8, with a helpful note on chronological discrepancies.

sometimes compelled to face about and fight off the Turkish attacks while marching backwards. On the very first day of the march the line became too extended, the rearguard under the duke of Burgundy lagged behind and the Turks swooped in, breaking through the line and attacking the wagon train. Richard himself rushed back from the van and saved the situation. A happy result of that first day was the healing of an old enmity. The French knight William des Barres fought with such gallantry that Richard decided to forget the grudge he had borne for so long.[9] But it was a useful lesson. From then on Richard's orders were rigidly obeyed and rearguard duties were normally performed either by the Templars or the Hospitallers – the soldiers with most experience of this hard school of warfare. Baha al-Din was particularly struck by the discipline of the infantry. 'I saw some of the Frankish foot-soldiers with from one to ten arrows sticking in them, and still advancing at their usual pace without leaving the ranks.... One cannot help admiring the wonderful patience displayed by these people, who bore the most wearing fatigue without having any share in the management of affairs or deriving any personal advantage.'[10]

Day after day the army toiled on, past Haifa, over the ridge of Mount Carmel, and on past Caesarea. Everywhere they found that Saladin's men had been there before them, razing fortresses to the ground and burning crops. But the presence of the fleet enabled Richard to keep his men supplied and rest the sick and exhausted aboard ship.[11] The heat was intense, and the Franks, heavily armoured in felt vests and coats of mail, suffered badly. Sunstroke claimed many victims. And every day the arrows of the Turks claimed many more. Richard himself was wounded by a spear-thrust in the side, not very seriously. Yet still the army, in close formation, moved doggedly on. It was not to be harassed into defeat. By early September Saladin realized that his only hope of stopping it lay in committing a much larger proportion of his troops than he had risked up till now. When Richard sought an interview with al-Adil, Saladin instructed his brother to spin out negotiations to give time for the reinforcements he had summoned to join him. However, Saladin's hopes were disappointed since Richard's peace terms were nothing less than the return of the whole Latin kingdom; the meeting of 5 September came to an abrupt end.[12]

By now Saladin had picked his battleground: the plain to the north of Arsuf. On 6 September the Franks were relieved to be unmolested as they marched through the forest of Arsuf; there had been a rumour that the forest would be set ablaze while they were in the midst of it. But as they

[9] Ambroise, 5756–808; Baha al-Din, 275; Ibn al-Athir, 49.
[10] Baha al-Din, 282–3.
[11] At one point the army halted for a day to allow the supply ships to land fresh provisions, Ambroise, 5936–42.
[12] Baha al-Din, 287–8.

emerged from the cover of the woods they saw why they had been left in peace. Saladin had spent the day drawing up a vast army – as it seemed to the crusaders – in battle array. The Franks, of course, had no choice but to advance in open ground towards the orchards outside Arsuf. On 7 September, Richard took even more care than usual in organizing his line of march. In the van he placed the Templars; next came the Bretons and the men of Anjou; then King Guy with the Poitevins; in the fourth division marched the Normans and English guarding the dragon standard; after them came the French contingents, and bringing up the rear, in the position of greatest danger, the Hospitallers. They were drawn up into such a solid and tight formation that it was impossible to throw an apple into the ranks without its hitting a man or a horse. Richard and the duke of Burgundy, with a retinue of picked knights, rode up and down the line of march observing Saladin's movements and checking and re-checking their own formation. As always the infantry had their vital defensive role to play. The only difference between the battle of Arsuf and the fighting of the last two and a half weeks was that, by committing his main force to the attack, Saladin would be giving Richard a chance to deliver one of the famous Frankish charges. If he could seize the moment, victory would be his.

Mid-morning Saladin made his move. The sight and sound of the Turkish cavalry as it swept towards them was something which Ambroise would never forget:

> With numberless rich pennons streaming
> And flags and banners of fair seeming
> Then thirty thousand Turkish troops
> And more, ranged in well-ordered groups,
> Garbed and accoutred splendidly,
> Dashed on the host impetuously.
> Like lightning sped their horses fleet,
> And dust rose thick before their feet.
> Moving ahead of the emirs
> There came a band of trumpeters
> And other men with drums and tabors
> There were, who had no other labours
> Except upon their drums to hammer
> And hoot, and shriek and make great clamour.
> So loud their tabors did discord
> They had drowned the thunder of the Lord.[13]

Although the spears and arrows of the Frankish infantry took heavy toll, the

---

[13] Ambroise, 6226–40, on whose account this narrative of the battle is based, ibid., 6091–13.

Turkish forces, supported by Bedouin and Nubian auxiliaries, seemed to be everywhere, their horsemen charging in, then wheeling round and charging again, pressing closer and closer. The rain of arrows was so thick that even the bright sunlight was dimmed. In the rearguard the Hospitallers came under terrible pressure. Several times during the day, the master of the Hospital begged for permission to charge. Each time Richard said no: they must wait until he gave the signal for a general assault – six clear trumpet blasts, two in the van, two in the centre, two in the rear – and that would not be until the Turkish army was closely engaged and their horses had begun to tire. The Hospitallers held on grimly. As the day wore on, the heat became more and more oppressive; so did the dust and the deafening noise of drums and cymbals. The Hospitallers began to feel that the signal would never come and that they would be branded as cowards for submitting so patiently to the unending onslaught. Moreover, they were losing horses at an alarming rate. Goaded beyond endurance, two of the knights, the marshal of the order and Baldwin Carew, lost their nerve and charged. At once the rest of the Hospitallers and the French knights galloped after them, scattering the infantry screen, which was unprepared for the rearguard's sudden move. This was the critical moment. The Hospitallers' counterattack, premature though it was, had to be supported at once otherwise the rearguard, having lost contact with the main army, would be gradually smothered by the superior numbers of the Turks. Without hesitation Richard and his own knights charged too, ordering the Bretons, Angevins and Poitevins to join them.

Baha al-Din witnessed the crisis of the battle.

> I myself saw their knights gathered together in a single body in the midst of a protecting screen of infantry, knowing that nothing but a supreme effort could save them from the defeat which we now flattered ourselves we could easily inflict upon them. They put their lances in their rests, uttered a mighty war-cry and the ranks of infantry parted to allow them to pass; then they swept out and charged, one division against our right wing, another against our left, and a third against our centre, throwing our whole force into confusion. I was in the centre and when that body fled in the wildest disorder, I tried to take refuge with the left wing which was nearer, but found that too was struck with panic. On turning to the right wing I found it in even greater confusion.[14]

But under an experienced captain like Saladin, whose standards were still flying and drums still beating, it was at precisely this moment that the Turks were most dangerous. If in their excitement the Franks pressed the charge too far, the knights, having lost their close order, might find that

---

[14]Baha al-Din, 290–1. They charged 'like one man', Ibn al-Athir, 49.

they had galloped headlong into a trap. Richard was well aware of the danger. The Normans and English had been held in reserve; the royal standard was to act as a rallying point. Thus when the Turks counterattacked in their turn there was a basis upon which the Franks could re-form their lines. Then in a fierce struggle which marked the climax of the battle, with both sides having thrown in their reserves, the day was won by a series of charges led by Richard and William des Barres. Saladin withdrew and the army continued on its southward march, though that night many returned quietly to the battlefield to plunder the bodies of the slain.

The march from Acre and the battle of Arsuf have been described as 'outstanding feats of the crusades', 'the last great triumph of the Christians in the Near East' – and all the more outstanding because they were achieved against so formidable a foe as Saladin.[15] First Acre, now Arsuf. Saladin's prestige had suffered a second great blow. 'We were all wounded,' wrote Baha al-Din, 'either in our bodies or in our hearts.'[16] Richard now stood at the height of his fame. Naturally his soldiers praised – and doubtless magnified – Richard's own part in the hand-to-hand combat. Ambroise imagined Saladin berating his beaten and demoralized troops until he was answered by an emir who put their defeat down to two causes, the quality of Frankish armour and the prowess of one of their knights. 'You never saw anyone like him. He will always be at the front, always at the place of greatest need like a tried and tested knight. They call him Melec Richard.'[17] Richard's bravery and prowess inspired the loyalty and admiration of his followers, but it was his generalship which had won the day. Although the Hospitallers had anticipated his signal, Richard's swift reaction and masterful handling of the next few minutes had conjured victory out of imminent confusion. Not for nothing has a recent study of Western warfare between 1000 and 1300 called him 'undoubtedly the greatest commander within this period'.[18]

Three days later, on 10 September, the Frankish army reached Jaffa. It had taken nineteen days to cover the 81 miles from Acre to Jaffa. The skirmishing and harassing had continued unabated, but the Franks could not be provoked into a charge nor were Saladin's troops willing to face them again in pitched battle. In destroying Jaffa's walls, Saladin had done so much damage that the army could find no lodging within the town; they camped in an olive grove outside. In Saladin's camp it was assumed that Richard was still heading for Ascalon. 'The enemy as soon as they had massacred its garrison,' wrote Baha al-Din, 'would probably make Ascalon the base of their operations in an

[15] Verbruggen, *The Art of Warfare*, 232.
[16] Baha al-Din, 293–4.
[17] Ambroise, 6799–834.
[18] J. France, *Western Warfare in the Age of the Crusades 1000–1300* (London, 1999), 142.

1a. (*above*) Reverse of first great seal of Richard I.
1b. (*below*) Reverse of his second great seal, used from 1198 onwards.

The design on the reverse sides of Richard's two great seals is the traditional one of a knight on horseback. There are however significant differences between the two. The second knight is wearing the (more advanced) barrel helm. Above all, whereas the design on the first shield shows a single lion *rampant*, the second shows three lions *passant guardant*. Richard was the first English monarch to adopt the coat which has ever since remained the royal arms of England: Gules, three lions *passant guardant or*.

2a. (*above*) Obverse (or 'majesty' side) of Richard I's second great seal.
2b. (*below*) Obverse of the seal of Philip II Augustus.

Weapons of war were part of the iconography of English kingship and here Richard follows tradition in showing the king seated, crowned and carrying a drawn sword. Philip, by contrast, follows Capetian tradition, showing the king with sceptre and staff – though this more peaceful message suited the political style of his father far better than it did his own.

3. Signet ring identified as Richard I's private seal. In the ring and setting of gold lies a late antique gem, plasma, engraved with the figure of Mercury. The legend, which has been systematically defaced – perhaps to invalidate it after the king's death – reads 'S Richard re[g?] p'. Since Roger of Howden refers to 'one of the king's seals', Richard evidently had more than one, and a ruler who sent out 200 letters in one night (see p. 96) is likely to have had a privy seal. If correctly identified this is the earliest known privy seal of a king of England.

4. A sixteenth-century woodcut showing Richard about to pull out a lion's heart. Naturally the mere fact that the story had always been recognised as a tall one did not stop it being told and re-told.

5. This scene from the fourteenth-century Luttrell Psalter shows Richard unhorsing Saladin. Although in reality the two never met, Richard's exploits at Jaffa gave rise to the romance of the *Pas de Saladin* where Richard and twelve peers hold a narrow pass against a whole Saracen army. The motif of Richard's duel with Saladin (a favourite of King Henry III) was to be a feature of many wall paintings and decorated floor tiles.

6. Richard is the first king of England of whom it was reported that he was buried with his coronation insignia. In this early thirteenth-century effigy at Fontevraud he is shown on a draped bier, crowned, sceptred and magnificently attired. His sword, unbuckled, lies at his side. Although he now lies beside his mother, the effigies have been moved many times – and the whereabouts of their bones are unknown.

7. The castle of Chalus-Chabrol. According to the contemporary local historian, Bernard Itier of Limoges, when the king of England laid siege to this small tower it contained just two knights and 38 others, men and women. According to local tradition the king's entrails were buried in the castle church.
(Photo: Howard Nelson)

8. A late seventeenth-century drawing of the effigy of Berengaria on her marble tomb in the choir of the abbey church of her Cistercian foundation, l'Epau near Le Mans. Like Eleanor she is shown holding a book but, unlike Eleanor, she is not shown reading it. On the cover of her book is an image of a queen holding a book and lying on a bier between two large candles. Her feet rest on a lion, and beneath the lion a small dog.

9. Her tomb – no longer of marble – is now in the chapter house of l'Epau. It contains a skeleton which may well be hers.

Victorian images

10a. (*facing page*) Carlo Marochetti's equestrian statue, first shown at the Great Exhibition of 1851, was cast in bronze and then – many would say inappropriately – placed in this focal point of English history (Westminster Palace Yard, between the Abbey and the Houses of Parliament). The costs were met by public subscription, to which Queen Victoria contributed £200.

10b. (*above*) *The Pedlar* by Charles Alston Collins, 1850 in Manchester City Art Gallery. The painting's alternative title, *Berengaria's alarm for the safety of her husband, Richard Coeur de Lion, awakened by the sight of his girdle offered for sale at Rome* gives Victorian colouring to the same legendary idea as that in the Blondel story – the romantic notion that when the king was captured he 'disappeared' and had to be tracked down.

11. Battle scene from an early thirteenth-century manuscript of the *Roman de Girard de Roussillon*. There is a touch of realism in the depiction of the sword rather than the lance as the knight's battle weapon *par excellence*.

12. Western image of Muslim cavalry, taken from a manuscript of the *Roman de Godefroy de Bouillon*.

13. This illustration, taken from the *Roman de Godefroy de Bouillon*, graphically demonstrates the role of siege artillery in bringing down high walls and towers such as those at Acre and Darum. Whether the besiegers of Acre in fact used the kind of counterweight trebuchet shown here is uncertain.

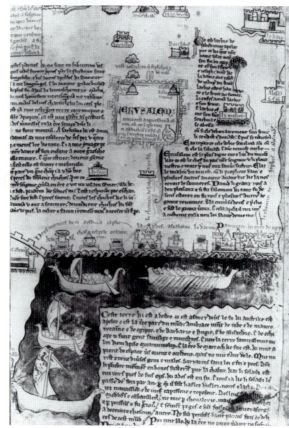

14. Part of one of Matthew Paris's maps of Palestine. This section of the map focuses on the fortresses of the coast — the great walls of Acre can be seen on the left — and on the road between Jaffa and Jerusalem.

15. Kantara, Cyprus. The easternmost of the castles on the strategically vital Kyrenia range of mountains. According to Ambroise it was here that Isaac held out against Richard until brought to surrender by the news of his daughter's capture.

16. Chinon. One of the strategic centres of Angevin power in France, the castle and treasure depository of Chinon, as in 1189 and 1199, was the scene of many of the decisive moments of the dynasty's history. When Anjou and the Touraine fell to Philip Augustus in 1203, this great stronghold overlooking the river Vienne held out until 1205.

17. Château-Gaillard. A view of the ruined Castle of the Rock (*castrum de Roka*), dominated by the keep with its curvilinear *enceinte*, and beyond, in the Seine, the island on which once stood the *castrum de Insula*. To the left is the chapel added by John, the weak link in the chain of defences.

18. This representation of Kaiser Heinrich is the opening image in
the great Heidelberger Liederhandschrift, reflecting the fact that
Henry VI too had several songs attributed to his authorship.

attack on Jerusalem, and thus cut off all communication with Egypt.' Saladin wanted to defend both Jerusalem and Ascalon but in the opinion of his emirs he did not have enough troops. After some discussion they came to the unanimous decision to demolish Ascalon. Leaving a force under al-Adil to keep an eye on Jaffa, Saladin took his army to Ascalon and stayed there from 11 to 23 September. It is clear from both Baha al-Din's and Imad al-Din's accounts that this was a deeply humiliating experience both for them and for their master. 'The inhabitants were overwhelmed by the news that their city – its walls strong, its buildings beautiful – was to be destroyed and that they would have to lose their homes.' Such were the pressures on Saladin that he was now beginning to think of surrendering 'all the cities of the coast to the Franks' in return for a negotiated peace. To add to his troubles Saladin's nerves were on edge throughout the work of demolition for fear that the Franks would learn what he was doing and, by attacking, force him to break it off.[19]

The Franks did indeed learn of it. According to Ambroise, when rumours came of what Saladin was doing at Ascalon, there were some who thought the stories must be false, a joke perhaps, since surely he would never, whatever straits he was in, behave so feebly. To ascertain the truth Richard sent the lord-designate of Ascalon, Geoffrey of Lusignan, in a galley to reconnoitre the situation from the sea.[20] On his return, a meeting of the army council was held. Richard argued for going straight to Ascalon, but the majority preferred to stay where they were and re-fortify Jaffa, on the grounds that it was the quicker way to complete their pilgrimage. For them, since they now held the port nearest Jerusalem, the obvious course, once they had rested, was to march inland and head directly for the Holy City. But did Richard have enough troops to lay siege to Jerusalem and protect his supply line? If Saladin succeeded in cutting his communications, he would be in serious trouble. During the march from Acre to Jaffa, Richard had had one flank protected by the sea and had relied heavily on his fleet for supplies; the Muslim army, although it had been defeated, was still intact and inland their Turkish harassing tactics would be far more effective. As always there was a divergence of views between those who saw the need to think in terms of military strategy, of holding terrain as well as winning it, and those who were essentially pilgrims and who wanted, above all, to enter the Holy City. Reluctantly Richard gave way to the majority view. This was, as Ambroise asserts, a mistake.[21] Had they taken Richard's

[19] Baha al-Din, 295–8; Imad al-Din, 345–6. In the latter's view Ascalon could – and should – have been held, but the events at Acre had made men cowards.

[20] Ambroise, 6960–86. Unfortunately Ambroise does not give a date for Geoffrey de Lusignan's reconnaissance. According to Baha al-Din, 299, the Hospitallers' Tower at Ascalon, a building that commanded the sea and was as strong as a castle, was still intact on 22 September. But see Lyons and Jackson, 340, for the view that Saladin had moved fast enough to prevent significant interference from Richard.

[21] Ambroise, 6957–7030.

advice they would have done what Saladin most feared. On crusade
Richard was in command of a precarious coalition, forced – as indeed
Saladin was – to take account of the feelings of the men on whose
co-operation he relied if he were to achieve anything. At least to stay at
Jaffa for a while would give the soldiers a rest that was very welcome after
the exertions on the road to Arsuf.[22] During September and October 1191
the Franks settled down to rebuild Jaffa's fortifications and enjoy the
comforts of the town and its surrounding orchards. Ambroise was less
happy about the women who travelled down from Acre to entertain them:

> Back to the host the women came
> And plied the trade of lust and shame.[23]

Despite the relaxed atmosphere, the enemy were never far away and foraging was inevitably a dangerous occupation – for both sides.

On 29 September a Frankish foraging party was attacked by the Muslim
advance guard. Baha al-Din described what he was told happened next. 'As
soon as the enemy was informed of this, they sent a detachment of cavalry
to their support. One of the prisoners said that the king of England had
ridden out with this detachment, and that a Muslim was about to pierce
him with his lance, when a Frank threw himself in between and received
the blow which caused his death; the king himself was wounded. That, at
least is what we were told, but God alone knows the truth.'[24] On the

---

[22] It has been argued that their best chance to take Jerusalem was to lay siege to it
immediately before Saladin had time to improve its defences, J. Prawer, *Histoire du
royaume latin de Jérusalem* (2 vols, Paris, 1969–70), ii, 83. However, there is no evidence that anyone advocated this course at the time. This suggests that even the
most enthusiastic Jerusalem pilgrims among the leaders appreciated the importance of fortifying what was for them the crucial bridgehead (i.e. the one nearest
Jerusalem) as well as the army's need for refreshment. While Saladin's field army
was intact it would have been an amazingly rash decision. In any event, even if
Jerusalem had fallen in September 1191, it is impossible to see how, without a well-
defended supply line, it could have been held. Significantly, Muslim accounts only
worry about the Franks making a rapid advance on Ascalon, not on Jerusalem, e.g.
Ibn al-Athir, 51–2.
[23] Ambroise, 7041–2. This doubtless added to his feeling that they stayed too long
at Jaffa, Ambroise, 7076–8.
[24] Baha al-Din, 302. According to Imad al-Din, 1347, Richard escaped because he
had ridden out incognito and the Muslims captured one of his men who managed
to deceive them into believing that he was the king. This suggests that this may be
the same incident as the one told by Ambroise, 7091–146, where William des
Préaux is identified as the knight who sacrificed his freedom for the king's.
According to Ambroise, the principal purpose of the patrol Richard was on was
reconnaissance – not quite what the two Muslim historians thought, though the
line between a patrol sent to protect foragers and one sent out to collect information is obviously a blurred one. Though he gives no precise date, Ambroise
appears to place it in the second half of October.

Frankish side people were alarmed by the narrow escape and did their best to dissuade Richard from taking the risk of going out on patrol. 'When you want to damage the Turks take a large company with you for our life is in your hands, for when the head of a body falls, the body cannot survive alone.' But like his ancestor William the Conqueror Richard both led by example and knew the value of accurate information. According to Ambroise, he continued to go out on patrol and whenever he saw a skirmish he flung himself into the fray.[25] Like many medieval campaigns this was a war of attrition in which there was a great deal of fighting – not pitched battles involving the main body of troops in a theatre of war but skirmish after skirmish, ambush after ambush. By 4 October the pressure which Richard's tactics exerted on Muslim foragers had increased to such an extent that Saladin withdrew from Ramla to Latrun, demolishing Ramla and Lydda before he left.[26]

By this date Richard had formulated a new plan of campaign. 'With God's grace we hope to recover the city of Jerusalem and the Holy Sepulchre within twenty days after Christmas and then return to our own dominions.'[27] This was written in a newsletter dispatched on 1 October 1191, when mid-January 1192 was still three and a half months away. It was not so much that he expected a long siege; rather that he knew it would take many weeks to advance so far inland. Without the fleet it would not be possible to replicate the fighting march which had taken them from Acre to Jaffa. A secure supply line had to be established, and this meant that the road over which they advanced would have to be well protected. Since Saladin had adopted a strategy of systematically destroying all strongpoints before he withdrew from them, this meant that they had, equally meticulously, to be rebuilt. This was a slow process.[28] But Richard was also thinking about what would be needed if they did take Jerusalem: more resources, more money and, above all, more people to settle and defend both it and the coastal towns they had already retaken or would soon retake. On the same date – 1 October – he sent a another letter, this one to the abbot of Clairvaux, spelling out this need and asking that the abbot would bend his mind to organizing the preaching which would lead to great numbers taking the cross and sailing with the next passage to the East, in spring 1192. In order to reinforce the urgency of the message he told the abbot that he, the duke of Burgundy and the count of Champagne, as well as all the other counts, barons and knights, were running out of money and would not be able to

---

[25] Ambroise, 7147–76. On the Conqueror's similar practice see 'William the Bastard at War' and 'Richard I and the Science of War in the Middle Ages', both reprinted in M. Strickland, ed., *Anglo-Norman Warfare* (Woodbridge, 1992).
[26] Baha al-Din, 303.
[27] *Chron.*, iii., 130.
[28] For the strategy see Gillingham, 'Richard I and the Science of War'.

stay in Syria after the following Easter.[29] Despite these words – words obviously intended to galvanize action in the West – in fact he was considering staying on for longer and had a grander strategy in mind.

Richard had been thinking about Egypt from – at the latest – early August 1191 when he set Ascalon as the goal of the march from Acre; at the very least the intention then was to interrupt the line of communication between Syria and Egypt. By October 1191 he was contemplating the conquest of Egypt. Throughout the twelfth century this had been a favourite scheme of the kings of Jerusalem – and possibly a mistaken one, since the end result of their attacks on Egypt was the unification of Egypt and Syria under one ruler, Saladin. But once this unification had been achieved, the project made good sense: Saladin's hold on Jerusalem was made possible by the wealth of the Nile valley. In the thirteenth century the maxim that 'the keys of Jerusalem are to be found in Cairo' became the principle on which crusade strategy was based. Richard announced his plan for an Egyptian campaign 'for the advantage of the holy land of Jerusalem' in letters sent to the Genoese on 11 October 1191. He asked them to come with a fleet and as much equipment as possible in time for a campaign to be launched the next summer; he would pay half the expenses of their galleys from the moment they left port, and they would acquire a share in the land gained proportionate to the size of fleet they brought.[30] His policy up until then had been one of alliance with the Pisans, since this had been the line taken by Guy of Lusignan, while Conrad of Montferrat and Philip of France looked to the Genoese. But difficult though it was to persuade those old and bitter rivals, Pisa and Genoa, to co-operate, it was also obvious that any military operation on the scale of an attack on Egypt would require maximum maritime support.[31] So, also in October 1191, we find Richard offering privileges to the Genoese, confirming privileges for the Pisans, and persuading his protégé, Guy of Lusignan, to do the same.[32] Whether Richard genuinely wanted to lead an invasion of Egypt we shall never know. He may have preferred to think of planning an attack on Egypt, 'the region in Saladin's empire most sensitive to pressure', rather as a way of 'applying sufficient pressure on Saladin to compel him to make an acceptable settlement'.[33] Richard was always

[29] *Chron.*, iii, 130–3, trans. in Edbury, 179–81.

[30] *Codice diplomatico della repubblica di Genova*, ed. C. Imperiale di Sant'Angelo (Fonti per la storia d'Italia, 89. 3 vols, Genoa, 1936–42), iii, 19–21. One of the letters is translated in Edbury, 181–2.

[31] In this context it is worth noting the construction of longships which Richard ordered in January 1192 – a shipbuilding operation which, Ambroise noted, came to nothing, 7930–2.

[32] M-L. Favreau-Lilie, *Die Italiener im Heiligen Land* (Amsterdam, 1989), 288–93.

[33] This is the assessment of a historian who had to think about such matters when at Bletchley Park during the second world war, Prestwich, 9; also J. O. Prestwich,

looking for a settlement with Saladin, and from October 1191, for a number of reasons, he did so with increasing intensity.

The letters to the Genoese were dispatched from Acre. According to Ambroise, Richard had gone there to bring back Berengaria and Joan as well as those who had preferred the bars of Acre to the routine of rebuilding Jaffa and laying in supplies.[34] Saladin's informants thought there was another reason. According to them Richard had discovered that Conrad of Montferrat had allied with the Muslims and was planning to attack Acre. Richard, Saladin was told, had gone to Acre to counter this threat. Undoubtedly Conrad had approached Saladin and had offered to attack Acre in return for the cession of Sidon and Tyre.[35] Richard's return to Jaffa on 13 October with a large fleet was interpreted by the disappointed Muslims to mean that the king of England was now confident of his hold on Acre, though they were still not sure whether he intended to march on Jerusalem or Ascalon.[36] Richard's own negotiations with al-Adil now intensified. In Baha al-Din's view, whenever the enemy (i.e. Richard) learned of contacts between Conrad and Saladin, 'they made fresh efforts to get the peace signed for they were in the greatest dread lest the Marquis should conclude a peace with the Muslims'.[37] Ambroise seems not to have been aware of the negotiations until after 6 November, and even then it is clear that he had no idea what terms were on the table, but both Baha al-Din and Imad al-Din were themselves involved in the high-level discussions and certainly did. On 17 October Richard asked al-Adil to send him a messenger. Al-Adil sent over his secretary Ibn an-Nahhal and, according to Baha al-Din:

Richard had long private talks with him to discuss the peace, assuring him that 'I shall not break my word to my brother and my friend'. He also sent a letter via Ibn an-Nahhal to the Sultan which said in effect that 'I am to salute you and tell you that the Muslims and the Franks are bleeding to death, the country is utterly ruined and goods and lives have been sacrificed on both sides. The time has come to stop this. The points at issue are Jerusalem, the Cross, and the land. Jerusalem is for us an object of worship that we could not give up even if there were only one

'Military Intelligence under the Norman and Angevin Kings' in *Law and Government in Medieval England and Normandy*, ed. G. Garnett and J. Hudson (Cambridge, 1994), 2–3, 21.

[34] Ambroise, 7051–78.

[35] Baha al-Din, 302–4. However, although Saladin would have liked to accept this offer, he would not return Beirut and Sidon until after Conrad had captured Acre and released all the prisoners he held. As with Richard and Saladin in August, neither trusted the other.

[36] Ibid., 306–7.

[37] Ibid., 325 (Gabrieli, 231); the same point made by Imad al-Din, 377.

of us left. The land from here to the other side of the Jordan must be
consigned to us. The Cross, which for you is simply a piece of wood with
no value, is for us of enormous importance. If you will return it to us, we
shall be able to make peace and rest from this endless labour.' When the
Sultan read this message he called his councillors of state and consulted
them about his reply. Then he wrote: 'Jerusalem is as much ours as
yours. Indeed it is even more sacred to us than it is to you, for it is the
place from which our Prophet made his ascent into heaven and the
place where our community will gather on the day of judgement. Do not
imagine that we can renounce it. The land also was originally ours
whereas you are recent arrivals and were able to take it over only as a
result of the weakness of the Muslims living there at the time [i.e. of the
First Crusade]. As for the Cross, its possession is a good card in our hand
and could not be surrendered except in exchange for something of outstanding benefit to Islam.' This reply was sent to Richard by the hand of
his own messenger.[38]

On 20 October Imad al-Din and Baha al-Din were among those whom al-
Adil sent for in order to discuss new proposals brought by the messenger
whom he had sent to the king of England (presumably his secretary Ibn an-
Nahhal).

These proposals have always caused puzzlement among historians, partly
because they are never mentioned by Latin Christian sources and partly
because they have been thought to be intrinsically implausible and so, if
made at all, then only as a joke. That they were made is, on the evidence
of Baha al-Din and Imad al-Din, beyond doubt. Richard had proposed that
if Saladin would grant Palestine to his brother, then he would arrange for
his sister Joan to marry al-Adil and provide her with a dowry consisting of
the coastal cities which he held. The new 'kingdom' would remain part of
Saladin's dominions. Al-Adil and Joan could live at Jerusalem, to which the
Christians should be given free access. The Cross would be returned to the
Franks; prisoners on both sides would be released. Imad al-Din took the
plan very seriously, and both he and Baha al-Din thought that al-Adil did
too. It was decided that Baha al-Din should pass it on to Saladin. He was
instructed to let him know that al-Adil would go along with the idea if that
is what the sultan wanted, but that if he was against it, then Baha al-Din was
to say: 'this is the final point reached in the negotiations for peace and it

[38] Baha al-Din, 307–9 (Gabrieli, 225–6). It doubtless suited Baha al-Din to present
Richard as the petitioner. But then at this stage the Franks were always asking for
more than the status quo. As early as June Richard's envoy had asked to hear
Muslim views and was told by al-Adil, 'It is not we who made advances to you: you
came to us; if you have anything to say, it is for you to speak; we are prepared to
listen', Baha al-Din, 257.

is he [i.e. Saladin] who has decided to bring them to nothing'. In fact when the idea was put to Saladin, he accepted it at once, somewhat to the surprise of his advisers. Saladin believed that the whole thing was just a trick and a joke on Richard's part and that he would not carry it through.[39] Sure enough, when al-Adil's envoy next saw Richard, the king told him that Joan had flown into a rage when she heard of her brother's plan, swearing that she would never consent to being an infidel's wife. Perhaps, Richard continued in the same vein, the best way of solving the problem would be for al-Adil to turn Christian. 'By this means,' commented Baha al-Din, 'he left the door open for future negotiations.'[40] Indeed since these marriage proposals – made by a man who talked 'half-seriously, half-jokingly'[41] – involved the partition of territory they proved to be a helpful point of entry for the later and ultimately successful discussions when the territorial arrangements finally made in August 1192 were very close to the ones proposed in October 1191. As so often, both sides had to continue the fight to the point of exhaustion before they could quite bring themselves to conclude a peace along lines which had seemed to be within reach long before. In the meantime all contacts were ways of assessing the mood in the Muslim camp – which was, of course, far from being united.[42] The setbacks suffered by Saladin in the last few months could reasonably be expected to have led to further tensions and rivalries. Richard's proposals may have been intended as probes in the hope of finding and widening splits at Saladin's court, perhaps above all between Saladin and the brother whom he admired, respected and trusted – yet who inevitably posed a threat to the peaceful succession of his own sons.[43] So Richard intensified diplomatic contacts while simultaneously pressing forward with preparations for advancing inland from Jaffa.

On 31 October 1191 Richard left Jaffa and occupied the two ruined fortresses of Yasur, the Casal of the Plains and the Casal Moyen.[44] Rebuilding them took two weeks while foraging and skirmishing continued

[39] Baha al-Din, 310–12 (Gabrieli, 226–8; a translation which makes al-Adil the author of the plan); Imad al-Din, 349–50.

[40] Baha al-Din, 312. Imad al-Din, 350–1 believed that Joan was happy enough with the idea but was browbeaten by churchmen into giving it up.

[41] See above, 21.

[42] Roger of Howden had reported that in July Saladin offered to make an alliance with the crusaders besieging Acre, giving them all they wanted if they would join him in a campaign against his Muslim enemies. *Gesta*, ii, 175–6. Of course this is only evidence of what some crusaders believed or hoped, not of Saladin's real priorities.

[43] Kessler, 205.

[44] On the castles, D. Pringle, 'Templar Castles between Jaffa and Jerusalem', in *The Military Orders*, ed. M. Barber (Aldershot 1994). The fact that, back in England, Howden mentions the rebuilding of these two castles is an indication of their importance, *Chron.*, iii, 174.

unabated. On 6 November a detachment of Templars guarding a foraging party ran into trouble. Richard, who was supervising building works at Casal Moyen, sent the earl of Leicester and the count of St Pol to help – only for them in their turn to be ambushed by a larger force. By the time Richard, having hurriedly armed himself, arrived on the scene with a small company the Franks were in great difficulties. Quickly weighing up the situation, his companions advised him not to intervene: 'You will not succeed in rescuing them. It is better that they die alone than that you risk death in this attack, and so endanger the whole crusade.' But, although Richard was familiar with the argument and doubtless appreciated it, he was also moved by another code of values: 'I sent those men there. If they die without me, may I never again be called a king.' In Ambroise's words, 'he kicked the flanks of his horse, gave him free rein and went in faster than a sparrowhawk, breaking through the Saracens and striking out with the power of a thunderbolt'.[45]

On 8 November, just two days after this knightly exploit, Richard spent the greater part of the day talking quietly with al-Adil, first in the latter's tent and then in his own quarters.[46] The ceremony and the gift exchange which accompanied this diplomatic episode meant that everyone now knew that talks were in progress.[47] Ambroise's account of these negotiations emphasizes both the extent of Richard's demands – the full restoration of the former kingdom and of its tribute from Egypt – and the right he had to make these demands. His right came, according to Ambroise, 'by inheritance since his lineage had conquered it'.[48] Since it is clear from the Muslim accounts that Richard and al-Adil had continued to discuss the marriage proposals, it may be that Richard did stress his dynastic rights. But Ambroise was also concerned that Richard might be deceived by Saladin's counter-offers, and by al-Adil's assurances that Saladin truly wanted peace. He was convinced – and so were many others – that the Muslims were merely playing for time while they continue to

[45] Ambroise, 7177–367. It looks as though Leicester and St Pol had come up against Saladin's own élite troop, though this time the Muslims – who claimed to have had the better of the affray – did not know that Richard himself was involved, Baha al-Din, 318–20; Imad al-Din, 352–3.

[46] Baha al-Din, 320; Imad al-Din, 353. According to Richard de Templo, on 7 November the king – who had just been bled – decided not to talk to al-Adil that day, but gave orders that he (al-Adil) should be served many different delicious dishes by Stephen of Thornham, *Itin.*, Bk. 4, ch. 31. Since lines 8705–8 show that Ambroise knew about Stephen's involvement in the negotiations with Saladin and al-Adil it seems probable that Richard de Templo obtained that additional information from a fuller text of Ambroise than the one extant.

[47] For the ceremony – including, at Richard's request, the concert of Arab music, see above, 21, 23.

[48] For discussion of Richard's right, Gillingham, 'Roger of Howden on Crusade', in *Coeur de Lion*, 144–6, esp. n. 27.

demolish castles, which the crusaders then had to rebuild at great cost in both time and money.[49] In order to dispel rumours that he was about to betray the cause, Richard liked to return from the patrols on which he continued to ride carrying the heads of Turks as a public demonstration of his devotion to the crusade. Ambroise – if he was ever worried – was convinced. The problem, he decided, was not caused by what Richard received, but by what he lost to those who robbed his purse – but for the latter, he would have rescued the land.[50]

On 9 November Saladin met Richard's ambassador, Humphrey de Toron. According to Baha al-Din:

The king says: 'your friendship and affection are dear to me. I told you that I would give these parts of Palestine to your brother, and I want you to be the judge between us in the division of land. But we must have a foothold in Jerusalem. I want you to make a division that will not bring down on your brother the wrath of the Muslims or on me the wrath of the Franks'.

Baha al-Din thought this message made a profound impression on Saladin. Even so, 'at the close of the audience the Sultan turned to me [Baha al-Din] and said: "If we make peace with these people, there is nothing to protect us against their treachery."' Imad al-Din was in no doubt. In his view Richard made proposals only to disown them. Dealing with him was dealing with a double-dealer. So it is hardly surprising that on the same day that he met Humphrey de Toron, Saladin was inclined to accept a treaty with Conrad 'on terms calculated to sow disunion among the Franks' – something of an understatement since the terms required the marquis to make war against his co-religionists.[51] None the less when two days later (11 November) Saladin's council considered the rival proposals put to them by Conrad and Richard they decided that if peace were to be made it should be with the king – 'since it was improbable that Franks and Muslims would live amiably side by side, and they had no security against treacherous attacks'. This suggests they preferred the relative security of partition to the hazardous uncertainties of a military alliance with a former enemy.[52] So negotiations with Richard over his sister's marriage to al-Adil continued, ambassadors coming and going. Eventually, however, Saladin received a message from Richard:

[49] Ambroise, 7371–418. Here too Richard wants peace with honour, 7413–14.
[50] Ibid., 7367–446. Ambroise believed that for Saladin negotiations were merely delaying tactics and that they broke down on the question of Crac de Montréal (Shaubak), a key castle on the kingdom's southern frontier. See *Itin.*, Bk. 4, ch. 31.
[51] Baha al-Din, 322–4 (Gabrieli, 229–30, but cf. Lyons and Jackson, 344); Imad al-Din, 354.
[52] Baha al-Din, 323–4 (Gabrieli, 230). On the council meeting and its date, Lyons and Jackson, 344.

The Christian people disapprove of my giving my sister in marriage without consulting the pope, the head and leader of Christianity. I have therefore sent a messenger who will be back in three months. If he authorizes this wedding so much the better. If not, I will give you the hand of one of my nieces, for whom I shall not need papal consent.[53]

This message suggests that, whatever Ambroise may have thought about Richard being deceived, he too was playing for time. It also shows how Richard dealt in disinformation since the silence of all the Christian sources on the subject of the proposed marriage shows that 'the Christian people' had not been given a chance to disapprove of it. Remarkably, this secret diplomacy had been kept secret – not only from Ambroise but also from Richard's many Christian enemies.[54] Conceivably it had even been kept from Guy of Lusignan, though he more than anyone apart from Joan herself on the Christian side would have been affected by the establishment of a Muslim 'kingdom of Jerusalem'. Whether he was in the know or not, this scheme must already have raised the question of how he could be honourably compensated.

Was such a marriage possible? There is nothing implausible about Richard suggesting – half seriously, half jokingly – that al-Adil convert to Christianity in order to marry Joan. Such ideas about Muslims converting were already in circulation in the West. According to one such report Saladin himself offered to convert when proposing a marriage between a son of his and a daughter of Frederick Barbarossa in 1173.[55] The 'good Saracen' or 'good pagan' was a stock figure in medieval literature – including, most brilliantly, the works of the great German poet Wolfram von Eschenbach.[56] Yet no fictional Muslims were admired more than Saladin and al-Adil (Safadin). Of Saladin's reputation Ambroise wrote, 'For in the world there was no court/Where he enjoyed not good report' and later he refers to him as 'the generous and valiant Saracen'. As for Safadin, he was, Ambroise thought, both wise and too honourable to make an alliance with Conrad of Montferrat; in Richard of Devizes's words he was 'very polished and wise' (*multum civilis et sapiens*).[57] According to Richard de Templo – though this is not in the only surviving text of Ambroise – Richard knighted a son of Safadin.[58] In Wolfram's *Parzival* the black heathen queen

---

[53] Baha al-Din, 324–5 (Gabrieli, 230–1).
[54] Kessler, 200.
[55] For this and other reports see Möhring, *Saladin*, 127–8.
[56] It has been argued, on the basis of Wolfram's *Parzival*, 'that so far as purely chivalrous values are concerned, heathens can be regarded as fully the equals of their Christian contemporaries', H. Sacker, *An Introduction to Wolfram's Parzival* (Cambridge, 1963), 14–15.
[57] Ambroise, 5497–500, 7390, 8692–700, 10,902; Devizes, 75.
[58] *Itin.*, Bk 5, ch. 12.

Belekane, a woman of great beauty and inner worth, marries the central character of the early chapters of the work: Parzival's father, Gahmuret of Anjou. It has become a commonplace of studies of medieval German literature to consider the question: was Richard 'of Anjou' the model for Gahmuret of Anjou?[59] Whether Richard 'was' Gahmuret or not, if his values had been shaped as much by secular literature as by ecclesiastical theory then it is not hard to imagine him proposing that his sister should marry Saladin's brother. The marriage of Christian and Muslim was readily imaginable and had occasionally, in eleventh-century Spain for example, occurred.

Once the Casals were re-fortified, Richard moved on again, 'on good horses, fed on barley', to Ramla, forcing Saladin to retreat to Toron des Chevaliers (Latrun). This was on 17 November.[60] According to Imad al-Din, Saladin now feared an advance on Jerusalem and patrols were sent out every day. At Ramla, only ten miles inland, the Franks waited for six weeks stockpiling supplies while the rains came down and the roads got steadily worse. Why the frustrating delay? Because in a war of attrition the question was, who could hold their army together the longer, Richard or Saladin? The difficulties of campaigning in this kind of weather meant that winter was traditionally the season when armies were disbanded and soldiers went home. Saladin kept his army together until 12 December, but he was at last compelled to give way before the pressure of his emirs and their troops and the threat of deteriorating morale. A forward post was left at Beit Nuba on the edge of the plain, but he and his staff including Imad al-Din and Baha al-Din withdrew to Jerusalem and the bulk of his army dispersed. As Ambroise saw it, 'they had abandoned the plains to us and taken to the mountains'.[61] Richard moved his headquarters up to Latrun. Here he spent Christmas and then ordered the main crusading army to advance up to Beit Nuba, only 12 miles from the Holy City and at the foot of the hill country. The weather was appalling: heavy rain and violent hailstorms; mud everywhere. Their food was soggy and rotten, their clothes wet through, and their arms and armour rusty. Yet they believed they had brought sufficient supplies to be able to lay siege to the city and the soldiers were in jubilant mood. They gave thanks to the God who had brought them so far:

> God may we now our voices raise
> In thanks, in worship and in praise!

[59] M. H. Jones, 'Richard the Lionheart in German Literature', 93–7.

[60] Ambroise, 7447–78. It was presumably at this time that Richard told Saladin he had sent a messenger to Rome, i.e. he had broken off negotiations – while trying to keep the door ajar.

[61] Imad al-Din, 354–5; Baha al-Din, 326–7. Ambroise, 7617–18. In view of the weather Saladin did not expect a serious attack until the next spring.

Now we shall see Thy Holy Tomb!
No man felt any grief or gloom,
Or any sadness or distress,
For all was joy and happiness.[62]

Not everyone was so optimistic. Saladin continued to send out patrols and
raiding parties, concentrating on the Jaffa road. Imad al-Din reports a particularly successful ambush on a Frankish caravan near Ramla on 3 January
1192; from Ambroise's account of the same incident it seems that Richard
himself lay in wait during the night in an attempt to ambush the ambush-
ers and did at least manage to inflict some losses.[63] Incidents such as this
only served to highlight the problems.

After Epiphany (6 January) a meeting of the army council was held.
Those who knew the country well, foremost among them the Templars and
Hospitallers, pointed out that if Richard laid siege to Jerusalem, he would
almost certainly be caught between the garrison and a relieving army.
What hope was there of escaping from that trap when they were so far from
the sea, and when their supply line would come under even heavier attack?
And if they did take Jerusalem, what then? The enthusiastic crusaders,
pilgrims to the Holy Sepulchre, would all go home, their pilgrimage
completed, their vows fulfilled. How many could be persuaded to live in
Jerusalem and defend it? The answers to these questions were obvious.
Instead the army should go, as Richard had originally wanted, to Ascalon.[64]

Observers on the Muslim side were well aware of the problems Richard
faced. 'Richard said to the Franks of Syria who accompanied him, "Draw
me a map of the city of Jerusalem for I have not seen it." They drew one
for him. He saw the valley which surrounded it on all sides except for a
small section in the north, and asked questions about the valley and its
depth.' Armed with this information he then demonstrated that, even dis-
counting the risk that the vital supply line to the coast would be broken by
Muslim attacks, a successful siege of the city was impossible while Saladin
was still active – at least according to Ibn al-Athir, who presents the reader
with what is said to be Richard's analysis of the situation.[65] On 13 January
Richard gave the order to return to Ramla. To most of the ordinary soldiers, the pilgrims, it was a bitter blow. Despite the mounting difficulties
they had never quite abandoned their dream of saving Jerusalem. The

[62] Ambroise, 7619–88.
[63] Imad al-Din, 356; Ambroise, 7661–6, 7717–60. Saladin had in fact been reinforced by Egyptian troops on 22 December.
[64] Ambroise, 7691–717, 7761–80. Richard de Templo added, perhaps on the
basis of his Ambroise text, that they advised postponing an advance on Jerusalem
itself precisely in order to keep as many pilgrims, vow unfulfilled, in the land for as
long as possible, *Itin.*, Bk 4, ch. 35.
[65] Ibn al-Athir, 55–6.

weather conditions, which had been bearable while they were marching forward to the Holy City, were now intolerable. Even the elements seemed to be mocking them:

> When they were burdened with a load
> Of goods and through the thick mud strode,
> They stumbled to their knees and fell.
> Then to the devil down in hell
> Men cursing gave themselves. My lords,
> Think not that these are idle words:
> Never was goodly company
> So deeply sunk in misery.[66]

Not since God created time, he wrote, was there ever seen an army so dejected.

From that day to this Richard's decision to accept the advice of locals has been fiercely debated. Those who believed that Jerusalem should have been besieged were strengthened in that conviction when they were later told, rightly or wrongly, that the Turks had been in such difficulties in Jerusalem that the city could have been taken.[67] That was one thing; whether it could have been retained was another. Richard de Templo's version of this section of the *Estoire* ends with an additional sentence: 'Yet it could not have been held by our people for long, because when the pilgrimage was completed the people would have gone home and there would not have been anyone left who could defend it.' [68]

---

[66] Ambroise, 7781–832.

[67] Ibid., 7799–810. As he makes clear, this was hindsight. They did not know it at the time. As he saw it later, moreover, Saladin's problems were caused by a shortage of supplies – in other words the strategy of attrition had been working.

[68] *Itin.*, Bk 5, ch. 1. The argument was, however, familiar to Ambroise (7707–16) and the additional passage could have been in the manuscript Richard used.

Chapter 12

ASCALON AND JAFFA

Taking and rebuilding Ascalon was sound military strategy but it was not for this that many soldiers had crossed the sea. At Ramla the army began to break up. Some of the French contingents, those who were said to have been in favour of laying siege to Jerusalem, retired to Jaffa – even to Acre and to Tyre. Those led by Richard's nephew Count Henry of Champagne, however, stayed with him.[1] Even so it was with a much-diminished army that Richard reached the deserted ruins of Ascalon, probably on 21 January.[2] They spent a gloomy first week there, the size of the task ahead magnified by supply problems caused by bad weather impeding shipping.[3] For the next four months Richard's forces remained there, making it the strongest fortress on the coast of Palestine. According to Ambroise, three-quarters of the building costs were met from Richard's own purse.[4] Right from the start of building operations he was able to threaten the road between Egypt and Syria. On one raid near Darum he attacked a caravan taking Christian prisoners to Egypt and was able to release them.[5] Not surprisingly, Conrad of Montferrat remained immune to the argument that since he enjoyed a share in the kingdom's revenues he ought to do his part in strengthening and extending it. The duke of Burgundy went to Ascalon

[1] From the moment of his arrival at the siege of Acre in August 1190 Count Henry had played an important role, partly thanks to his position as nephew of both kings of England and France.

[2] For the date, Imad al-Din, 373. This implies a stay of some days at Ramla before the march via Ibelin to Ascalon. Richard de Templo's date (20 January) is probably an inference from his text of Ambroise. On his calculation of dates see H. E. Mayer, *Das Itinerarium Pereginorum* (Stuttgart, 1962), 145. It may be that those days were needed for the sick and depressed to recover, cf. Ambroise, 7830–9.

[3] Ambroise, 7897–932.

[4] Ibid., 8073–7. D. Pringle, 'King Richard I and the Walls of Ascalon', *Palestine Exploration Quarterly*, cxvi (1984). At the same time Saladin was strengthening the defences of Jerusalem, setting an example by carrying stones on his saddle-bow as well as using the slave labour of 2,000 Frankish prisoners of war and the services of 50 skilled masons sent from Mosul, Imad al-Din, 356, 367–8, 371; Lyons and Jackson, 346–7.

[5] According to Ambroise he freed no fewer than 1,000 captives. For this and another profitable raid on a caravan travelling between Egypt and Syria, an indication that the fortress would soon be self-sufficient, Ambroise, 8089–138, 8286–304; however it was not all one-way traffic, Imad al-Din, 373–5.

for a while in early February but then returned to Acre as soon as Richard made it plain that he could not afford to lend him any more money.[6]

Acre was now sliding into chaos. Allegedly the Genoese and Burgundy's French tried to seize control of the city on behalf of Conrad of Montferrat but were driven out by the Pisans, still loyal to Guy of Lusignan, shortly before a flotilla of galleys under Conrad's command arrived. For three days the Pisans defended the city against Conrad's attacks.[7] As it happened Richard, still trying to persuade Conrad to join the common enterprise, was at Caesarea on his way north to meet him when he received the Pisan appeal for help. He reached Acre on 20 February to find that the news of his approach had forced Conrad and Hugh to beat a hasty retreat to Tyre.[8] Richard managed to bring about a temporary reconciliation between Pisans and Genoese before going north to see Conrad. The two men met at Casal Imbert on the road to Tyre. On both sides angry words were spoken and Conrad again refused to join the army at Ascalon. Richard then presided over a council meeting at which Conrad was formally deprived of his share of the revenues of the kingdom of Jerusalem. However, since the marquis had the support of most of the local baronage and the French, it was extremely difficult to put this judgment into effect.

From Acre Richard renewed diplomatic contact with Saladin. Once again he sought a meeting with 'his brother', al-Adil. The latter was instructed by Saladin to conclude a peace if he could and, if not, to spin out negotiations to give more time for the army to be brought together from outlying provinces. Al-Adil insisted that a document be drawn up putting in writing the utmost limits of the concessions he was empowered to make in order to reach a settlement.[9] It soon transpired that Richard was thinking of a partition of the land based on the status quo and with Jerusalem divided, leaving the Rock and the Citadel in Muslim hands but

[6] He had earlier loaned him 5,000 marks, Ambroise, 5351–6, 7967–94, 8158–76.

[7] However since Ambroise 8157–270, Ambroise translated and interpreted by Richard de Templo, *Itin.*, Bk 5, chs 10–14 and Roger of Howden, all of them deeply prejudiced against Conrad and the duke of Burgundy, are the only sources for these events caution is clearly required. Howden adds that Burgundy and the French wished to make Conrad king. He may have obtained this analysis of the politics of the struggle for Acre from Robert of Thornham; dating these events to 'after Easter' was probably just a slip for 'before Easter', *Chron.* iii, 180–1. For discussion see Favreau-Lilie, *Die Italiener*, 294–5.

[8] The date 20 February is not in Ambroise's text as we have it, but in the form 'the day after Ash Wednesday' may have been in the version used by his translator. Alternatively it might have been calculated by Richard de Templo on the basis of other information Ambroise supplied, Mayer, *Das Itinerarium*, 145.

[9] Al-Adil's insistence on having a document drawn up suggests that he thought peace was a realistic possibility and that he was anxious to avoid being blamed for its terms. This in turn suggests that the discussions he had had with Richard on 8 November 1191 had been serious ones since it is clear they were very similar to the ones now proposed.

returning the rest to Christian control. When Saladin put this proposal to his emirs it was thought to be acceptable – indeed in some respects al-Adil had been authorized to go further than this. In Baha al-Din's judgement, 'we were induced to make such concessions by the condition of our troops, worn out by the fatigues of constant war, harassed by lack of money, and pining at their long absences from home'.[10] It seemed that peace was close, but on 27 March Saladin was informed that Richard, despite his recent accommodating frame of mind, had left Acre without seeing al-Adil. This seemed to signal an aggressive intent. At any rate by mid-April Saladin was persuaded that Richard had heard enough of Saladin's own domestic political problems to believe that by increasing the military pressure he could dictate terms.[11] Conceivably this was what Richard wanted Saladin to think.[12] Doubtless for a crusader king it was important to celebrate the great festivals of the Christian year together with his front-line troops, but he arrived at Ascalon on 31 March, and since Easter was not until 5 April he probably could have waited a little longer.

There was bad news waiting for Richard at Ascalon. Envoys from Conrad and Hugh had arrived before him, reminding those of King Philip's subjects who were still there that their lord had been Conrad's ally and had instructed them to obey Hugh. Despite Richard's pleas and his offer to pay their expenses, no fewer than 700 French knights decided to leave for Tyre.[13] The French, according to Ambroise, were going to enjoy themselves at Tyre:

> Those who were present there assured
> Us that they danced through the late hours
> Of night, their heads bedecked with flowers
> Entwined in garland and in crown;
> Beside wine casks they sat them down
> And drank until matins had rung;
> Then homeward made their way among
> The harlots ...[14]

[10] Baha al-Din, 327–9. The Muslims were informed of Richard's latest proposals by al-Adil's chamberlain, Abu Bekr, who told Saladin that he had had several interviews with the king and persuaded him to modify his demands.

[11] Ibid., 331. These problems were the consequences of Nasir al-Din, the son of Taqi al-Din, fearing that Saladin was likely to deprive him of *iqtas* (revenues) held by his father and so acting in such a way since the death of his father (news of which had reached Saladin on 1 November 1191) as to give rise to the suspicion that he was about to join Saladin's Muslim enemies.

[12] The observations of al-Mashtub, the former commander of the Acre garrison, just released from captivity on payment of a ransom, helped Saladin to reach this conclusion.

[13] Richard gave instructions that they were not to be admitted to Acre, Ambroise, 8305–80.

[14] Ibid., 8458–65. But according to Sicard of Cremona the French barons and 500

Immediately after Easter Richard went on reconnaissance patrols to Gaza, which Saladin had demolished in the previous year, and to Darum, which he had not. In order to see how Darum could best be attacked, he walked all around it, within range of the archers and crossbowmen in the garrison, but evidently with some kind of protection against their shot.[15]

Before laying siege to Darum, however, he took advantage of the arrival of news from home to sort out the troubled internal politics of the Latin kingdom. The prior of Hereford, presumably sent by William Longchamp, arrived at Ascalon; he reported that John had overthrown the chancellor and was seeking to take over the government. He advised that Richard should return. As yet Richard had no intention of going back, but the message must have forced him to think about what would happen in Outremer when he did go. Conrad was not prepared to co-operate with Guy of Lusignan. If their feud continued, Saladin would almost certainly be able to recover the ground he had lost in the last twelve months. Indeed Saladin had been continuing the obvious policy of negotiating with Conrad as well as Richard, holding out the possibility of a military alliance with Conrad, even offering to let him retain any cities which they captured jointly. The kingdom desperately needed a king whose authority was undisputed and who as a politician and soldier was a match for Saladin. It had to be Conrad, recognized by Baha al-Din as 'the most energetic leader, most experienced warrior and cleverest counsellor of the Franks'.[16] Compared with this harsh fact the question of who had the better legal right was a matter of secondary importance. With this in mind, Richard called a meeting of the army council for the next day.[17]

After much argument, the council opted for Conrad.[18] Although it used to be said by Richard's biographers and historians of the crusades that this decision came as a shock to the king, this is hardly likely. It is true that up till then he had consistently taken Guy's side. In practice, however, this had simply meant that Richard had been king of Jerusalem, not Guy. If Richard

---

knights left Ascalon 'because Richard held them cheap' and at Tyre launched highly profitable raids on Muslim settlements, Sicard, 23.

[15] *Itin.*, Bk 5, ch. 19. It seems probable that this was in Richard de Templo's text of Ambroise. Cf. Imad al-Din, 378.

[16] Baha al-Din, 318. 'He was the greatest devil of all the Franks – god damn him', Ibn al-Athir, 58 (Gabrieli, 24).

[17] Since Ambroise, and following him, Richard de Templo merely say that the prior arrived after Easter, the meeting cannot be precisely dated, Ambroise, 8519.

[18] Ibid., 8519–648. Ambroise described it in terms of a choice between just two men, Conrad and Guy. According to Sicard of Cremona, however, some had expressed a preference for a third candidate, the count of Champagne, Sicard, 25. If this is not just a guess made in the light of subsequent events, it would help to explain the speed with which Count Henry was recognized a few weeks later. For the moment, however, Henry was not much more likely than Guy to get the marquis's loyalty.

had wanted Guy to take over the direction of affairs when he was gone, there would have been no need to call a meeting of the army council and offer it a choice of kings. Richard's army already recognized a king, Guy, and this meeting only made sense if a policy change was being considered. In all probability Guy's formidable brother, Geoffrey of Lusignan, had already decided to renounce the lordships of Ascalon and Jaffa and return home to Poitou. Once he had left, Guy's position would become even more vulnerable. While Richard was king in reality, Guy could perfectly well be king in theory. But not even Richard had been able either to defeat Conrad of Montferrat or to secure his co-operation, and, left to his own resources, Guy had little or no chance against this clever and unscrupulous opponent. If Guy had succeeded in recapturing Acre it might have been different but, as it was, in the eyes of the barons of Outremer he was still the man who had lost the battle of Hattin. All this must have become crystal clear to Richard during the six weeks he spent at Acre – if not earlier. Indeed he may already have raised the matter with Conrad himself. According to Baha al-Din, in negotiating with Conrad Saladin had agreed that if the king of England were to grant Conrad the government of the country then, with the exception of Ascalon, he – Conrad – would be entitled to enjoy the benefit of any peace treaty concluded between Richard and Saladin. Since the envoy taking this proposal back to Conrad seems to have left Saladin's court before 13 April, it could be that Conrad already had a shrewd suspicion that he was about to be promoted.[19]

Fortunately Richard was in a position to compensate Guy in magnificent style. He had earlier sold Cyprus to the Templars, but they were clearly happy to re-negotiate. According to the later Old French Continuations, the Templars had so far paid 40 per cent of the purchase price of 100,000 bezants and their attempt to raise the rest of the money by imposing dues on the Greek Cypriot population had provoked a rebellion. It looked as though Cyprus was going to be more trouble than it was worth. If Richard were already thinking about transferring Cyprus to Guy, this was the moment to act. (The implication of the plan for a marriage between al-Adil and Joan is that Richard must have been thinking about appropriate potential compensation for Guy for several months.)[20] Guy reimbursed the

[19] Baha al-Din, 329–30. Saladin's reservation highlights yet again the strategic importance of Ascalon.
[20] No source gives a date for the grant of Cyprus to Guy, but several, including Ambroise and Howden, *Chron.* iii, 181, imply that it was not until after Conrad's death. Although the deal was not formalized until then, it is not easy to believe that there can have been an interval of several weeks during which Guy de Lusignan was left entirely out in the cold; he and his brother would surely have had a great deal to say about that. According to Greek sources the Cypriot revolt broke out on 5 April. It may be that if the Templars soon afterwards expressed doubts about their ability to hold Cyprus that it was this, i.e. the opportunity to compensate Guy, quite

Templars the 40,000 bezants and in return received Cyprus; perhaps he acknowledged that he owed Richard the balance of 60,000 marks. If so, both probably assumed that it was unlikely ever to be paid. In that case, from Richard's point of view, he had in effect given Cyprus to Guy.[21] The Lusignans were to rule Cyprus for the next 300 years, until 1489.

Meanwhile, Conrad of Montferrat had to be told of his good fortune, so Richard sent Count Henry of Champagne to take the news to Tyre. When he heard, Conrad fell on his knees and thanked God, praying – or so Ambroise heard – that he should not be permitted to be crowned if he were not worthy to be king.[22] There was great urgency, so it was agreed that he should be crowned at Acre within the next few days. Count Henry returned there to make preparations for the coronation. A few days later, on 28 April, Conrad was assassinated at Tyre. Both Muslim and Christian contemporaries told in essence the same story. After dining with the bishop of Beauvais, the marquis was on his way home when he was stabbed to death by two men. One of the murderers was killed at once; the other was questioned and confessed that they were Assassins before he too was put to death.[23]

The Assassins were followers of Rashid al-Din Sinan or – as he was popularly known in the West – 'The Old Man of the Mountain'. The description of the Assassins given by the late twelfth-century German chronicler Arnold of Lübeck, illustrates very well the impact which the Old Man of the Mountain made on the European imagination:

> This Old Man has by his witchcraft so bemused the men of his country that they neither worship nor believe in any God but him. He entices them with promises of an afterlife in which they will enjoy eternal pleasure and so he makes them prefer death to life. He only has to give the nod and they will jump off a high wall, breaking their skulls and dying miserably. The truly blessed, so he tells them, are those who kill others and are themselves then killed. Whenever any of his followers choose to die in this way, he presents them with knives which are, so to speak,

as much as news from England and Normandy, that precipitated Richard's decision to call a council meeting.

[21] *Itin.*, Bk 5, ch. 38 says that Richard granted him rule over Cyprus gratis. Although Richard de Templo is clearly following Ambroise here, the surviving text gives no indication of whether Guy paid for it or not, Ambroise, 9119–23. According to the Old French Continuations, Richard treated Guy with courteous generosity; cf. Edbury, 112–13 and the discussion in P. Edbury, 'The Templars in Cyprus', *The Military Orders: Fighting for the Faith and Caring for the Sick*, ed. M. Barber (Aldershot, 1994), 190. At the French court it was believed that Richard 'sold' Cyprus to Guy, Rigord, 118; so too Sicard of Cremona, though he put the price at 20,000 bezants, Sicard, 25.

[22] Ambroise, 8715–46.

[23] Ibid., 8780–818; Baha al-Din, 333.

consecrated to murder. He then gives them a potion which intoxicates them, plunging them into ecstasy and oblivion. Thus he uses his magic to make them see fantastic dreams, full of pleasures and delights. He promises them that they will live in such dreams for ever if they die when killing at his command.[24]

From 1169 until his death in 1193 Sinan was the leader of the Syrian branch of a revolutionary religious movement which had been founded in Persia at the end of the eleventh century. The orthodox Muslims who ruled Persia looked upon the followers of the new teaching as heretics and tried to suppress them. But these heretics did not submit meekly to persecution. They created a secure base for themselves in the great mountain fortress of Alamut, and they struck back at those who attacked them. Their chosen weapon was the dagger. In the early twelfth century the new teaching was carried into Syria and it was here that its devotees were given the name by which they are remembered: Assassins – the word coming from the Arabic *hashish*. Their enemies accused them of taking hashish; to outsiders it seemed the easiest way of explaining why they acted the way they did. There is no good evidence of this, but there is no doubt at all about the fact that they used murder as a political weapon. Thus, in the course of the twelfth and thirteenth centuries, a new word entered the languages of Europe: assassin, a dedicated killer.

Because many of their deeds were done by stealth, the power of the Assassins was easily magnified. There was no way of knowing where they would strike next. A story involving Saladin tells us much about the nature of the power attributed to Sinan. According to this tale the Old Man of the Mountain sent a messenger to Saladin with instructions to deliver the message only in private. Naturally Saladin had the messenger searched, but no weapon was found. Then Saladin dismissed everyone but a few trusted advisers. The messenger refused, however, to deliver his message. So Saladin sent everyone away except his two personal bodyguards. Still the messenger was reluctant, but Saladin said: 'These two never leave my side. I look upon them as my sons. Deliver your message or not, as you choose.' Then the messenger turned to the two bodyguards and said: 'If I ordered you in the name of my master to kill Saladin, would you do so?' They said they would, and drew their swords saying, 'Command us as you wish.' The messenger ordered them to sheathe their swords and all three left the sultan's camp. Sinan's message had been delivered. We have to remember that Saladin, the champion of Muslim orthodoxy, was prepared to order the crucifixion of heretics so was in much greater danger of assassination

---

[24] B. Lewis, *The Assassins* (London, 1967), 4–5. For the 'Old Man of the Mountain' and the stories of his relations with Saladin, ibid., ch. 5. Ambroise sees the Assassins as fanatics 'brainwashed' when children, Ambroise, 8519–46.

than were most Christians. At one stage he is said to have been able to sleep only in a specially constructed wooden tower. In 1176 he seems to have reached an accommodation with the Syrian Assassins. But before that date there were at least two attempts on his life.[25]

But why should the Assassins have wanted to kill Conrad of Montferrat? Muslim sources all report that the murderer's confession implicated Richard. Hence the Franks, as Ibn al-Athir noted, blamed Richard. His own opinion was that Saladin had bribed Sinan to kill both Richard and Conrad, but the Old Man preferred to kill only Conrad because he knew that, if he killed Richard, it would have given the sultan a free hand to turn against the Assassins.[26] There is no strong reason to think Ibn al-Athir blamed Saladin on the basis of information rather than prejudice; his imagined reconstruction of the Old Man's priorities does, however, reinforce his own high opinion of Richard's abilities. Neither of the authors close to Saladin say who they thought was behind the killing, though both by implication clear their master, Imad al-Din by writing that it was 'of little benefit to us', and Baha al-Din by saying that Saladin had just (on 24 April) agreed to a treaty with the marquis.[27] According to Baha al-Din, on 21 April Saladin learned that the marquis was on the point of coming to an agreement with the Franks, who would then embark for their own country. If this means that Saladin thought Conrad and Richard were about to end the quarrel which had always been so much to his advantage, it is worth noting that he dispatched a message from Jerusalem to Tyre on 24 April and the marquis was dead on 28 April.[28]

The evidence is much too inadequate to enable us to decide whether the murder was carried out by the Old Man for reasons of his own, or whether he was bribed by Richard, Saladin or any one of the other candidates for the role of unseen hand. What is certain is that the finger of suspicion was very firmly pointed at Richard. It was standard Assassin technique to provide the killer with a misleading 'cover story' in order to spread mistrust and suspicion in the opposing camp. In view of the tension between Richard and Conrad, the king of England was the obvious candidate. In any case if there was anyone who knew what the murderer(s) had said before he/they died, it was those who interrogated them at Tyre, people working for the most powerful men on the spot, Philip, bishop of Beauvais and/or Hugh of Burgundy.[29] Since they were the people whom Ambroise

[25] Lyons and Jackson, 87–8, 105–6.

[26] Baha al-Din, 333; Imad al-Din, 376; Ibn al-Athir, 58 (Gabrieli, 239, 241).

[27] Imad al-Din, 377 (Gabrieli, 240); Baha al-Din, 332. If Imad al-Din did write that Richard, once the marquis was dead, realized that he had been wrong to support Guy by giving him Cyprus, this would mean that Imad al-Din assumed that Richard had no foreknowledge of the murder, Gabrieli, 240; however, see Grousset, *Histoire des croisades*, iii, 89–91, for a plausible emendation to the text.

[28] Baha al-Din, 330, 332. See Kessler, 230.

[29] See Kessler, 214.

characterized as 'the envious, those who belittled everything Richard did', it was inevitable that they would seize the opportunity. 'They said that King Richard by bribery had sought the death of the marquis. They sent to the king of France, advising him to be on his guard against the Assassins because they had killed the marquis and Richard had sent four of them to sweet France to kill him. God! What a foul thing to say! What an evil deed! Because of this evil deed the king was later treacherously imprisoned out of envy for the deeds he had performed in Syria.'[30] William of Newburgh reported that 'on account of his recent dispute with the marquis, many people were inclined to blame Richard. The French, who were on the marquis's side, were his principal defamers and they raised a great scandal against him on the subject of Conrad's murder throughout the whole Western world. As soon as the king of France heard the news he joyfully seized the opportunity to defame the king of England. In order to increase prejudice against him, and contrary to the custom of his ancestors, he never went anywhere without an armed guard, as if he was in fear of assassins paid by Richard.'[31]

This charge at least Richard was eventually able to rebut fairly successfully. He was explicitly cleared of it in a letter allegedly sent to Leopold of Austria by the Old Man of the Mountain himself. This asserted that Sinan and Conrad had a quarrel of their own, and that it was as a consequence of this, and for no other reason, that the Assassins were sent to Tyre.[32] Although this was presumably a forgery concocted by Richard's men in an attempt to dispel the rumours, it does look as though the message it contained, whether true or false, got through. Rigord, writing in 1195, reports that when Philip received the warning that Richard's hired Assassins were on the way, he both took measures to protect himself and sent envoys to the Old Man of the Mountain to ascertain the truth. When they returned they brought letters absolving Richard of all blame.[33] Whatever King Philip may have thought or been told by his cousin the bishop of Beauvais in 1192–3, by 1195 he was concerned to deny those rumours. Hence it was the approved version of Conrad's murder which found its way into the mid-thirteenth-century Old French Continuations of William of Tyre. They report as rumour the widespread story that Richard had arranged for the Assassins to kill Conrad and had persuaded the lord of the Assassins to send men to kill the king of France, but only after they have already said that Conrad had offended Sinan by an act of piracy and that his death was

[30] Ambroise, 8879–908.
[31] Newburgh, Bk 4, ch. 25.
[32] Diceto, ii, 127–8. Longchamp sent a copy to the dean of St Paul's so that he could include it in his history – which he did under the year 1195.
[33] Rigord, 120–1. According to William of Newburgh, Philip decided in 1195 that he could make a treaty with Richard after listening to a reading of some such letters, Newburgh, Bk 5, ch. 16. On these forged letters, see Gillingham, 'Royal Newsletters, Forgeries and English Historians'.

the Old Man's revenge.[34] Unfortunately for Richard, it was not until 1195 that Philip found it convenient to call a halt to the propaganda campaign. By then the king of England and his subjects both in England and on the continent had paid dearly.

Conrad's death threw the political situation into a state of confusion. According to Ambroise, the French, led by the duke of Burgundy, tried to seize Tyre on behalf of the king of France, but Conrad's pregnant widow, Isabella, shut herself up in the castle, saying she would gladly hand it over when he returned from France; otherwise she would obey her husband's dying words and give the keys only to Richard or to the rightful lord of the land.[35] But who was the rightful lord? Was Guy of Lusignan now king again? Some later stories suggest that the Pisans may have encouraged him to renew his bid for the throne.[36] Presumably he would have done if he had not just been granted Cyprus. Where did Isabella's first husband, Humphrey of Toron, stand now? Or could Isabella, the twenty-one-year-old, twice-married heiress to the kingdom, find a third husband? At this point, with the struggle for Tyre still going on, Count Henry returned from Acre and 'the people' begged him to marry the widow and take the crown. He said he would need his uncle's consent and at once sent messengers to Richard. Richard encouraged him to accept the kingdom but had, according to Ambroise, reservations about the marriage. After all, if Isabella's marriage to Conrad had been invalid, was she not still married to Humphrey of Toron? Whether or not Richard did have doubts on this score, Henry married Isabella. According to Diceto, the marriage was celebrated on 5 May.[37] If Diceto's date is correct there was barely time for Henry to leave Acre for Tyre on hearing the news of Conrad's murder, and then for an envoy to get from Tyre to see Richard, perhaps at Jaffa, and back again to Henry at Acre.[38] In the last few days events had moved with

---

[34] Edbury, 114–15. They also say that some people, not surprisingly, pointed the finger at Guy of Lusignan.

[35] Ambroise, 8856–64, 8910–24.

[36] Edbury, 115–16, 120. Although the Pisans may have floated the idea for a day or two – according to Sicard of Cremona, Count Henry barred Guy from entering Acre (Sicard, 25) – the story as developed in the Old French Continuations is fundamentally implausible. It has Richard planning to replace Guy as ruler of Cyprus within a few days of granting it to him; this, together with its legendary aspects – Guy is said to have asked Saladin for advice on how to rule Cyprus – means that I am not inclined to regard it as a reliable source; contrast Favreau-Lilie, *Die Italiener*, 304–10. Möhring has argued, to my mind convincingly, that the letter in which al-Fadil reports that the ruler of Cyprus had broken with Richard (see Lyons and Jackson, 349) refers to Isaac in May 1191, not to Guy in May 1192, Möhring, *Saladin*, 187.

[37] Diceto, ii, 104. No other source dates the wedding.

[38] According to Ambroise, 8951–6, Richard was campaigning 'in the plains of Ramla' when he heard the news of Conrad's death. Presumably he would at once

bewildering speed. From Richard's point of view, the outcome of it all was that, for the first time, he had all the forces of the kingdom at his disposal. If he had wished to put Henry on the throne he would have had to get rid of Conrad and placate Guy – which is what happened. Either he had reacted in a remarkably sure-footed way to the twists and turns of events, or some of them had been foreseen and, at the least, contingency plans had been laid. This surely applies to the decisions to recognize Conrad as king of Jerusalem and Guy as lord of Cyprus. Not surprisingly the Old French Continuations attribute the decision to arrange the marriage to Richard rather than to any of those at Tyre, whether Isabella, Henry or the French, and they say that he took others unawares by the speed with which he moved after Conrad's death.[39]

After Richard's departure Henry became an effective ruler of the coastal kingdom, though he never assumed the title of king – either because he could not be crowned in Jerusalem or because of worries about the validity of his marriage. In 1197 he accidentally stepped backwards through the open window of an upper room and was killed. Isabella then married, as her fourth husband, Guy of Lusignan's brother, Aimery, who died of a surfeit of fish in 1205.[40] In part Ambroise took a romantic view of the count's motives in 1192:

> My soul, I should have done the same,
> For she was fair and beautiful
> And so, may God be merciful
> To me, the Count, unless I err,
> Was well disposed to marry her.

But he also believed that the French strongly favoured the match, noting that Henry was King Philip's nephew as well as Richard's.[41] It made good

---

have started for Tyre. *Itin.*, Bk 5, chs 30–3 relate a number of episodes dated between 16 April and 1 May which concern patrolling, foraging and skirmishing in the countryside between Ascalon, Darum and Jerusalem. In several of these Richard was prominent; in one, displaying brilliant horsemanship, he killed a wild boar. I suspect that these too were in Richard de Templo's fuller version of Ambroise, but see Mayer, *Das Itinerarium*, 150, for the suggestion that they were taken from another source.

[39] Edbury, 115–16. According to this version, Henry was reluctant to marry Isabella because if the baby she was carrying turned out to be a son his own future prospects would be uncertain. Allegedly Richard reassured him by promising to return one day to conquer the whole kingdom of Jerusalem together with some unspecified pagan lands as well as the empire of Constantinople!

[40] By the time she was thirty-three, Isabella had been divorced once and widowed three times.

[41] Ambroise, 8987–9102. Imad al-Din, by contrast, was scandalized by the fact that at the time Isabella was pregnant with Conrad's child: cf. Sicard of Cremona's assertion that she was married against her will, Sicard, 25.

political sense and ushered in a period of unusual co-operation between Richard's followers and Burgundy's French.

Richard now summoned Henry and the French army to join him in an attack on the fortress of Darum, 20 miles south of Ascalon. Its capture would add to the length of the coastline in Christian hands, and increase the pressure on Saladin's line of communication between Egypt and Syria. Without waiting for Henry and the French to arrive, however, Richard moved to Darum with just his household troops to take possession of the beach and clear a landing place for his ships. Well aware of its importance and of Richard's intentions, Saladin, though short of troops at the time, had sent 'Alam al-Din Qaisar to its asssistance, but he and his troops preferred to stay outside Darum rather than shut themselves within its walls.[42] They seem to have done little, either to harass Richard when he arrived on Sunday, 17 May or to impede the subsequent unloading and reassembling of three siege machines sent down from Ascalon by ship; Ambroise was impressed by the way both king and nobles put their backs into the work of moving the sections almost a league from beach to castle. Although they were too few to invest the castle on all sides, it seems that Richard's earlier close reconnaissance had revealed a weakness in the principal tower.[43] There then followed three days and nights of well-directed artillery assault and sapping. From their different perspectives both Baha al-Din and Ambroise emphasize the importance of the sappers' work. On the fourth day, Friday 22 May, the defenders offered to surrender on condition that they, their wives and property were spared. Richard rejected the offer, and that same day the castle was taken by assault, Ambroise recording the names of those otherwise unknown men who were the first to fight their way in. The surviving members of the garrison surrendered unconditionally and were taken prisoner.[44]

Next day Henry and the duke of Burgundy arrived. In a fine gesture, Richard at once handed the captured town to the new lord of Jerusalem. Now that there was a new spirit of co-operation among the Christians they would surely succeed. Leaving a garrison behind in Darum, they advanced to al-Hasi, 'Cane Brake of Starlings', on 28 May and from there they carried out operations which Baha al-Din described as 'beginning to over-

[42] Imad al-Din, 378.

[43] Above, 195.

[44] Ambroise, 9160–370. According to Richard de Templo, 300 prisoners plus women and children were taken, *Itin*, Bk 5, ch. 39. Ambroise gives the following list of those whose banners waved over Darum: Pisans, Genoese, Stephen de Longchamp, Robert earl of Leicester, and Raymond, heir to Antioch. Both Baha al-Din, 337 and Imad al-Din, 378, date the fall of Darum to 23 May, a Saturday. The capture of Darum made a big impression on Howden, though none of his details, except that Richard laid siege to it on a Monday and took it by storm on a Friday, can be relied on, *Chron.* iii, 180.

run the open country'.[45] Then an envoy, John of Alençon, arrived with the
disquieting news of a conspiracy between John and Philip Augustus.
Richard was now caught in a terrible dilemma: which mattered most – the
crusade or the Angevin empire? It would have taken John of Alençon
about eight weeks to bring the news. What had happened in those weeks?
If he left now, what would happen in the next two or three months?
Jerusalem at least was near at hand. Should he try again to take it? It was a
forlorn hope, if ever there was one, but did he want to be known as the
king who did not even try? This time, moreover, they would not be hampered by the winter mud and rain. If by some miracle he took Jerusalem,
it would put an end to the conspiracy. Philip and John would find no one
to support them against the conqueror who had restored the Holy City to
Christendom. But suppose he failed, and then came home too late? While
Richard fretted and rumours about his intentions spread, the barons –
French, Norman, Poitevin, English, Manceaux, Angevin – met and decided
that, whatever Richard did, they would attack Jerusalem. When this news
was leaked to the soldiers their joy was so great

> That they went not to bed, but danced
> Till after midnight, still entranced.[46]

By this time Saladin's reinforcements had joined him, so he ordered an
advance against the Franks, who then withdrew to Ascalon on 31 May and
1 June.[47] It looked like a retreat but it was in fact to assemble supplies and
muster more troops. The mood in the army remained optimistic – but this
was not shared by Richard. The decision to lay siege to Jerusalem had been
taken against his advice. According to Ambroise he withdrew to his tent
and stayed there for several days, troubled and despondent, until one of
his chaplains, William of Poitiers, managed to revive his spirits. He
reminded the king of all the past triumphs which God had allowed him to
enjoy, of all the dangers which he had, by God's grace, escaped. Now that
he had been brought to the verge of the ultimate victory, it would be a
shameful thing to retreat.

> Now it is said by great and small
> Who wish you honour, one and all,
> How unto Christendom have you
> A father been, and brother, too,
> And if you leave it without aid
> 'Twill surely perish, thus betrayed.

---

[45] For very different views of the success of these operations, Imad al-Din 379;
Baha al-Din, 337–9; Ambroise, 9395–432.

[46] Ambroise 9436–508.

[47] Imad al-Din, 379; Baha al-Din, 339; Ambroise, 9509–18.

Richard listened in silence and even after the chaplain had finished he still said nothing, but next day he announced that he would stay in Palestine till the following Easter and that all should at once prepare for the siege of Jerusalem.[48]

On 6 June Saladin was informed that a large Christian force had moved out of Ascalon and had camped 19 miles (31 kilometres) inland at Tell al-Safiya (Blanchegarde).[49] From there they moved north and on 9 June they camped beyond Latrun, taking by surprise a Muslim raiding party returning from Jaffa. Next day they advanced to Beit-Nuba. It had taken five days to accomplish the journey which the previous year had taken them two months. According to Ambroise, who describes the happy and confident mood, their only losses were two soldiers who died of snake bites. Henry of Champagne had gone to Acre to fetch reinforcements and Richard ordered his men to wait for their arrival. Apart from the usual skirmishing between foraging and reconnaissance patrols the main army was left in peace. Ambroise reports that in the course of one skirmish the king rode to the top of a hill from where he had a clear view of Jerusalem: this may well have been the hill known as Montjoie, the spot from which the men of the First Crusade first saw the Holy City.[50] It was the nearest Richard ever came to Jerusalem. In thirteenth-century legend this moment was given a more dramatic turn: when the king realized that he was within sight of Jerusalem he flung up his shield to cover his eyes and, weeping, begged God that he might not have to look upon the city if he could not deliver it.[51]

To the soldiers kicking their heels at Beit Nuba, Count Henry seemed an interminable time coming. Meanwhile they had to endure dawn raids and ambushes. Ambroise describes two skirmishes in detail, from close up. Baha al-Din makes the strategic position clear. 'The road from Jaffa to the enemy's camp was permanently crowded with convoys of provisions for the Franks, and Saladin ordered our forward troops to take every opportunity of attacking them.'[52] As so often in the history of the crusades the convenient discovery of a relic helped to keep up morale. Apparently a fragment of the Holy Cross was in the neighbourhood, buried in order to keep it out of infidel hands. Richard and his knights were led to the spot by the man who had hidden it:

---

[48] Ambroise, 9550–720. Only Richard de Templo provides a date for his announcement, 4 June, *Itin.*, Bk 5, ch. 46.

[49] Baha al-Din, 340; Imad al-Din, 379.

[50] Ambroise, 9748–884. Imad al-Din, 380 reports an unsuccessful Frankish sortie to within five miles of Jerusalem.

[51] Joinville, *Histoire de Saint Louis*, English trans. M. R. B. Shaw, *Chronicles of the Crusades*, 304–5.

[52] Ambroise, 9885–10,088; Baha al-Din, 341–42.

Abbot of Saint Elias, who fed
On nothing more than roots and bread.
With his great beard that grew untrimmed
A very holy man he seemed.[53]

Finding this piece of the Cross comforted some, but as far as the leaders of the crusade were concerned nothing had changed. They were back where they had been six months earlier. Once again the French were for pushing ahead with a siege of Jerusalem, and Richard against it, pointing out that once they were in the hill country around Jerusalem Saladin would be able to cut the supply line to Jaffa. According to Ambroise, he added that he knew there were people in France who would love to be able to report that he had led the army into a disastrous trap, but he had no intention of putting his reputation so foolishly at risk. As previously, he emphasized the importance of relying on local advice. Eventually it was decided to put the matter to a committee of twenty: five Templars, five Hospitallers, five French barons and five from the Latin kingdom.

The committee opted in favour of an Egyptian campaign – as Richard undoubtedly knew it would, since fifteen of its twenty members were local experts and he was always careful to work in close consultation with them. His fleet was lying moored at Acre, ready to transport all their supplies to the Nile Delta. He himself was ready to lead an army of 700 knights and 2,000 men-at-arms, paid out of his own resources, along the coast road into Egypt. Here, it seemed, was the fruition of the idea which had long been in the back of his mind. The duke of Burgundy and the French contingent, however, refused to co-operate. For them it was Jerusalem or nowhere. Richard was prepared to go to Jerusalem, he said, if the army insisted, but he would not lead them there. He would go as their comrade, their fellow-pilgrim, but not as their commander.[54] It was at this point, on 21 June, that news arrived which, for the moment, reunited them all around a common enterprise of great strategic importance – and one, moreover, which called for immediate action.

Saladin was expecting reinforcements and supplies from the army of Egypt, commanded by al-Adil's half brother, Falak al-Din. Richard, whose whole strategy was based on an understanding of the place of Egypt in Saladin's empire, knew how important this army was and had taken steps to ensure that he was kept well informed. When the Egyptian army, accompanied by a great caravan of camels, mules and merchants, left Bilbeis for Jerusalem, it never suspected, wrote Baha al-Din, that 'Arab miscreants' were keeping the enemy informed of its movements. Throughout it had

---

[53] Ambroise, 10,089–139.
[54] Ibid., 10,140–252. In Ambroise's view, to besiege Jerusalem then would have been 'great folly', 10,263–6.

been a war in which both sides knew a great deal about their opponents' plans. Fought in a country where the overwhelming bulk of the population either was Muslim or spoke Arabic and dressed in Arab fashion, at the 'civilian' level it was impossible to tell friend from foe. Scouts and spies moved freely from one side to the other. According to Ambroise, 'Bernard the spy, a man born in Syria', and two other well-paid 'barbarians' indistinguishable in dress and speech from the Muslims, brought the crucial information to Richard on 21 June.

He left the camp at Beit Nuba that same evening, taking 500 knights and 1,000 sergeants with him, and accompanied, in return for a one-third share of the plunder, by the duke of Burgundy and the French. They made a forced march, most of the way by moonlight, to Galatie, where they waited until refreshed with food and drink brought from Ascalon.[55] On the same day (22 June) Saladin received intelligence that Richard had moved off southwards. He promptly sent a force under high-ranking officers to warn and reinforce the caravan. However, on the 23rd, while Richard moved to al-Hasi, Falak al-Din decided to take the shortest route and then camp for the night at Tell al-Khuwialifia (The Round Cistern), 14 miles from al-Hasi, rather than risk a night march in which they might lose cohesion. When Richard's scouts reported this he was sceptical and sent out another patrol, disguised as Bedouin, to check the information.[56] It was confirmed. His troops ate and, more important, the horses were given a feed of barley. Then they rode the 14 miles to attack just after daybreak when the camels were being loaded up. Ambroise dwells on the fighting – in which 'the noble and the most fearless king / surpassed them all in everything' – and then with delight on the immense variety and quantity of booty that was gained and distributed.[57] The greater part of the army scattered into the desert and managed to get back to Egypt. Baha al-Din commented that 'those Egyptian soldiers who passed for brave men were happy to owe their lives to the speed of their horses'. He estimated that about 500 men, 3,000 camels and as many horses were captured. Richard's contemporaries rightly regarded this as one of his greatest military enterprises. Strategically it was an important strike, seriously disrupting the army of Egypt and depriving Saladin of the massive reinforcement in men, arms and transport on which he had been counting. 'This was a most disgraceful event; it was long since Islam had suffered so serious a disaster. . . . I was in the Sultan's tent when one of the young mamluks attached to

---

[55] Ibid., 10,269–312.

[56] Baha al-Din, 343–4. For his view of this night reconnaissance patrol see above, 17.

[57] Ambroise, 10,509–96. The loot included notes made by the geographer al-Harawi. On this see above, 23.

the stables came in and told what had just happened. Never was the Sultan more grieved or rendered more anxious.'[58]

His response was to order that cisterns around Jerusalem be destroyed and wells filled in. Baha al-Din gives a graphic picture of the alarm at Saladin's headquarters – the emirs urging that rather than allow themselves to be cooped up in Jerusalem they should seek a battle in the field. Victory in battle would turn the tide. If defeated they could at least escape; the fate of Acre still weighed heavily. By Friday, 3 July it was decided that the situation was so dangerous that Saladin himself ought no longer to remain there, and that command in the city should be handed over to his great-nephew. Saladin performed the Friday prayer in the Aqsa mosque with tears pouring down his cheeks.

But that evening his forward troops informed him that the Franks had moved out of the camp and then back again, a manoeuvre which shouted of indecision.[59] Although by the time (29 June) Richard's troops, glorying in their triumph and new-found wealth, returned to their bases at Ramla and Beit Nuba, Count Henry had arrived there, the basic situation remained unaltered. Exciting though these episodes were, for the pious they were no substitute for a siege of Jerusalem; indeed the grumblers moaned at the rise in barley prices caused by the demand from so many captured animals. The army was hopelessly split into two camps and condemned to ineffectiveness.[60] Saladin's destruction of the cisterns had added a new problem for any besieging force. The French grumbled about the delay which – they somewhat heatedly claimed – had given him time to do this.[61] Hugh of Burgundy composed an insulting song about Richard, and his troops relieved their feelings by singing it loudly; Richard replied in a similar vein.[62] However, apart from this minor contribution to the troubadours' art the army achieved nothing.

On 4 July the withdrawal began. For Richard it must have been a day of misery. In agreeing to stay on in the Holy Land he had risked far more than the rest. For all he knew, he might already have succeeded in losing the Angevin empire. By various routes the army returned to the coast. Saladin was worried that Richard might invade Egypt, especially now that he had so

---

[58] Baha al-Din, 344–5.

[59] Ibid., 346–51.

[60] Ambroise's references to the First Crusade (8494–518) are to contrast the harmony which he believed existed in the Christian army then with the divisions he saw now; it was not, *pace* Markowsi, 'Richard Lionheart', 362, in order to advocate any particular military strategy.

[61] The question of water for men and animals was central to Baha al-Din's reconstruction of the debate between the enthusiastic French and the realistic Richard, Baha al-Din, 14, 351–2. Had they advanced directly to Jerusalem from Beit Nuba they would not have been able to take the army of Egypt by surprise.

[62] Ambroise, 10,593–662.

many camels and pack animals.[63] From a military point of view, even at this juncture an invasion of Egypt would have been a far graver threat to Saladin than an attack on Jerusalem. The problem was, as Lyons and Jackson point out, that 'the crusading force was too deeply disunited and too urgently in need of a quick solution to follow the dictates of grand strategy. Its discipline and unity depended on the prospect of an attack on Jerusalem and when this finally vanished the initiative had at last returned to Saladin.'[64] Should Jerusalem have been besieged, since the prospect of doing so gave the crusader army what fragile unity it possessed? Some modern historians would still answer yes. According to this line of argument, 'the point is not that Richard could have taken Jerusalem, but rather that any good crusader should have done what the army expected, what the pope and crusade preachers expected, and what Saladin expected: make the attempt to enter the city.'[65] But what the prospect of a siege could do, the realities of a siege could undo. Saladin and his advisers naturally preferred to see the crusader army break up and return home without laying siege to Jerusalem, but although the Muslims had been disheartened by the events of the last twelve months there is little doubt that, for all their present alarm, they would have taken heart again had they seen the crusaders caught in the hills of Jerusalem, short of supplies and water and exposed to attacks by reinforcements from al-Adil, al-Afdal and the easterners.[66] The coastal strip could be reconquered by exclusively military methods, exploiting the crucial advantage that their mastery of the sea gave the Christians, but only by negotiation was there any realistic hope of recovering Jerusalem itself. For negotiations from a position of strength there were only two possible scenarios: either military pressure on Egypt, sending war galleys and supplies up the river Nile, or the death of Saladin followed by succession disputes and the break-up of his empire. Either way, a substantial crusader army would be required, not the rump that would be left behind after the pilgrims had prayed at the holy places of Jerusalem and then gone home, their vows fulfilled. It was for this reason that the local military experts advised that an attack on Jerusalem should remain a prospect, and only a prospect.

It was a profoundly unpopular decision, and throughout the West people looked around for someone to blame. Roger of Howden asserted that Richard wanted to besiege Jerusalem but was prevented from doing so because the duke of Burgundy, on the instructions of the king of France,

---

[63] Baha al-Din, 352. See the discussion of the problems Saladin would face if Richard marched on Egypt, Lyons and Jackson, 352–3.

[64] Lyons and Jackson, 355.

[65] Markowski, 'Richard Lionheart', 363. Markowski, 360 also argues that Richard could have taken Jerusalem. Unluckily he uses the analysis by Lyons and Jackson in support of this contention – despite the fact that they were emphasizing the difficulties for Saladin caused by an advance on Egypt, not by an advance on Jerusalem.

[66] Lyons and Jackson, 355.

would not follow him there.[67] For a long time this explanation was widely accepted – even by non-English historians. In the Old French Continuations of William of Tyre the finger of blame was again pointed at Burgundy – this time out of an allegedly misguided concern for the honour of Philip and the kingdom of France which would suffer if the king of England won it 'after the king of France had fled'.[68] According to Joinville, the duke of Burgundy prevented a siege taking place 'because he did not wish it to be said that the English had taken Jerusalem'.[69] What emerges from the later consensus that it was Burgundy's fault is the belief that such a failure could not be attributed to the heroic Richard. But as Ambroise and other contemporary commentators make plain, in Richard's own day there were many, above all in France and Germany, who did not regard him as a hero – despite his heroics both before and after the second retreat from Jerusalem. In their eyes Richard was to blame; hence he returned home, his many victories tarnished with the brush of failure. This he recognized and he vowed to return.[70]

In resuming negotiations with Saladin – negotiations about which Ambroise seems to have heard nothing – Richard did his best to recover the initiative; as early as 6 July he asked al-Mashtub to take a private message to Saladin. 'Do not be deceived by my withdrawal. The ram backs away in order to butt.' Yet by saying 'You and I can go on no longer', he acknowledged his own war-weariness.[71] They were quickly able to come close to a settlement. By playing upon Saladin's reputation for generosity of spirit – 'On many occasions monks who have been turned out, have petitioned you for churches, and you have never shown yourself niggardly, now I beg you to give me a church' – Richard brought him to allow pilgrims into Jerusalem and to offer them the Church of the Resurrection. Saladin also agreed to cede the coast to Henry, 'your sister's son'. According to Baha al-Din the message they sent back to Richard was: 'Since you trust us with such trust, and since one good turn deserves another, the Sultan will treat your sister's son like one of his own sons.'[72] But there was a proviso: Richard had to demolish Ascalon. He, however, refused to consider the

---

[67] And he subsequently applied this same explanation to the withdrawal of January 1192 as well. *Chron.*, iii, 175, 183.

[68] *Chronique d'Ernoul*, ed. L. de Mas-Latrie (Paris, 1871), 278–9.

[69] *Histoire de Saint-Louis*, in *Chronicles of the Crusades*, 304.

[70] Coggeshall, 52, 91. Even Coggeshall, though lost in admiration for Richard's extraordinary courage and prowess and recognizing that he had recovered a very great part of the Holy Land, none the less (after Richard's death) pointed out that he had failed to complete the pilgrimage.

[71] Baha al-Din, 353. Al-Mashtub claimed that when he talked with the king of England after the council had left, Richard said: 'Act as mediator between the Sultan and me'.

[72] Ibid., 355.

demolition of a fortress on which he had spent so much time and money; instead he sent more troops there to remind them of the threat to Egypt.[73] He told Saladin that unless the terms of the peace allowed the Franks to hold on to the coast from Antioch to Darum, they would not accept it and, though both sides were weary of war and bloodshed, he would not be able to resist their insistence that he stay and fight on.[74] 'See the cunning of this accursed man,' wrote Baha al-Din. 'To obtain his ends he would first employ force and then smooth words; and even now, although he knew he was obliged to depart, he maintained the same line of argument. God alone could protect the Muslims against his wiles. We never had to face a craftier or a bolder enemy.'[75]

While the argument about Ascalon continued, Richard moved to Acre, arriving there on 26 July. He had for a while been contemplating a strike to the north, against Beirut. This promised two benefits. It would put an end to the disruption caused to sea communications with Tripoli and Cyprus by ships from Beirut; it might draw Saladin north, leaving Jerusalem to be attacked by forces from Jaffa and Ascalon. But if that was Richard's plan, it could not work because his intentions had been read by Saladin's advisers as early as 22 July.[76] In response, Saladin planned a surprise attack on Jaffa. His position was getting stronger as reinforcements came in from Aleppo and from east of the Euphrates (the latter under al-Adil) and if he could recapture Jaffa he would win back all the ground lost since the previous September. The day after Richard reached Acre a large Muslim army appeared outside the walls of Jaffa. Next day (28 July) the attack began. The events of this and the following days are best described in the words of Baha al-Din, an eyewitness. As the artillerymen and miners went to work, 'everyone thought the city would be taken that same day'. But they were first surprised and then discouraged by the 'hardy valour and determined resistance' with which the defenders held breaches made by artillery and mining. 'O what fine soldiers they were, how brave and how courageous.' Early in the morning of 31 July mines and fire of five mangonels combined to bring down a large section of wall: 'the wall fell with a fall like the end of all things ... a cloud of dust and smoke arose that hid the light of day. When it dispersed it revealed that the gap had been closed by a wall of lances and bills. Then indeed we beheld a terrifying sight, – the spectacle of the enemy's unwavering constancy, as they stood undaunted, unflinching, self-controlled in all their movements.' But that human wall too was brought down by stones from the mangonels. The garrison offered

---

[73] Ibid., 356.
[74] Darum cannot have been in a fit state to stand another siege so soon after the battering he had given it in May. Shortly after this he had it demolished.
[75] Baha al-Din, 353–9.
[76] Imad al-Din, 384; Baha al-Din, 360. See Lyons and Jackson, 355–7.

to surrender; they were granted terms and told to retreat into the citadel while the town was given over to the orgy of killing and plundering that constituted a sack. At this point Saladin received a message from his troops stationed near Acre telling him that Richard was on his way to relieve Jaffa. Saladin immediately tried to arrange a peaceful evacuation of the citadel so that he would control it before Richard arrived, but could not get his troops to obey orders. 'It was a long time since our troops had taken any booty or won any advantage over the enemy; they were therefore eager to take the citadel by storm.' A combination of heat, smoke, noise, their wounds, their excitement and their exhaustion meant that for the remainder of that day they would do nothing but continue the sack. While the town was pillaged, the citadel survived intact. Next morning at daybreak 'we heard the sound of Frankish trumpets'.[77]

Richard had received the news at Acre on the evening of 28 July and had at once embarked together with the Pisans and Genoese. Burgundy's French refused to help but Henry of Champagne with a force of Templars and Hospitallers took the land route south, only to be halted at Caesarea by a report that the road was blocked by a second Muslim army. Richard's galleys were held up by contrary winds off Mount Carmel, so it was not until the night of 31 July/1 August that his first ships reached Jaffa.[78] When dawn came, it looked as though Richard had arrived too late. Muslim standards were floating over every quarter of the town; the noise of the waves, the yells of the combatants and the shouts of 'There is but one God' and 'God is great' meant that those on board could not hear their countrymen's calls for help. For all they could tell, the citadel had already fallen. Saladin was still confident. 'The Sultan sent for me at once and said: "A force has come by sea to relieve them, but we have enough troops on the beach to prevent them landing."' Baha al-Din was instructed to supervise the evacuation of the citadel. As the hours went by and no landing was attempted, those inside began to give up hope; some of them laid down their arms and left the citadel. Eventually someone in the citadel realized why Richard was being so cautious. 'One of the besieged committed himself to the keeping of the Messiah and jumped from the citadel; he came down unhurt for it was sandy. He ran into the water, was picked up by a boat and taken to the king's galley. To him he explained how things stood. As soon as the king heard that the citadel was still holding out he made all speed for the shore, and his galley – it was painted red, its deck was covered with red awning and was flying a red flag – was the first to land. In less than

---

[77] Baha al-Din, 361–6. Inevitably Ambroise dwelt on other aspects of the days of smoke, chaos and killing in Jaffa (10,858–68, 11,040–66, 11,271–86). However, he too represents Saladin as trying to spare lives.

[78] Ambroise, 10,958–11,028. According to Baha al-Din, 370 he came with 15 swift galleys and 35 other ships.

an hour all the galleys had landed their men under my own eyes. They then charged the Muslims, scattering them in all directions and driving them out of the harbour. I galloped off to tell the Sultan.'[79]

According to Ambroise's more detailed account of the landing, crossbow fire had helped to clear the shore. Richard himself had been among the first to take off his leg-armour, jump into the water and wade ashore.[80] On that day, wrote the *jongleur*, the king's prowess exceeded Roland's at Roncesvaux. Once they had got a toehold on the shore, some of the troops were detailed to seize all the timber they could lay their hands on and barricade a beachhead. The others, led by Richard, pressed forward and entered the town. The Muslims were apparently still confident and entirely confused: some still had their minds bent on plunder rather than war; others believed that the garrison had already surrendered and were taken by surprise when it sallied out in support of Richard. In no time at all they were either dead or in flight. Saladin withdrew inland, his retreating forces harried by crossbowmen.

> The king gave his command to pitch
> his tent on the same spot in which
> Saladin had not dared to wait;
> And there encamped Richard the Great.[81]

Saladin's attack on Jaffa had been a brilliant and unexpected thrust. If it had succeeded it would have effectively cut the coastal strip of the reborn kingdom of Jerusalem into two separate parts, and it had come within inches of success. It had failed because the extraordinary courage of the garrison enabled them to hold out for, as it turned out, just long enough. Richard had arrived in the nick of time; and against him, his knights and his crossbowmen, there were no Muslim troops who fought in expectation of victory. Only a few hours later, and he would have found Saladin securely in control of Jaffa. More important still, having seized the initiative in this dramatic fashion, Saladin would have been well on the way to winning back his reputation of 1187 and to reasserting his authority over his emirs.

Negotiations were resumed at once – with Richard, as usual, making the first approach. That same afternoon he invited al-Adil's chamberlain,

---

[79] Baha al-Din, 368–70. The man who jumped was an unnamed 'mass-singing priest', Ambroise, 11,111.

[80] Cf. the leap which won him a place in Paradise (according to the fourteenth-century El Conde Lucanor discussed by Hook, 'The Figure of Richard I', 129–39).

[81] 'Richarz li maines', Ambroise, 11,128–238. The speed of the Muslim retreat meant they left their plunder behind – including, a particularly exasperating point, much that had, they thought, been recovered from the plunder of the Egyptian caravan.

Abu Bekr, and other leading Muslims to visit him. Once again Baha al-Din's report of the visit shows us a Richard very different from the stereotype. They found him in the company of several of the prisoners captured at Acre, high-ranking Mamelukes 'who were treated with great cordiality by the king, and whom he often summoned to his presence. He spoke half seriously and half in jest. Among other things he said: "This sultan is mighty, and there is none mightier than him in the land of Islam. Why then did he run away as soon as I appeared? By God I was not even properly armed for a fight. See, I am still wearing my sea boots". Then again he said: "Great and good God, I did not think he could have taken Jaffa in two months, and yet he did it in two days". He then turned to Abu Bekr, and addressed him as follows: "Greet the Sultan from me, and tell him that I beseech him, in God's name, to grant me the peace I ask. This state of things must be stopped. My own county beyond the sea is being ruined. There is no advantage either to you or to me in allowing the present condition of things to continue.'[82] Envoys went to and fro with great rapidity, Saladin still demanding the cession of Ascalon. Next day, 2 August, Richard announced through a messenger that if he were allowed to retain Ascalon, then peace could be concluded within a week and he could return to his own country without having to spend another winter here.

> Without a moment's hesitation, the Sultan replied: your king will have to stay the winter anyway, since if he goes everything he has conquered will fall into our hands. Yet if he, who is vigorous and at an age when he could be enjoying himself, can manage to stay here, far from his own people, two months' journey from his native land, then he should consider how much easier it is for me to stay here winter and summer, in the heart of my own country, surrounded by my household and my children. The soldiers who serve me in winter will be replaced by others who will serve me in summer. And, above all, I know that in acting thus I am doing God's will and furthering His cause. I shall not stop.[83]

These, as Richard must have known, were powerful arguments. Yet he still would not give up Ascalon, the key to any future Egyptian campaign.

Saladin therefore decided to try a surprise attack on Richard's camp outside Jaffa's walls before the army coming by land could link up with Richard's amphibious force, and while he was still desperately short of horses. Richard had too few men to defend Jaffa's battered and broken walls, and he could maintain the cohesion of his force better outside than

[82] Baha al-Din, 371–2.
[83] Ibid., 373–4.

in.[84] But his camp was a tempting target, and Saladin saw the opportunity. During the night of 4 August his cavalry moved quietly forward. From Ambroise's account it seems that the attempt to take the crusaders by surprise very nearly succeeded. Luckily Richard received just enough warning of their approach to be able to get his troops into battle array, though some of his soldiers were still only half dressed at the time of the first attack. The front rank knelt down, each man protected by his shield and pointing a lance at the enemy. Behind them were the crossbowmen, working in pairs; while one discharged his bolt, the other wound a second crossbow. When they saw by how much they were outnumbered, all were afraid. The king went amongst his knights, speaking words of encouragement and exhortation. The Muslims charged but stopped and veered away as soon as they saw that this formidable defensive hedgehog would not break and run. According to both Ambroise and the Cistercian abbot, Ralph of Coggeshall (who claimed he was told what happened by Hugh de Neville, one of the handful of mounted knights), this happened on a number of occasions. Both authors also say that the Muslims broke into the town, and had to be cleared out – according to Abbot Ralph, Richard and six knights being more than a match for 3,000 Saracens.[85] After confrontation and fighting from the first hour of the day to the ninth, the Christians moved over to the attack and the Muslims fled. That day Richard and his tiny band of heroes – Count Henry of Champagne, Robert earl of Leicester, Andrew de Chauvigny, Raoul de Mauléon, William de l'Étang, Hugh de Neville, Bartholomew de Mortemer, Gerard de Furneval, Roger de Saci, Henry le Tyois (the German) who bore the king's lion banner – performed prodigies of valour.

What of the king, one man surrounded by many thousands? The fingers stiffen to write of it and the mind is amazed to think of it. Who has heard of anyone like him? I do not know how he remained invincible and invulnerable among all his enemies, perhaps by divine protection. His body was like brass unyielding to any sort of weapon. His right hand brandished his sword with rapid strokes, slicing through the charging enemy, cutting them in two as he met them, first on this side, then on that.[86]

---

[84] Count Henry had come by ship from Caesarea, but left the rest of the land army there. There was also the problem of disease in a town full of bodies; it was to this that Ambroise attributed the illness from which Richard and many were soon to suffer, Ambroise, 11,318–20, 11,338–40, 11,683–90. Cf. Coggeshall, 51.

[85] Coggeshall, 50. According to Richard de Templo, two knights and some crossbowmen were sufficient for the job, *Itin.*, Bk 6, ch. 22; this is evidently based on a better text of Ambroise, which as it survives has a line missing after the mention of two knights, 11,579.

[86] This is Richard de Templo surpassing even Ambroise in his enthusiasm, *Itin.*, Bk 6, ch. 23.

Ralph of Coggeshall was just as enthusiastic, taking seven pages of printed text to describe the 'battle', and using the word 'incredible' four times.[87] People soon came to think of the confrontation outside the walls of Jaffa on 5 August 1192 as 'the great miracle at which the whole world wonders'.[88]

It may well be that the victory was won not by the charge of a heroic few into a mass of Saracens, but by the professional competence with which Richard arrayed his troops and by the poor morale of the Muslims, still suffering from the effects of their ejection from Jaffa and critical of Saladin's leadership. The terms granted on the surrender of Jaffa (for which Ambroise praised Saladin's generosity) had been a cause of great annoyance throughout the Muslim army for the soldiers felt they had been deprived of plunder which they richly deserved. Allegedly one of the emirs now told Saladin that if he wanted anyone to attack he should send for those servants of his who had beaten the men on the day they captured Jaffa, and had taken their booty from them. But for Baha al-Din too, 5 August was the day that Richard rode into legend. 'I have been assured by men who were there that on that day the king of England, lance in hand, rode along the whole length of our army from right to left, and not one of our soldiers left the ranks to attack him'.[89]

We are in the world of legend. One of the favourite stories told in subsequent centuries about Richard was how he dealt with a gift of horses sent to him by either Saladin or Safadin. According to Ambroise, Safadin 'the bold, the generous and the courteous' was so impressed by Richard's courage and prowess outside Jaffa that he sent him two fine Arab steeds.[90] There is nothing implausible about the gift in itself, but nothing is more improbable than that it should be made in the thick of the fighting. Doubtless there were occasions in which a man as much admired as al-Adil, could have been drawn into making such a gesture – but not when his brother Saladin was desperately trying to get recalcitrant troops to attack; in any case Baha al-Din implies that al-Adil was ill and hence somewhere else (since he could not have ridden through the night) at the time.[91] However improbable, it is none the less significant that Ambroise places his version of the story – the earliest known version – precisely here, on the occasion of 'the incredible victory'.

Again Richard reopened negotiations at once. On 8 August his envoy returned to Jaffa in the company of Abu Bekr who was bringing a letter

[87] Coggeshall, 44–50.

[88] Ambroise, 11,345–6.

[89] Baha al-Din, 375–6. And for his – rather more plausible – version of the 'battle' of Jaffa see above, 18–19.

[90] Ambroise, 11,544–64. For subsequent development of the gift-horse story, see 'Some Legends of Richard the Lionheart', Gillingham, *Coeur de Lion*, 183.

[91] Baha al-Din, 376.

(and two horses?) from al-Adil. Abu Bekr told Saladin, 'The king would not allow me to enter Jaffa, but came out to see me, and these are the words he used. "How long am I to go on making advances to the Sultan that he will not accept? More than anything I used to be anxious to return to my own country, but now the winter is here and the rain has begun. I have therefore decided to remain." '[92] But fresh troops came to Saladin, from Mosul on 8 August, from Egypt on 20 August, and more troops under his nephew al-Mansur on the 22nd. By this time Richard was ill and had a great longing for pears and peaches. He asked Saladin for fruit and snow, which the Sultan willingly supplied as a way of discovering what was going on in Jaffa. He found out that there were at most 300 knights there, perhaps as few as 200, that they were repairing the walls of the citadel but not of the town (presumably this is one reason why Richard had decided to do Abu Bekr the honour of going out to meet him) and that despite Count Henry's best efforts, the French had decided to go home. The chance of taking Jaffa was still there. His emirs agreed, all the more so when it was reported that a foray into the countryside around Jaffa had been opposed by a paltry force of no more than 300 riding on mules. But on the night of 27 August, as Saladin's augmented forces closed in around Jaffa, and Saladin himself moved up to Ramla, Abu Bekr gave Saladin the gist of an earlier conversation: 'when he had happened to be alone with the king', Richard had said, 'Beg my brother, al-Adil, to think hard about how he can induce the Sultan to make peace. Ask him to let me keep Ascalon. Then I shall leave, and then he with little effort will be able to recover the rest of Frankish territory. My only object is to retain the position I hold amongst the Franks. If he insists on his claim to Ascalon, then let al-Adil find me some indemnity for the expenses I have incurred in fortifying Ascalon.' For the first time Saladin learned that Richard might be willing to give up Ascalon.

Saladin halted the projected attack and seized the diplomatic opportunity. On 28 August he secretly sent a confidential servant to al-Adil. 'If they will give up Ascalon, conclude a treaty of peace, for our troops are worn out by the length of the campaign and have consumed all their resources.' That same day Hubert Walter approached the commander of the Muslim advance units, Badr al-Din Dildirim, one of Saladin's most influential emirs and known to be on friendly terms with Richard, and let him know that the king was willing to yield Ascalon without compensation. In the light of this, the next day Saladin's council approved the terms he proposed to offer: Richard could keep Jaffa and its dependent territories except for Ramla, Lydda, Yubna and Majdal Yaba; also Caesarea, Haifa and Acre with all their dependent territories except Nazareth and Sepphoris. On 30 August Richard denied that he had renounced his demand for

---

[92] This and the next two paragraphs are taken from Baha al-Din, 376–87. For Richard's radically new approach to Frankish–Muslim diplomatic relations, see Köhler, *Allianzen und Verträge*, 347–54.

compensation, but eventually said he would accept the terms, and that he relied on Saladin's generosity. On 1 September the final terms were agreed and a document drawn up. Al-Adil came to Jaffa, and waited in a tent outside the town until Richard, who was very sick, was brought to see him.[93] Richard was handed the draft but was too ill to be able to read the treaty terms and said: 'I have made peace. Here is my hand.' There was to be a truce for three years and eight months from 2 September 1192, the date when the treaty of Jaffa was formally sworn by the leaders on both sides. It was to include Antioch and Tripoli and the neighbouring territories of the Assassins. Muslims and Christians were granted free passage through each other's lands. The walls of Ascalon were to be demolished. The revenues of Ramla and Lydda were to be shared equally between Muslims and Franks. Richard had been given some measure of compensation.

It is clear from the circumstances in which the decision to attack Jaffa was made on 27 August that, setting aside the question of morale, Saladin possessed a huge strategic advantage.[94] He recognized this and emphasized the point to his emirs. But he still had to bow to their preference for a peaceful settlement. According to Imad al-Din – and he was one of the drafters of the treaty document – they pointed out that were his troops to disperse then all the advantages of which he made so much would disappear. The implied threat is plain. The question of morale could not be set aside. Baha al-Din's analysis of Saladin's reluctant acquiescence in making peace was all in terms of the needs and state of mind of his troops.

> The Sultan thought it desirable to make peace, because his troops had suffered a great deal, and their funds were exhausted; he knew that they were very anxious to return to their homes, and he did not forget the unwillingness they had shown before Jaffa when he had ordered them to attack, and they had refused to move. He felt obliged therefore to give them time to rest, and to forget the state to which they were now reduced; otherwise when he needed them, he might find that they had simply gone away.[95]

Although he feared that making peace might be a mistake in the longer term, 'he saw that at this juncture it made sense, for the troops had lost heart and were abetting each other in disobedience'. Coming on top of the defeats they had suffered at Acre, Arsuf and the Round Cistern, the failures to drive home the overwhelming superiority they had possessed at Jaffa at the end of July and the beginning of August were disastrous blows. Despite

---

[93] That Richard denied he dropped his demand for compensation until persuaded by Hubert Walter that he had done so, may have been a consequence of his fever.

[94] For a clear appreciation of the strategic situation, Lyons and Jackson, 358–60.

[95] Baha al-Din, 383.

the fact that the crusaders had twice marched away from Jerusalem, the courage, determination and fighting spirit, in short the morale, of the troops who fought under Richard's command was infinitely better. 'If they fail to obtain a truce,' argued Saladin's emirs (according to Imad al-Din), 'they will devote all their energies to consolidating their position; they will face death with high courage, and for the love of their faith will refuse to submit.'[96] Unquestionably this high courage had something to do with Richard's style of leadership. According to Ambroise, when he was ill he wanted to go for treatment to Acre, but Count Henry and the Military Orders told him that without him they could not hold Jaffa against Saladin, whose large army was ominously close.[97] His subjects may have praised him to the skies and beyond, but it is the words of those who had to fight against him which carry weight. Even when they knew he was very ill, they preferred to make peace rather than prolong the war.

Most Western contemporaries, however much they lamented the loss of Ascalon, seem not to have blamed Richard for it. Some, such as Arnold of Lübeck and even an extremely hostile observer, the Austrian 'Pseudo-Ansbert', explained why it could not be retained.[98] But the terms in which Ambroise defended the truce show that there were critics and who they were. Since everyone else was making for their boats Richard preferred a truce to leaving the land in danger. If he had continued the war Ascalon would certainly have been lost anyway, and perhaps Tyre and Acre too. He who seeks honour chooses the lesser of two evils. The French would not help, yet they were the ones who blamed him.[99] Inevitably then, Rigord, Philip's official historian, asserts that Ascalon was demolished because Richard was bribed; and in this he was followed by Andreas of Marchiennes and William the Breton.[100] Richard of Devizes adopted a different strategy in order to exonerate Richard from this French-inspired blame. His line was that the Christian position was so bad as a result of Richard's illness that Hubert Walter and the key members of the king's household saw that only a truce could save them from disaster. Hence although they were concerned to give the Muslims the impression that they were reluctant to make 'a most hateful and unwanted truce', they were in fact desperate to get it

[96] Imad al-Din, 389–91; Gabrieli, 234–7. Indeed at times during this last flurry of negotiation 'we', wrote Baha al-Din, 'were afraid that these talks were like the former ones – nothing but a means employed by the king to gain time – and by this time we were well acquainted by his methods', 383–7.

[97] Ambroise, 11,731–48, 11,795–8. Throughout these days 'each army could see the fires of the other. We heard the sound of their bells; they heard our call to prayer', Baha al-Din, 23.

[98] Arnold of Lübeck, *Chronica Slavorum*, ed. J. M. Lappenberg, MGH, SRG, 1868, 1930, Bk 4 ch.16 (146); Ansbert, 99.

[99] Ambroise, 11,719–24, 11,756–64, 11,843–4.

[100] *Sig. Cont.*, 429; *Philippidos*, IV, 382–6. See also Aubri des Trois Fontaines, MGH SS, 869 for the continuation of this tradition among French historians.

at any price; he further defended his king's reputation by putting into the mouth of the 'noble Safadin' a request that the terms of the truce be kept secret from the sick man.[101] According to Ralph of Coggeshall, Richard was now running out of money since, through an excess of generosity, he had held an army of Frenchmen and other foreigners together for a year.[102] Little of this, of course, is evidence one way or another for the realities on the ground in Palestine.[103] But it is evidence for the realities of the gathering storm of the propaganda war in the West.

Although the truce allowed Muslims to visit the market of Jaffa and Christians to visit Jerusalem as pilgrims, Richard did not go. Nor, when he was given the opportunity, did St Louis. According to Joinville, Louis IX's counsellors quoted the example of Richard's decision, advising their lord that if such a king as he went on pilgrimage to Jerusalem without delivering the city from God's enemies, then all other kings coming after him would be content to do the same, and would make no effort to recover the Holy City.[104] Whatever Richard's motives may have been, Saladin's advisers believed he was reluctant to see many pilgrims completing their vow precisely because he feared that if they did so they would be less concerned to take the cross again, in order to try again, as he announced he was determined to do. For this reason, they explained, Richard asked that Saladin should let through no one who did not have a letter from him or Count Henry; and for exactly the same reason Saladin rejected Richard's request, instead encouraging as many Christians as possible to take the opportunity.[105] Obviously Richard could not command his followers not to visit Jerusalem; instead he did his best to put the trip to Jerusalem on an organized basis in three parties under three experienced commanders, and he encouraged them to make offerings not to the holy places but to the fund for the fortification of Jaffa.[106] On the other hand it may simply be that he was too ill to travel to Jerusalem. Baha al-Din reported that his illness grew worse and it was rumoured he had died.

When his followers had fulfilled their vows, it was time to leave, though he was still far from well. He agreed to free ten high-ranking Muslim pris-

---

[101] Devizes, 74, 78–9.

[102] Coggeshall, 51–2.

[103] According to Richard de Templo, as late as August 1192 in order to stop people drifting away from the crusade Richard offered wages to all who entered his service: fifty knights and 200 infantry did so, *Itin.*, Bk 6, ch. 27. This passage too may well have been in his Ambroise text. See n. 85.

[104] Joinville, *Chronicles of the Crusades*, 304.

[105] Baha al-Din, 388–9; Imad al-Din, 394. On being informed of Richard's request, the French were furious, believing it was aimed at them. According to Ambroise, 11,839–62, most of them left at once; according to Baha al-Din, it only made them the more eager to perform the pilgrimage.

[106] Ambroise, 11,868–83.

oners in exchange for William des Préaux who had saved him from captivity the year before. Then he announced that he would pay all outstanding debts, and, according to Ambroise, did so.[107] Finally on the feast of St Denis, 9 October 1192, he set sail.[108] The Third Crusade – his crusade – was over. In that it had not taken Jerusalem it was a failure, but given the political and military problems with which Richard and his fellow-commanders had to cope, it is amazing that they achieved as much as they did.[109] According to Baha al-Din, Saladin left Jerusalem for Damascus on 14 October as soon as he had confirmed the news that Richard had sailed. Certainly Saladin feared that the coastal towns might be used as bases from which the rest of Palestine would be conquered. While Saladin was alive there was not much chance of that, but after the great Muslim leader was gone, who could tell? Saladin himself had grave misgivings. It was already obvious that his death would be followed by a struggle for power within his family. Had Richard stayed in the Holy Land until the next Easter – as he had once said he would, and as he nearly did, since 9 October was just about the latest date in the year at which it was safe to sail – he might have achieved his ambition. By one of the ironies of history, Saladin died on 4 March 1193, more than three weeks before Easter. But by that time Richard was a prisoner in Germany.

[107] Ibid., 12,263–88.

[108] Diceto, ii, 106, from where Richard de Templo got both this date, and the date – the feast of St Michael, 29 September – when Berengaria and Joan set sail. According to Howden, Richard sailed on 8 October, *Chron.*, iii, 185.

[109] The treaty of Jaffa was an 'almost incredible success which prolonged the life of the crusader states for another century', H. E. Mayes, 'Henry II of England and the Holy Land', *EHR*, xcvii (1982), 739.

Chapter 13

A CAPTIVE KING

On 28 December 1192 the Emperor Henry VI wrote to King Philip of France.

Because our imperial majesty has no doubt that your royal highness will take pleasure in all of those providences of God which exalt us and our empire, we have thought it proper to inform you of what happened to Richard, king of England, the enemy of our empire and the disturber of your kingdom, as he was crossing the sea on his way back to his dominions. His ship was driven by winds onto the Istrian coast and there it was wrecked at a place between Aquileia and Venice. By God's will he and a few others escaped. A loyal subject of ours, Count Meinhard of Görz, and the people of the district, hearing that Richard was in their territory and calling to mind the treason, treachery and mischief of which he had been guilty in the Holy Land, went to arrest him. They captured eight knights from his retinue but he escaped. He reached a town called Friesach in the archbishopric of Salzburg, where Friedrich of Pettau arrested six more of his knights. Richard himself escaped yet again, this time with just three companions, and rode hard in the direction of Austria. But the roads were watched and guarded, and our dearly beloved cousin, Leopold duke of Austria, captured the king in a disreputable house near Vienna. He is now in our power. We know that this news will bring you great happiness.'[1]

In tone and contents it is an extraordinary letter; one sovereign ruler writing to another about the capture of a third. Not so long ago the Third Crusade had witnessed the German emperor and the kings of France and England engaged on a common Christian enterprise; now the rulers of France and Germany rejoiced in the capture of their common enemy, the king of England, and they called to mind 'the treason, treachery and mischief of which he had been guilty in the Holy Land' – at first sight an odd way to refer to the commander who had defeated Saladin at Arsuf and Jaffa. How had it come to this?

---

[1] *Chron.*, iii, 195–6. The contents of the letter were drawn upon by both French and German 'official' sources, Rigord, 121–2 and *Annales Marbacenses*, ed. H. Bloch, MGH SRG (1907), 165. On the status of the Marbach Annals see W. Wattenbach and F.-J. Schmale, *Deutschlands Geschichtsquellen im Mittelalter*, i (Darmstadt, 1976), 120–4.

The fact was that too many of those who had left the crusade earlier than Richard had returned home humiliated – and blaming him for their humiliation. Foremost among them was, of course, Philip Augustus – Richard's enemy from the moment he had shamed Philip's sister, Alice. Philip made his way back to France towards the end of 1191. Roger of Howden travelled with him, and thanks to the historian's pen we can trace Philip's itinerary in remarkable detail.[2] At Rome Pope Celestine III absolved him and all who returned with him and after him from their oaths as Jerusalem pilgrims. But, according to Howden, Philip hoped for more from the pope than this concession.

> In an attempt to conceal the manifest wickedness of his nature, and setting aside the oath which he had sworn to Richard before leaving the land of Jerusalem, he complained about Richard to the pope and all the cardinals, saying much about him that was unfitting: that it was he who had driven him from the land of Jerusalem, and that he had never wanted to do anything for him. And he sought the pope's permission to invade Richard's dominions. But the pope forbade him to do any such thing, knowing that he was motivated only by envy, and told him he would be excommunicated if he touched him or his lands.[3]

Philip's propaganda war had begun. Disappointed by the pope's response, Philip left Rome and moved into northern Italy, imperial territory. Initially Henry VI regarded him with grave suspicion; as well as earlier tensions between the two there was the matter of Philip's friendship with Tancred of Sicily while on his way to the Holy Land. A well-informed Austrian chronicler tells us that Philip met Henry VI at Milan, and that they became allies.[4] Howden knew that in order to obtain a safe-conduct to pass through imperial territory Philip had had to promise fidelity to Henry, and swear that he had not helped, nor would he help, Tancred. However, he does not appear to know of a meeting with Henry VI, or at any rate he does not mention it. Nor does he appear to know of the alliance as late as the summer of 1192, when he stopped work on his *Gesta Ricardi*. Not until later in the 1190s when he produced a revised version of Philip's homecoming in his *Chronica*, and when he was writing in the knowledge of what had happened, does Howden assert that the emperor promised Philip that he would arrest

---

[2] *Gesta*, ii, 192–8, 203–4, 206, 227–30. He reached Otranto on 10 October.
[3] Ibid., 229.
[4] Ansbert, 100; Otto of St Blasien, *Chronica*, ed. A. Hofmeister, MGH SRG (1912), 56. This was probably in early December, see P. Csendes, *Heinrich VI*, 104. On Ansbert and Otto of St Blasien, Wattenbach and Schmale, *Deutschlands Geschichtsquellen*, 99–101, 113–14.

Richard if he travelled through his land.[5] This suggests that in 1191 the king of France succeeded in keeping his alliance with Henry VI a secret.

A second humiliated crusader was Leopold of Austria. When Acre was captured, Leopold of Austria had claimed a share in the triumph, and this meant a share in the plunder. His claim had been rejected. At the time it had seemed, at least to the English and Normans, a fairly unimportant incident; it is mentioned by neither Ambroise nor Roger of Howden. The earliest extant accounts of the episode, written by Richard of Devizes and Gervase of Canterbury, were composed after Leopold had taken Richard prisoner. According to Richard of Devizes, Leopold entered Acre with his banner, the signal of his claim, carried before him, but it was then thrown down and insulted – if not on Richard's direct orders, at least with his consent. The duke for the moment concealed his anger and withdrew to his tent. But as soon as he could, still full of wrath, he sailed back home.[6] What was it that lay behind the incident of the standard? Why did Richard humiliate Leopold? To understand what it was all about we have to look more closely at Leopold of Austria's position in the crusader camp. Leopold had reached Acre in the spring of 1191, somewhat earlier than the two kings. From the moment of his arrival he found himself cast in the role of leader of the German contingent. This was because Frederick Barbarossa had never reached the Holy Land; in June 1190 he had been drowned in a river in Asia Minor. After his death the great German crusade broke up.[7] Only a pitifully small remnant of Barbarossa's army managed to struggle on to Acre. They arrived in October 1190, carrying with them some bones from the body of the dead emperor – bones which they hoped would one day find a fitting resting place in Jerusalem. In command of this contingent was Barbarossa's second surviving son, Duke Frederick of Swabia. In January 1191, however, Frederick's name was added to the long list of those who succumbed to the diseases of the camp. Thus, when Leopold arrived, he found himself the most important German noble present. But despite his splendid family connections – he was related to both the Hohenstaufen and the Comneni – Leopold did not have the resources to make his presence felt in the Frankish camp. There were not many Germans at Acre; Leopold's own retinue was tiny; and he did not have the cash to attract other men to his banner as Richard had been doing ever since he reached Marseille. The duke of Austria remained an unimportant

---

[5] *Gesta*, ii, 228; *Chron.*, iii, 167. It was, *pace* Stubbs, at least a remote possibility that Richard would return through imperial dominions since they included northern Italy.

[6] Devizes, 46–7. Other accounts differ in detail, but all, whether English, French or German, agree on the central points, e.g. Gervase, 514, Rigord, 118, Otto of St Blasien, *Chronica*, 54.

[7] It had, however, contributed to the siege of Acre since news of its approach had worried Saladin and prevented him from concentrating his resources on the siege.

outsider in a camp which had split into two factions.[8] For him to raise his standard in Acre was totally unrealistic.[9]

If the kings of France and England had allowed Leopold's standard to remain there they would, in effect, have publicly acknowledged that the duke of Austria was entitled to share the plunder with them. Yet right from the start of the crusade, Richard and Philip had acted on the assumption that they would each take one half of their conquests. The two kings were being acquisitive, but not only that. For some years now the barons of Outremer, faced by a succession of political and military crises, had made it plain that if a king from Western Europe came to their aid he could expect to be able to wield power within the kingdom of Jerusalem – and to wield power he would have to be able to draw upon the kingdom's financial resources.[10] Since these resources now had to be reconquered, the agreement between Richard and Philip fitted perfectly naturally into the prevailing framework of political and legal custom. The problem arose in part as a result of Leopold's awkward position in the crusader camp; partly owing to the fact that the two kings were late-comers to the siege of Acre. The duke of Austria was certainly not the only one to resent the way in which the newly arrived kings monopolized the rewards. There were many barons and knights who, having endured the rigours of the siege for a year or more, now found themselves out in the cold. Robbed of their just reward, they were too poor to do anything but return home. Naturally they complained bitterly and, in a sense, Leopold was acting as their spokesman: he had found a role at last.[11] Undoubtedly, throughout the whole of this affair, Philip had taken the same line as Richard, but it was Richard who acted – and acted in a characteristically direct and high-handed fashion. An incident such as this can only have happened as the victors marched into Acre, or very soon afterwards. It follows from this that King Philip must also have been involved. But he was able to avoid a share

[8] The best-informed Austrian source admitted that Leopold's presence at Acre was not as splendid as was appropriate to his rank, Ansbert, 98

[9] This was first fully appreciated by Heinrich Fichtenau, 'Akkon, Zypern und das Lösegeld für Richard Löwenherz', *Archiv für österreichische Geschichte*, cxxv (1966). This is not how Otto of St Blasien presented it. For him Richard, Philip and Leopold were three equals, Otto of St Blasien, *Chronica*, 53–4. Similarly, so far as the Marbach annalist was concerned, Acre was captured by a triumvirate, *Annales Marbacenses*, 165.

[10] See R. C. Smail, 'The International Status of the Latin Kingdom of Jerusalem, 1150–92', in *The Eastern Mediterranean Lands in the Period of the Crusades*, ed. P. M. Holt (Warminster, 1978), 23–43.

[11] Richard of Devizes, 46, calls Leopold 'one of the old besiegers of Acre'. The kings of England and France were clearly 'young besiegers', but since Leopold himself only arrived in the spring of 1191 it seems that he had indeed become a spokesman for all those who had been there much longer.

of the blame. All accounts, even the English ones, hold only Richard responsible.[12]

The incident, minor as it may have seemed at the time, symbolized something. Richard's wealth, fame, generalship and military prowess were all enviable, and were envied. He made everyone else feel inferior. According to Ansbert, Richard usurped lordship over all, despised all others, lacked all respect for his own lord, the king of France, held cheap the marquis of Montferrat, and regarded the duke of Austria as a nobody.[13] According to Otto of St Blasien, after Philip had returned home – his lands were threatened! – Richard and Leopold continued the siege. When Acre fell Richard arrogantly claimed the victory as his alone; he insulted the duke, distributed the plunder amongst his men only and decided everything as he thought best. The Germans and Italians would not have put up with this had not they given way to the authority of the Templars. At last, however, detesting English perfidy and disdaining being subjected to the English, they and Leopold embarked for home.[14] Philip was at one with all the others on this subject. Everyone felt slighted. Richard 'was always suspicious of German courage', wrote an annalist at Cologne.[15] Leopold had good cause to hate the king of England.[16]

A third influential figure who returned from crusade before Richard was the bishop of Beauvais. He may not have been humiliated, but he had been Conrad of Montferrat's close associate. As he came back, according to Richard of Devizes:

> At every stage of his journey he spread the word that that traitor, the king of England, had arranged to betray his lord, the king of the French, to Saladin; that he had the marquis's throat cut, that he poisoned the duke of Burgundy; that he was an extraordinarily savage man, thoroughly unpleasant and as hard as iron, adept at deceit, a master of dissimulation.[17]

The Winchester historian can hardly be regarded as an impartial source, but the gist of what he says on this subject is confirmed by Rigord of St Denis. According to Rigord, Philip was so alarmed by a report that Richard

---

[12] Rigord, 118. Gervase, ii, 88 dates the episode to after Philip's departure, while Coggeshall, 59, places it at Jaffa.

[13] Ansbert, 98. For a similar impression of Richard at Acre, *Chronicon Magni Presbiteri*, MGH SS, xvii, 520.

[14] Otto of St Blasien, *Chronica*, 54–5.

[15] *Chronica Regia Coloniensis*, ed. G. Waitz, MGH, SRG (1880), 154.

[16] Not in William of Newburgh's opinion. According to him Leopold remembered a slight and forgot that he had been funded by the king of England, Newburgh, Bk 4, ch. 23.

[17] Devizes, 80.

had sent Assassins to France to kill him that he had bodyguards watch over him night and day.[18] William of Newburgh put it less kindly: 'the king of France joyfully seized the opportunity to defame the king of England ... the French raised a great scandal throughout the whole western world'. In Ambroise's words, 'God! What a foul thing to say! What an evil deed! Because of this evil deed the king was later treacherously imprisoned out of envy for the deeds he had performed in Syria.'[19]

By the time that Richard, homeward bound, reached Corfu – if not before – he must have learned of the extent of the propaganda war being waged against him, and of the threat this posed to his safe return. According to Diceto he was at Corfu at about Martinmas, 11 November.[20] If he had kept up this kind of pace on the overland route from Venice to Normandy he would have been back in his own dominions in January 1193. If he had returned at that date it would have been obvious to all, both contemporary writers and modern historians, that the arrangement he had made for the government of his lands in his absence had worked extremely well. He would have returned to an undiminished Angevin empire.

There had been some difficulties – as was inevitable when Richard had a brother as ambitious and as crooked as John; and Richard had certainly not helped matters when he named Arthur as his heir in the treaty he made with Tancred in October 1190.[21] None the less, for almost a year after the sealing of that treaty, Richard's chief official in England, William Longchamp, bishop of Ely, papal legate, justiciar and chancellor of England, remained in control of the situation.[22] His relations with John had been tense, and Richard had heard something of this in February 1191 while he was still in Messina. He had provided Walter of Coutances, archbishop of Rouen, with letters authorizing him, if need be, to take charge of affairs. But there was clearly no crisis, no sense of urgency. Walter of Coutances waited at Messina until Eleanor and Berengaria arrived there on 30 March, and then he returned with Eleanor at a leisurely pace, not reaching England until the end of June. Longchamp meanwhile had achieved an uneasy compromise with John, chiefly by agreeing to do all he could to help him to the throne should Richard die on the crusade. (In that event this was what any sensible politician would have done anyway; nothing would be gained by supporting the claims of a child as young as Arthur.) Throughout the summer of 1191 Longchamp continued to rule

[18] Rigord, 120–1.
[19] Newburgh, Bk 4, ch. 25; Ambroise, 8879–908.
[20] Diceto, ii, 106.
[21] Above, 136.
[22] For the events in England in 1191 see the narrative in Appleby, *England without Richard* and the account in F. J. West, *The Justiciarship in England*, 69–77.

England and John was accepted as the heir apparent. But in September the chancellor made a fatal mistake, giving John a chance which he was quick to exploit. Richard and John's half-brother, Geoffrey, now consecrated archbishop of York, decided to return to England in defiance of his oath to remain out of the country for three years. He landed at Dover, where Longchamp's brother-in-law was the constable of the castle. Discovering that the constable's men intended to arrest him, he took refuge in St Martin's Priory. Here he was besieged for four days until, on 18 September 1191, Longchamp's men went in after him and dragged him outside by his arms and legs, his head banging on the pavement as they pulled him away from the altar of the priory church.

   This act of violence reminded men of the death of Thomas Becket, with Longchamp in the part of Henry II. Almost to a man the English clergy turned against him; from that day there was no act of tyranny, no offence, whether political, sexual or financial, of which they did not think him capable. John and his partisans had no difficulty in stirring up such strong feeling against him that he was forced to flee the country in ignominy. Some idea of the propaganda techniques used by John's friends can be obtained from the widely circulated account of the scene on Dover beach one day in October as Longchamp, described by his enemies as being small, ape-like and excessively fond of boys, looked about for a boat in which he could cross the Channel. It is best left in the immortal, if unreliable, words of Hugh of Nonant, John's chief propagandist and, in his spare time, bishop of Coventry – a man of whom it was said (again by his enemies) that when he confessed a lifelong catalogue of sins on his deathbed in 1198, no confessor could be found who was willing to absolve him.

> Pretending to be a woman – a sex which he always hated – he changed his priest's robe into a harlot's dress. The shame of it! The man became a woman, the bishop a buffoon. Dressed in a green gown of enormous length, he hurriedly limped – for the poor little fellow was lame – from the castle heights to the sea-shore, and then sat down to rest on a rock. There he attracted the attention of a half-naked fisherman who was wet and cold from the sea and who thought that the Bishop was the sort of woman who might warm him up. He put his left arm round Longchamp's neck while his right hand roamed lower down. Suddenly pulling up the gown he plunged unblushingly in – only to be confronted with the irrefutable evidence that the woman was a man. The fisherman then called his mates over to have a look at this truly remarkable creature.[23]

According to Hugh of Nonant, Longchamp's servants eventually managed to rescue him from the fisherman but after further adventures of this kind

---

[23] *Gesta*, ii, 215–20.

the chancellor ended up in Dover gaol, where he was left to cool his heels for a week before being released and finding his way to Flanders. But although John's friends could assassinate a man's character, they could not secure for their patron the power which he coveted. As envisaged by Richard, the chancellor's place at the head of the administration was taken by Walter of Coutances – to John's intense disappointment, as he made clear by his conduct when King Philip returned to France.

By Christmas 1191 Philip was at Fontainebleau, 'safe and sound and impudently boasting that he was going to devastate the king of England's lands'.[24] On 20 January 1192 Philip Augustus met the seneschal of Normandy, William FitzRalph, at a conference between Gisors and Trie. There he produced a forged version of the treaty of Messina of March 1191. According to this document the Norman Vexin had been intended as Alice's dowry and since Richard had married someone else, Philip claimed that it should now be handed back to him, together with his sister. William FitzRalph and the barons of Normandy refused to comply with this demand. Philip left the conference in anger, swearing he would take the Vexin by force. His first step was to invite John to Paris. It was believed that he would offer to make John lord of all the Angevin lands in France if he would step into Richard's shoes and marry Alice (the fact that John was married already was evidently not a problem). At this point Eleanor of Aquitaine intervened. Hitherto she had stayed in Normandy but now she crossed hastily to England to confront her youngest son, who was just about to leave for France. Under pressure from his mother and Walter of Coutances, above all swayed by the threat that if he went to see Philip they would confiscate all his estates, John did as he was told. King Philip tried to organize an invasion of Normandy, but his nobles refused to join in an attack upon the lands of an absent crusader, so this plan too came to nothing.[25] Philip in any case had the vital business of the Flanders inheritance to arrange and consolidate. By early 1192 he had recognized Baldwin, count of Hainault as the heir to Flanders itself, accepted Eleanor of Beaumont as heir to Valois and Vermandois (for which she immediately conceded Péronne), and had himself taken possession of Artois. Since Artois included Arras, Bapaume, St Omer and Aire as well as the county of Lens, and the homage of the counts of Guines, Saint-Pol, Lille and Boulogne, this transformed the position of the crown in the north-east of France. These were rich lands and strategically valuable – well worth coming back from crusade for.[26]

---

[24] Ibid., 235.

[25] Devizes, 60–1; *Gesta*, ii, 236–7. According to Howden Philip also demanded Aumale and Eu. Otherwise his account of Philip's demands in January 1192 conforms to his account of the treaty of March 1191. Had he been shown a copy of the treaty as prepared by Philip's clerks?

[26] J. W. Baldwin, *The Government of Philip Augustus* (Berkeley, California, 1986),

Inevitably Philip's return meant that throughout the Angevin empire Richard's castles were put into a state of readiness.[27] These preparations achieved the desired effect. Only in Aquitaine did Philip succeed in shaking the loyalty of any of Richard's vassals. Taking advantage of the fact that Élie de la Celle, the seneschal of Gascony, was incapacitated by illness, a number of lords rose in rebellion. Chief among them were the count of Périgord and the viscount of Brosse. But once he had recovered his health, the seneschal lost little time in regaining the initiative. He captured the castles of the chief rebels and either destroyed them or kept them in his own hands. Behind the revolt lay not only the intrigues of Philip Augustus but also the natural desire of the count of Toulouse to recover the lands of which he had been deprived in 1188. It was here that the Navarre alliance, cemented by Richard's marriage to Berengaria, proved its worth. Berengaria's brother, Sancho of Navarre, brought a large force of knights to the seneschal's aid and together they took the war into Count Raymond's lands, advancing right up to the walls of Toulouse itself.[28] Thus, at the end of 1192, it was apparent that the Angevin empire, despite Philip's best endeavours, had held firm. The only real trouble was not in England but in Aquitaine, and even here Richard's arrangements – his choice of officials, his diplomatic marriage – had proved more than adequate to cope with the situation.

But in view of 'the scandal raised against him throughout the whole western world', just how was Richard to reach his own dominions? Because of Count Raymond's enmity any plan of disembarking at a north Italian or south French port and returning to Aquitaine through Provence would now have to be shelved. To travel by a road further east through France or the Rhineland would be to run the risk of capture by Philip or Henry VI. At Corfu the officials of King Tancred of Sicily would have supplied him with the latest news. Tancred, who watched all of the emperor's movements with great care, would undoubtedly have known of the Milan meeting between Philip and Henry VI, and of their alliance.[29] Richard's October 1190 treaty with Tancred, and the marriage alliance between the two families, was in any case sufficient to incur Henry VI's hostility. After the failure of his 1191 campaign, when his wife Constance fell into Tancred's hands, the emperor was planning a new invasion of Sicily and his diplomatic and naval preparations included treaties with both Pisa and

---

80–1. It was also agreed that he would have Valois and Vermandois if Eleanor of Beaumont died childless – a fairly safe bet since she was still childless after four marriages. Andreas of Marchiennes took a very jaundiced view of Philip's dealings with Count Baldwin in 1192, *Sig. Cont.*, 428.

[27] Devizes, 59.

[28] *Chron.*, iii, 194.

[29] Though Richard might have learned of it much earlier – from, for example, a visit which Andrew de Chauvigny made to Rome in March 1192, *Chron.*, iii, 193.

Genoa. For Richard to coast westwards towards Barcelona in the hope of returning home through Aragon and Navarre was to run the risk of being sighted and intercepted by forces sent out by Pisa, Genoa or Toulouse. Moreover, north-western Italy was Montferrat territory. The Mediterranean winter was closing in, and the longer he stayed at sea, the greater the risk of shipwreck; seaborne commerce normally came to a halt during the winter months. (The twelfth-century customs of Pisa went so far as to forbid all maritime activity after 30 November.) He could not return via the Atlantic. According to the great twelfth-century Arab geographer Edrisi this ocean was a forbidding sea of darkness, its sombre-hued waters torn by gales in which the waves rose to frightening heights; the English, he wrote, were the chief of the audacious sailors who ventured upon it, but even they sailed only in the summer. In any case it was impossible to reach the Atlantic. Sailing west through the Straits of Gibraltar was out of the question. Wind, current and the fact that the coasts on both sides of the Straits were held by Muslim powers combined to rule this out.[30] Richard was in a very awkward position. All the obvious routes home were blocked.

It seems probable that his aim was to head for the lands of his brother-in-law, Henry the Lion, in the north-east of Germany.[31] He may have planned to go through the territory of the king of Hungary.[32] If so, stormy weather and perhaps shipwreck meant that he came to land further west, between Aquileia and Venice, than he had intended. According to the most detailed story of his journey into captivity, that told by Ralph of Coggeshall, at Corfu he left the great ship on which he had been sailing hitherto and hired two galleys.[33] He now took with him only a few loyal

[30] Pryor, *Geography, Technology and War*, 13, 92, 196. Kate Norgate wrote that 'it is difficult to guess why he did not proceed through the Pillars of Hercules direct to England', Norgate, 265; but when she wrote historians had hardly begun to study such matters.

[31] According to a history written *c.* 1220 by an author attached to the Béthune family, probably reflecting tradition handed down by Baldwin de Béthune, he was aiming for Saxony, *Histoire des ducs de Normandie*, 87. Andreas of Marchiennes believed he wanted to reach his nephew the duke of Saxony, *Sig. Cont.*, 430; cf. *Continuatio Admuntensis*, MGH SS ix, 587.

[32] Arnold of Lübeck, *Chronica Slavorum*, Bk 4, ch. 16. He may have wanted to travel via Dalmatia and Hungary to Moravia. On the other hand Bela III of Hungary was married to Margaret, Alice's half–sister, and he may well have felt that Margaret would resent the treatment given Alice. For the feud between Leopold and Bela, *Annales Marbacenses*, 164. Both Coggeshall and Howden report Richard landing at Zara, in Hungarian territory – perhaps this is what he had intended, Coggeshall, 54; *Chron.*, iii, 185.

[33] Coggeshall, 53–4. His great ship was later seen at Brindisi, *Chron.*, iii, 194. It used to be thought, by me amongst many others, that the ship was called the *Franche Nef*. However, in a fine piece of detective work it has now been shown that this identification derived from confusion with Frankfurt am Main! H. E. Mayer, 'A Ghost Ship Called Frankenef: King Richard I's German Itinerary', *EHR* (forthcoming).

knights such as Baldwin of Béthune and William of L'Étang, some Templars and his most trusted clerk, Master Philip of Poitou, suggesting that he had already resolved that if his enemies would not grant him safe-conduct through their territories, he would try to get back without inform-ing them.[34] It was unfortunate that the shipwreck brought Richard to land in a region about as dangerous for him as it was possible to be; Meinhard of Görz was not only 'a loyal subject of ours', as Henry VI called him, he was also a nephew of Conrad of Montferrat. What Henry VI in his letter to Philip Augustus described in terms appropriate to police action – with Richard fleeing arrest – was seen rather differently by the contemporary Bavarian chronicler Magnus of Reichersberg. According to him, Richard's party was set upon and despoiled by local nobles who killed and wounded some of them, but the king himself and a very few followers managed to escape. He travelled through Carinthia, not knowing where he was going until, without realizing it, he entered the land of the duke of Austria. He was arrested by the duke's oficers at Vienna, where he was found hiding in a poor man's dwelling while preparing food for himself and his compan-ions.[35] Roger of Howden tells a different story. According to him, although Richard and his followers were disguised as pilgrims, their lavish expendi-ture meant they soon fell under suspicion. Realizing the danger Richard left Baldwin de Béthune and the rest of his household behind to draw attention to themselves while he and just one companion rode day and night until they reached a small village near Vienna. Unluckily, while the king was sleeping, his companion shopping for food was recognized by one of the duke of Austria's officers.[36] The small village is identified by an annalist from Zwettl – a house with close ties to Hadmar II of Kuenring, the lord of Dürnstein, and hence likely to be well informed on local detail – as Erdburg (now within the city of Vienna).[37] Most other contemporary or near-contemporary versions contain variations on Howden's theme of an attempt at disguise being undermined by conspicuous wealth or expendi-ture. According to an anonymous Salzburg annalist who was deeply impressed by Richard's fight against Saladin, the king was arrested on the Feast of St Thomas the Apostle (21 December); the same date is given in a

---

[34] Coggeshall, 54. In a marginal addition Anselm the chaplain is also named as one of his companions. Most of 54–5 is a later addition.

[35] *Chronicon Magni Presbiteri*, 519–20. A journey in the Alps in winter presented huge problems. Possibly he was now heading for Bohemia, since by this time he would have learned that Henry VI and Ottokar of Bohemia were at odds. Csendes, *Heinrich VI*, 113, n. 70.

[36] *Chron.*, iii, 185–6. Howden could have obtained his account from one of those who escaped the shipwreck, Peter of Poitou, later bishop of Durham. Coggeshall, 54–5 later came across a particularly dramatic account of the chase, which he claimed to have had from Anselm the chaplain.

[37] MGH SS, ix, 679, though curiously placed under the year 1212.

marginal addition in Coggeshall.[38] For those who thought in religious terms it was a judgment of God. For his revolt against his dying father, said Diceto. God only knows why, said Coggeshall. For insulting Duke Leopold at Acre, and for wrongs done to Leopold's kindred, Isaac of Cyprus and his wife, and for the suspicion that he had been behind the murder of Leopold's cousin, Conrad of Montferrat, said Ansbert.[39]

Leopold sent Richard to a castle built high on a rocky slope overlooking the Danube: the castle of Dürnstein, held by one of the duke's most power-ful servants, Hadmar II of Kuenring.[40] According to legend, Richard's faithful minstrel, Blondel, travelled the length and breadth of Germany in search of his missing lord. He visited castle after castle and outside each one sang the first lines of a song which he and Richard had composed together. At last, at Dürnstein, he heard the refrain. In its earliest known form, the legend was told by a Rheims minstrel in the second half of the thirteenth century.[41] There is not a shred of evidence to indicate that there is any truth in the story – but it was good publicity for minstrels. There was, in fact, very little mystery about Richard's captivity. Both Leopold of Austria and his lord, the Emperor Henry VI, were keen to take full advan-tage of their victim and this was best done by trumpeting to the world that they held the king of England prisoner. By 28 December Leopold had informed the emperor, and the emperor had written to the king of France. 'We know that this news will bring you great happiness.'[42] In no time, all of Christendom had heard the astonishing news that a king so much admired had been captured in humiliating circumstances.[43] Philip wrote at once to

---

[38] Ibid., xiii, 240; Coggeshall, 54–6. Diceto gives 20 December, Diceto ii, 106. Both Coggeshall and Diceto then moved to expatiate on the barbarity of the Austrians. After this time no one in England had a kind word for the Austrians: 'they are sav-ages who live more like wild beasts than men,' wrote the dean of St Paul's.

[39] Diceto, ii, 107; Coggeshall, 56–7; Ansbert, 102.

[40] *Annals of Zwettl*, MGH SS, ix, 679. Ansbert, 102.

[41] *Récits d'un ménestrel de Reims*, ed. N. de Wailly (Paris, 1876), 41–4; trans. E. N. Stone, *Three Old French Chronicles of the Crusades* (University of Washington Publications in the Social Sciences, x, Seattle, 1939). B. B. Broughton, *The Legends of King Richard I* (The Hague, 1966), 126–8; Gillingham, *Coeur de Lion*, 184–5. In recent decades a sexual element has been introduced into the relationship between Richard and Blondel, e.g. N. Lofts, *The Lute Player* (London, 1951) and A. L. Rowse, *Homosexuals in History* (London, 1977), 3. See below, 254, 265.

[42] *Chron.*, iii, 195–6. However, even Philip's biographer, Rigord of St Denis, strong critic of Richard though he was, believed that the king of England was unjustly held prisoner by the emperor, Rigord, 122. The annalist of Saint–Aubin reports the belief that in holding Richard, Henry was acting on Philip's advice, *Annales angevines*, 26. This was believed at Limoges too, *Chroniques de Saint–Martial*, 192.

[43] Ansbert, 105 writes of *fama velox* (rapid rumour). A copy of Henry VI's letter 'found its way' to the justiciar, Walter of Coutances, who had more copies made and circulated. Howden used the one sent to the bishop of Durham.

Leopold, reminding him that Richard had had his kinsman Conrad assassinated and asking him not to release Richard without consulting him.[44]

To Henry VI the news came as a godsend. He was in deep political
trouble. His Sicilian ambitions had, so far, proved to be both expensive and
disastrous. Within Germany itself he was facing fierce opposition.[45]
Germany was a kingdom ruled by princes. Although the Staufen king was
by far the greatest of the princes, for him to try to impose his own will in
every corner of his vast kingdom was to invite rebellion. But making concessions and compromises did not come easily to Henry VI. He was
inclined to insist upon his rights as king, come what might. In 1191 the
election of a new bishop of Liège had led to quarrels between two local
princes: the duke of Brabant and the count of Hainault. Henry's response
to the dispute was to try to impose a third candidate of his own, and by the
autumn of 1192 he seemed to have had some success. But then, on 24
November 1192, one of the rival candidates, Albert of Brabant, was
murdered by a group of knights who were widely believed to have been
carrying out Henry's orders.[46] The result of the storm of protest which
followed was that the emperor found himself faced with two major theatres
of rebellion: the Welfs and their allies in the north and east; and the
princes of the Lower Rhineland, led by two formidable churchmen, the
archbishops of Cologne and Mainz, in the north-west. With something like
half the princes of Germany in open revolt there was a very real threat that
Henry would be deposed; the name of Henry duke of Brabant, the
murdered man's brother, was being mentioned as a possible alternative
king. It was at this critical juncture that fortune delivered Richard into his
hands. He at once summoned the duke to bring Richard to his court at
Regensburg. The bargaining was about to begin.

For more than a year kings and princes haggled over Richard's body, the
body of a man who was a crusader and supposedly, therefore, under the protection of the Church.[47] But in the eyes of politicians the most valuable piece
on the chessboard of Europe had come on to the market and the bidding
for him was correspondingly fierce. Events in the Byzantine empire as well
as in England, France and Germany would depend upon the outcome of the

---

[44] Ansbert, 105–6. Whether or not this letter is genuine its place in this Austrian
narrative is clear: to explain who – i.e. not Leopold – was responsible for the accusation, later accepted as false, that Richard had murdered Conrad, Kessler, 258–9.

[45] P. Csendes, *Heinrich VI*, 106–14; J. Ahlers, *Die Welfen und die Englischen Könige
1165–1235* (Hildesheim, 1987), 158–9.

[46] R. H. Schmandt, 'The Election and Assassination of Albert of Louvain, Bishop
of Liège 1191–2', *Speculum*, (1967), 653–60.

[47] That Leopold was well aware of what the Church's view of his conduct would be
is made clear by the fact that when he agreed with the emperor the terms on which
Richard would be released, he included a requirement that Richard should get the
pope to absolve him from excommunication.

auction. The first deal to be negotiated was the sale of Richard to Henry VI –
a complicated matter since both emperor and duke were pursuing designs
of their own and neither trusted the other an inch. On 6 January 1193
Leopold of Austria and Meinhard of Görz arrived at Regensburg, bringing
their prisoners with them. The first meeting between Henry VI and Richard
I, the two rulers who dominated Europe in the 1190s, was a brief one.
Fearing that the emperor intended to kidnap Richard, Leopold sent him
back to Austria for safe-keeping. It then took six weeks of bargaining before
Henry VI and Leopold finally agreed terms, at Würzburg on 14 February.[48]
The word 'ransom' was not, of course, employed. But they decided that
Richard should pay 100,000 marks, of which the duke would have half. This
sum was disguised as a dowry for Eleanor of Brittany, Richard's niece, who
was to marry one of Leopold's sons the next Michaelmas. In addition
Richard was to release, without ransom, two prisoners he had taken in
Cyprus, Isaac Comnenus and his daughter. On his mother's side Leopold
was related to the Comneni and by helping them he could cover a good
piece of business with the veneer of a good deed. (Isaac was, in fact, released.
No sooner was he out of prison than he made a bid to seize the throne of
Constantinople. But sudden death – he may have been poisoned – put an
end to his hopes of a new empire.)[49] Leopold and Henry VI also agreed that
Richard should both provide Henry with 50 fully armed and equipped
galleys (with 100 knights and 50 crossbowmen) and come himself with
another 100 knights and 50 crossbowmen to assist the German king on his
next invasion of Sicily, staying until the conquest was complete or Henry let
him go. On these conditions Leopold was willing to hand Richard over to
the emperor, but in exchange he demanded 200 hostages from Henry VI as
a guarantee that he would keep his side of the bargain. It was agreed that
Richard should hand over 200 hostages to the emperor, who would pass fifty
of them on to Leopold.[50] All this had been a matter for Henry and Leopold
to settle; Richard himself had no say in any of it.

By now Philip had passed the information on to the man he believed
could make the best use of it. By mid-January 1193 Count John was already
on his way to France.[51] At Paris he did homage to Philip for Normandy and

[48] The text of the treaty is given by Ansbert, 103–5. This and other relevant documents are conveniently assembled in *Urkundenbuch zur Geschichte der Babenberger in
Österreich*, ed. H. Fichtenau and E. Zöllner, iv, Part 1 (Vienna, 1968).

[49] For this and for the later history of Isaac's daughter, Fichtenau, 'Akkon', 25–31.

[50] *Chron. Magni Presbiteri*, 520; Ansbert, 102–5.

[51] For the rest of this paragraph, Gervase, i, 514–15, *Chron.*, iii, 196–7, 204–5.
When John got to Normandy he found that the Norman seneschal, William
FitzRalph, had already summoned the Norman barons to a council at Alençon to
consider Richard's release. When they refused to accept John as their lord he went
on to Paris. Philip invaded Normandy but, according to Howden, the Normans, led
by the recently returned crusader earl of of Leicester, put up a sturdy resistance.

all of Richard's other lands including – or so it was said in England –
England. He promised to marry Alice (with Philip's new acquisition of
Artois as her dowry) and to hand over Gisors and the Norman Vexin to
Philip. As ruler of Artois Philip was lord of the coastal counties of Guines
and Boulogne. With the help of an accommodating count of Boulogne a
Capetian king of France was for the first time in history in a position to
threaten England from the sea. At Wissant in the county of Boulogne an
invasion fleet was assembled.[52] Meanwhile John returned to England to stir
up rebellion. He asked for help from William, king of the Scots, but
William would have nothing to do with such treacherous schemes. The
politic generosity with which Richard had dealt with the Scots in 1189 (the
Quitclaim of Canterbury) now reaped its reward. In England Eleanor and
the justiciars mustered levies to defend the south-east coast and, apart from
a few rash troops who were promptly captured, the invasion never materi-
alized. The best that John could do was to levy some Welsh and Flemish
mercenaries and use them to garrison the castles of Windsor and
Wallingford. He then claimed the kingdom, asserting that his brother
Richard was dead. A few believed him, but Eleanor, the justiciars and the
barons did not. They knew John and they knew that Richard was alive; a
copy of Henry VI's letter to Philip had come into the hands of Walter of
Coutances. They also knew that the bishop of Bath, Savaric de Bohun, had
seen the emperor – to whom he was distantly related – and had already
opened the question of Richard's release while Henry was still negotiating
with Leopold. Walter summoned the great council of the realm to a meeting at Oxford on 28 February 1193.

The council sent two Cistercians, the abbots of Boxley and
Robertsbridge, to Germany to seek further information.[53] On 19 March
they found Richard at Ochsenfurt, a small town on the river Main not far
from Würzburg. Duke Leopold was taking him to Speyer to hand him over
to the emperor. According to Howden, Richard received the two abbots
'affably and cheerfully'. They were the first visitors able to give him reliable
information on recent events in England and Normandy, so he questioned
them closely. Although he grieved over his brother's treachery, a poor
return for the estates and titles which he had showered upon him, he consoled himself with the observation that 'my brother John is not the man to
win lands by force if there is anyone at all to oppose him'. The abbots
accompanied Richard on the last three days of his journey to Speyer.
Presumably it is on their report back to the council in England that
Howden based his description of the king's conduct during this difficult

---

[52] Gervase, i, 514. Renaud of Dammartin had abducted and married the heiress to
Boulogne; in 1192 Philip recognized him as count of Boulogne, acquiring in the
process a powerful claim on Renaud's loyalty, Rigord, 138.
[53] The principal source for the next two paragraphs is *Chron.*, iii, 198–9, 205–6.

time: active, courteous, prudent, a man whose capacity to rise above the vicissitudes of fortune won the admiration of all who met him; he would have made a worthy emperor.

At an Easter court held at Speyer Richard had to undergo the ordeal of a show trial at the hands of the man who was emperor. Howden asserts that on 21 March Henry, through intermediaries, made demands which Richard, though in danger of his life, refused to accept. In reality, as Richard presumably realized, whatever Henry may or may not have threatened, his life was not in danger. The terms of the treaty of Würzburg meant that the outcome of the trial had been decided in advance. He would be condemned to fulfil its terms and this meant that Henry and Leopold needed him alive and even, up to a point, co-operative, otherwise the money would not be raised. None the less, since he was not a prisoner of war to be ransomed, some formality was required which would at least appear to legitimize the payment of a king's ransom. Next day, 22 March, before an assembly of princes of the empire loyal to Henry VI, he was accused of betraying the Holy Land (presumably by making peace with Saladin in return for a bribe), of plotting the death of Conrad of Montferrat (one of Henry VI's most loyal supporters was Conrad's brother, Boniface of Montferrat) and of breaking agreements he had made with the emperor. Roger of Howden does not specify what these breaches were, but Henry VI was almost certainly referring to Richard's alliance with Tancred of Sicily.[54] Two of these three charges reflect the war of propaganda waged by the king of France from the moment of his departure from crusade. To all accusations, however, Richard replied so forcefully and persuasively that he won the court round to his side.[55] Even William the Breton, Philip's court poet, was impressed. 'When Richard replied he spoke so eloquently and regally, in so lionhearted a manner, that it was as though he had forgotten where he was and the undignified circumstances in which he had been captured and imagined himself to be seated on the throne of his

---

[54] According to the Marbach annalist, an author close to Henry VI's court, Richard had sworn to do no harm as he passed through imperial territory on his way to the Holy Land, but he had lied, and had made an evil treaty with Tancred; later, having been bribed by Saladin, he had demolished Ascalon, noblest of cities, MGH SS, xvii, 164–5. This was presumably the 'treason, treachery and mischief' of Henry VI's letter. The Marbach annalist does not mention the assassination of Montferrat; perhaps by the time he wrote this charge had been 'disproved'. Cf. Peter of Eboli, *Liber ad honorem Augusti*, ed. G. G. Siragusa (Rome, 1905–6), 75 for the perception of Richard's dealings with Tancred as an infringement of imperial rights. According to Coggeshall, 59, Richard's treatment of Leopold and Isaac was added to the charges against him; but even if the insult offered to Leopold and the Germans at Acre was his 'real crime', it is unlikely that this matter was raised in the formal proceedings.

[55] Coggeshall reveals how much he was impressed by Richard's dialectical skill and eloquence, which he believed he displayed to the full at Speyer, *ut est facundissimus*, Coggeshall, 59–60.

ancestors at Lincoln or at Caen.'[56] Sensing the mood of the meeting, Henry VI dropped his accusations and instead praised Richard, giving him the kiss of peace and promising to bring about a reconciliation between him and King Philip. This scene moved the onlookers to weep with joy. On 23 March Leopold formally gave Richard into the emperor's custody.[57] Kiss or no kiss, he still had to pay the emperor for his freedom. On 25 March he agreed to pay 100,000 marks and supply Henry with the services of 50 galleys and 200 knights for a year. This, it was said, was the fee due to Henry for his trouble in reconciling the kings of England and France, a fee arranged by the good offices of the duke of Austria.[58] If seriously meant, this would certainly have caused Henry plenty of trouble. No sooner had the peace been agreed than envoys from Philip Augustus arrived and, in their master's name, formally defied Richard.[59]

To assist in the government of England and to accelerate the business of raising England's share of the ransom, Richard decided to appoint Hubert Walter archbishop of Canterbury. Hubert had been with the English advance party which went to Acre in the autumn of 1190 in the company of Baldwin of Canterbury. After the archbishop's death on 19 November 1190 he took charge of the English contingent at the siege until the arrival of Richard himself. From then on he had been one of the king's inseparable companions in Outremer and had won a great reputation as a soldier, diplomat and administrator. He had probably been left at Corfu when Richard began his bid to return home in disguise. At any rate he was still in the kingdom of Sicily when he heard the news of Richard's capture. He at once went to Rome, presumably to ask Pope Celestine III to excommunicate Leopold of Austria and to do everything possible to obtain the king's release, and he then hurried on, though beset with difficulties and dangers, to Germany where, said Richard in a letter written to his mother on 30 March 1193, he had worked hard and effectively on the emperor and princes to obtain Richard's release. The king now showed his gratitude and good judgement by asking Eleanor to see that Hubert was elected to the archbishopric of Canterbury, which had remained vacant ever since Baldwin's death; nothing, he wrote, apart from his own freedom,

---

[56] *Philippidos*, iv, 393–6, and William then gives Richard's words in direct speech. Presumably William heard about Richard's bearing from Philip's envoys to Speyer who, if they were not present on 22 March itself, were there very soon afterwards, and would have been told.

[57] Diceto, ii, 106.

[58] Consequently Henry agreed that if he failed to reconcile them, he would release Richard without payment. From Richard's point of view he had at least negotiated terms of military service slightly better than those in the treaty of Würzburg.

[59] For an expression of shock that a captive crusader could be defied in this manner, *Annales angevines*, 26.

mattered more to him than this.[60] Hubert and the two Cistercian abbots then took their leave and headed for England.

Richard sent to England for hostages and for ships to take him back.[61] This suggests he expected a release as soon as he had supplied the hostages which the emperor required. But Henry VI had no intention of letting this trump card slip out of his hand so quickly. Nor, indeed, did he have any reason to trust Richard. Despite the theatrical gesture he had made at Speyer he saw no reason why he should not listen to further approaches from Philip and play one king off against the other. He sent Richard, under close guard, to the castle of Trifels, in the mountains west of Speyer. This was to remove him from the German political arena where, as the proceedings at Speyer had shown, he had many sympathizers and, in effect, to place him in solitary confinement.[62] He was rescued from Trifels by the diplomacy of another old friend, William Longchamp, who despite being driven out of England had forfeited neither Richard's trust nor his office as chancellor. Longchamp persuaded Henry VI to allow Richard to return to the imperial court, which by now had moved on to the palace at Hagenau, and he also negotiated a date for the king's release: as soon as 70,000 marks had been paid and hostages for the rest handed over. Longchamp was then sent back to England with letters from both Richard and Henry VI exhorting the prisoner's subjects to find the money as quickly as possible. Richard's letter suggested various ways of raising money, urged the justiciars to set an example, and added that he would like to know how much each magnate contributed, 'so that we may know how far we are bound to return thanks to each'. As soon as Eleanor and the justiciars in England received this letter they issued orders levying a 25 per cent tax on income and on the value of moveable property, and appropriating the year's wool crop from the Cistercian monasteries as well as gold and silver plate from churches throughout the country.[63] Similar letters were sent to the other parts of Richard's dominions and similar measures taken – though possibly, except in Normandy, not with that high degree of bureaucratic thoroughness which characterized English government.

Inevitably, while all this was going on, Philip and John had not been idle. War had broken out in three different parts of the Angevin empire. In

---

[60] *Epistolae Cantuarienses*, 362–3. The text of this letter helps to explain how Gervase came to portray Richard as a captive king agonizing over Canterbury's lack of an archbishop as well as his own lack of freedom, Gervase, i, 516.

[61] *Chron.*, iii, 206.

[62] See Diceto, ii, 106–7 for the dark reputation which Trifels enjoyed.

[63] The texts of letters sent by Richard to Eleanor and the justiciars, and by Henry to the people of England, both dated 19 April 1193, are given by Howden, *Chron.*, iii, 208–11. The king promised to return to the churches plate to the same value. Cf. *Epistolae Cantuarienses*, 362, to the same effect. In 1195 the promise was kept, *Chron.*, iii, 290, *Itin*, Bk 6, ch. 37.

England John was able to benefit from the continuing uncertainty about Richard's future – according to Howden, John constantly asserted that Richard would never return – but even so he gained very little ground. The justiciars repaired and garrisoned royal castles, raised armies and succeeded in driving John's forces back into the castles of Windsor and Tickhill, where they were besieged. They were believed to be on the point of capitulation when Hubert Walter arrived from Germany on 20 April and suggested, presumably acting on Richard's instructions, that a six months' truce be made. If a great deal of money was to be raised quickly with John's estates in England and Normandy contributing their share, then domestic peace was essential. The justiciars, naturally hesitant about taking extreme measures against a man who might soon be king, agreed at once. By the terms of the truce John was allowed to retain the castles at Nottingham and Tickhill but had to hand over Windsor, Wallingford and the Peak (Derbyshire) to his mother for the duration of the truce.[64] In Aquitaine Ademar of Angoulême, claiming to hold his county as a fief of France – i.e. not subject to the duke of Aquitaine – began to raid the duke's estates in Poitou. But here too Richard's officials stood firm. Ademar's troops were beaten back and he was captured.[65] In the third theatre of war, Normandy, there was a different story to tell. Here Philip himself took charge of operations and succeeded in delivering a shattering blow to the duchy's defences. On 12 April the great frontier castle of Gisors and its near neighbour Neaufles were surrendered to the king of France.[66]

The decisive weakness here was political, not military. Henry II and Richard had spent huge sums on the fortifications of Gisors and the other castles of the Norman Vexin, but Philip did not have to try his strength against this massive bulwark. Gisors was not blockaded or battered into submission. When Philip laid siege to it, the castellan, Gilbert de Vascœuil, yielded without a blow being struck. English and Norman writers were unanimous in condemning him as a traitor.[67] Unquestionably he did betray his lord's trust, but he was in a very awkward position and must have found it hard to weigh present against future loyalties. Gilbert had been in Sicily during the winter of 1190–1 and he was well aware that neither Henry VI

---

[64] *Chron.*, iii, 206–7; Gervase, i, 516 for Hubert's role.

[65] This is reported by the annalist of St Aubin, *Annales angevines*, 26, and inferred from one of the clauses of the subsequent treaty of Mantes, *Chron.*, iii, 218.

[66] Philip naturally argued that all he was doing was recovering the Norman Vexin so long unjustly held by Henry II and Richard, Rigord, 123. On this question see above, 77. This was a matter of great interest to a monk of St Denis since Philip's campaign resulted in the restoration of Châteauneuf to St Denis – in Rigord's opinion, its rightful owner.

[67] *Chron.*, iii, 206; Coggeshall, 61; Newburgh, Bk 4, ch. 34; Ambroise, 1166–7; *Annales de Jumièges*, 75; *Le très ancien contumier de Normandie*, ed. E. J. Tardif (Rouen, 1881), 108.

nor Philip Augustus had any cause to love Richard. If Richard were not released, what would happen to Gisors? On the day that John, with Philip's help, became duke of Normandy, Gisors would become a Capetian possession. No one else in the whole Angevin empire was as exposed as the castellan of Gisors. Many other frontier lords succumbed to the pressure which Philip exerted in the spring of 1193: the lords of Aumâle and Eu, Hugh of Gournay, William of Caïeux, Count Robert of Meulan and Count Geoffrey of Perche.[68] At least three of these men had been on crusade with Richard – William of Caïeux, Hugh of Gournay and Geoffrey of Perche; and to Count Geoffrey, Richard had given a niece in marriage. Yet these associations did not prevent them from making their castles available to Philip's troops. Their problem was that as Marcher lords they held estates on both sides of the border and could rarely afford to be unambiguously loyal to one lord only. They were always walking a political tightrope between the king of France and the duke of Normandy. It had been these same lords who had joined the revolt of 1173–4 against Henry. If they did not leap on the bandwagon in time they were always likely to be run down. Following Philip's acquisition of Artois the lords of north-eastern Normandy were in a particularly vulnerable position. It was hardly surprising that some of them won an unenviable reputation as turncoats in those difficult times when Richard was in prison or John was on the throne. But morally and militarily there were differences as well as similarities between their case and that of Gilbert de Vascœuil. They could claim that they had a duty to protect their ancestral estates whereas Gilbert, though a wealthy Norman landowner, had no estates around Gisors and Neaufles: there purely as Richard's castellan, his only duty was to his lord.[69] In military terms, moreover, the fall of Gisors and the other castles of the Vexin might have been crushing, for it opened the road to the heart of Normandy, to Rouen itself.

Without hesitation Philip advanced to lay siege to the ducal capital. He was at the head of a large army, including a Flemish contingent under Count Baldwin VIII of Flanders and Hainault, and – according to Roger of

[68] The Gournay, Perche and Meulan changes of allegiance can be inferred from clauses of the treaty of Mantes, *Chron.*, iii, 218; that by William is an inference from Richard's poem, below, 243; for Aumale, Newburgh, Bk 4, ch. 34.

[69] On Gilbert see Powicke, 96 and D. J. Power, 'Between the Angevin and Capetian Courts: John de Rouvray and the Knights of the Pays de Bray, 1180–1225', in *Family Trees and the Roots of Politics*, ed. K. S. B. Keats–Rohan (Woodbridge, 1997), 375–9. His main estates lay in the Andelle valley, far enough from the Epte frontier for his surrender of Gisors to be regarded as highly treacherous. By contrast the lords of Gisors were essentially a French family with some Norman and English estates; so there was nothing remarkable about John of Gisors opting for Philip in 1193. See J. Green, 'The Lords of the Norman Vexin' in *War and Government in the Middle Ages* (Woodbridge, 1984), ed. J. Gillingham and J. C. Holt, 58–9. And below, 273.

Howden's information – no fewer than twenty-three siege machines. At first there was confusion and uncertainty in Rouen, but the arrival of another of Richard's crusading companions, Robert, earl of Leicester, stiffened the resolve of the defenders. When Philip called upon the city to surrender he was told that the gates were open and he could enter any time he liked. The king of France was not the man to walk into an obvious trap. He settled down to a siege but seems to have been disconcerted by this obvious display of confidence on the part of the defenders. In what seemed to Andreas of Marchiennes to be an angry gesture typical of the man, Philip set fire to his siege machines and beat an 'inglorious retreat'.[70] In fact he had moved off in search of easier game. Verneuil held out against him but he soon captured two more border castles, Pacy and Ivry – and since Pacy belonged to Robert of Leicester its fall was particularly satisfying. Despite the setback before the walls of Rouen, April and May 1193 were wonderfully good months for Philip. From now on the castle of Gisors was to be a thorn in Richard's flesh.

It was probably soon after this that Richard composed his best-known song, 'Ja nus hons pris' while the desertion of some of those barons who had been on crusade with him was still fresh in his mind.

> Feeble the words, and faltering the tongue
> Wherewith a prisoner moans his doleful plight;
> Yet for his comfort he may make a song.
> Friends have I many, but their gifts are slight;
> Shame to them if unransomed I, poor wight,
> Two winters languish here!
>
> English and Normans, men of Aquitaine,
> Well know they all who homage owe to me
> That not my lowliest comrade in campaign
> Should pine thus, had I gold to set him free;
> To none of them would I reproachful be
> Yet – I am prisoner here!
>
> This have I learned, here thus unransomed left,
> That he whom death or prison hides from sight,
> Of kinsmen and of friends is clean bereft;
> Woe's me! but greater woe on these will light,

---

[70] *Chron.*, iii, 207; *Sig. Cont.*, 430; Gislebert of Mons, *Chronicon Hanoniense*, ed. L. Vanderkindere (Brussels, 1904), 285; *Annales angevines*, 26; *Annales de Jumièges*, ed. J. Laporte (Rouen, 1954), 75. Rigord does not mention a siege of Rouen in this year, see below, n. 98. Gervase, i, 515–16 was clearly delighted to write about the confusion of 'vaniglorius ille rex' – a total reversal of his former positive view of Philip.

Yea, sad and full of shame will be their plight
If long I languish here.

No marvel is it that my heart is sore
While my lord tramples down my land, I trow;
Were he but mindful of the oath we swore
Each to the other, surely do I know
That thus in duress I should long ago
Have ceased to languish here.

My comrades whom I loved and still do love
The lords of Perche and of Caïeux
Strange tales have reached me that are hard to prove;
I ne'er was false to them; for evermore
Vile would men count them, if their arms they bore
'Gainst me, a prisoner here!

And they, my knights of Anjou and Touraine
Well know they, who now sit at home at ease,
That I, their lord, in far-off Allemaine
Am captive. They should help to my release;
But now their swords are sheathed, and rust in peace,
While I am prisoner here. [71]

In a very real sense the events of these months were to cast a shadow over the rest of Richard's reign.

The defences of Normandy had been undermined by the possibility that Richard would never be freed. Normans may well have remembered another twelfth-century duke of Normandy, Robert, captured by Henry I in 1106, and still in prison when he died nearly thirty years later. Both John and, to greater effect, Philip played upon this theme for all they were worth. Philip, of course, did his best to turn possibility into reality. He arranged to meet Henry VI at a conference on 25 June.[72] Ostensibly Henry was going in order to reconcile the two kings, but Richard was convinced that if this meeting took place he would soon find himself in a French prison from which there would be no escape. Philip could offer the emperor either cash or political help, or a combination of the two. With Philip's assistance, for example, Henry VI might be able to attack the rebels of the Lower Rhineland from two sides at once.[73] At all costs Richard had to prevent this alliance. The prisoner became diplomat. Throughout the early summer of

---

[71] Translation based on that in Norgate, 278. For an assessment of the song, see below, 255.
[72] *Chron.*, iii, 212, 214–17.
[73] Newburgh, Bk 4, ch. 37.

1193 he was busy and eventually he succeeded in reconciling Henry with
some of the rebels. Owing to their vital commercial links with England and
Normandy the princes of the Lower Rhineland were inclined to listen carefully to what Richard said, while Henry was prepared to make peace if the
settlement included the money he needed to finance his Sicilian campaign.
The June meeting between Philip and the emperor did not take place.
Instead, with Richard as mediator, Henry came to terms with the Rhineland
rebels. He swore that he was innocent of complicity in the murder of Albert
of Brabant and allowed a new episcopal election to take place at Liège.[74] As
part of this same political process the terms of the king's ransom were re-
negotiated yet again and finally settled at Worms on 29 June. Richard
would be freed when the emperor had received 100,000 marks plus
hostages for an additional payment of 50,000 marks, which would have to
be made within seven months of Richard's release. Within the same period
Eleanor of Brittany would have to be sent to Austria to marry Duke
Leopold's son. The additional sum of 50,000 would, however, be remitted
if Richard were able to make good a promise he made concerning Henry,
the former duke of Saxony: Henry the Lion.[75] In other words, Richard had
managed to thwart Philip's plans but only at considerable financial cost to
his own subjects – though there was, at least, no longer any obligation to
provide expensive military assistance for Henry's Sicilian campaign.

   When Philip heard of this latest treaty between Henry and Richard he
sent John a message: 'Look to yourself; the devil is loose.'[76] Acting on this
belief the King of France made peace with Richard's agents in Normandy
in order to consolidate the gains he had already made. The first clause of
the treaty made at Mantes on 9 July 1193 simply stated that Philip could
keep all the lands he had taken.[77] Arrangements were made to enable John
to be restored to his estates on both sides of the Channel. After his release,
Richard was to pay Philip 20,000 marks in four instalments. As security for

---

[74] *Chron.*, iii, 214. Howden notes that the duke of Saxony (as he continues to call
Henry the Lion) was not included in the peace; if the price of peace had been that
he should renounce his duchies he would presumably have refused.

[75] It is not clear what this clause refers to, since it is couched in opaque terms,
doubtless deliberately so. One possibility that has been much canvassed is that
Richard promised to persuade Henry the Lion's son, Henry of Brunswick, to call
off his betrothal to Agnes, heiress to Conrad of the Palatinate, see Ahlers, *Die
Welfen*, 162–3. If Richard did promise to try, he is unlikely to have wanted to succeed later that year when Philip sought her hand in marriage. But it is more likely
that Richard promised to try to persuade the reluctant duke to accept the loss of
his duchies and make peace. See below, 247.

[76] *Chron.*, iii, 216–17.

[77] Howden gives the text of the treaty, ibid., 217–20. Loches and Châtillon were
to be given into Philip's keeping; Drincourt and Arques into the custody of the
archbishop of Reims. The costs of garrisoning all four were to be borne by the king
of England. For comment see *Annales angevines*, 26.

this payment four major castles were handed over: Loches, Châtillon-sur-Indre, Drincourt and Arques. The count of Angoulême was to be freed and neither he nor his vassals were to be in any way penalized for their war against the duke of Aquitaine. From Richard's point of view these were harsh terms but probably he now knew better than Philip did that it would be many months yet before he was free. In these circumstances it was worth agreeing to almost anything so long as a halt was called to Philip's advance.

The invasion of Normandy was only one aspect of Philip's war against Richard. On the diplomatic front the struggle continued. It was obvious that once released Richard would immediately begin the fight to recover lost territory. Philip still harboured hopes of launching an invasion of England and to this end had entered into negotiations for a marriage alliance with Denmark. On 15 August 1193 he married Ingeborg, the daughter of King Cnut VI. As a successor of the famous Cnut, the eleventh-century conqueror and king of England, Cnut VI possessed both a tenuous claim to the throne of England and a fleet.[78] Philip was interested in both of these assets but, unfortunately for Ingeborg, he had lost interest by the morning after the wedding.[79] He repudiated his new wife and tried to return her to the custody of the Danish envoys who had escorted her to France. They refused to take her back and departed in haste, leaving Ingeborg to her fate. For years Philip was to endure the condemnation of the Church rather than have Ingeborg as his queen. His dream of a new Danish invasion of England had became a domestic nightmare. In his pursuit of Richard, however, Philip was not a man to be put off by minor disappointments. On 5 November 1193 he had his marriage dissolved on the spurious grounds of consanguinity, by some pliant Capetian bishops – among them, of course, his cousin the bishop of Beauvais, who had performed a similar service on behalf of Conrad of Montferrat during the siege of Acre. The pope disapproved, but Philip felt himself free to look around for a new wife. Hoping to create some kind of counterweight to Richard's influence among the princes of Germany he proposed himself as a husband for Agnes, heiress of Henry VI's uncle, Conrad of Hohenstaufen, count palatine of the Rhine.

By 20 December 1193 so much money had been collected from Richard's subjects in England and in all his continental lands that Henry VI fixed 17 January 1194 as the day of Richard's release. The emperor also announced that he planned to make Richard king of Provence and had set 24 January as coronation day.[80] This plan, if it had been carried out, would

---

[78] On memories of the Danish claim in late twelfth-century England, Gillingham, 'Gaimar, the Prose *Brut* and the Making of English History', in *L'Histoire et les nouveaux publics dans l'Europe médiévale*, ed. J–P. Genet (Paris, 1997).

[79] *Chron.*, iii, 224–5. For a convenient summary of the extraordinary story of Philip and Ingeborg's marriage see Bradbury, *Philip Augustus*, 177–85.

[80] *Chron.*, iii, 225–7, including copies of letters sent by Richard from Speyer and by Henry VI from Gelnhausen.

have made Richard ruler of a kingdom stretching from the Alps to the river Rhône, and including the port of Marseille. Although this territory was in theory a part of the empire, in practice Henry VI did not have the power to impose a king over the heads of the local magnates. Richard would have been king in title only.[81] Yet since one of his vassals in this new 'kingdom' would have been the marquis of Provence, who was also the count of Toulouse, even this would have given Richard a legal lever which might have come in useful in his relations with this neighbour whose county he claimed. So far as Henry VI was concerned it would certainly add to the dignity of his empire, and might conceivably be a diplomatic asset, if the king of England, in his role as king of Provence, owed him homage.

But in the north Richard's continuing attempts to bring about a reconciliation between himself and his brother went badly wrong. When John, at Richard's invitation, left the French court to take possession of the castles of his Norman honours, he found that so little did the keepers of those castles trust him that they refused to obey Richard's writs ordering them to hand the castles over. He returned in anger to Philip and was consoled by being put in possession of Drincourt and Arques – those castles which, according to the terms of the treaty of Mantes ought to have been held by the archbishop of Reims.[82] John was now a desperate man. In a treaty made with Philip in January 1194 he showed why no one trusted him. He surrendered the whole of Normandy east of the Seine except for the city of Rouen and its environs; also Vaudreuil and the lands south of the river Itun, including Verneuil and Evreux. Further west he granted Moulins and Bonsmoulins to the count of Perche, whose ancestors had held these castles until 1168. Vendôme was granted to Louis of Blois. He recognized the validity of Count Ademar's claim that Angoulême was independent of the duchy of Aquitaine. Perhaps most serious of all, he surrendered the key fortresses of the Touraine: Tours, Azay-le-Rideau, Amboise, Montbazon, Montrichard, Loches and Châtillon-sur-Indre.[83] In the hope of ousting Richard he was prepared to undo all his father's and his brother's work and be content with an Angevin empire which was not only much truncated but also seriously weakened by the loss of vitally important frontier regions. This was conduct which can only have led Philip to despise John, a view which was to be of critical importance in 1199 and after.[84] For the moment, however, the two of them were bound together more closely than ever. Pooling their resources they approached Henry in mid-January 1194 with

---

[81] At any rate according to the realistic Roger of Howden, *Chron.*, iii, 225–6.
[82] Ibid., 227–8.
[83] *Foedera*, i, 57. For the date of the treaty see Powicke, 97, 99; Landon, 205, n. 6.
[84] 'Ille dolo plenus, qui patrem qui modo fratrem prodiderat, nec non et regis proditor esset', *Philippidos*, iv, 449–50. He had betrayed his father; now his brother and also King Philip. Writing *c.* 1196 Rigord, 126 too described John's treaty with Philip as 'in dolo'. See *HGM*, 10,163–70 for the view that Philip despised John.

a new bid. They offered him either £1,000 a month for as long as he cared to keep Richard captive, or 80,000 marks if he would detain Richard until the autumn (i.e. until after the end of the next campaigning season), or 150,000 marks if he would either keep him a whole year or hand him over to them. 'See how they loved him!' commented Roger of Howden.[85]

Henry was tempted. He may even, for the moment, have been feeling some sympathy for Philip Augustus. The king of France's marriage plans had been dramatically thwarted. Agnes's mother, believing that Philip's record as a husband left something to be desired, connived at her secret marriage to Henry of Brunswick, Henry the Lion's son and Richard's nephew.[86] Agnes's clandestine marriage did not amuse her cousin, the emperor, and their shared anger may have drawn the two kings closer together. Henry postponed the date of Richard's release and summoned the princes of the empire to another meeting, at Mainz on 2 February.[87] To this assembly came not only two of Richard's most trusted advisers, Archbishop Walter of Rouen and Chancellor Longchamp, but also his mother. Henry gave Richard the letters he had received from Philip and John for him to read. There were, as Walter of Rouen put it, 'anxious and difficult' discussions.[88] By then, however, it is unlikely that Richard was in any real danger of staying a prisoner much longer. A few days earlier at an assembly of princes at Würzburg the emperor had already decided to accept Henry of Brunswick's marriage.[89] This step in the direction of rec-onciliation between Welf and Hohenstaufen brought Richard a little nearer to freedom. Also at Würzburg in late January were Richard's old friends among the Rhineland princes, the archbishop of Mainz and Adolf, archbishop elect of Cologne, together with the duke of Austria, presum-ably keen to get his hands on the money and impatient of any further delays. Hence a coalition of German princes was already in place to per-suade the emperor to reject the advances made by Philip and John.[90] Even

---

[85] *Chron.*, iii, 229.

[86] William of Newburgh, who clearly enjoyed telling the tale of Philip's disap-pointment, believed that Henry VI had welcomed Philip's proposal, Newburgh, Bk 4, ch. 32. Cf. Arnold of Lübeck, *Chronica*, Bk 5, ch. 20 ; *Annales Stederburgenses*, MGH SS, xvi, 227. Ahlers, *Die Welfen*, 164–5.

[87] *Chron.*, iii, 229. It has indeed been suggested by some German historians that Henry blamed Richard for failing to prevent the marriage.

[88] Diceto, ii, 112 – from a letter written by the archbishop to Ralph himself.

[89] Indeed, according to Arnold of Lübeck, Henry of Brunswick had finally despaired of his father recovering his honours by military means and decided to try the path of a risky marriage. It seems to have been the failure of his mission to obtain armed assistance from the court of Denmark – presumably he went there after learning of Philip's repudiation of Ingeborg – that brought Henry of Brunswick to this point. H.-J. Freytag, 'Der Nordosten des Reiches nach dem Sturz Heinrichs des Löwen', *DA*, xxv (1954), 517–20. Jordan, *Henry the Lion* (Oxford, 1986), 197. Csendes, *Heinrich* VI, 142 comments on the speed with which Henry VI accepted the marriage.

[90] G. Baaken, *Die Regesten des Kaiserreiches unter Heinrich VI, Regesta Imperii* IV/3

so, Henry VI succeeded in further tightening the screws on Richard. On his mother's advice, Richard resigned the kingdom of England to Henry VI in order to receive it back as a fief of the empire.[91] He was to pay his overlord £5,000 a year. Richard was now a vassal of Philip for his continental lands and a vassal of Henry VI for his island kingdom, but it seems that in England few, if any, were willing to acknowledge this, and that this part of the agreement was hushed up.[92] At Henry's court, of course, it was regarded as the jewel in the crown.[93] And so, on 4 February, on completing the payment of 100,000 marks and giving hostages for the 50,000 marks still outstanding, the archbishops of Mainz and Cologne brought Richard to his mother. He was at long last a free man.[94]

According to Howden's calculations he had been in prison for one year, six weeks and three days. On his release he sent an envoy to Henry of Champagne and the other rulers of Outremer telling them that he would return at the agreed time to help them against the infidel – if he had peace and if God allowed him vengeance against his enemies.[95] On the day of his release Henry VI and the princes of the empire had sent Philip and John a letter telling them that they would do all they could to help Richard if everything that had been taken while Richard was in captivity was not restored at once. In return for pensions from his seemingly inexhaustible treasure chest

---

(Cologne, 1972) nos 331–2. The archbishop of Rouen, in a letter to Dean Ralph, highlights the part played by the archbishops of Mainz and Cologne in the negotiations between the emperor, the king and the duke of Austria, Diceto, ii, 112–13.

[91] The anonymous Salzburg annalist who was so impressed by Richard's prowess against Saladin (see above, 232) also emphasized both the investiture of Richard by the emperor and the presence at Mainz of Eleanor of Aquitaine, 'desirous of freeing the son whom she especially loved', MGH SS, xiii, 240. For the archbishop of Salzburg's presence at Mainz in early February, *Chron.*, iii, 232.

[92] The dean of St Paul's gives no details at all, but waxes indignant about some unspecified agreements made, Diceto, ii, 113. The details are given by Howden, *Chron.*, iii, 202–3, but only in a later interpolation in his own hand, added probably as late as 1201 (see Corner, *EHR*, xcviii (1983), 'The Earliest Surviving Manuscripts of Roger of Howden's *Chronica*', 309), and certainly after Henry VI's death, i.e. after the emperor on his deathbed had, or so Howden claimed, released England from its state of dependence.

[93] *Annales Marbacenses*, MGH SS, xvii, 165. Cf. the Salzburg annalist, MGH SS, xiii, 240. For Richard's oath remembered by Archbishop Siegfried of Mainz at the Fourth Lateran Council, S. Kuttner and A. Garcia y Garcia, 'A New Eyewitness Account of the Fourth Lateran Council', *Traditio*, xx (1964), 115–78.

[94] *Chron.*, iii, 231–3. Among the hostages left behind – in some cases not for very long – were the archbishop of Rouen, the chancellor, Savaric bishop of Bath, Ferdinand, son of King Sancho of Navarre, two of Henry the Lion's sons (Otto and William), Robert of Thornham, Baldwin Wake and a son of Roger de Tosny. Presumably ransom payments continued to be made after Richard's release, but when, in November 1195, the emperor pardoned the payment of 17,000 marks, this was probably all that was still outstanding, *Chron.*, iii, 303.

[95] Ibid., 233–4.

Richard received the homage of the archbishops of Mainz and Cologne, the bishop of Liège, the duke of Brabant, the duke of Limburg, count of Holland and several other lords from the Lower Rhineland, as well as from the duke of Austria, Boniface, marquis of Montferrat, the duke of Swabia and the count palatine of the Rhine.[96] Since Richard obtained no direct military aid from these alliances they have sometimes been judged to be expensive luxuries, but they were to become part of a coalition which was intended to hem in Philip Augustus and deprive him of his own most valuable ally, the count of Flanders – as was explicitly recognized at the time by the writer who knew the politics of this region better than any other contemporary historian: Baldwin VIII of Flanders's chancellor, Gilbert of Mons.[97] Philip, conscious that his last opportunity had come, set his armies in motion in order to take possession of the territories which John had surrendered to him in the treaty of January 1194. As yet, of course, John's grants existed only on paper. It was up to the beneficiaries to turn them into reality. Philip began in Normandy. In February he captured Evreux, Neubourg, Vaudreuil and 'many other strongholds some of which he demolished', thus gaining control of both banks of the Seine to within easy striking distance of Rouen. He threatened the ducal city for a second time before withdrawing.[98] He then went south to Sens, where he received the homage of two more of Richard's Aquitanian vassals, Geoffrey de Rancon and Bernard, viscount of Brosse.

While these further inroads were being made into his dominions Richard was on his way back to England. He went first to Cologne, where he spent three days with the powerful archbishop. In the cathedral the archbishop, as one of the choristers, on 12 February sang the mass for 1 August, 'Now I know that God has sent his angel and taken me from the hand of Herod.'[99] From there Richard travelled to Louvain (16 February)

---

[96] Ibid. For some princes at least these were in part promises of payment in return for help received in obtaining his release, ibid., iv, 37–8. For the whole subject of these pensions and alliances, A. L. Poole, 'Richard the First's Alliances with the German princes in 1194', in *Studies in Medieval History Presented to F. M. Powicke*, ed. R. W. Hunt, W. A. Pantin and R. W. Southern (Oxford, 1948), 90–9.

[97] Gislebert of Mons, *Chronicon*, 284–5. Richard, he said, promised to help the duke of Louvain (or Brabant) in his feud against Baldwin VIII, count of Flanders and Hainault and the marquis of Namur. It is hardly surprising that Baldwin's chancellor did not like the league, nor Richard, especially since one of those who received a pension was none other than Baldwin VIII's son.

[98] Rigord, 125–6. According to Rigord it was on this occasion that Philip, in an excess of anger, set fire to his siege machines. According to the annals of Jumièges, the citizens of Rouen, helped by the rest of the Normans, had put up a vigorous defence, *Annales de Jumièges* 75.

[99] Diceto, ii, 114; *Chron.*, iii, 235. Archbishop Adolf, then provost of Cologne, had attended the assembly at Speyer in March 1193, and may well have been one of those who had spoken up so effectively on Richard's behalf.

and Brussels (25 February).[100] At Antwerp, the main port of Brabant, he was met by a fleet sent from England. There he boarded the galley of Alan Trenchemer and sailed to Zwin, where he stayed five days. Not until 12 March did he decide to cross the Channel. This seems remarkable dilatoriness for a ruler whose lands were being invaded. Coggeshall noted the delay and explained it in terms of the weather.[101] Perhaps – but Richard was certainly doing more than just waiting and hoping for fair weather. Each night, Howden reports, Richard slept aboard a big and beautiful ship from Rye, and each morning he returned to his galley 'so that with her he could move more easily between the islands'.[102] Was this a pleasure cruise – or a reconnaissance of the Zwin and Scheldt estuaries and their islands? His brother's surrender of Normandy east of the Seine in January 1194 had allowed the king of France to take possession of Arques and Eu with their ports of Dieppe and Tréport. Philip and his allies were now in control of the ports of Flanders, Boulogne and eastern Normandy.[103] Richard, already more experienced in naval and amphibious warfare than any other king of England, must have been well aware that he faced a naval as well as a land-based threat. Some years later, in 1213 when King John faced a French invasion, it was precisely in the waters cruised by Richard's galley in 1194 that the English were to win one of their earliest naval victories, the battle of Damme.[104] Moreover, as Howden noted, 'Zwin is in Flanders, in the land of the count of Hainault.' Presumably the presence of Richard's fleet there (just downstream from Bruges itself) in March 1194 was meant to intimidate Count Baldwin of Flanders and Hainault and so to take pressure off the duke of Brabant who in late February had been facing an attack by Flemish and French troops.[105] If this is so, then Gilbert of Mons was wrong when he wrote that Richard's promise to help Brabant was one of those covenants which went unobserved. 'No wonder,' he commented,

[100] J. Falmagne, *Baudouin V, comte de Hainaut 1150–95* (Montreal, 1966), 278–9.

[101] Coggeshall, 62. Cf. 'Il est à noter qu'à cette époque de l'année, surviennent les grandes marées d'équinoxe qui rendent la traversée de la Manche quasi impossible pour une dizaine de jours', Falmagne, *Baudouin*, 279.

[102] *Chron.*, iii, 235. Howden probably got information from Philip of Poitou, Landon, no. 394.

[103] Coggeshall, 61, summarizing Philip's acquisitions in 1193–4 'usque ad Diepe'. Gervase of Canterbury reported a rumour that Philip was planning to ambush Richard at sea, Gervase, 524.

[104] And later, in these same waters, Edward III's great naval victory at Sluys in 1340.

[105] For the military operations against Brabant see Gislebert of Mons, *Chronicon*, 291. Although the chancellor of Hainault explains his lord's setback in terms of the weather, it is hard to see how his calculations can have been unaffected by the presence of Richard's fleet at Antwerp and Zwin. Andreas of Marchiennes also noted the presence of Richard's ships at Antwerp, *Sig. Cont.*, 431.

'since the king of England never kept faith or pact with anyone, nor were those with whom he made treaties accustomed to observe their covenants.'[106]

Richard landed at Sandwich on 13 March. The return of the king was greeted with great joy.[107] For William the Marshal the sad news of the death of his brother John was more than compensated for by the news of Richard's return; he decided to miss the funeral in order to hurry to meet him. 'Such joy have I in the king's coming that I can withstand the grief that I did not believe I could bear.'[108] At the shrines of Canterbury and Bury St Edmunds Richard gave thanks for his freedom.[109]

The long captivity in Germany had cost him and his subjects dearly. On the other hand, the provisions he had made for defending and governing his dominions during his absence on crusade had worked well. For more than two and a half years, from July 1190 to March 1193, the Angevin institutions of government functioned remarkably well, in Aquitaine, in Anjou, in Normandy and – despite the bit of trouble between John and Longchamp – in England.[110] Some of the credit for this must go to the seneschals and justiciars who were left in charge of affairs while Richard was away, and some also to the king who had chosen and appointed them. While Richard was on crusade, even though there were some observers

---

[106] Gislebert of Mons, *Chronicon*, 285. The jaundiced tone in which Gilbert condemned all parties – who just happened to be opposed to his master – should have warned historians to treat his words with caution.

[107] *Sig. Cont.*, 431; Newburgh, Bk 4, ch. 42; Diceto, ii, 114, on his reception at St Paul's; even the heavens rejoiced, according to Coggeshall, 62–3. *Philippidos*, iv, 428. *HGM*, 10,012–16. *Annales angevines*, 28.

[108] *HGM*, 10,018–86. The episode is nicely elucidated in Crouch, *William Marshal*, 72–4.

[109] Gervase's note, that Richard did not want to enter any English church until he had visited the mother church of Canterbury, suggests that Richard had learned how to handle the monks of Canterbury, Gervase, i, 524. Visit to St Edmunds, Coggeshall, 62.

[110] The system of itinerant justices continued to function in 1191 and 1192, but was brought to a halt by John's rebellion in 1193. Of course if an administration is judged solely, or even primarily, by the amount of revenue it collects then the government of England had done badly in 1191–2. English revenues audited at the exchequer had sunk to £12,418 in 1191, £9,857 in 1192, £10,506 in 1193. It may be that a respite was needed after the extraordinary effort made in 1190 (no less than £31,089, see above, 116 n. 64), but the revenue for those three years was very much less than had been collected in the latter years of Henry II's reign and would be in the remaining years of Richard's. (I owe these figures to the kindness of Dr N. Barratt.) But it has to be remembered that in the king's absence there was much less need to spend money; it would have been a gross political error to try to keep revenue up to 'average' levels. Although only £10,506 went through the exchequer between Michaelmas 1192 and Michaelmas 1193, very much more must have been raised once collecting for the ransom started in the spring of 1193. None of the accounts kept by the separate exchequer of the Ransom survive.

who feared that he might not return, it was possible – and simplest – to go on behaving as though he would. But his imprisonment provoked a totally unforeseeable crisis. The exploitation of this crisis by his most ruthless enemy, Philip of France, twisting John's ineffectual and treacherous ambition to his own purposes, forced men to face up to the possibility that Richard might never return.[111] With Philip on the move they could no longer just wait and see; they were compelled to weigh up the probabilities, consider their loyalties and choose sides. Since the leader of one side was in prison while the other rode with his knights it is hardly surprising that many of those who lived in exposed frontier positions chose as they did. Compared with the loss of support which King Stephen suffered in Normandy while he was in captivity – from February to November 1141 – Richard's continental possessions survived quite well. None the less Philip had encouraged some of the more restless lords of Aquitaine to rise in revolt and he himself had made strategically important gains in the Loire and Seine valleys, as well as in the north-east of France. On his return Richard was faced with a daunting task – and one that would inevitably involve heavy expenditure on war, to add still further to the already unprecedented financial burdens placed upon his subjects. One hundred thousand marks was a vast sum, a king's ransom, more than twice his total annual income from England.[112] Most of it had clearly gone into the coffers of Henry VI. In 1193 and 1194 there seemed no end to the emperor's good fortune. On 20 February 1194 King Tancred of Sicily died, and the heir to the throne was a small child. In May Henry marched across the Alps, his war chest full of Angevin silver. On 22 November 1194 he was crowned king at Palermo.

Of Richard's enemies there were two who had little cause to celebrate. The first of these was John. Once Richard had been released it was evident that John's gamble had failed miserably. His castles in England were besieged and were certain to fall. It was said that the castellan of St Michael's Mount in Cornwall died of fright when he heard the news that Richard had landed. In Normandy Philip had granted him custody of Arques, Drincourt and Evreux but even if he managed to hold them against his brother they could in no way compensate for the loss of the

---

[111] Twice Gervase described the king's return as *ex insperato*, 'unexpected', Gervase, i, 525, 526–7.

[112] Of course it did not come only from England. The abbey of St Martial raised 50 marks from its own estates, and 50 marks from tenants, *Chroniques de Saint-Martial*, 192, with the observation that contributions were required from all the monasteries 'of his kingdom' – by which the author certainly did not mean just the kingdom of England. For the large ransom payments noted on the Norman Exchequer Rolls see V. Moss, 'The Norman Fiscal Revolution 1193–98', in *Crises, Revolutions and Self-Sustained Fiscal Growth*, ed. R. Bonney and M. Ormrod (Stamford, 1999).

estates which Richard had given him in 1189. Even before Richard reached England, the council of the realm had declared John's estates forfeit and the bishops had excommunicated him.[113] The best he could do was to throw himself on his brother's mercy. He had achieved nothing except to cause some damage to the empire which he still had a chance of inheriting and to give the world further evidence of his ineptitude and treachery.

The second was Richard's captor, Leopold of Austria. For daring to imprison a crusader he was excommunicated and ordered to pay back the ransom money. He refused. He had spent a great deal (probably 26,000 marks) and expected another 20,000 when Eleanor of Brittany arrived to marry his son.[114] But seven months passed from the day of Richard's release and there was still no sign of the promised bride. He threatened to execute his hostages unless Richard sent his niece to Austria, and one of the hostages, Baldwin of Béthune, was given the task of carrying this news to the king. The threat worked. In December 1194 Baldwin of Béthune set off again for Austria, escorting both Eleanor and the daughter of Isaac Comnenus. But on 26 December, while Leopold was out riding, his horse fell and crushed his foot. By the next day the foot had gone black. The surgeons advised amputation but Leopold could find no one who had either the strength of mind or the heart to perform the painful operation. Despite the duke's pleadings not even his son and heir could steel himself to the task. Eventually Leopold himself had to hold an axe close to the bone of his leg and order a servant to drive the axe through with a mallet. After three blows the gangrenous foot was removed. But it was too late. On the last day of the year Leopold died, after having made his peace with the Church and promised to make full restitution to Richard. The hostages returned home.[115] In the eyes of the Angevins, God's justice had been done. But in the eyes of one early thirteenth-century German commentator, it was the sin committed in imprisoning Richard which explained why the Holy Land had not yet been liberated.[116]

[113] *Chron.*, iii, 236–8.

[114] That he regarded 20,000 (plus 1,000) as still unpaid at the time of his death is reported in the letter of Adalbert of Salzburg, *Chronicon Magni Presbiteri*, 522. For discussion, Kessler, 260–1, 301–2.

[115] *Chron.*, iii, 276–8. A letter written by Archbishop Adalbert of Salzburg who attended Leopold's deathbed shows that in essentials Howden's story is accurate. By 25 January 1195 Richard had written to the archbishop, thanking him for his efforts, and asking him to see to the return of the money, *Chron. Magni Presbiteri*, 521–3. However, it had not been refunded by May 1198, *Selected Letters* 4–5.

[116] Arnold of Lübeck, *Chronica*, Bk 4, ch. 20. See B. U. Hucker, 'Die Chronik Arnolds von Lübeck as "Historia Regum"', *DA*, xliv (1988), 98–119, esp. 105.

Chapter 14

THE CHARACTER OF A LIONHEART

In captivity for so long, Richard must have been thrown back on his own resources. Ultimately unknowable though his character is, it was then that it must have been most severely tested. Even William the Breton was impressed by Richard's bearing in misfortune. The two Cistercian abbots who visited Richard saw in him a man whose ability to rise above the vicissitudes of fortune won the admiration of all. It may have been from information supplied by them that Abbot Ralph of Coggeshall formed his judgement on the king in prison: 'No tribulation could cloud the countenance of this most serene prince. His words remained cheerful and jocund, his actions fierce or most courageous as time, place, reason or person demanded.'[1] In captivity as well as on crusade, Richard became a figure of romance. The legends that cluster about his imprisonment are legends which relate to his 'private' personality: his musicality and his sexuality.

According to the earliest known version of the Blondel legend, Blondel was the minstrel who discovered the whereabouts of Richard's prison 'in a lofty castle'. He heard the king's voice answering when, in a garden adjoining a tower, he sang the first portion of a song which they had composed and which was known only to the two of them.[2] Two songs are attributed to Richard in early troubadour manuscripts: the *rotrouenge* said to have been composed in captivity and a sirventes aimed at Dauphin of Auvergne.[3] It is impossible to be absolutely certain that Richard did write them, but the evidence that he was unusually interested in music is overwhelming. Although nothing is known of Richard's education, two things are clear. First that the education of a young noble would have included music; second, that Richard was very well educated – and it is worth remembering the place of south-west France in the history of music. In the Anglo-Norman *Romance of Horn* composed *c.* 1170 – which Richard would almost certainly have known – the author, Master Thomas, presents the hero Horn as the model of an accomplished prince. He was a master of the

---

[1] *Philippidos*, iv, 393–6; *Chron.*, iii, 199; Coggeshall, 58.
[2] *Récits d'un ménestrel de Reims*, 41–4; trans. Stone, *Three Old French Chronicles*.
[3] Text in F. Gennrich, *Die altfranzösische Rotrouenge* (Halle, 1925), 20–1; C. A. F. Mahn, *Die Werke der Troubadours*, i (Berlin, 1846), 129–30.

arts of hunting and hawking, of swordsmanship and horsemanship. Above all, 'there was no musical instrument known to mortal man in which the princely lord Horn did not surpass everyone'. When he took a harp, 'anyone who watched how he touched the strings and made them vibrate, sometimes causing them to sing and at other times to join in harmonies, would have been reminded of the harmony of heaven'.[4] Richard was presumably not in this class, and there is no explicit evidence for him playing an instrument. However, that he did write songs like those attributed to him, songs with a political content, is shown by Ambroise's report of Richard's riposte in kind to a song written by the duke of Burgundy.[5] He evidently enjoyed music of all kinds. The Cistercian Ralph of Coggeshall observed the pleasure he took in church music. When the clerks of his royal chapel were singing in the choir, he would often walk among them, urging them with voice and hand to sing with greater gusto.[6] Most striking of all is Ibn al-Athir's picture of Richard asking if he could listen to some Arab songs and enjoying what he heard – or at least saying that he had.[7] This wide-ranging interest in music makes the attribution of these particular songs to Richard reasonably plausible. The song written in captivity, 'Ja nus hons pris' (No man who is in prison), has been admired by good judges. 'The poetry is so unobtrusive that at first we might think, this man is not specially talented; his tone is quiet, slow and rueful, but then we notice the glint in his eye, a flicker of pride and a flicker of sardonic humour, and we realise that this poetic voice is very much his own, and that a most uncommon personality has penetrated our imagination.'[8] The qualities detected here – a flicker of pride, a flicker of sardonic humour – correspond curiously closely to the qualities which Baha al-Din reported.

Perhaps even Master Thomas would have acknowledged Richard as Horn's equal when it came to horsemanship and swordsmanship. Where he acquired his expertise is not known. Although he appreciated the value of tournaments as training for war (see below, 278) there is very little evidence of his own participation in these war games. That he had participated is implied by Roger of Howden's statement that in 1178 Geoffrey of Brittany engaged in tournaments in order to match the

[4] 'Romance of Hern', in *The Birth of Romance*, trans. J. Weiss (London, 1992), 9, 59, 66. The arts of hunting and hawking included training dogs and birds.
[5] Ambroise, 10,660–2. The fact that Ambroise was a *jongleur* himself adds to the value of this evidence, just as the fact that particular songs were attributed to Richard is, at the very least, evidence of the prestige he enjoyed among troubadours and *trouvères*, P. Bec,'Troubadours, trouvères et espace Plantagenêt', *CCM*, xxix (1986), 10–11.
[6] Coggeshall, 97. This is almost certainly an eyewitness observation.
[7] Ibn al-Athir, 53.
[8] P. Dronke, *The Medieval Lyric* (2nd edn, London, 1978), 212. Kessler suggests the 'popular' form of the *rotrouenge* may have been chosen in hope of reaching a wide audience, to help raise ransom, 356 n. 639.

military fame enjoyed by both his older brothers, 'since the *ars bellandi* has to be game-played if it is to be there when needed'.[9] None the less Richard's only known 'tournament' is the mock-joust with canes against William des Barres in Sicily when time was hanging heavy on everyone's hands. Similarly with hunting. Richard de Templo applauds Richard as a brilliant horseman and courageous and skilful hunter when suddenly confronted by a wild boar – but in this episode Richard is portrayed as being out on patrol, not out hunting.[10] Although he went hawking, perhaps sometimes, in the manner of his ancestor William the Conqueror, combining it with reconnoitring, he was not a celebrated huntsman.[11] He was neither a tournament addict, like his brother Henry, nor an addict of the hunt, like his father. Gerald de Barri, writing in the late 1180s, noted that whereas the Young King went in for war games, Richard went in for real wars.[12] The one time Roger of Howden mentioned Richard hunting was when he was waiting to set sail and very frustrated by the delay.[13] Hawking must have helped to pass the waiting time in captivity.[14]

Another evident outcome of Richard's education was that he was highly literate – sufficiently well educated to be able to crack a Latin joke at the expense of the grammar of a less learned archbishop of Canterbury.[15] He deeply impressed Ralph of Coggeshall with his dialectical skill and his eloquence.[16] His forceful way with words comes out very vividly in the description of his confrontation with a papal legate in the *Histoire de Guillaume le Maréchal*.[17] Of course this particular scene may reflect the author's way with words rather than Richard's, but even the king's enemies were struck by the way he spoke.[18] Why did Bertran de Born call Richard 'Yea and Nay' (Oc e Non)?[19] Was it because he was fickle, said first one thing and then another? Or because he said one thing and meant another? Or because he decided quickly and spoke his mind tersely and to the point:

[9] *Gesta*, i, 207; *Chron.*, ii, 166.

[10] *Itin.*, Bk 5, ch. 31. This is not in Ambroise.

[11] Ibid., Bk 4, ch. 28 – if this is not just a flight of imagination on Richard de Templo's part, for there is no reference to hawking in the relevant lines of Ambroise.

[12] Gerald, *Top.*, 198; *Princ.*, 248. Cf. Bertran de Born's song 'Rassa, mes sison primier' where he envisages Richard turning to dogs, greyhounds, hawks and falcons now that peace has come, Born, no. 18, 244–7.

[13] He recorded Richard's pleasure in viewing Sherwood Forest for the first time, but made no mention of him hunting there, *Chron.*, iii, 240, 251

[14] PR 5 Richard I, 2 for the expenses incurred in sending his birds to Germany. They were then sent to Normandy, PR 6 Richard I, 213.

[15] Gerald, *De Invectionibus*, ed. W. S. Davies (London, 1920), 100–1.

[16] 'ut est facundissimus', Coggeshall, 59–60.

[17] See below, 319.

[18] For William the Breton's admiration see above, 237; for Baha al–Din's, 21.

[19] For examples and some comments, Born, nos 2, 20, 30, 32, 34, 37, 40.

'let your communication be, Yea, yea: Nay, nay: for whatsoever is more than these cometh of evil' (Matthew, 5: 37)? Since the mid-twentieth century the third of these has been the generally accepted interpretation of the name.[20] Another possibility might be that Richard liked to hear words that were brief and to the point. When the abbot of Crowland put his side of his dispute with Spalding Priory to Richard, he felt that 'the brevity of his argument seemed to please the king'.[21]

The number of jokes and *bons mots* which he is recorded as making continued to impress historians for many centuries to come. Few – if any – of the 'witty remarks' attributed to him by contemporaries appear to strike modern readers as particularly amusing – perhaps on a par with the one line attributed to him in Walt Disney's *Robin Hood* (1973): 'It seems I now have an outlaw for an in-law.'[22] However, the evidence of Baha al-Din demonstrates that Richard's bantering conversational style – half serious, half joking – did cross cultural frontiers. Writing soon after Richard's death Coggeshall not only remembered the king's ferocious look when interrupted at work, he remembered too seeing him with the members of his private household, happy and relaxed, enjoying jokes and games. The same historian believed that in prison Richard had kept his spirits up by making his guards drunk and playing practical jokes on them.[23]

One of Richard's most celebrated cracks was his rejoinder to Fulk of Neuilly, the great preacher of the day, when the latter accused him of having three wicked daughters: pride, avarice and sensuality: 'I give my pride to the Templars, my avarice to the Cistercians and my sensuality to the Benedictines.' These reminders of some of the notorious weaknesses of various monastic orders amused his courtiers and Gerald de Barri – though not Roger of Howden – but they reflected the views of church reformers rather than of those who were hostile or indifferent to the Christian religion.[24] Moreover, despite this comment on the Cistercians, Richard retained a Cistercian abbot as his almoner and was a notably generous benefactor to that order, as was pointed out by Ralph, later abbot of the Cistercian house at Coggeshall in Essex and by Aubri des Trois Fontaines in France. His gift of 120 marks a year to the Cistercian General

---

[20] Though it may be that the pseudonym carries different meanings in different contexts. It has been pointed out that in one lyric (Born, no. 34) Sir Yes and No is said to be loading the dice, so here trickery, saying one thing and meaning another, seems a fair interpretation.

[21] 'The Case concerning the Marsh lying between the Abbey of Croyland and the Priory of Spalding, 1189–1202', in D. M. Stenton, *English Justice between the Norman Conquest and the Great Charter 1066–1215* (London, 1965), 178

[22] Though I should admit I quite like that one.

[23] Coggeshall, 58, 92.

[24] *Chron.*, iv, 76 Gerald, *Opera*, iv, 54; he included the same story in a later edition of his *Journey through Wales*, trans. L. Thorpe (Harmondsworth, 1978), 104–5.

Chapter may well have encouraged the Cistercian order, as an order, to look favourably upon him and to ensure that letters he wrote to the abbots of Clairvaux were given wider circulation.[25] More conventionally, he founded a Cistercian house at Bonport in Normandy, a Premonstratensian abbey (Le-Lieu-Dieu-en-Jard) and a Benedictine priory (Gourfailles) in the Vendée.[26] Nor was the old order of the Benedictines made to feel left out in the cold. At St Albans in the mid-thirteenth century there was a strong tradition of a close relationship between the abbey and the king.[27] Richard was evidently drawn to the shrine of St Edmund at Bury. This may have reflected an Aquitanian view of England; as an enthusiastic crusader he may also have been attracted by a cult which celebrated a king who died in the struggle against pagans.[28] In view of his delight in music and ceremony there is every reason to believe that he enjoyed the liturgy of the Church. He was assiduous in his attendance at mass, except – Howden implies (see below, 264) – first thing in the morning. His behaviour during church services was exemplary.[29] As king he was normally accompanied by the clerks of the royal chapel so he had plenty of opportunities to indulge in the pleasures of ritual. It was, after all, a ritual which exalted kings.

Adam of Eynsham, the biographer of St Hugh of Lincoln, gives us a revealing description of Richard in the last summer of his life. Richard had ordered the confiscation of the estates of the see of Lincoln and Bishop Hugh decided to go himself to Normandy and protest. He found the King in the chapel of his new castle of the Rock of Andeli [that is, Château-Gaillard] hearing High Mass on the feast of St Augustine, and immediately greeted him. The King was on a royal throne near the entrance, and the two Bishops of Durham and Ely stood at his feet. ... A good omen had

[25] Coggeshall, 97–8; Aubri des Trois Fontaines, *Chronicon* MGH SS, xxiii, 876. Caesarius of Heisterbach thought of Richard as both a very generous patron of the Cistercian (his own) order and a man of outstanding faith, Caesarius of Heisterbach, *Dialogus Miraculorum*, ed. J. Strange (2 vols, Cologne, 1851), ii, 249–50. See also A. D. A. Monna, 'Diagnose van een omstreden 13e eeuwse kalender uit de Servaasabdij te Utrecht', *Archief voor de Geschiedenis van de Katholieke Kerk in Nederland*, xxv (1983).

[26] A. Gosse-Kischinewski, 'La fondation de l'abbaye de Bonport', *Connaissance de l'Eure*, lxxxix–xc (1993). See also E. M. Hallam, 'Henry II, Richard I and the Order of Grandmont', *JMH*, i (1975) and, for the architecture of his churches at Bonport and Petit Andelys, L. M. Grant, 'Gothic Architecture in Normandy *c.* 1150–1250' (unpub. Ph.D. thesis, University of London, 1986). He may also have paid for the sumptuous chancel and transepts of the chapel of St Thomas, now Portsmouth Cathedral (cf. below, 273). For his patronage of Le Pin near Poitiers, see below, 323.

[27] *Chron. Maj.*, ii, 403, 413–16.

[28] He found time to go there in both 1189 and 1194; cf. *Gesta*, ii, 164; and he gave the banner of Isaac of Cyprus to Bury, see above, 147. Bertran de Born called England 'the land of St Edmund', Born, no. 23, 288–9.

[29] Coggeshall, 97; *Chronicon Turonense Magnum*, ed. A. Salmon, *Recueil des chroniques de Touraine* (Tours, 1854), 144; *Roberti canonici S. Mariani Autissiodorensis Chronicon*, MGH SS, xxvi, 259.

encouraged Hugh for just as he reached the chapel steps he heard the choir in full voice chanting the words 'Hail renowned bishop of Christ'. When Richard did not respond to his greeting except by frowning and then turning away, Hugh remained undismayed.

> He said to him, 'Lord King, kiss me.' But Richard turned his head even further and looked the other way. Then the Bishop firmly gripped the King's tunic round his chest and shook it violently, saying again, 'You owe me a kiss because I have come a long way to see you.' The King answered, 'You deserve no kiss from me.' He shook him more vigorously than before, this time by his cloak, and said boldly, 'I have every right to one'; adding, 'Kiss me.' Richard, overcome by his courage and determination, after a little while kissed him with a smile.

Later on, in discussion with the members of his household, the King referred to Hugh. 'If the other bishops were like him,' he said, 'no king or ruler would dare raise up his head against them.'[30] Like his father, who had appointed him bishop, Richard could only admire the courage and saintliness of Hugh of Lincoln.

But the episode tells us more than Adam of Eynsham intended. It shows Richard enthroned amidst his choir and his bishops – in all there were two archbishops and five bishops present in his chapel on this occasion. The king was a central figure in the ritual of the Church. Moreover the two bishops standing at the foot of the throne had both been appointed for administrative work done in the king's service. Before becoming bishop of Durham in 1197, Master Philip of Poitou had been a clerk of the king's chamber and his constant companion. He had gone with Richard on crusade and had shared with him the hazards of the perilous journey home.[31] Master Eustace, consecrated bishop of Ely in 1198, had been vice-chancellor and keeper of the king's seal since 1194. Both men were typical members of the new class of civil servants, who had been educated at university and styled themselves 'master'. For all his reverence for Hugh of Lincoln, Richard had always been determined that other bishops should not be like him. Unremarkably he looked upon bishoprics as rewards which he could bestow upon clerks who served him loyally and efficiently. Even in captivity ambitious clerks went to him in the hope of preferment, and he responded – or, as in the case of Hubert Walter, saw to it that men of his own choice were appointed.

---

[30] *Magna Vita*, ii, 101–2, 105–6. The same scene is more briefly described by Gerald de Barri in his *Vita Hugonis*, though Gerald gives rather more weight to the humility and patience with which 'the almost tyrannical' Richard suffered Bishop Hugh's homilies and criticisms, *Opera*, vii, 103–6.

[31] On Philip's career in the chancery, H. E. Mayer, 'Die Kanzlei Richards I von England auf dem Dritten Kreuzzug', *Mitteilungen des Instituts für Österreichische Geschichtsforschung*, lxxxv (1977), 22–35.

Richard's fame was such that he came to be regarded as the founder of
both an English military order – the order of St Thomas at Acre – and of
an English order of chivalry – the order of the Garter.[32] If he visited the
shrine of St Edmund at Bury, he also inspected the body of Renaud de
Montauban and his brothers at Naples. There is no reason to doubt the
sincerity of Richard's religious beliefs, but in the crises of his life he lived
by another set of values: that 'secular code of honour of a martially
oriented aristocracy' now known as chivalry. Chivalry, in Maurice Keen's
words, 'conflated in its ideal of honour, principles of personal integrity
with the title to social respect'.[33] Probably no one ever felt more entitled to
'social respect' than a king who was also 'the finest knight on earth'.[34] In
one of Bertran de Born's songs, 'Nostre seingner somonis el mezeis' –
almost certainly composed in 1188 – we are told that Richard 'desires
honour (*pretz*) more than any man, Christian or infidel. He seeks honour
and success so intently that his reputation constantly grows and improves.'
As observed above, in this single stanza Bertran applied the word *pretz* to
Richard no fewer than seven times in nine lines.[35] Perhaps most revealing
is Baha al-Din's report of what Richard said to al-Adil's chamberlain, Abu
Bekr, in August 1192 as peace talks reached crisis point: 'my only object is
to retain the position I hold among the Franks'.[36]

To retain the desired social respect imposed obligations. It obliged
Richard to share some of the dangers of his soldiers. Even a witness as hostile as William the Breton saw Richard in that light. In the space of thirteen
lines of Latin verse describing the king of England's decision to risk,
against the odds, an attempt to rescue a beleaguered garrison, William
three times refers to him preferring honour (*honor*) to advantage (*utilitas*),
calls him 'noble' twice, and a 'lion' twice.[37] Richard was, of course, often
called a lion, several times by Bertran de Born: 'Tell Sir Richard that he is
a lion, and that King Philip looks like a lamb to me.' In another song, 'Ar
ven la coindeta sazos', he wrote,'I like the way of the lion, who is proud
against pride but not cruel to a defeated creature'.[38] This is not what the
ordinary soldiers of the defeated garrison of Acre would have thought.[39]
Christian parsons such as Roger of Howden or monks such as Gervase of
Canterbury also had serious reservations about the scope of Richard's

[32] A. J. Forey, 'The Military Order of St Thomas at Acre', *EHR*, xcii (1977). The
notion that he was inspired by St George to found the Garter was rightly dismissed
by the first serious historian of the Order, E. Ashmole, *The Institution, Laws and
Ceremonies of the Most Noble Order of the Garter* (London, 1672), 181.

[33] M. Keen, *Chivalry* (London, 1984), 252–3.

[34] Ambroise, 12, 135–6.

[35] Born, 386–7; and see above, 105.

[36] Baha al-Din, 380.

[37] *Philippidos*, v, 194–206.

[38] Born, nos 42, 43.

[39] For discussion of the massacre of Acre, above, 167–70.

mercy.[40] Chivalry, however, was a status-specific form of humanity. By that code of values it was common for prisoners of humble rank to be slaughtered and for those of high status to be spared.[41] Apart from one or two probable exceptions Richard lived by that code. At the siege of Nottingham, for example, he had sergeants hanged, but not knights.[42] After the capture of Acre he spared high-ranking Muslims. Doubtless there was an element of mercenary calculation in this, but it was a set of priorities that was understood and appreciated by other high-ranking Muslims with whom he was soon to get on well – suspiciously well, as it seemed to serious-minded Christians.

Where Richard was perceived as notably merciful was in his treatment of John. In a scene in the *History of William the Marshal* we see John keen to seek his brother's forgiveness, but nervous about entering the king's presence. He is reassured with the words: 'The king is straightforward and merciful, and kinder to you than you would be to him.'[43] And once again it is the comment of a hostile witness that is most telling. According to William the Breton, although Richard hated John's odious conduct (William had in mind a treacherous surprise attack on Evreux and the slaughter that resulted), he was his brother and so did not withhold from him the love due to a brother.[44] Except in such terms it is hard to explain the consistent generosity of Richard's treatment of his younger brother.

Among the values admired by the chivalric rather than the specifically Christian code was largesse. Although critics described Richard as greedy for money, no one ever accused him of hoarding it. Aubri des Trois Fontaines wrote: 'As he was strenuous in arms so he is said to have been lavish in gifts.'[45] In the words of Richard FitzNigel in the preface to the *Dialogue of the Exchequer*, a king's glory lies not in hoarding treasure but in spending it as it should be spent. Richard spent and gave lavishly. According to Roger of Howden, in February 1191 he distributed gifts so generously 'that many said that not one of his predecessors had given away as much in a year as he gave away in that month'.[46] A

---

[40] See below, 329–30.

[41] See M. Strickland, *War and Chivalry*, 180–1, 223.

[42] *Chron.*, iii, 239; iv, 14–15. For the implementation of the code and a probable exception see below, 269 n. 2. For some other possible cases, Strickland, *War and Chivalry*, 202. In this respect Richard's conduct mirrors that of his father.

[43] *HGM*, 10,397–99. The scene is well described and set in context in P. Hyams, 'What Did Henry III of England think about in Bed and in French about Kingship and Anger?', in *Anger's Past*, ed. B. Rosenwein (Ithaca, New York, 1998), 115.

[44] *Philippidos*, v, 471–80. 'Sed quia frater erat, licet illius oderit actus/Omnibus odibiles, fraterne federa pacis/Non negat indigno, nec eum privavit amore/Ipsum qui nuper sceptro privare volebat.'

[45] MGH SS xxiii, 876.

[46] See above, 140.

mid-thirteenth-century author writing in the Christian East believed that such was Richard's reputation for largesse and gifts that during the crusade as many as 300 Mamelukes entered his service and that 'he took 120 of them with him overseas when he left this land'.[47] His nephew Henry III had painted over the door to the Painted Chamber in his palace at Westminster the words: 'He who does not give what he has, will not get what he wants.'[48] To no king, it might be thought, did this apply more than to Richard. His generosity to King William of Scotland in 1189 paid rich dividends in 1193–4. In the opinion of his contemporary, the great German poet Walther von der Vogelweide, it was precisely Richard's generosity which made his subjects willing to raise a king's ransom to free him, and made it possible for him to get what he most wanted when he needed it most. In the poem in which he made this point, Walther paired Richard with Saladin, two idealized and ideally generous rulers.[49] Unquestionably Richard and Saladin shared values. 'My feeling,' said Saladin, according to Imad al-Din, 'is to reject the truce and, in preferring war, to prefer my honour and make it my guide.'[50]

Except in the cases of his brothers, however, Richard's generosity did not extend to the lenient treatment of those whom he regarded as having let him down. Not for nothing did Coggeshall remember the king's angry look. In 1196 Robert de Ros, later a significant enough figure to be one of the committee of Twenty-Five established by Magna Carta, was given custody of an important French prisoner. When the prisoner escaped, allegedly with the connivance of the sergeant to whom Robert had entrusted him, Richard imprisoned Robert de Ros and fined him 1,200 marks – a massive sum. The sergeant, adjudged to have betrayed his lord, was hanged.[51] During the financial year 1195–6 the sheriff of Lincolnshire and one of the most prominent landowners in the shire, Simon of Kyme, was fined at least 1,000 marks for allowing ships and merchants to leave St Botolph's Fair; Richard treated this as a serious breach of the embargo which he had imposed as part of the war against King Philip of France.[52]

[47] Edbury, 118. See below, 295 for the evidence of Muslims in his service in Normandy.

[48] P. Binski, *The Painted Chamber at Westminster* (London, 1986), 13.

[49] See M. H. Jones, 'Richard the Lionheart in German Literature', 85–88.

[50] Gabrieli, 235.

[51] *Chron.*, iv, 14–15. On Robert's estates and career, J. C. Holt, *The Northerners* (Oxford, 1961), 24–6.

[52] PR 8 Richard I, 248–9. In 1197–8 Walter de Lacy agreed to pay 3,100 marks in order to recover his estates and the king's grace, though how he had lost it is unknown: possibly because of some shortcoming *vis-à-vis* the Welsh, PR 10 Richard I, xxix, 213.

The second legend of Richard's captivity is one that bears on the question of his sexuality. According to a verse romance which survives only in a four-teenth-century version but which probably dates back to the thirteenth, while Richard was in prison the king of Germany's daughter Margery fell in love with him, and they spent some happy nights together before her father Modred found out. Outraged, he planned to murder Richard by having a hungry lion released into his cell. But our hero was able to kill the lion by thrusting his arm down the beast's throat and pulling out its heart. This was easier than it sounds since his arm was protected by forty of Margery's silk handkerchiefs wound around it. Then, pausing only to give thanks to God, Richard strode up to the great hall, sprinkled the heart with salt and ate it before the astonished gaze of King Modred and his court.[53] The assumption of this tale is that Richard's tastes were heterosexual and carnivorous. Many other stories, including contemporary ones, point in the same directions. His Aquitanian enemies accused him of sating his own lust on his subjects' wives and daughters before he handed them on to his soldiers. According to Richard of Devizes, Saladin was told that Richard ate his enemies alive.[54] A thirteenth-century tale links Richard with a nun of Fontevraud. As told by Stephen of Bourbon, a Dominican friar and a popu-lar preacher, Richard wanted one of the nuns so badly that he threatened to burn down the abbey unless she was delivered to him. When the nun asked what it was that attracted him so much and was told that it was her eyes, she sent for a knife and cut them out, saying, 'Send the King what he so much desires.'[55]

It is possible that Richard got on better with the fictional Margery than with the real Berengaria. After the end of the crusade Richard and his wife do not seem to have spent much time together. There were times when force of circumstance gave them no choice in the matter, but there were times also when Richard preferred to do without her. According to Adam of Eynsham, Bishop Hugh of Lincoln told Richard that his unfaithfulness to his wife was a matter of general gossip. Roger of Howden, writing in Richard's lifetime, reports an incident, apparently in 1195, when a hermit came to the king and rebuked him for his sins. 'Remember the destruction of Sodom and abstain from illicit acts, for if you do not God will punish you

---

[53] *Der mittelenglische Versroman über Richard Löwenherz*, ed. Brunner, ll. 880–1100.

[54] *Gesta*, i, 292 (see above, 66); Devizes, 77.

[55] *Anecdotes historiques ... d'Etienne de Bourbon*, ed. A. Lecoy de la Marche (Paris, 1877), 211, 431. The same story had been told by a contemporary of Richard, Peter the Chanter, a famous master in the schools of Paris, but in his writings he refers only to a king of the English, giving no name. Possibly he was just being cau-tious; we do know that Stephen of Bourbon claimed to have listened to Peter's ser-mons; J. W. Baldwin, *Masters, Princes and Merchants: the Social Views of Peter the Chanter and his Circle* (2 vols, Princeton, 1970), i, 245; ii, 183–4. For the story of the nun's eyes see Broughton, *Legends*, 132–6.

in a fitting manner.' At first Richard ignored the warning but when, some time later, he was struck by an illness, he recalled the hermit's words. He did penance and, says Roger of Howden, tried to lead a better life. This meant regular attendance at morning church – and not leaving until the service was over; it meant distributing alms to the poor. It also meant avoiding illicit intercourse; instead he was to sleep with his wife, a marital duty which he had been neglecting.[56] Whatever he did or didn't do, their marriage remained childless and this, given the desire of most kings to have a son to succeed them, is generally taken as evidence for one kind of failure. But Richard acknowledged a child. Indeed his illegitimate son is a central figure in one of Shakespeare's plays.[57] Philip Faulconbridge, the personification of sturdy English virtues, is doubtless a far cry from the Philip to whom Richard gave the lordship of Cognac as part of his campaign to hold the counts of Angoulême in check.[58] Even so, were *King John* as good a play as *King Lear* then Philip might have become as well known as Edmund, Gloucester's son. Unfortunately it is not. Inevitably we are in the realm of speculation but the probability is that Berengaria was barren. An annulment might have been considered but in political terms the Navarre alliance was probably too important to be put at risk, at any rate until the 'diplomatic revolution' of 1196.[59] Berengaria did not remarry. What she thought about all this is unknown; except in one respect no contemporary or near-contemporary writer thought her feelings worth mentioning. According to Adam of Eynsham, after Richard's death Bishop Hugh of Lincoln, speaking wonderfully to the heart, was able to comfort a grieving widow close to breakdown.[60]

Although there is some evidence that Richard committed adultery, there is no evidence that he was homosexual – or bisexual – either before or after marriage. We simply do not know. Naturally we can speculate or, if we prefer, 'unnaturally'. Roger of Howden's report that, in 1187 Philip Augustus and Richard shared a bed was meant to be understood in political, not sexual, terms.[61] When men exchanged kisses or held hands in

[56] *Magna Vita*, ii, 104. *Chron.*, iii, 288–90. A story very similar to this also came to the ears of William of Newburgh (Bk 5, ch. 9). The content of the next few paragraphs is considered in greater detail in Gillingham, 'Richard I and Berengaria of Navarre'.

[57] See Olivier de Laborderie, 'L'Image de Richard Coeur de Lion dans *La Vie et la mort du roi Jean* de William Shakespeare', in Nelson, *Coeur de Lion*, 141–65.

[58] 'Comptes d'Alfonse de Poitiers', in *Archives historiques du Poitou* (Poitiers, 1875), iv, 21–2; PR 3 John, 283. Howden has Philip kill the viscount of Limoges in revenge for his father's death, *Chron.*, iv, 97. However, I know of no confirmation of this report, and it fits rather well into Howden's motif of vengeance taken despite the dying king's wishes (see below, 329 n. 29).

[59] See below, 306. For the evidence of problems by 1196, Gillingham, *Coeur de Lion*, 137–8.

[60] *Magna Vita*, ii, 136.

[61] *Gesta*, ii, 7. See above, 84.

public we are dealing with political gestures of peace or alliance, not of erotic passion. In 1198 Philip was dismayed when he saw Richard hand in hand with the counts of Flanders and Boulogne, not because he was offended by a public display of homosexual attachment, but because he feared the powerful alliance which that act symbolized.[62] Thus when Coggeshall wrote that in prison Richard was so closely guarded that none of his own followers was allowed to spend the night with him, he was commenting on his political predicament, not his sexual one.[63] Philip's 'bedding' of Richard in 1187 and the hermit's warning of 1195 are the two main planks on which the case for Richard's supposed homosexuality is based. But references to 'the destruction of Sodom' are generally just that – allusions not so much to the nature of the offences as to the terrible and awe-inspiring nature of the punishment, the apocalyptic image of whole cities being overwhelmed by fire and brimstone. In the days when people listened to more sermons, this was well understood. For example, the seventeenth-century Anglican bishop, Thomas Fuller, on reading this passage noted that Richard 'amended his manners, better loving his Queen Beringaria, whom he slighted before: as soldiers too often love women better than wives'.[64]

One or two eighteenth-century authors may have thought Richard was homosexual. Laurence Echard associated the hermit's warning with 'unnatural impurity' (which is not in Howden) and wrote of Richard and Philip that 'such a great intimacy grew between them, that one Table and one Bed *usually* [my italics] serv'd for both'.[65] In this Echard was followed by his great admirer, the Huguenot historian of England, Rapin de Thoyras, who wrote of 'sins against nature' and has Philip 'admit Richard to his bed' in order to suggest that 'these caresses wrought a sudden effect in the mind of the English prince who never once suspected the motive'.[66] Yet if homosexuality is what Echard and Rapin had in mind, it is curious that their readers, such as David Hume, do not, so far as I can tell, appear to have fastened upon it. What King Richard's alleged sins were in 1195 – as opposed to the heterosexual offences of which he was accused in 1182 (see above, 84) – Roger of Howden does not tell us, and any guess is bound to reflect upon ourselves and upon our age rather than upon Richard's behaviour. For example, when the German scholar who wrote a monumental life of Philip Augustus in six volumes and, in the process, came to study Richard's career with great thoroughness, read Howden's account of Richard's act of contrition in Sicily (see above, 89) he believed that he must have

---

[62] *HGM*, 8984.
[63] Coggeshall, 58.
[64] Thomas Fuller, *The Historie of the Holy War* (3rd edn, Cambridge, 1647), 131.
[65] Laurence Echard, *The History of England* (London, 1707), 211, 226.
[66] Paul de Rapin-Thoyras, *History of England* (London, 1732), 241, 257.

'abandoned himself entirely to the pleasures of Messina where the women seemed very seductive to warriors from the North'.[67] Thus in 1948 when J. H. Harvey asserted that Richard was homosexual, he claimed to be 'breaking the conspiracy of silence surrounding the popular hero Richard'.[68] With extraordinary rapidity Harvey's reading of the evidence became the orthodox view, supported in curious ways. For example, women as well as Jews were barred from attending Richard's coronation. This, it was once suggested, showed that Richard was a homosexual who preferred to turn his coronation banquet into a bachelor party.[69] Unfortunately for this theory, what little evidence we have for earlier coronations makes it perfectly plain that women always were excluded. One twelfth-century author, Geoffrey of Monmouth, believed that this was a tradition which went back to the earliest days of the island's history when the Britons 'observed the ancient custom of Troy'. The argument of the 'bachelor party' would have slightly more force if it were used to suggest that all the kings of legendary Britain and early medieval England were homosexual.[70]

We can at least, if we are of a romantic turn of mind, picture Richard at his coronation banquet. We have a description of his appearance on that occasion. 'He was tall, of elegant build; the colour of his hair was between red and gold; his limbs were supple and straight. He had quite long arms which were particularly suited to drawing a sword and wielding it to great effect. His long legs matched the rest of his body.'[71] But this was written by Richard de Templo long after the king's death, probably between 1217 and 1220, when he had already passed into legend, and had perhaps been provided with a suitably heroic physique. It might be more accurate to say that he was overweight and pale of face.[72] The evidence is too fragmentary to be sure. The effigy on 'his' tomb is of uncertain date and there is no reason to think it a realistic likeness – any more than Eleanor's is the like-

---

[67] A. Cartellieri, 'Richard Löwenherz', in *Probleme der englischen Sprache und Kultur: Festschrift Johannes Hoops zum 60 Geburtstag überreicht*, ed. W. Keller, (Heidelberg, 1925), 136. A similar view was taken at the beginning of this century by A. Richard, *Histoire des comtes*, ii, 330.

[68] J. H. Harvey, *The Plantagenets* (London, 1948), 33–4.

[69] Brundage, *Richard Lionheart*, 257.

[70] Geoffrey of Monmouth, *The History of the Kings of Britain*, trans. L. Thorpe (Harmondsworth, 1966), 229. Since two of his 199 British kings are explicitly criticized for homosexuality, Geoffrey – great liar and joker though he was – presumably did not expect people to draw this inference. For more detailed consideration of the evidence from earlier coronations, Gillingham, *Coeur de Lion*, 135.

[71] *Itin.*, Bk 2, ch. 5.

[72] This according to William of Newburgh (who probably never saw him), supported by the assertion of Ralph of Coggeshall (who almost certainly had) that when he was mortally wounded 'too much fat' made the surgeon's task difficult, Newburgh, Bk 4, ch. 5. Coggeshall, 95.

ness of an eighty-year-old woman.[73] Judging by the number of doctors who attended him at one time or another Richard took good care of his health, although it was a subject on which, according to William of Newburgh, contemporaries speculated wildly. Some said he suffered from a feverish ague. Others claimed that he had over a hundred ulcers in his body through which corrupt humours drained. Still others said that he was broken and enfeebled by premature and excessive soldiering.[74] Fat or not, he continued soldiering with – as some said – excessive courage until the unexpected end.

All that Gerald de Barri, the twelfth-century's most accomplished master of the pen portrait, had to say about Richard's appearance in a character sketch composed in 1189, shortly before he succeeded his father on the throne, was that he was above average height.[75] On the prince's political personality, however, he poured lavish praise. He presents a prince who had already achieved much. He had restored Aquitaine's ancient boundaries and had brought good order to a previously ungovernable province.[76] In his burning zeal for peace and justice (*pacis et justitiae zelo defervens*) he had been happy to take up arms and to walk through bloodshed, undeterred either by precipitate slopes or by hitherto impregnable towers. For this reason the rigour of his rule had led to his being accused of cruelty. However, once severity had achieved its purpose, he approached the golden mean by showing himself to be possessed of both forbearance (*mansuetudinem*) and mercy (*clementiam*).

But to restrain the fiercest impulses of his nature this our lion – and more than lion (*hic leo noster et plusquam leo*) – is vexed like a lion by a quartan ague. Hence he trembles almost continuously – though not through fear – and his trembling makes the whole world tremble and fear. Above all he possesses three fine qualities: first, exceptional courage and energy (*strenuitas et animositas eximia*); second, great generosity and courtliness (*largitas et dapsilitas immensa*); and thirdly, what is most praiseworthy in a prince, adorning all other virtues, firmness of purpose both in thought and word (*superlaudabilis in principe, ceterasque adornans virtutes, tam animi quam verbi firma constantia*).[77]

[73] Even if the effigy traditionally identified as his *is* his, as opposed to his father's.
[74] Newburgh, Bk 4, ch. 5.
[75] This was in the second edition of his *Topographia Hibernica*. Unfortunately the English translation of the first edition in Penguin Classics, J. O'Meara, *Gerald of Wales. The History and Topography of Ireland* (Harmondsworth, 1982), does not include Gerald's subsequent additions.
[76] Similar praise is put into the mouth of the much admired and allegedly well-informed Safadin, Devizes, 76. This was written in 1193.
[77] Gerald, *Top.*, 195–6.

What are we to make of this panegyric? Gerald later confessed that he had produced too flattering a picture of Richard's father in this work. Had he done the same for Richard? Undoubtedly he was writing what he thought Richard would like to hear, in the expectation that Richard would soon be king and in the hope that the new king would see his merits. He completed his new book on *The Conquest of Ireland* in the summer of 1189 and dedicated it to Richard, suggesting that the new ruler might like to employ a man of Gerald's talents as his own historian.[78] In his later book, the *De Principis Instructione* (On the Instruction of Princes) – on which he continued to work long after Richard's death – when he was deliberately contrasting the 'good' Capetian kings of France with the 'bad' Angevin kings of England, Gerald might have been expected to take a much more hostile line, especially since it was under Richard that he was forced to give up his dreams of promotion through government service.[79] Despite this disappointment, about which he subsequently wrote at length, the consistency of his view of Richard is remarkable. He chose to retain the whole of this passage; indeed he amplified it with some praise for Richard's crusading deeds. His conclusion was that if only Richard had been willing to put pride aside and give humble thanks to God for his achievements, then he would have been the most distinguished of all the rulers of our time.[80] This was to praise with faint criticism.

[78] Gerald, *Expug. Hib.*, 20–5.

[79] On the reasons behind Gerald's failure to win promotion in England, Bartlett, *Gerald*, 19, 65; Gillingham, 'Henry II, Richard I and the Lord Rhys', 235.

[80] Gerald, *Princ.*, 247–50 (Bk 3, ch. 8). Later in this work he touches on Richard's death and sees it, inevitably, as God's punishment for his 'tyrannical pride', *Princ.*, 326 (Bk 3, ch. 30); cf. above, n. 30. William the Breton took a similar view. For him Richard, *invictissimus*, was the invincible king than whom England could never have had a better ruler (if only he had been Philip's good subject!), *Philippidos*, iv, 393–424.

Chapter 15

ENGLAND, 1194-9

By the time Richard had returned to England most of the castles held in John's name had already capitulated. The only two still holding out against the siege operations mounted in mid-February by Hubert Walter, now archbishop of Canterbury and chief justiciar, were Tickhill and Nottingham. The garrison of Tickhill sent two knights to see if Richard was indeed in the country and when they confirmed the truth of the stories, the castle was surrendered. The garrison of Nottingham was made of sterner stuff. Richard arrived there on 25 March 1194 to the accompaniment of 'a great blowing of horns and trumpets'.[1] But the defenders were convinced that the fanfare was just a trick and fought on. Some men who were standing close to Richard were hit by archery fire from the battlements, so the king gave the order for an immediate assault on the castle. Richard himself took part in the attack, wearing only a light coat of mail and an iron head-piece but protected by large, strong shields carried in front of him. They took the outer bailey and then the barbican. The coming of darkness put an end to the fighting. During the night the garrison burned down the castle's outer works, calculating that since they could no longer hold them it was better to deprive the besiegers of as much cover as possible. Next day Richard pressed the attack by other means. He brought up his siege artillery and had gallows erected in full view of the garrison. Some of the soldiers captured on the previous day were hanged. The message was clear: if they continued to hold out they would all suffer the same fate. On 27 March two of the defenders were given a safe-conduct to visit the camp of the besiegers. 'Well,' said Richard, 'what can you see? Am I here?' When the two knights reported back, fourteen members of the garrison left the castle at once and all the rest surrendered unconditionally on the next day. The lives of most of them were spared, but they had to pay stiff ransoms.[2]

---

[1] This account of the siege of Nottingham is based on *HGM*, 10,177–289 (William Marshal had met the king on his way to the siege, see above, 25); *Chron.*, iii, 237–40. PR 6 Richard I 175 suggests that preparations included the provision of Greek Fire.

[2] According to a marginal addition in Coggeshall, Richard treated one prisoner more severely: Robert Brito, who he ordered should be starved to death in prison, Coggeshall, 33. Robert Brito has been identified (Carpenter, 'Abbot Ralph', 1223, n. 1) as the brother of Hugh de Nonant who had angered Richard in Germany by refusing to be a hostage for the ransom on the grounds that he was John's man,

From 25 March to 3 May it is possible to follow the king's activities unusually closely. Roger of Howden had evidently returned to court, probably in the entourage of the bishop of Durham, Hugh du Puiset, and for that period he mentions every day but one.[3] His court diary gives a good impression of a king's daily routine. After a day trip to admire Sherwood Forest which – Howden observed – he had never before seen, and which was the nearest he ever came to the legendary figure of Robin Hood, Richard returned to Nottingham and to an important, four-day council meeting.[4] On the first day of the council (30 March) a number of new shrieval appointments were made. Nineteen of the twenty-eight shires which rendered account at the exchequer received new sheriffs. The opportunity was taken to introduce a new exchequer policy. Sheriffs had to pay increments over and above the hitherto customary payment of the 'sheriff's farm', i.e. they were required to hand over rather more of their profits to the treasury. By this innovation Richard 'more effectively tapped the escalating but unrealized wealth of the shires'. On the other hand the idea that the overhaul of shrieval appointments was nothing more than a money-raising exercise has been convincingly rebutted. His brother Geoffrey offered 3,000 marks to be sheriff of Yorkshire. There was very little chance that he would actually pay the money, but having him obliged to the king and in debt might be a way of disciplining a royal and very unruly archbishop.[5] The recent study of Richard I's sheriffs by Dr Heiser concluded: 'Because the King was involved in the appointment process when possible, shrewd in selecting and placing those he employed, and wise in knowing how to turn his resources into revenues, Richard's reputation as an indifferent and even reckless sovereign needs to be reassessed.'[6]

On the second day of the council, legal proceedings were begun against John and his partisans, chief among them Hugh of Nonant.[7] In consequence so many estates were confiscated that an administrative experiment

and who died in prison at Dover in 1195, *Chron.*, iii, 232–3, 287. Andreas of Marchiennes also heard that one of John's closest associates, his dapifer, was flayed to death, *Sig. Cont.*, 431.

[3] Corner, 'The *Gesta Regis*', 243. Howden was also involved in arrangements for the visit of King William of Scotland.

[4] On the council's agenda, *Chron.*, iii, 240–3.

[5] As Howden put it, 'he became the king's servant and placed himself in the king's power', *Chron.*, iii, 241. See D. M. Stenton's discussion, PR 6 Richard I, xxix–xxxii.

[6] Heiser, 'Richard I and his Appointments to English Shrievalties', 1–19, developing the argument of both an earlier article, 'The Sheriffs of Richard I' and his thesis 'The Sheriffs of Richard Lionheart'. For the significance of 1194 in the history of sheriffs see D. A. Carpenter, 'The Decline of the Curial Sheriff in England, 1194–1258', *EHR*, 91 (1976), 3–7.

[7] Hugh of Nonant was restored to grace in 1195 in return for 5,000 marks, *Chron.*, iii, 287.

first tried in 1189–90 was revived: two escheators, Hugh Bardolf in the north and William de Ste Mère Eglise in the south, were appointed to supervise the management of the forfeited estates. On the third day of the council (1 April) money and troops were the principal items on the agenda. Richard imposed a tax (a carucage) at the rate of 2 shillings a hide and ordered that a third of the knights due from each fee should accompany him to Normandy. Those who went were excused payment of scutage. In this financial year, to Michaelmas 1194, the scutage brought in just over £2,000.[8] How much the carucage raised is unknown, but in the months after Richard's return, as in 1189–90, the greatest yield came from innumerable deals made either with individuals seeking office or favour, or with communities like the Jews or the citizens of Lincoln, who wanted protection or privilege.[9] Men who may have thought they had bought their offices in 1189 were informed that, in reality, they had only leased them for a term of years, and that the term had now expired.[10] If they wished to remain in such lucrative positions they would have to make new financial arrangements. The Cistercians paid heavily for their exemption from the demand that they contribute the year's wool clip. Despite this it must have been in 1194–5 that the Cistercian historian, Ralph of Coggeshall, composed his adulatory account of Richard on crusade and in prison. Revenue audited at the exchequer for the year ending Michaelmas 1194 totalled £25,292, roughly two and a half times as much as in the previous year.[11]

On the fourth day of the council it was decided that there would be a solemn crown-wearing at Winchester on 17 April. Coggeshall believed that it was rather against his will that Richard was persuaded of the need for some kind of public demonstration of the fact that the king had returned with his sovereignty unimpaired either by the long imprisonment or by the homage paid to the emperor.[12] His reluctance may have been caused by worries about the length of time it would take to organize such a ceremony. Although, as Gervase of Canterbury pointed out, there was a precedent for it in the crown-wearing at Canterbury after King Stephen's release from captivity in 1141, in 1194 a crown-wearing would require

---

[8] PR 6 Richard I, xxiv.

[9] York gave 200 marks 'out of joy at the king's return from Germany'. So at least an exchequer clerk said, PR 6 Richard I, 163. Conceivably in view of the city's part in the massacre of the Jews, there was some deliberate irony here. The next line in the roll deals with Richard Malebisse's offer of 300 marks to be pardoned his offences, including his involvement in the massacre.

[10] For the case of Godfrey, bishop of Winchester, *Chron.*, iii. 246, discussed PR 6 Richard I, xxii.

[11] All figures for Richard's English revenues come from N. Barratt, 'The English Revenues' (forthcoming). However, none of these figures includes any of the large sums audited separately by the exchequer of the ransom.

[12] Coggeshall, 64.

some research. In Stephen's time kings of England had been accustomed
to wear their crowns two or three times a year – but Henry II had dropped
the practice.[13] However, since it would also take time for a fleet and army
to assemble at Portsmouth, there was probably little point in him objecting
strongly. The rest of the final day of the council was spent on what was
probably the most arduous and, at times, exasperating part of a king's job:
dispute settlement – hearing petitions and complaints against and between
powerful men.[14] Over the next few weeks quarrels between Archbishop
Geoffrey and Hubert Walter, between Archbishop Geoffrey and the
chancellor, between the bishop of Durham and King William of Scotland
were to take up a great deal of time.[15] At least Hubert Walter was still
enjoying a honeymoon period with the monks of Canterbury, so that one
recurring dispute remained quiescent for the moment.

From Nottingham Richard went to Southwell where he met King
William of Scotland on 4 April. Until the 22nd the two kings spent a good
deal of time together. William had a claim to Northumbria, which was well
worth pursuing, and Richard had very good reason to be grateful to him.
He had to find a way of refusing William's requests without so angering
him that the safety of the northern border was put in jeopardy. In this he
succeeded, principally by finding more or less plausible reasons for postponing a decision.[16] On the Sunday after Easter, 17 April, in full regalia
and wearing a crown, with the king of Scots and two earls carrying swords
before him, he walked in procession from his chamber in Winchester
Cathedral priory (St Swithun's) into the cathedral church, preceded by the
prelates and followed by earls, barons, knights and a great crowd of people.
His mother and her ladies waited for him in the north transept. After a
great banquet in St Swithun's priory he returned to Winchester castle for
the night.[17]

[13] Hence, Gervase observed, the church of Canterbury, and presumably Gervase
himself, was consulted about the arrangements proper to such a ceremony, which
he then gives in some detail, Gervase, i, 524–7.

[14] Howden records complaints – by many – against Archbishop Geoffrey, and
against Gerard de Camville instigated – he believed – by the chancellor, complaints
which were then extended to include the charge of treason, Chron., iii, 242. In due
course Gerard's offer of 2,000 marks to recover the king's good will and the restoration of his lands was accepted, PR 6 Richard I, 118, 120.

[15] Chron., iii, 246–50. As parson of a Durham church and a royal clerk deeply
involved in Scottish business Roger of Howden was exceptionally well informed
about the quarrel between Hugh du Puiset and King William, and well placed to
observe Richard's irritation with the bishop, ibid., 245–6.

[16] Ibid., 243–5, 249–50. William offered 15,000 marks for Northumbria with its
castles while Richard was only prepared to offer Northumbria without the castles.
So William went home depressed – but not breathing threats. Indeed next year he
was to suggest making Richard's nephew Otto his heir.

[17] Ibid., 247–9. One striking difference between 1141 and 1194 is that in the
former case Stephen's queen, who had done so much to obtain her husband's

On 22 April King William went north, while Richard prepared to cross the Channel; he had heard bad news from Normandy.[18] He arrived at Portsmouth on the 24th and, with two brief exceptions, stayed there until 12 May. From Howden's journal it is evident that Richard found the delay extremely frustrating. On 28 April he went to Stansted and spent the day hunting.[19] In his absence fighting broke out between his Brabançon and Welsh troops. On 2 May preparations were at last sufficiently advanced for him to be able to order the loading of the fleet. Against the advice of the sailors he boarded a longship and put to sea in a storm, but the rest of the fleet would not leave harbour in these conditions. Next day he was forced back to Portsmouth, and he had to wait there for more than another week. Not until 12 May did the fleet of 100 heavily laden great ships sail for Barfleur.[20]

Despite the anxieties and frustrations, the long delay was put to good use: the naval base of Portsmouth was created.[21] When Richard arrived he found not just the old castle at Porchester and the superb harbour which had long been used by his predecessors for the muster of fleets; he also found, at Portsmouth itself, an embryonic new town recently founded by Jean, lord of Gisors. As a major landowner in the Vexin, Jean de Gisors had virtually been forced to give his allegiance to Philip and hence to John. His estates, including his new town, were now among those forfeited to the crown and being managed by William de Ste Mère Eglise. On 2 May, just before putting to sea, Richard approved the grant of Portsmouth's first royal charter. William de Ste Mère Eglise stayed in charge of Portsmouth until Christmas 1196, supervising the building of a new royal palace in the town. In 1194 more than £160 was spent on works at Portsmouth, the greater part of it on the palace. On the basis of the sums recorded in the Pipe Rolls more money was spent on this than on any other civil building in England in Richard's reign, more even than on the palace of Westminster. By 1212 the role of Jean de Gisors had been forgotten: Portsmouth was Richard's town. The scale of investment in Portsmouth indicates that a new focal point of royal power was being created, in that place where treasure and arms and troops were regularly brought from all over England and Wales before being shipped across the Channel to Normandy. This has been called 'a treasure route as essential to the fortunes of the Angevin house as the

release, also wore her crown in state; in 1194 Berengaria was not in England, and Richard owed his release more to his mother than his wife.

[18] Ibid., 250.

[19] See above, 256.

[20] *Chron.*, iii, 250-1.

[21] See my article, 'Richard I, Galley-Warfare and Portsmouth: the Beginnings of a Royal Navy', in *Thirteenth Century England VI*, ed. M. Prestwich, R. H. Britnell and R. Frane (Woodbridge, 1997), 12-14.

bullion fleets from America were to the cause of the Hapsburg kings of Spain'.[22]

In 1194 – unlike 1189 – it never occurred to anyone that Richard would not return to England. But the overriding imperative to recover his lost territories meant that he stayed on the continent for the next five years – as it turned out, for the rest of his life. He had left his kingdom in the care of one of the most outstanding government ministers in English history, Hubert Walter. As a nephew of Henry II's justiciar Ranulf Glanville, Hubert gained his early administrative experience under the Old King, but it was on crusade with Richard that he had really come to the fore. In the first flush of enthusiasm after the fall of Jerusalem several bishops had taken crusader's vows, but only two of them, Baldwin of Canterbury and Hubert of Salisbury, had fulfilled them. When Hubert returned from the Holy Land he was a famous and much-respected man. There were plenty of influential candidates for the archbishopric, vacant since Baldwin's death at Acre in November 1190, but Hubert was unquestionably the king's man and, as such, was elected archbishop in May 1193. At Christmas he was appointed chief justiciar in succession to Walter of Coutances and eventually, in March 1195, he was also made papal legate.[23]

This cluster of the great offices of church and state in the hands of one man, combined with the king's steady support for his minister, gave Hubert Walter an unassailable position. There were, of course, critics — whether disappointed and bitter men such as Gerald de Barri or austere saints such as Hugh of Lincoln, who, on his deathbed, asked for God's and Hubert Walter's forgiveness for not rebuking the archbishop as often as his conscience told him he should have done.[24] Both critics in their different ways expressed the strict official line of the Church: churchmen should not become involved in worldly affairs. Since the Church was unwilling to renounce its wealth and privileges a degree of involvement was unavoidable, but the sight of a clerk as deeply immersed in secular business, financial, judicial, even military, as Hubert Walter was, often made ecclesiastics uncomfortable, whether they attacked him for it or whether they went out of their way to justify him, as Ralph of Diceto did. It seems to have made the archbishop uncomfortable too: in 1198 he resigned his justiciarship, and his place was taken by a layman. Yet despite this he continued to work at Richard's side and, under a new king, took high office again as chancellor. Without government business to occupy his mind he felt – or so Gerald de Barri said – 'like a fish out of water'.[25] From the king's point

---

[22] Holt, 'Ricardus rex', 29.

[23] C. R. Cheney, *Hubert Walter* (London, 1967) remains by far the best and most balanced short biography.

[24] *Magna Vita*, ii, 188–9; Gerald, *Opera*, iii, 164.

[25] Gerald, *De Invectionibus*, ed. W. S. Davies (London, 1920), 97. But for Hubert's

of view, however, it was a very comfortable arrangement. Since the sheer size of his dominions inevitably meant that for most of the time he was an absentee ruler it was convenient and reassuring to know that all important business, whether of church or state, went through one pair of trustworthy hands. This is what Henry II had hoped to achieve when he appointed his chancellor Thomas Becket as archbishop of Canterbury; and what Richard had hoped from Longchamp. Becket was a disaster; Longchamp failed but might not have done in less unfavourable circumstances; Hubert Walter was a resounding success. No king had a better servant.

None the less, admiration for Hubert Walter has sometimes gone too far, particularly from those who regard administrative development as praiseworthy in itself. There is no evidence to support such statements as: 'The great administrative measures of Richard's reign are to be wholly attributed to the genius of Hubert Walter; King Richard had no part in formulating them.'[26] They are based on the old, and still widely held, belief that Richard was not interested in government and administration. But he was ultimately responsible for picking the justiciars and seneschals who administered justice and finance on the his behalf, and the fact that he did this consistently well for all his dominions, with the exception of England before his departure on crusade, suggests he had some understanding of the tasks these men were going to undertake. Moreover it is a mistake often made by historians of administration, particularly of financial administration, to forget that government is as much about spending money as about collecting it, and all the evidence is that Richard spent money efficiently. Wars then as now were won in large part by sheer administrative competence, by the ability to transform economic resources into military supplies and ensure that they were in the right place at the right time. As Prestwich has put it, 'To be a *bellator* in Richard's eyes involved an understanding of the importance of wheat, barley and meat'.[27] The history of Richard's crusade is very much the history of his concern for supplies – above all at the times when he had the most difficult and controversial decisions to make. All of this seems so obvious that it is hard to see how people ever came to accept ideas such as that Richard 'had no practical interest in administration' [28] – unless it is that historians of English government used to hold as an article of blind faith the notion that a king of England who rarely stays in 'well-governed' England must *ipso facto* have no interest in government.

piety and support for the cults of two English saints, Gilbert of Sempringham and Wulfstan of Worcester, see R. Bartlett, 'The Hagiography of Angevin England', in *Thirteenth Century England V* (Woodbridge, 1995), 51–2.

[26] Appleby, *England without Richard*, 223.

[27] Prestwich, 13. Cf. 'He had also been a man of business and through his choice of officials he proved an able as well as an heroic king', M. T. Clanchy, *England and Its Rulers 1066–1272* (London, 1983), 142.

[28] H. G. Richardson and G. O. Sayles, *The Governance of Medieval England* (Edinburgh, 1963), 328–9.

Fortunately in face of the analyses published by Sir James Holt and other scholars since 1985 it has now become impossible to hold such an absurd position.[29] In the key article, Holt, while reinforcing the view that Hubert Walter was 'one of the greatest royal ministers of all time', pointed out that 'even during his justiciarship the stream of *brevia regis* reflects that Richard intervened frequently and persistently in the control of English affairs'. In particular he showed that the 'teste me ipso' (myself as witness) formula on royal charters can serve as a register of Richard's personal interest and intervention. He also demonstrated that Richard gave especially close attention to what he termed 'the administrative heart of England' – the region between London/Westminster and Winchester/Southampton/Portsmouth from and to which treasure and troops and supplies were taken before being shipped across the Channel.[30] Since then other studies have taken the matter further. Ralph Turner, for example, on the basis of a study of episcopal elections demonstrated that 'Richard I, despite his almost constant absence from England, wielded a strong hand over the English church'; that in placing his own men on the bench of bishops he 'had a greater success than his father or his brother'.[31] Similarly it has been argued that the evidence crediting Henry II with a close personal interest in the legislation promulgated in his reign is no better than the evidence for Richard's interest in the legislation issued in his. Richard's assizes were the naval laws of 1190, the instructions to the judges promulgated in 1194, the 'royal edict' of 1195 (a set of instructions relating to the keeping of the peace), the revised Forest Assize and the Assize of Weights and Measures, both of 1197. Although most of these are documents long familiar to students of English constitutional history it was always assumed that it was the royal ministers, not Richard, who were responsible for them. However, since no new assizes were promulgated while the king was on crusade and in prison, it seems that – as might be expected – administrative innovation required the king's authorization.[32]

---

[29] I argued this in general terms in *Richard the Lionheart* as long ago as 1978, but historians of administration tend to be impressed only by the evidence of administrative documents. For this reason a crucial moment in the historiography of Richard's reign came in 1985, when an article by Holt originally published in 1981, but not in a place readily accessible to students in the U.S. or Britain, was reprinted. This article (Holt, 'Ricardus rex') used precisely the 'right sort' of evidence – charters, Pipe Rolls and the judicial records of the king's court – to investigate Richard's management of business, including the business of patronage.

[30] Holt, 'Ricardus rex'. Even if, as has generally been assumed, it was a chancery clerk, perhaps the chancellor, William Longchamp, who devised the actual words 'teste me ipso', it would still be the king who took responsibility for their use in a particular document. Cf. C. Fagnen, 'Le vocabulaire du pouvoir', 89–90.

[31] R. V. Turner, 'Richard Lionheart and English Episcopal Elections', *Albion*, xxix (1997), 10–11. This reinforced the view long ago expressed that Richard was 'forever busy with the English church', C. R. Cheney, *From Becket to Langton: English Church Government 1170–1213* (Manchester, 1956), 10.

[32] Gillingham, *Coeur de Lion*, 105–18.

The most important administrative and fiscal innovation of Richard's reign was the introduction of a royal customs system – something so exasperating to merchants specializing in foreign trade and yet so central to the king's prosecution of the war against Philip Augustus and his allies that it must have been at his insistence that it was pushed through. By 1194–5 the exchequer accounts reveal that a customs duty levied on overseas trade at the rate of one-tenth had been introduced. In that year William of Yarmouth accounted for £537 14s 2d from the tenth levied in the ports of Norfolk and Lincolnshire.[33] Although, as with virtually all revenue raised from new sources, customs revenue was not subjected to the bureaucratic process of an exchequer audit, and so its yield is unknown, other incidental Pipe Roll entries show that it continued to be raised until after the end of Richard's reign. Collection of the duty required setting up a system of port management which facilitated military (economic warfare) as well as fiscal policy.[34] By 1198 the duty of supervising and checking the performance of the port managers had been laid upon the itinerant justices.[35] Since royal officers were involved not only in bulk buying of food and materials for the prosecution of the war but also in selling the prizes they captured from the king's enemies, it is not surprising the government issued an Assize of Weights and Measures.[36] Given the large sums of money which had gone to Germany to pay the ransom (of which there is no surviving record since the documentation of the specially constituted 'Exchequer of the Ransom' has vanished), the steady flow of cash into the treasury after 1194 is fairly impressive: more was received in the later 1190s than in the early years of John's reign.[37] Yet revenue audited at the Norman exchequer in the late twelfth century climbed much faster than revenue audited at the English exchequer and it may have been this that led Richard to send Abbot Robert of St Stephen's at Caen, a senior official of the Norman exchequer, together with his confidential agent Philip of Poitou, to carry out a thorough enquiry into the workings of its English counterpart in 1196. Abbot Robert, however, was taken ill while dining with Hubert Walter and he died five days later, on 11 April 1196.[38] Some time during

---

[33] PR 7 Richard I, 79. T. H. Lloyd describes this as 'a tax strangely overlooked by historians', *The English Wool Trade in the Middle Ages* (Cambridge, 1977), 8.

[34] For payments to those who 'kept' the port of London and their purchase of a *navicula* (presumably a police/customs launch), PR 8 Richard I, 18; for discussion of the fines imposed for selling corn to the king's enemies, PR 10 Richard I, xiv–xv.

[35] *Chron.*, iv, 62.

[36] Ibid., 33–4. Much to Howden's disgust, in John's reign merchants were no longer required to conform to the standards laid down in Richard's statute, Ibid., 172.

[37] N. Barratt, 'The English Revenues'.

[38] *Chron.*, iv, 5; Newburgh, Bk 5, ch. 19. Newburgh believed that Hubert Walter – understandably – was not pleased at having his exchequer investigated in this way. For background on Robert of Caen's mission I am grateful to Vincent Moss.

the same year, probably later, Hubert informed Richard that he had sent
him 1,100,000 marks in the last two years – a fantastic total which is either
a chronicler's error or a minister's pardonable exaggeration.[39]

One measure which historians have always been happy to ascribe to
Richard's initiative was his innovative – indeed unique – decree relating to
the holding of tournaments in England. According to William of
Newburgh, when mock battles had been held in England they had always
led to real quarrels. Hence tournaments had been prohibited on the
orders of Henry II, following in the footsteps of his grandfather, Henry I.
Those Englishmen who wished to try their hand at tournaments had to go
abroad.

> Therefore the famous king Richard, observing that the extra training
> and exercise of the French made them correspondingly fiercer in war,
> wanted the knights of his own kingdom to be able to train in their own
> lands so that they could learn from tourneying the art and customs of
> real war and so the French would no longer be able to insult English
> knights as crude and lacking in skill.[40]

In August 1194 Richard designated five places in England as official tournament sites: the fields between Salisbury and Wilton in Wiltshire, between
Warwick and Kenilworth in Warwickshire, between Brackley and Mixbury
(Northants), between Stamford and Warinford (probably Suffolk) and
between Blyth and Tickhill in Nottinghamshire. A fee was charged for
licence to hold a tournament and each participant was charged a fee
according to rank, from earl down to landless knight.[41] Richard appointed
William, earl of Salisbury as 'director of tournaments' and Hubert Walter
appointed his own brother Theobald as collector of fees.[42] How popular
and how profitable this unique system of 'nationalized' tournaments was,
it is impossible to say. William of Newburgh, writing a few years later, was
still able to think of tournaments as occasions at which, 'even to the pres-

[39] *Chron.*, iv, 12–13. According to Howden, Hubert had been thinking of resign-
ing the justiciarship.

[40] Newburgh, Bk 5, ch. 4.

[41] J. Barker, *The Tournament in England 1100–1400* (Woodbridge, 1986); R.
Barber, *The Knight and Chivalry* (revised edn, Woodbridge, 1995), Part III 'Chivalry
in the Field'. R. Barber and J. Barker, *Tournaments. Jousts, Chivalry and Pageants in
the Middle Ages* (Woodbridge, 1989). Though he sadly underestimates the intelligence of William Marshal, there is a good analysis of the value of tournaments as
training for war in G. Duby, *Guillaume le Maréchal* (Paris, 1984), 111–36. Cf. G.
Duby, *The Legend of Bouvines* (Berkeley, 1990), 84–97, Gillingham, 'War and
Chivalry in the *History of William the Marshal*', in *Coeur de Lion* and Strickland, *War
and Chivalry*, 104 ff., 149 ff.

[42] For the text, Diceto, ii, lxxx–lxxxi, and *Foedera*, i, 65; Howden gives the gist,
Chron., iii, 268.

ent day, repeated papal prohibitions were treated with contempt by the fervour of young knights who were keen to acquire military fame and the favour of kings' – phrases which suggest that the fees charged had not been set so high as to discourage participation. Many years later William Marshal reminisced about the days towards the end of Richard's reign when thirty English knights were worth forty French.[43]

For all his overriding concern with the wars on the frontiers of his continental dominions, Richard did not forget England's frontiers. His reign stands out as a time of peace in relations with Scotland.[44] Whether or not William the Lion had already consulted Richard when, in 1195, he announced his intention of marrying his daughter Margaret to Richard's nephew Otto and making the latter heir to the Scottish throne is not stated in the only source for this scheme – Roger of Howden. Despite some opposition in Scotland, William pressed ahead and Richard responded, sending an envoy (almost certainly none other than Howden himself) to carry out preliminary negotiations on his behalf. By the end of the year matters were sufficiently far advanced for Hubert Walter to spend Christmas at York on his way to speak to the Scottish king. William was to endow his daughter with Lothian, and Richard was to endow Otto with Northumbria and the county of Cumberland. In the meantime the king of England would have custody of Lothian and its castles and the king of Scotland would have the custody of Northumbria and Cumberland with theirs. However, the scheme was dropped when William's queen became pregnant, and he hoped for the birth of a male heir.[45] Although it came to nothing this radical scheme was clearly intended to lay to rest the most serious cause of tension and war between the kings of England and Scotland: the latter's claim to Northumbria. In Ireland John's justiciar was removed and replaced by John de Courcy and Walter de Lacy. In 1195 they met the king of Connacht, Cathal Crobderg Ua Conchobar, at Athlone and made peace.[46]

After Richard's return from crusade and captivity, 'a greater energy', according to Sir John Lloyd, 'was undoubtedly shown by the English in their dealings with Wales'. Whether this was to be attributed to Hubert Walter (Lloyd's view) or, ultimately, to the king is not a question which

---

[43] *HGM*, 11,064–67.

[44] See above, 9, 113.

[45] *Chron.*, iii, 298–9, 308. See A. A. M. Duncan, *Scotland. The Making of the Kingdom* (Edinburgh, 1975), 239–40 and D. D. R. Owen, *William the Lion* (East Linton, 1997), 83–5. Earlier there had been a short-lived scheme to make Otto earl of York, *Chron.*, iii, 86; PR 3 Richard I, 61. On Roger of Howden's journey to the Scottish court in the autumn of 1195 see my 'Travels of Roger of Howden and his Views of the Irish, Scots and Welsh', *ANS*, xx (1997), 157–8.

[46] M. T. Flanagan, *Irish Society, Anglo-Norman Settlers, Angevin Kingship* (Oxford, 1989), 282–3. Both Walter de Lac and William Marshal obtained possession of their lordships in Ireland while Richard took over from John as lord of Ireland.

concerned contemporaries – at least not so far as can be ascertained from surviving sources. The two men who led English expansion into Maelienydd (east-central Wales) and to St Clears (in the south-west) in 1195, Roger Mortimer and William de Briouze, were both high in royal favour.[47] The defeat which Hywel Sais (Lord Rhys's son) suffered at St Clears persuaded him to set his father free, and it may have been the news that this elderly but still great Welsh leader had been set at liberty that explains the concern for the Welsh frontier which Richard showed in a letter to Hubert Walter in April 1196. In this he pressed for troops to be sent urgently to Normandy but at the same time insisted that William de Briouze, William d'Albini and the barons of the March of Wales should stay where they were.[48] After this, first Hubert Walter and then his successor as justiciar, Geoffrey FitzPeter, gave Welsh affairs a rather higher priority.

In December 1197 Hubert Walter summoned a council meeting at Oxford and passed on Richard's requirement that the barons of England should supply him with a force of 300 knights prepared for a year's service at their own expense, while the towns should provide 500 men-at-arms. Royal demands for which there was no exact precedent always provoked opposition but, according to Howden, only Hugh of Lincoln refused to comply. [49] Other churchmen were unhappy, notably the bishop of Salisbury, but in the end they were browbeaten or persuaded to do as the king asked.[50] Abbot Samson of Bury St Edmunds went to Normandy but, according to his biographer, he was for a long time unable, 'despite the many gifts he made to our lord the king', to come to terms with a king who said he wanted soldiers, not gold and silver. Eventually Samson hired four knights for forty days at a cost of 36 marks and paid an additional £100 to be exempted from the expense of maintaining them for the rest of the year.[51] Saints such as Hugh of Lincoln had, in the last resort, other priorities but on the whole the

[47] J. E. Lloyd, *History of Wales* (3rd edn, London, 1939), ii, 579–80; J. J. Crump, 'The Mortimer Family and the Making of the March', in *Thirteenth Century England VI* (Woodbridge, 1997), 119–20.

[48] Diceto, ii, lxxix–lxxx.

[49] *Chron.*, iv, 40. Howden mistakenly dates the council to 1198 – probably because he was in Rome at the time. For accounts written some fifteen years later which emphasize Bishop Hugh's brave resistance to an 'oppressive' demand, see *Magna Vita*, ii, 98–100, Gerald, *Opera*, vii, 103–4. See above, 258–9.

[50] According to the annals of Winchester, both the bishops of Winchester and Salisbury went to Normandy early in 1198, the latter under very heavy pressure of the sort which only a saint such as Hugh of Lincoln could withstand, *Annales Monastici*, ii, ed. H. R. Luard (RS, 1865), 67. For the whole question see PR Richard I, xix–xxiv.

[51] *The Chronicle of Jocelin of Brakelond*, ed. H. E. Butler (London, 1949), 85–7. The knights were sent to Eu.

English historians of the time seem to have shared Abbot Samson's values. Much as they disliked the level of Richard's demands, they sympathized with the policies which made them necessary. To them it seemed right and proper that a king should strain every nerve to recover the lands of which he had been treacherously deprived.[52]

Unquestionably Hubert Walter was in a situation which must have taxed his great abilities. Even if he had been a layman without the responsibilities and obligations of an archbishop and papal legate, it would not have been easy to represent both the king to the English political establishment and the English political establishment to the king. Having talked of resignation on and off since 1194, he eventually resigned in 1198.[53] In an open letter to his English subjects dated 11 July 1198 Richard announced the appointment of Geoffrey FitzPeter as justiciar and emphasized just how much he had appreciated Hubert's labours:

> He has often earnestly begged us to release him from office, and to this end has alleged many cogent reasons, bodily weakness, illness and other inconveniences. But we, for our sake and yours, and because of the peace in which he maintained the kingdom, have hitherto refused to grant his request. At last, however, considering his infirmity and the intolerable burden of his labours, we have agreed to release him from the office committed to him.[54]

During the five years between his return from captivity and his death Richard spent most of his time in Normandy. Gaps in his itinerary as it is known at present make it impossible to give anywhere near as precise a picture of his movements as can be done for John's reign.[55] In 1195 he probably spent about five months in Normandy and five months in Anjou. But as the struggle between him and Philip Augustus came to be concentrated on the Vexin and north-eastern Normandy so he spent more and more time in Normandy – about ten months in 1196, nine months in 1197 and ten months in 1198 – and increasingly in that 'capital region' on the 20-mile stretch of the Seine between Rouen and Les Andelys.[56] From here it was no harder for him than it would be for

---

[52] 'It would not be honourable for the king of England to make peace when his dominions, when he was in prison and in defiance of the law of nations, had been so mutilated by the king of France', Newburgh, Bk 5, ch. 15.

[53] Gervase, i, 527; *Chron.*, iv, 12–13.

[54] *Foedera*, i, 71.

[55] See Landon. This itinerary contains many gaps – some quite large, such as the months of September and October 1194. The discovery and publication of more charters by Dr Vincent will almost certainly help to fill in many of these gaps.

[56] Gillingham, *The Angevin Empire*, 56 (repr. in *Coeur de Lion*).

another masterful king, Henry V, to control English business. Those who
resisted his justiciar were summoned to Normandy. As Richard wrote to
Hubert early in 1196, 'If there is anyone who is reluctant to obey our
orders sent in writing, send him to us at once and we will give him that
order *viva voce*.'[57]

[57] Diceto, ii, lxxx.

Chapter 16

FRANCE, 1194-6

William Marshal long remembered the jubilation with which Richard was greeted on landing at Barfleur. Everywhere he went he received a tumultuous welcome. Old and young joined in the dancing and singing: 'God has come again in His strength. It's time for the French King to go.'[1] But the unwelcome fact was that Richard faced massive problems. Everywhere from Aquitaine to Normandy the security of his continental dominions had been shattered. In the twelve months since the surrender of Gisors in April 1193 he had suffered one damaging loss after another.[2] Philip held much of Normandy east of the Seine, including the lordships of Arques and Eu with their ports of Dieppe and Tréport. His acquisition of Artois from Flanders in 1192, coming on top of his acquisition of the Amienois in 1185, meant that Philip was infinitely richer and more powerful in the north-east of France than any king of France since Carolingian times.[3] West of the Seine he had occupied a tongue of land reaching deep into Normandy, from Tillières on the Avre northwards to Beaumont-le-Roger, Neubourg and Vaudreuil. On both banks of the Seine he was now within easy striking distance of Rouen itself. As count of Mortain John was able to carry with him many in south-west Normandy, and in February 1194 Philip had given him charge of the important town of Evreux.[4] Inevitably the great Norman Marcher lords like William of Caïeux, Hugh of Gournay, Richard de Vernon, Count Robert of Meulan and Count Geoffrey of Perche had gone over to Philip.[5] They had had little choice if they did not

---

[1] *HGM*, 10,429-52.

[2] According to a contemporary Crowland source, 'King Philip had fraudulently rather than violently stolen the greatest and best part of Normandy', 'The Case concerning the Marsh lying between the Abbey of Croyland and the Priory of Spalding 1189-1202', in D. M. Stenton, *English Justice between the Norman Conquest and the Great Charter* (London, 1965), 176-8.

[3] It was in this region that he had made the gains which led to Rigord christening him Augustus, Rigord, 6.

[4] The accounts (or lack of them) for the *bailliages* (bailiwicks) of Mortain, Tinchebrai, Gavray and Avranches in the Norman exchequer Rolls all point to damaging military activity by John in this region, *MRSN*, i, 215-16; ii, 292-3.

[5] For Richard de Vernon, ibid., i, 148, 153. Geoffrey of Perche had a family claim to Moulins and Bonsmoulins and it was doubtless the costs incurred in defending these important frontier castles against his attacks that are recorded in Exchequer

want to share the fate of Earl Robert of Leicester. His loyalty to Richard cost him the castle of Pacy. In Touraine and Berry the loss of Loches and Châtillon-sur-Indre were grievous blows. In Aquitaine, the counts of Angoulême and Perigueux, the viscount of Brosse, and Geoffrey de Rancon were all in revolt. Here at least Richard had friends. The Navarre alliance had yielded troops led by Berengaria's brother, Sancho.[6] But Richard's most powerful ally, the emperor, was marching south, bent on the conquest of Sicily. In France itself all the great princes either kept their distance or fought on Philip's side, at their head the counts of Toulouse, Flanders, Boulogne and Ponthieu. If this were not enough, many modern scholars have argued that Capetian financial resources were now greater than Richard's. Given the difficulty of the task facing him, the extent of his success is astonishing. It would be even more so if these modern guesstimates were right.

In fact in May 1194 Philip's advance was not yet over. Although there was supposed to be a truce until Whitsun, Philip alleged that it had been broken by disturbers of the peace coming over from England, and took up arms again.[7] On 10 May he laid siege to Verneuil, a strongly defended and strategically sited castle. The garrison had already withstood one siege in 1193 and were confident of repeating that success. They mocked Philip, first by opening the gate and inviting him to enter; then by drawing on it a caricature of him holding a mace for him to look at when it was shut.[8] Presumably they owed much of their confidence to the belief that Richard was already on the way to relieve them. In reality he was still at Portsmouth on 10 May, held up by storms in the Channel. As a result Philip was given one last chance to score a major victory. His siege machines succeeded in bringing down a section of the castle wall.[9] According to the *History of William the Marshal*, by the time Richard reached Lisieux, worry about Verneuil meant he was unable to sleep. One of Philip's allies, however, chose not to wait to see the outcome of the siege before changing sides.

Roll for 1195: *MRSN*, i, 244–6. Cf. D. J. Power, 'What Did the Frontier of Angevin Normandy Comprise?', *ANS*, xvii (1994), 189. The absence of a considerable part of the 1195 account for the *bailliage* of Alençon might reflect disruption caused by the count of Perche. This and the similar point in the previous note I owe to Vincent Moss.

[6] *Chron.*, iii, 252–3.

[7] *Sig. Cont.*, 431. Was this the bad news which Richard heard at Portsmouth?

[8] A story known to Andreas, who also noted Verneuil's strength, ibid. This must have made a very good story since it was even mentioned (after Bouvines, when it was safe to do so) by William the Breton, *Philippidos*, iv, 481–5. According to the later French verse chronicler Guillaume Guiart, *Branches des royaux lignages*, ed. J. A. Buchon (Paris, 1820) ll. 1820–53, it was intended as an allusion to the armed men Philip employed to guard him against assassination – and whom he was still employing when William the Breton wrote his prose chronicle, WB, 194.

[9] Rigord, 127.

John went to Lisieux, to the house of John of Alençon where Richard was staying, and fell at his brother's feet, begging forgiveness. It was given at once; generously, said Richard's admirers, but also casually and contemptuously. 'Don't be afraid, John, you are a child. You have got into bad company and it is those who have led you astray who will be punished.' It was some time before he received some of his estates back, and even then the castles were withheld from him. Even so the 'child' (now twenty-seven years old) had been treated better than he deserved – and, as John of Alençon told him to his face, very much better than he would have treated Richard.[10]

From Lisieux Richard hurried on to reach Tubœuf, some 20 kilometres west of Verneuil, on the morning of 21 May. Here he was met by a knight from the Verneuil garrison who had managed to ride through the French lines, presumably in search of aid. In his haste Richard had gone on well ahead of the large army he had brought across from England. Instead of advancing to challenge Philip to battle – a tactic which always alarmed the French king – he dispatched one force of knights, men-at-arms and crossbowmen to break through the French lines and reinforce the garrison (which they did), while ordering other troops to ride round to the east of Verneuil to cut Philip's supply lines. After being on the brink of success Philip's position began to deteriorate. On 28 May he received the news that John had returned to Evreux, had killed the French in the town and announced that he now held it for Richard, not for Philip. It is no wonder that Capetian as well as Angevin writers looked upon him with distaste.[11] At once the French king rode off in the direction of Evreux. Although he left sufficient forces at Verneuil to maintain the siege, they decided to withdraw next day (Whitsun Eve). Philip's sudden departure had been the last straw for his troops, already demoralized by the threat to their supplies and by the knowledge that Richard's main armies were now well on their way from Normandy and Anjou. Philip had to endure the humiliation of learning that his siege train had fallen into enemy hands.[12] It may have been this which led him to sack John's Evreux, destroying churches and relics, but it was also an acknowledgement of the fact that he could no longer hope to

---

[10] *HGM*, 10,365–419. Diceto places their meeting at Brix, ii, 114. Howden, though he does not locate it, adds that they were reconciled on Eleanor's advice, *Chron.*, iii, 252, followed in this by Newburgh, Bk 5, ch. 5. In 1195 John recovered Mortain, Eye and Gloucester, but without the castles, and £2,000 per annum in place of all the other counties he had once possessed, *Chron.*, iii, 286.

[11] According to William the Breton, John acted like Hengist and Horsa (i.e. the 'first Englishmen') by inviting the unsuspecting French to a meal and then having them killed, *Philippidos*, iv, 452–69. On William's perception of Richard's attitude to this, see above, 261.

[12] The humiliation of the French retreat from Verneuil was lovingly dwelt on by the dean of St Paul's, Diceto, ii, 114–18, including Latin verses attributed to Geoffrey (probably Geoffrey Vinsauf). See also *Annales angevines*, 26 for a similar view from St Aubin at Angers.

hold on to the town.[13] After harassing the retreating French, Richard entered Verneuil on 30 May, in triumph and in joy. To show his appreciation of the garrison's courage and loyalty he kissed each man in turn and promised them rich rewards.[14] The tide of war had turned.

Nevertheless Philip was far from being a beaten man. After venting his fury on Evreux he was still able to get close to Rouen and he made this plain for all to see by crossing the Seine and attacking the castle of Fontaines, a bare four or five miles from the ducal capital. John and the earl of Leicester were at Rouen but had nothing like enough strength to challenge the French royal army, which was able to press the siege uninterrupted. Even so it took Philip four days, from 10 to 14 June, to capture what was a very small castle, which he then demolished before withdrawing.[15] The dean of St Paul's was very scornful of Philip's boldness in taking on a tiny castle with a royal army.[16] But as he withdrew he won a much greater prize, capturing the earl of Leicester who had ridden out to raid the lands of Hugh de Gournay.[17] Having secured so valuable a bargaining counter Philip at once began to make peace overtures, beginning with a proposal for a three years' truce, but this fell through because Richard would not agree that those who had deserted him should enjoy the protection of a truce. After this, commented Howden, the war became fiercer.[18]

By this time Richard's forces had captured three castles, all more important than Fontaines, and one of them, Loches, a major fortress. The great army which mustered at Verneuil had been divided. Forces from Anjou

[13] Even Rigord and William the Breton regretted Philip's fury, Rigord, 127; WB, 196; *Philippidos*, iv, 497–8. Andreas of Marchiennes dates Philip's furious sack of Evreux and its churches to 'the feast of Holy Spirit', *Sig. Cont.*, 431–2. It was a shocking event: see Newburgh, Bk 5, ch. 2 and *Annales angevines*, 26. The date implied by Howden – though he should have been very well infomed (see n. 18) – is therefore probably wrong.

[14] *Chron.*, iii, 252; Rigord, 127; *HGM*, 10,456–508. As Vincent Moss points out, financial rewards for the defenders of Verneuil bulk large in the 1195 Norman exchequer Roll, i, 236–9.

[15] According to Howden, he attacked Fontaines while a delegation headed by the seneschal of Normandy and Walter of Coutances waited in vain at Pont de l'Arche in the expectation of meeting his envoys to discuss peace, *Chron.*, iii, 253.

[16] Diceto, ii, 116. He probably owed his knowledge of this minor event, and his attitude towards it, to his friend Walter of Coutances.

[17] Tellingly the Capetian historians mention the capture of the earl – 'vir fortis et magnanimus', Rigord, 127, 'strenuissimus', WB, 196, but not Fontaines. For his liberty the earl later offered £1,000 and his right to Pacy.

[18] *Chron.*, iii, 253–5. As David Corner has shown, the historian was himself at Rouen in mid-June 1194, Corner, 'The *Gesta Regis*', 143–4; hence his detailed knowledge of the abortive truce proposals. Perhaps he placed the sack of Evreux at this point in order to illustrate his general theme of the growing nastiness of the war with a notorious example.

and Maine went to the Maine–Perche border where they 'besieged, captured and completely demolished' the castle of Montmirail.[19] An Anglo-Norman contingent went north and took Beaumont-le-Roger, a castle belonging to Robert of Meulan, one of the Marcher lords who had declared for Philip.[20] Richard's chief concern now was for his lands further south where Sancho of Navarre with a large force, including 150 cross-bowmen, was busy laying waste the lands of Ademar of Angoulême and Geoffrey de Rancon.[21] Although Sancho himself was called back to Navarre by the news that his father, King Sancho VI, was dying, his army moved into Touraine to besiege Loches, where it had been arranged that Richard would join them. The loss of Loches may have triggered a general collapse of the Angevin position in Touraine. When Richard reached Tours on 11 June, he not only confiscated the houses and goods of the canons of St Martin's, he also allowed himself to be offered 2,000 marks by the towns-people – which suggests that they felt that they too had done something to incur his wrath.[22] By the time he arrived at Loches next day, the Navarrese troops had been there for a while without making any perceptible progress; probably they had not brought the equipment needed to crack a nut of this size and could do no more than blockade the castle. But on 13 June, in one fierce and prolonged assault, Richard took the castle by storm.[23]

After reasserting his authority in Touraine, Richard's next task was to subdue the rebels in Aquitaine. Following the breakdown of truce talks the French king marched south in an attempt to curtail Richard's freedom of movement in what had now become the main theatre of the war. It was not easy for Philip to do this without giving his opponent the chance to bring

[19] *Chron.*, iii, 252; Diceto, ii, 116–17. The latter identifies it as the castle of William of Perche Gouet. The phrase in quotation marks is common to both accounts and may indicate a common source of information. The annalist of St Aubin was notably proud of the prowess of the men of Anjou, *Annales angevines*, 27.

[20] *HGM*, 10,545. Although the capture of Beaumont is not mentioned by Rigord, Diceto or Howden, it is also placed here by William the Breton, WB, 196, 'castrum munitissimum'. Cf. *Philippidos*, iv, 526.

[21] Diceto, ii, 117; *Chron.*, iii, 252–3.

[22] *Chron.*, iii, 252; Diceto, ii, 117. Since both historians explicitly note that the payment was voluntary, it presumably wasn't. At St Denis there was no doubt that Richard oppressed the canons of St Martin's, Rigord, 127–8. For some amends made later by Richard, Diceto, ii, 122.

[23] The annalist of St Aubin was especially impressed, reporting that Richard took a massively fortified stronghold 'boldly and manfully in one assault, with few companions, in the space of two or three hours', taking 220 prisoners, *Annales angevines*, 27. According to Howden (from whom this date is derived), he captured five knights and twenty-four (*quatuor et viginti*) sergeants, *Chron.*, iii, 253; Diceto says it had been garrisoned by fifteen knights and eighty (*quater viginti*) sergeants, ii, 117. What looks like Howden's mistake suggests a common source. See Gillingham, 'Royal Newsletters'.

him to battle, and this was precisely the opportunity Richard was waiting
for. Early in July he moved up to Vendôme (another town surrendered by
John in January) and pitched camp outside the town – as secure in his
tents, boasted Howden, as if he had been behind walls – barring the road
that Philip would have to take if he wanted to make his presence felt in the
Loire valley. As soon as Philip's scouts reported that Richard's army lay just
in front of them, the French king sent word that he would attack in the
morning and then promptly made off in the opposite direction. Near
Fréteval on 4 July Richard caught up with the French rearguard and soon
the whole of Philip's army was in flight to Châteaudun. Richard led a determined pursuit in the hope of catching Philip himself. According to
Howden, when one horse tired, Mercadier was at hand to provide Richard
with another. Although Philip managed to elude his pursuers, the French
wagon train did not. The rich booty included horses, tents, siege engines
and much of Philip's treasure. In addition, by capturing the French king's
chapel, Richard had captured the royal archives, including documents
giving the names of those of his subjects who had been prepared to join
the enemy.[24]

Despite his eagerness to hunt down the man whom he had learned to
hate, Richard had not forgotten elementary tactics. One of his most experienced captains, William Marshal, had joined neither the pursuit nor the
plundering of the wagon train, but had, on Richard's orders, held his
troops together ready to deal with any attempt by the French to rally and
counterattack. That evening, as Richard's men celebrated, boasting of
their great deeds, the knights they had captured and the booty they had
won, the king praised William, and, by implication, praised himself: 'The
Marshal did better than any of you. If there had been any trouble he would
have helped us. When one has a good reserve, one does not fear one's
enemies.'[25] Within the space of forty days Philip had suffered two humiliating retreats, once at Verneuil where he lost his artillery and once at
Fréteval where he lost his whole wagon train.[26] Philip had been driven
from the field and Richard now had a free hand in Aquitaine.

From Vendôme Richard moved south. We know nothing about the campaign except what Richard himself wrote in a brief letter to Hubert Walter:

Know that, by the grace of God, who in all things upholds the right, we
have captured Taillebourg and Marcillac and the whole land of Geoffrey

---

[24] *Chron.*, iii, 255–6; Diceto, ii, 118; *Annales angevines*, 26–7. According to Philip's
historians, Richard launched a surprise attack, Rigord, 129; WB, 196–7; *Philippidos*,
iv, 530–42. And so he may have done. Where the historians on both sides reflect
the party line, it is often impossible to know what 'really happened'. Only the outcome is not in doubt.
[25] *HGM*, 10,583–676.
[26] As gleefully pointed out by Diceto, ii, 118.

de Rancon; also the city of Angoulême, Châteauneuf-sur-Charente, Montignac, Lachaise and all the other castles and the whole land of the Count of Angoulême in its entirety; we captured the city and citadel of Angoulême in a single evening; in the lands which we took in those parts we captured up to 300 knights and 40,000 soldiers. Myself as witness at Angoulême, 22 July.[27]

Evidently Richard had been busy in the two and a half weeks since Fréteval. The old and formidable alliance of Geoffrey de Rancon and the count of Angoulême had apparently been overwhelmed in a campaign of shattering power and decisiveness, thanks in part to the fact that the groundwork had already been laid by Sancho of Navarre. The capture of Angoulême was the culmination of two months of remarkable military success; the relief of Verneuil, the taking of Loches, the pursuit at Fréteval and the capture of Taillebourg. As Ralph of Diceto observed, 'from the castle of Verneuil to Charles's Cross [in the Pyrenees] there was no one to stand out against him'.[28]

North of Verneuil, however, less had been achieved. It was Normandy which had felt the weight of King Philip's main thrusts in 1193 and 1194. In the truce talks of June 1194 and in the events of the next two weeks Philip had tried to maintain his threat to Richard's position in the Loire valley and beyond, but when he turned and ran at Fréteval it became clear that his priorities lay further north. Although he was prepared to make gestures of support for rebels in Richard's southern lands – as he had been doing since 1182–3 – he would not put up a determined fight on their behalf. In Normandy it was different. Economically and strategically the Seine valley was vitally important to the king of Paris. Philip would fight tooth and nail to hold on to the gains he had made here; when he did his best to stir up trouble in Aquitaine it was only in an attempt to distract Richard's attention. In the end Philip's strategy worked and Richard was killed in Aquitaine. This, however, does not alter the basic pattern of the last four years of Richard's rule – a struggle for dominance in the region between Paris and Rouen, a struggle which revolves around castles and bridges across the Seine, a struggle which concerns control of territory and the flexible deployment of resources within that territory.[29]

After Fréteval, while Richard went south to the Saintonge and Angoumois, Philip sped back north. In his absence a Norman army commanded by Count John and the earl of Arundel had laid siege to

---

[27] *Chron.*, iii, 257. The dean of St Paul's also saw a copy of this newsletter, Diceto, ii, 118–19. The number '40,000' is pure rhetoric.

[28] Ibid., ii, 119.

[29] As indeed was perceived by William the Marshal in his summary of the 'great war', *HGM*, 10,564–80.

Vaudreuil.[30] After the loss of the Norman Vexin in 1193, the castle of Vaudreuil had become the key fortress on this border, controlling access to the Seine bridge at Pont de l'Arche, only ten miles south of Rouen. Vaudreuil's importance in the eyes of the Norman dukes is indicated by the fact that, together with Rouen, Caen and Falaise, it was one of those castles where they stored their treasure. Its fall in February 1194 had been a bitter blow – and to Philip, of course, a great triumph. He did not intend to let it slip out of his grasp. It throws a sharp light on John's career if we remember that the prince who besieged it in July 1194 was the same man who had granted it to Philip just six months earlier. From Châteaudun to Vaudreuil was a journey which Philip accomplished in three days – a marvellous feat, according to his biographers, since it normally took a week for an armed force to cover the 100 miles. Certainly it was quick enough to take John and the earl of Arundel by surprise. The French king then attacked John's camp at dawn and won a thoroughly convincing victory. While the Norman cavalry rode to safety, most of the infantry, together with John's siege artillery, were captured.[31] Philip's success at Vaudreuil in mid-July showed that the spectacular gains which Richard was still registering elsewhere could not be repeated on the Norman–French frontier. Here it was going to be a hard slogging match, with each forward push requiring methodical and expensive preparation.

The intensity and pace which had characterized the campaigning since 10 May could not last, and Richard must have given his representatives in Normandy, headed by Chancellor Longchamp, authority to make a truce. The truce of Tillières, sealed by Philip's representatives on 23 July 1194, was due to last until 1 November 1195 and, like all truces, was based on the principle of status quo.[32] Both sides were to keep what they held on the day of the truce. This meant that Philip kept Vaudreuil with the dependent fortifications at Louviers, Acquigny and Léry, as well as Gisors and the Norman Vexin, Vernon, Gaillon, Pacy, Illiers-l'Evêque, Marcilly-sur-Eure, Louye, Tillières-sur-Avre and Nonancourt. Other lands which Richard acknowledged to be held by his enemies included much of north-east Normandy: the lordships of Eu, Arques, and Drincourt now held by Philip himself; Aumâle and Beauvoir (held by Hugh de Gournay); Mortemer (held by William de Caïeux) and Neufmarché (held by William de Garland). Despite his loss of Beaumont-le-Roger Count Robert of Meulan still sided with Philip. The terms of the truce make plain the size of the task

---

[30] According to William the Breton, William the Lion's brother, Earl David of Huntingdon, and Geoffrey of York were also present: WB, 197; *Philippidos*, v, 18–50.

[31] Rigord, 130. Not surprisingly neither Howden nor Diceto mentions this setback.

[32] Howden gives its text, *Chron.*, iii, 257–60. In addition the prisoners taken at Vaudreuil were ransomed, Rigord, 130.

confronting Richard. Not only had he lost control of a large part of eastern Normandy but there was also a band of countryside further west where Philip's troops had devastated the land and demolished the fortifications. According to the terms of the truce Richard was only allowed to rebuild four castles: Drincourt in the north-east, and Neubourg, Conches and Breteuil to the west of Evreux. Two of the rebels in Aquitaine were also included in the truce: the viscount of Brosse and the count of Angoulême. Since the truce was agreed on 23 July 1194 it was negotiated by Richard's representatives in Normandy in ignorance of the most recent developments in Aquitaine. None the less, since Richard had completed his conquest of the lands of Geoffrey de Rancon and Ademar of Angoulême by 22 July, he may have been content with the status quo of 23 July. Even in Normandy there had been some recovery since the nadir of February 1194. Philip may well have tried to hold on to some places which he finally chose to destroy. Evreux and Drincourt certainly came into this category; Conches, Breteuil and Neubourg probably did. A story, reported by Roger of Howden, that the terms displeased Richard may well reflect his displeasure at 'turncoats' being permitted to enjoy the benefits of the truce.[33]

There was very little chance, however, that the truce would be observed for long. In part this was because the complicated criss-cross of allegiances in the Marches was bound to lead to argument, and thus to an outbreak of skirmishing.[34] The truce had not tried to resolve any of the problems in this region, as a peace – if it hoped to achieve any sort of permanence – would have had to do. It had simply left the situation as it happened to be on one day. The position within the lordship of Drincourt, for example, was clearly unstable. Philip counted the tenants of Drincourt among his followers since he insisted that they should be included in the truce, but Richard's Norman supporters presumably held Drincourt itself since this was one of the four fortresses that Richard was expressly permitted to rebuild. But the position was not only unstable, it was also basically intolerable. Truce or no truce, the duke of Normandy was bound to seize any opportunity of lessening the dishonour of knowing that Capetian banners were waving over his castles. Even the Augustinian canon, William of Newburgh, felt that while it was doubtless prudent for Richard to agree to the truce, it was not honourable so long as Philip held lands that were more justly his.[35] Richard was bound either to prepare for another burst of

---

[33] *Chron.*, iii, 267, cf. ibid., 255 for Richard's attitude a month earlier. Howden's report that, as a consequence of his irritation, Richard had a new seal made and all acts under the old one annulled, has caused much debate, see Landon, 177–80. It may be that the making of a new seal was threatened in the summer of 1194 as part of Richard's grumbling about aspects of the truce, but not yet implemented.

[34] *Chron.*, iii, 276; cf. Diceto, ii, 120.

[35] Newburgh, Bk 5, ch. 3.

all-out war or to attempt to negotiate a proper peace – or, most likely, simultaneously do both. That he did this to good effect seems clear from the peace negotiations of the summer of 1195, since Philip was then prepared to hand back all of his conquests except the Norman Vexin, Gaillon and Vernon (on the Seine), Ivry and the earl of Leicester's castle of Pacy. It is hard to imagine why Philip would be so generous unless his other conquests were either already lost or on the point of being lost. This must mean that the war had been continued by other means.[36]

According to Howden, Philip denounced the truce after he discovered that Henry VI, newly returned in triumph to Germany from his conquest of Sicily, was encouraging Richard to invade France with the promise that he would lend him support. This led the king of France to take the unpleasant kind of decision that Richard had taken over Ascalon. 'Seeing that he had no hope of defending them against Richard, he had many Norman castles demolished.'[37] The two kings met near Vaudreuil in July 1195. Philip had already decided to destroy the great castle and, according to the English version of events, was using the conference simply as a device to gain time to enable his engineers to complete the job of undermining the walls. Only when Richard heard the crash of the walls did he understand what Philip was up to. Swearing that by God's legs he would see to it that saddles were emptied that day, he at once gave the order to attack. Philip beat a hasty retreat across the river Seine and then had the bridge at Portjoie broken down after him. Cheated of his prey, Richard returned to Vaudreuil and took possession of both it and those of the French king's army who had been left behind. Although this was a memorable episode, told in vivid terms by writers on both sides, it cannot be precisely dated.[38] But if the incident on the day of the Vaudreuil conference had been an isolated event, Philip's decision to undermine the castle would have been an act of folly. In fact charter evidence demonstrates that on at least two occasions before July 1195 Richard's chancery was issuing charters from Vaudreuil, in January 1195 and in June. What this suggests is that on more than one occasion Richard had been able to hold court right at the gates of the castle, that he had, in other words, already reduced the Vaudreuil garrison to impotence.[39] A garrison that can no longer dominate the terri-

[36] As early as August 1194, as part of his long-term preparations for the renewal of war, Richard had organized the holding of tournaments in England. See above, 278.

[37] *Chron.*, iii, 300–1. According to this account Richard was much more sceptical of the value of the emperor's promise. However, there is little doubt that Philip feared German intervention. Rigord, 130, without going into details, says it was Richard who, in July, put an end to the truce.

[38] Wherever he possibly can Roger of Howden likes to give a precise date, but in this case he says only that it happened 'on a certain day'; *Chron.*, iii, 301; Rigord, 130–1; *HGM*, 10,534–58; Newburgh Bk 5, ch. 15.

[39] The Norman exchequer Roll (*MRSN*, i, 138) records the payment of the large sum of 85 *livres angevines* (four to the pound sterling) to transport a palisade from

tory around its castle is an expensive luxury, which Philip might well have chosen to do without.

The records of the Norman exchequer for the financial year ending in September 1195 show that Richard spent large sums on the castle at Pont de l'Arche only three or four miles north of Vaudreuil, close to the Cistercian monastery that he founded at Bonport, and controlling the bridge across the Seine which carried the road to Rouen. As long as the bridge at Pont de l'Arche was in Richard's hands he could at will bring across forces, mustered at Rouen and supplied from that city's ample resources, which were large enough to ensure that the Vaudreuil garrison stayed behind their castle walls. The same source records further expenditure at nearby Orival and Moulineaux, and although theoretically the money could have been spent after the fall of Vaudreuil, the *History of William the Marshal* refers to work at Orival and Pont de l'Arche by way of prelude to the Vaudreuil incident.[40] Pressure of this kind, exerted over a long period, though it might lead to skirmishing, was unlikely to explode into a stirring military action of the type to attract the attention of chroniclers; so long as it did not, it did not constitute an undeniable breach of the truce. Yet it could be an extremely effective means of waging war. The truce between July 1194 and July 1195 was probably also a war of attrition, of sustained military pressure against some of Philip's Norman castles, gradually robbing them of their function, depriving them of the revenues and resources they would normally expect to draw from the countryside around them.

By the summer of 1195 Philip was ready to cut his losses on Normandy's north-eastern frontier as well as at Vaudreuil. Events there are even more obscure than in the Seine valley. But if Richard's problem in the Marches of Normandy had been caused by the uncertain allegiance of the Marcher lords then one obvious course was to install men of proven loyalty in these lordships. One family which was committed to Richard's cause throughout the 1190s was the Lusignan family: in Outremer, in Cyprus and in Poitou. The head of the family, Hugh IX le Brun, had a younger brother, Ralph of Exoudun, and to him Richard granted the hand of the heiress to the county of Eu. Ralph first appears as count of Eu in August 1194. Another rich lady whose estates lay in the same region, the widowed countess of Aumâle, was given in marriage to Baldwin of Béthune, recently returned from Austria. The date of the wedding is uncertain; we know only that Richard paid all or part of the expenses and that it happened between January and September 1195.[41] There is, of course, a very big difference

Rouen to Vaudreuil, probably for a temporary fortification. It may have been from here that the charters were issued. I owe this reference and suggestion to Vincent Moss.

[40] Ibid., 136-8; *HGM*, 10,528-532.

[41] *MRSN*, i, 210, after Baldwin's return from Germany and before the end of the exchequer year.

between being given a countess and being given the countess's estates. The terms of the truce of Tillières show that Philip had granted the lordship of Aumâle to Hugh of Gournay and that he himself held Eu and Arques. In August 1195 he was to give them together with his sister Alice – now at last returned to him – to Count William of Ponthieu.[42] There were always, in other words, two claimants for both Eu and Aumâle, one recognized at Richard's court and one at Philip's. Obviously it would not be surprising if Ralph of Exoudun and Baldwin of Béthune were keen protagonists of an unrecorded war of attrition in north-eastern Normandy; they had much to win. And the evidence of the peace negotiations of 1195 suggests that they had, in fact, been winning. Later events suggest that Dieppe also had been recovered – but not yet the great fortress of Arques, a few miles inland.

That Richard held the military initiative during the truce of 1195 can be seen from the evidence of another campaign. At his accession to the throne in 1189 Richard had surrendered all his rights over Auvergne and the lordships of Issoudun and Graçay. But since Philip, in Richard's eyes, had stolen parts of Normandy he felt justified in looking for compensation on another front. According to William of Newburgh, the only English writer to give any account of this campaign, Richard's Brabançons first captured Issoudun and some other fortresses in Berry and then advanced into Auvergne, capturing the count and his castles. William of Newburgh looked upon this as a splendid extension of Angevin power, but apart from implying that it took place during the summer when Vaudreuil fell, he gives no date for the campaign.[43] A charter in Richard's name was issued at Issoudun on 3 July 1195 and the Norman Exchequer Roll for that year includes a payment of 1440 *livres* 'to barons and knights, going to the king at Issoudun in wartime'.[44] The king may well have left Mercadier in charge when he returned to Vaudreuil but it looks as though Richard himself supervised the early stages of the successful campaign in Berry.

Peace talks were resumed off and on throughout this period. War and diplomacy went hand in hand and chroniclers often found the schemes put forward at peace conferences more interesting than the routine of warfare. Ralph of Diceto, for example, reports a Capetian suggestion made at some date in 1194 that the dispute should be settled by a duel between five champions on each side and says that Richard was delighted with the idea – on condition that he and Philip should take part; the scheme was

---

[42] Rigord, 131 gives the date of marriage. For the terms of the grant of dowry, *Recueil des actes de Philippe Auguste*, i and ii, ed. H-F. Delaborde, C. Petit-Dutaillis and J. Monicat (Paris, 1916–43), no. 508, dated August 1195, in which the king clearly signalled his interest in the possibility of taking Eu and Arques back into his own hands, evidence of his perception of their strategic importance.

[43] Newburgh, Bk 5, ch. 15. The *routiers* were commanded by Mercadier: Rigord, 132.

[44] Landon, no. 454; *MRSN*, i, 136.

dropped.[45] Plans of this nature were simply propaganda exercises – public statements to show that both sides believed that they were in the right and were prepared to prove it by due process of law. Equally, both sides were anxious to show that they were genuinely concerned about the outcome of the struggle between Christian and Muslim and so, when bad news came from Spain at the end of July 1195, it was obviously appropriate to talk again about patching up their quarrel. At a peace conference in August Richard returned Alice to her brother and Philip seemed to be willing to renounce a large part of his conquests in Normandy. According to Howden's summary of this proposed settlement, if Richard's niece Eleanor married Philip's son Louis he would be willing to bestow the Norman Vexin, Ivry and Pacy and Vernon and 20,000 marks upon them; in return Philip would concede everything Richard claimed in Angoulême, Aumale, Eu, Arques and 'many other castles'. But Richard's ally Henry VI needed to be consulted, so a short truce, to last until 8 November, was agreed to give him time to ratify the terms.[46] It could also be that Alice's husband, the count of Ponthieu, was too eager to gain possession of his newly acquired rights in Eu and Arques for a peace along the lines mooted in August 1195 to be feasible. But the idea of a permanent cession of the Norman Vexin as a dowry for Prince Louis's bride was to run and run. To judge from William of Newburgh's account, it was at about this time, when Philip was looking for a way of making peace with Richard, that he publicly exonerated the king of England from the charge of murdering Conrad of Montferrat.[47] Yet although this may have freed Richard from the suspicion of arranging for Assassins to kill King Philip, it is worth noting that he appears not to have worried about the scandal or fear that might have been caused by the employment of Muslims in Western Europe; according to the records of the Norman exchequer, he employed Saracens at Domfront and in the forest of Le Passeis.[48]

With the expiry of the truce the war boiled up to a new climax. This had certainly been anticipated. Another large English army had arrived at Barfleur on 28 August and when Abbot Henry of Crowland, who crossed the Channel with them, disembarked he decided to postpone seeing Richard for a while when made aware that, although it was a truce, the king 'could attend to nothing but campaigns, the organisation of army camps and the custody of castles'.[49] Howden alleges that some sharp practice on

---

[45] Diceto, ii, 121. On this and similar challenges see M. Strickland, 'Provoking or Avoiding Battle? Challenge, Judicial Duel, and Single Combat in Eleventh- and Twelfth-Century Warfare', in *Armies, Chivalry and Warfare in Medieval Britain and France*, ed. M. Strickland (Stamford, 1998), 317–43.

[46] *Chron.*, iii, 302–3.

[47] Newburgh, Bk 5, ch. 16; cf. Rigord, 120–1. See Gillingham, 'Royal Newsletters'.

[48] *MRSN*, i, 221, ii, 350.

[49] Stenton, *English Justice*, 176–7. On this text and on Abbot Henry – William Longchamps's brother and a model abbot – Bartlett, 'Hagiography', 49–51.

the French part at talks scheduled for 8 November showed that they were determined on war; two days later they launched simultaneous attacks on several of Richard's territories.[50] If true, it shows their capacity to exploit the advantage of interior lines of communication. Much the most memorable of these attacks was a raid on Dieppe which Philip himself led and which ended with the town sacked and some ships in the harbour going down in flames after being hit by Greek Fire. Since Howden also says that Richard had only recently rebuilt Dieppe, the town had probably been damaged, or deliberately slighted, when Philip withdrew from it, perhaps in July. None the less it seems that the French king still had possession of Arques when he bestowed it on the count of Ponthieu in August since, according to Rigord, Richard was besieging Arques when Philip led 600 élite knights on the highly successful Dieppe raid.[51] Although the evidence is too slight to be sure exactly what happened, 1195 clearly witnessed a fierce and damaging struggle for possession of Arques and Dieppe, one that was in the end, as the peace treaty of January 1196 shows, won by Richard.

At this point Philip, perhaps counting on Richard's attention being distracted by events in Normandy, made a bid to recover the ground lost in Berry. He may have hoped that the levies of Aquitaine would have their hands full with a war against the new count of Toulouse, Raymond VI, and possibly also with a rebellion in the Périgord. At any rate the coast seemed to be clear when Philip laid siege to Issoudun and he succeeded in capturing the town. The castle, however, held out and the defenders managed to get a message through to Richard. When the news came he was at Vaudreuil. Immediately he sent orders for his armies to converge on Issoudun while he himself, travelling at breakneck speed – covering three days' journey each day, says Howden – went on ahead. On reaching Issoudun he broke through Philip's lines and entered the beleaguered castle. Since Richard had only a small force with him, the French king pressed on with the siege but over the next few days more and more Angevin troops appeared on the scene. It soon became apparent that it was not Richard but Philip who was caught in the trap. He was now outnumbered and in no position even to flee as he had at Fréteval. He had no alternative but to accept Richard's conditions and this he did on 5 December 1195.

---

[50] *Chron.*, iii, 304, where he names the bishop of Beauvais as guilty of sharp practice.

[51] Ibid.; the loss of shipping suggests a combined sea and land operation against Dieppe, perhaps at the instance of the count of Ponthieu for whom Dieppe would be the chief local rival to his own port of St Valéry. Rigord admits that on the way home the French rearguard suffered casualties when Richard launched a surprise attack from the forest, Rigord, 131–2; WB, 198. As perceived at the Capetian court, Richard's capacity to wage 'forest warfare' owed much to his employment of terrifyingly fierce Welsh troops.

The two kings then separated, agreeing to meet again after Christmas to ratify the peace terms. In the meantime a short truce was to be observed.[52]

The peace conference took place, as arranged, near Louviers in the Seine valley between Vaudreuil and Gaillon. By comparing the terms of peace of January 1196 with the truce of July 1194 we can see that Richard had made tremendous gains. In Normandy he had recovered everything except the Norman Vexin and the castles of Neufmarché, Vernon, Gaillon, Pacy, Ivry and Nonancourt. Crucially, the French threat to the Channel had been thrown back. In Berry he had regained Châtillon-sur-Indre (one of the castles surrendered in July 1193), La Châtre, Saint-Chartier, Châteaumeillant, Issoudun and Graçay. In Aquitaine Philip formally recognized that the count of Angoulême, the viscount of Brosse and the count of Périgueux owed homage and service to the duke of Aquitaine. Philip also agreed to abandon his ally, the count of Toulouse, if the latter did not want to be included in the peace. All in all the Peace of Louviers marked a considerable step forward on Richard's part; a victory too for Ralph of Exoudun and Baldwin of Béthune, his counts of Eu and Aumale.[53] It was also agreed that the Norman estates of Hugh of Gournay would revert to the duke after Hugh's death – or earlier if Hugh chose to return to Richard's allegiance. Hugh of Gournay's position had been seriously undermined, since the Peace of Louviers reveals that some of his knights had been fighting on Richard's side. So it is not surprising to find him back in the Angevin camp by the following year. The Peace of Louviers could only be an interim settlement; while Philip held a foot of the land which Richard considered to be rightly his, a permanent peace was impossible.[54] However, it was a peace, and from the French point of view it marked Richard's recognition that the kings of England had lost the Vexin for ever. Rigord saw this as a triumph – which is how Philip presented it when, soon afterwards, he paid St Denis a ceremonial visit.[55]

Although the peace with Philip could be no more than a breathing space, Richard now felt strong enough to risk stirring up war on a new

[52] *Chron.*, iii, 304–5; Newburgh, Bk 5, ch. 17; Rigord, 133, preferred to dwell on the fact that in sight of the two armies Richard did homage for Normandy, Poitou and Anjou – a miracle of peace when they had been on the verge of shedding blood. WB, Cf. 199; *Philippidos*, v, 56–9. For the date of the truce, Powicke, 107, n. 69.

[53] Text in *Recueil des actes*, no. 517. Summary in Landon, 107–9.

[54] Newburgh, Bk 5, ch. 18 emphasized the determination of both kings to renew the war, indifferent alike to religious festivals and to bad weather and famine. Gervase does not mention the Peace of Louviers. All he saw was a truce to last until the feast of John the Baptist on 24 June, Gervase, i, 532.

[55] Rigord, 133. Of course when Richard renounced his right to the Norman Vexin, he was lying. Indeed the peace terms prepared the ground for a future advance since he had been able to insist that one of the castles of the Vexin, Baudemont, should be held by a partisan of his, Stephen of Longchamps.

front. In the spring of 1196 he summoned Constance of Brittany to attend his court. After the death of her first husband, Richard's brother Geoffrey, she had been given in marriage to Ranulf, earl of Chester. She, however, stayed in Brittany while he preferred to live in England or Normandy and in general it seems that the duchy had gone very much its own way after Henry II's death. Although Richard held Constance's daughter, Eleanor, in his custody and had, more than once, arranged marriages for her, he needed more than this if he were to reassert the traditional Norman ascendancy over the Bretons: he needed custody of the heir. Arthur was now nine years old and it was time he left his mother's care. Unfortunately the situation very quickly became hopelessly confused. No sooner had the Duchess Constance set foot on Norman soil than she was kidnapped by her husband and carried off to his castle at St James-de-Beuvron. Alarmed and, rightly or wrongly, holding Richard responsible for this, Constance's Breton advisers, who had Arthur in their charge, appealed for help to Philip and threw off all allegiance to the duke of Normandy.[56] Brittany in enemy hands posed a serious threat to English and Norman sea communications with Aquitaine and Richard's response was to invade. The rebels were forced to bow before his superior military resources and – according to William the Breton – before the ruthlessness with which he waged war, not stopping even for Good Friday.[57] But although Richard won his war, he lost the dispute. Arthur's guardians took him first into hiding and then to the safety of the court of King Philip. In granting Arthur asylum at his court Philip made a public declaration of hostile intent against Richard. From Brittany, on 15 April (four days before Good Friday), Richard wrote to Hubert Walter, asking him to send knights to Normandy by 2 June ready to serve in a long campaign: he expected war with the king of France.[58]

He was right. In June 1196 the counts of Flanders, Boulogne and Ponthieu were all to be found at the French court.[59] Despite the treaty of Louviers's concessions in north-eastern Normandy, Philip had held the old coalition together remarkably effectively. In June he provided compensation for the count of Ponthieu, vital if Alice's new husband was to remain content with a wife who had been scandalously used then discarded by the Angevins.[60] Philip was also successful in persuading the new count of Flanders and Hainault, Baldwin IX, to follow in his father's footsteps and fight at Philip's side. The ground had been well prepared for the attack

[56] *Chron.*, iv, 7. Newburgh, Bk 5, ch. 18. According to Howden the Bretons raided Normandy.

[57] *Philippidos*, v, 147–68.

[58] Landon, no. 464; Diceto, ii, appendix to preface, lxxix–lxxx. Send all the money and treasure you have as fast as possible, was Richard's message.

[59] Rigord, 135. A. Teulet, *Layettes du trésor des Chartes,* i (Paris, 1863), 188–9.

[60] Teulet, *Trésor des Chartes,* i, 189; cf. *Recueil des actes,* no. 541, n. 1.

Philip launched against Aumâle in July.[61] Philip had a large army, includ-ing a contingent led by Count Baldwin, and plenty of siege machines. But Aumâle was stoutly defended and Richard struck back by capturing Nonancourt; according to the French chroniclers, its castellan surren-dered without a fight and then, repenting of his treason, went to the Holy Land and became a Templar.[62] From Nonancourt Richard marched to the relief of Aumâle; and there, in an attack on the French camp, he was defeated. Only the French chroniclers give any details; the English either say nothing or hint that Richard, anxious to avoid a bloody battle, turned away and sent his troops to devastate Capetian territory instead.[63] Either way, Richard tried to relieve Aumâle and failed. To some extent, the story that he was reluctant to fight is supported by William the Breton's account of Richard giving the order to attack only after some hesitation, having weighed the likelihood of defeat against the certain dishonour if he were to withdraw without even attempting to help the defenders.[64] Richard was not in the habit of publicizing his defeats, so the evidence is unsatisfactory, but in all probability he had been forced to attack a well-entrenched French camp and had been driven off with some losses. A week or so later, on about 20 August, Aumâle surrendered. Richard had to pay 3,000 marks in order to ransom the garrison he had been unable to save. The French artillery had given the castle such a severe battering that Philip decided to complete the job of demolition rather than repair and try to hold it.[65] A monk of Jumièges consoled himself with the thought that Philip's own losses had been heavy.[66] The rest of the summer went badly for Richard. He laid siege to Gaillon and was wounded in the knee by a crossbow bolt.[67] Philip re-took Nonancourt, in what Rigord saw as a splendid

---

[61] According to Rigord, 135, however, Philip besieged Aumâle because Richard had treacherously seized and destroyed the castle of Vierzon in Berry. Cf. WB, 199 and *Philippidos*, v, 90–8. Since a set of brief notes on the lords of Vierzon, *Breve Chronicon Virzionis Coenobii*, *RHF*, xviii, 246–7, places Vierzon's destruction by the king of England under the year 1197, it looks as though Rigord may have been trying to shift the blame for the renewed outbreak of war.

[62] *Philippidos*, v, 111–17; Rigord, 135; *Sig. Cont.*, 433.

[63] William of Newburgh's interpretation, Bk 5, ch. 25.

[64] *Philippidos*, v, 168–257. On this see above, 260.

[65] *Chron.*, iv, 5 on the 3,000-mark ransom; among the prisoners was Gui de Thouars. Capetian sources are naturally much fuller on the siege itself, which lasted over seven weeks, Rigord, 135–6; WB, 200. An entry in some annals from St Stephen's, Caen puts the ransom at 2,500 marks and notes the strenuous defence put up by the garrison, *RHF*, xviii, 349.

[66] *Annales de Jumièges*, 77.

[67] *Philippidos*, v, 258–68. This is mentioned by no other source, but an injury to Richard 'not long after' (as William the Breton put it) the failure of his attempt to relieve Aumâle might explain why he apparently did little later that year.

assault.[68] The one bright spot was the capture of Gamaches, one of the castles of the Norman Vexin, by John.[69]

In the Peace of Louviers Philip had restored much, but the heavily fortified Vexin, so close to the centre of Philip's power, was going to be a much more difficult nut to crack. The setbacks of 1196 were a sign that it would take more than the resources and generalship which Richard alone could muster if he were to recover it as his subjects' and his own sense of right insisted he should. Diplomacy would be needed as well as war.

[68] Rigord, 136. It was captured together with fifteen knights and eighteen crossbowmen after a day and night artillery bombardment and then given into the keeping of Robert of Dreux; WB, 200. William of Newburgh thought it inadequately defended at the time, Bk 5, ch. 25.

[69] This is reported only by Howden, *Chron.*, iv, 5.

Chapter 17

FRANCE, 1197–8

In order to reconquer the Norman Vexin Richard set himself two tasks. The first was to build a secure forward base from which he could put French garrisons under constant pressure. The second was to deprive Philip of his two most valuable allies, the count of Toulouse and the count of Flanders.

His base camp was to be Château-Gaillard, or rather that whole complex of fortifications on the Seine at Andeli (now Les Andelys) crowned by the castle on the Rock of Andeli which is his most famous monument. It is evident that the desirability of fortifying this site had occurred to both kings, since it was expressly forbidden in the Peace of Louviers.[1] The island and manor of Andeli belonged to the church of Rouen and the archbishop had built a toll-house there for the collection of dues from ships passing up and down the Seine. This was one of Rouen's prize possessions – all the more so since many of its other properties had suffered badly in the war. Indeed Archbishop Walter's attempts in December 1195 to obtain compensation had resulted in him feeling persecuted by both kings and in consequence fleeing from his see. In the archbishop's absence Richard visited the Isle of Andeli in March 1196 and he returned there in April, May and June. He had presumably already begun to negotiate with the church of Rouen with a view to acquiring the site.[2] By the time the archbishop returned to Rouen (7 July) Philip had laid siege to Aumâle. Now in the teeth of the archbishop's resolve to hang on to one of his most lucrative assets, the king lost patience.[3] He seized the manor and began to build. The archbishop protested. Richard took no notice. Eventually on 7 November 1196 the archbishop set out for Rome in

---

[1] Indeed, according to Howden, Philip demanded Andeli, *Chron.*, iv, 3–4. I use 'Andeli' to refer to what was there before 1196, 'Les Andelys' to refer to the whole new complex.

[2] Landon, nos. 462, 463, 466, 468. The dean of Rouen, Archbishop Walter's nephew, was elected bishop of Worcester, doubtless at Richard's behest: Diceto, ii, 139.

[3] According to his envoys at Rome, Richard had 'repeatedly offered much', *Chron.*, iv, 17–18. The tone of Walter's letter to Dean Ralph, written soon after 7 July, and the letter's silence on the subject, indicate that Richard had not then taken possession of Andeli, Diceto, ii, 144.

order to lay his grievances before the pope.[4] In response Richard sent an embassy of his own.[5]

Meanwhile, he fortified the Isle of Andeli and built the palace there which became his favourite residence during the last two years of his life. Opposite on the right bank he laid out a 'most attractive' new town (now Petit-Andelys). Behind the town and linked to the Seine by two substantial water-courses, each spanned by a bridge, lay what William the Breton called 'a deep and most capacious pool'.[6] On the 300-foot limestone crag overlooking Petit-Andelys and the Seine and linked to both by a series of outworks, there rose what he himself called either his 'fair castle of the Rock' (*bellum castrum de Rupe*) or his 'saucy castle' (Château-Gaillard).[7] The whole complex of defences was completed by a stockade built across the river on the south side of the rock. Richard himself supervised the entire operation and allowed nothing to stop it. Among his other protests the archbishop of Rouen had imposed an interdict on the duchy. This meant that most church services were banned and, in consequence, said Roger of Howden, 'the streets and squares of the towns of Normandy were littered with the unburied bodies of the dead'.[8] But at Les Andelys the hodmen, the water carriers, the lime-workers, carpenters, quarrymen, stone cutters, woodmen, miners, watch-men, warders and smiths worked on. In April 1197 Pope Celestine lifted the interdict and sent the archbishop and his fellows back to Normandy to final-ize the settlement between king and archbishop which had been negotiated before the pope and cardinals. Both Howden and William of Newburgh believed that the curia took a sympathetic view of the military needs of a cru-sader-king whose lands had been occupied in his absence.[9]

---

[4] In his letter to the dean of St Paul's, Diceto, ii, 148–50, the archbishop tells Ralph that he is going to Rome to oppose one of his own suffragans, the bishop of Lisieux, who has taken the king's side against him. An entry in Rouen annals shows that another suffragan, the bishop of Evreux, was also on the king's side, *RHF*, xviii, 358.

[5] William Longchamp, who died *en route*, and Philip of Poitou, bishop elect of Durham, were, together with the bishop of Lisieux, the principal members of Richard's delegation to the curia, *Chron.*, iv, 14, 16–17. Roger of Howden probably went too, attached to Philip of Poitou's staff, serving both Durham and the king: see Gillingham, 'The Travels of Roger of Howden', 165.

[6] The remarkable description of what Richard built at Les Andelys by William the Breton is the best evidence of the impression it made upon contemporary observers – especially, of course, precisely those whom it was meant to impress, WB, 208–9; *Philippidos*, v, 48–85. There are good descriptions in English in Powicke, 190–5; Norgate, *England under the Angevin Kings*, ii, 375–80, 411–23. Archaeological excavations by Dominique Pitte, begun in 1991 and continuing, are starting to throw new light on the site. See D. Pitte, *Château-Gaillard* (Vernon, France, 1996); also his report in *Archéologie médiévale*, xxiii (1993).

[7] 'He called it Gaillard, which is French for "impudence" ', WB, 209.

[8] *Chron*, iv, 16,

[9] Ibid., 17–19,; William was himself sympathetic to Richard's side of the argument,

In May 1198, says William of Newburgh, a shower of blood fell from the sky, spattering the unfinished walls. Some of Richard's advisers were alarmed, taking it to be an evil omen, but the king was unmoved. Not for a moment would he allow the masons and engineers to slacken the pace of their work. 'He took such pleasure in the building that, if I am not mistaken, if an angel had descended from heaven and told him to abandon it, that angel would have been met with a volley of curses and the work would have gone on regardless.'[10] Richard's close personal involvement with Château-Gaillard makes it possible to use its design as evidence – if evidence were needed – of his deep practical knowledge of the craft of siege warfare. The increasing, and increasingly effective, use of siege machines in the twelfth century had made military architects more sharply aware than ever of the threat posed by 'dead angles', spots which could not be reached by the defenders' missiles. Château-Gaillard's most distinctive feature, still visible today, is the elliptical inner citadel with its remarkable curvilinear enclosing wall. Here there is no dead angle to be found; the fire of the garrison could cover all approaches. The choice of site, the overall structure of the fortifications, stockade, island town, castle, each element a harmonious part of the whole – and the details of the design of walls and towers – all indicate the hand of a master builder.[11] Untroubled by modesty, Richard claimed that it was so perfectly designed that he could hold it even if its walls were made of butter.[12]

Impressive though they are, the ruins of Château-Gaillard give no real indication of the importance of this whole fortified complex. There are other castles whose ruins seem to be equally formidable. But this is misleading because, taken as a whole, the fortifications at Les Andelys are quite extraordinary. In the first place the modern appearance of most castles, whether they are reasonably intact or in a ruined state, reflects the labour of generations: castles, like cathedrals, were generally a long time a-growing. The ruins of Château-Gaillard, however, are the ruins of a fortress built in just two hectic years – and built only five miles distant from Philip's castle at Gaillon. We can get some idea of the importance Richard attached to this work from the settlement he reached with Archbishop Walter. In exchange for the one manor of Andeli he gave the

and believed that Rouen had been given generous compensation, Newburgh, Bk 5, ch. 28, 34.

[10] Newburgh, Bk 5, ch. 34. These are the last words of William's history; probably he died soon afterwards. At any rate he gives no sign of knowing that Richard would die in April 1199. The dean of St Paul's merely noted the fall of a rain of blood on 8 May 1198, Diceto, ii, 162.

[11] It fell in 1204 partly owing to John's inadequate attempts to relieve it, and partly because the one extension to the castle built by John contained a fatal flaw: a window accessible to an acrobatic French squire, WB, 219.

[12] Gerald, *Princ.*, 290.

church of Rouen not just two manors but also the flourishing seaport of Dieppe.[13] An even better picture of its importance comes from the fortunate survival of the account of expenditure on Les Andelys in the two years ending September 1198. In this period recorded expenditure was approximately £12,000.[14] In order to obtain some inkling of what this means it is necessary to compare it with expenditure on other castles. On rebuilding the walls of the town of Eu – the next largest piece of construction work recorded in the 1198 account roll – Richard spent about £1,250.[15] Turning to English castles, for which the surviving financial evidence is much more complete, we find that Richard spent just over £7,000 on all of them during the whole of his reign. By far the most that was spent on any one English castle in the later twelfth century was the £7,000 spent on building Henry II's great new fortress at Dover – and that was spread over the thirteen years from 1179 to 1191.[16] Measured in these terms Château-Gaillard completely dwarfs every other castle in the Angevin empire, probably in Europe. The vast sums that Richard was prepared to spend show beyond all doubt that the building of Château-Gaillard was of overwhelming importance to him. The question has to be asked: why? Why so much money on one site?

The conventional answer is that Les Andelys was intended to plug the gap in the Norman defences which had been caused by the fall of Gisors. Seen in this light the role of Château-Gaillard was a defensive one: its function was to block the direct route to Rouen.[17] Obviously there is something to this – but it is by no means the whole story. This was the role which, as it turned out, the fortress was called upon to play in John's reign when there was a general collapse of the Angevin position in Normandy. In the demoralized atmosphere of distrust and uncertainty created by that king, the six months' defence put up by the isolated garrison of Château-Gaillard was one of the few creditable episodes.[18] But it does not follow from this that Richard intended Château-Gaillard to perform a primarily defensive function. In the years 1196–9 he was thinking less about defending Normandy and more about recovering the Vexin.[19] A place has to be found for Château-Gaillard

---

[13] *Chron.*, iv, 18–19. On the fame of Dieppe, Newburgh, Bk 5, ch. 34.

[14] The audited account of the clerks in charge of expenditure over two years totalled 48,878 *livres angevines*; *MRSN*, ii, 309–10, repr. in Powicke, 204–6.

[15] *MRSN*, ii, 386 (5,000 *livres*).

[16] R. A. Brown, 'Royal Castle-Building in England 1154–1216', *EHR*, lxx (1955), 353–98; idem, *English Castles* (London, 1954), 160–1.

[17] And this, of course, is how the seizure of the property of the church of Rouen was justified at the time, as a measure necessary for the defence of Normandy against French aggression, Newburgh, Bk 5, ch. 34; *Chron.*, iv, 18.

[18] The amount of money Richard spent on the site, and the amount of time that Philip was to spend reducing it, are two compelling quantitative indicators of the crucial military importance of the whole complex overlooked by the Castle of the Rock.

[19] As was recognized by William the Breton. See his comments on the fortress at

within the framework of a strategy of reconquest. Château-Gaillard protected the forward base from which Richard was to deliver hammer blows against Philip's castles. Men and supplies could be sent here from the main Norman arsenal at Rouen. They could go by the well-defended Seine valley road, via Pont de l'Arche, Vaudreuil and then over the bridge at Portjoie to Les Andelys. Richard's interest in this route was shown when he built himself a residence at Portjoie and rebuilt the Seine bridge after Philip had fled across it in July 1195, breaking it down behind him. Or men and supplies could go by river. An entry in the 1198 Exchequer Roll records a payment of 12 *livres* 'for taking the king's galleys from Rouen to the Isle (of Andeli) and back to Rouen'; even more significantly, another entry records a payment of 166 *livres* to a master carpenter named Galfridus of Bayonne and four others, 'for making four galleys'.[20] In the thirteenth and fourteenth centuries Bayonne was to be the main source of expertise drawn upon by the kings of England when building galleys. The king who knew Bayonne better than any other king of England was already putting that expertise to good use – a king who in the Mediterranean had already proved himself a master of galley warfare. According to William the Breton Richard built a fleet of seventy ships of a type he called *cursoria* (cursors or runners) – slender and shallow-hulled ships built for speed.[21] This design suggests war rather than merely transport. The war for the Vexin was to be in part a river war – as the war for Egypt would have been. William the Breton's 'deep and most capacious pool' (*stagnum amplissimum et profundum*) was surely intended as a well-protected river port.[22] At the other end of the strategic lifeline linking England with the Norman frontier Richard was building a palace, a new town and a port at Portsmouth, close to Porchester Castle. Here, sheltering below Château-Gaillard, lay the palace, new town and port of Les Andelys.[23]

Portjoie: 'ut terram suam quocumque modo recuperaret' and on Boutavant: 'the name meaning "I thrust forward in order to recover my land"', WB, 208–9. Archbishop Walter's letter to Dean Ralph, telling him of the final deal, describes Andeli as 'ad acquisitionem et defensionem terrae suae valde congruum', Diceto, ii, 154. Howden dated the fortification of Boutavant, and Philip's opposing fortification of Le Goulet, to 1198, *Chron.*, iv, 78.

[20] *MRSN*, ii, 307.

[21] *Philippidos*, vii, 173–4. Though it may well be that in terms of shipbuilding technique these were descendants of Viking warships rather than Mediterranean-type skeleton-built 'galleys proper'; on this see N. A. M. Rodger, *The Safeguard of the Sea* (London, 1997), 64–7. Unfortunately for the tidy classifications of scholars, contemporaries called them galleys, presumably recognizing that they were used in the same ways as the 'galleys proper' they had got to know so well on crusade.

[22] Perhaps as a development of the port at Andeli which existed already – as demonstrated by the reference in a papal letter of 1131 to 'oppidum quod dicitur Andeleium ... cum portu', *MRSN*, i, xli.

[23] The argument is further developed in my article, 'Richard I, Galley-Warfare and Portsmouth'.

In that same summer of 1196 when Richard laid his plans for the fortification of Les Andelys, he also entered into negotiations with Count
Raymond VI of Toulouse, negotiations which were to end in a diplomatic
revolution. Ever since 1159 the Angevin dukes of Aquitaine had been in a
state of almost permanent war with the counts of Toulouse. The dukes
argued that Toulouse was theirs by hereditary right and although they were
unable to make good this claim, they had generally been successful in
holding on to the Quercy. But no self-respecting count of Toulouse could
resign himself to the loss of this valuable region around Cahors and so
whenever the duke of Aquitaine was in difficulty or had his hands full elsewhere, the count of Toulouse stepped in and did his best to take advantage
of the situation. This was an essential element in the standard political pattern of the 1180s and 1190s and obviously it was one which suited Philip
Augustus down to the ground. In 1195 Richard was given the chance to
reshape the pattern because late in the previous year Raymond V had died,
and was succeeded by his son, Raymond VI. But Philip was able to retain
the allegiance of the new count and the terms of the Peace of Louviers
make it clear that 1195 had been yet another year of war between
Aquitaine and Toulouse – though it was a war which no one chronicled.
However, the terms also indicate that Philip made peace without consulting Raymond and was prepared to abandon the count if he found these
terms unacceptable.[24] Here was Richard's opportunity. Moreover, the
death of Alfonso II of Aragon in April 1196 may have suggested that the
time had come to reshape the diplomatic configuration of south-western
Europe, particularly since King Sancho of Navarre had now immersed himself in a war with Castile and could no longer be Richard's reliable ally in
the south.[25] Even so it may have taken the setbacks which he suffered in
Normandy in the summer of 1196 before Richard was willing to pay the
price required by the count of Toulouse.

By October 1196 all was settled. Raymond VI came to Rouen and there
married Richard's sister Joan. Richard renounced his claim to Toulouse,
restored the Quercy and gave them the county of Agen as Joan's dowry.

---

[24] *Recueil des actes*, ii, no. 485 (the grant of Figeac to Raymond VI in February
1195), ii, no. 517, clauses 11–13 of the Peace of Louviers.
[25] A document dated March 1196, recording a treaty between Sancho of Navarre
and Arnold-Raymond, viscount of Tartas, singles out Richard as, at the least, a
potential enemy of Navarre, *Documents des archives de la Chambre des Comptes de
Navarre 1196–1384* ed. J-A. Brutails (Paris, 1890), 1–3. This has implications for
Berengaria's position. In a letter written in May 1198 Pope Innocent III promised
Richard that he would try to persuade Sancho of Navarre to return the castles of St-
Jean-Pied-de-Port and 'Rocca bruna', which Sancho's father had given to Richard
as Berengaria's dowry, *Selected Letters*, 5. This suggests that a question mark was
already hanging over Richard's childless marriage with Berengaria. There were few
positions more precarious than that of a queen who bore no heir and who represented an alliance which was no longer needed.

Agen was to be held as a fief of the duchy of Aquitaine in return for the service of 500 knights for a month should there be war in Gascony.[26] These were generous terms, calculated not simply to neutralize a former enemy but to turn him into a friend and ally. From a financial point of view it made sense for the lord of Bordeaux to be at peace with the lord of Toulouse, so that the river-borne trade of the Garonne could flourish and be a source of profit to them both. At least one English historian, William of Newburgh, recognized the significance of this marriage alliance. It marked, he said, the end of forty years of exhausting war, the end of the old hatred – and it meant that whereas Richard had been fighting on three fronts, against France, Toulouse and Brittany, he could now focus all his attention on the struggle with King Philip.[27]

Even more important than the alliance with Toulouse was the diplomatic revolution which brought Flanders into his camp.[28] Close as were the economic ties between Bordeaux and Toulouse, the ties between Flanders and eastern England were even closer and more vital. Flanders was the most densely populated and highly industrialized region in north-western Europe. Bruges, Ypres, Ghent and Lille were great manufacturing centres, with more mouths than the fields of Flanders could feed. For their very existence they depended upon imported foodstuffs, and also, since their chief industry was cloth manufacture, upon the import of wool. England supplied both grain and huge quantities of high-quality wool. All this meant that the count of Flanders was a prince of great wealth – but also one who was unusually vulnerable to economic pressure. At least as early as 1194 an embargo on trade with Flanders had been imposed. Some English merchants who were detected exporting corn were heavily fined.[29] Count Baldwin VIII died in December 1195 but, as with the new count of Toulouse, his successor, Baldwin IX, at first remained true to the French alliance, giving Philip material aid at the siege of Aumâle in the summer of 1196.

The first indication that Richard was winning back the initiative in the north-east came in the spring of 1197 – perhaps an early benefit of the peace with Toulouse. In April he renewed the war with a raid on Ponthieu and on the count's port of St Valéry. He burned the town and carried off much booty, including the relics of the saint. In the harbour he found some English ships loaded with grain and other foodstuffs. The sailors

---

[26] *Chron.*, iv, 13, 124–5, where Howden gives the terms on which Raymond VI did homage to John in 1200.

[27] Newburgh, Bk 5, ch. 30. For the whole subject see Benjamin, 'A Forty Years War'.

[28] The phrase 'diplomatic revolution' was used by G. G. Dept, *Les Influences anglaise et française dans le comté de Flandres* (Ghent, 1928), 24–32.

[29] For this economic warfare see Lloyd, *The English Wool Trade*, 8–9; PR 10 Richard I, xiv–xv.

were hanged, the ships burned and their cargoes seized.[30] The king intended to see that his economic sanctions were properly enforced; there was an implied message here for the merchants of Flanders. In May 1197 Richard was at Gournay and from there he led a raid into the Beauvaisis, capturing the castle of Milli. According to the *History of William Marshal*, the hero of the assault on Milli was none other than William himself, and when it was all over he was reproved by Richard. 'Sir Marshal, a man of your station ought not to risk his life in adventures of that kind. Leave them to the young knights who still have a reputation to win.' Yet Richard himself had had to be forcibly restrained from plunging into the thick of the fray.[31] While Richard and William Marshal were at the storming of Milli, another Angevin contingent, led by Mercadier, brought off a still greater coup: they captured Philip's cousin, the bishop of Beauvais. According to William of Newburgh, he had sprung to arms on hearing that the castle was being attacked and had suffered the fate he deserved. His capture was widely and gleefully reported by English historians.[32] In the opinion of William the Marshal, Philip of Beauvais was 'one of the men Richard hated most in all the world'.[33] Richard put the bishop in prison and refused to release him. Protests on the grounds that this was no way to treat a churchman were countered by the argument that Philip had been captured not as a bishop but as a knight riding to war, for he had been fully armed and helmeted. The bishop of Beauvais was a notoriously militant bishop and this was a great propaganda coup which Richard played for all it was worth. It was in this context that the *History of William the Marshal* put into Richard's mouth the claim that God was showing who was right and who wrong.[34] After this

---

[30] Diceto, ii, 152; *Chron.*, iv, 19; Newburgh, Bk 5, ch. 31. The brief reports in the sources give no indication of the involvement of ships in the attack on St Valéry, though I would be surprised if it were not a combined operation.

[31] *HGM*, 11,105–264.

[32] Newburgh, Bk 5, ch. 31; Gervase, i, 544; Annals of Winchester in *Annales Monastici*, ii, 65. The dean of St Paul's and William the Marshal gave the credit to Mercadier, Diceto, ii, 152, *HGM*, 11,265–9. Only Howden associates John with Mercadier, and he does so in a passage which may have been written after John had come to the throne. At any rate it was added later, which helps to explain why he dated the bishop's capture, unlike every other English source, to 1196, *Chron.*, iv, 16. Rigord, by contrast, places it a year too late, in the autumn of 1198, perhaps because this enables him to present it as part of God's punishment of King Philip for allowing the Jews back to Paris, Rigord, 141–3.

[33] *HGM*, 11,265–310. According to Newburgh (Bk 5, ch. 31), the conditions in which Richard had been held prisoner in Germany worsened considerably on the morrow of a visit from the bishop of Beauvais. Diceto credits Hubert Walter with improving the conditions in which Bishop Philip was held, Diceto, ii, 158.

[34] *HGM*, 11,297–300. Papal letters condemning the soldier bishop were forged, *Chron.*, iv, 21–4. Bishop Philip was later to take an active part in the battle of Bouvines, striking down several men with his mace — though William the Breton said that it was only by chance that he happened to have a mace in his hand, which,

highly successful raid Richard returned to Normandy, where he took Dangu, a Vexin castle only four miles away from Gisors.[35] According to William the Breton, he even threatened the outskirts of Paris.[36]

By the early summer of 1197 the tide of war was flowing Richard's way again.[37] Richard's envoys to Flanders doubtless played upon the sense of grievance felt by Baldwin's family since 1192 when Philip had deprived them of Artois, including towns as rich as Arras, St Omer and Douai – 'nearly half their inheritance', in William of Newburgh's opinion.[38] Now, if Baldwin IX came over to the Angevin side, not only would the crippling trade embargo be lifted, but he would receive full payment of the arrears of his pension, as well as a substantial gift: 5,000 marks, according to Roger of Howden.[39] Count Baldwin's advisers and kinsmen were also to be given a taste of the benefits to be gained from an alliance with the rich king of England.[40] In June or July 1197 Baldwin came to Normandy and a formal treaty was drawn up.[41] Richard and Baldwin agreed that neither would make a truce or peace with the king of France without the other's consent. The alliance was a triumph for Richard's wine and cash diplomacy. The momentous shift in the balance of power which it implied is shown by the presence of three Norman Marcher lords – Count Robert of Meulan, William of Caïeux and Hugh of Gournay – among those who stood surety for Richard's observance of the treaty.[42] In 1197 they were just as sensitive to the way the wind was blowing as they had been when they joined Philip in 1193. In the estimation of Rigord of St Denis, the

so long as it was for defence, was excusable, *Philippidos*, xi, 538–58. In the same vein William added to Rigord's account of the bishop's capture the explanation that he had ridden out 'to defend the patria', WB, 202.

[35] *Chron.*, iv, 20. It was surrendered by its constable, William Crispin. On the Crispin family see Green, 'Lords of the Norman Vexin', 54–6.

[36] WB, 202. It seems more likely, however, that this was a memory of 1198 rather than 1197.

[37] By now (*pace* Powicke, 110) – if not indeed immediately after the demolition of the castle by Philip – Richard and/or Baldwin of Béthune had probably recovered possession of Aumâle.

[38] Newburgh, Bk 5, ch. 32; Coggeshall, 77.

[39] *Chron.*, iv, 20; PR 9 Richard I, 62, 164, discussed by Poole, 'Richard the First's Alliances', 96–7.

[40] William of Hainault, the count's uncle, received a pension of 160 *livres* on the farm of Bonneville-sur-Touque, *MRSN*, ii, 369.

[41] For the text of the treaty (which is not in Howden), Diceto, ii, 152–3; *Foedera*, i, 67–8; Landon, 118–19. *MRSN*, ii, 307 for a payment of 100 *livres* to meet the count's expenses at Drincourt.

[42] Howden notes that men of Champagne, Flanders and Brittany switched to Richard, swayed by his gifts, *Chron.*, iv, 19–20. On the dilemmas of Robert of Meulan, *Philippidos*, iii, 77–89. After Philip's conquest of Normandy he lost all his lands.

defection of the count of Flanders was a serious blow to the French king and his land.[43]

By 20 July Baldwin had invaded Artois, while Richard made his move in the south, in Berry.[44] The two-pronged strategy which would be employed by John in 1214 was here carried through with success. Philip, however, began by coolly ignoring both threats; his overriding concern remained the Vexin. Only after he had recaptured Dangu did he turn north.[45] By this time Douai and other castles had fallen and Arras was under siege. When Philip advanced with a great force to the relief of Arras, Baldwin retreated and the king of France chased after him, determined to punish his disloyalty. In his indignation Philip went too far. In a series of skilfully executed manœuvres Baldwin broke down the bridges behind and in front of Philip's army and cut off his supply routes. The French troops were forced to live off the land, to send out foraging parties which inevitably became targets for Baldwin's men – indeed according to Coggeshall, the French became so disheartened that they even suffered the indignity of being beaten by bands of Flemish women. Eventually Philip realized that he had been drawn into a trap from which there was no escape and he sued for peace, offering to give Baldwin what he wanted if he would break with Richard. The count of Flanders would not do this, and instead it was agreed that there should be a conference of all parties in September between Les Andelys and Gaillon. Andreas of Marchiennes (near Douai) wrote that those who had feared Philip's coming, laughed as he departed.[46] Baldwin and Richard met at Rouen and then went to the conference together. Richard certainly was not yet ready for a final peace but he was willing to agree to a truce for a year from the Feast of St Hilary (13 January) on the basis of the status quo, a restoration of trade and the ransoming or exchange of prisoners.[47] While Baldwin and Philip had been busy in Artois he had captured several castles – as many as ten, according to Roger of Howden – in Berry and/or the Auvergne.[48] It was probably on this campaign that Richard destroyed the castle of Vierzon in Berry.[49] In the Vexin, moreover, despite the failure to retain Dangu, there seems to

[43] Rigord, 137–8.

[44] Landon, 119.

[45] *Chron.*, iv, 20. He ransomed the knights and sergeants of the garrison for 500 marks.

[46] Detailed account in Coggeshall, 77–9; Newburgh, Bk 5, ch. 32; *Sig. Cont.*, 434; *Chron.*, iv, 20–1. The campaign is omitted altogether by Philip's historians.

[47] *Chron.*, iv, 24; Newburgh, Bk 5, ch. 32.

[48] *Chron.*, iv, 20; Coggeshall, 77; Newburgh, Bk 5, ch. 32.

[49] According to Rigord, 135, he captured it by treachery in 1196. The date of the fall of Vierzon is something of a puzzle. According to William the Marshal's memories (at this point chronologically vague), Richard sent the Marshal to Flanders after entering Vierzon, *HGM*, 10,679–87. The Vierzon annals (see 289, n. 61) date the castle's destruction to 1197 and the three English historians were all convinced

have been some advance. The records of the Norman exchequer show that Richard was spending money on the castles of Gamaches and Longchamps; the frontier between him and Philip was gradually being pushed back.

In theory the truce made in September 1197 was meant to last until January 1199. Inevitably it did not. Equally inevitably, the months of peace were filled with preparations for war. Richard pressed on with his two main tasks: castle-building and coalition-building. His search for further allies in the struggle with Philip became entangled with another vital question of European diplomacy – the election of a new German king to succeed Henry VI, who died of a fever at Messina on 28 September 1197, aged only thirty-two.[50] Since Henry's son, the future Emperor Frederick II, was less than three years old it was a golden opportunity for the enemies of the Hohenstaufen to reassert themselves. At their head were Richard's allies from 1194, the princes of the Lower Rhineland, led by Archbishop Adolf of Cologne. At the end of the year they sent envoys to Rouen to invite Richard to take part in the business of choosing a new king. Rather than go himself, Richard sent a powerful delegation headed by the bishop of Durham, Philip of Poitou, and the count of Aumâle, Baldwin of Béthune.[51] The election became, in part, an aspect of the struggle between Richard and Philip Augustus. In England there were rumours that these two were themselves candidates for the throne. An author from Béthune even believed that Richard was chosen, but turned the offer down.[52] In fact he supported the candidature of his nephew, Henry of Brunswick. This might have caused a rift between Richard and Archbishop Adolf, who was naturally uneasy at the thought of Henry the Lion's heir as emperor. As it happened, however, Henry was away on crusade and the news that an assembly of princes had already (in March 1198) elected Henry VI's younger brother Philip of Swabia as the Hohenstaufen candidate, made it impossible to argue for a delay until he returned. Adolf and his allies quickly agreed on Henry of Brunswick's younger brother Otto, who was still in Aquitaine at the time and who, from the point of view of the archbishop's territorial claims, was far less threatening than his older brother. Moreover an 'English' candidate

that Richard campaigned successfully in Berry or (Howden) Auvergne while Philip was being outmanoeuvred by Count Baldwin.

[50] According to Howden, in his last illness Henry offered to compensate Richard for the ransom and Pope Celestine forbade his burial until the money had been restored, *Chron.*, iv, 30-1. Richard obviously took this up, but in May 1198 the new pope, Innocent III, allowed Henry's body to be buried and circumspectly chose not to require his brother, Philip of Swabia, to hand the money back, *Selected Letters*, 4-5; Csendes, *Heinrich VI*, 193.

[51] *Chron.*, iv, 37-9. Philip of Poitou was doubtless the source of Roger of Howden's information on the imperial election.

[52] Gervase, I, 545, Coggeshall, 88; *Histoire des ducs de Normandie*, 90.

could count on support from the businessmen of Cologne.[53] Otto had spent most of his youth at the Angevin court and had been count of Poitou since 1196.[54] For a while indeed he may have been Richard's preferred heir.[55]

In June 1198 Otto was elected king at Cologne and next month crowned at Aachen.[56] Among those present at his coronation were Count Baldwin of Flanders and his brother.[57] At the end of June Philip of France and Philip of Swabia made a treaty of alliance in which Hohenstaufen promised to help Capetian against all his enemies, specifically naming King Richard, Otto, the archbishop of Cologne and the count of Flanders. Rigord's understanding of his king's alliance with Philip of Swabia was that it was intended to undermine the position of Baldwin of Flanders.[58] This only serves to highlight the fact that Richard gained more from his German allies than Philip did from his, since Richard's friends – Dietrich, count of Holland, Henry, duke of Limburg, Henry, duke of Brabant, as well as Adolf, archbishop of Cologne – were strategically clustered in the Lower Rhineland, precisely where they could ensure the security and friendship of the count of Flanders. Moreover Richard's support for Otto meant that his envoys could count on a friendly reception at Rome.[59] The new pope, Innocent III, elected on 8 January 1198, though at this stage doing his best to preserve a façade of neutrality, in fact preferred a Welf to a Hohenstaufen emperor; and this is how his stance was perceived at the Capetian court.[60] Not surprisingly, in the eyes of the annalist of Jumièges, the election of Otto was one of Richard's magnificent achievements.[61]

[53] Chron., iv, 38. For analysis of the electoral politics see Ahlers, Die Welfen, 180–4; B. U. Hucker, Kaiser Otto IV (Hanover, 1990), 22–35; Natalie Fryde, 'King John and the Empire', in King John: New Interpretations, ed. S. Church (Woodbridge, 1999).

[54] For his early career see Ahlers, Die Welfen, 169–78 and Hucker, Kaiser Otto, 4–15. Philip Augustus was later to complain to Innocent III of the damage he had suffered at Otto's hands while the latter was still count of Poitou.

[55] See A. V. Murray, 'Richard the Lionheart, Otto of Brunswick and the Earldom of York: Northern England and the Angevin Succession, 1109–91', Medieval Yorkshire, xxiii (1994), 5–12. But, as pointed out by Landon, a document issued by John on 8 September 1197 implies that by then he was Richard's heir, Landon, 121–2. After 1199 Otto (and his brothers) may have come into the reckoning again until 1207 when a son was born to John, Hucker, Kaiser Otto, 17–19.

[56] On Richard's spending to get Otto elected see Caesarius of Heisterbach, Dialogus Miraculorum, ed. J. Strange (2 vols, Cologne, 1851), i, 102f. and the doubtless exaggerated report of Arnold of Lübeck, Chronica, 50.

[57] Chron., iv, 39. Gervase, 545, thought Baldwin supported Otto in order to please Richard. Baldwin visited Canterbury in autumn 1197, Chron., iv, 24.

[58] Rigord, 143.

[59] On Richard's representations on Otto's behalf at the curia, Ahlers, Die Welfen, 190–6.

[60] Ibid., 192; Rigord, 138. Innocent was also, of course, at odds with Philip of France over the latter's repudiation of Ingeborg.

[61] 'O splendid deed of a splendid man, who acquired the empire of the whole world for his nephew', Annales de Jumièges, 77. This author's consistently favourable view of Richard makes it unlikely that this remark was intended ironically.

But to judge from the tone of the Capetian chroniclers, the alliance that really hurt was Richard's alliance with Count Renaud of Boulogne. In part this was due to the count's reputation as a military man. Ralph of Coggeshall described him as 'the standard bearer in every conflict, outstanding in every aspect of knightly prowess'.[62] As late as April 1198 Renaud still acknowledged Philip's authority – though the evidence for this comes from a document couched in terms which shout of the king of France's suspicion and distrust.[63] The tone in which William the Breton wrote about him – using phrases such as 'long may he rot in the donjon of Le Goulet where he now rots' – is doubtless due to his prominent role in the Bouvines campaign, but it is already clear from Rigord's much earlier comments that Renaud's defection was bitterly resented. According to Rigord, it was at the devil's instigation that Renaud joined Richard, and that subsequently he and his *routiers* did much damage to the French kingdom.[64] The *History of William the Marshal* says that King Philip was dismayed and angry when Richard went to a conference between Vernon and Boutavant hand in hand with the counts of Boulogne and Flanders.[65] Others joined the Angevin bandwagon in 1198: the counts of Guines, of Brienne, Hugh, count of St Pol, Geoffrey of Perche and Louis of Blois.[66] William the Breton was to paint an even gloomier picture of Philip's position in 1198. Not only the counts of Flanders and Boulogne, he wrote, defected from their proper allegiance, but so too did Louis of Blois and almost all the princes of the kingdom, some secretly, some openly. For this reason Richard was so confident and so aggressive that he threatened even Paris itself.[67] Naturally Philip did not remain idle. He almost certainly struck back in traditional fashion by entering into an alliance with two of Richard's Aquitanian vassals: Aimar of Limoges and Ademar of Angoulême.[68]

---

[62] Coggeshall, 136.

[63] *Recueil des actes*, no. 580. It also reveals how close was the association between Renaud and the count of St Pol.

[64] *Philippidos*, iii, 90–5. WB, 202, 205; cf. Rigord, *instigante diabolo*, 138. According to William the Breton, Renaud held no lands from Richard which might have excused his change of allegiance. In fact there was the inheritance of his wife both in Normandy and England for which he received royal confirmation charters (Landon, 526 and 526a). The Pipe Roll for 1197–8 shows he recovered property in England during that exchequer year.

[65] *HGM*, 10,688–740.

[66] *Chron.*, iv, 54. According to Howden, the Bretons and men of Champagne had joined in 1197, *Chron.*, iv, 19–20.

[67] WB, 202–3. On 1 September 1198 Counts Thibault of Champagne and Louis of Blois were still publicly avowing that they had not joined the ranks of Philip's enemies. The fact that they did so indicates deep suspicion about their real alignment, Landon, 133.

[68] Based on documents which bear the date April 1199 – which, by our reckoning, means April 1198. For the detailed argument see Gillingham, *Coeur de Lion*, 175–6.

But in this diplomatic warfare it was Richard who held the upper hand. A number of contemporaries – William the Breton, Roger of Howden, Lambert of Ardres, Caesarius of Heisterbach, the Anonymous of Béthune – who offered explanations for Richard's diplomatic triumphs were unanimous. It was his great wealth and generosity which drew so many allies to his side. In the words of the Anonymous of Bethune 'King Richard was a good deal richer, both in land and money, than the king of France'.[69]

The war began again in early September 1198 when Baldwin invaded Artois, the land which he believed Philip had taken unjustly. He captured Aire without a fight and then, together with Renaud of Boulogne, laid siege to St Omer. The citizens of St Omer, with Baldwin's consent, sent a message to Philip, saying that they would have to surrender unless he came to their aid. Philip wrote back, promising to come by 30 September; if he did not, they were at liberty to make the best terms they could. In fact, as before, the allies had opened a war on two fronts and Philip was detained in the Vexin throughout September. After a six-week siege Baldwin marched into St Omer on 13 October.[70] Meanwhile, in Normandy, the king of France had been defeated twice. On the earlier occasion he had led his army on a raid into the Norman Vexin. Richard's forces were dispersed, so at first he could do no more than shadow the French with a few men until he was joined by 200 knights and Mercadier's troop – by which time the French had burned some eighteen places. As they withdrew he attacked from the rear, inflicting a number of casualties and capturing thirty knights and sergeants and 100 horses.[71]

---

[69] Anonymous of Béthune, 'li rois Richars estoit trop riches de terre et d'avoir, asés plus que il rois de France n'estoit', *RHF* xxiv, pt 2, 758. Cf. Howden,'the gifts of his bounteous hand surpassed all other gifts', *Chron.*, iv, 19–20. Caesarius of Heisterbach, *Dialogus*, i, 102; *Philippidos*, iv, 590–7; Lambert of Ardres, *Chronique de Guines et d'Ardres*, ed. M. de Godefroy Menilglaise (Paris, 1855), 371.

[70] This is based on the account written from close at hand by Andreas of Marchiennes, *Sig. Cont.*, 435, supplemented by Gervase, i, 573 who gives the date for the town's surrender and signals the presence of the count of Boulogne in what Andreas had merely called a very large army. At the later stages of the siege it may well have included a contingent commanded by William the Marshal and his nephew John, Peter des Préaux and Alan Basset, none of whom witnessed royal charters between 18 September and November 1198. At some date in the financial year ending at Michaelmas 1198 William and Peter were dispatched to Flanders armed with 1,730 marks to spend on the king's behalf, PR 10 Richard I, 172. Although traditionally ascribed to 1197, the episode in William's Flemish campaign described in the *History of William the Marshal* seems to fit the siege of St Omer, with news of Philip's withdrawal being taken to Richard at Courcelles, better than any alternative event in 1197. Naturally it was Marshal's wise advice which led to Philip beating a retreat, *HGM*, 10,783–840. But given the extent to which Philip was committed in the Vexin, he could hardly have afforded to send a substantial force to the relief of St Omer.

[71] This assumes that Roger of Howden, our only source for this incident, has

The second occasion, an altogether more serious affair, was described in a triumphant letter dictated by Richard himself and given the widest possible circulation. On 27 September Richard forded the river Epte at Dangu and invaded the French Vexin. He captured Courcelles and Boury on that day and then returned to Dangu, while another force took Sérifontaine. The capture of Dangu (implied by this account) together with these three other fortresses meant that a net was closing around Gisors. Philip received news of the attack on Courcelles and with a considerable French army (300 knights, plus sergeants and urban contingents), set out to its relief next day, not knowing that it had already fallen. As his army moved north from Mantes it was detected by patrols which Richard had sent to reconnoitre the land east of the Epte while the bulk of his forces rested at Dangu. Richard, as so often, was out with the patrols himself. As soon as it became clear that Philip was not planning to attack the Angevin army at Dangu but intended to continue on his northward path, apparently still unaware of what was happening, Richard decided to use the advantage won by good reconnaissance and attack the French army while it was in marching order.[72] He sent orders for the troops at Dangu to join him as quickly as possible. As Philip carried on marching, however, Richard could see his advantage slipping away. The French king was bound to realize what was going on when he reached Courcelles – if not before – and so Richard gave the order to attack while some of his reinforcements were still on the way. According to the *History of William the Marshal* he led the attack like a starving lion which catches sight of its prey. For the second time Philip took to his heels, galloping northwards to the one place of refuge left to him, the castle of Gisors.

> We so pressed them to the gate of Gisors that the bridge broke beneath them, and the king of France, as we hear, drank of the river. Up to twenty other knights were drowned. With our own lance we laid low Matthew de Montmorenci and Alan de Rusci and Fulk de Gilerval and held them captive. Over one hundred of his men were taken. We send you the names of the most important and will forward the rest when we have them. Mercadier also took thirty knights whom we have not seen. Mounted sergeants and foot sergeants were also captured, but these have not yet been counted; and 200 chargers were seized, of which 140

described it twice, counting French losses in a different way each time, but making clear that it happened a little earlier than the famous pursuit to Gisors, *Chron.*, iv, 55, 59.
[72] The account of this incident in the *History of William the Marshal* refers to Richard's presence on patrol and emphasizes that he rejected Mercadier's advice in order to follow that of a knight who knew the area well, *HGM*, 10,933–56, 10,967–71.

were armoured. It was thus that we defeated the French king at Gisors. It was not our might, but God's and the justice of our cause, which triumphed, for in this deed, against the advice of all our men, we placed at hazard both our head and our reign. We tell you of these things that you may rejoice along with us. Witness ourselves at Dangu, 30 September.[73]

According to Angevin sources, Richard had attacked a numerically superior army – though one which had been taken unawares before it could get into battle formation. Richard did not have the equipment to lay siege to Gisors, so he returned with his prisoners to Dangu; only the fact that Philip himself had escaped – helped, it was said, by the clouds of dust kicked up on the dry roads – diminished his triumph. The war, however, continued. Philip took his revenge by mustering another army and raiding Normandy south of the Seine, burning Evreux.[74] Richard retaliated by sending Mercadier to plunder the town of Abbeville, where many French merchants had gathered for the fair. It may be that Howden's comment on the war of 1198, that it was waged more fiercely than ever, with Philip blinding prisoners and Richard, unwillingly, retaliating in kind, applies to the aftermath of the French king's dip in the waters of the Epte.[75]

Did the fact that Philip had been able so soon afterwards to raid and burn Evreux mean that he had not, after all, suffered a serious defeat at Gisors?[76] Clearly English historians believed he had. The rout was given no fewer than seventy lines in the *History of William the Marshal* – and this though the poem's hero was not even there! After this, wrote the *jongleur*, thirty of ours could take on forty Frenchmen.[77] But perhaps English sources accepted all too readily the gloating tone of Richard's widely circulated newsletter.[78] On the other hand non-English sources, such as the

[73] *Chron.*, 58–9, the copy sent to Philip of Durham. In addition Howden obtained, presumably also from Philip of Durham, the list of prisoners mentioned in the letter. The translation here is based on that in Holt, 'Ricardus rex', 31. In these words, as he points out, 'the soldier–poet seems to break through the formalities of epistolary composition'.

[74] And soon afterwards Philip is alleged to have lost another seventeen knights and many sergeants when he sent a force to prevent 'Novum Burgum' being burned down – by John, according to Howden, *Chron.*, iv, 60. (In the context of the fighting of September 1198 it is hard to see why John should have burned Neubourg. I would guess that Howden meant Neufchâteau-sur-Epte.)

[75] *Chron.*, iv, 54, 60. William the Breton very properly said that it was Richard who started the atrocities, *Philippidos*, v, 309–27.

[76] Bradbury, *Philip Augustus*, 124.

[77] *HGM*, 10,907–11,067.

[78] According to Roger of Wendover, Richard sent copies to all his friends (prelates and barons) in England, *Chron. Maj.*, ii, 449. In addition to Howden, evidence for its circulation can be found in *Magna Vita*, ii, 109 (using copy sent to Bishop Hugh of Lincoln); Diceto, ii, 164; Gervase, i, 574 (perhaps); Annals of Winchester, *Ann. Mon.*, ii, 70, and (perhaps) Annals of Margam, *Ann. Mon.*, i, 23.

history of Andreas of Marchiennes, also report the personal humiliation of Philip's fall into the river Epte.[79] William the Breton admitteded that ninety – or ninety-two – knights were captured.[80] The loss of ninety knights and 200 warhorses (140 armoured) would always have been a heavy blow.[81] What made it especially so was the fact that these were distinguished knights, men of note. The *History of William the Marshal* made the point that those captured were the best knights, who on such an occasion fought in the rearguard.[82] But the best evidence for the scale of the defeat comes from Capetian sources. Both Rigord and William the Breton do their best to save French honour. According to their version Richard had taken Philip by surprise by invading the Vexin with 1,500 knights, many *routiers* and a huge army of foot; when Philip made for Gisors he had a much smaller force than that (500 knights, according to Rigord; only 200 according to William the Breton). In this way they imply (without explicitly stating) that the French were outnumbered by at least three to one on 28 September – and they then fought so bravely that the honour of the day belonged to the few against the many.[83] But both make it plain that Philip suffered a major defeat. Rigord writes that many were captured, names four of them and then says he can't bring himself to name any more because he is so upset. Both authors felt that the defeat was so severe as to require special explanation and they found it in the view that God was punishing Philip for allowing the Jews into his domains and for oppressing the Church.[84]

That Richard continued to gain ground is suggested by other events which Roger of Howden happens to mention. First, two days' fighting around Pacy, at the end of which the earl of Leicester, though he did not recover his castle, came off the better. Then a little later, but still in October, William le Queu, the castellan of Lyons-la-Forêt, captured eighty mounted sergeants and forty foot sergeants whom Philip had sent to garrison Neufmarché – in itself not a major confrontation but doubtless

---

[79] *Sig., Cont.*, 435.

[80] WB, 202 gives ninety; *Philippidos*, v, 428, 437 gives ninety-two.

[81] In their treaty of 1186 King Alfonso II of Aragon and Richard had agreed to aid each other in the war against Toulouse to the tune of 200 knights. See above, 81.

[82] *HGM*, 11,022–30. Here the number of captured knights is given as ninety-one. Roger of Wendover plausibly explains the capture of so many élite knights as the outcome of the rearguard's desperate struggle to allow Philip himself to escape, *Chron. Maj.*, ii, 448.

[83] Rigord, 141–2; WB, 201–2; *Philippidos*, v, 355–440.

[84] Rigord, 141; WB, 202; *Philippidos*, 440–89. In William's poem the action at Gisors represented the pinnacle of Richard's military success, creating in him the vainglory and pride, the failure to understand that all good things came from God, that led inexorably to his death. Whatever Richard may have thought (and William the Breton may of course be right), in his letter he explicitly wrote that 'it was not us but God and our right that overcame the French king at Gisors'.

typical of the dozens of unrecorded incidents which must have marked Richard's advance into the Vexin.[85] Howden's was a partial view, but Philip's own assessment of the situation can be deduced from the peace terms which he offered in the autumn of 1198.[86] He simply did not have the resources to stand the strain of a war on two fronts and if he were to recover the territory he had lost in Artois then he would have to make peace with Richard, even if this meant renouncing his conquests. So he offered to hand back everything he had taken, except Gisors. But Richard refused to make a peace which did not include the count of Flanders and all those who had switched their allegiance to him.[87] Finally in November a truce was agreed, to last until 13 January 1199.[88] On 13 January Richard sailed up the Seine to meet Philip as arranged. The two kings talked. Philip was on horseback while Richard remained on board ship – presumably one of his galleys. They agreed to meet again; and this time, with a papal legate and magnates from both sides acting as mediators, they agreed to a five-year truce, based on the status quo.[89] But since no documentary record of the terms of the truce survives, it is hard to know precisely what was meant by 'status quo'. One definition of it is given by the *History of William the Marshal* – which, though an unofficial and later source, is based on the old marshal's very vivid memories.

As he saw it, Philip, though cunning as a fox, was losing. He had spent all his money, and whichever way he turned, he found himself opposed by Richard. Many of his men went over to Richard; his only hope was to appeal to Rome. The papal legate, Peter of Capua, arrived on the scene at about Christmas 1198.[90] Innocent III had proclaimed a new crusade and was anxious to see an end to the Angevin–Capetian quarrel.[91] So far as William Marshal was concerned the legate was a smooth-talking tool of France, with a complexion as yellow as a stork's foot, and a nauseating pose of humility.[92] Many years later he still retained vivid memories of a stormy interview between Peter and Richard.[93] Richard was willing to make peace

[85] *Chron.*, iv, 60, 78.

[86] That is if Howden accurately reproduces the gist of Philip's proposals; there is no Capetian source for them.

[87] *Chron.*, iv, 61.

[88] Ibid., 68.

[89] Ibid., 79–80.

[90] *HGM*, 11,311–57; Rigord, 143–4.

[91] Howden gives the text of Innocent's crusade letter (dated 13 August 1198) in which, among much else, he announced the sending of Cardinal Peter to make peace, or a five years' truce, between the kings, *Chron.*, iv, 70–5.

[92] Hardly fair given the fact that twelve months later Peter of Capua presided over the council which imposed an interdict on Philip's kingdom.

[93] *HGM*, 11,373–688. In the passages given here in direct speech I have taken advantage of the translation in Jessie Crosland, *William the Marshal* (London, 1962), 78–81.

and forgo compensation for the damage done by Philip, if Philip restored all the lands he had taken. Otherwise while he could still get into the saddle he would give Philip no peace. When the legate tried to talk him into a more compromising frame of mind, arguing that all the time their war continued the kingdom of Jerusalem remained in danger, Richard angrily reminded him of the circumstances in which Philip had invaded his lands. 'If it had not been for his malice, forcing me to return, I would have been able to recover the whole of Outremer. Then, when I was in prison he conspired to keep me there so that he could steal my lands.' From Richard's point of view, as he forcefully said, it was wrong to make either peace or a long truce while his enemy still held land and castles taken unjustly. 'Ah, sire', the legate is represented as saying, 'how true it is that no one can have everything he wants', and he continued to play, as indeed his script demanded, on the needs of the Holy Land until eventually Richard offered a five-year truce, allowing Philip to keep the castles he held – 'but not a foot more'.

Peter of Capua said he would take this proposal back to Philip but then drove Richard to fury by asking him to release the bishop of Beauvais. 'It is wrong to keep under lock and key a man such as he who is both anointed and consecrated.' 'By my head!' said the king, 'he is de-consecrated for he is a false Christian. It was not as bishop that he was captured but as a knight fighting and fully armed, a laced helmet on his head. Sir hypocrite, what a fool you are! If you had not been an envoy I would send you back with something to show the pope which he would not forget. Never did the pope raise a finger to help me when I was in prison and wanted his help to be free. And now he asks me to set free a robber and an incendiary who has never done me anything but harm. Get out of here, Sir traitor, liar, trickster, corrupt dealer in churches, and never let me see you again.' The legate fled back to the king of France, afraid that if he stayed a moment longer he would be castrated. Richard retired to his chamber, angry as a wounded boar, had all the shutters closed and threw himself on the bed, refusing to see anyone. Not until the Marshal arrived did anyone have the nerve to disturb him. William calmed the king by pointing out that he had more reason to laugh than to boil with anger. Let Philip keep the castles which he holds. Without the land surrounding them, far from being an asset, they would become a drain on his already overstretched resources. All Richard would have to do would be to ensure his captains prevented the Capetian garrisons from coming out to collect provisions and revenues from the surrounding countryside. According to the *History of William the Marshal*, William le Queu carried out this policy so effectively that it was he, not Philip's castellan, who collected the rents from Gisors, while the garrison of Baudemont was afraid even to draw water from the spring just outside their castle.[94] This may be

---

[94] *HGM*, 11,727–44.

poetic exaggeration, but it would none the less be true that on terms such as this Philip would find peace as expensive as war.

The point, of course, was to show how no one but William could calm the king. But if the story accurately reflects the terms of the truce, then it was the king who must have seen, just as clearly as the Marshal, the advantage gained by these terms because it was he – not William – who proposed them. Indeed it was presumably methods such as these which had led to the recovery of castles such as Vaudreuil in 1195.[95] But in that case, why so angry? Was it a stage-managed anger? Of course it was. All that slamming of shutters. After all, if the French could be made to believe that he was unhappy about the outcome of the legate's mediation, they were all the more likely to accept the deal. On the other hand Richard *was* angry with the king of France who had invaded his lands. If Richard were anywhere near as shrewd and cunning a ruler as hostile sources say he was, then the anger was both genuine and calculated.[96] So William the Marshal's assessment of the situation early in 1199 was that Richard was winning. The Capetian assessment is that Richard thought he was winning – and that he was. According to Rigord, the truce was not properly ratified because Richard cunningly avoided doing this – i.e. he believed that continuing the war suited his interests.[97] And the whole tone of Rigord's and William the Breton's narratives of 1197–8 is one of despair as the tide of war flowed strongly against them.

[95] See above, 292–3.
[96] White, 'The Politics of Anger' for a discussion of lordly anger which incorporates, without 'merely politicizing', that emotion into eleventh- and twelfth-century political processes.
[97] Rigord, 144.

Chapter 18

DEATH AND REPENTANCE, 1199

Richard's death came as a great shock. In the words of Abbot William of Andres, 'at a time when almost the whole world either feared the king of England or praised him, he was snatched suddenly from this life'.[1] A lament composed by Geoffrey of Vinsauf – and one which came to be very well known since Geoffrey included it in his *Poetria Nova*, the most popular handbook on the art of writing Latin poetry – gives a sense of the suddenness, and does so at some length.[2]

O death! Do you realise whom you snatched from us? To our eyes he was light: to our ears melody; to our minds an amazement. Do you realise, impious death, whom you snatched from us? He was the lord of warriors, the glory of kings, the delight of the world. Nature knew not how to add any further perfection; he was the utmost she could achieve. But that was the reason you snatched him away. If heaven allow it, I chide even God. God why do you fail? If you recall he alone defended your Jaffa against many thousands; Acre too he restored to you. The enemies of the cross bear witness – all of them Richard, in life, inspired with such terror that he is still feared now he is dead. O Lord, if it is permissible to say it, let me say – with your leave – you could have done this more graciously, and with less haste, if he had bridled the foe at least (and there would have been little delay, he was on the verge of success). He could then have departed more worthily to remain with you. But by this lesson you have made us known how brief is the laughter of earth, how long are its tears.[3]

[1] *RHF*, 18,572.
[2] Hence Chaucer's teasing allusion to it in the 'Nun's Priest's Tale'. 'O Geoffrey, thou my dear and sovereign master/Who, when they brought King Richard to disaster/And shot him dead, lamented so his death,/Would that I had thy skill, thy gracious breath', *Canterbury Tales*, trans. N. Coghill (Harmondsworth, 1951), 244.
[3] The translation here is based on that in *Poetria Nova of Geoffrey of Vinsauf*, trans. M. F. Nims (Toronto, 1967), 28–31. The lament begins: 'Once defended by King Richard's shield, now undefended, O England [or in some versions, 'O Normandy'],' and in this form – 'O Neustria' – the lament was copied into the Vitellius E xvii manuscript of Howden's *Gesta Regis*, see *Gesta*, i, xxiv.

321

For William the Breton, who naturally took a different view, Richard's death meant that in 1199 God had come to save France.[4] Yet the year had begun much like the last four years. Although, as a gesture of help for the projected crusade, the two kings had agreed on a five years' truce, it was extremely unlikely that it would last for as long as five months. Almost immediately Richard accused Philip of breaking the truce. He had sent Mercadier south to help his seneschal cope with the Limoges–Angoulême revolt, but *en route* his company was ambushed by some French counts. Philip denied that he was responsible, and it may well be – in view of the general loathing for bands of mercenaries – that the four counts had acted on their own account. But when Richard himself moved off southwards, Philip took the opportunity to begin building a new castle on the Seine between Gaillon and Boutavant. Warned by Richard's chancellor, Eustace of Ely, that unless he demolished it the truce would be at an end, and urged by the legate to comply, he agreed to do so.[5] But obviously in this atmosphere of mutual suspicion and recrimination, hostilities were likely to start again at any moment.

One more attempt was made to find a peace settlement which would leave Gisors in Philip's hands and yet which Richard could accept. The King of France's rights over the church of Tours had been a constant source of irritation to the Angevins; perhaps if he were to give these up then Richard might reconcile himself to the loss of Gisors. So, with the legate's help, a treaty on these lines was drafted. Philip's son, Louis, would marry one of Richard's nieces, a daughter of the king of Castile, and Richard would grant them Gisors and 20,000 marks as a dowry. As well as giving up his rights in Tours, Philip would also agree to abandon his ally Philip of Swabia and instead help Richard's nephew, Otto of Brunswick, in his fight to win undisputed possession of the German crown.[6] Whether or not Richard would have ratified these terms we shall never know. For the moment he remained in Maine and Anjou, leaving these preliminary discussions to his officials. Philip – 'the sower of discord', as Howden called him – turned to the kind of tactic that had worked so well in the past. He let Richard know that John had reverted to the Capetian allegiance and showed him what purported to be John's charter. Astonishingly, wrote Howden, Richard believed this and ordered the seizure of John's estates on both sides of the Channel. However when John sent two of his knights to Philip's court to deny the charge formally, no one there was prepared to

---

[4] 'Anno incarnationis Dominice MCXCIX visitavit Deus regnum Francorum. Nam Richardus rex occiditur in pago Lemovicensi', WB, 204.

[5] *Chron.*, iv, 80. By 2 February 1199, when Richard's court was at La Suze in Maine, the vice-chancellor is sealing charters instead of Eustace, so the latter had presumably left to deliver the warning to Philip. See Landon, 142–3.

[6] *Chron.*, iv, 80–1.

stand by the accusation, so Richard restored his brother's estates and gave less credence to the king of France's words.[7]

Soon after 15 March 1199 Richard left Chinon and went to join Mercadier in Aquitaine. Philip's allies, the count of Angoulême and the viscount of Limoges, had not been included in the truce, so Richard was free to move against them. On and off since 1176 he had been at odds with these two magnates. Their semi-permanent hostility was a major political problem. Late that month Richard brought up his troops to lay siege to the viscount's castle at Chalus-Chabrol, not far south of Limoges. In Coggeshall's words:

> during Lent King Richard took advantage of the opportunity of peace with King Philip to lead an army of his own against the Viscount of Limoges, who had rebelled against him during the time of war and had made a treaty of alliance with Philip. Moreover there are some people who say that a treasure of incalculable value was found on the Viscount's lands; that the King ordered it to be handed over to him; and that when the Viscount refused the King's anger was further aroused. Then he devastated the Viscount's land with fire and sword, as though he did not know that arms should be laid aside during Lent, until at last he came to Chalus-Chabrol ...[8]

The detailed account of the siege which then follows may well derive from the story told to Abbot Ralph by someone who was there: Milo, the king's almoner, and abbot of the Cistercian house of Le Pin near Poitiers. Indeed it was Milo who, according to Coggeshall, heard Richard's last confession, ministered extreme unction and then closed the dead man's mouth and eyes.[9] For three days Richard pressed the attack hard. He and his crossbowmen forced the defenders to keep their heads down, while the sappers concentrated on undermining the castle walls. Every now and then a piece of stonework came crashing down over the heads of the besiegers, but the sappers, protected by specially constructed covers, worked steadily on. Threatened by the imminent collapse of the castle walls, the forty men and women within were clearly on the verge of surrender.

---

[7] Ibid., 81. It should be noted that Howden's version of this episode was almost certainly written after John had come to the throne. For confirmation of renewed distrust of John at the end of the reign see *Magna Vita*, ii, 137; Coggeshall, 99.

[8] Coggeshall, 94.

[9] That Milo attended Richard's funeral at Fontevraud is shown by his presence in the witness list of a charter issued then, *Calendar of Documents preserved in France*, ed. J. H. Round (London, 1899), 389. According to Coggeshall, 97, Richard found the Cistercian abbey of Le Pin (14 kilometres from Poitiers and close to the ducal castle of Montreuil-Bonnin) in a ruined state and endowed it richly. For his charters to Le Pin, see Landon, nos 107, 144, 433, 469. Milo was abbot of Le Pin from 1190 to 1226.

After supper on the evening of 26 March 1199, although daylight was beginning to fade, Richard left his tent in order to observe the progress of the siege and to exercise (as he often did) his own skill with a crossbow. Because he was not riding into battle he wore no armour except an iron headpiece, relying for protection on the rectangular shield which was carried before him. That day only one member of the garrison, a cross-bowman using a frying pan as a shield, was brave enough to show himself on the ramparts. It was a splendidly makeshift gesture of defiance but to the professional soldiers under Richard's command his occasional shots could be nothing more than a minor irritant. The lone figure of the cross-bowman with the frying pan was still visible on the parapets of the doomed castle and Richard could not help applauding as the man sent a well-aimed bolt in his direction. As a result he was fractionally late in ducking behind the shield and was struck on the left shoulder. Not wishing either to alarm his own men or to give heart to the defenders, he made no sound. Calmly he returned to his tent as though nothing had happened. Once inside he tried to pull out the bolt but succeeded only in breaking off the wooden shaft, leaving the iron barb, the length of a man's hand, deeply embedded in the flesh. Then a surgeon arrived. Working by the flickering light of torches he managed to remove the bolt; but the shoulder was badly hacked about. The wounds from the bolt and the surgeon's knife were then treated and bandaged up. The king's wound turned gangrenous and daily the infection spread. Richard had seen too many men die not to know what was happening to him. He wrote to his mother, Eleanor of Aquitaine, and she came in haste. To keep the news from getting out Richard stayed in his tent, allowing only four of his most trusted associates to enter.[10] Soon after-wards Chalus-Chabrol fell. But it was no longer a victory. Richard forgave the man who had shot him, then confessed his sins and received extreme unction. At Chalus on 6 April, as evening came, he died.[11]

According to Roger of Howden, the king's body was then disposed of according to his instructions. His brain and entrails were buried on the Poitou–Limousin border at Charroux – an abbey which claimed none

[10] According to a note added to the lower margin of the earliest manuscript of Coggeshall, as he lay in the tent Richard behaved without self-control, flouting the advice of his doctors, Coggeshall, 96. This may indicate that the stories about Richard having sex as he lay dying, whether true or not (see, e.g., *The Chronicle of Walter of Guiseborough* ed. H. G. Rothwell, Camden Society, 3rd series, lxxxix, 1957, 142) did not come from Milo. William the Breton also portrays the dying Richard preferring the 'joys of Venus' to 'salubrious counsel', *Philippidos*, v, 604–5. A modern version has him 'making love to some of the youths around Chaluz for a few days', M. Mitchell, *Berengaria* (Burwash Weald, 1986), 88.

[11] This account of the siege and of Richard's death is based on Coggeshall, 94–6. But the date is Howden's, *Chron.*, iv, 84. As an ex-chancery clerk he ought to have been precise about such matters; Coggeshall gives 7 April.

other than Charlemagne as its founder. His heart went to Rouen, where it was buried next to his elder brother. According to Gervase of Canterbury it was an unusually large heart; a little bigger than a pomegranate, said others.[12] The rest of him, together with the crown and regalia he had worn at Winchester, reported the Winchester annalist, was buried at Fontevraud, at his father's feet, on Palm Sunday, 11 April.[13] The effigy on a tomb shaped like a draped bier shows him crowned, sceptred and magnificently attired, his sword by his side.[14]

As his body went north so too did the stories which attempted to make sense of so unexpected an event. At their focal point was the discovery of a treasure and Richard's attempt to seize it for himself. As is plain from his own account of Richard's motives in going to the Limousin, the well-informed Coggeshall had heard a story of buried treasure, though he had also taken the trouble to identify it as a story – 'there are some people who say' – separate from his report of a campaign against Philip's Limousin allies.[15] It may be that there was no treasure.[16] Certainly no treasure appears in the account of Richard's death by the author who was much better placed to know the background to the story than anyone else. This is Bernard Itier. In 1199 Bernard was in his mid-thirties, a monk in the great

[12] Gervase, i, 593; Annals of Winchester, in *Annales Monastici*, i, 71. A silver shrine and a tomb effigy of the king were subsequently erected near the high altar. There is a fascinating account, with line drawings, of the then recent rediscovery of effigy and heart by A. Way in *Archaeologia*, xxix (1842), 202–16. When I last saw the heart (if that is what it was), in Rouen's city museum, it was indeed, as described there, 'withered to the semblance of a faded leaf'.

[13] Richard is the earliest king of whom it is explicitly reported that he was buried in the coronation insignia, though his father may also have been. See D. A. Carpenter, *The Reign of Henry III* (London, 1996), 436. If his father was, then presumably this was on Richard's instructions. 'Bury richly the king my father,' he commanded, according to William Marshal, *HGM*, 9358–60.

[14] J. Martindale, 'The Sword on the Stone: Some Resonances of a Medieval Symbol of Power', *ANS*, xv (1993), 219–30 for some of the implications of this innovatory practice. The effigy itself, together with those of his parents, can only be dated roughly – to the early thirteenth century, E. M. Hallam, 'Royal Burial and the Cult of Kingship in France and England, 1060–1330', *JMH*, viii (1982), citing the opinion of Andrew Martindale. I do not know on what evidence, if any (apart from later tradition), one effigy is identified as Henry II's and one as Richard's.

[15] Only in one other place in his long description of the siege of Chalus-Chabrol does Coggeshall use the phrase 'as people say' and that is where he writes that for almost seven years Richard had abstained from communion 'because of the mortal hatred which he bore in his heart for the King of France', 96. But there is a great deal of evidence to show that Richard was assiduous in his attendance at mass. On the other hand, refusal to take mass belongs in the world of the Angevin legend of their descent from the devil. (See above, 24, 258.)

[16] Tales of the discovery of hidden treasure have often been used to explain the apparently inexplicable, K. Thomas, *Religion and the Decline of Magic* (London, 1971), 279–82.

Benedictine abbey of St Martial in Limoges, where he later became librarian. Relations between the viscounts of Limoges and St Martial's, though often tense, were also extremely close; the viscounts' castle stood cheek by jowl with the abbey, and the abbey was the traditional burial place of the viscounts. Much of Bernard's historical writing took the form of brief marginal notes or memoranda jotted down here and there among the manuscripts in the library of St Martial's. Very often these notes began with a phrase such as 'Written by Bernard Itier'. His account of Richard's death was written in a note of this kind added to the library's copy of the chronicle of Geoffrey de Vigeois.

> Bernard Itier wrote this on the Friday before the feast of St John the Baptist in the year that King Richard, known as Coeur de Lion, died and was buried with his father in the abbey of Fontevraud, to the joy of many and the sorrow of others. In the year of our Lord 1199 Richard, the most powerful (*fortissimus*) king of the English, was struck in the shoulder by an arrow while besieging a keep at a place in the Limousin called Chalus-Chabrol. In that keep there were two knights with about thirty-eight others, both men and women. One of the knights was called Peter Bru, the other Peter Basil, of whom it is said that he fired the arrow which struck the king so that he died within twelve days, that is to say, on the Tuesday before Palm Sunday, on 6 April, in the first hour of the night. In the meantime while on his sickbed he had ordered his forces to besiege a castle called Nontron belonging to Viscount Aimar and another fortress called Montagut. This they did, but when they heard of the king's death they withdrew in confusion. The king had planned to destroy all the viscount's castles and towns.[17]

Not only does this not mention any treasure, it also makes plain that we are not dealing with the siege of just one, rather minor, castle. Richard attacked three of the viscount's castles and, in Limoges, men believed that he had intended to attack them all.[18] It seems that Coggeshall was right when he wrote of the king 'devastating the viscount's land with fire and sword'. But by an extraordinary chance, as the result of an apparently trivial slip of the pen, Bernard Itier's version of events happened to escape the attention of nearly all modern historians. The Saint-Martial copy of Geoffrey de Vigeois's chronicle no longer exists, but in the early seventeenth century it – or possibly a copy of it – was transcribed by a rather

---

[17] Text printed in F. Arbellot, *La Vérité sur la mort de Richard Coeur-de-Lion* (Paris, 1878) 61–4 – a study of the subject which was ignored for far too long.

[18] In another note in another St Martial's manuscript Bernard Itier listed fourteen places besieged in 1199, including Chalus-Chabrol, Nontron and (probably) Montagut, *Chroniques de Saint-Martial*, 66.

incompetent copyist. He misread the opening words of this note and instead of 'Scripsit B. Iterii' he put down 'Scripsit Beati'.[19] This was complete nonsense and, as a result, when the seventeenth-century French antiquarian, Père Labbe, printed Geoffrey of Vigeois he decided to omit the first sentence of the note, with its incomprehensible beginning. As Labbe printed it, the note began with the words 'In the year of our Lord 1199'.[20] In consequence, as an anonymous note of uncertain provenance, no one took it very seriously. If historians had realized that it had actually been written by Bernard Itier, the story of treasure-trove would long ago have been relegated to the wings, and its place centre stage would have been taken by the rebellion.[21] A rebellion, moreover, which was encouraged by Philip Augustus and which Richard had good reason to take seriously since it occurred in precisely that part of Aquitaine where revolts against ducal authority had been most common: in 1176–9, 1182–3, 1192, 1194, and now again in 1198–9. This was, in effect, the soft underbelly of the Angevin empire – as Philip has always known.

Instead of a rebellion the tale of treasure-trove has dominated accounts of Richard's death. It has seemed to be an altogether appropriate end for a king who was thought to be a negligent, adventurous and brutal warmonger. The king of England, the greatest crusader of his age, had been killed in a trivial quarrel in Aquitaine when nothing of any significance was at stake; arrogance, greed and short-sightedness had brought about his downfall in an obscure side-show over buried treasure. 'Continuing concern to make good any chance of immediate gain is characteristic of his whole career; and so he sold off Cyprus. So too, the final scene of his life was played out in pursuit of a gaudy bauble.'[22] In the words of Sir Maurice Powicke, whose *Loss of Normandy* remains in many ways the standard version of that subject, 'It is sad to reflect that Richard died in such a sordid quarrel. Yet he was fighting for his *regalia*, and the incident is symbolic of his whole career; his mind had burned with the same enthusiasm to rescue the Holy Sepulchre. In this case his imagination was kindled by a useless relic of antiquity.'[23] Once established as a king who had devoted his life to

---

[19] For further detail on all the matters in this and the next paragraph, Gillingham, *Coeur de Lion*, 155–80.

[20] P. Labbe, *Novae Bibliothecae Manuscriptorum Librorum*, ii (Paris, 1657), 342. Labbe's text of this note was simply reprinted in the *Recueil des historiens des Gaules et de la France*, xviii (Paris, 1879), 239, n (a).

[21] The treasure, if it existed at all, was thus of subsidiary importance. It was not for this that Richard went south again. Other historians of the time who refer to a rebellion without mentioning any treasure are the author of William the Marshal's memoirs, *HGM*, 11,573–5; *Magna Vita* ii, 130–1; and *Chron. Maj.*, ii, 451–2. The last two, with sound reason, represent the count of Angoulême as the leader of the rebellion.

[22] Brundage, *Richard Lionheart*, 254.

[23] Powicke, 126.

sterile deeds of knightly prowess, as a brave soldier, but no statesman, a leg-endary warrior but an irresponsible king who understood little of the true art of government, this was the final scene which brought the drama of his life to a satisfying conclusion.

True or not, appropriate or not, stories of the treasure circulated rapidly and widely; they repay investigation for the light they shed on the judge-ments which men came to on the king. As Rigord tells the story, when Richard demanded the treasure which an unnamed knight had unearthed, the knight took refuge with his lord, the viscount of Limoges. Despite the fact that it was Lent, when war was prohibited by the Church, Richard laid siege to Chalus-Chabrol and there he was shot by an unnamed crossbow-man.[24] In his verse epic, the *Philippidos*, William the Breton takes up these themes and develops them. Fifty lines devoted entirely to moralizing about Richard's false pride and the wrong he is committing in making war against his overlord, the king of France, set the scene. Then we hear of a wonder-ful event which happened near Limoges. A peasant ploughing his fields stumbled across a hoard of coins and took them to his lord, Achard of Chalus. The rumour of this reached Richard and, putting everything else aside, he determined to possess the treasure. In the face of Richard's over-whelming military might, Achard begged for a truce during the holy days of Lent and offered to submit the quarrel between them to the court of the king of France. Infuriated by this suggestion, Richard pressed on with the siege and very soon the walls of Chalus began to crumble. At this point William interrupts his narrative of the siege in order to introduce his readers to the Fates, the three Old Sisters who control man's destiny, either spinning out the thread of his life or deciding to cut it short. Into the mouth of one of the three, Atropos, he puts a thirty-line speech explaining why it was that Richard no longer deserved to live: he is greedy, has no respect for God or for holy days, he has broken treaties made with his lord and, by making war against his own father, has offended against the law of nature.[25] Having convinced her sisters that it was time to stop their spinning, Atropos herself then took a hand in the siege. She showed Achard where he could find a bolt and told him to give it to a crossbowman called Dudo. 'This is how I want Richard to die, for it was he who first introduced the crossbow into France. Now let him suffer the fate he has dealt out to others.'[26] This is obviously not history in the sense of an attempt to give a more or less accu-rate idea of what happened; it is history in the higher sense of moral drama, a genre in which even the obviously nonsensical, such as the notion that Richard introduced the crossbow into France, was used to make a point.

[24] Rigord introduced his description of the treasure with the phrase *ut ferebatur*, 'according to the story which I have heard', Rigord, 144–5.

[25] Note the nature of his unnatural act.

[26] *Philippidos*, v, 440–620.

The story of treasure-trove cannot, however, be dismissed as mere black propaganda put out by the French court. The treasure and the fact that Richard attacked the viscount's castle in Lent are the main points in the brief report of the king's death in the Margam annals. Although the annalist wrote in the mid-1230s, it is possible that in Margam Abbey men remembered stories told by William de Briouze (died 1211) – and charter evidence shows that William was at Chalus on 5 April 1199.[27] Although the story in the Margam annals is both late and of uncertain provenance, these are not qualifications which can readily be made of the version told by Roger of Howden. One of his main informants was Robert of Thornham – a man who certainly ought to have been very well informed about the circumstances of Richard's death since he had custody of the great castle at Chinon in 1199 and was a key player in the events that followed Richard's death.[28] In Howden's version, Viscount Widomar of Limoges sent Richard a considerable part of the large treasure of gold and silver which was found on his land, but the king demanded it all, and came to Chalus-Chabrol with an army in order to take it by force. The garrison offered to surrender on condition their lives, limbs and weapons were spared, but Richard would have none of it. He swore to hang them all. That same day he was shot by a crossbowman called Bertrand de Gurdon and retired, mortally wounded, to his tent. When the castle fell all the defenders were hanged on Richard's orders, excepting only Bertrand de Gurdon, whom he would have condemned to a miserable death had he recovered. When the king knew he was dying he sent for Bertrand. 'What wrong have I done you that you should kill me?' 'With your own hand you killed my father and two brothers, and you intended to kill me. Take your revenge in any way you like. Now that I have seen you on your deathbed I shall gladly endure any torment you may devise.' Upon this Richard forgave him and ordered him to be released.[29]

[27] Annals of Margam, in *Annales Monastici*, i, 23–4, Landon, no. 418. For the date of the Margam annals, see C. Petit-Dutaillis, *Le Déshéritement de Jean sans Terre et le meurtre d'Arthur de Bretagne: etude critique sur la formation et la fortune d'une légende* (Paris, 1925), 84–7. Robert Patterson has identified the hand of the compiler as that of a Margam Abbey scribe active from *c.* 1225 to mid-century, 'The Author of the Margam Annals', *ANS*, xiv, (1991), 203. Alternatively the compiler could have heard stories told by a member of William de Briouze's staff while with his lord in exile – at the French court.

[28] *Chron.*, iv, 86. See D. Corner, 'The Earliest Surviving Manuscripts', and J. Gillingham, 'Historians without Hindsight: Coggeshall, Diceto and Howden on the Early Years of John's Reign', in *King John: New Interpretations*, ed. S. Church (Woodbridge, 1999), for the identification of Robert of Thornham as one of Roger's main informants.

[29] The clemency of the dying king was to become one of the most familiar images of Richard, a favourite subject for nineteenth-century artists. But according to Howden, *Chron.*, iv, 82–4, the dying king's orders were disobeyed. Bertrand was held a prisoner and after Richard's death Mercadier had him flayed alive. A similar

In this version we hear neither about Lent nor about an appeal to the court of the king of France. There is, none the less, a moral in this story of a ruthless man of blood who, in the end, as he lay dying, redeemed his sins by showing mercy. There is the same moral in Gervase of Canterbury's account of Richard's death. Here too Richard refused to grant life in return for an offer of surrender; as the crossbowman prepared to shoot he asked God to direct his aim so that the innocent might be freed from the king's oppression. Here too the dying Richard forgave his killer – and, an especially admirable point, repented for any harm he might have done to the church of Canterbury.[30] It is possible that at Chalus Richard did insist on unconditional surrender and that he subsequently pardoned the man who shot him. In the light of his conduct of the sieges of Darum (1192) and Nottingham (1194), it would seem that he often insisted on unconditional surrender and then, but only then, showed mercy.[31] However, this is not really the point. Until quite recently English scholarship traditionally saw Howden as the historian whose 'passionless, colourless narrative' provided 'the great store of facts' for the reigns of Henry II and Richard I.[32] It is partly for this reason that Howden's version of Richard's death is the one that has had by far the greatest impact on subsequent historical writing. It is certainly hard to imagine the history of those reigns without the evidence of his narrative, but it is equally certain that Howden was not just a purveyor of facts.

As a deeply religious man – and seemingly more so as he got older – Howden was also, like William the Breton, a purveyor of moral dramas. His treatment of Richard's death was of a piece with his earlier treatment of Richard's life and reign. It was he who first told the story of the flow of blood from Henry's nose when Richard approached his father's corpse. It was he who told how in front of the assembled archbishops and bishops in the chapel of Reginald de Moyac at Messina, Richard, inspired by God's grace, flung himself naked to the ground and, holding three scourges in his hands, confessed the filthiness of his life. 'The father of mercies who wisheth not for the death of a sinner, but rather that he may turn from his wickedness and live, called him to repentance. O happy the man who after repentance does not fall back into

story was told at Winchester. Although Richard forgave him, Mercadier sent him secretly to Joan, and she had him condemned to a horrible death, Annals of Winchester, *Ann. Mon*, ii, 71

[30] Gervase, i, 592–3. Although Gervase locates these events at Nontron, a castle – he says – belonging to the count of Angoulême, he mentions neither treasure nor rebellion.

[31] Kessler, 318–20. In his imaginary account of Richard's siege of Jerusalem, Howden wrote that the king refused to accept a conditional offer of the city's surrender, *Gesta*, ii, 231.

[32] Stubbs in *Chron.*, i, xiii, lxix.

sin.'[33] Again it was Roger of Howden who told how in 1195 Richard remitted his anger and ill-will against Bishop Hugh of Coventry, and against Geoffrey of York, how he remitted his anger and ill-will against John and forgave him, and then how 'the Lord visited him with a rod of iron and scourged him with a severe illness' so that he remembered the hermit's warning (see above, 263–4) and amended his life. 'Truly great and inexpressible are the works of the Lord, and his mercies are over all his works. For this king turning from his wickedness unto the Lord, was received by Him as a son. For God, in whose hands are the hearts of kings, and who turneth them whichever way He thinketh fit, instilled it into the heart of the king that he changed his life and company for the better. O happy the son whom in this pilgrimage the father's severity chastens for his correction not for his destruction.'[34] It is in the light of this repeated concern for the wickedness of Richard's life and for his soul that we must read Howden's story of the king's death. In this case the wickedness would be the less if the garrison of Chalus-Chabrol were portrayed as rebels. As the historian knew very well, the proper penalty for those who took up arms against the king was that they should be at the king's mercy; it would have been right for him to insist on unconditional surrender. By setting the king's last good deed in the context of a merciless treasure hunt rather than in the context of suppression of rebellion, Howden ensured that the point he wanted to make emerged all the more sharply. At the end of his life, however wicked he has been, by true contrition a man can save himself.[35] Roger of Howden then rounded off his narrative of Richard's reign by quoting – if not writing – four or five verse epigrams. One four-line epigram is a catalogue of sins – avarice, unbounded lust, blind desire, brutal pride – which after reigning for ten years have been brought down by a crossbow. The three or four other epigrams, comprising eighteen lines of verse, lament the death of a hero, the lion slain by the ant. They reveal the awe in which Howden still held the king. 'His valour could no throng of mighty labours quell, his onward advance no obstacles restrain; no rage of sea, no abysses of the deep, no mountain heights', etc. etc. ...[36]

In the long obituary composed by Ralph of Coggeshall we can see the same line of thought. Not long after Richard's death, probably in 1201, Coggeshall decided to write up a history of the years after 1195. In what he had written in 1195 he had had little but praise for Richard, and for

[33] Gesta, ii, 146–7; Chron., iii, 74–5. Very likely Richard did sin again. The point here is only that Howden chose to include the incident in his history.
[34] Chron., iii, 286–9.
[35] The story was told, as Galbraith pointed out, 'to illustrate Richard's stern unforgiving character': V. H. Galbraith, 'Good and Bad Kings in History', History, xxx (1945), 126. But not only to illustrate that.
[36] Chron., iv, 84–5. No epigrams of any sort follow his account of Henry II's death.

his extraordinary exploits on crusade.[37] Hence he was puzzled by
Richard's captivity and acknowledged that he could not understand why
God had decided it should happen.[38] Richard's death had also, of course,
been decreed by God, and in a long and remarkable section of his history
Coggeshall set out to explain just what it was that had led Richard to
deserve the final punishment of being slain, not – as he thought befitted
a warrior-king – in a great battle, but in some obscure little place.[39] Now
he decided that Richard had been ill advised to return too soon from crusade, his pilgrimage not yet complete. He wrote of his insatiable cupidity,
his harsh financial demands including – and this he described as 'the
summit of all evil' – the change of royal seal and consequent insistence
that property owners had to pay up again to have their charters
renewed.[40]

> No age can remember, no history can record any preceding king, even
> those who reigned for a long time, who exacted and received so much
> money from his kingdom as that king exacted and amassed in the five
> years after he returned from captivity. He could to some extent be
> excused. The money had been used to win over the great men of the
> kingdom of France, to put his nephew on the imperial throne, to defend
> his own lands, and to subordinate other lands to his rule.[41]

But Richard continued to breathe threats against subjects and rebels, and
so God's justice struck him down lest he go on to commit further evil deeds
and earn a yet more severe punishment. So he was mortally wounded, was
able to confess his sins and receive extreme unction.[42] As a Cistercian it
was inevitable that Coggeshall would explain Richard's death as a punishment for sins. In essence his past sins amounted to oppressive exaction of

[37] Though as an English patriot he felt Richard had been too generous in supporting French and other foreigners on crusade, Coggeshall, 51–2.
[38] Ibid., 56–7.
[39] Ibid., 93–4. This has been well analysed by David Carpenter, 'Abbot Ralph',
1210–30. Gerald de Barri interpreted Richard's sudden death similarly – if with
uncharacteristic brevity – as divine punishment for his 'tyrannical pride' (see
above, 268).
[40] For Rigord of St Denis 'the summit of all evil' was King Philip's imprisonment
of Ingeborg, the wife whom he had repudiated, Rigord, 147. Coggeshall expected
God to strike Philip down for the suffering he had caused by launching an unjust
war by deceit and treachery; but at least God the Englishman had seen to it that
Philip's subjects suffered more than Richard's from the famine of the late 1190s,
Coggeshall, 74,76.
[41] Coggeshall, 93. It was also his view that since his release from captivity Richard
had taken more castles from Philip by siege and assault than he had lost to Philip
by deceit and treachery, ibid., 76–7.
[42] Ibid., 91–6.

money which he had spent in a just cause. But it was the certain knowledge that he would go on to future – less just – wars that made God, in his mercy, decide to cut him down now.

However, the Cistercian monk did not leave it there. He went on to write that Richard gave a fine example to all other rulers by quickly filling ecclesiastical vacancies rather than – as previous rulers had done – prolonging vacancies in order to fill his own coffers. He drew attention too to Richard's enthusiasm for church music and to his respectful behaviour during mass.[43] Finally he turned to Richard's devotion to St Edmund, to his generous benefactions to the Church, above all to the Cistercian order. This enabled him to conclude with the hope that Richard's pious deeds, together with his final confession and contrition, would be enough to ensure his salvation.[44] In this respect the Cistercian's approach was like that adopted in the closing lines of 'Fortz chausa es', the famous lament on Richard's death composed by the troubadour Gaucelm Faidit, 'Ah! Lord God! You who are merciful, true God, true man and true life, have mercy. Pardon him for he has great need of your compassion. Do not consider his sins, but remember how he was going to serve you.'[45] Overall it is clear that Coggeshall was favourably impressed by Richard, but saw no way of explaining his unexpected death other than by recalling his endless demands for money.[46]

Historians have often noted that Coggeshall used the same phrase, *satis laboriose*, to sum up both Richard's and John's rule. In the past this has been translated as 'indefatigably' or 'with reasonable energy' (in the latter case damning with faint praise). What has not been noted is that another contemporary made exactly the same comment on Richard. 'He reigned for 10 years *satis laboriose*.' This was the anonymous author of the annals of Jumièges who, from his other comments, was clearly a great admirer of Richard's. As Prestwich has pointed out, a more accurate translation of *satis laboriose* is 'with a good deal of difficulty'. It 'refers not to what these rulers did but to what their enemies did to them'.[47] Thanks to the efforts of Saladin, Leopold of Austria and Philip Augustus, few rulers can have

[43] Ibid, 97. These were digs at Henry II whose treatment of vacancies and habit of talking business at mass were both alike notorious.

[44] Ibid., 97–8. In 1232, according to Roger of Wendover, the bishop of Rochester announced that he had seen three visions of Richard leaving purgatory for heaven, *Chron. Maj.*, iii, 212, 216.

[45] *Les Poèmes de Gaucelm Faidit*, ed. J. Mouzat (Paris, 1965), no. 50, 'Fortz chausa es que tot lo major dan'. This was Gaucelm's most famous song; it circulated in both French and Occitan versions.

[46] As Carpenter points out, he was to take a very different view of John, for whom he held out no hope that he would escape the torments of hell, 'Abbot Ralph', 1229–30.

[47] J. O. Prestwich, 'Mistranslations and Misinterpretations in Medieval English History', *Peritia: Journal of the Medieval Academy of Ireland*, x (1996), 326–7.

faced greater difficulties than Richard. In the words of another trouba-dour, Giraut de Borneil, 'in many trials (*mains assais*) he proved himself more virtuous (*plus pros*) and more valiant (*plus valens*) than all other mortal men'.[48] In the end, in the words of an anonymous contributor to the annals of Vendôme, 'he was defeated only by the Supreme Judge'.[49]

[48] R. V. Sharman, *The* Cansos *and* Sirventes *of the Troubadour Giraut de Borneil: A Critical Edition* (Cambridge, 1989), 475, 478.
[49] 'solo a summo judice superatus', *Annales angevines*, 74.

Chapter 19

IN RICHARD'S SHADOW

According to Howden, Richard named John as his successor and ordered that he should be given possession of all his castles and three-quarters of his treasure; the remaining quarter was to be divided between his servants and the poor.[1] Whatever the dying king may have wanted, there can be no doubt that his mother and his household decided in favour of his younger brother. When John arrived at Chinon on 14 April, three days after his brother's funeral, they went through the formal ritual of an election.[2] Robert of Thornham, the seneschal of Anjou, delivered the castle of Chinon and its treasury to him.[3] Inevitably John faced immediate problems. As soon as he heard the good news of Richard's death, Philip invaded Normandy and occupied the Evrecin.[4] The barons of Anjou, Maine and Touraine declared for Arthur.[5] But John acted with impressive speed and determination to get his authority recognized in Normandy and England. On 25 April he was invested as duke at Rouen.[6] On 27 May he was crowned king at Westminster. A month later he was back in Rouen with a large army and arranged a truce with Philip. He used the time very effectively to secure the alliances he had inherited from Richard. According to the annals of Jumièges, 'on a single day 15 counts came to his court, among them were the count of Bar, the count of Flanders and the count of Boulogne, and they all swore an oath against the French king.'[7] This was in

---

[1] *Chron.*, iv, 83. His jewels were to go to Otto.

[2] *Magna Vita*, ii, 137.

[3] *Chron.*, iv, 86; Coggeshall, 99.

[4] 'Statim, eo mortuo, Philippus magnanimus post Pascha capit Ebroicum et munit, et municipia circum adjacentia', WB, 204. Howden said the same: 'statim', *Chron.*, iv, 85.

[5] By 20 April John had lost control of Le Mans, *Magna Vita*, 147. Philip took over the towns, castles and fortifications of Anjou, Maine and Touraine while Arthur himself was taken to Paris. All that John's forces, under his mother and Mercadier, could do was ravage Anjou, *Chron.*, iv, 87–8.

[6] *Chron.*, iv, 87–8.

[7] *Annales de . . . Jumièges*, 77. Howden also noted that the French counts and barons who had supported Richard did homage to John and swore to aid him against Philip, *Chron.*, iv, 93,95. Cf. *Rotuli Chart arum 1199–1216*, ed. T. D. Hardy (London, 1837), 30–1 for John's treaties with Renaud of Boulogne and Baldwin of Flanders; the former is dated 18 August.

August.[8] In the same month an embassy arrived with a promise of support from Otto IV; and Otto, it was known, was Innocent's preferred candidate for the imperial throne.[9] With Richard's system of alliances still intact, John was in a strong position. As Sir James Ramsay put it, 'John had an extraordinary opportunity for a coalition, with, for once in a way, both pope and emperor in accord and on his side'.[10] He advanced into Maine, driving Philip back before him, and by 22 September he had recovered Le Mans. There Arthur and his mother, Constance of Brittany, were brought to him by William des Roches, the commander of Arthur's forces, and there they submitted to him. Why did William des Roches do this? According to Howden, he had been exasperated by Philip's high-handed behaviour. This may well be true but presumably he had also, astute politician that he was, decided that the tide was flowing in a way that made it sensible to break with King Philip.[11] Whatever William's motives, John's rival for the succession had been brought to submit to him. This was a great triumph.[12]

Yet by the end of the year John's position had crumbled. Soon after Christmas he met Philip and conceded the terms which were to be enshrined in the treaty of Le Goulet, formally sealed in May 1200. This treaty was, in Jacques Boussard's words, 'a great success for Philip Augustus'. In some respects it was based on the settlement provisionally worked out in January 1199 (see above, 322). But there were also highly significant modifications, all to John's disadvantage: he allowed Philip to keep all his recent gains in Normandy, he made important territorial concessions in Berry, agreed to pay Philip 20,000 marks and promised to abandon his alliance with Otto IV.[13] What had gone wrong? The clue lies

---

[8] By this time Poitou also had been secured. Philip had accepted Eleanor's homage for Poitou and she then issued a charter (probably on 31 July) declaring John as her heir – presumably all this was to counter Arthur's claim to be her heir, Rigord, 146. For 31 July as the date of Eleanor's charter, Richard, *Histoire des comtes*, ii, 352–4. For the legal implications of Eleanor's charter and John's own counterpart to it see J. C. Holt, 'Aliénor d'Aquitaine', 95–100.

[9] *Chron.*, iv, 95.

[10] J. H. Ramsay, *The Angevin Empire* (London, 1903), 383.

[11] For a summary of William's background and career, N. Vincent, *Peter des Roches* (Cambridge, 1996), 23–6.

[12] *Chron.*, iv, 94–6. The moment of triumph can be dated from John's chancery records to 18–22 September 1199 (*Rotuli Chartarum*, 30) and not, as Howden mistakenly wrote, to October. According to Howden, Philip captured Conches in September. If he did, he presumably lost control of it almost at once since he had to capture it again in 1203.

[13] *Chron.*, iv, 106–7; J. Boussard, 'Philippe Auguste et les Plantagenêts' in *La France de Philippe Auguste: Le temps de mutations*, ed. R. H. Bautier (Paris, 1982), 279; Bradbury, *Philip Augustus*, 134. I now think I was wrong to see the treaty as 'something of a triumph for John's diplomacy', *Coeur de Lion*, 67, largely because I compared the situation in 1200 with John's later predicament instead of with the strength of his position in the summer of 1199.

in the ending of the alliance with Otto. Whereas in January 1199 it had been envisaged that Philip would abandon his alliance with Philip of Swabia and instead support Otto, now the position was reversed. The system of alliances created by Richard had fallen apart.

According to Rigord, 'following the death of Richard king of England of glorious memory, many barons of France, that is Baldwin of Flanders, Louis of Blois, Stephen of Perche, the marquis of Montferrat and many other great men and fine warriors took the cross'.[14] In William the Breton's formulation the princes who took the cross were 'the count of Flanders and those others who had deserted Philip'.[15] Rigord, as we have seen, associated their decision with the death of Richard. That is how he remembered it, but in fact none of them did take the cross in the immediate aftermath of Richard's death. Pope Innocent had proclaimed a new crusade in August 1198, but was long to be bitterly disappointed by the lack of response. Not until November 1199 did the enlistment of a real crusading army of knights finally begin. This was at the famous tournament held by Count Thibaut of Champagne at Ecry-sur-Aisne, when he and his cousin, Count Louis of Blois, and many of their followers, put down their weapons and committed themselves to the crusading cause.[16] In subsequent weeks and months more of the nobles of northern France followed their example, among them the counts of Perche and Flanders. Richard's friends in France who as late as August 1199 were to be found paying court to John at Rouen, were now abandoning him.

What had happened to trigger this desertion, this first 'betrayal' of King John beginning in November 1199? Absolute certainty is impossible, but a plausible explanation is provided by an incident full of intense personal drama. According to Roger of Howden, on the very day that William des Roches brought Arthur to John at Le Mans, Arthur was warned that the king of England would put him in prison. On the same day John compelled Aimeri, viscount of Thouars to hand over Chinon. So that night Arthur, his mother Constance, the viscount of Thouars and many others slipped away and took refuge in Angers.[17] The story was told by Kate Norgate in 1902, but since then historians have not thought it worth telling.[18] Despite its omission by all of John's more recent biographers, the story is critically important. It reveals a king who, at the beginning of his reign, was not trusted and who, in consequence, suffered a severe setback. John's record

---

[14] Rigord, 153.

[15] WB, 205.

[16] D. E. Queller, *The Fourth Crusade* (Leicester, 1978), 1–3 and n. 46.

[17] *Chron.*, iv, 96–7. And Constance married Gui de Thouars.

[18] Norgate, *John Lackland* (London, 1902), 70–1. She noted that John 'acted with less than his usual caution'; but otherwise made little of it. It was mentioned in 1913 by Powicke, 138–9, but discussed in a curiously opaque fashion and with complete disregard for chronology.

of treachery – treachery to his father in 1189, treachery to his brother in 1193–4, treachery to the king of France in 1194 – was a bad one, and it was all too easy to fear that he would behave treacherously again. Precisely this episode was recalled, much later, by the author of the *Histoire de Guillaume le Maréchal*, who believed that John refused the requests made by William des Roches in 1202 because he remembered how Arthur had behaved in 1199.[19] Of course this was written with the loss of Normandy in mind, when incidents to which people at the time paid little heed might have seemed, in retrospect, to have had a previously unsuspected significance. But this cannot be the case with the episode of Arthur's flight from John in the autumn of 1199. Not only did Howden tell the story – and he died in 1201 – but the other experienced English historian of the time, the dean of St Paul's, also clearly thought that John got something wrong in his dealings with Arthur in 1199 – and he was dead by 1202. Between John's return to Normandy in June 1199 and the end of the year Diceto mentions only two matters: one was John's divorce and the second was this episode of Arthur's flight. In the former instance John acted, he wrote, 'on the advice of evil men' (*consilio pravorum*); in the latter, after Arthur had submitted to him, John acted 'less than prudently' (*minus caute*) and Arthur returned to the king of France.[20] Whatever John had done or not done, said or not said, the sudden flight of Arthur, Constance and their friends from Le Mans in late September 1199 must surely have reminded many of John's past and reactivated old fears. At any rate later that autumn his French allies discovered a new enthusiasm for the crusade and slipped away.[21] John was now virtually isolated and had to make peace on terms which compelled him to abandon his one remaining ally: his nephew Otto IV.

What happened in the autumn of 1199 is also significant in the context of the debate surrounding John's loss of Normandy and Anjou in 1203–4. It has often been argued that the fault was not really John's, that Philip Augustus was the richer ruler, and that in the end it came down to a question of resources. The orthodoxy of 1999 is that by 1199 the Angevin empire was incapable of paying for its own defence, and not even Richard's warlike spirit could have sustained it for much longer. It is difficult, however, to see how the hypothesis of failing resources can be made to explain how it was that John was in so strong a position in mid-September 1199 that William des Roches chose to bring Arthur to him, and so much weaker just three months later.[22] In any case the debate over financial resources,

---

[19] *HGM*, 12,472–92.

[20] Diceto, ii, 166–7. I have discussed Diceto's and Howden's views of John in more detail in 'Historians without Hindsight'.

[21] Precisely when Baldwin of Flanders made up his mind to seek a peace with Philip – the treaty of Péronne was sealed in January 1200 – is not known.

[22] It is similarly hard to see how the question of resources relates to the sudden deterioration in John's position between August and September 1202.

as hitherto conducted, has left a crucial factor out of account – the resources of the allies. Because no Capetian financial accounts earlier than 1202–3 survive, the argument has principally been conducted in terms of the relative wealth of Philip and John in 1202–3. On this basis it has been claimed that Philip enjoyed a financial superiority which meant that the resources he could deploy in the war zone were already far greater than anything John could bring to bear – and this conclusion has then been confidently applied to the latter years of Richard's reign.[23] Calculation based on existing financial accounts (or in the case of Anjou and Aquitaine, non-existing) of the relative wealth of Philip and John is an extraordinarily hazardous enterprise, involving, as Holt has put it, 'a structure of guesswork of Byzantine complexity'.[24] The most recent comparative analysis of Philip's and John's finances argues that if higher wages paid to Capetian soldiers are taken into account so that 'revenue totals are expressed in military terms' then the Angevins actually retained a slight advantage.[25] But even if it were true that in 1202–3 Philip was richer than John – which I doubt – the situation in Richard's reign and at the time of John's accession in the spring and summer of 1199 was entirely different. In 1193–4 Philip was probably much richer. While treasure from Richard's dominions was flowing into Germany to pay the ransom, Philip could focus his expenditure on war – and count on help from the resources of his allies, headed by the count of Flanders and the count of Toulouse. By 1197–8, however, Capetian resources, depleted by the open or secret attitude of so many French princes, were now pitted against not only the resources of Normandy and whatever could be sent from England, Anjou, Poitou, Gascony and (perhaps) Ireland, without any longer having to meet the burden of the ransom, but also against the resources of Richard's allies. In 1197 and after, this meant the resources available to Count Baldwin of Flanders and Hainault; in 1198 and after, also the resources of at least the counts of Boulogne, Guines and St Pol.[26] For Philip the loss of the rich towns of north-eastern France – Arras, Douai, St Omer and Aire – must have had a considerable impact upon his revenues.[27] In terms of resources the collapse of Richard's coalition was a disaster for John.

---

[23] For the most recent statement of this orthodoxy see R. V. Turner, 'Good or Bad Kingship? The Case of Richard Lionheart', *HSJ*, viii (1996, pub. 1999), 78.

[24] Holt, 'The Loss of Normandy and Royal Finance', in *War and Government in the Middle Ages*, ed. J. Gillingham and J. C. Holt (London, 1984), 99.

[25] N. Barratt, 'The Revenues of John and Philip Augustus Revisited', in *King John: New Interpretations*, ed. S. Church (Woodbridge, 1999).

[26] 'At least' because this list takes no account of potential resources from Brittany and elsewhere.

[27] Perhaps it was these losses as well as Philip's losses in Berry which led Coggeshall to the view that by the time of his death Richard had taken more castles from Philip than he had lost while in prison, Coggeshall, 76–7.

The collapse is much more plausibly attributed to the question marks against John's personality than to any structural reasons – except perhaps one. That one is the fact that traditionally the French princes owed a higher allegiance to the king of France than to any other lord, and they may have felt a little uncomfortable when at war with him – though it was a discomfort which many of them, in recent centuries, had seemed to bear with equanimity.[28] From 1196 onwards Richard was able to persuade more and more of them to support him against their king. John W. Baldwin, the historian of Philip Augustus, has explained why. 'Richard benefited both from his deserved reputation for open-handed generosity and from Philip's unsavoury reputation as a violator of the property of crusaders and a tyrannical husband to spin a web of alliances around the French king'.[29] With John's accession there came to the throne a king whose reputation was even more unsavoury than Philip's. Once reminded of this reputation by the stories of Arthur's 'narrow escape' which presumably came to their ears just as quickly and at least as theatrically as to Howden's and Diceto's, the princes of northern France preferred to revert to their traditional allegiance and seek safety in crusade.

What was the basis of Richard's reputation for generosity? That Richard won powerful allies by giving bigger gifts than Philip is asserted both by Roger of Howden on the Angevin side and by William the Breton on the Capetian.[30] Was it because he was prepared to invest a higher proportion of his income in diplomacy than Philip was? In this case the events of 1197–8 showed that Philip miscalculated badly. Or was it partly for no better reason than that Richard disposed of greater resources than Philip and was able to outbid him – as he had so evidently outbid him when on crusade? Certainty here is impossible, but it is hard to get away from the impression that contemporaries and near-contemporaries thought Richard the wealthier king. That there is any doubt at all is very largely a consequence of one passage in one work, Adam of Eynsham's *Life of St Hugh*. According to Adam's account of the meeting in December 1197 at which Hubert Walter put Richard's request for the service of 300 knights for a year, 'the archbishop explained the king's needs. With smaller resources and forces he was struggling against a very powerful king who was straining every nerve to disinherit and ruin him.'[31] Two points should be

---

[28] However, see D. Bates, 'The Rise and Fall of Normandy, *c.* 911–1204', in *England and Normandy in the Middle Ages*, ed. D. Bates and A. Curry (London, 1994), 34–5.

[29] Baldwin, *Government of Philip Augustus*, 91. Our best hope of understanding the diplomatic style of Richard the 'spider–king' probably lies with the Muslim historians quoted above, 19–23.

[30] *Chron.*, iv, 19–20; *Philippidos*, iv, 588–97.

[31] *Magna Vita*, 98. That Norman resources alone were smaller than those available to Philip is not in dispute – and may be what Adam had in mind.

borne in mind here. The first is that Adam was imaginatively reconstruct-ing a speech making a case for aid, hence a speech which emphasized the size of the problem facing Richard; Adam was not actually saying that this was his own view of the relative wealth of the two kings. The second is that he was writing in about 1213, and if the words put into the archbishop's mouth did reflect Adam's own view, his perception of Philip's power may have been shaped by the additional resources which the king of France enjoyed after his conquest of Normandy in 1203–4.[32] Despite these quibbles, if Adam's story were the only evidence for contemporary or near-contemporary perception it would have to be taken very seriously indeed. But it is not. Not only is there the impression created by Howden's and William the Breton's account of Richard's gifts. There is also the explicit opinion that John's defeats in 1203–4 were not caused by money problems – with the implication this carries for Richard's position in 1197–8. A monk from Clairmarais near St Omer believed that when John left Normandy 'he was struck down by cowardice rather than lack of money'. Much more explicit is the bald assertion by the Anonymous of Béthune that 'Richard was richer in land and money than the king of France'.[33] Moreover Lambert of Ardres, writing before the loss of Normandy, believed that Richard had won over Baldwin of Flanders with barrels full of gold and silver, so that the count 'had an infinite amount of sterling' at his disposal.[34] Much as it might enhance Richard's heroic image to have him fighting against a richer enemy, the balance of evidence, from a variety of political allegiances and much of it written in that part of the world – St Omer, Béthune, Ardres – where the two kings competed most fiercely for allies, appears to point in the other direction.

Is it possible that Richard bought his allies at so high a price that his own realms, in particular Normandy and England, were impoverished as a result? It is commonly said that the Norman Exchequer Rolls for 1195 and 1198 reveal 'a duchy squeezed to the limit'.[35] Unquestionably the Rolls show that Richard was getting more out of Normandy in 1198 than he had in 1195, and that in 1195 he was getting far more than his father had in 1180. This Vincent Moss has dubbed the 'Norman fiscal revolution'.[36] But it is far from obvious that this resulted in Normandy's impoverishment. The destructive aspect of war was limited both in time and place. Campaigning was constantly interrupted by truce and peace. The war was

---

[32] Of course this may cut both ways since an English author writing in 1213 would have known about the amount of money which John extracted from England after 1208. See below, 343.

[33] *RHF*, xxiv, part 2, 758; MGH SS, ix, 330.

[34] Lambert of Ardres, *Chronique de Guines et d'Ardre*, 371.

[35] Most recently Turner, 'Good or bad kingship', 73.

[36] V. Moss, 'The Norman Fiscal Revolution 1193–98'. Cf. Moss, 'Normandy and England in 1180: the Pipe Roll evidence'.

fought in bursts: at a rough estimate ten weeks in 1194; ten weeks in 1195; perhaps ten weeks, including the Brittany campaign, in 1196; six months in 1197; eight weeks in 1198 – an average of roughly three months a year. It was very largely fought in the frontier zones. By far the larger part of Normandy was untouched by the direct ravages of war. On the other hand, spending on preparations for war went on throughout the periods of truce and peace, which meant that the duke-king was constantly purchasing all sorts of goods and services. It involved major building projects such as the creation of a new town as well as a fortress at Les Andelys, the building of the walls of Eu, of a new town at Pont de l'Arche. If anything, this kind of expenditure stimulated the Norman economy. As long ago as 1913 Powicke took the view that by 1203–4 'Normandy as a whole was probably not impoverished and did not feel the strain which was put upon England by the constant exportation of men and treasure'. This was because 'the money drawn from England and from the king's creditors' was spent in Normandy.[37] When Abbot Samson came to Normandy in 1198 he not only made available £124 to pay for knights who were sent to garrison Eu, and who presumably spent their wages there, he also took back with him a cross of gold and a precious gospel book valued at 80 marks. If these were bought in Normandy, as is implied in Jocelin of Brakelond's account, this meant more English money and more work for Norman craftsmen and artists; it also means, of course, that in the abbot's business judgement – a famously sound business judgement – the abbey of St Edmund's was not teetering on the edge of 'bankruptcy' in 1198 as it had been in 1180.[38]

Did other great churches share the prosperity of Bury St Edmunds – or was Samson's abbey an exception under an exceptional abbot? Was, as Powicke implied, the English economy as a whole under strain – whatever that might mean – and if so, to what extent were economic problems the consequence of the war on the Norman frontier?[39] Since England was generally at peace, money raised in England was sent to the continent; it would be curious if it were not. But was war taxation responsible for 'impoverishing England'? Roger of Howden famously wrote of England in 1198 that 'by these and other vexations, whether justly or unjustly, the whole of England from sea to sea was reduced to poverty'.[40] The 1198 Pipe Roll shows that revenue audited by the exchequer in that year came to

[37] Powicke, 239. Future studies by Dr Vincent Moss should considerably amplify the point.

[38] *The Chronicle of Jocelin of Brakelond*, ed. H. E. Butler (London, 1949), 87. It is just possible that he bought these precious objects in England on his way back, in that case probably in London, but there is no doubt at all that Jocelin associates these expensive purchases with the abbot's trips abroad. 'As often as he returned from across the sea, he brought back some ornament with him.'

[39] For the English economy *c.* 1200 see the essays by J. L. Bolton and P. Latimer in Church, *King John*.

[40] *Chron.*, iv, 66.

£25,405, to which might be added another £1,000 or so as the yield from the carucage (in total about average for the years from 1194). But this total was dwarfed by the size of the sums which John was able to raise a dozen years later. Revenues audited at the exchequer in 1210, 1211 and 1212 came to £51,913, £83,291 and £56,612 (all figures which exclude considerable amounts of income from other sources in those years).[41] The history of taxation in England under John does not suggest that he had succeeded to an impoverished kingdom. Poverty, obviously, is and was a very relative concept, and whether or not the revenues collected by the state impoverish society depends very largely on what those revenues are spent on.

None the less Howden's expression of opinion shows that he felt unhappy about Richard's fiscal demands in 1198. Since he sandwiches this comment between a text of the agenda of the justices in eyre and a text of the Assize of the Forest it would appear to be principally these two institutions which he had in mind when he used the words 'these and other vexations'. Careful analysis of the Pipe Roll totals has shown that Howden had cause for concern. In 1198 Richard had reverted to his father's practice of raising money from fines imposed by the itinerant justices. Fines levied for offences against forest law had long been very unpopular, especially with Howden, but not until this year did Richard send out a forest eyre. The combined profits of the judicial and forest eyres totalled £1,588 in 1197–8, significantly higher than in any preceding year in Richard's reign – though not as high as the £2,800 yielded from these two sources in 1187–8, the last exchequer year of Henry II's reign.[42] In 1198 there were other fiscal demands. Howden went on to mention the carucage imposed (against opposition from the monastic orders) in that year and the king's insistence that charters must be re-sealed under the new seal. By the end of 1198 – the earliest date for Howden's composition of this complaint – there was undoubtedly discontent in England at the weight of the king's financial demands. It is particularly strongly reflected in Coggeshall's obituary notice on Richard, and his assertion that no previous king of England had ever raised so much money (see above, 332).

William of Newburgh, writing in 1197 or 1198, had his own opinion on the level of the demand and the level of discontent. According to him, although Richard taxed more heavily than his father, people complained less. 'This foolish people make less complaint now that they are chastised with scorpions than when they were chastised with whips.' Looking back

---

[41] N. Barratt, 'The English Revenues'; idem, 'The Revenues of King John', *EHR*, cxi. Similarly the fact that ambitious bidders offered on average 1,158 marks for wardships under Richard did not prevent them offering an average of 3,068 marks under John, S. L. Waugh, *The Lordship of England: Royal Wardships and Marriages in English Society and Politics 1217–1327* (Princeton, 1988), 157–8.

[42] N. Barratt, 'The English Revenues'.

from the late 1190s it seemed to William that Henry II had been a great and, in most respects, an admirable ruler, but several times he observed that in his own day Henry had been deeply unpopular. People had had eyes only for his bad qualities and shortcomings.[43] The evidence for English opinion in the late 1190s suggests that complaints against the level of taxation were coupled with an acceptance that the money was properly spent on a just war by a ruler who, unlike his father, was admired by his own subjects. Howden, Coggeshall and Newburgh were all fiercely hostile to Philip Augustus and believed that it would be wrong to allow him to retain the territorial gains he had so treacherously made. Hence, as David Carpenter has observed, 'all the [English] chroniclers regarded Richard as a hero' – including those who criticized him for financial oppression.[44]

Norman opinion is harder to judge. Had the war undermined the loyalty of Richard's Norman subjects? Despite the almost total lack of evidence for Norman opinion, many historians have answered this question with a confident yes. According to Warren, 'John's mustering of forces in 1199 was impressive . . . But behind them lay an economy at full stretch and a Normandy suddenly weary of war.'[45] It has been argued that 'it appeared to Norman clerics that Richard had grown more oppressive, especially in his financial demands' and that 'by the end of the twelfth century many Normans, clerical and lay, longed for peace even at the price of annexation by the French king'.[46] But, except in one respect, the evidence hitherto cited in support of this proposition is fragmentary and fragile. That one respect is the case of Walter of Coutances. He was extremely unhappy – and with very good reason. His own diocese of Rouen was virtually co-extensive with what was by far the most devastated war zone – the Vexin (both Norman and French) and north-east Normandy. For the estates of the church of Rouen the war of the kings was a disaster.

But the attitude of the rest of the Norman clergy may well have been quite different. When the archbishop of Rouen went to Rome to protest against Richard's seizure of Andeli, the king's embassy to the pope included two of the archbishop's own suffragans: the bishop of Evreux and the bishop of Lisieux. The Rouen annalist makes it plain that both the bishops of Lisieux and Evreux opposed Archbishop Walter 'because they wanted to please the king'.[47] In Normandy four episcopal elections

---

[43] Newburgh, Bk 3, ch. 26.

[44] Carpenter, 'Abbot Ralph', 1222.

[45] W. L. Warren, *King John* (London, 1961), 72. At present this remains the orthodoxy. See, for example, the review by T. K. Keefe in *Speculum*, lxxi (1996), 716–17; Turner, 'Good or Bad Kingship?', 72–8.

[46] Turner, 'Richard Lionheart and the Episcopate in His French Domains', *French Historical Studies*, xxi (1998), 525, 539; cf. idem, 'Good or Bad Kingship?', 74.

[47] *RHF*, xviii, 358. This means that the bishop of Lisieux's offer of 2,000 marks as recorded in the Norman Exchequer Roll cannot possibly be taken as evidence of

occurred during the reign, and in each case men loyal to Richard were chosen.[48] The episcopate and cathedral chapters remained what they had long been, 'ducal-dominated' – without, however, Richard giving Philip Augustus the kind of propaganda gold mine that John did with his heavy-handed harassment of Sées cathedral in 1202.[49] The one Norman contemporary who wrote slightly more than very scrappy notes was the anonymous annalist of Jumièges. He described Richard at the time of his coronation as a 'man of great prowess'; enthused over his performance on crusade; praised the sturdy defence which the citizens of Rouen put up against King Philip; described Richard's acquisition of the empire for his nephew as 'the praiseworthy action of a praiseworthy man'; and finally noted the grief felt at the king's death.[50] The paucity of Norman historical writing in the 1190s means that expressions of opinion are hard to come by – but what little there is suggests that Richard was popular rather than unpopular with most Norman clerics.

More than anyone else in Normandy and England the archbishop of Rouen had good cause to yearn for peace. But he was far from being the only one. Two passages from William of Newburgh and Roger of Howden have often been cited as evidence of war-weariness and of the damage done by war. Newburgh wrote of 'recently flourishing provinces devastated by fire and sword'. The precise context of the generalization is worth noting. In the next sentence he described how Philip laid siege to Aumâle in 1196, eventually capturing it 'with great loss to his army', while Richard concentrated on devastating the lands of the king of France.[51] Roger of Howden wrote eloquently and in general terms on the ravaging, plundering and burning caused by war in 1198 (and, naturally, this is the passage quoted). When he descended to the specifics of 1198, he noted that the war did not re-start until September because it had been agreed that the truce should last until both sides had gathered in the grain harvest. The campaigning

hostility to the duke, *MRSN*, i, 253. In general, such payments and offers of payment may mean the reverse of hostility.

[48] Turner, 'Richard Lionheart and the Episcopate', 524–5.

[49] This is based on the systematic analysis by D. Spear, 'Power, Patronage and Personality in the Norman Cathedral Chapters, 911–1204', *ANS*, xx (1997), 205–21. Within the Norman Church, as Spear has shown, only the see of Coutances had a tradition of independence from the duke so it is probably significant that the one payment made by an ecclesiastic and recorded in the Norman Exchequer Rolls which almost certainly was resented was the fine of 266 *livres* 13s 4d paid by William, bishop of Coutances because his men withdrew from the army without permission, *MRSN*, ii, 477. William had been bishop of Coutances since *c.* 1180.

[50] *Annales de Jumièges*, 73–7. 'O laudabilis viri laudabile factum qui totum mundi imperium nepoti suo comparavit.' There is little that is remarkable about the expression of grief at Richard's death. Henry II's, however, was recorded without comment of any kind, even the most perfunctory.

[51] Newburgh, Bk 5, ch. 25.

that followed was restricted to the Evrecin, where Philip burned Evreux, and to the Vexin, both Norman and French, except that Mercadier raided the fair at Abbeville, plundering the French merchants there. When he returned, in Howden's words, 'he filled Normandy with spoil taken from the French'.[52] What the specific content of both these passages reveals is that the destruction of war affected Philip's subjects at least as much as it affected Richard's.

If there was war-weariness on the Angevin side, then also on the Capetian. If there was discontent on the Angevin side at the level of 'war taxation', then also on the Capetian. Comments made by Newburgh or Howden or Coggeshall can be used as evidence that the Angevin empire 'was experiencing stresses that would have caused increasing problems for any English king, even Richard if he had lived'. They cannot be used as evidence that 'the fall was bound to come'.[53] This would depend just as much upon the increasing level of stresses experienced within Philip's realm. Indeed all three of these historians, as well as Ambroise, felt that Richard was winning in 1197–8. Coggeshall took the view that by the time of his death Richard had taken more castles from Philip than he had lost while in prison; William of Newburgh observed that in 1197 'the king of France began now to defend his borders with decreasing energy, while the king of England gradually increased in power and prosperity'.[54]

According to William of Newburgh, John archbishop of Lyon told some English friends that the financial demands which Philip made on the churches of his kingdom were far more oppressive than those of Richard. 'I tell you that your king is a hermit compared with the king of France.'[55] This may have been of some slight comfort to the archbishop's listeners, but on its own it could hardly be regarded as a solid indicator of the performance of the two kings. Much more revealing is the fact that although Rigord of St Denis and William the Breton were both much more closely aligned with the interests of Philip than any English historian was with Richard's interests, they acknowledge that Philip too was regarded as an oppressive ruler. Rigord, for example, wrote that after his return from crusade Philip gathered in treasure with the double purpose of freeing Jerusalem and defending the kingdom of France against the attacks of its enemies; 'however some rather less than sensible people, ignorant of the king's intentions, accused him of excessive ambition and avarice'. By 1198 Rigord may even have been tempted to join the ranks of the less than sen-

[52] *Chron.*, iii, 301; ibid., iv, 54, 59–60.
[53] Keefe, *Speculum* (1996), 716–17. Keefe regarded the view that the fall was inevitable as one confirmed by very recent research.
[54] *Chron.*, iv, 19, 54–61; Coggeshall, 76–7; Newburgh, Bk 5, ch. 31, and a similar point in ch. 32; Ambroise, 12, 333–40.
[55] Newburgh, Bk 5, ch. 3. John had previously been treasurer of York and bishop of Poitiers.

sible, since under that year he referred to Philip's 'grave persecution of God's churches'.[56] Even William the Breton, who hardly ever referred to his king without the epiphet *magnanimus*, admitted that by 1197–8 Philip had been oppressing some churches.[57] From the point of view of opinion in Capetian France at this time, Philip's fiscal record seemed a great deal worse – more stressful – than Richard's. This was because it was apparent to all Philip's subjects, but particularly to those who lived near the Norman and Flemish frontiers, that Philip was losing the war. Nothing makes this plainer than the anguished tone with which Rigord and William relate the events of 1197 and 1198, and the relief with which they greeted the death of Richard.

It does not, of course, follow that the Angevin empire would have become a permanent or near permanent feature of the political map of Europe if only Richard had lived longer – outlived Philip Augustus, for example. The empire was a family firm.[58] The interests of the family counted for more than any notion of keeping the empire intact under a single ruler; a partition was always on the cards.[59] Although after the massive losses of 1203–4 the remaining dominions of the English king tended to be treated as a single indivisible inheritance, this might not have happened if the kings of England had retained control of the lands of the dukes of Normandy and counts of Anjou. In these circumstances the kings of France, possessors of an indivisible crown, would always have used their position as overlords of the Angevin lands in France to press for partition of the empire, and doubtless there would often have been members of the Angevin dynasty to whom, for one reason or another, this idea appealed. It was the partibility of the empire, inherent in its structure from its beginning under Henry II, which was virtually certain to be its undoing. There is no reason to think Richard would have grieved over this prospect. After his return from crusade and captivity he fought for two inextricably linked goals: for honour and for the recovery of his inherited lands – but not, so far as we can tell, for their permanent survival under one ruler. In the treaty of Messina (1191) he had envisaged partition in the event of him having more than one legitimate son. As it happened, of course, the empire was weakened in 1199 and collapsed in 1203–4. This was because John's shortcomings as a ruler enabled King Philip to take advantage of the empire's old structural 'weakness', its partibility. It was not because the empire had recently been 'exhausted' by the costs and stresses of war –

---

[56] Rigord, 129, 141.

[57] WB, 202.

[58] For contemporary use of the term 'empire' applied to Henry II's dominions, see the phrase 'les baruns de tun empire' in *The Song of Dermot and the Earl*, ed. G. H. Orpen (Oxford, 1892), 22.

[59] On this see Holt, 'The End of the Anglo-Norman Realm', Gillingham, *The Angevin Empire*, ch. 3; Turner, 'The Problem of Survival'.

costs and stresses which had hit Philip's realm more than they had hit Richard's.

In 1198–9 Richard was winning the war against Philip. This was in part because, as he demonstrated in Cyprus and in Palestine, he was a highly competent ruler, unusually effective across the whole range of a king's business, administrative, diplomatic and political as well as military. In Ibn al-Athir's judgement, 'his courage, cunning, energy and patience made him the most remarkable man of his time'.[60] When material resources and willing allies gave him a strong hand, he could play it well. But he was also winning because of the way he played a weak hand – as he had at Jaffa in 1192 or at Aumale in 1196. The qualities which he displayed on these occasions – prowess, valour and the sense of honour which impressed William the Breton – were the qualities which made him a legend. They endangered his life, but while he lived they contributed greatly to his successes. After his death they ensured that his reputation lived on.

[60] Ibn al-Athir, 43. And see above, 15–23, for a fuller assessment of the perception of Richard by his Muslim opponents.

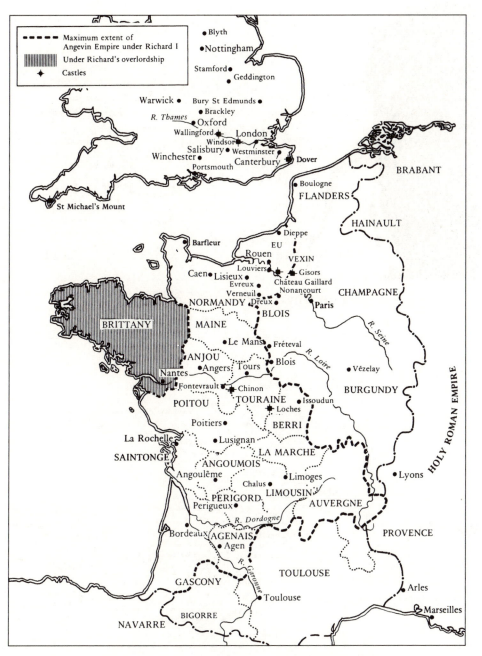

The Angevin Empire under Richard I

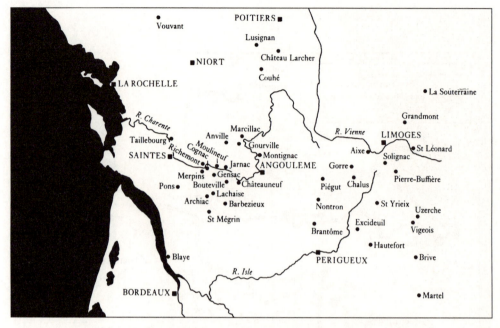

The Angoumois and Limousin

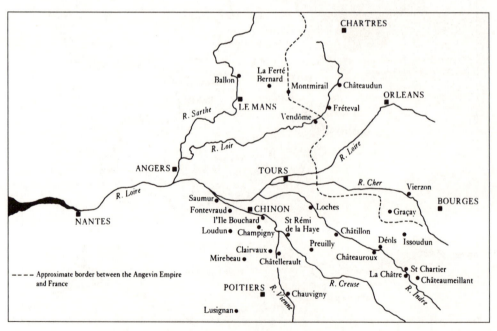

The Lower Loire Valley

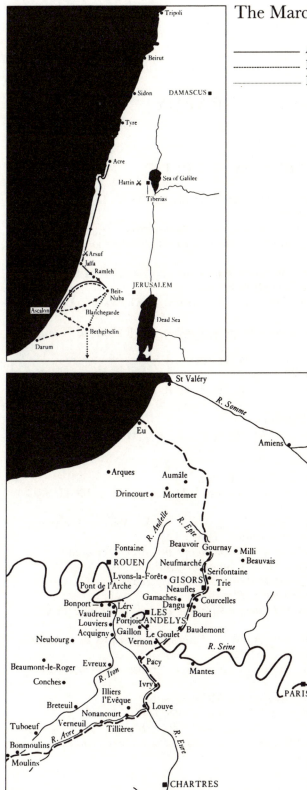

The Marches on Jerusalem

——————— August 1191–January 1192
------------------- May–June 1192
.... Raid on caravan

Tripoli

Beirut

Sidon   DAMASCUS ■

Tyre

Acre

Hattin ✕   ■ Sea of Galilee
Tiberias

✕ Arsuf
Jaffa
Ramleh

JERUSALEM

Beit-Nuba
Ascalon
Blanchegarde
Dead Sea

Bethgibelin

Darum

Eastern Normandy

Captured by Philip by March 1194:
Dieppe, Arques, Eu, Aumâle,
Mortemer, Drincourt, Gournay,
Neufmarché, Pont de l'Arche,
Vaudreuil, Louviers, Léry,
Acquigny, Neubourg, Evreux,
Beaumont-le-Roger, Conches,
Breteuil, Tillières, Nonancourt,
Illiers l'Evêque, Louye, Ivry, Pacy,
Vernon, Gaillon, and the Vexin.

Held by Philip Christmas 1195:
Neufmarché, Neaufles, Gisors,
Dangu, Gaillon, Pacy, Ivry,
Nonancourt, Vernon, Gamaches.

——————— Rivers
------------------- Border between
Normandy and the Kingdom of
France

St Valéry

R. Somme

Eu   Amiens ●

● Arques   Aumâle ●

Drincourt ●   ● Mortemer

R. Andelle   R. Epte

Fontaine   Beauvoir Gournay ● Milli
              Dangu   ● Beauvais
■ ROUEN   Neufmarché
Lyons-la-Forêt GISORS Serifontaine
Pont de l'Arche Neaufles Trie
Bonport ●   Gamaches ● Dangu Courcelles
Léry   LES   ● Bouri
Vaudreuil   ANDELYS
Louviers   Portjoie
Neubourg ●   Acquigny Gaillon Le Goulet Baudemont
                        Vernon
Beaumont-le-Roger Evreux Pacy
Conches ●   R. Iton   Mantes

                    Ivry   R. Seine
Illiers   ● PARIS
l'Evêque
Breteuil ●   Nonancourt Louye
Tuboeuf ● Verneuil
Bonmoulins R. Avre Tillières   R. Eure
Moulins ●

■ CHARTRES

BIBLIOGRAPHY

I PRIMARY SOURCES

ADAM OF EYNSHAM, *Magna Vita Sancti Hugonis*, ed. D. L. Douie and H. Farmer (2 vols, Edinburgh, 1962).

AMBROISE, *L'Estoire de la Guerre Sainte*, ed. G. Paris (Paris, 1897). Trans. by M. J. Hubert and J. La Monte as *The Crusade of Richard Lionheart* (New York, 1941).

ANDREAS OF MARCHIENNES, *Sigeberti Continuatio Aquicincta*, MGH SS 6.

——, *Historia regum Francorum*, MGH SS xxvi.

ANDREAS CAPELLANUS, *De Amore*, ed. and trans. P. G. Walsh (London, 1982).

Annales de l'Abbaye Royale de Saint-Pierre de Jumièges, ed. J. Laporte (Rouen, 1954).

Annales Marbacenses, ed. H. Bloch, MGH SRG (1907).

Annales Stederburgenses, MGH SS xvi.

Annals of Margam, in *Annales Monastici*, i, ed. H. R. Luard (RS, 1864).

Annals of Rouen, *RHF*, xviii.

Annals of Salzburg, MGH SS xiii.

Annals of Winchester, in *Annales Monastici*, ii, ed. H. R. Luard (RS, 1865).

Annals of Zwettl, MGH SS ix.

ANONYMOUS OF BÉTHUNE, *RHF*, xxiv, Part 2.

ARNOLD OF LÜBECK, *Chronica Slavorum*, ed. J. M. Lappenberg, MGH, SRG (1868, 1930).

BEHA ED-DIN, *What Befell Sultan Yusuf*, trans. C. W. Wilson (Palestine Pilgrims Text Society), xiii (London, 1897).

BERTRAN DE BORN, *The Poems of the Troubadour Bertran de Born*, ed. W. D. Paden, Jr, T. Sankovitch and P. H. Stäblein (Berkeley, 1986).

BLONDEL, *Die Lieder des Blondel de Nesle*, ed. L. Weise (Dresden, 1904).

Breve Chronicon Virzionis Coenobii, *RHF* xviii.

CAESARIUS OF HEISTERBACH, *Dialogus Miraculorum*, ed. J. Strange (2 vols, Cologne, 1851).

Cartulaire de l'abbaye de Noyers, ed. C. Chevalier, *Mémoires de la Société archéologique de Touraine*, xxii (1872).

CHRÉTIEN DE TROYES, *Arthurian Romances*, trans. W. W. Kibler (Harmondsworth, 1991).

Chronica Albrici Monachi Trium Fontium, MGH SS xxiii.

Chronica Monasterii de Melsa, i, ed. E. A. Bond (RS, 1866).

Chronica Regia Coloniensis, ed. G. Waitz, MGH SRG (1880).

Chronicon Turonense Magnum, ed. A. Salmon, *Recueil des Chroniques de Touraine*, (Tours, 1854).

Chronique d'Ernoul, ed. L. de Mas-Latrie (Paris, 1871).

Chroniques de Saint-Martial de Limoges, ed. H. Duplès-Agier (Paris, 1874).

Chroniques des Comtes d'Anjou, ed. L. Halphen and R. Poupardin (Paris, 1913).

Codice Diplomatico della repubblica di Genova, ed. C. Imperiale di Sant' Angelo (3 vols, Genoa, 1936–42).

Continuatio Admuntensis, MGH SS ix.

La Continuation de Guillaume de Tyr (1184–1197), ed. M. R. Morgan (Paris, 1982). English trans. in P. W. Edbury, *The Conquest of Jerusalem and the Third Crusade. Sources in Translation* (Aldershot, 1996).

Crusade and Death of Richard I, ed. R. C. Johnston (Anglo-Norman Texts, xvii, 1961).

Documents des archives de la Chambre des Comptes de Navarre 1196–1384, ed. J. A. Brutails (Paris, 1890).

Epistolae Cantuarienses, in *Chronicles and Memorials of the Reign of Richard I*, ii, ed. W. Stubbs (RS, 1865).

Foedera, conventiones, litterae, i, part 1, ed. T. Rymer, A. Clarke, F. Holbrooke and J. Caley (London, 1816).

GAUCELM FAIDIT, *Les Poèmes de Gaucelm Faidit*, ed. J. Mouzat (Paris, 1965).

GEOFFREY OF VIGEOIS, 'Chronica', in *Novae Bibliothecae Manuscriptorum Librorum* ed. P. Labbe (2 vols, Paris, 1657), ii, 279–329. For Book 1 of Geoffrey see P. Botineau, 'La Chronique de Geoffroi de Breuil, prieur de Vigeois', (unpub. diss., Paris, 1964); for Book 2 *RHF*, xviii, 211–23.

GEOFFREY OF VINSAUF, *Poetria Nova*, trans. M. F. Nims (Toronto, 1967).

GERVASE OF CANTERBURY, *Opera Historica*, ed. W. Stubbs (2 vols, RS, 1879–80).

GIRALDUS CAMBRENSIS., *Expugnatio Hibernica. The Conquest of Ireland*, ed. and trans. A. B. Scott and F. X. Martin (Dublin, 1978).

GIRALDUS CAMBRENSIS, *Opera*, ed. J. S. Brewer, J. F. Dimock and G. F. Warner (8 vols, RS, 1861–91).

GIRAUT DE BORNEIL, *The* Cansos *and* Sirventes *of the Troubadour: A Critical Edition*, ed. R. V. Sharman (Cambridge, 1989).

GISLEBERT OF MONS, *Chronicon Hanoniense*, ed. L. Vanderkindere.

GUILLAUME GUIART, *Branches des royaux lignages*, ed. J. A. Buchon (Paris, 1820).

Histoire de Guillaume le Maréchal, ed. P. Meyer (3 vols, Société de l'histoire de France, Paris, 1891–1907).

Histoire des ducs de Normandie et des rois d'Angleterre, ed. F. Michel (Paris, 1840).

Historia de expeditione Friderici, ed. A. Chroust, MGH SRG (1929).

IBN AL-ATHIR, *el-Kamil*, in *Recueil des historiens des croisades: historiens orientaux*, ii, part 1 (Paris, 1887).

IMAD AL-DIN, *Conquête de la Syrie et de la Palestine par Saladin*, trans. H. Massé (Paris, 1972).

INNOCENT III, *Selected Letters of Pope Innocent III concerning England*, ed. C. R. Cheney and W. H. Semple (London, 1953).

Itinerarium Peregrinorum, ed. H. E. Mayer (Stuttgart, 1962).

Itinerarium Peregrinorum et Gesta Regis Ricardi, in *Chronicles and Memorials of the Reign of Richard I*, i, ed. W. Stubbs (RS, 1864). English trans. by Helen Nicholson, *Chronicle of the Third Crusade* (Ashgate, 1997).

JAQUES DE VITRY, *History of Jerusalem.*

JEAN DE JOINVILLE, *Histoire de Saint Louis*, ed. N. de Wailly (Paris, 1868). English trans. M. R. B. Shaw, *Chronicles of the Crusades* (Harmondsworth, 1963).

JOCELIN OF BRAKELOND, *The Chronicle of Jocelin of Brakelond*, ed. H. E. Butler (London, 1949).

JOHN OF SALISBURY, *Letters of John of Salisbury*, ed. W. J. Millor , H. E. Butler and C. N. L. Brooke (2 vols, London, 1955–79).

Jordan Fantosme's Chronicle, ed. R. C. Johnston (Oxford, 1981).

LAMBERT OF ARDRES, *Chronique de Guines et d'Ardres*, ed. M. de Godefroy Menilglaise (Paris, 1855).

Magni Rotuli Scaccarii Normanniae, ed. T. Stapleton (2 vols, London 1840–4).

MAGNUS OF REICHERSBERG, *Chronicon Magni Presbiteri*, MGH SS xvii.

Der mittelenglische Versroman über Richard Löwenherz, ed. K. Brunner (Vienna, 1913).

Œuvres de Rigord et de Guillaume le Breton, ed. H. F. Delaborde, (2 vols, Société de l'histoire de France, Paris, 1882–5).

OTTO OF ST BLASIEN, *Chronica*, ed. A. Hofmeister, MGH SRG (1912).

PETER OF EBOLI, *Liber ad honorem Augusti*, ed. G. G. Siragusa (Rome, 1905–6).

Great Roll of the Pipe for the First Year of the Reign of Richard I, ed. J. Hunter (London, 1844); for the rest of the reign, ed. D. M. Stenton (Pipe Roll Society, London, 1925–33).

Radulfi Nigri Chronica, ed. R. Anstruther (London, 1851).

RALPH OF COGGESHALL, *Chronicon Anglicanum*, ed. J. Stevenson (RS, 1875).

RALPH OF DICETO, *Radulfi de Diceto Decani Londiniensis Opera Historica*, ed. W. Stubbs (2 vols, RS, 1876).

Récits d'un ménestrel de Reims, ed. N. de Wailly (Paris, 1876), 41–4; trans. E. N. Stone, *Three Old French Chronicles of the Crusades* (University of Washington Publications in the Social Sciences, x, Seattle, 1939).

Recueil d'Annales angevines, ed. L. Halphen (Paris, 1903).

Recueil des actes de Philippe Auguste, i and ii, ed. H.-F. Delaborde, C. Petit-Dutaillis and J. Monicat (Paris, 1916-43).

RICHARD OF DEVIZES, *Chronicon*, ed. and trans. J. T. Appleby (London, 1963).

RICHARD THE POITEVIN, *RHF*, xii.

ROBERT OF AUXERRE, *Roberti canonici S. Mariani Autissiodorensis Chronicon*, MGH SS xxvi.

ROBERT OF TORIGNY, *The Chronicle of Robert of Torigni*, in *Chronicles of the Reigns of Stephen, Henry II and Richard I*, ed. R. Howlett, iv (RS, 1889).

ROGER OF HOWDEN, *Chronica*, ed. W. Stubbs (4 vols, RS, 1868–71).

ROGER OF HOWDEN, *Gesta Henrici II et Ricardi I*, ed. W. Stubbs, (2 vols, RS, 1867).

ROGER OF WENDOVER, *Flores Historiarum*, iii, ed. H. G. Hewlett (RS, 1886-9).

Romance of Horn, trans. J. Weiss, in *The Birth of Romance* (London, 1992).

Rotuli Chartarum 1199-1216, ed. T. D. Hardy (London, 1837).

RYMER, T., *Foedera, Conventiones, Litterae*, i, part 1, ed. A. Clarke and J. Caley (London, 1816).

SALIMBENE DE ADAM, *Cronica*, ed. G. Scalia (Bari, 1966).

TARDIF, *Coutumiers* I, i.108.

TEULET, A., *Layettes du trésor des Chartes*, i (Paris, 1863).

'The Case concerning the Marsh lying between the Abbey of Croyland and the Priory of Spalding, 1189-1202', in D. M. Stenton, *English Justice between the Norman Conquest and the Great Charter 1066–1215* (London, 1965).

Urkundenbuch zur Geschichte der Babenberger in Österreich, ed. H. Fichtenau and E. Zöllner, iv, 1 (Vienna, 1968).

WALTER MAP, *De Nugis Curialium. Courtiers' Trifles*, ed. and trans. M. R. James, C. N. L. Brooke and R. A. B. Mynors (OMT, Oxford, 1983).

Die Werke der Troubadours in provenzalischer Sprache, ed. C. A. F. Mahn, i (Berlin, 1846).

WILLIAM OF NEWBURGH, *Historia Rerum Anglicarum*, ed. R. Howlett, in *Chronicles of the Reigns of Stephen, Henry II and Richard I*, i and ii (RS, 1884).

II SECONDARY WORKS

ABULAFIA, D., *The Two Italies* (Cambridge, 1977).

AHLERS, J., *Die Welfen und die Englischen Könige 1165–1235* (Hildesheim, 1987).

AILES, A., *The Origins of the Royal Arms of England* (Reading, 1982).

ANDRIEU, J., *Histoire de l'Agenais* (Agen, 1893).

APPLEBY, J. T., *England without Richard* (London, 1965).

ARBELLOT, F., *La Vérité sur la mort de Richard Coeur-de-Lion* (Paris, 1878).

AUBRUN, M., 'Le Prieur Geoffroy du Vigeois et sa chronique', *Revue Mabillon*, lviii (1974).

AUDOUIN, E., *Essai sur l'armée royale au temps de Philippe Auguste* (Paris, 1913).

BAAKEN, G., *Die Regesten des Kaiserreiches unter Heinrich VI. Regesta Imperii IV/3* (Cologne, 1972).

BALDWIN, J. W., *The Government of Philip Augustus* (Berkeley, California, 1986).

——, 'La Décennie décisive: les années 1190–1203 dans le règne de Philippe Auguste', *Revue historique*, cclxvi (1981).

BARBER, R. W., *The Knight and Chivalry* (revised edn, Woodbridge, 1995).

BARBER R. W. and BARKER, J., *Tournaments. Jousts, Chivalry and Pageants in the Middle Ages* (Woodbridge, 1989).

BARKER, J. R. V., *The Tournament in England 1100–1400* (Woodbridge, 1986).

BARRATT, N., 'The English Revenues of Richard I' (forthcoming).

——, 'The Revenues of John and Philip Augustus Revisited', in *King John: New Interpretations*, ed. S. Church (Woodbridge, 1999).

——, 'The Revenues of King John', *EHR*, cxi (1996).

BARTLETT, R., *Gerald of Wales 1146–1223* (Oxford, 1982).

——, 'The Hagiography of Angevin England', in *Thirteenth Century England*, v (Woodbridge, 1995).

BATES, D., 'The Rise and Fall of Normandy c. 911–1204', in *England and Normandy in the Middle Ages*, ed. D. Bates and A. Curry (London, 1994).

BAUTIER, R.-H., 'La Collection de chartes de croisade dite "Collection Courtois", in *Comptes rendus des séances de l'Académie des Inscriptions et Belles-Lettres* (Paris, 1956).

——, *La France de Philippe Auguste – Le temps des mutations* (Paris, 1982).

BEC, P., 'Troubadours, trouvères et espace Plantagenêt', *CCM*, xxix (1986).

BEECH, G. T., *A Rural Society in Medieval France: the Gâtine of Poitou in the Eleventh and Twelfth Centuries* (Baltimore, 1964).

BENJAMIN, R., 'The Angevin Empire', *History Today*, xxxvi (February 1986).

——, 'A Forty Years War: Toulouse and the Plantagenets, 1156–96', *Historical Research*, lxi (1988).

BENTON, J. F.,'The Court of Champagne as a Literary Center', *Speculum*, xxxvi (1961).

BERESFORD, M., *New Towns of the Middle Ages* (Gloucester, 1988).

BEZZOLA, R.R., *Les Origines et la formation de la littérature courtoise en occident*, Part 3, *La Société courtoise* (2 vols,).

BILLORÉ, M., 'La Noblesse Normande dans l'entourage des Plantagenêt', *CCM* (forthcoming).

BISSON, T. N., *The Medieval Crown of Aragon* (Oxford, 1986).

BOSWELL, J., *Christianity, Social Tolerance and Homosexuality* (Chicago, 1980).

BOURGAIN, P., 'Aliénor d'Aquitaine et Marie de Champagne mises en cause par André le Chapelain', *CCM*, xxix (1986).

BOUSSARD, J., *Le Comté d'Anjou sous Henri Plantagenêt et ses fils 1151–1204* (Paris, 1938).

——, *Le Gouvernement d'Henri II Plantagenêt* (Paris, 1956).

——, 'Philippe Auguste et les Plantagenêts', in *La France de Philippe Auguste: Le temps de mutations*, ed. R. H. Bautier (Paris, 1982).

BRADBURY, J., *Philip Augustus, King of France 1180–1223* (London, 1998).

BRIDGE, A., *Richard the Lionheart* (London, 1989).

BROUGHTON, B. B., *The Legends of King Richard I* (The Hague, 1966).

BROWN, R. A., *English Castles* (London, 1954).

——, 'Royal Castle-Building in England 1154–1216', *EHR*, lxx (1955), 353–98.

BRUNDAGE, J. A., *Richard Lionheart* (New York, 1974).

CARPENTER, D. A., 'Abbot Ralph of Coggeshall's Account of the Last Years of King Richard and the First Years of King John', *EHR*, cxiii (1998).

——, 'The Decline of the Curial Sheriff in England, 1194-1258', *EHR*, xci (1976).

——, *The Reign of Henry III* (London, 1996).

CARPENTIER, E., 'Les Historiens royaux et le pouvoir Capétien', in *L'Historiographie médiévale en Europe* (Paris, 1991).

CHAMBERS, F. M., 'Some Legends concerning Eleanor of Aquitaine', *Speculum*, xvi (1941).

CHAUVENET, F., 'L'Entourage de Richard Coeur de Lion en Poitou Aquitaine', *CCM* (forthcoming).

CHENEY, C. R., *From Becket to Langton: English Church Government 1170–1213* (Manchester, 1956).

——, *Hubert Walter* (London, 1967).

CHURCH, S., *King John: New Interpretations* (Woodbridge, 1999).

CLEMENTI, D., 'The Circumstances of Count Tancred's Accession to the Kingdom of Sicily', in *Mélanges Antonio Marongiù* (Palermo, 1967).

——, 'Some Unnoticed Aspects of the Emperor Henry VI's Conquest of the Norman Kingdom of Sicily', *Bulletin of the John Rylands Library*, xxxvi (1954).

CLOULAS, I., 'Le Douaire de Bérengère de Navarre, veuve de Richard Coeur de Lion et sa retraite au Mans', *CCM* (forthcoming).

COLKER, M. L., 'A Newly Discovered Manuscript Leaf of Ambroise's *L'Estoire de la Guerre Sainte*', *Revue d'histoire des textes*, xxii (1992).

CONTAMINE, P., 'L'Armée de Philippe Auguste', in *La France de Philippe Auguste: Le temps de mutations*, ed. R-H. Bautier (Paris, 1982).

CORNER, D., 'The Earliest Surviving Manuscripts of Roger of Howden's *Chronica*', *EHR*, xcviii (1983).

——, 'The *Gesta Regis Henrici Secundi* and *Chronica* of Roger, Parson of Howden', *BIHR*, lvi (1983).

COULSON, C., 'Fortress Policy in Capetian Tradition and Angevin Practice. Aspects of the Conquest of Normandy by Philip II', *ANS*, vi (1983).

CROSLAND, J., *William the Marshal* (London, 1962).

CROUCH, D., *William Marshal* (London, 1990).

CRUMP, J. J., 'The Mortimer Family and the Making of the March', in *Thirteenth Century England VI* (Woodbridge, 1997).

CSENDES, P., *Heinrich VI* (Darmstadt, 1993).

DANIEL, S., *The Collection of the Historie of England* (London, 1621).

DEBORD, A., *La Société laïque dans les pays de la Charente X–XII siècles* (Paris, 1984).

DEPT, G. G., *Les Influences anglaise et française dans le comté de Flandres* (Ghent, 1928).

DEVAILLY, G., *Le Berry du Xe siècle jusqu'au milieu du XIIe siècle* (Paris 1973).

DION, R., *Histoire de la vigne et du vin en France des origines au XIXe siècle* (Paris, 1959).

DOBSON, R. B., *The Jews of Medieval York and the Massacre of March 1190* (Borthwick Papers, xlv, York, 1974).

DOUIE, D. L., *Archbishop Geoffrey Plantagenet and the Chapter of York* (York, 1960).

DRONKE, P., *The Medieval Lyric* (2nd edn, London, 1978).

DUBY, G., *William Marshal. The Flower of Chivalry* (London, 1986).

——, *The Legend of Bouvines* (Berkeley, 1990).

DU GARDE PEACH, L., *Richard the Lionheart* (Ladybird History Book, London, 1965).

DUNBABIN, J., *France in the Making 843–1180* (Oxford, 1985).

EDBURY, P., *The Kingdom of Cyprus and the Crusades 1191-1374* (Cambridge, 1991).

——, 'The Lyon *Eracles* and the Old French Continuations of William of Tyre', in *Montjoie: Studies in Crusade History in Honour of Hans*

Eberhard Mayer, ed. B. Kedar, J. Riley-Smith and R. Hiestand (Aldershot, 1997).

——, 'The Templars in Cyprus', in *The Military Orders: Fighting for the Faith and Caring for the Sick*, ed. M. Barber (Aldershot, 1994).

EDWARDS, C., 'The Magnanimous Sex-Object: Richard the Lionheart in the Medieval German Lyric', in *Courtly Literature: Culture and Context*, ed. K. Busby and E. Kooper, (Utrecht Publications in General and Comparative Literature, xxv, Amsterdam, 1990).

EVERARD, J., 'The Justiciarship in Brittany and Ireland under Henry II', *ANS*, xx (1997).

FAGNEN, C., ' Le Vocabulaire du pouvoir dans les actes de Richard Coeur de Lion, duc de Normandie', in *Actes du cent cinquième congrès national des sociétés savantes, Caen 1980* (Paris, 1984).

FALMAGNE, J., *Baudouin V, comte de Hainaut 1150–95* (Montreal, 1966).

FAVREAU, R., 'Les Débuts de la ville de la Rochelle', *CCM*, xxx (1987).

FAVREAU-LILIE, M-L., *Die Italiener im Heiligen Land* (Amsterdam, 1989).

FICHTENAU, H., 'Akkon, Zypern und das Lösegeld für Richard Löwenherz', *Archiv für österreichische Geschichte*, cxxv (1966).

FLANAGAN, M.T., *Irish Society, Anglo-Norman Settlers, Angevin Kingship* (Oxford, 1989).

FOREY, A.J., 'The Military Order of St Thomas at Acre', *EHR*, xcii (1977).

FRANCE, J., *Victory in the East: A Military History of the First Crusade* (Cambridge, 1994).

——, *Western Warfare in the Age of the Crusades 1000–1300* (London, 1999).

FREYTAG, H-J., 'Der Nordosten des Reiches nach dem Sturz Heinrichs des Löwen', *DA*, xxv (1954).

GALBRAITH, V. H., 'Good and Bad Kings in History', *History*, xxx (1945).

GIBB, H. A. R., 'The Arabic Sources for the Life of Saladin', *Speculum*, xxv (1950).

GILLINGHAM, J., *The Angevin Empire* (London, 1984), repr. in *Richard Coeur de Lion*.

——, 'The Art of Kingship: Richard I', *History Today*, xxxv (April 1985); repr. in *Richard Coeur de Lion*.

——, 'Conquering Kings: Some Twelfth-Century Reflections on Henry II and Richard I', in *Warriors and Churchmen in the High Middle Ages: Essays Presented to Karl Leyser*, ed. T. Reuter (London, 1992), repr. in *Richard Coeur de Lion*.

——, 'Henry II, Richard I and the Lord Rhys', *Peritia: Journal of the Medieval Academy of Ireland*, x (1996), 225–36, repr. in J. Gillingham, *The English in the Twelfth Century* (Woodbridge, 1999).

——, 'Historians without Hindsight: Coggeshall, Diceto and Howden on the Early Years of John's Reign', in *King John: New Interpretations*, ed. S. Church, (Woodbridge, 1999).

——, *Richard Coeur de Lion. Kingship, Chivalry and War in the Twelfth Century* (London, 1994).

——, 'Richard I and Berengaria of Navarre', *BIHR*, liii (1980), repr. in *Richard Coeur de Lion*.

——, 'Richard I and the Science of War in the Middle Ages', in *War and*

Government in the Middle Ages. Essays in Honour of J. O. Prestwich, ed. J. Gillingham and J. C. Holt (Woodbridge, 1984), repr. in *Richard Coeur de Lion.*

——, 'Richard I, Galley-Warfare and Portsmouth: the Beginnings of a Royal Navy', in *Thirteenth Century England VI*, ed. M. Prestwich, R. H. Britnell and R. Frame (Woodbridge, 1997).

——, *Richard the Lionheart* (2nd edn, 1989).

——, 'Roger of Howden on Crusade', in *Medieval Historical Writing in the Christian and Islamic Worlds*, ed. D. O. Morgan (London, 1982), repr. in *Richard Coeur de Lion.*

——, 'Some Legends of Richard the Lionheart: Their Development and Their Influence', in *Riccardo Cuor di Leone nella storia e nella leggenda* (Accademia Nazionale dei Lincei, problemi attuali di scienza e di cultura, ccliii, 1981), repr. in *Richard Coeur de Lion.*

——, 'The Travels of Roger of Howden and his Views of the Irish, Scots and Welsh', *ANS*, xx (1998), repr. in Gillingham, J., *The English in the Twelfth Century* (Woodbridge, 1999).

——, 'The Unromantic Death of Richard I' *Speculum*, liv (1979), repr. in *Richard Coeur de Lion.*

——, 'War and Chivalry in the History of William the Marshal', in *Thirteenth Century England: II*, ed. P. R. Coss and S. D. Lloyd (Woodbridge, 1988) repr. in *Richard Coeur de Lion.*

——, 'Royal Newsletters, Forgeries and English Historians: Some Links between Court and History in the Region of Richard I', *CCM* (forthcoming).

GOLB, N., *The Jews in Medieval Normandy* (Cambridge, 1998).

GOSSE-KISCHINEWSKI, A., 'La fondation de L'abbaye de Bonport', *Connaissance de l'Eure*, lxxxix–xc (1993).

GRANSDEN, A., *Historical Writing in England, c.550–c.1307* (London, 1974).

GRANT, L., 'Gothic Architecture in Normandy, c. 1150–c.1250' (unpub. Ph.D. thesis, University of London, 1986).

GREEN, J., 'The Lords of the Norman Vexin' in *War and Government in the Middle Ages*, ed. J. Gillingham and J. C. Holt (Woodbridge, 1984).

GROUSSET, R., *Histoire des croisades*, iii (Paris, 1936).

HAJDU, R., 'Castles, Castellans and the Structure of Politics in Poitou 1152–1271', *JMH*, iv (1978).

HALLAM, E. M., 'Aspects of the Monastic Patronage of the English and French Royal Houses c. 1130–1270' (unpub. Ph.D. thesis, University of London, 1976).

——, *Capetian France 987–1328* (London, 1980).

——, 'Henry II, Richard I and the Order of Grandmont', *JMH*, i (1975).

——, 'Royal Burial and the Cult of Kingship in France and England, 1060–1330', *JMH*, viii (1982).

HARVEY, J. H.,*The Plantagenets* (London, 1948).

HEISER, R., 'Richard I and His Appointments to English Shrievalties', *EHR*, cxii (1997).

——, 'The Royal *Familiares* of King Richard I', *Medieval Prosopography*, x (1989).

——, 'The Sheriffs of Richard I: Trends of Management as Seen in the Shrieval Appointments from 1189 to 1194', *HSJ*, iv (1992).

——, 'The Sheriffs of Richard Lionheart: A Prosopographical Survey of Appointments, Politics and Patronage, 1189–99' (unpub. Ph.D., thesis, Florida State University, 1993).

HIGOUNET, C., *Bordeaux pendant le haut moyen âge* (Bordeaux, 1963).

——, 'La Rivalité des maisons de Toulouse et de Barcelone pour la prépondérance méridionale', in *Mélanges d'histoire du moyen âge dédiés à la mémoire de Louis Halphen* (Paris, 1951).

HILL, G., *A History of Cyprus*, i (Cambridge, 1940).

HIVERGNEAUX, M., 'Aliénor d'Aquitaine: le pouvoir d'une femme à la lumière de ses chartes', *CCM* (forthcoming).

HOFFMAN, H., 'Französische Fürstenweihen des Hochmittelalters', *Deutsches Archiv*, xviii (1962).

HOHLER, C., 'A Note on Jacobus', *Journal of the Warburg and Courtauld Institute*, xxxv (1972).

HOLT, J. C., 'Aliénor d'Aquitaine, Jean sans Terre et la succession de 1199', *CCM*, xxix (1986).

——, 'The End of the Anglo-Norman Realm', *Proceedings of the British Academy*, lxi (1975), repr. in *Magna Carta and Medieval Government*.

——, *King John* (London, 1963) repr. in *Magna Carta and Medieval Government*.

——, 'The Loss of Normandy and Royal Finance', in *War and Government in the Middle Ages*, ed. J. Gillingham and J. C. Holt (London, 1984), repr. in *Magna Carta and Medieval Government*.

——, *Magna Carta and Medieval Government* (London, 1985).

——, *The Northerners* (Oxford, 1961).

——, 'Ricardus rex Anglorum et dux Normannorum', in *Riccardo Cuor di Leone nella storia e nella leggenda* (Accademia Nazionale dei Lincei, problemi attuali di scienza e di cultura, xxliii, 1981), repr. in *Magna Carta and Medieval Government*.

HOLT, J. C. AND MORTIMER, R., *Handlist of the Acta of Henry II and Richard I in British Repositories* (London, 1986).

HOOK, D., 'The Figure of Richard I in Medieval Spanish Literature', in *Richard Coeur de Lion in History and Myth*, ed. J. L. Nelson (London, 1992).

HUCKER, B. U., 'Die Chronik Arnolds von Lübeck als "Historia Regum"', *DA* xliv (1988).

——, *Kaiser Otto IV* (Hanover, 1990).

HYAMS, P., 'What Did Henry III of England Think about in Bed and in French about Kingship and Anger?', in *Anger's Past*, ed. B. Rosenwein (Ithaca, New York, 1998).

JAMISON, E.M., *Admiral Eugenius of Sicily* (London, 1957).

JONES, M. H., 'Richard the Lionheart in German Literature of the Middle Ages', in *Richard Coeur de Lion in History and Myth*, ed. J. L. Nelson (London, 1992).

JORDAN, K., *Henry the Lion* (Oxford, 1986).

KEDAR, B. Z., 'The Battle of Hattin Revisited', in *The Horns of Hattin*, ed. B. Z. Kedar (London, 1992).

——, 'The Patriarch Eraclius', in *Outremer: Studies in the History of the Crusading Kingdom of Jerusalem Presented to J. Prawer*, ed. B. Z. Kedar, H. E. Mayer and R. C. Smail (Jerusalem, 1982).

KEEFE, T. K., Proffers for Heirs and Heiresses in the Pipe Rolls: Some Observations on Indebtedness in the Years before the Magna Carta (1180–1212), *HSJ*, v (1993).

KEEN, M., *Chivalry* (London, 1984).

KESSLER, U., *Richard I. Löwenherz. König, Kreuzritter, Abenteurer* (Graz, 1995).

KIBLER, W. W., *Eleanor of Aquitaine: Patron and Politician* (Austin, Texas, 1976).

KÖHLER, M. A., *Allianzen und Verträge zwischen fränkischen und islamischen Herrschern im Vorderen Orient* (Berlin, 1991).

LABANDE, E-R., 'Pour une Image véridique d'Alienor d'Aquitaine', *Bulletin de la société des antiquaires de l'ouest* 4th series, ii (1952).

LABORDERIE, O. DE, 'Du Souvenir à la réincarnation: l'image de Richard Coeur de Lion dans la *Vie et Mort du Roi Jean* de William Shakespeare', in *Richard Coeur de Lion in History and Myth*, ed. J. L. Nelson (London, 1992).

LANDON, L., *Itinerary of King Richard I* (London: Pipe Roll Society, new series, xiii, 1935).

LEES, B., 'The Letters of Queen Eleanor of Aquitaine to Pope Celestine III', *EHR*, xxi (1906).

LEJEUNE, R., 'Le Rôle littéraire d'Alienor d'Aquitaine', *Cultura Neolatina*, xiv (1954).

——, 'Le Rôle littéraire de la famille d'Alienor d'Aquitaine', *Cahiers de civilisation medievale*, i (1958).

LE PATOUREL, J., 'The Plantagenet Dominions', *History*, l (1965).

LEWIS, B., *The Assassins* (London, 1967).

LEYSER, K., 'The Angevin Kings and the Holy Man', in *St Hugh of Lincoln*, ed. H. Mayr-Harting (Oxford, 1987).

——, 'Frederick Barbarossa, Henry II and the Hand of St James', *EHR*, xc (1975).

LLOYD, J. E., *History of Wales* (3rd edn, London, 1939).

LLOYD, S., *English Society and the Crusade, 1216–1307* (Oxford, 1988).

LLOYD, T. H., *The English Wool Trade in the Middle Ages* (Cambridge, 1977).

LYONS M. C. and JACKSON, D. E. P., *Saladin. The Politics of the Holy War* (Cambridge, 1982).

MCCASH, J. M. H., 'Marie de Champagne and Eleanor of Aquitaine: a Relationship Re-examined', *Speculum*, liv (1979).

MARKOWSKI, M.,'Richard Lionheart: Bad King, Bad Crusader?', *JMH*, xxiii (1997).

MARTINDALE, J., '"Cavalaria et Orgueill" Duke William IX of Aquitaine and the Historian', in *The Ideals and Practice of Medieval Knighthood*, ii, ed. C. Harper-Bill and R. Harvey (Woodbridge, 1988), repr. in *Status, Authority and Regional Power*.

——, 'Eleanor of Aquitaine' in *Richard Coeur de Lion in History and Myth*, ed. J. L. Nelson (London, 1992), repr. in *Status, Authority and Regional Power*.

——, *Status, Authority and Regional Power. Aquitaine and France, 9th to 12th Centuries* (Aldershot, 1997).

——, 'Succession and Politics in the Romance-speaking World *c.*1000–1140', in *England and her Neighbours: Essays in Honour of Pierre Chaplais*, ed. M. Jones and M. Vale, (London, 1989), repr. in *Status, Authority and Regional Power.*

——, 'The Sword on the Stone: Some Resonances of a Medieval Symbol of Power', *ANS*, xv (1993).

MASON, E., '"Rocamadour in Quercy above All Other Churches": the Healing of Henry II', in *Studies in Church History*, xix, ed. W. Sheils (Oxford, 1982).

MATTHEW, D., *The Norman Kingdom of Sicily* (Cambridge, 1992).

MAYER, H. E., *The Crusades* (2nd edn, Oxford, 1988).

——, 'A Ghost Ship called Frankenef: King Richard I's German Itinerary', *EHR* (forthcoming).

——, 'Henry II of England and the Holy Land', *EHR*, xcvii (1982).

——, *Die Kanzlei der lateinischen Könige von Jerusalem* (2 vols, Hannover, 1996).

——, 'Die Kanzlei Richards I von England auf dem Dritten Kreuzzug', *Mitteilungen des Instituts für Österreichische Geschichtsforschung*, lxxxv (1977).

MAYER H. E., and FAVREAU, M. L., 'Das Diplom Balduins I. für Genua und Genuas goldene Inschrift in der Grabeskirche', *Quellen und Forschungen aus italienischen Archiven und Bibliotheken*, lv/lvi (1976).

MÖHRING, H., *Saladin und der dritte Kreuzzug* (Wiesbaden, 1980).

MONNA, A. D. A.,'Diagnose van een omstreden 13e eeuwse kalender uit de Servaasabdij te Utrecht', *Archief voor de Geschiednis van de Katholieke Kerk in Nederland*, xxv (1983).

MOORE, O. H., *The Young King Henry Plantagenet 1155–1183 in History, Literature and Tradition* (Columbus, Ohio, 1925).

MOSS, V., 'The Norman Fiscal Revolution 1193–98', in *Crises, Revolutions and Self-Sustained Fiscal Growth*, ed. R. Bonney and M. Ormrod (Stamford, 1999).

——, 'Normandy and England in 1180: the Pipe Roll Evidence', in *England and Normandy in the Middle Ages*, ed. D. Bates and A. Curry (London, 1994).

——, 'Normandy and the Angevin Empire. A Study of the Norman Exchequer Rolls 1180–1204' (unpub. University of Wales Ph.D. thesis, 1996).

MURRAY, A. V. 'Richard the Lionheart, Otto of Brunswick and the Earldom of York: Northern England and the Angevin Succession, 1190–91', *Medieval Yorkshire*, xxiii (1994).

NELSON, J. L., ed., *Richard Coeur de Lion in History and Myth* (London, 1992).

NORGATE, K., *England under the Angevin Kings* (2 vols, London, 1887).

——, *John Lackland* (London, 1902).

——, *Richard the Lionheart* (London, 1924).

NORWICH, J. J., *The Kingdom in the Sun* (London, 1970).

NOWELL, C.E., 'The Old Man of the Mountain', *Speculum*, xxii (1947).

ORME, N., *From Childhood to Chivalry. The Education of the English Kings and Aristocracy 1066–1530* (London, 1984).

OWEN, D. D. R., *Eleanor of Aquitaine* (Oxford, 1993).

PACAUT, M., *Louis VII et son royaume* (Paris, 1964).

PAINTER, S., 'The Houses of Lusignan and Châtellerault, 1150–1250', *Speculum*, xxx (1955).

——, 'The Lords of Lusignan in the Eleventh and Twelfth Centuries', *Speculum*, xxxii (1957).

——, *William Marshal* (Baltimore, 1933).

PARTNER, N., *Serious Entertainments. The Writing of History in Twelfth-Century England* (Chicago, 1977).

PATERSON, L., 'Military Surgery: Knights, Sergeants, and Raimon of Avignon's Version of the *Chirurgia* of Roger of Salerno (1180–1209)', in *The Ideals and Practice of Medieval Knighthood II*, C. Harper-Bill and R. Harvey, (Woodbridge, 1988).

PATIER, P., *Le Siège de Chalus-Chabrol par le Roy Richard Coeur de Lion, l'an 1199. Étude des deux châteaux de Chalus* (Limoges, 1973).

PHILLIPS, J., *Defenders of the Holy Land* (Oxford, 1996).

PITTE, D., *Château-Gaillard* (Vernon, France, 1996).

POOLE, A. L., *From Domesday Book to Magna Carta* (2nd edn, Oxford, 1955).

——, 'Richard the First's Alliances with the German Princes in 1194', in *Studies in Medieval History presented to F. M. Powicke*, ed. R. W. Hunt, W. A. Pantin and R. W. Southern (Oxford, 1948).

POWER, D. J., 'Between the Angevin and Capetian Courts: John de Rouvray and the Knights of the Pays de Bray, 1180–1225', in *Family Trees and the Roots of Politics*, ed. K. S. B. Keats-Rohan (Woodbridge, 1997).

——, 'What Did the Frontier of Angevin Normandy Comprise?', *ANS*, xvii (1994).

POWICKE, F. M., *The Loss of Normandy* (2nd edn, Manchester, 1961).

PRAWER, J., *Histoire du royaume latin de Jérusalem* (2 vols, Paris, 1969–70).

——, *The Latin Kingdom of Jerusalem* (London, 1972).

PRESTWICH, J. O., 'Military Intelligence under the Norman and Angevin Kings', in *Law and Government in medieval England and Normandy*, ed. G. Garnett and J. Hudson (Cambridge, 1994).

——, 'Mistranslations and Misinterpretations in Medieval English History', *Peritia: Journal of the Medieval Academy of Ireland*, x (1996).

——, 'Richard Coeur de Lion: *Rex Bellicosus*', in *Riccardo Cuor di Leone nella storia e nella leggenda* (Accademia Nazionale dei Lincei, Problemi attuali di scienza e di cultura, ccliii, Rome, 1981); repr. in *Richard Coeur de Lion in History and Myth*, ed. J. L. Nelson (London, 1992).

PRINGLE, D., 'King Richard I and the Walls of Ascalon', *Palestine Exploration Quarterly*, cxvi (1984).

——, 'Templar Castles between Jaffa and Jerusalem', in *The Military Orders: Fighting for the Faith and Caring for the Sick*, ed. M. Barber, (Aldershot, 1994).

PRYOR, J. H., *Geography, Technology and War. Studies in the Maritime History of the Mediterranean 649–1571* (Cambridge, 1988).

QUELLER, D. E., *The Fourth Crusade* (Leicester, 1978).

RAMSAY, J. H., *The Angevin Empire* (London, 1903).

REGAN, G., *Lionhearts. Saladin and Richard I* (London, 1998).

RENOUARD, Y., *Études d'histoire médiévale* (Paris, 1968).

RICHARD, A., *Histoire des comtes de Poitou 778–1204* (2 vols, Paris, 1903).

RICHARD, J., *The Latin Kingdom of Jerusalem* (London, 1979).

RICHARDSON, H. G., *The English Jewry under Angevin Kings* (London, 1960).

——, 'The Letters and Charters of Eleanor of Aquitaine', *EHR*, lxxiv (1959).

RICHARDSON H. G. and SAYLES, G. O., *The Governance of Medieval England* (Edinburgh, 1963).

RILEY-SMITH, J., *The Feudal Nobility and the Kingdom of Jerusalem 1174–1277* (London, 1973).

——, *The Knights of St John in Jerusalem and Cyprus c. 1050–1310* (London, 1967).

RODGER, N. A. M., *The Safeguard of the Sea* (London, 1997).

ROGERS, R., *Latin Siege Warfare in the Twelfth Century* (Oxford, 1992).

RUNCIMAN, S., *A History of the Crusades*, iii (Cambridge, 1954).

SAYERS, J., 'English Charters from the Third Crusade', in *Tradition and Change. Essays in Honour of Marjorie Chibnall* (Cambridge, 1985).

SCAMMELL, G. V., *Hugh du Puiset* (Cambridge, 1956).

SCHMANDT, R. H., 'The Election and Assassination of Albert of Louvain, Bishop of Liège 1191–2', *Speculum*, xlii (1967).

SIBERRY, E., *Criticism of Crusading 1095–1274* (Oxford, 1985).

SMAIL, R. C., *Crusading Warfare 1097–1196* (Cambridge, 1956).

——, 'The International Status of the Latin Kingdom of Jerusalem, 1150–92', in *The Eastern Mediterranean Lands in the Period of the Crusades*, ed. P. M. Holt (Warminster, 1978).

——, 'The Predicaments of Guy of Lusignan, 1183–87', in *Outremer – Studies in the History of the Crusading Kingdom of Jerusalem Presented to J. Prawer*, ed. B. Z. Kedar, H. E. Mayer and R. C. Smail (Jerusalem, 1982).

SPEAR, D., 'The Norman Empire and the Secular Clergy, 1060–1204', *Journal of British Studies*, xxi (1982).

——, 'Power, Patronage and Personality in the Norman Cathedral Chapters, 911–1204', *ANS*, xx (1997).

SPUFFORD, P., *Money and its Use in Medieval Europe* (Cambridge, 1988).

STENTON, D. M.,'Roger of Howden and "Benedict"', *EHR*, lxviii (1953).

STRICKLAND, M., *War and Chivalry. The Conduct and Perception of War in England and Normandy 1066–1217* (Cambridge, 1996).

——, ed., *Anglo-Norman Warfare* (Woodbridge, 1992).

——, 'Provoking or Avoiding Battle? Challenge, Judicial Duel, and Single Combat in Eleventh- and Twelfth-Century Warfare', in *Armies, Chivalry and Warfare in Medieval Britain and France*, ed. M. Strickland (Stamford, 1998).

STUBBS, W., *Historical Introductions to the Rolls Series*, ed. A. Hassall (London, 1902).

THOMAS, H., 'Portrait of a Medieval Anti-Semite: Richard Malebisse', *HSJ*, v (1993).

TUCOO-CHALA, P., *La Vicomté de Béarn et le problème de sa souveraineté* (Bordeaux, 1961).

TURNER, R. V., 'Eleanor of Aquitaine and her Children: an Inquiry into Medieval Family Attachment', *JMH*, xiv (1988).

——, 'Good or Bad Kingship? The Case of Richard Lionheart', *HSJ*, viii (1999).

——, 'The Households of the Sons of Henry II', *CCM* (forthcoming).

——, 'The Problem of Survival for the Angevin "Empire"', *American Historical Review*, c (1995).

——, 'Richard Lionheart and English Episcopal Elections', *Albion*, xxix (1997).

——, 'Richard Lionheart and the Episcopate in His French Domains', *French Historical Studies*, xxi (1998).

TYERMAN, C., *England and the Crusades 1095–1588* (Chicago, 1988).

——, *The Invention of the Crusades* (London, 1998).

VERBRUGGEN, J. F., *The Art of Warfare in Western Europe during the Middle Ages* (Woodbridge, 1997).

VERYNAUD, G., *Histoire de Limoges* (Limoges, 1973).

VIELLIARD, J., *Le Guide du pèlerin de St Jacques de Compostelle* (Macon, 1938).

VINCENT, N., *Peter des Roches* (Cambridge, 1996).

VINCENT, N., 'The Poitevins in the Household of Henry II', *CCM* (forthcoming).

——, 'William Marshal, King Henry II and the Honour of Châteauroux', *Archives* (forthcoming).

WARREN, M., 'Roger of Howden Strikes Back: Investing Arthur of Brittany with the Anglo-Norman Future', *ANS*, xxi (1998).

WARREN, W. L., *Henry II* (London, 1973).

——, *King John* (London, 1961).

WATSON, R. C., 'The counts of Angloulême from the ninth century to the Mid-Thirteenth Century', (unpub. Ph.D. thesis, University of East Anglia, 1979).

WATTENBACH, W. and SCHMALE, F-J., *Deutschlands Geschichtsquellen im Mittelalter*, i (Darmstadt, 1976).

WAUGH, S. L., *The Lordship of England: Royal Wardships and Marriages in English Society and Politics 1217–1327* (Princeton, 1988).

WAY, A., 'Effigy of King Richard Coeur de Lion in the Cathedral of Rouen', *Archaeologia*, xxix (1842).

WERNER, K. F., 'Andreas von Marchiennes und die Geschichtsschreibung von Anchin und Marchiennes in der zweiten Hälfte des 12. Jahrhunderts', *DA*, ix (1952).

——, 'Kingdom and Principalities in 12th-Century France', in *The Medieval Nobility*, ed. and trans. T. Reuter (Amsterdam, 1979).

WEST, F. J., *The Justiciarship in England 1066–1232* (Cambridge, 1966).

WHITE, S. D.,'The Politics of Anger', in *Anger's Past*, ed. B. H. Rosenwein (Ithaca, New York, 1998).

INDEX